Twayne's American Literary
Manuscripts Series

Joel Myerson, Editor

Edward Taylor's
"Church Records" and Related Sermons

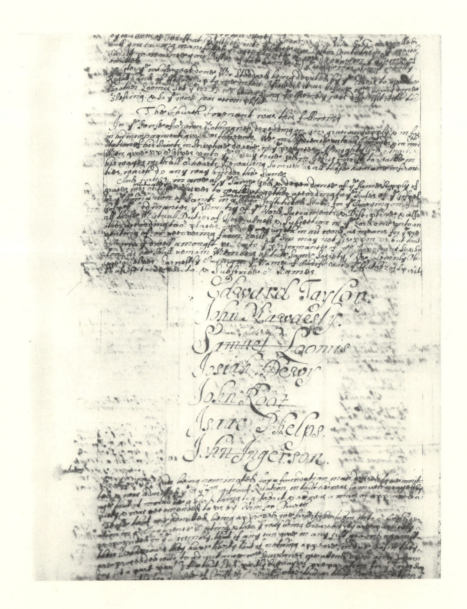

The Church Covenant: "Church Records," Manuscript p. 101

Edward Taylor's

"Church Records" and Related Sermons

Volume 1 of the Unpublished Writings of Edward Taylor

Edited by Thomas M. & Virginia L. Davis

TWAYNE PUBLISHERS • BOSTON

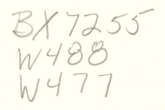
Copyright © 1981 by G.K. Hall & Co.
All rights reserved

Published in 1981 by Twayne Publishers
A Division of G.K. Hall & Co.
70 Lincoln Street, Boston, Massachusetts 02111

Printed on permanent/durable acid-free paper and bound
in the United States of America

Book design by Barbara Anderson

First Printing

Taylor, Edward, 1642?–1729.
    Edward Taylor's "Church records," and related
sermons.

    (Twayne's American literary manuscripts series)
(The Unpublished Writings of Edward Taylor)
    Includes bibliographical references.
    1. Westfield Church, Westfield, Mass. 2. Taylor,
Edward, 1642?–1729. 3. Congregational churches—Sermons.
4. Sermons, American. I. Davis, Thomas Marion.
II. Davis, Virginia L.   III. Title.   IV. Title: "Church
records," and related sermons.   V. Series: Taylor,
Edward, 1642?–1729. Unpublished writings of Edward
Taylor; v. 1
BX7255.W488W477   285'.9'0974426   80–72925

ISBN 0-8057-9650-9

> *In Memoriam*
>
> **Mary Lois Eaton**
>
> *1902 – 1975*

CONTENTS

Acknowledgments

T HE MANUSCRIPT OF THE WESTFIELD "CHURCH RECORDS" IS here published by courtesy of the Directors of the Westfield Athenaeum and Franklin P. Taplin, Head Librarian. Our work in Westfield was made especially enjoyable by the unfailing enthusiasm and assistance of Sophie Kareta, Assistant Librarian, and Frances B. McMahon, Curator of the Edwin Smith Historical Museum. We owe them, and the entire staff of the Athenaeum, a special debt.

The manuscripts of the three sermons are published by courtesy of the Trustees of the Boston Public Library and the Deacons of the Old South Church, the Reverend Frederick M. Meek, Pastor. James Lawton, Curator of Manuscripts, and John Alden, Keeper of Rare Books, deserve particular thanks for making our work in the Boston Public Library so effortless.

The material from Taylor's "Commonplace Book" included in this volume is published by courtesy of the Massachusetts Historical Society, Malcom Freiberg, Editor of Publications. The "Petition for support of heirs of the Rev. Edward Taylor of Westfield," in the Jonathan Edwards Collection of the Andover Newton Theological School, is published by courtesy of Ellis E. O'Neal, Jr., Librarian. We are also indebted to Duke University Press and the Editorial Board of *American Literature*, Arlin Turner, Editor, for permission to reprint material which has been previously published in that journal.

We owe particular thanks to the staffs of the Houghton Library of Harvard University, especially Carolyn E. Jakeman and Joseph McCarthy, and of the Beinecke Rare Book and Manuscript Library of

Yale University, particularly Marjorie G. Wynne and Christina M. Hanson, who have responded to our requests and assisted us in many ways.

The work on this edition has been facilitated by support from the Research Council of Kent State University, and the special assistance of Martin Nurmi, Chairman of the Department of English. Cleatus Hinds, John Parks, Jeff Hammond and Walter L. Powell have aided us in our research.

During the time we have worked on this edition, we have incurred special indebtedness to the following friends, who—if for no other reason—have apparently been willing to listen to us talk about Taylor: Susan and Mason Lowance, Sharon and Ken Silverman (who read and offered valuable criticism of the manuscript), Thomas Schafer, Wilson Kimnach, Sandy and Nora Marovitz, and, especially, Katherine and Everett Emerson.

Introduction

IN SPITE OF RECENT STUDIES, OUR VIEW OF EDWARD TAYLOR REMAINS incomplete. At each point when we think we are beginning to grasp the man himself, he again eludes us. We know something of his reverence for orthodoxy, of his staunch reaction to Solomon Stoddard's innovations, of his autocratic direction of the Westfield Church, a little about his wives and children, friends and acquaintances— and we have, of course, much of his poetry. But at very few points in his life are we able to make that essential synthesis which tells us who the whole man was.

This is true in part because the materials we have, with few exceptions, tend to reveal only one aspect of him. For no other major colonial figure, for example, is so little biographical information available: what we know of his years spent in England is scant, and of his life in this country we know little more. Except for a few dates—of their marriage, and the births and baptism of their children—we have discovered almost nothing of the relationship with his second wife, Ruth Wyllys Taylor. There is no record that she ever entered into Full Communion with the Westfield Church, and the only reference to her in all of his writing is the oblique, slightly wry comments of the fifty-year-old poet in their "epithalamium":

> Nay, may I, Lord, believe it? Shall my Skeg
>   Be ray'd in thy White Robes? My thatcht old Cribb
> (Immortall Purss hung on a mortall Peg,)
>   Wilt thou with fair'st array in heaven rig?[1]

The same is true in relation to the basic role of his life, Westfield's minister. We know almost nothing of his pulpit character, whether he preached from notes or sermon booklets, whether the sermons we have are pulpit copies or revisions, or what stage, if revisions, the sermons are in. One suspects that the reason why we have so few of his sermons is that he preached only from rough notes, and that the extant copies are considerably revised and expanded. In the eight sermons of the *Treatise Concerning the Lord's Supper*, for example, one is not dated, four are dated on Sundays, two on Thursdays, and one on a Saturday. The longest sermon in the series, Sermon 4, is so long that it is hardly likely to have been delivered in one session, though it is headed, "preacht 18th 12^m 1693/4."[2] To point out these matters is simply to note that we do not have even the most basic information about the man's primary role in life.

And part of the problem results from certain aspects of Taylor's own character. Only rarely, and then not clearly, do the man, minister, and poet come together in a single whole. This is not to say that the poems exist apart from his theology, or that the earthiness of the man and his penchant for the striking image do not appear in the sermons. When, in describing the last judgment, Taylor seizes upon the image of the "Most Curious perfumed Rose that should be as big as the Whole Creation of God from the Centre of the earth to the Circumference of the Highest heaven...,"[3] one senses that the passionate nature of the man, the poetic care he lavishes on the image, and the dedicated minister have coalesced—we see Taylor entire. But this is rarely the case. And while the poetry itself is the basis on which his reputation will rest, our understanding of that poetry and the intelligence behind it will benefit by knowing more about the Reverend Edward Taylor of Westfield, Massachusetts.[4]

To this end, this edition of the Westfield "'Church Records' and Related Sermons" will contribute a partial beginning. The manuscript of the "Church Records" contains a rather full account of Taylor's pastoral activities: the founding of the church; the "Profession of Faith" of the Westfield congregation; the Public Relations of Taylor and the foundation men; the sermon Taylor preached that day; a record of those admitted to full membership; baptismal records; and accounts of the disciplinary cases which came before the church for nearly half a century. The initial disagreements with his Northampton neighbor, Solomon Stoddard, implicit in much Taylor says in the founding sermon, are extended in the carefully revised and expanded version of that sermon, "A Particular Church is Gods House," also included in this edition. Finally, the two disciplinary sermons, which make up the remainder of this volume, focus upon a major disturbance in the Westfield Church which Taylor fully documents in the "Church Records." These sermons explicate Taylor's views concerning Congregational polity, as well as reveal his unquestioning allegiance to the principles of New England's founders.

The major interests of Taylor's public life, then, dominate these manuscripts. Though these records extend over fifty years, there are no surprises in this man: the principles which motivate him in 1675 are still the basis for his view of the world in 1725. But, of course, the world changed much in these years, and, in large part, in ways that were distasteful to Taylor. And while one may regret the occasional harshness of his public actions, he "kept the faith," at least as he saw it. That to him would have been a better epitaph than poet.

The Gathering of the Westfield Church

Taylor was addicted to order and process, and it is characteristic of him that he would keep one of the most complete extant accounts of the organization and development of a church. In addition, he was also recording the "acts" of God in the furthermost western settlement in the New England wilderness. Such a record would be important to future generations, for they would see that even in the earliest stirrings of apostacy in the Connecticut Valley, God's children in Westfield—under Edward Taylor's direction—had kept themselves pure. Taylor was clearly aware that the Federal experiment in New England no longer possessed the homogeneity initially achieved by those "Worthy, & Renowned men of God, that laid the Foundation here" (p. 191); the Half-Way Synod was already history when he entered Harvard, and the Westfield Church was organized in the hysteria of the Jeremiad which preceded the Reforming Synod. He knew that the Westfield Church would live out its life in a crucial time. And so, sometime after the formal organization of the Church, he began recording the ecclesiastical history of the orthodox of Westfield.[5]

Taylor's disagreements with Solomon Stoddard began shortly after he arrived in Westfield; in the exchange of letters during the early seventies, Stoddard was clearly impatient with Taylor's reluctance to gather the Westfield brethren.[6] While Stoddard's position seems justified—Taylor's near petulance must have been quite irritating—the paternalistic tone which Stoddard employed could not have pleased Taylor. After protracted delays, however, the General Court authorized the organization of the Westfield Church in the summer of 1678; Taylor was not ready, and the intervening year was still not enough time for him to complete the preparations. As he notes, he "had both hands full," and yet still "must go down into the Bay before the time" (p. 7). He may have wanted to consult with Increase Mather, who was emerging as Stoddard's major opponent; or he may have wanted to seek Mather's advice about the sermon he intended to preach on the day the church was organized. For whatever reason, the trip was apparently necessary, and the day of gathering, in light of Taylor's procrastination and his disagreement with the views Stoddard was beginning to express, did not promise to be a smooth one.

The visiting Elders, apparently led by Stoddard, "did not well approove" of the planned order of the day's ceremonies; and when they discovered that Taylor had not prepared a creedal statement, they "did stickle more [than] was meet" (p. 8). Taylor clearly attached little importance to a formal profession of faith, wanting simply to profess the "Doctrine laid down in the Catichisme of the Assemblies of Divin[es at West]menster so far as it goes, and where it is deficient, to acknowledge the Platform of C[hurch Disci]pline put forth" by the Cambridge Synod of 1648 (pp. 7–8). The visiting Elders, however, would not accept this offhand acknowledgement; the ceremonies were apparently delayed until Taylor wrote out some kind of statement of belief, which seems to have taken up most of the morning. Taylor then wanted to deliver the foundation sermon; the Elders insisted that the public relations be given next. The six foundation men and Taylor had written out their statements, intending to read them entire. Such a plan of proceeding would have focused the services on the significance of a public confession of faith, emphasizing by the very order of the service Taylor's disagreement with Stoddard. But the "Elders & Messenger of Northampton, & Hadly Churches drove on to the Contrary," and though the relations were "personally given," they were not read but delivered extempore. Had they been read, as Taylor notes, "it would have been to more edification" (p. 97).

How much of the Foundation Day Sermon was actually preached is not clear. The hour was late, and Taylor's lack of preparation had caused the ceremonies to consume more time than was expected. Taylor notes that since time was short, he went over only "the Choise heads" of the sermon, suggesting a shorter version than the one he later copied into the "Church Records." The Moderator then "propounded the Brethren to the Elders, & Messengers for their approbation," Taylor and the founding men "entered into the Covenant," and Stoddard was selected to proffer the "right hand of Christian Fellowship." Stoddard's brief welcome—"I do in the Name of the Churches give you the Right hand of Fellowship"—was not "altogether approved on" (p. 159), at least by Taylor, and perhaps others who were present as well. The Reverend Pelatiah Glover's statement of ordination also did not please Taylor, for the "charge was almost wholly omitted" (p. 160). One suspects that the visiting dignitaries were as much disturbed by Taylor's inadequate preparation—after nearly a decade of delay—and the lateness of the hour, as they were by anything Taylor may have said in the sermon. In any case, the proceedings finally ended, Psalm 122 ("I was glad when they said unto me, Let us go into the house of the Lord") was set, and the "Assembly was dismisst with the Blessing. & so the work was accomplisht."

THE PROFESSION OF FAITH

The version of the Westfield creed which Taylor drew up for the visiting Elders was no doubt considerably shorter than the one he finally copied into the "Records." Although he notes that in transcribing the general headings into the ledger, "some little addition is Set down," the manuscript indicates that he intended to develop the major headings in even more detail: more than half of the pages have only a few lines of script (see page 54), leaving most of the leaf blank. This final version, and the version Taylor presented to the visiting Elders, is apparently based on the earlier "Heads of Divinity" which he began in 1673, shortly after he arrived in Westfield: ". . . when I had served some two years here, we set up Conference me[eting in] which I went over all the Heads of Divinity unto the means of the Application [of Re]demption, in order to prepare them for a Church State. . ." (p. 4). These "heads" are the ones recorded in the untitled "Notebook," a manuscript of some two hundred pages with theological headings in Taylor's hand at the top of most of the pages.[7]

In large part the early "Heads of Divinity" is Taylor's paraphrase of the "Shorter Catechism" of the Westminster Assembly. The "Catechism" begins with the familiar "What is the chief end of Man?" and answers: "Man's chief end is to glorify God, and to enjoy him for ever." Taylor's heading reads: "Mans End ultimate Gods Glory." The second question of the "Catechism" reads: "What rule hath God given to direct us how we may glorify and enjoy him?" The response is that "the word of God, which is contained in the scriptures of the Old and New Testaments, is the only rule to direct us how we may glorify and enjoy him." Taylor's version is: "Mans Rule to this End: The Word of God, Isa. 8.20."

Yet Taylor does not follow the "Catechism" consistently. He often ignores some sections completely, and radically condenses others. Questions 23–26 (those dealing with Christ's office as Prophet, Priest, and King) become a single statement in the "Heads": "The Offices of the Redeemer Godward as his Priesthood, Manward, a Propheticall, Kingly Office."[8] He occasionally expands the question and answer sequences of the "Catechism" into larger units;[9] and there are a number of headings, particularly in the latter part of the "Notebook," which do not have parallels in either the Westminster Confession or the Cambridge Platform: such topics, for example, as "Dancing," "Stageplayes," "Foolish Songs," "Gluttony," "Fornication," "Beastiality," "Cheating," and so on. These exist as a single word or phrase at the top of each page, suggesting Taylor's initial concern with a comprehensive moral code, not simply a creedal statement. Though the "Notebook" generally includes the standard fare of most catechisms and creeds, Taylor also expands it to include matters ordinarily not found in such works.

By the time Taylor came to copy the version of the "Profession of Faith" into the "Church Records," however underdeveloped most of the headings are, he had received a copy of James Fitch's *The first Principles* (Boston, 1679), and the abbreviated entries in the "Heads of Divinity" are replaced by a series of neatly ordered categories, Ramistically structured, which generally follow the order of his father-in-law's catechism. In 1675, when Philip's War seemed imminent, Fitch's congregation, interpreting the impending calamities as a clear indication of God's displeasure with New England, "Solemnly renewed" their original covenant. As a part of their rededication, the group at Norwich established frequent catechetical instruction until the unregenerate children of members came to the "enjoyment of full Communion with the Church." Later, as Fitch notes, he was urged to make the catechism available for the benefit of others.[10] Increase Mather wrote a preface to the work, commending it and noting that ". . . if endeavours of this sort were more diligently attended, it would be one good means to prevent Degeneracy in the succeeding Generation."

The first Principles begins with the question, "What is Religion?"; it is, Fitch answers, "a Doctrine of living unto God, and consists of two parts, Faith and Observance." Taylor's "Profession" begins, "CHRISTIAN-ITIE, or the CHRISTIAN RELIGION, OR DIVINITIE, IS THE Doctrine OF LIVING UNTO GOD, consisting in $\begin{cases} \text{FAITH \&} \\ \text{OBEDIENCE.} \end{cases}$" Fitch discusses the name and general nature of Christianity, as does Taylor, and in much the same terms. Both writers discuss the nature of God, his "attributes," how God is made known by his attributes (which Taylor calls his "Communicable Properties"), the work of God in Creation, God's Providence, Man's apostasy, and so on. These sections in Taylor's "Profesion" are not as complete as his father-in-law's discussions, though from the blanks left Taylor apparently intended to expand them. Often he follows Fitch's order, but introduces a slightly different emphasis: in the special acts of God's Providence, for example, he is more concerned with the covenant relationship and the consequences of man's disobedience. And at times Taylor simply paraphrases Fitch's comments.[11]

The "Profession of Faith," however, is not completely derivative. Fitch generally provides the order of the various categories, and Taylor's statement of doctrice in indebted to this order, and to some particulars as well. But there are a number of sections which indicate Taylor's developing doctrinal concerns, passages which clearly set him off from Fitch's approach. Fitch discusses at some length, for example, the requirements of the Ten Commandments, a section invariably included in such catechisms. Taylor, however, omits any discussion of the Commandments, focusing instead on the "Seals of the Covenant of Grace." Unlike his father-in-law, Taylor is quite specific in relating his discussion of the Seals of Baptism and the Lord's Supper to his concern with the public acknowledgment of the work of saving grace. The "Primarie End of the Sacraments" is a sign and seal of the covenant; but the secondary, and just as meaningful end, is "the publick Profession of our Faith in God, & Communion of Saints" (p. 57). If there is no "publick Covenanting," according to Taylor, the seals are misused. The same impulse underlies his discussion of the "Use of the Keyes." It makes no sense to

Taylor if the discipline of the Church is not used both for expelling the unworthy and prohibiting their entrance in the first place. These extended discussions are related to Taylor's sense of the centrality of the Lord's Supper, and his disapproval of a more liberal admissions policy.

But the major difference between Fitch's work and Taylor's creed is the expanded section on the "Day of Judgment." Short sections on the Last Day commonly appear in creedal and catechetical statements; none however is developed to the length and degree of intensity Taylor manages to invest this section with. That he chose to include it in the "Church Records," and develop it as he does, while leaving underdeveloped more central concerns—at least more central in the standard creedal statement—indicates clearly the imaginative importance it possessed for him. Much of the reality of the golden sea of grace lies in the vividly literalistic intensity with which he views the punishments of Hell:

> . . . Oh! the body is all over tortured. Its Sunk down into a lake of burning fire & brimstone. It Swims in rappid Flames. If the whole Earth was all of a glowing fire Coale & the four winds of heaven were from all quarters blowing as so many bellows of a furnace upon it with all their fury to force its burning to the highest degree of intencness up & into the Center from every Side, & thou fixt in the very Centre thereof to have all this burning heat blown upon thee, & under the same kept alive by the power of God to beare this torment would not this be an unconceivable torment? but yet it would not be So much as a fleabiting compared unto the torments of Hell. (p. 84)

THE DEVELOPMENT OF THE
TAYLOR-STODDARD CONTROVERSY

Much of the discussion of the disagreements between Taylor and Stoddard—the "poet vs. the pope," to use Norman Grabo's felicitous phrase—tends to be inaccurate, partly because Stoddard's practice of a freer admissions policy has been dated much too early, and also because comments about their disagreements have been based upon the revised version of the Foundation Day Sermon, a different document from the one Taylor originally delivered.[12] The sermon Taylor preached the day the church was organized—assuming that he preached most of what is copied into the "Church Records"—cannot accurately be described as an "impassioned defense" of his views.[13] As it stands, it is a reasoned defense of the Half-Way Covenant, compromising in tone, and impersonal in its assertions. Taylor admits that in evaluating the validity of the Relation, the church's judgment must be "extended as far as the Rules of Christian Charity...can reach out its hand," and he acknowledges that since the judgment is made "from the Appearance of things, it is a fallable judgment"; such "... humane infirmities, as are to be found in the best of Gods people doth sway our judgment to hope & therefore to pass the Sentence of Christian Charity Concerning the reallity of Such a Persons Holiness..." (p. 126). Taylor's most stringent attack is upon those who do not content themselves with the "Revelation of Gods will in this matter," and he identifies, as an example of this perversion, the ecclesiastical hierarchies of the Roman and Anglican faiths, and "such like human devised stuffe" (pp. 145–46). It is true that much of what he says may reflect Stoddard's initial proposals for modifying the stipulations of the Half-Way Covenant. But Taylor does not attempt to force the issue, and the sermon ends with a clear statement of warning against contention, urging all to be "knit together in love." To express his position clearly on this day—and thus his allegiance to the proclamations of New England's synods—was no doubt expected of Taylor; but at this point in his relationship with Stoddard their differing views called for persuasion, not disputation. Stoddard's practice, whatever he may have argued for at the time, is still more than a decade away. The abrasive language and patronizing tone which characterize Taylor's later rejections of Stoddardism are not a part of the sermon he delivered on the day the Westfield Church was organized.

By early spring of 1688, however, Stoddard had taken concrete steps to initiate the practices he had been advocating. Taylor records in his "Commonplace Book" a copy of the letter he sent to Stoddard at this time: "A Letter sent to the Rev. Mr. Solomon Stoddard Pastor Church of Christ at Northampton when he was about to bring all Civilized & Catechised above 14 years old to the Lords Supper & throwing away all relations of the account of their hope to the Church; Westfield 13: 12ᵐ 1687/88".[14] Taylor notes that he presumes to "trouble Stoddard with a few lines upon a Report that comes very hot to us upon some occasions afoot in your Church with you." Stoddard may have begun, in sermons or weekday lectures, to urge his views upon the Northampton congregation. *The Safety of Appearing at the Day of Judgment* (Boston, 1687), published earlier in the same year, contains for the first time in print the principle of Stoddard's freer admission standards. The Lord's Supper, he asserts, is one of a number of guarantees which believers have and which qualifies them for the "safety of appearing." He then adds:

> ...but God no where requires a faith of assurance in those that partake of that Ordinance: this Ordinance is a special help to those that are in the dark with a good conscience: and though it must be granted that to partake of it without Faith is a sin: and so deserves damnation, and so it does to pray or hear without Faith: yet when the Apostle says that *he that eateth and drinketh unworthily, eateth and drinketh damnation or judgment on himself*..., he intends particularly that evil of not distinguishing this eating and drinking from common eating or drinking: doing it either ignorantly or profanely. (pp. 38-39)

After this publication, Stoddard apparently began to press his congregation to accept open admission; he had, Taylor says in the letter, "held one day of Debate...& hath fixt upon another." Given Stoddard's comments in *The Safety of Appearing*, Taylor no doubt kept himself informed of what went on in Northampton, and the "hot report" is more than likely an account of the first day of debate, and the scheduling of a second.

Taylor's letter goes to some length, however, to insist on the friendliness of his intentions. He confesses that he does not like "meddling in other men's matters," yet he believes that "Friendship will not permit" Stoddard to be offended. He insists again that he writes in friendship, and that he does not "design Disputation." Taylor then presents a series of reasons why he feels that the practice of bringing "all Civilized & Catechised above 14 years old" to the Supper will be a disturbing influence among the churches, how it will be slanderous to those "that brought us hither in this wilderness," and how it is "not according to the Foundation, nor Expectation" of Stoddard's own church. Taylor implies that Stoddard's proposals had not met with complete agreement in the Northampton congregation, and warns that "it's not a matter without hazzard of peace of your own Church, & people. & the Glory of your ministry is Gone, if your Church [is] tore to pieces." And he concludes: "God's faithfull ones in following ages will be ready to date the begining of New Englands Apostacy in Mr. Stoddards motions." Taylor's disapproval is clearly enunciated, but the letter is conciliatory in tone, and ends with an explicit attempt to avoid an open break with Stoddard.

Stoddard's reply, some three months later, is in the same tone. He accepts Taylor's letter as a "Fruite" of his "Zeale for the Cause of God,

& love to mee . . . ." But Stoddard makes clear that he is not to be dissuaded: "I have been abundantly satisfied these many years, that we did not attend the Will of God in this matter; & that to our neglect therein is the occasion of the greate prophaness, & corruption that hath over spread the land & therefore thought it both necessary for myselfe, that I might be found doing the Will of God; & necessary for the Country, that we might not go on further to forsake God. If in this matter I be under any mistake I should be glad of better Light." This exchange of letters indicates that however strongly both men felt, neither was willing at this time to force the matter to an open break. They were both aware of the potential for disturbance among the churches, and both seem to want to avoid that if possible. When Stoddard insists on pressing his views, however, when he has not found "better light," Taylor will be less charitable.

At some point between this interchange of letters and the fall of 1690, however, Stoddard provided Taylor with a complete statement of his reasons for "espousing" the extension of the Sacrament to Half-Way members. Taylor records this manuscript in his "Extracts" volume with the following heading: "Mr. Solomans Stoddard, Pastor to the Church of Christ at Northampton . . . being Contrarily opinionated, touching Admission into a Church State, hath Composed his thoughts in this matter in Arguing for this Proposition following, as he resolves it thus. All Such as do make a Solemn Profession of Faith & Repentance, & are of Godly Conversation, having Knowledge to Examine themselves, & discerning the Lords Body, are to be admitted to the Lords Supper." In his reply to Taylor's letter in 1688 Stoddard had noted that it was not "convenient to undertake to write a particular answer to all you say," and he had suggested that at some later time they might "discourse the matter at large." Taylor may have asked him to explain his position, and Stoddard obliged; the nine "Arguments for the Proposition" which Taylor copied in his manuscript book are clearly Stoddard's views, and Taylor specifically attributes them to him.[15]

Stoddard's manuscript begins with a series of questions and answers explaining the terms of the "proposition" that if men fulfill certain requirements—not including a public profession of saving grace—they are to be admitted to the Lord's Supper. Taylor's strategy in his response to Stoddard's "Arguments," the "Animadversions," is to quote each of these arguments, granting what seems to be acceptable— which is very little—but attacking Stoddard's reasoning, and particularly his misreading of scripture. If, Taylor asserts, by visible saints Stoddard means those who have an "Experimentall Knowledge of Spirituall things," then there can be no disagreement with his first argument; but if they do not possess this life, to "sett food to such as are dead, is paganish, who sett a mess of Beans in the Grave with their dead" (p. 93). Higher qualifications than simple moral behavior are required; a profession of "Faith and repentance," Taylor continues, is not simply an "assent to Doctrine," but a profession of the "evidence of Grace in the heart" (p. 95). As to Stoddard's assertions about the requirements of the Jewish Church, Taylor notes that the Hebrews were a "Visibly Perverse, Wicked, Murmuring, Mutinous, Rebellious, Idolatrous, untractable people," that the typological nature of the Old Testament did not contain the higher spiritual qualifications of the antitypical nature of the New. They were, he asserts, only types—and hence incomplete—of the "Good things to Come..." (p. 96). Taylor agrees that those who are qualified for membership are also qualified for Full Communion, if by that qualification Stoddard means more than "Doctrinall Knowledge," for such knowledge alone does not make an individual a "Member in the Mysticall Church."

Taylor then moves to Stoddard's sixth argument, that persons fit to be baptized are fit for the Lord's Supper. The "object" of the two ordinances, Taylor insists, is quite different: one is a seal of initiation, the other of confirmation; admission to baptism is by "Federall Holiness onely," while admission to the Lord's Supper is by "Sanctifying Grace." It does not follow, he argues, that because baptism is an initial stage in the growth of grace that the Supper is upon the same level: different qualifications, as the scriptures demonstrate, are required. Taylor further discusses Stoddard's assertion that excluding non-scandalous believers from the Sacrament is a form of excommunication. Such individuals may not be "well qualified" for Full Communion, but that, Taylor asserts, is not to say that they are so "Ill-Qualified" as to be laid under censure. All are members of the Catholic church, "Tag, Rag , & Bobtail"; but not all are qualified to be members of particular churches. Citing from Origen and Augustine, Taylor insists that the practice of the early churches demonstrates the absurdity of Stoddard's position. Finally, Taylor argues that the practice of confirmation, neither scripturally nor historically, was for admittance to the Lord's Supper as Stoddard had argued. Confirmation in Taylor's view, was simply a ceremony in which believers baptized in their infancy were confirmed when they "offrd themselves to be catechized." There is, Taylor concludes, "not one argument given to make it probable," nor is there any evidence in the "Practice of the Church both the Primitive & the Protestant," which indicates that confirmation was preparatory to admission to Full Communion.

Before Taylor had completed the "Animadversions," however, and by October 1690, Stoddard had clearly gone beyond arguing for the simple extension of Communion privileges to Half-Way members. The specific sermon which he preached calling for a radically different view of the nature of the Lord's Supper—radical in the context of New England Congregationalism at any rate—is transcribed in Taylor's "Extracts" volume, partly in his hand and partly in the hand of someone else: "Some notes of the said Mr. Stoddards touching the Lords Supper as a Converting Ordinance preacht before he urged his Church to the Practice thereof which motion he urged them to Oct. 5. 1690."[16] Whatever Stoddard's views may have been between 1677 and 1690, Taylor indicates that his revised position on the nature of the Supper itself was not advanced until the "Winter of 1690." Taylor's proximity, his concern with his neighbor's innovations, his obtaining notes of the specific sermon, and so on, make it almost certain that whatever the Mathers and others thought—and he would have surely kept them informed—he was not much disturbed about Stoddard's actions during the 1680s because whatever he may have proposed, he did not actually begin the practice of "unregenerate" communion until 1690.

Stoddard's sermon on Galatians 3.1 presents arguments for extending the right of the Lord's Supper to non-scandalous persons who have reached the age of majority. The doctrine which Stoddard draws from the text is that "the Lords Supper is appointed by Jesus Christ, for the begetting of Grace as Well as for the Strengthning of Grace." Stoddard argues, in the first place, that although the Lord's Supper may be viewed as limited to visible saints, given the nature of fallen man and the fallacy of human judgment, some who partake are not in fact saints. As a result, since "many must be admitted by Gods Institution to participate in the Lords Supper that are not reall Saints," it follows that the "Lords Supper is for the begetting of Grace."[17] Stoddard argues that God would not design an ordinance which was not for the "good, & Salvation of men"; hence, like the other ordinances, the Lord's Supper "hath in its own Nature a tendency to the Begetting of Faith." Christ commands all men to "Take, Eate," which demonstrates, Stoddard asserts, that ". . . there is a sure liberty, Sufficient warrant, & that its no presumption to come to him. Here is a Divine Command which shews that its a Duty to come: & that its dangerous to stay away from Christ. & this Offer is made in the Lords Supper absolutly, not upon Condition that they have believed already, but whether they have, or have not, they are invited..." (p. 133). He further insists that if the Supper is only for the strengthening of Grace and not for the begetting of it, then men must possess certain knowledge of their spiritual state, which, in point of fact, is not within man's capabilities. And if a man awaits absolute certainty, Stoddard says, "he becomes guilty & procures a curse instead of a blessing, hee would be bound in conscience to forbeare..." (p. 135). Stoddard's final two arguments follow from this basic assumption that certain knowledge of a right to the Table is impossible to attain: if, for example, one misleads himself and finds after he has taken the Sacrament that he is not converted, then he must abstain, unless it is indeed a converting ordinance. And, finally, Stoddard argues that all ordinances are provided as much for the begetting of grace as they are for the sustenance of it: "...the word is to be preached to all, baptisme is to be applyed to all Church members, the censures to offending members, the Supper is to be given to members that are adult, & without offense..." (p. 137).

These early manuscript interchanges, then, provide the context in which Taylor revises the sermon he preached on the day the Westfield Church was organized.[18] In discussing the manuscript of the revised sermon, Grabo notes that in the course of the argument it is "as if Stoddard himself were speaking,"[19] which of course is the case; for Taylor quotes directly from Stoddard's "Arguments for the Proposition" and refers explicitly to the major assertions of the Galatians sermon. The added material in the second version of the Foundation Sermon focuses mainly on the doctrine of the converting nature of the Supper, but large sections from the "Animadversions," particularly those concerned with the necessity of a public relation of saving grace, are also included. Stoddard had not commented upon the right of the particular congregation to evaluate its members, focusing primarily upon the duty of self-examination. In the "Animadversions" and the additions to the Foundation Sermon, Taylor insists that the responsibility of fitness for Full Communion lies not only in self-examination, but also in the "judgment to be passt by the Church upon those she admitts into a Full State..." (p. 316). Hence he begins his revisions by insisting that "every Distinct Society of men have a power essentiall to itselfe... in its right exercise for its own preservation." Having established that the Church has the responsibility to apply the "Keyes of Binding, & Loosing," Taylor then turns to the points Stoddard had raised in the "Arguments." Stoddard had indicated, for example, that there were three qualifications for admission to the Lord's Supper: "a solemn Profession of Faith & Repentance"; "godly Conversation"; and "Knowledge to examine a mans Selfe." Taylor had established his position on the first and third matters in the first version of the sermon; he then begins the section added to the revised version by quoting a "theoretical" objection, which is in fact Stoddard's second qualification: "Let the Life, & Conversation Speake. This is Obvious to all." And Taylor replies: "So let it; and let it be heard too...for a Profession, & Faith without it are vain..." (p. 317). However, he adds, this is not enough. Stoddard had defined "godly Conversation" as walking in "all the Commandments of God, not living in the Practice of any known Sin, or Omision of any Duty."[20] To accept this view, Taylor asserts, "would open the Church doore & let even Socrates, & Cato in as suitable matter of the Church." And in the first part of this added material, he quotes and answers a series of possible objections, which in fact are the positions Stoddard defends in the "Arguments."

But Taylor's primary concern in the revised version of the Foundation Sermon is to refute the doctrine of Stoddard's Galatians sermon that the "Lords Supper is appointed by Jesus Christ, for the begetting of Grace as Well as for the Strengthning of Grace," a view Taylor could not have considered when he first preached the sermon. Nor, except incidentally, in the "Animadversions." Stoddard had tentatively stated this view in the "Arguments," asserting that to deny visible saints access to the Lord's Supper is to hinder the "increase of Grace." Taylor is aware that a Public Relation is hardly to the point if the Supper is viewed as converting, and he develops a series of "Artificiall" and "Inartificiall" proofs designed to demonstrate the fallacy of Stoddard's view. He argues, first of all, that there are "absolutely necessary" antecedents preparatory to participation in the Sacrament: Baptism, a "full State of Churchhood," and self-examination, which, Taylor insists, involves more than the superficial examination Stoddard requires.

Taylor then moves, in his second major argument, to distinguish between the Lord's Supper and other ordinances designed for conversion. The properties of a converting ordinance, he argues, are that it is to be extended to those in sin (such as the preaching of the word and prayer); that the unconverted are under a "Duty to attend these means"; that converting arguments have gracious promises as well as "threatonings"; and that there is clear evidence that converting ordinances do convert. The Lord's Supper, he asserts, "hath none of these Adjuncts attending upon it." In the third place, he argues that that ordinance which requires Saving Faith for its benefits can be no converting ordinance; when Christ said, Take, Eat, he had intended only those who could benefit from the Sacrament, not those who would drink damnation upon themselves. Taylor reiterates his stand that the ordinances seal different things: Baptism is a "Seale of Initiation, the Lords Supper of Confirmation." That ordinance, Taylor says in his fifth argument, which, if attended unworthily, "makes guilty of the Body & Blood of Christ," does not have the characteristics of a converting ordinance. He then concludes this series of arguments by discussing the absurdities which "unavoidably follow" by viewing the Supper as a converting ordinance, as, for example, that a person in a state of sin can worthily partake of the Lord's Supper.

The second part of these additions to the Foundation Sermon focuses upon "inartificial" arguments, scriptural passages and testimonies from the Church Fathers and Protestant leaders, which demonstrate that the requirement of a public relation and "regenerate" communion were the practice of the early Church, and of orthodox Protestants from the beginning. Taylor also adds at this point a discussion of the proper role of church censures, insisting that in the administration of censure, as well as in admittance to Full Communion, it is incumbent upon the individual "fully to satisfy the Charity of the Church." And he concludes this section: "But here are Still some piddling objections that some disaffected Spirits cast out, as bolts shot against the Case, which I shall endeavour to Obviate thus..." (p. 342). The last of these objections is one of Stoddard's major arguments in the Galatians sermon: "...these Relations Discourage many good Christians from seeking Full Communion." In his response in the "Animadversions," Taylor had called this a "pitiful" objection; here, in the material added to the Foundation Sermon, he comments that if "this was Good arguing, then we might bring Gods Laws to mans Will, & make them Suite every man: or as a Taylor doth the Cloath, Cut out of the Piece a garment that he fits to the back of his Customer. Such Commands as are too Streat, wreath them, as on the Tyrants iron Bed. Such as are too wide, or large, Cut them shorter.... What Divinity is this?" (p. 343). When the hearts of men are against it, Taylor says, then it is surely God's law; though such individuals may be "Good Christians," they are not "Good enough for Full Communion: For they are so humorsom, that they are not like either to receive benefit from, nor be beneficiall to, the Fellowship."

Except for minor stylistic changes, then, Taylor's design in revising the Foundation Day Sermon is to take into account the additional arguments Stoddard had presented in the "Arguments for the Proposition" and the Galatians sermon. The main thesis of the sermon Taylor preached on the day the Church was organized had been based on the right and obligation of a particular church to require a public relation for admission to full fellowship; in the additions to the second version, however, Taylor introduces material in response to Stoddard's additional arguments, particularly that the Lord's Supper may be viewed as a converting ordinance. For Taylor as well, however, is the necessity of defending the practices of the founders of New England. Near the end of the "Arguments" Stoddard had acknowledged that "tho' the practice was taken up at first, but as a usefull thing: yet many now make it an Ordinance; there is as much weight laid on it, as if it were a Divine Institution.... This people came from their Native Country to injoy the Pure Institutions of Christ. And we should be the more Carefull to keep ourselves exactly to them" (p. 84). To this Taylor responds: "Our authour would now insinuate a Warping from what was the Principles laid down by the leaders of this people...."[21] Such a view to Taylor is simply incomprehensible.

But Taylor was not through with the subject. In the second version of the Foundation Sermon, in a minor aside, he had insisted that the unconverted could not come to the Sacrament because they "wanted the Wedden Garment."[22] In the fall of 1693, then, he initiated a series of eight sermons, the *Treatise Concerning the Lord's Supper*, ordering them around the parable of the guest who lacked the "Wedden Garment." In the fourth and longest sermon in the series, in addition to other arguments, Taylor incorporates much of the material from the "Animadversions" and the revised Foundation Sermon. He refers to Stoddard's sermon on Galatians 3.1 in specific terms, citing from it, and framing his response in the terms he had used in the revised Foundation Sermon. In the course of his *Treatise* arguments, for example, Taylor notes: "Another argument is this: the Lord's Supper hath in its nature a tendency to the begetting of faith" (p.135). This is, of course, the doctrine of Stoddard's Galatians sermon. Taylor then adds, "I have laid down proofs to the contrary. See them among the arguments," referring to the revised Foundation Sermon. "But," he continues, "how is this made out?" Stoddard had asserted in the Galatians sermon that when Christ said, Take, Eat, this was a "Divine Invitation to come to Christ which shews that there is a sure liberty, Sufficient warrant, & that its no presumption to come to him" (p. 133). Taylor cites this passage directly in the *Treatise* sermon: "Here is a divine invitation, which shews that here is true liberty, sufficient warrant, and no presumption to come" (p. 136). Such an argument, Taylor insists in both the "Animadversions" and revised Foundation Sermon, as he does in this passage in the *Treatise*, would lead to administering the Supper to "infidels and unbelievers"; such an argument is not only "sick of the lax," but is also a perversion of Christ's invitation, which was "made only to them in full communion that appear at the particular celebration of the Lord's Supper" (p. 137).

The result of Taylor's more than ten years of thought and study, of re-examination of his position in light of Stoddard's views as presented in the "Arguments" and the Galatians sermon, then, reaches its culmination in the eight sermons which make up the *Treatise Concerning the Lord's Supper*, particularly Sermon 4, the longest one of the series. The plot to make the Lord's Supper a converting ordinance had "budded and blossomed" in New England, and Taylor explicitly identifies Stoddard's views, citing passages from the two Stoddard manuscripts he possessed. The *Treatise* sermons, however, are more successful, because— apart from devoting eight sermons to the subject—the image of the "wedden garment" permits Taylor to order and structure his arguments more forcefully than before. The Feast and the guest who comes without the proper garment become the controlling metaphor for the sanctity of the Supper, and so allows Taylor to distinguish more precisely between central and peripheral matters. Quoting from Stoddard's two manuscripts, incorporating revised material from the "Animadversions" and second version of the Foundation Sermon, Taylor manages to control and clarify his own deepest convictions. He discusses again the requirements of a meaningful profession of faith (Sermon 2, p. 28), the implications of "godly Conversation" (2, pp. 28, 46), the proper reading of the requirements of the Jewish ceremonies (2, pp. 73–74; 4, pp. 99, 126–28, 132–35; 6, p. 169), the practice of the New Testament church (2, pp. 30ff.; 4, pp. 67, 78), the examples of the Church Fathers and Protestant reformers (2, pp. 31ff.; 4 pp. 67, 89–90, 94–95, 111–16, 125), and—in more detail than any other subject—the inconsistencies of Stoddard's view that the Lord's Supper is a converting ordinance (2, pp. 41ff.; 4, pp. 64, 65, 72–146).

The disagreements with Stoddard do not end of course with the *Treatise Concerning the Lord's Supper*; Stoddard was not to be dissuaded. He repeated his position in *The Doctrine of Instituted Churches* (London, 1700), defended himself again in *The Inexcusableness of Neglecting the Worship of God, under A Pretence of being in an Unconverted Condition* (Boston, 1708), and acquitted himself well in response to Increase Mather's *A Dissertation, wherein the Strange Doctrine...is Examined and Refuted* in the reasoned *An Appeal to the Learned...Against the Exceptions of Mr. Mather* (Boston, 1709). Taylor does not seem to have been involved in these interchanges, but he responds again to Stoddard's arguments in a manuscript in the "Extracts" volume, "The Appeale Tried." And at about this same time, in Meditations 102–111, composed in 1711 and 1712, Taylor was apparently again preaching against Stoddardism. Their personal relationships had also suffered, for the disciplinary cases in the "Church Records" indicate that Stoddard's importance in the area often led Taylor's disaffected parishioners to appeal to the authority of the "pope."[23]

Yet while they disagreed on much, both men seem to be motivated by what they perceived to be the decline of piety in New England churches. Stoddard, however, is willing to re-think the assumptions of the founders, acknowledging that while it may "possibly be a fault and an aggravation of a fault, to depart from the ways of our Fathers," it may "also be a vertue...to depart from them in some things." If, he notes, "we be forbidden to Examine their practices, that will cut off all hopes of Reformation."[24] From as early as the Reforming Synod of 1679, one of Stoddard's most insistent laments is his belief that there "has not been one Sin generally reformed these twenty years. Instead of growing better and better, the Country grows worse and worse." Stoddard may have been impelled by his anti-democratic sentiments, or his preference for Presbyterian policy,[25] but the impetus behind his innovations seems more than likely to be his intensely personal response to the degeneracy he found about him. He writes that

> the design of our Fathers in Planting this Country, was that their Posterity might fear and serve the Lord. They would not have left *England* meerly for their own quietness; but they were afraid that their Children would be corrupted there. But what advantage will the Planting of this Land be, if we should grow a corrupt People

here? as good have been bad in Old *England* as in New: what great matter is it, if we be delivered from Superstition, if we carry in other respects wickedly. The Planters of the Country might even repent that ever they came over into the Land . . . .[26]

In order to combat the sins he found on every hand, Stoddard intended to bring as many "sinners" as he could under the discipline and control of the church, even if it meant "unregenerate" communion. And this, of course, Taylor would not—could not—excuse. "I cannot but be grieved," Taylor wrote, "to see such a worthy pen make such a mangling work of the holy oracles of God."[27]

The Problems of Church Discipline

The majority of the disciplinary cases Taylor records in the "Church Records" are fairly standard fare in New England churches— fornication, land disputes, backbiting, drunkenness, and so on[28]—but the case which leads to Taylor's suspension of an unruly member (and calls forth the two disciplinary sermons) touches on more central issues, and seriously disturbs the peace in his congregation. Taylor's actions do not reveal him in a completely flattering light, and the repeated justification of his position seems somewhat strident. On the other hand, it is too easy to label him a "strict, haughty, and domineering minister when the circumstances seemed to call for it, willing to honor the *vox populi* only so far as it agreed with his own decisions."[29] He could be inflexible and jealous of his authority, and aware of his prerogatives; but he was also fulfilling the explicitly defined responsibilities incumbent upon him as sole leader of his congregation. Given the commitments he expresses in the controversy with Stoddard, and his untiring devotion to the pronouncements of New England synods, he could have done little else.

In brief, the case involves attempts by various members of the Church to have one of Westfield's original settlers, Walter Lee, declared incompetent and made a ward of the court.[30] Taylor refused to sign a petition drawn up by Benjamin Smith, a member of the congregation, requesting the court to place Lee under "guardians," though Taylor later drew up one himself with other members of the Church, which seems to have been used in the court hearing to effect what Smith desired. When Taylor accused Smith of distorting his petition, "angry words passt on both sides." Taylor then forbade Smith's appearance at the Lord's

Supper until he had given "satisfaction." At the next Church meeting, Smith refused to do so, and after further harsh words, Taylor attempted to force the Church to vote Smith an offender. Because there was some confusion about Lee's legal status, and because Smith also asked time to reconsider, the Church postponed action until the next conference day.

When they met again, Smith attempted to give in a grudging confession, Taylor pressed him, more harsh words were exchanged, and—though this is not too clear—the congregation apparently refused to vote on the matter. Taylor, forced to "New Methods," laid Smith under a "Pastoral admonition," leaving the impression with some members of the Church that he had also suspended them from the Lord's Table. Either at this meeting, or a subsequent one, Taylor finally persuaded the Church to support his suspension of Smith, though under questionable voting procedures. In the meantime, Smith had appealed to his uncle, Samuel Partridge, Justice of the Hampshire Sessions, Solomon Stoddard, and the ministers of the Springfield churches. To further complicate matters—and increase Taylor's ire—without Taylor's knowledge some of the membership, under the leadership of Isaac Phelps, the local schoolmaster, attempted to resolve the matter by arranging for Smith to observe the Lord's Supper at the West Springfield Church. Taylor would not accept this as a valid action of the membership, although he met with Smith and the two neighboring ministers and grudgingly accepted a confession written out at that session. Taylor then lectured the Church on their failings, and called for a fast day preparatory to administering the Supper. Four months after the trouble began Taylor administered the Sacrament; five months later he preached the two disciplinary sermons justifying his actions.

The Westfield Church had never had but one of the three ruling officers stipulated in the Cambridge Platform of 1648, and Taylor was accustomed to exercising the authority designed to be divided among the pastoral, teaching, and ruling elders.[31] And, as far as the Records reveal, his authority had never been significantly challenged. That authority, however much some ministers may have tempered it in actual practice, was quite comprehensive:

> The powr which Christ has committed to the Elders, is to feed & rule the church of God, & accordingly to call the church together upon any weighty occasion, when the members so called, without just cause, may not refuse to come: nor when they are come, depart before they are dismissed: nor speak in

the church, before they have leave from the elders: nor continue so doing, when they require silence, nor may they oppose nor contradict the judgment or *sentence* of the Elders,
without sufficient & weighty cause, becaus such practices
are manifestly contrary unto order, & government, & in-lets
of disturbance, & tend to confusion.[32]

New England congregations were not unaware—no matter what gestures
were made toward the liberties of the brethren—where authority
resided in a particular church:

This *Government* of the church, is a mixt Government.... In
respect of *Christ*..., & the Soveraigne power residing in him, &
exercised by him, it is a *Monarchy*: In Respect of the body, or
Brotherhood of the church, & powr from Christ graunted unto
them, it resembles a *Democracy*, In respect of the *Presbyetry* & powr
comitted to them, it is an *Aristocracy*.[33]

The Reforming Synod had defined in even more precise detail than the
earlier assemblies the extent of ministerial power. In the "Propositions"
assembled in the second session of that Synod, for example, the framers
had explicitly stated that "the pastor of a church may by himself *authoritatively* suspend from the Lord's-table a brother accused or suspected
of a scandal...."[34] The "Propositions" also define the Elder's authority
as an absolute "*negative* on the votes of the brethren."[35] As might
be expected, Taylor was quite conscious of the power which resided
in his office, and within the framework of that authority, he acted within
his rights.

Moreover, the justification of his actions in the disciplinary
sermons is impeccable. In his reading of scripture and his citations from
the various Synod documents, he has no difficulty in demonstrating the
rightness of his procedures. The first sermon has as its text Christ's
instructions for dealing with an offender: treat with the individual
privately, and if that is not successful, "tell it to the Church." The
fraternity—within the limitations imposed by the Elder's authority—
have the responsibility for "binding and loosing" (Matthew 18. 17–18).
Taylor's argument is quite direct: Christ is a king, kings have subjects
"liable to offend his Law"; therefore, he has established a court to
enforce his laws. That court is the "Particular Society of believers in
Covenant together to attende upon all Gospell ordinances of Divin
worship & Discipline" (p. 385). The society of believers, however, is
ruled by the Elders, "the highest Authority that Christ hath in the

Church"; the "Right of Rule [is] in the hand of the Rulers" (p. 399). The fraternity, therefore, are not to shirk the responsibility they have to enforce Christ's laws—subject, of course, to the determination of the Elders. The major emphasis in the second disciplinary sermon is to demonstrate that the Elders have an authority to "binde & loose" distinct from that of the body of the church. Such power is not the "Peculiar Priviledge of the Church," but of the church acting under the direction and in consort with their Elders. It is at this point in the second sermon, then, that Taylor refers specifically to the Benjamin Smith case. The Westfield congregation, he asserts, avoided their scriptural responsibilities in two specifics: they refused to act when he as Elder first brought the case before them; and they then acted without his knowledge, thereby subverting his office authority.

Of course the matter was not that simple. Taylor was "right," but by insisting on his prerogatives he created a situation out of all proportion to the original incident. Smith was insulting, but his initial response may have been the result of the unproved accusation that he had misused the petition Taylor sent to the court. Taylor would not drop it at that point, but insisted on "satisfaction." In addition, his "petition" to authority, and his earlier disagreements with Smith during a visit as Westfield's physician,[36] suggest that Taylor's reaction was personal as well as principled. In any case, the bickering and charges and counter-charges—so characteristic of New England infighting—seriously marred the peace of the Church.

Edward Taylor's "history" of the acts of God's Chosen in Westfield indicates a clear awareness of the importance of his role in that history, and in the larger context of New England as well. There were, of course, the daily tasks that any minister faced. Children had to be catechized, crops tended, families comforted, wood supplies obtained, sinners counseled, herbs harvested, and so on. And in these matters—as well as in his service as the town's physician—he seems to have been as effective as any other minister. His relationships with his parishioners reveal a man careful of high standards of morality, but understanding of the human weaknesses of his church family. Stephen Kellog, for example, cited several times before the Church for public drunkenness, is treated by Taylor more gently than by some of the members, who declined to accept Kellog's confession of remorse.[37] And the major disciplinary problem in the Church came about because Taylor insisted that Walter Lee—

not the most sainted of the church family—be treated fairly. Firm, and only occasionally rigid, fair and understanding, his long tenure as Westfield's minister, even in his later more irascible years, is remarkable for the relatively few serious problems which occurred. At no time during the more than fifty years, for example, is there any indication that his church family "came to blows," as is reported of Stoddard's Northampton congregation.[38]

Beyond his daily pastoral responsibilities, Taylor also seems to have been a minister who exemplified to his people the joy of faith. The exuberance and delight, passionate devotion and spiritual buoyancy which his faith provided, and which we sense in the sermons and recognize in his poetry, were surely a central part of his ministry. What from our viewpoint seems dogmatic may have been viewed by his congregation as an admirable defense of the beliefs which brought them—and him—into the wilderness. Whatever the case, in the days of New England's relative decline, his spiritual leadership was more than ordinarily effective. When the Church was gathered in 1679, for example, about thirty percent of the adult population were admitted to full communion; by 1689, nearly forty percent were members in full standing, and, at a time when, as Edmund Morgan notes, the "proportion of church members to congregation seems to have been seldom more than one in five and usually less...."[39] Even at the turn of the century, one in three inhabitants of the town were church members in full standing. A number of factors may have contributed to the relatively large number of full members, but certainly one of them must have been the quality of Taylor's ministerial influence. His warmth and sensitivity, devotion to spiritual values, and his conscientious care of his people must have been widely influential in the lives of the congregation.

In addition to Taylor's sense of the importance of the orthodox behavior of the Westfield Church in the Connecticut Valley, however, he was also aware of the larger context in which the "acts" of God's Westfield Elect were carried on. Throughout his writing—and especially in these Records—Taylor's sense of the historical importance of the New England experiment is always evident. The unfolding of God's determinations in Westfield was of course important in itself; but it was also significant in the history of the errand which had brought them all into western Massachusetts. God's displeasure with the failings of his New England followers had been clearly expressed in the ravages of Philip's War. In quite specific ways, Satan had attempted to thwart the designs of Westfield's faithful. And when they had survived the warfare, and were gathered into a church state the month before the Reforming Synod met in Boston, none could have been unaware of the importance of this newly gathered congregation, and the necessity for it to reflect the regeneration of New England's ideals.

Hence Stoddard's attempts to modify the decisions of previous synods, and his suggestion that the founders may have been mistaken in their views, must have heightened Taylor's—and his congregation's—resolve to be found among the faithful. They were gathered according to the principles enunciated by the founders, and as long as Taylor was an active minister, those principles were the standards by which the congregation lived. Had he not been so personally involved, Taylor would have still opposed Stoddard's views, for his sense of Reformed history centered on New England's crucial role in that history. The beliefs which God's New England faithful had exhibited for all to see were not simply the expression of an out-of-the-way provincial society, but the culmination of the central impulses of the Reformation. However much those beliefs were challenged, and however much individuals and congregations failed to live up to them, the principles remained the same. Whatever the society at large or neighboring ministers and churches did, Westfield, ministered to by Edward Taylor, would be found among the saving remnant. His life, as the inscription on his tombstone aptly puts it, was to serve faithfully his generation by his service to God:

Here Rests ye Body
of ye Revd Mr Edward
Taylor, ye Aged,
Venerable, Learned,
& Pious Pastor of ye
Church of Christ in
this Town, who after
He had served God
and his Generation
Faithfully for many
Years, fell asleep
June 24, 1729 in ye
87 year of his age

T.M.D.

Notes to the Introduction

[1]Meditation 46, Series I. See also *The Poems of Edward Taylor*, ed. Donald E. Stanford (New Haven: Yale University Press, 1960), p. 74. Here, and throughout, we cite from our own transcriptions. We are indebted to the Yale University Library for permission to cite from the Taylor manuscripts in their possession.

[2]See *Edward Taylor's Treatise Concerning the Lord's Supper*, ed. Norman S. Grabo (East Lansing: Michigan State University Press, 1966), p. liv.

[3]See below, pp. 80–81. Subsequent references to the present edition will be made parenthetically in the text.

[4]Much of the early critical disagreement about Taylor's orthodoxy, for example, was uninformed about the material in the "Church Records." For a convenient summary of these varying views, see Stanford, "Edward Taylor on the Lord's Supper," *American Literature*, 27 (May 1955), 172–78.

[5]The handwriting of these Records indicates that they were written out as early as 1680–1682, and, except for the disciplinary cases, and baptismal and admissions records, completed by the mid-1680s.

[6]See the letters quoted below, CR, note 6. Paul R. Lucas's account of these events is grossly inaccurate, as these manuscripts make clear; see "A New Moral Order," *Valley of Discord: Church and Society along the Connecticut River, 1636–1725* (Hanover, N.H.: University Press of New England, 1976), especially pp. 121ff.

[7]For a discussion of this manuscript, see Charles W. Mignon, "Another Taylor Manuscript at Yale," *Yale University Library Gazette*, 41 (October 1966), 72–73.

[8]This statement comprises headings on four consecutive pages.

[9]See, for example, Questions 30–32 of the "Catechism" dealing with the "Application of Redemption." These three questions provide headings for six pages in Taylor's "Notebook."

[10]Fitch's account of these incidents appears in the introduction to *An Explanation of the Solemn Advice Recommended by the Council . . .* (Boston, 1683).

[11]One should note, however, that the statements by both men are fairly conventional definitions of doctrine. The "Shorter Catechism," for example, defines Justification as "an act of God's free grace, wherein he pardoneth all our

sins, and accepteth us as righteous in his sight, only for the righteousness of Christ imputed to us, and received by faith alone." Fitch's definition reads: "Justification is that whereby the Righteousness of Christ being imputed to a believer, and by Faith applyed, God is reconciled to him, and he is absolved from the guilt of sin, and pronounced righteous and worthy of eternal life, in and for the sake of Christ" (p. 48). And Taylor's: "Justification is a gracious sentence of God passt upon a true believer in Christ, whereby on the account of Christs Righteousness, he being freed from guilt of Sin, is pronounced truely Righteous in the sight of God eternally" (p. 50).

[12]Perry Miller wrongly asserts that Stoddard had begun to admit the unregenerate to the Supper as early as 1677; see his statements in "Solomon Stoddard, 1643-1729," *Harvard Theological Review*, 34 (October 1941), 277-320, and *The New England Mind: From Colony to Province* (Cambridge: Harvard University Press, 1967), pp. 226ff. For a discussion of some of Miller's inaccuracies, see James P. Walsh, "Solomon Stoddard's Open Communion: A Reexamination," *New England Quarterly*, 43 (March 1970), 97-114.

Grabo's analysis of the early disagreements between Stoddard and Taylor, though accurate in general points, would have benefited by a comparison of the two versions of the Foundation Sermon; see "Edward Taylor on the Lord's Supper," *Boston Public Library Quarterly*, 12 (January 1960), 22-36; and *Edward Taylor* (New York: Twayne, 1961), pp. 31-39. For an analysis of the differences between these two versions, see Dean Hall and Thomas M. Davis, "The Two Versions of Edward Taylor's Foundation Day Sermon," *Resources for American Literary Study*, 5 (Autumn 1975), 199-216. A full analysis of the disagreements between Stoddard and Taylor appears in the introduction of *Edward Taylor vs. Solomon Stoddard: The Nature of the Lord's Supper* (Boston: Twayne, 1981).

[13]Robert G. Pope, *The Half-Way Covenant: Church Membership in Puritan New England* (Princeton: Princeton University Press, 1969), p. 254.

[14]This interchange of letters was first printed in Grabo, "The Poet to the Pope: Edward Taylor to Solomon Stoddard," *American Literature*, 32 (May 1960), 197-201. We cite from our own transcriptions.

[15]Further reference to these nine arguments will be titled "Arguments for the Proposition" or "Arguments." This manuscript has been previously published in "Solomon Stoddard's 'Arguments' Concerning Admission to the Lord's Supper," *Proceedings* of the American Antiquarian Society, 86 (April 1976), 75-111.

An earlier version of these same arguments, incorporated in an Increase Mather rebuttal, has recently been edited by Everett Emerson and Mason I. Lowance. This manuscript, in Cotton Mather's hand, but clearly Increase's work, was written about 1680; internal evidence establishes that Mather compiled—but did not publish—this early response to Stoddard's views shortly after the 1679 Synod (see "Increase Mather's Confutation of Solomon Stoddard's Observations Respecting the Lord's Supper 1680," *Proceedings* of the American Antiquarian Society, 83 [April 1973], 29-65).

During the abortive debate at the Synod meetings, Stoddard apparently drew up a series of propositions designed to convince the Elders to credit his freer admissions policy; Mather must have obtained a copy at that time or shortly after. Taylor's manuscript copy represents a more fully developed defense of Stoddard's views, indicating that Taylor's copy represents substantial development on Stoddard's part.

In the "Confutation," for example, Mather includes only one direct citation from Stoddard's text, other than the nine propositions. Stoddard had argued that the stipulation of a public relation was a recent phenomenon, and had not been required by New England's founders. In his refutation, Mather states that "there is one expression I cannot but sett a remark upon. The words are these. *It will hardly be made to appear that one divine from the Apostles dayes till within these forty years did plead for relations....*" In Taylor's version, the phrase is altered from "forty years" to "fifty years" suggesting that approximately a decade had passed since Stoddard first drew up a defense of his views.

[16]Taylor refers to the doctrine of this sermon in Argument 6 of his "Animadversions," indicating that he was still working on his response to Stoddard's "Arguments" when he received a copy of the Galatians sermon. The sequence of the manuscripts in this early stage of the controversy is:

> Foundation Day Sermon, 24 August 1679;
> Taylor's letter to Stoddard, 12 February 1688;
> Stoddard's reply, 4 June 1688;
> Stoddard's "Arguments for the Proposition," ca 1689–1690;
> Taylor's "Animadversions," ca. 1690;
> Stoddard's sermon on Galatians 3.1, 5 October 1690;
> Revised version of the Foundation Sermon, 1692–1693;
> A series of six anti-Stoddard syllogisms Taylor copied in his "Commonplace Book," ca. 1693; and
> The eight sermons of *The Treatise Concerning the Lord's Supper*, from early fall of 1693 to spring of 1694.

Taylor's introductory comments to the six syllogisms (which might have been written after the *Treatise* sermons), determine in part this chronology:

> Mr. Stoddard having preached up from Gal. 3.1 that the Lord's Supper was a Converting Ordinance (Some Animadvertions on which Sermon Se among my manuscrips) & urged till on an Occasion of the Ruling Elders absence by reason of Sickness, & many if not almost all of the Ancient members of the Church were dead then he calls his Church to New Covenanting & among other Articles presented gains a major part to this Article to bring all to the Lords Supper that had a knowledge of Principle[s] of Religion, & not scandalous by open Sinfull Living. This done in the Winter of 1690. Which being done on the account that the Lords Supper is a Converting Ordinance, hath occasioned still further thoughts about this matter besides those laid down in my Manuscript on Eph. 2.22 [the revised Foundation Sermon]. Some of which thoughts I have here dropt as they dropt in upon my thoughts upon various occasions & at various times.

The syllogisms then follow. This heading, of course, mentions all of Taylor's anti-Stoddard manuscripts to this date, except the *Treatise* sermons.

[17]Taylor's copy of the Galatians sermon is not paginated; we have provided pagination for our citations. This sermon was originally published in "Solomon Stoddard's Sermon on the Lord's Supper as a Converting Ordinance," *Resources for American Literary Study*, 4 (Autumn 1974), 205–24. This sermon is included in *Edward Taylor vs. Solomon Stoddard: The Nature of the Lord's Supper* (Boston: Twayne, 1981).

[18]It is unlikely that this revised version was ever preached; Taylor seems to have wanted to incorporate all of his arguments in a single manuscript.

[19]"Edward Taylor on the Lord's Supper," p. 26.

[20]At the beginning of the "Arguments" Stoddard answers three questions relating to a Profession of Faith, "godly Conversation," and self-examination. This definition is Answer 2.

[21]"Animadversions," *Edward Taylor vs. Solomon Stoddard*, p. 124.

[22]See below, p. 326. George Gillespie, whom Taylor approvingly cites on a number of occasions, also makes use of the same image: "That Ordinance unto which one may not come without a wedding garment, is no converting ordinance" (*Aarons Rod Blossoming, or the Divine Ordinance of Church-Government Vindicated* [London, 1646], p. 510).

[23]See below, for example, the disciplinary cases titled "Suffield Concerns," "Steven Kellog & Sergeant Joseph Mawdsly," and the "Benjamin Smith Case."

[24]"Preface," *The Inexcusableness of Neglecting the Worship of God....*

[25]The first view is Miller's, most clearly expressed in "Solomon Stoddard," pp. 311ff. Walsh argues that in contrast to Stoddard's Presbyterianism, his "open-communion seems almost like an afterthought..." (p. 106). Stoddard's statements in these manuscripts demonstrate just the opposite.

[26]*The Danger of Speedy Degeneracy* (Boston, 1705), pp. 23–24.

[27]*Treatise*, p. 131.

[28]Emil Oberholzer, Jr., provides a broad context of the disciplinary problems of New England churches in his *Delinquent Saints: Disciplinary Action in the Early Congregational Churches of Massachusetts* (New York: Columbia University Press, 1956).

[29]Grabo, *Treatise*, p. lviii.

[30]For specific details, see below, CR, note 83.

[31]See Chapters 6 and 7 of the Cambridge Platform of 1648, reprinted in Williston Walker, *The Creeds and Platforms of Congregationalism* (Boston: Pilgrim Press, 1960), pp. 210–14.

[32]Walker, *Creeds and Platforms*, p. 219.

[33]Walker, *Creeds and Platforms*, pp. 217–18.

[34]Cotton Mather, *Magnalia Christi Americana* (New York: Russell & Russell, 1967), II, 249.

[35]For the full text of this "Proposition," see below, CR, note 95.

[36]For this letter to Justice Partridge, and Taylor's account of his relation with Smith as physician, see below, pp. 227ff., and CR, note 93.

[37] See below, CR, pp. 236ff.

[38] Cf. Sereno E. Dwight, *The Life of President Edwards* (New York: G. & C. & H. Carvill, 1830), pp. 463–64.

[39] "New England Puritanism: Another Approach," *William and Mary Quarterly*, 18 (April 1961), 236–42.

For these statistics, I am indebted to Walter L. Powell's unpublished study, "Edward Taylor of Westfield, Massachusetts," pp. 3ff.

A Note on the Text

THE MANUSCRIPT OF "THE PUBLICK RECORDS / of the Church at Westfield / Together / With a briefe account of our proceeding in order to / our entrance into that State," a folio volume, measuring 9½" by 11⅝", is in the possession of the Westfield Athenaeum. The volume was first bound during the 1780s; the Reverend Noah Atwater, who was ordained on 21 November 1781, entered the following note at the beginning of the "Church Records":

> For the information of those who will come after me I leave in writing the following—
> When I became the Pastor of this Church I found these Records without a Binding, in a form irregular and inconvenient. I sent them away to be bound. The Binder by inattention misplaced and inverted a number of leaves and in paring the whole took off too much of the writing. When he returned them to me I marked the pages without any reference to the inverted leaves. This is the reason of their appearing in their present form.
> Attest: Noah Atwater

The volume was rebound in 1929, at which time the leaves were encased in silk or linen layers. The pages in Taylor's hand are noted at the appropriate places in the text.

The manuscripts of "A Particular Church is Gods House" and the two untitled "Disciplinary Sermons" are described in *The Prince Library: A Catalogue of the Collection of Books and Manuscripts . . . Now Deposited in the Public Library of the City of Boston* (Boston, 1870), p. 159. The title of this collection of manuscripts, in a hand other than Taylor's, is written on the front cover in ink: "Extracts, by Rev. Edward Taylor, Westfield." In this volume, which contains fourteen items, including the eight sermons called the *Treatise Concerning the Lord's Supper,* the expanded version of the Foundation Sermon, here called "A Particular Church is Gods House," is Item 5; the Disciplinary Sermons are Items 6 and 7. For reasons we discuss in the "Introduction," and on the basis of the handwriting itself, we believe that this copy of "A Particular Church" was made between 1691 and 1693; the handwriting of the Disciplinary Sermons indicates that the copies were made shortly after they are dated, 2 December 1713 and 31 January 1713/14.

Because these manuscripts are the only ones known, this edition is based exclusively upon them. In most particulars we have followed the principles established in the "Report on Editing Historical Documents," *Bulletin of the Institute of Historical Research,* 1 (London, 1923), 6–25. We have, however, modified the Anglo-American "Report" in the following ways.

We have regularized Taylor's method of citing scriptural passages (he ordinarily uses commas to set off citations, but occasionally he will use periods or dashes—or a combination of periods, commas, and dashes—or no punctuation at all), his punctuation of "etc" and "viz," his punctuation of numerical headings, his abbreviations for "Chapter" (C., Ch., Cha., and Chap.), and his abbreviations for such titles as "Captain," "Lieutenant," "Sergeant," "Major," "Governour," "Senior," "Bishop," "Doctor," and "Esquire." We have also spelled out his "y" contractions (y^e for "the," y^{er} and y^{ir} for "their," y^t for "that," y^r for "your," y^m for "them," y^y for "they," and—infrequently —y^n for "than"), such abbreviations as *Ch* and *Chch, sd, foresd, bec,* $w:^{ch}, w:^n, w:^{th}$ (for "Church," "said," "foresaid," "because," "which," "when," and "with"), and the following infrequent abbreviations: $G:^l C:^o$ for "General Court," *N:E:* for "New England," *Engl* for "England," $K:^ndom$ for "Kingdom," S^{ts} for "Saints," *H: Gho:* for "Holy Ghost," $w:^bout$ for "without," *Ld* for "Lord," *Hon:*^{d} for "Honored," p^t for "part," those which use ξ as an abbreviation for *er, or,* and *our* spellings: e.g., favξ, Pastξ, and so on. We have also modernized *v* used initially and *u* medially.

We have let stand, however, abbreviations noted by an apostrophe, as in *tho'* and *altho'* (and regularized the use of the apostrophe). Taylor occasionally uses brackets both for parentheses and quotation marks; we have modified both uses as the context requires, and indicated such changes in the Textual Notes. He often uses the circumflex, as is the practice of early Latin texts, to indicate the double consonant (e.g., comûnion); we have doubled the consonant only in those cases where he uses the circumflex, even though his practice is not consistent.

Except where noted in the Textual Apparatus, we have let stand Taylor's spelling, capitalization, and use of the ampersand. Taylor's capital S is inconsistent, if not capricious. Our practice has been to consider as a capital only those S's in which the lower downward stroke terminates on the line *and* closes with the initial upward stroke, unless the size and shape of the character itself suggest that he intended it for a capital. (We should add, however, that neither this method nor those proposed by previous editors is entirely satisfactory.) Taylor forms a capital *T* in two different ways: at the beginning of paragraphs or headings, it is normally formed similar to the Hebrew *teth;* within paragraphs the cross stroke is perceptibly lower than the top of the vertical stroke even when it is the initial letter of a sentence and follows a period. The ampersand has been retained because Taylor often seems to use it—though not invariably—in specific rhetorical patterns. It often functions within a paragraph as a kind of semicolon (which he uses infrequently), indicating grammatical relationships between units of thought; it is also used within a paragraph in a series of statements, culminating in a final assertion, introduced by shifting to "and." (We should note, however, that at times, especially at the end of a line, he uses the ampersand simply to save space; and he often spells out the conjunction to justify the right-hand margin.) We have also retained the blank spaces in the text where Taylor apparently intended to enter scriptural citations; where possible, we have tried to identify the passage he seems to have had in mind.

The Textual Apparatus section is organized as follows. Editorial emendations and authorial alterations are included in the same section, followed by the Textual Notes. Conjectural readings are identified by "conj." Where Taylor has revised, we have attempted to determine the original reading (marked by "orig."). All modifications of the text (e.g., the addition of a period) are indicated by the following form:

80.29 Strains.] Strains

The portion to the left of the bracket is the emended reading in the text; the portion following the bracket is the manuscript reading. All such emendations are identified (except as noted here), either in the Apparatus or by brackets in the text itself.

Because of the "paring" of the edges of the leaves when the "Church Records" manuscript was bound in the 1780s, the top line or two, the bottom line or more, and the last (or initial) word or two on many leaves were cut off. The conjectural readings in these cases are enclosed in square brackets, as are all emendations not identified in the Textual Apparatus. To indicate words or phrases which are illegible, and all lacunae, we have used three asterisks; for a full line or more trimmed or worn away, we have used six asterisks. Special problems in relation to these matters are identified in the appropriate footnotes and recorded in the Textual Notes. (These same principles also apply to the sections of the Westfield "Town Records" and Hampshire "Court Records," as well as Taylor's other manuscripts that we have edited for this volume, except that we have not provided textual notes for this additional material.)

Finally, Taylor's marginal annotations have been dropped from the text to the footnotes. In identifying these references, we have tried to determine the specific editions which Taylor used; when that was not possible (as was too often the case) we have used only those editions which could have been available to him. In entering these references, we have identified publishers only for works issued after 1800. We have also identified in the footnotes the titles which appear in the inventory of Taylor's library (itemized in Thomas H. Johnson, *The Poetical Works of Edward Taylor* [Princeton: Princeton University Press, 1966], pp. 204–20). If Taylor translates or closely paraphrases his source, we have not cited the complete passage in the footnote (although he normally does in the margin), but identified the exact reference. In those cases where he simply refers to a source without paraphrase or citation, we have quoted the passage in full in the note. Taylor makes use of Greek characters no longer in use; we have modernized in accordance with the Erwin Nestle text, *Novum Testamentum Graece* (Stuttgart: Württ Bibelanstalt, 1952). We have also dropped the italics (except for individual words or phrases) from those Latin sources which are printed completely in italics; we have, however, italicized Taylor's Latin citations.

In these matters our debt to Norman S. Grabo's meticulous edition of the *Christographia* sermons (New Haven: Yale University Press, 1962) is extensive; we are pleased to acknowledge it here.

PART ONE

The Publick Records
of the Church at Westfield

The Publick Records
of the Church at Westfield
Together

With a briefe account of our proceeding in order to our entrance into that State.

arronnoko (or-kee) (the Indian name of the place,) being upon petition to the [General] Court granted to be a township by the Court was by reas[on of the][1] Rivers upon which it was situated, first calld Streamefield; but after upon bett[er con]sideration, arising from the cardinall Point of it's situation, as being al[most] if not wholly due West From Boston, the Matropolis of the Colony, as also [it be]ing the most westerly plantation in all the Colony was called WESTFIELD the name being Stated & fixt by the General Court.

Westfield, then, Warronnokee, comming to be an English Plantation, [had at] first Mr. John Holyoake, Son to the Godly, Capt. Elizur Holyoake of S[pring]field, to dispense the word of life amongst them, Ano Dni 1667 about h[alf] a yeare, but in the begining of winter following, he as finding the Mini[sterial] work too heavie for him desisted. From which time till the beginning of Winter [following they] had no minister. But then the town, being increased, sent down to [the Bay] to seek for one, and were supplied by the Reverend Mr. Moses Fisk, son to the [Reverend John] Fisk, Pastor of the Church of Christ at Chelmsford here in New England. Bu[t he be]ing here in their beginnings met with many temptations, so that [*after he*] had Served the Lord amongst them about 3 years he left them.[2]

The Town now being Destitute of a Minister sent into the B[*ay with*] an eye to the now Reverend Mr. Adams, Pastor of the Church at Dedham, my Clasmate, [*but*] yet designing to attend the advice of the Reverend Elders in the Bay about this [*matter*] & finding the said Mr. Adams not as yet movable from the Collidge, their Messeng[*er*] advised to myselfe, (the meanest of those that labour in Christs vinyard) & who [*upon ad*]vice did adventure to go with him home, & upon the Lords day following 3[d] of the 10[m] Ano Dni 1671 preached my first Sermon amongst them from Ma[tt. 4.17,] Repent, for the Kingdome of Heaven is at hand.[3]

I being now brought amongst them, did not determine any Settlement [*at once*] but when I had served some two years here, we set up Conference me[*eting in*] which I went over all the Heads of Divinity unto the means of the Application [*of Re*]demption, in order to prepare them for a Church State before we did [*enter.*][4] Tho' we began this Course, yet I was not determined within myselfe [*what to do.*] But at length my thoughts being more settled, I determined within [*myself that*] in case things could go comfortably on, to Settle with them: & in [*order thereto*] Changed my Condition, & entred into a married State; hop[*ing that the following*] Summer would open a doore to l[*et*] us into a Church State. [*But the summer coming*], opened a doore [*to*] that De[*solating*] war began by Philip Sac[*hem of the Pakanoket*] Indians, by which [*this handful was sorely pressed yet sovereignly preserved.*]

[*But yet not so as that we should be wholly exempted from the fury of—for our soil was moistened by the blood of three Springfield men, young Goodman Dumbleton, who came to our mill, and two sons of Goodman Brooks, who came here*] [1/2] to look after the Crop on the land, he had lately bought of Major John Pynchon Esquire, who being perswaded by Springfield folk went to accompanie them; but fell in the way, by the first assault the Enemies made upon us, at which time they turn'd Mr. Cornish's house to ashes, & also John Sackets with his barn, & what was in it, being the first snowy day of winter: they also at this time lodged a bullet in George Grangers leg, which was the next morning taken out by Mr. Bulkly, & the wound soon heald; It was judged that the Enemy did receive some losse this time, because in the Ashes of Mr. Cornishes house, were found pieces of the boanes of a man, lying about the length of a man in the Ashes. Also in winter some Sculking Rascolds upon a Lords day, in the time of our After noon Worship fired Ambrose Fowlers house & barn & in the week after Wa[l]ter Lees barn; but in the latter end, & giving up of winter, the last snowy day we had thereof, we discovering an End of Indians did send out to make a full discovery of the same, designing onely three, or four, to go out with order that they should not assalt them: but to our woe, & smart there going 10, or 12, not as scouts, but as assailants, rid furiously upon the Enemy, from whom they received a furious Charge, whereby Moses Cook an Inhabitant, & Clemence Bates a souldier, lost their lives, Clemence in the place, & Moses at night. Besides which we lost none of the town, onely at the Fall Fight at Deerfield there going nine from our town, 3 Garison Souldiers fell.[5] Thus tho' we lay in the very rode of the Enemy were we preserved; onely the war had so impoverisht us that many times were we ready to leave the place, & many did, yea many of those that were in full Communion in other places, for their number in all being but nine, four of them removed. & worse than this, a sore [tem]ptation was thrust in amo[n]gst us by the Adversary that seem'd to threaten the overthrow of all proceedings unto a Church state, by those on whom that intrest was before, most apparently devolved.[6] But God, whose designs shall never fall to the ground, hath not [only] shew'd himselfe gratious in the one respect, but also in the other. & therefore after [he had] stilled the noise of war, hath in some measure restrain'd the Adversary of the Gospell, & hath [recoll]ected that little strength that he hath preserved so far, as that this Spring 1679 we [came] to determine an Entrance into a Church State the latter end of the sixt moneth. [& ab]out the 4th or 5th month we came to determine it upon the last fourth day of [the si]xt moneth, after many prayers, & adresses unto the Almighty on this account.

And now Coming to fix on the day, we also determined what Churches to send unto to desire their assistance, & Fellowship there in; & So we fixt on this Conclusion, viz, to Send to Norwich, to Windsor, to Springfield, to Northampton, & Hadley unto whom we brake our Desires in the form of this letter following.

Our Letter that we sent to
the Church of Christ at
{
Norwich
Windsor
Springfield
Northampton
Hadley
}

Honored & Reverend Sir, together with the Much Respected Church of Christ at N,   etc., in which you serve.

[Af]ter the manifold Temptations, & Experienced Difficulties, of one nature, & an other, that we the Pro[p]osed Servants of Christ, in this place, have met withall, & been delayed thereby, with respect unto the [Inter]est of Christ in a Gospell instituted Order; it hath graciously pleased the Divine Omnipresent [*Preserv*]er, the Father of Spirits, & the God of All Mercy, in Christ, so far to shine forth upon us, as to [le]ad us by the hand, so, through the same as to bring us to a Conclusion among ourselves to fix upon [the] last fourth day of the sixth Moneth next ensuing, for the mannagement of that Solemn, & Holy [*work of*] Entrance into a City Frame, a Church Instituted State. And thereupon in Sense of our [own Insuff]iciencie for it, need of Advice, Directions, & Assistance, as also the Right Hand of Fel[lowship in] & about the same; as also con[sid]ering the Result of Civill Authority in this matter; [*& that it*] behooveth us, as our Master, [to] ful[*fill all*] Ri[*ghteousness:*] & also the Custom of the Churches of Chri[*st (which in all commendable things is greatly to be adhered unto)*] harmonizing herein, we have fixt on [*certain churches in this business*] * * * [2/3] [*also desire that you would accept of such a burden of Christ in the Gospell put upon you by us in this de*]sire, a[s that] you would send your Reverend El[*ders & Messengers to*] help, & in[*courage us in this*] worke, that is to be carried on by us upon the day above mentioned.

Thus earnestly desiring the Everlasting Father, the Prince of Peace, & the Ete[rnall Sp]irit of Love, that sitts between the Cherubims, that is in the middest of the Golden Candle[sticks,] & that speakes unto the Churches, to prevent all impediments obstructive [*to our moti*]on; to Stir you up to all readiness of minde to accept thereof; to give his graci[ous Pre]sence to you; & by, & with you unto us, we remaine, subscribing ourselves

Your Neighbours, Friends,

Companions, & Brethren [in the

com]mon Intrest of Christ

Westfield
July 1679

Edward Taylor
John Mawdsley
Ensign Samuel Loomis

Josiah [Dewy]
Isaak [Phelps]
John [Root]

6

These for the Reverend Mr. J. F. pastor of, together with the Church of Christ at N[orwich].⁷ *Sin de Caeteris.*

These then being Sent, our work came on a pace, for temptations having attended our seasons time after time before, I for my part was altogether unhearted untill now to prep[are] & therefore now I had both hands full. & must go down into the Bay before the time Wherefore having often in private sought God together in order unto this matter, n[ow] upon the 20th day of August, that day se'night unto the day of our Coalenscence, [we set apart] for a fast to [be] kept by the whole town in order to the great work of the day of imbodying. On which da[y I] preached from that I Kings 8.57, the Lord our God be with us, as he was with our Fathers. * * * it were made out, & applied That those that Succeed, an Ordinance Erecting p[rocess] ought, when they are about to erect Gods Ordinances amongst them to pray ha[rd to] God that he would be present with them, as he was with their Fathers. & as [for the] duty of prayer, two of the brethren did help carry it on.

The day being come, we had none came from Norwich, Capt. Daniel Cla[rk and] Benjamin Newbery onely from Windsor, Mr. Chauncy their Teaching Officer, tho' [those] be sent, durst not adventure from home, Mrs. Chauncy being waiting for her [hour. From] Springfield came Cousen Glover, teaching Elder, Mr. John Holyoake, Deacon Bu[rt, Dea]con Parsons messengers. From Northampton Mr. Stoddard Pastor, Mr. Strong [Teaching] Elder, & Capt. Aaron Cook, & Lt. Clark Messengers; & From Hadly there [came] Mr. Russell Pastor, Lt. Smith, Deacon Tilton, & Mr. Younglough messenger[s]. [Here] was the Worshipfull Major John Pynchon of Springfield, & the Rev. Mr. [Samuel Kerr] Pastor of the Church of Christ at Farmington, Guesse.

The Elders, & Messengers comings all over night, except such as came from Sp[ringfield] Church, consulted our preparation; which in some things they did not well approove of, [as we] had not drawn up a profession of our Faith, & in that I had prepared to preach [in the after]noon, & not to begin the worke with preaching. The reasons of which were these, viz, as [to our Pro]fession of Faith, Temptations had so often encountered, in our proceeding formerl[y as] I could not tell how to go about that labour, as thinking it might be in vain, unt[ill we] wrote unto the Churches, & then finding our worke so much that I could not well [get through] it, concluding to do it by a professing the Doctrine laid down in the Catichisme of the Assemblies of Divin[es at West]menster

7

so far as it goes, & where it is deficient, to acknowledge the Platform of C[*hurch disci*]pline put forth by the Rev. Elders & Messengers in a Synode held at Cambridge in [*Anno Domi* 1647], if this would not be acceptible, then to give an account of our profession, the which I did at last, they not accepting of the former; & indeed did stickle more [*than*] was meet, till Cousin Glover came. & for the other my preaching in the after part [*of the day*] was principally to gain time; for otherwise there would be two intermissio[ns.] * * * & an other after the relations were given: the which I judged would be * * * * * * [3/4]

[*I then*] gave [*an account of the work*] of the day & [*I inquired into the*] order of our mo[*tions*] hitherto, & our [*liberty for the same*] from
{ Civil Authority
{ Church Dismission of members.

As for the answer unto the first, this following order which was granted the foregoing yeare, was presented, & read.

August 9th 1678

These doe signifie, that we approve, the Christian people of West-field in the Colony of Massachusetts, to enter into a Church State, according to the Rules of Christ, & Lawes of the Countrey, in that case provided; & in particular the Persons here undernamed, viz, Mr. Edward Taylor, Minister, John Mawdsley, Samuel Loomis, Isaak Phelps, Thomas Gun, Josiah Dewey, & John Root, who have made Application to us, who together with such others living in that place, whom God hath fitted as living stones for that spirituall Building (having testimony of their professed Subjection into the Gospell of Christ) we do allow to enter into Church State, & Commend them to the Lords Gracious blessing. Signed the day, & yeare above written

> John Leverett   Governor
> Simon Broadstreet ⎫
> Daniel Gookins, Sr. ⎪
> Thomas Danforth ⎬   Assist.
> John Pynchon ⎪
> Edward Ting ⎪
> Joseph Dudley ⎭

As for the last, the Elders, & Messengers of the Churches there present, to which they belonged, then testified that the Churchs respectively had recomended them unto the business in hand. And the severall Dismissions given would testifie the same, which I had in my hand, tho' we read them not, in form as follows

The Recommendation of the Brethren
from Windsor Church unto this work
writ to myselfe

Honored Reverend & Beloved,
The Lord who appoints the place of our habitations, having cast the dwellings of our Brethren Thomas Gun, John Mawdsly, Samuel Loomis, & Isaak Phelps at Westfield (whereby the Good hand our God upon them, they are planting of a Church, for the injoyment of Fellowship with Christ in his Ordinances amongst themselves) they have desired their Dismissions from us, which we have accordingly granted to them; & desire they may be received as becometh Saints, to Communion in all the Ordinances of Christ, that they may be further built up in their most holy Faith & new Obedience to the praise of him that hath called them. Thus desiring the good Lord to be with you, assisting, & blessing your Endeavours to build a house among you for himselfe to dwell in, commending you to the grace of God we remain
Yours in our Common Saviour

Windsor	Nathaniel Chauncy in the name & with
Aug: 22–79	the Consent of the Church

The Recommendation Farmington
Church gave Brother Root.

[Dear] Sir
By our beloved Brother John Root, we are informed, that your purpose of incorporat[in]g into a Church State is come, * * * its birth; on which account * * * * * * [4/5] House, * * * you may * * * & flourishin[g] bring forth much fruit to shew that he is upright. [I]n him I remain

Yours to Serve,
Aug. 25–79   Samuel Hooker.

Northampton Church's Recommendation
of their Brethren.

Brother Josiah Dewey, & Brother John Ingerson, having desired their Dismissions to the worke of gathering a Church at Westfield, the Church hath readily granted the same, [as] is attested by us

N:hampton	Solomon Stoddard
Aug. 27.79	John Strong

Thus the proceeding being cleared, the next thing attended on, was the Relations, which were then called for, & made; yet this not being according to my Moddle wherein I accounted it most meet to have given the Profession of our Faith in the first place, & then our Experiences of Gods grace upon our Spirits, I shall first give an account of our Faith & then of our Experiences.

Now as for the Profession of our Faith, it was held out in these general Heads following; onely some little addition is Set down.

CHRISTIANITIE, OR THE CHRISTIAN RELIGION, OR DIVINITIE, IS THE DOCTRINE OF LIVING UNTO GOD, consisting in $\begin{cases} \text{FAITH \&} \\ \text{OBEDIENCE.} \end{cases}$

1. For explication we have the $\begin{cases} \text{Name} \\ \text{Nature} \end{cases}$ to weigh.

1. The Name of the thing Described, & this is variously laid down, viz, Christianity, or the Christian Religion, or Divinity. As to the words these Names are ἄγραφα unscripturall: But as to the Spirit, Matter, or Intent thereof, they are ἔγγραφα Scripturall, drawing their pedigree from Christ, as Christianity from Christ the Author of it. Or the Christian Religion, as that which having its Spring Head in Christ runs with Christ-like influences from Christ into the Soul tinging of it with a Smack of Christ, & as Spirituall Magnetick attracting of the heart & affections to God in Christ with a devout Design there to abide. & hence it is called Divinity in that it is the Lesson the Divine Nature Reads to us; & in our Learning of it, we shall come to attain Divine Communication of Light from the Divine Minde, & of Grace from the Divine Goodness of this Minde, John 17.3. And here all are used as the Names of the thing that is Described.

2. The Nature of the thing described thus, Is the Doctrine of Living to God.

The thing is Described from its $\begin{cases} \text{General Nature} \\ \text{End.} \end{cases}$

1. Its Generall Nature, thus Its the Doctrine, Deut. 32.2, Prov. 4.2, Isa. 28.9, 29.24. So Christ calls it his Doctrine, John 6.16,17. Doctrine not negatively, as if Divinity was not an Art, or Science, as well as other Arts, But Emphatically its a Doctrine in that, whereas there are such clear footsteps of other Arts, & Sciences imprinted in the Fabrick of Nature leading blinde Nature to gather up the Systems of the Rules thereof, & to hold out the same without any supernaturall teacher, yet Divinity cannot be so learned; But God himselfe must teach it himselfe, or else it had never been Discovered. Hence is the promise, Isa. 54.13, * * * 6.45. & Such as receive it are called * * * * * *

2. Its end, viz, to live to God, hence its also a Doctrine according to godliness, I Tim. 6.3.

Now this living to God lieth in these things, viz,

1. In the right improovment of those gracious Influences which we receive from him, so as to bring up the Exercise of the inward, & outward man into a Conformity unto him. This is to live to God indeed, I John 2.6, I Thess. 4.1. & this is indeed to glorify God & that which we are called to in all these calls, whereby we are called to glorify, or give glory & honour to God, I Cor. 10.31, Ps. 22.23, Isa. 24.15, etc.

2. In the right improovment of those gracious Influences comming from him upon our Souls so as to draw out the Soule Satisfying delight of God in them to the felicitating of our Souls with the Divine Sweetness therein. Oh this is Sweet indeed, Cant. 1.3. This is called the injoying of God, Ps. 73.25. Hence se Paul, as Phil. 3.7,8,9.

2. For Confirmation, we have $\begin{cases} \text{Scripture} \\ \text{Reason.} \end{cases}$

1. Scripture as those already laid down to which I might adde many more, as Matt. 5.16, Acts 9.31, Rom. 6.4, 8.1, 13.13, Eph. 4.1-17, so 5.8, Col. 1.10, Ps. 50.15, *ult.*

2. Reasons to proove this are these Drawn

1. *Ab absurdo è Contrà.* From the Absurdity in Case the Contrary be asserted, or this Description denied, for then there is no Doctrine of Living unto God. For there is no Doctrine teaching us to live to God, if Divinity doth not. Grammar, Rhetorick, Logick, are peculiarily conver-

sant about the Essence, Grace, & Argumentative Strength of Speech. Physick, Metaphysick, & Methamatick peculiarily treate upon the Principles, Notions, & Affections of Being. & therefore nothing about living to God. And as for Ethicks they onely lay down unto us the Dictates of Naturall Theologie, & can rise no higher. So that it onely teacheth us morallity. & hence none teach us to live to God of all these. & therefore if Divinity do not, there is no Doctrine teaching us to live to God * * * will not this be very * * * [5/6]
* * * * * *

Doctrines, etc. teaching us in other matters which are but of low concern indeed, & no such thing respecting the matters of the greatest moment which is, viz, a right glorifying of God, & receiving of the greatest concern to the Soul which is, viz, its injoying of God? Surely this is very absurd to assert, therefore to avoid this, Divinity well claims the nature of the Doctrine of Living to God.

2. *Ab Efficiente.* Because its a Doctrine immediately delivered by Christ, as he is the Mediator. & therefore it is called his Doctrine, John 7.16,17. Now what ever comes to us from Christ, as Mediator, is designed as a means to bring us up to God, for he came for this end himselfe, Heb. 2.10. & all he did was for this end. As light held out to the Understanding, Luke 2.32, Grace to the heart, II Cor. 12.9, Rom. 8.29, Holiness in the life, I Cor. 1.30. & hence the whole Communication of the minde of God to us is to bring us to God, John 6.38,39,40, Chap. 14.6. & Therefore Divinity is the Doctrine of Living to God. * * * The Nature * * * Religion prooves it, for the Parts of Divinity hold it out. For the first part peculiarly [te]nds to bring up the inward Man unto God, inlightening of it how to frame its beliefe on God, on his works, on its own State by Creation, by the fall, & on the works of Redemption, & the Application thereof & the benefits thence accrewing. & the Other part containing clear Rules leading our Life to the Glory of God in the Duties of Piety towards God, & Charity towards man. Ergo

4. *A Fine.* The End of Divinity prooves it. The *Finis Intentionis*, or Design of its Author, was to bring men by it as the Rule, Isa. 8.20, to live up unto God, hence its called the Doctrine according to Godliness, I Tim. 6.3, Titus 2.10. Se also II Pet. 1.19. The *Finis Attentionis*, or design of attention unto it is the coming into a Conformity unto the Will of God, Gal. 6.16, Rom. 12.1,2, & So the glorifying of God, & the injoying him for Ever, as I Cor. 10.31, John 10.28. Hence it appeareth that the Christian Religion is the Doctrine of Living to God.

Faith is the first part of Christianitie which teaches us what we are to believe concerning God. Where we are to consider its $\left\{\begin{array}{l}\text{Principles} \\ \text{Object.}\end{array}\right.$

The Principles of it are [6/7]

* * * Father, & the Son.

Thus much of the Nature of God, he is a Spirit, considered simply in his Essence, & Relatively, in its Subsistances.

2. The Properties of God are those Divine Perfections attributed to God, in the Scriptures, by which he makes himselfe known, as Infinit, etc.

Those Properties, or Attributes fall under our Consideration some as { Habits in ther Subjects as that he is, Infinite, Eternall, etc. Act exerted by their Subjects, as that according to's pur- pose, etc. [7/8]

Gods Incommunicable Properties are those whose nature he doth not communicate to any one, as his $\begin{cases} \text{Infinities} \\ \text{Eternities.} \end{cases}$

Infinitie is one of Gods Incommunicable Properties, whereby God is without all bounds, hence he is infinite.

From Gods Infinitie follows his $\begin{cases} \text{Immensitie} \\ \text{Unitie.} \end{cases}$ [8/9]

Eternitie is one of Gods Incommunicable Properties whereby hee is without beginning, & ending. Hence Unchangeable.

Thus much concerning the Incommunicable Properties. The Communicable follow, as Truth, Goodness, Holiness, Righteousness, Wisdome, & Power. [9/10]

Truth is a Communicable Propertie of God rendering him infinitly, &
Eternally Conformable unto his own Understanding, whereby he
being absolutly true in everything, is the object of our trust. [10/11]

[Goodness is a Communicable] property of God consisting in the infinite & eternal Ex[cel]lency of his own Nature, whereby it yields a compleat satisfaction to his own Will in a[ll] things.

Holinesse is a Communicable Property of God, consisting in the infinite, & eternall Puritie of his own nature, whereby he is most Holy, & acts holily. [11/12]

[Righteousness is a Communicable Property of God, consisting in the infinite,] & eternall Exactnesse of his own Nature unto the Law of his own Will, whereby being most Righteous he doth most Righteously.

Wisdome is a Communicable Property of God, consisting in the infinite, & eternall Light of his own Understanding, whereby he being most Wise, doth most perfectly see all things. [12/13]

Power is a Communicable Property of God, consisting in the infinite, & eternall virtue of his own Nature, whereby he being Omnipotent, doth irresistible effect whatere he Wi[lls.]

Thus much for the Communicable Attributes of God. & So we have done with those Properties of God which are considered as habits in their Subjects.

Such Properties of God considered as Acts, Exerted by their Subjects, are the works of God, as his $\begin{Bmatrix} \text{Internall} \\ \text{Externall} \end{Bmatrix}$ works, thus added in the Description, who according to his own Purpose hath created, & doth despose of all things.

The Internall Works of God, are the Proper Acts which God from all Eternity carried on within his own minde; expressed thus in the Description of God, viz, His own Purpose. [13/14]

Gods Purpose is either, General as the Decree, or Particular, as the Covenant of Redemption.

The Decree is an Internall Act of God, whereby hee hath for his own Glory appointed whatsoever shall come to passe, from all eternity. [14/15]

The Covenant of Redemption is an Internall Act of God

The Externall Workes of God are those Proper acts of God whereby he doth accomplish his Decrees as the Workes of
$\begin{cases} \text{Creation, thus expresst, who hath created.} \\ \text{Providence, thus expresst, \& doth despose [all] thin[gs.]} \end{cases}$

Creation is an Externall Worke peculiarly Proper unto God whereby according to his Decree hee gives being unto all things. & it is to be considered in $\begin{cases} \text{General} \\ \text{Particular. [15/16]} \end{cases}$

Creation in Generall is an Externall Worke of God, whereby God hath made all things of nothing by the word of his Power in the space of six dayes, & all very Good.

Creation in Particular is Gods particular making Angels, & Men that we shall treat of.

Angels are compleat Spirits created, probablie in the morning of the first day, with Intellectual faculties, to attend the glorious Throne of God, & to be sent out for the good of Gods elect. [16/19]

The Providence of God is an Externall Worke of God whereby he doth most expediently dispose of a[ll] things, according to his own Purpose. & this is considered as it is { Generall / Particular.

Providence in General is an externall worke of God whereby he disposeth of all things with all their Actions.

The Particular Providence of God is an Externall worke of God whereby he disposeth of particular things, the which is more especially considerable as it respects { Angels & / Men.

With respect unto Angels, & Men Gods Particular Providence is Considerable as to its { Sorts as Actually & Permissive / Special Acts. [19/20]

The Speciall Acts of Providence towards Angels, & Men are Gods dealings with them in a Covenantall way where we are to consider the

$$\left\{\begin{array}{l} \text{Covenant itselfe, \&} \\ \text{Consequents thereof. [20/21]} \end{array}\right.$$

The Covenant of works with Angels, & Men is Gods transacting with them, upon their Creation, in puting them into his service, Whereby he gave them his Law, as the condition of injoying life, binding of them to perfect Obedience upon pain of deadth, & for the confirmation of mans faith therein, he instituted the tree of nowledge, & Life to be the Sacramentall Seales thereof.

The Consequences of this Covenant are considered as falling under Gods $\begin{cases} \text{Permissive,} \\ \text{Actual Pro[vi]den[ce.]} \end{cases}$

Those that fall under the eye of Gods Permissive Providence respect $\begin{cases} \text{Angels \&} \\ \text{Men.} \end{cases}$

Those that respect Angels are to be found respecting the $\begin{cases} \text{Elect or} \\ \text{Reprobat Angels.} \end{cases}$

That that Respect the Elect Angels, is their Persistency in the Covenant & it is a Conseque[nce] of their being in Covenant with God, consisting in a volentary conformity of themselves with most exact Obedience, unto the duties required in the Covenant whereby they are confirmed in their good Estate. [21/22]

That Permissive Consequence Respecting the Reprobat Angels, is their Apostacy which is a Consequence of their being in Covenant with God consisting in a volentary refusall of obedience, from an Affectation of being above Gods command, whereby they fell from their happy estate into an estate of Damnation irrecoverably.

Those Consequences of the Covenant of worke falling under the eye of Permissive Providence respecting man are the $\begin{cases} \text{Fall itselfe} \\ \text{Fallen State. } [22/23] \end{cases}$

The Fall itselfe is a Consequence of the Covenant of Workes consisting in a volentary disobedience unto the Command, through the instigation of Satan, by eating the forbidden fruit, whereby all mankinde fell from God into a State of Sin.

A Fallen State is a consequence of the covenant of works consisting in
$\begin{cases} \text{Sin, \&} \\ \text{Sorrow.} \end{cases}$

Sin is to be considered with respect unto its $\begin{cases} \text{Constitution, \&} \\ \text{Affections.} \end{cases}$

The Constitution of Sin declares what it is from its $\begin{cases} \text{Nature, \&} \\ \text{Propagation.} \end{cases}$

Sin therefore in it's nature, is a Spirituall Evill Consequente upon the Covenant of works, consisting in any want of Conformity unto, or any transgression of the Law of God. [23/24]

The Propagation of Sin is that whereby Sin is carried on in the world, &
its { Originally
{ Actually.

Originally by Originall Sin, which is the want of Originall Righteousness together with a Strong inclination unto all actuall evill flowing from the guilt of Adams first Sin over all his posterity descending from him by ordinary generation, & is the spawn and spring of all Actuall transgressions. [24/26]

Actually by actuall Sin, which is any actuall transgression. [26/27]

The Affections of Sin are those Speciall Properties arising from the nature of Sin as it respects Man its author, or God its Object.

As it Respects Man its affections are $\begin{cases} \text{Guilt} \\ \text{Filth.} \end{cases}$

Guilt is an Affection of Sin binding the Sinner down under the Condemning Sentence of the Law.

Filth is an Affection of Sin which, arising in opposition unto the Image of God, doth defile the Soule, whereby he is made abominable in the sight of God. [27/28]

The Affections of Sin as they respect God, are $\begin{cases} \text{Dishonoure to God, \&} \\ \text{Displeasure to God.} \end{cases}$

Dishonour of God, is an Affection of Sin arising from Sins opposition against the Dignity of God.

Displeasure unto God is an affection of Sin consisting in an opposition unto the good will of God whereby God is provoked to wrath against the sinner. [28/29]

Sorrow is another property of a Fallen State; but it properly falls under Gods Actuall Providence. & there I shall speake to it.

Those Consequences of the Covenant of Workes which fall under the hand of Gods Actuall Providence respect Angels, & Men.

Such as respect Angels are considerable in respect unto the
{ Elect Angels
Reprobate Angels.

That which respects the Elect Angels is their Confirmation in their happy state, which is a gracious Act of Gods Righteous Providence communicating unto them all the benifits of the Covenant whose Condition they have observed, whereby being confirmed in their happy state, they are everlastingly supported in their Obedience, unto Gods Glory. [29/30]

That which respect the reprobate Angels is their Finall Rejection, which is a Righteous Act of Gods holy Providence, powering down upon them the curses of the Covenant which they have violated, whereby they were wholy stript of every spark of holiness, being carried on with finall Obstinacy against God, are banisht eternally out of their first habitation from the holy Angels, as accursed exiles, rageing here in these lower Regions fast bound in hellish chains of darkness to sustain eternall vengeance at the day of judgment. [30/31]

Those Consequences of this Covenant falling under the hand of Gods Actuall Providence respecting man, are such as are carried on by him as he is $\begin{cases} \text{A Righteous Judge as the Cur[se]} \\ \text{A Gracious Lord as the Recover[y.]} \end{cases}$

The Curse, is a Consequence of the Covenant of work as broken, proceeding from God as a Righteous Judge, inflicting all sorts of Sorrows on man for his Sin, as Death $\begin{cases} \text{Temporall} \\ \text{Eternall.} \end{cases}$

Temporall Death is the Curse of God inflicted, as a Righteous Judge, in this life, & its $\begin{cases} \text{Spirituall} \\ \text{Corporall.} \end{cases}$

Spirituall Death is the Curse of God, as a Righteous Judge, inflicted upon the Soule, & the Facultie[s] attending it in its conjunct State, whereby it, & they, being separated from Communion with God, do die away from God under Sin & Sorrow. [31/32]

Corporall Death is the Curse of God as a Righteous Judge, inflicted upon the Body and what apperta[i]ns thereto, on the account of Sin whereby it being deprived thereof is worn down under Pain untill by the separating of the Soule, & body a sunder it fall into the grave.

Eternall death is [32/33]

Those Consequences of the Covenant of works broke falling under the hande of Gods Actuall Provedence, as he is a Gracious Lord are the Recovery or Anastasis, which is a Consequence of the Covenant of works broke mannag'd by the hand of Gods Actuall Providence, as he is a Gracious Lord, whereby he recovers his Elect out of a fallen State into a State of Salvation.

& its Parts are $\begin{cases} \text{Redemption} \\ \text{Application. [33/34]} \end{cases}$

Redemption is the first part of the Recovery of the Elect out of the Fall by the Redeemer, Who laying down for them the full price satisfactory to justice itselfe, hath purchased them unto eternall Salvation. & here we are to consider the $\begin{cases} \text{Redeemer himselfe, \&} \\ \text{Nature of Redemption.} \end{cases}$

The Redeemer himself is to be considered in respect unto his $\begin{cases} \text{Person \&} \\ \text{Medi[a]tion.} \end{cases}$

The Person of the Redeemer is the Lord Jesus Christ, the eternall Son of God, who by an extraordinary Conseption in the womb of the virgin Mary by the power of the Holy Ghost, assuming humane Nature, abides two distinct natures God-Man, in one person for ever. [34/39]

The Mediation itselfe, is Christs appearing before his Father on the account of his people who by making full Satisfaction to Justice itselfe, hath purchased them unto Eternall Salvation. & in this Mediation we are to consider the $\begin{cases} \text{Offices performed \&} \\ \text{State in which they were carr'd [on.]} \end{cases}$

The Offices themselves comprehend the whole worke of Christs Mediation in Satisfying for, & Purchasing of, the Elect unto life; & they are transacte $\begin{cases} \text{Godward as his Priesthood} \\ \text{Manward as his} \end{cases}$ $\begin{cases} \text{Prophetical Offi[ce]} \\ \text{Kingly Office.} \end{cases}$

Christs Priestly Office is the part of his Mediation transacted Godward on mans account whereby offering up himselfe a Sacrivise once to Satisfie divine Justice, he hath purchased them to Salvation, & makes continuall Intercession for them. [39/40]

Christs Propheticall Office is that part of his Mediation transacted manward on Gods account Whereby he reveals by his Spirit the Will of God unto us so far as it is necessary for our Salvation.

Christs Kingly Office is that part of his Mediation, transacted manward on Gods account, whereby * * * Gathering us unto himselfe into his Kingdome State, he arming us with his Spirit, gives us the victory unto eternall Salvation; but doth destroy utterly all his Enemies. [40/41]

The State wherein Christ carri'd on these Offices, is the State of {Humiliation & Exaltation. But these belonging to the nature of Redemption, I shall speak of them there.

The Nature of Redemption is that wherein redemption doth consist in respect unto The thing itselfe, & in Respect unto its parts.

In respect unto the thing itselfe Redemption is the first part of the Recovery of the Elect consisting in Satisfaction unto Justice & Purchaseing Salvation. [41/42]

Redemption in respect unto its parts co[n]sists in Christs $\begin{cases} \text{Humiliation, \&} \\ \text{Exaltation.} \end{cases}$

Christs Humiliation is the first part of Redemption whereby yielding obedience unto the whole Law of God perfectly satisfactory to justice itselfe, he hath purchased eternall Salvation for his People. [42/43]

Christs Exaltation is the other part of Redemption, whereby he rising from the dead up into heaven to transact the conserns of his people, doth sit down on the right hand of his father in the Throne of his glory, & shall judge the world at the last day. [43/44]

APPLICATION is the other part of the Recovery of the Elect out of the fall, whereby the Redemption purchased by Christ is made theirs & we are to consider it $\begin{cases} \text{Absolutly, \&} \\ \text{Relatively.} \end{cases}$

The Absolute consideration of the Application of Redemption consist[s] in $\begin{cases} \text{Union to Christ,} \\ \text{Communion with him.} \end{cases}$

Union to Christ is the first work of Application whereby the Soule is joyned unto Christ, by Effectual Calling, in a Covenant of Grace, that it may be made Partaker of the benefits of Redemption.[8]

The Covenant of Grace [44/45]

Effectuall-Calling is the Regenerating work of the Spirit of God in the means of Grace upon the Soule, whereby the Soule turning from Sin, is inseparably joyn'd unto Christ in a new Covenant, this regenerating work of Effectuall-Calling therefore consists in $\begin{cases} \text{Convicti[on]} \\ \text{Repentan[ce.]} \end{cases}$

Conviction is the first work of the Spirit in effectuall Calling, on the Soule, which upon the understanding, is called Illumination, and in the Will, & Affections is properly called Conviction. [45/46]

Repentence is the next work in Effectuall Calling carried on upon the Soule whereby the Soule turns from Sin unto God; & it consists in $\begin{cases} \text{Aversion from Sin, \&} \\ \text{Reversion to God.} \end{cases}$

Aversion from Sin is the first part of Repentance consisting in the turning of the Soule from sin in its preparation for God, by the work of $\begin{cases} \text{Contrition, \&} \\ \text{Humiliation.} \end{cases}$

Contrition is that part of Aversion from Sin, whereby the will, & Affections are broken off from sinfull Objects. [46/47]

Humiliation is that part of aversion from Sin, whereby the Soule, on the account of Sin doth lie low in its own eyes mourning before God.

Reversion to God is the secondary part of Repentance, consisting in the returning of the Soule unto God in Christ * * * where consider its
{ Principall &
{ Acting. [47/48]

The Principall of the Souls returning to God is the Passive Principle of Grace wrought upon the Will by the free grace of God.

The Actings of Reversion are those wherein its nature lies as
$\begin{cases} \text{Faith \&} \\ \text{Its Concomitants.} \end{cases}$

Faith is the First Saving Act of Reversion, wrought in the heart by the Spirit of God in its effusing the Principle of Grace therein, whereby the Soule doth inseparably cleave unto Christ Jesus its Saviour, for life, & Salvation. [48/49]

The Concommitants of Faith in the Souls Return are the turnings back again of the Affections unto God in Christ, as Love, Hope, Joy. [49/50]

Communion is the other Worke of Application whereby the Soule is made Partaker of the benefits of Redemption, & it consists in a Change
$\begin{cases} \text{Relative} \\ \text{Real.} \end{cases}$

The Relative Change is an absolut putting of the Soule into a new Relation as $\begin{cases} \text{Justification} \\ \text{Adoption.} \end{cases}$

Justification is a gracious sentence of God passt upon a true believer in Christ, whereby on the account of Christs Righteousness, he being freed from guilt of Sin, is pronounced truely Righteous in the sight of God eternally. [50/51]

Adoption is a gracious Act of God, passt upon a true believer in Christ, whereby, translating him out of Satans famaly, as a Childe into his own houshould, he constitutes him a rightfull heire of all the Privilidges of his own child.

The Reall Change of State is a progressive renewall of the Qualities of man in the likeness of God, consisting in $\begin{cases} \text{Sanctification, \&} \\ \text{Glorification.} \end{cases}$

Sanctification is a Reall Change of State whereby the Person being cleansed from the filth of sin, is renewed in the likeness of God by the graces of the Spirit. [51/52]

Glorification is a Reall Change of State, whereby a Person is translated out of a State of misery into a State of felicity that shall be compleated in the full fruition of heavenly Glory to all eternity. [52/53]

The Relative consideration of the Application of Redemption is that whereby it is treated of as it respects its
{ Subject unto which it is applied &
{ Investing its Subject with it.

The subject of the Application of Redemption is the Church
{ Generall, &
{ Particular.

The Church Generall, or Catholick, is

A Particular, or Instituted Church is a Companie of believers united together among themselves by a speciall Covenant to carry on the Ordinances of Divine Worship in the Communion of Saints, for their own edification, to the glory of God. [53/54]

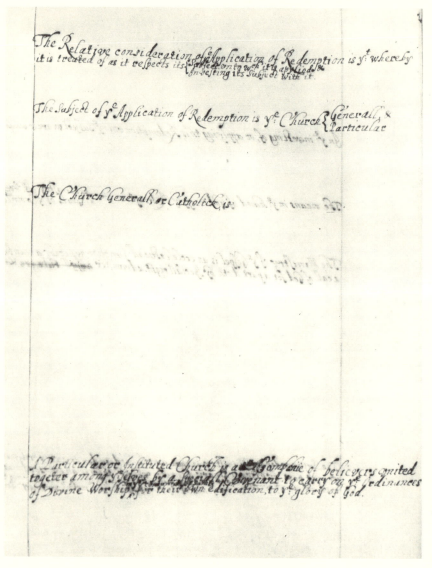

Profession of Faith, manuscript p. 53.

In the investing of, or applying this Redemption unto the Subject we are to weigh the $\begin{cases} \text{Means } \& \\ \text{Manner thereof.} \end{cases}$

The means in the hand of God to apply Redemption are the $\begin{cases} \text{Ministry of the Covenant } \& \\ \text{Seals of the Covenant of Grace} \end{cases}$ Adjuncts.

The Ministry of the Gospel is an ecclesiasticall function whereby a man being by a call of God set apart doth by speciall right administer Gospell Charges, & it is $\begin{cases} \text{Extraordinary} \\ \text{Ordinary.} \end{cases}$

The Extraordinary Ministry is performed under an extraordinary call for the most part, by extraordinary assistance whereby there is an extraordinary work carried on, as the work $\begin{cases} \text{Under the Old Testament of} \\ \text{Under the New, of Apostles,} \end{cases}$ Prophets & Apostolicall persons $\Big\}$ in gathering of the Church & writing the Scriptures. [54/55]

The Ordinary Ministry is that which is performed under an ordinary call in all things according to the Scriptures unto the edification of the Church as $\begin{cases} \text{Elders \&} \\ \text{Deacons.} \end{cases}$ [55/56]

The Seales of the Covenant of Grace (called the Sacraments) are means instituted of God, whereby the benefits of Redemption by outward signs represented, are sealingly applied unto believers, as in $\left\{\begin{array}{l}\text{Baptisme \&} \\ \text{the Lords Supper.}\end{array}\right.$

Explication

1. Here is Something of the Name to be considered, & this is the Seale of the Covenant of Grace; so God calls it Gen. 17.11 אלת ברית we English it a token, but it might better be rendered a Sign, or Seal. Sometime it is used for a bare Sign, as Jer. 6.1. Sometime its a Commemorative Sign, as Ex. 13.9, Josh. 4.6: Sometime its a Remonstrating Sign, as Ex. 4.8. & Sometime a Confirming Sign, as Isa. 7.11, so Chap. 38.7, 22. & a Covenant Confirming sign, as Gen. 9.12, 13, & therefore by a Synecdoche as much as חלתם , a Sealing Sign & hence called a Seal, Rom. 4.11. & hence Calvin *Obsignatio justiciae fidiei, ut nobis quoque credentibus justicia imputetur, in loc.*[9]

As for the word Sacrament its' not scripturall, but a military word denoting that Oath of faithfulness that Souldiers were bound withall unto their Generall:[10] & brought thence by the Church of Christ to import the Seals of the Covenant of Grace which all Christians are publickly obliged by unto the Captain of Their Salvation.

2. Here is the Nature of the thing laid from its Causes & from its Subject recipient.

1. From its Causes $\left\{\begin{array}{l}\text{Externall as its Efficient \& finall} \\ \text{Internall or Essentiall.}\end{array}\right.$

1. Its Efficient Cause, as it is the principall is Expresst thus, God, in that it is said to be a means instituted of God, hence God calls this his Covenant unto which this is the Sign, Gen. 17.11. & Christ said this is my body, Matt. 26. & he commanded it, Matt. 28.19, I Cor. 11.24. The Author of the Covenant must needs be the Instituter of the Seals. But the Instrumentall Efficient is the Officer under Christ whether pastor, or Teacher, as Matt. 28.18,19, I Cor. 10.18.

2. Its finall cause for which it is instituted is $\left\{\begin{array}{l}\text{Primary \&} \\ \text{Secundary.}\end{array}\right.$

The Primarie End of the Sacraments is to Seale the Covenant & hence they are called Seals from the finall Cause. Hereby God Sealeth unto the believer the truth of the promises: & the Believer Seals unto God his Faith, & Obedience. The Secundary End is the publick Profession of our Faith in God, & Communion of Saints. Both which Final

Causes are comprehended in these words in the Description, whereby the blessings of the Covenant represented, are Sealingly applied.

The Internall, or Essential Causes of the Sacrament do give Essence thereto, as the $\begin{cases} \text{Matter \&} \\ \text{Form.} \end{cases}$

1. The matter of the Seals is thus Expressed, viz, Means instituted whereby by outward Signs, wherein there is the generall matter held forth, wherein the Seales are of the Same Nature that other Ordinances are, viz, Means of Grace instituted of God; the Institution is before proved. & that they are Means of Grace appear in that they are the Seals of the Covenant of Grace. & so also in that they are for Confirming Seales as also in that they are commemoratory Signs. & thereby stir up grace unto its exercise. & also there is the particular Matter held out in these words, viz, Outward Signs, the which are both ἄδηλος & Visible, where there is Some thing Substantiall, as Water in Baptism, or Bread, & wine in the Lords Supper & Something Rituall, as the Speciall acts in using them as Washing, or breaking, pouring out, giving eat & drinking: & also νοῆτα, & Spirituall which are the things Signified. The other were the Sign. & those things are either, Substantiall as Christ with all his benefits, I Cor. 11.26: & something Rituall as the doing a way of Sin by Christs blood. *Spanh: Synt.*[11]

2. The Formall Cause, & this is that which makes this Matter a Sacrament, & this lies in that Spirituall Relation, or Union in the Sign, unto the thing Signified, implied in these words, viz, whereby the benefits of Redemption by out ward Signs represented are Sealingly applyed.

Now this Relation is Constituted betwixt the Sign & the thing Signified by pronouncing the words of the Institution in the administring of the Same. & in the right using thereof. & hence no more is Sacramentall than what is rightly used thereunto. Now upon this relation is grounded those various forms of Speech in this busines as When

1. The Sign is used for the thing Signified, as Circumcision for Sanctification, Jer. 4.4. 2. When the thing Signified is the name upon the * * * Bread & Wine is said to be Christs Body and Blood, Matt. 26.26,28. 3. When the Effect of the thing Signified is ascribed to the Sign, as Regeneration the effect of the Washing in Christs blood is ascribed to Baptism, as Titus 3.5. 4. When the property of the Sign is ascribed to the thing Signified, as the breaking the bread, unto Christ. & so John 6.16. & when 5. the property [of] the thing Signified is ascribed to the Sign, as When the Bread Sacramental is used for Spirituall.

Thus much of the Causes of Sacraments.

2. It is described from the Subject, viz, believers. This they must be unto whom these Seals are applied. For Christ & the Soule must συμφωνήσας Matt. 20.2, come both together in one voice, which is an agrement before they article & Seal & this agreement makes the Soule a Covenanter: & therefore a believer. & hence is that Heb. 8.9, without this the Soul doth but mock God in the Sacraments; & is thereby Seald under judgment, I Cor. 11.27,29.

Confirmation

Now it will appeare that there is ground for this that there are Seals to the Covenant of Grace.

1. From the Necessity thereof this appears, as, 1. That the Covenant of Grace may not be Counterfeted, & God's people deceived by others. For where things are not Signd & Sealed there is a danger of forgery: but where they are Signd, & Seald there is a Sure making. Now God is this & hence it cannot be counterfeted. & therefore those Covenants that have other Seals than his are not his. 2. For the Confirmation of his peoples faith in the Covenant. Parties concerned in Covenants, are in fear & doubt of the good they aim at, while the Covenant is unseald but when its Seald it is not So. So if Gods people had no Seales unto this Covenant there would be doubting. But now God hath Seald it, he hath excluded doubting & So Confirmed their faith therein.

2. From the End of these Seals this appears to be So, as 1. That every Soule believing may come into a publick Covenant with God: God greatly requires this, for in this publick Covenanting there is a Great Solemnity & awe of God upon the Soule, but now in Sealing there is this publick Covenanting. But where this is not, there is no publick, if any, covenanting. & therefore it is so.

2. That there may be a publick profession of God to be ours. [56/57]

The onely Adjunct of the Ministry of the Gospell is the Discipline of the Churches which is a means of Grace annext unto the ordinances, applying the Will of God personally in the use of the Keyes for the keeping out offences or putting them out of the Churches of Christ pure.

Explication.

First. We are to Consider the thing Described. & this is the Discipline of Christs Churches. Discipline is set out by various titles, as sometimes ἐξουσίας authority, II Cor. 10.8, from the Authority of Christ exerted by it; sometimes κανών, a rule, as v. 13, 15. From the peculiar manner of Mannaging Christs Authority & Church proceedings hereby: sometimes κυβερνήσεις government, as I Cor. 12.28, as being the Speciall Actings of Christ in the mannagement of his churches, Sometimes it's called ταξιν, order, I Cor. 14.40, from the effect or use of it as keeping all things in order by it in the Churches: & sometimes ῥάβδῳ, a rod, as I Cor. 4.21, either as being the emblem of Government, Ps. 2.9, & a Scepter, Ps. 45.6, so called, & Heb. 1.8. Or else to import the chastisment given unto the Offender by it, hence it is Called מוּסַר, Job 36.10, & παιδεία, instruction, II Tim. 3.16. But the same thing as is set out by these various terms Considered as peculiarly carried on among Christs disciples is called Discipline, importing the peculiar manner of Christs mannaging althings among his Disciples. Hence Discipline.

Secondly. We are to consider the description given which is in these words laid down, viz, A means of Grace annext to Gospell Ordinances consisting in a personall Application of the Will of God by the Use of the Keyes of Christs Kingdom whereby the Churches are kept pure, in which words we have it shown
1. The generall Nature of it, & that is this, its a Means of Grace. & it must needs be so, because herein God convays much Grace unto his people for edification, II Cor. 10.8, for repentance, I Cor. 5.5, & opening the doores of the Kingdom of heaven to the worthy, & to out the unworthy, Matt. 16.19.
2. Its Speciall Nature thus, viz, annext unto Gospel Ordinances consisting in a personall application, etc. in which words the Speciall nature of it is set out
    1. From its Formall Property, in these words, viz, its annext to the Gospell Ordinances; it cannot be without them, nor they without it, but they are as the Substanciall, & it with them the Circumstantiall means of Grace. Hence saith Christ, Ile build my Church & then I give the Keyes.
    2. From its Formall Act, viz, a personall application, it is that wherein a thing is brought down to the Object thereof. Now the formall act is set out

3. From its *formale Actuatum*, or thing applyed, & that is in generall thus, the Will of God. So Matt. 28.29. So that Such discipline that is not in the word of God erected is not Gods, as the Hierarchy. & So all more particularly in the use of the Keyes of the Kingdom of heaven.

Wherein we are to Consider two things, as the $\left\{\begin{array}{l}\text{Using}\\\text{Users}\end{array}\right\}$ thereof.

1. The Using of the Keyes, is in the Opening into, or o[ut]ing from the Kingdom, in respect unto the Opening in[to] the Kingdom; this is called loosing Sins, Matt. 16.19, or remitt[ing] which is done in judging the person worthy, Matt. 10, either on entrance into a Church State, & so receiving him, as II Cor. 7.8, Rom. 14.1, or unto Office in the Kingdome.

Or the use is by way of Outing from the Church State wh[ich is] called a binding, Matt. 16.19. Which is done by locking the doore ag[ainst] the unworthy, either in keeping, or Casting out either from a C[hurch] State, as I Tim. 3.3, 6, Rev. 2.2, or from Church State, as I Cor. 5 * * *

2. The Users of the Keyes. Now the First subject recipient is [the] Church: For so it appears I Cor. 5, Matt. 16.19, etc. 18, for oth[er]wise an Inorganick Church hath no power, her Officers r[e]moving, have removed away her power. Nay further Chri[st's] Churches have no reliefe in Case of Male Administration. But the secondary subject, or the Ministeriall Subject of the K[eyes] are the Officers in the churches.

4. From its Formall Object. & the formall Object of discip[line] is the particular person treated with, hence its cald a perso[nal] appli-cation of the will of God. & its applied both prepar[ati]vely, & this is privatly, Matt. 18.15,16. And Consummatively, & [this] is pub-lickly, which in Case of Outing from Christs Kingdom is done gradually, as first in Admonition. & in case of impenitence Excom-munication, Matt. 18.17, I Cor. 5.5.

Thirdly, Here is this Description the finall Cause or benefit hereof, in these word[s] whereby Christs Churches ar[e] kept pure, as they should, Matt. 3.10,11, I Cor. 5.6,7, hence as port[ers] were set at the gates of the Temple that none that were ceremon[i]ously unclean should enter, I Chron. 23.19, So Christ hath set 12 Angels * * *

Confirmation

1. By Scripture that Christ hath Discipline in his Churches, as Matt.

2. From Reason grounded on Scripture as following
    1. From the Excellencies of Christ the King of the Church. & s[o] I argue thus he that is most excellent hath all his Concerns carried on most excellently: for it is a disparigment unto his excellence to have his Concerns mannaged & not excell[en]tly. & hence the excellency of Solomons wisdom was illustr[i]ously dignified by the excellent mannagment of his concer[ns,] as I Kings 10.4,5. But now Christ Jesus is most excellent, [&] there is none may compare with him, Cant. 5.10–16. & the church is his Concerns he calls it his house or Church, Matt. 16.18, I Tim. 3.15, Heb. 3.3. & this excellent carrying on of things ther[ein] lies in the Discipline thereof as shall appeare by & by.
    2. From the Faithfulness of Christ, he that is faithfull perform[s] all things committed to his Charge. For faithfulness, & universal[l] obedience are equally extended, Jas. 2.10. But Christ is faith[full] in his house, Heb. 3.2: & the Concerns of the Churchs are Christs * * *
    3. From the Discipline in the Leviticall Ministry which was who[ly] exacted of God even unto the very garment of Service, as we[ll as] to the judging between the clean & unclean. Ergo Gospel Disci[pline.]
    4. From the beauty & glory of Christs Kingdom, for this is ve[ry] glorious, hence she is cald the beauty of holiness, Ps. 48.1,2, 150.3, & a bride adorned for her husband, Rev. 21.2: But now this shou[ld] not be without discipline for this brings althings in order, hen[ce] I Cor. 14, last, hence its a well Ordered Kingdom, Ps.   pearls tum[bled] together on a heap though they are pretious are little glori[ous] * * * [57/58]

The Manner how Redemption is applied is considerable as it was
{ Before Christs
  After Christs Passion.

From the beginning of the World untill Christs time it was applied by
dark Shaddows. [58/59]

The Object of Faith is God, who is to be evidenced * * *

2. What God is, so far as it is meet to inquire after him, may be [seen] in this Description, God is, a Spirit, Infinit, & Eternall in Tr[uth,] Goodnesse, Holinesse, Righteousnesse, Wisdom, & Power; who acco[rding] to his own Purpose, hath Created, & doth despose of, all things.

In this Description God is considered in Respect unto his { Nature & Properties.

1. As to his Nature, this is expressed by the word, Spirit, which is one of the highest expressi[ons] by which God Sets out his nature unto us in the Scripture, John 4.24, with respect his { Essence, & Subsistance.

1. The Essence of God is that thereby he is absolutely the first Being. [59/60]

* * * the whole Essence.
* * * three of them in Godhead.

[The Fat]her is the first Person in the Trinity, who hath begot the Son.

2. God the Son is the second Person, who is begotten of the Father.
[60/61]

From Christs time it is considered in respect of it[s] manner
{ Untill, &
{ In the [end] of the Wor[ld.]

From Christs time untill the end of the World it is applied in a cleare & Spirituall Dispensation of Gospel Grace.

In the end of the world it is applied by the transactions of the day of Judgment the which we shall consider { What } it is.[12]
{ That }

> What the day of Judgment is you may se in this Description, viz, The day of Judgment is the Generall Assise of Jesus Christ, who summoning all Sinners to appeare before his Tribunall, shall in a glorious manner render to every one exactly according unto their Deeds.

Explication

First, Here is something to be Spoke of the Name, the Day of Judgment. This is the thing described, its called a day, not because it shall be accomplisht in the limits of one Single day, for that is not the Reason why men's Courts are called Court dayes; for they are oft of many dayes duration: but because it hath its fixt date and that in the duration of time before eternity commence, & put time to periods. & its end shall be at the beginning of Eternity, Matt. 25.41,46. & a day of Judgment, from the work of the day, because then all things shall be judged, Eccl. 12.14, according to Rule of judging called judgments, Ps. 119.7, & by the judgment of Christ or his Determinative Faculty, John 5.22,27, whereby the wicked fall under punishment called Judgments, Jas. 2.13; hence it is called the Day of Judgment, Matt. 11.22,24.

Secondly. Here is the thing itself described from its

First, Generall Nature thus, the Generall Assise. Its an Assise day because it is a day of Calling & trying all actions Sinfull, as Eccl. 12.14: its the generall assise because all Sin defiled shall then appeare, II Cor. 5.10, & all Sinfull action then reviewed, Matt. 12.36.

Secondly. The Particular nature in the Rest of the Description, as it is
laid down from its {Authour
Transaction.

1. Its Author. Thus Jesus Christ, which words are not to be taken
exclusively to exclude the Other persons of the Trinity, for they are also
concern'd there in, hence the whole undivided * * * undistinctly hath
determined it, & doth transact it, as Acts 17.31, Eccl. 12.14: But
Emphatically. Because Christ Jesus, as he is the Son of man hath it
peculiarly conferred on him to transact the whole, John 5.22,27, hence
its calld the Judgment Seat of Christ, II Cor. 5.10.

2. The Transactions of this day are in the {Summo[ns]
Sessio[ns.]

1. The Summons lieth in these words, Who Summon[s] all Sinners to
appear before his Tribunall, in which words we are to Consider the
{Parties concernd in it
Summons itselfe.

The parties in this Summons are the {Agents
Objects} there[of.]

1. The Agents lie intimated in this pronoun Relative Who, which
discovers unto us the Principall Agent of the Summon, by looking back
to finde out unto whom it doth relate, & that is unto Christ Jesus, &
hence he gi[ves] this Summon, hence is that Matt. 13.41. But the In-
stru[m]entall Agents giving this Summon, are the Holy Angels, as Matt.
13.41. The trumpet shall be sounded by them, II Thess. 4.

2. The Objects of this Summons, are those that are Summoned, & these
are expressed by this Qualification, viz, Sinners. The reason is given, I
Tim. 1.9. The Law [is] not made for a Righteous, but for Lawless, &
disobedient, for the ungodly, & Sinners, etc. Now these Sinners are
{M[en]
An[gels.]} Hence the holy Angels are not to be called out to judgme[nt]
for they are onely Sinners that are to be judged. & those glorious Beams
of the morning are to attend upon [the] Glorious Judges person, in their
Sparkling Colours.

1. Mankind defiled with Sin must be Summond wh[e]ther at the day
of Judgment they shall be found De[ad] or a Live, for the voice shall be
given to both, I Cor. 15.52. So that neither shall be secure from this
Summon.

2. The Fallen Angels, these shall be Summoned f[or] all their Subtilty
shall not Secure them from this Summons. & therefore they lie now
bound in chains for Judgment of this day, II Pet. 2.4, Jude 6. [61/62]

* * * * * * & in it we are to take notice of the $\begin{cases} \text{Sitement} \\ \text{Influence.} \end{cases}$

1. The Sitement of Appearance. & this is variously called in Scripture, as a Shoute from its nature, but from the excellency of this tryumphant Shoute, the Sounding of a trumpet, I Cor. 15.52. As God in the giving of the Law sited the people to appear by the Sound of a trumpet, so now in coming to judge his people according to his Law he Sites them to appear by the Sound of a trumpet, which for its excellency is calld the Trumpet of God. & still from the Instrument of this Citement its called the Voice of the Archangel, I Thess. 4.16. But what this is that the Scripture set out this unto us is not known. But its probable it will be some most transcendently Powerfull voice wherein the power of God shall appear, that is here called by the Sounding of the Trumpet.

2. The Influence of this Summons is that whereby the Objects are brought before the judgment Seat, & it is considered as it hath respect unto Fallen $\begin{cases} \text{Man} \\ \text{Angels.} \end{cases}$

1. Upon Fallen Man the Influence is graduall, & to be distinguisht as they are found at the Day of Judgment whether $\begin{cases} \text{Alive or} \\ \text{Dead.} \end{cases}$

Upon those that then shall be found alive it will be a change equavolent to Death itselfe glorious unto those that are in Christ, & thus it consists in the Destruction of this naturall life, & in the renewall of them with an Immortal nature Spirituall, & an eternall Life & so a carrying of them up to Christs Bar, I Cor. 15.51–2, I Thess. 4.17. But Dreadfull to the Wicked securing of them under all their Sins in an impenitent State So that Repentance, & the means of Grace are out of Season. & then dragging of them unto the Judgment Seat of Christ.

Upon the dead the influence is as the dead in Christ or the dead out of Christ.

1. Upon the Dead in Christ the Influence of this Summons on those found * * * hereby is Considered as to their $\begin{cases} \text{Resurrection} \\ \text{The Manner thereof.} \end{cases}$

1. As to their Resurrection, here this Influence is graduall as that it is gradually Carried on; for first there is the Collection of the outward man all together, the flesh, & bones that are rotted to dust, & all dispersed is gathered together again, dust to its dust, & each bit of to its

proper place & bone to bone to constitude the humane body of the very matterialls that lay down, Job 19.26, which probably may be the work of the holy Angels, Matt. 13.39. & then the Soule shall be brought out of that Mansion, where it hath been gloriously welcomed ever Since its departure, probably by the holy Angels, who carried it there from the bodie, Luke 16.22, into its own proper body again. & oh! that Joy that the bodie shall now be wrapt up in at their meeting, whereby it shall as it were leap out of the grave at the Resurrection.

2. As for the manner of the Resurrection, it is as follows (& it will be the same to both those of Christ's saints that are Dead, or found alive at the Resurrection) consisting of absolute Perfection,

First Negatively, all imperfection shall be done away, with respect to the $\left\{ \begin{array}{l} \text{Body} \\ \text{Soule} \end{array} \right\}$ 1. The body as

1. There shall be noe dregs of the fall in mans nature then, Originall Corruption shall never rise out of the grave, it rises in incorruption, I Cor. 15.42, there is no dishonour in it, v. 42, no sinfull Stain shall be in it.

2. There shall be no sting of the Curse in it, no scratching briar, nor pricking thorn, no pains, nor aches, no tang of sickness, or Calamity then. Death then hath lost her Sting, & is Swallowed up in victory, as I Cor. 14.55.

3. There is no lameness nor want of any member, of part or in degree. He that dies a Child shall rise in a full Stature, he that at his death wanted finger, hand, arm, toe, foot, leg, eye, or the like, shall at his Resurrection meet with the want of none of these.

4. There shall be neither Spot nor wrinckle upon it, all frowns or freckles shall be left behinde in the grave, as it may appeare Eph. 5.27.

5. There shall be no weariness, nor tiring, then the back shall not bow, nor the foot blister. The Organs shall not weary in their work, the most glorious object which is ware out, the Organ of sight, the Eye shall not weary in beholding all the glory in heaven, nor the Eare be deadened by all that hart ravishing Musick or Melody there, etc. So that the body shall rise an unweariable body & hence

6. It shall be an immortall body it shall dy no more.

Secondly Affirmatively. The Positive perfection of the Bodies of the Saints in the Resurrection is unspeakable but in one word, they are raised Spirituall, I Cor. 15.43. Not that the Essence of their bodies shall be turn'd into a Spirit, for that is inconsistant with the Identity of the body rising unto the body dead to be raised but

1. In respect unto their Support, & Duration, they shall now indure as long as the Spirits, are as much now eternall; & have Support from any Creature without themselves as Angels, they neither marry nor are given in marriage, they neither eat, nor drink, they have as little compared as Angels with those things.

2. Spirituall in respect unto their Strength, I Cor. 15.43, the whole body shall be So strengthened as that it shall be able to Carry out the highest degree of Exercise that the Soule shall Mannage in it: the highest transportation of joy shall not be above the strength of the body to beare it with an inravishing influence. The most transcendent sparkling rayes of glory shall not breake or hurt, but felicitatingly Irradiate the Organ of Sight. The more transcendent Sound the Last trumpet shall make, the more heart-ravishing Melody shall it fill the eare withall, the most terrible voice shall not make eare to tingle.

3. Spirituall in respect unto nimbleness, & agility of the body. Now the body is unto the Soule like a golden prison to confine it. It breaks this prison, & flies to heaven, but at the Resurrection it shall be as golden wings unto the Soule for the Soule to fly about Gods Service withall, here it is the pinion of the Soule, but then it shall be the Souls wing. & with the Soule shall mount up to heaven, I Thess. 4.19.

4. Spirituall in respect unto Glory, I Cor. 15.42, if a few broken rayes of Gods glory striking in Moses's face made Moses's face shine as the Sun, what a Shine shall there be in the bodys of the Saints at the Resurrection, when as the Graces of the Spirit shall Shine within them. & all the glory of heaven shall shine upon them. Oh then the very bodies of the Saints Shall Shine like the Sun in the firmament, Matt. 23.43, nay like the glorious body of Christ, Phil. 3.21. Thus shall they be raised in Glory & be like Angels, Matt. 22.29. & thus they shall be Spirituall.

Secondly, respecting the Soule & the Affections.

1. Negative perfection in the Affections & Soule that the Saints shall arise withall is as follows.

1. In the Understanding there shall be no cloud or darkness therein, it shall see clearely.

2. Upon the Will there shall be no perversness there, no stubbornness.

3. In the Affections, here shall be no disorder, nor fretting Passion; no anger, nor galling envy, no Sorrow, etc.

2. Affirmative perfection of the Soule, etc., at the resurrection is that which render it compleatly excellent, as

1. A Perfect light Shining into the understanding, I Cor. 13.12.

2. A Perfection of Life in the Will. The Will is as full of Spirituall Life as ever it can contain.

3. A Perfection of Grace in the Affections. All the Graces ot the Spirit in the highest degree in the Soule sanctifying of it, & making of it holy. & thus both the inward, and outward man are repaired. Hence the resurrection is called the regeneration, Matt. 19.26, when all the parts of man are regenerated, & renewed perfectly into the Image of God out of which it fell by Sin.

Thus much for the Resurrection of the just. [62/63]

1. The Second act of this Summons upon the Dead in Christ is the gathering of them unto the Court, called in Scripture a gathering the Sheep upon the Right hand, as Matt. 25.33.

Secondly, the Influence of this Summons upon those Sinners out of Christ, these are Such as die in a State of Sin whether $\begin{cases} \text{Alive} \\ \text{Dead.} \end{cases}$

1. Upon those that shall be found alive at the Day of judgment & this will be that Change that they shall undergo equivolent unto Death, whereby their day of Grace shall be ended, & they put into an Eternall State. Now this Summons on them shall be such as shall reduce them out of this Chang unto the Bar of Jesus Christ.

2. Upon those then in a State of death. & it shall be such as shall
$\begin{cases} \text{Raise them} \\ \text{Present them.} \end{cases}$

1. As shall Raise them from the dead. & here we are to Consider
the $\begin{cases} \text{Resurrection itself} \\ \text{Manner thereof.} \end{cases}$

1. As for the Resurrection itselfe this as to the Worke its the very same with that of the Saints. But as to the Workers it may probably be

thought that they are not the Same, theirs being mannaged wholy by the Holie Angels; these by the Evill Angels probably that of theirs more probably attended upon by the Good Angels, but this of these by the bad as it is probable that the Good Angels attend the Souls of the Righteous unto their own Bodies again from Paradise unto the Judgment Seat.—So its probable that the Divels drag the Souls of the Wicked from their Dungion in hell unto their own bodies, & So to Christs Tribunall. They are not the Same as to the ground of the Resurrection, for the Ground of the Resurrection of the Righteous is the Grace of Redemption, & the Merits of Christ. The ground of the wickeds rising is the Absolute Power of the vindictive Justice of Christ. But in other things its the Same with theirs as the $\begin{cases} \text{Body} \\ \text{Soul.} \end{cases}$

1. As to the Body, the very Same body that Died shall rise again, & not a new one made, but its onely made a new, & therefore all its dust sought out, & every dust put to its place to make the whole a new. And the very Same Soule that departed & not an other shall enter into the very Same body out of which it departed. & oh the Surprisall, the Dreadfull Surprisall of feare that this old cottage now cottered together again shall be rapt up with all; it shall make every joynt to tremble again, & if it were possible, to fly to dust again, it would.

2. As to the Manner of the Resurrection of the Wicked.

Therefore, first in particular the manner in which the parts shall come forth as the $\begin{cases} \text{Body} \\ \text{Soule.} \end{cases}$

1. As for the Body it shall rise under a Perfectly compleat fallen State as

1. It shall rise totally deprived of all those naturall Excellencies which it were indowed with in this life unless they do remain to be instruments of Gods Righteous judgments for ever. Now that this shall be so read Matt. 25.28,29, take from him that had one talent, his talent. Hence altho' the Soule was for beauty the Paragon of his Age, the Ornament of his Sex, & the glory of the world all shall be taken away, it shall arise stript naked of all, & * * * So all Strength shall be taken, no more rema[in than] what will serve to keep Soule & body together * * * Ease, & rest shall be taken away, not so much [a shad]dow thereof remaining.

2. It shall arise totally acomplisht for * * * wrath, as universally as can be, as arising * * *

1. In as ugly, & ilfavoured appearance * * * all ugly, all overugly. Oh that gasterly, ghostly, * * * Hellish appearance that the body of the wicked shall * * *

2. In as weake, & trembling as possible can be * * * reeling, oh the trembling, oh the horrid trembling * * * limbs, the Joynts, the body as it peeps out of the Gr[ave.]

3. In as receptible a way of tortures as its po[ssible.] All the doores of the Senses standing wide open * * * they run to receive all tortures whatever. * * * passage of the being as wide open to admitt pa[in and tor]ment as may be. The Looking Glass of the Memo[ry] * * * all Sin and Guilt on the one hand, & hell & damna[tion] on the other hand before the face. The nimble distu[rbing] fancy dashing a Quaver of hell fire on every cir[cum]stance of the Same.

2. As for the Soule in the Resurrection it shall re[turn] unto its own bodie, where we are to Consider it,

1. As to the Understanding, & judgment & this will be s[uch] as that there shall be as Hellish darkness, & ignoran[ce] therein as possible there can, all litterall know[ledge] of the truths of Christ that any man did in this life inligh[tening] the Soule shall be utterly extinguisht, not any peeph[ole] of light to relieve the Soule shall remain unstop[ped.]

2. As for the Will & Affections, these shall be as pe[rverse] as pervers can be; as having not so much as an in[cli]nation against Sin, or for Sanctity, or the want of the * * * dram of love to Sin, or hatred to God, as also bein[g] Surprized with the highest Surprisalls of Fear brea[th]ing in upon the Soule in a fresh flushing Conquest of * * * Hope, for what ever tend to support the Soule in * * * manner doth it inter into the body. & therefore

2. As for the manner of the Whole Person when the B[ody] shall be raised.

1. It will Rise compleatly under the power & guilt [of] all Sin it ever Committed: Sin will not lose its life [with] the Sinners death, nor will it any whit be deadned b[y] the Sinners living again, but it will rise in its full p[o]wer in the poore Soule when [it] rises from the Dead; & hence you s[ee] it acting in him, Matt. 25.24, Charging Christ with un-ri[gh]teousness. Neither will the guilt of Sin be deadoned by [the] grave but the Soule will Stand formally under the guilt of all Sin committed by him, & of Originall Sin.

2. It will arise compleatly under the filth & ugliness of a[ll] Sin. Not one blot shall be taken of[f] by the Grave. But the whole Ugliness of Sin

Shall appeare. So that the Soule having all his excellence done away he is as filthy, ugl[y] & as unlike God as ever he can appeare by the contagion of Sin.

4. This Summons shall be Such as shall present them before the Judgment in this State that they rise in, & oh how ugly, how lamentable? how tremblingly shall they now Stand before the bar of Christ, hence Matt. 25.32.

Now that there is a resurrection of the dead appears

1. From Scripture, as Matt. 19.28,22, 30.32, Job 19.25,26, I Cor. 15 through out, Matt. 28.6, Rev. 20.

2. From Reason. 1. *Ab Absurdo.* If there be no resurrection then Gods creating this nether world, & man, as also all Religion is a meer fable, for there is no end why they are; man comes & goes & there is the conclusion. & religion is a toy. But what blasphemy is this to think? 2. From the righteousness of God, for how should this be if there is no resurrection seing the wicked are the prosperous in this world, & the Godly afflicted. [63/64]

Secondly. The Sessions or Court itselfe comes to be considered as to the $\left\{ \begin{array}{l} \text{Access to} \\ \text{Process in} \end{array} \right\}$ the Court, both which in the Rest of the Description are laid out to be in a most glorious manner.

1. The Access unto the Court or Sessions, this is Christs coming to the Bench in a most glorious way, where the Glory is to be considered as with respect unto the $\left\{ \begin{array}{l} \text{Courtiers} \\ \text{Throne of Judgment.} \end{array} \right.$

1. The Glory of the Courtiers as

1. The Glory of the Judge. He shall now come in transendent Glory, for he shall come to be admired at, II Thess. 1.10. Then he shall come in his glory, Matt. 25.31. If the bodies of the Saints shall at the Resurrection Shine like the body of the Sun, what shall the body of Christ the Son of God Shine like, it is called a body of glory now, Phil. 3.21, if he appeared so glorious in the Vision among his churches, Rev. 1.12—what shall his glory be now he comes to appear in his glory? if his description, Cant. 5.10—shows his glory to be so transcendent: what shall he show himselfe to be when he shall appeare in a more transcendent Glory then there is in that? If in the government of the world, Ezek. 1.26, 17, he appeare so glorious what will the glory of his appearance in his judging of the world be? Surely if he appeared in a vision to Daniel

having his body like unto byrill, his arms & feet in Colour like unto polisht brass, his eyes like Lumps of fire, his face like a flash of Lightening, & his voice like a clap of thunder, as Dan. 10.6 & 9, oh then what glory shall he now appear in?

2. The Glory of the Judges Attendants, those glorious waiting men of heaven, those sparkling beams of the morning, the heavenly hosts of holy Angels, Matt. 25.31. & thousands thousands of them in their flashing mantles of glory sparkling about him, & tenthousand times tenthousands ministring unto him, as Dan. 9.10, are the attendants. Those Courtiers of heaven Shall wait upon Christ in this Court.
Thus for the glory of the Courtiers.

2. The Glory of the Throne of Judgment. If the judge be so glorious, his throne must have an answerable glory. If Solomon had such a glorious Throne of Judgment, What a throne of Judgment shall the Lord Jesus have? If Solomon who in all his glory was not arrayed like the Lilly, Matt. 6.28,29, had such a Magnificient Throne, what a throne shall he have who hath clothed all things with glory that are glorious. Well let us compare them together a little. Solomons Throne, II Chron. 9.17,18,19, probably was set upon Some Stately Pavement: But Christs probably is set up[on] a Saphirine Pavement, or the Crystalline Fermament, Ex. 24.10, Ezek. 1.22, I Thess. 4.17, Matt. 24.30. Solomons throne was of Ivorie overlaid with pure gold. But this is of a Saphire having round about it the appearance of Amber, Ezek. 1.26,27. Solomons was a golden Ivory throne, this is a Firy Saphirine Throne, Dan. 11.9. Solomons had Six Stares to it with Lyons curiously wrought standing as Banisters upon each Step. But Christs is high & lifted up with Shining Angels attending on it, Isa. 6.2. Solomons was a yellow throne but Christs a White Throne, as Rev. 20.12. Solomons was a glorious throne. But Christs a Throne of Glory, Matt. 25.31. Oh what glory is here? Christs Throne then doth so far out shine the glory of Solomons Throne, that the glory of Solomons Throne is onely darksome in Comparison unto the glory of Christs Throne. & thus much for the glory of the throne. & So we have done with the glory of the Court respecting the Access unto it, & as for the glory further it will appear in the Process thereof.

2. The Process in the Sessions or Court. This lies in these words, "he shall render unto all exactly according to their deeds."

Now this Process shall be with the $\begin{cases} \text{Saints} \\ \text{Wicked.} \end{cases}$

1. With the Saints, it begins with them, begin at my Sanctuary, Judgment must begin at the house of God. [I] Pet. [4.17], Matt. 25.34, I Thess. 4.16, & here we are to consider both the $\begin{cases} \text{Triall} \\ \text{Judgment.} \end{cases}$

1. The Triall which consists of the $\begin{cases} \text{Inditment} \\ \text{Plea.} \end{cases}$

The Inditment runs against all that are under the Tryall & there is in it

1. The arrainment, those that have an interest in Christ shall be arraigned at the Bar: because the triall is a Capitall Case & hereby the Impartiality of the Judge, & the Righteousness of the Court will appeare: hence they Cannot Speak a word against the Court for arreigning them because they shall Se those that are Christ's own called out & arreign'd & not one of them escape, altho' they arose in such Excellent & Perfect Glory, & Stand as gloriously arrayed in Christs milke white Righteousness at the Bar, yet there they shall Stand & be tried, II Cor. 5.10, we must all appeare before the Judgment seat of Christ.

2. The Charge itselfe, & this shall be of all things done in the Flesh whether $\begin{cases} \text{Good} \\ \text{Bad} \end{cases}$ as II Cor. 5.10, not any thing shall be omitted whether good, & here nature, manner, & degree of the deed shall be searched out, & so the failing in any Circumstance presented among their Bad deeds, & the rest considered & weighed in the Ballence of Righteousness, which is called a judging out of the Book, as Rev. 20.12, or Whether they be their bad deeds, & those shall all of them with all their Circumstances be laid before the Soule. Thus all things done in the flesh according as they are done shall be charged home upon the Soule & he called to answer whether guilty or not guilty?

2. The Plea to this Charge respects the things that are bad, or their Sins, & unto these they plead guilty as to the Fact or Charge. & hereby they own the Righteousness of the Court, & acknowledge that they for their part deserve to be sunk down into hell. & this tends to the condemning of the Wicked. But yet as to the guilty, or Judgment they plead not guilty. & for a further triall of the Case they desire to by tryed by the Court or Throne of Grace where their Plea is, viz, Who shall implead Gods Elect? Its God that Justifieth. Who shall Condemn? it is Christ that died & is risen again, Rom. 8.32,33. & as for their Good they did, or obedience with an holy humility they cry out [64/65] When did we ever do anything worth taking notice of, Matt. 25.37,38,39. Not unto us

Lord, not to us but to thy Name be the Praise. & So leave all to the tryall of the Throne of Grace.

2. The Judgment that is brought in upon the case thus tryed consists in the $\begin{cases} \text{Sentence} \\ \text{Execution.} \end{cases}$

1. The Sentence that is given upon the Case is an accepting of the Plea of not guilty as to Judgment on the account of Christ to be found valid at the Throne of Grace. & therefore pronounces the Soule Righteouse on that account, Rom. 8.1. & as to the other part of the Charge respecting the duties of obedience the Judge weighing the Actions with all the Circumstances of the Same having perfumed them with his own merits to make them passe doth according to their Degree proportion by his Sentence an exact recompence unto the Soule in Eternall glory, II Cor. 4.18, Saying Come ye blessed of my Father, inherit the Kingdome prepared for you before the foundation of the world, Matt. 25.34. This is the judging out of what was * * * Rom. 20.

2. The Execution of this Sentence, & that lieth in the Actuall instating of the Soul in Glory & happiness which is to be considered as to the $\begin{cases} \text{Nature &} \\ \text{Duration} \end{cases}$ thereof.

1. As for the Nature of this recompence or Glory & happiness, it may be Illustrated as it is unto the Saints $\begin{cases} \text{Extrinsical} \\ \text{Intrinsicall.} \end{cases}$

1. The Glory of the Saints in heaven which is Extrinsicall is that which is properly the Glory of heaven, & it consists in the $\begin{cases} \text{Place itselfe} \\ \text{Inhabitants therein.} \end{cases}$

1. The Glory of the Place which for its building is most Glorious. Kings Palaces are adorn'd with Royall glory. If the firmament is Such a Silver arch adorn'd with golden Bosses of Sparkling twinkling Stares over the head of the terrestriall Creatures which is but as it were the under pavement of our Saviours Pavilion what shall we think of the inside Glory, where are horded up all Sorts of Excellencies the Conceptions of which have not entred into the thought of mans heart, Isa. 64.4, I Cor. 2.9. If the Palace Garden Court of the King of Persia Court was so gorgeously glorious as to have beds of Gold upon a Pavement of Red, blew, White, & Black Marble, What shall we think of the glory, that unconceivable Glory of the Court of Heaven! Rev. 21.1.

2. The glory of the Inhabitants of heaven, as of the $\begin{Bmatrix} \text{Society} \\ \text{Owner} \end{Bmatrix}$ of it.
The Society $\begin{cases} \text{Saints} \\ \text{Angels.} \end{cases}$

1. The Saints. Every Saint is in Scripture called a Precious Stone, they are called the Stone of a Crown, Zech. [9.16.] Saphires, Agats, Isa. 54.11,12, Rev. 21.14 & the 18 compared. Now if ever Saint is as a shining Carbuncle in the Ring of Glory, every ones Glory falling upon every one in glory Will be a glory unto every One. Oh then what a glory will here be arising from the Societie of the Saints upon every Saint in glory.

2. The Angels, the blessed, & glorious Angels, Heb. 12.22. The Saints shall be intred into the Society of Angels: & therefore they shall share with them in their glory. & here in Some respect I may say, that looke how much the glory of [the] Soule out shines the glory of [the bo]dy so much will the glory of Angels outshine the * * * the Saint. & therefore in that the Saints shall be * * * into the Society of Angels of those Glorious Angels * * * shall this Contribute to their glory? Oh! what Sp[arkling] Angelicall glory shall light upon the glorified w[hen the] Saints shall be received as members into that Sh[ining] Society of Glorious Angels, Matt. 28.30.

2. The Owner of it, & this is God himselfe. All the * * * glory would be a Cloud were it not for this glor[ious] glory is so bright, that the brightness of it doth make the other appeare li[ke a] darke cloud in the Sons glorious Shine in compa[rison] unto it. Oh! the glory of the Humane Nature of * * * Oh! the glory of that unconceivable union of [Hu]mane nature & the Divine in the person of the Son [of God.] Oh! the Glory of the Divine Nature in itselfe! Oh! [the glory] of the Persons in the Trinity, of three in One, & [One] in Three! Of three that are but one Eternall Essen[ce.] One Eternall Essence which is three Distinct Persons * * * glory of God in his Attributes & Operations! how * * * Sparkle forth! Look upon the glory of all the world, & [it is] but as a darke Smoke compared to the glory of the S[un,] looke upon the glory of the Sun, & this is probably b[ut] Smoking fog compared to the glory of heaven, & lo[ok] on the glory of Heaven, & probably its but as a fog[gy] Vapor compared unto the glory of the Saints & An[gels.] But look upon the glorified Saints, & glorious An[gels] & these are not so much a vapour or cloude in the [sky] compared with the glory of the Lord who dwels in * * * inaccessible, & full of glory. Thus much for their [Ex]trinscick glory of the Saints in glory.

2. The Intrinscick Glory of the glorified Saints * * * which is the influence of this extrinscick Glory upon * * * the which in respect unto the Degree of it is proportion[ate] unto the degree of their Graces, & Obedience in this li[fe,] & it is poured out upon them in a way of

1. Glorifying of them. You se what glory they were r[apt] up in. & how by the Resurrection they were wonderfully fi[tted] for glory in heaven. & now they have the glory of heaven * * * unto them falling upon all their other glory by t[heir] intring into heaven, making that intrinscicall gl[ory] of theirs, give a far more transcendently transcend-[ent] glory. & now their whole Soule, & body are filled fu[ll] of Glory.

2. Felicitating of them. Filling of them as full of h[ap]piness as ever they can hold. One cannot hold so mu[ch] as another not being so largly expatiated by the gro[wth] of Grace as another, yet every nature shall be filled as full [as] ever it can hold. Now the intrinsick felicity of the Saints flowing from that extrinscicall glory into their Souls is both $\begin{cases} \text{Immediate} \\ \text{Ultimate.} \end{cases}$

1. Immediate Influences & Such as doth felicitate t[he] person to the full as they light upon the outward ma[n] they render it compleatly happy, pouring out th[ere] upon, all those inravishing Influences as are always involving of it in new raptures of perfect happiness, & as in its Resurrection it was capacitated to receiv[e as] much, & its Senses throughly freed from all imperfection, & fitted with all Perfection. So that the Eye is fitted to behold with full heart ravishment the Glory, & the Eare to heare with all Soule solacement the Seraphick Melod[y] of Glory in heaven; etc. So now this Glory of heaven shall be poured in Such heart inamouring Influen[ce] as shall swallow up the Outward man in felicity. So the eye shall be filled unto the utmost of it[s] extent in beholding of all heart ravishing Glory and yet alwayes in the highest act of Contentment & never weary nor hurt by the Same & So for the eare, etc.

But as these influences fall upon the Inward man they are no less felicitating it, as they are poured out upon the Inward Senses. Now the Memory alwayes bears her bright looking [glass] before the Soule with * * * [65/66] inravishing incounter, so that more fresh, & felicitating acts of memory cannot be, & alway fresh & felicitating. & on the Fancie, oh how will the Influence of heavens Glorie upon the Fancy, that nimbly & heart-inflaming faculty make it set its Soule inamouring & felicitating Pauses, & Quavers over all Gods work & wayes. & to make the golden Strings of the Soule to tryumph for joy.

Or as this Influence falls upon the Soule as upon the Understanding. Oh that light of grace therein being now filled full with that light of Glory! what transporting contentment will it yield? to Se God face to face, to se Jesus Christ, to Se the wayes of God in the World! to Se the Golden Checker work of the Draw net of Providence hung open before the view of the Soule, To behold how in the Meshes of the Same the Saints are Caught, & carried to Glory, & the Sinner caught, & Cast into hell; etc., to See the glorious out going of Gods Essentiall Properties! etc. Oh how will this anoint the Soule. So also upon the Will, & Affections. Oh the pourings forth of heavens Glory here, will make all heaven within. Now it will make all life & liveliness heare. Love will be elevated with the Beams of Glory to inflame the Soule in the highest degree of Content, & always acting in the highest Imbraces. Joy will be mounted upon the Wings of Glory to give the Soule the highest transport of Delight that may be, & alwayes it is injoying fresh incomes, so that its Joyes never Cease. & thus it bathes itselfe in fulness of Joyes, & Pleasures, Ps. 16.12, & all those filling Influences of the Will & Affections break out in

2. The Ultimate Influence of heavenlie Glory upon the Soule. & that is this it sets the Soule a Singing forth the Praises of the Lord. God having made the Soule Such a glorious Musicall Instrument of his praises, & the holy Ghost having so gloriously Strung it with the golden wyer of grace, & heavenly Glory having Skrew'd up the Strings to Sound forth the Songs of Zions King, the pouring forth of the Influence of Glory play upon the Soule Eternall praises unto God. & Now the Soule beg[inn]ing to Sing forth its endless Hallelujahs unto God. If it were possible it would fly in pieces under its glory if this glory got no vent. & therefore it being filled with glory for Gods glory it falls to singing most heart-ravishingly out the Glory of God in the highest Strains.

Thus much for the Glory & Happiness itself.

2. The Duration of it. & this is Eternall, these are Everlasting Joys, & Pleasures for ever more, Ps. 16.11, Matt. 25.46. So that the Soule is alwayes inrapt in fresh Surges of Glory. The Glory never dims, the happiness never dies, the Soule never wearies, the wyers never breake, the Pins never Slip, the tunes or Musick never fail. But the flower is always in the flowrish, its Eternall Glory, II Cor. 4.18. Oh! its Eternall.

Suppose we then that this Glory of heaven conferred upon the Saints was Compared unto a Most Curious perfumed Rose that should be as big as the Whole Creation of God from the Centre of the earth to the Circumference of the Highest heaven, set with so many folds of flowers one in an other & one upon another as should fill it from the Centre to the Circumference with leaves no bigger than the fourth part of a leafe of a Rose flower, & on every of these leaves there were printed in figures of Gold as many milians of years as minuts from the begining to the end of the world & that then when all those years were expired that were figured in gold upon all those Rose leaves, the glory of heaven should be at an End, one would thinke the end would be so far off that it would be almost endless. But yet it would not be endless but would most certainly come to an End should it be run over & over again. But yet this Eternal glory shall have no end but shall be as far off from any end when all those years are ended as it was at the first, oh then what a glory is here that the Execution of this Sentence of Christs Judgment day shall bring the Saints into.

But this much Concerning the Process of the day with those that have an intrest in Christ.

2. The Process of the Day of Judgment with the wicked follows. These must come to be judged in the last place & the Divels themselves after the Saints because they shall be judged by the Saints; the Saints therefore being acquitted in the Judgment Shall be taken up unto Christ & joyn with him in judging these, Matt. 19.28, I Cor. 6.2.

3. Wicked men, & Divels shall be judged by the Saints & by the Law & Rule the Saints are acquitted the other shall be damned, & therefore we are to Consider in this Process the $\begin{cases} \text{Tryall made} \\ \text{Judgment thereon.} \end{cases}$

1. The Tryall of the case consists in the $\begin{cases} \text{Inditment} \\ \text{Plea.} \end{cases}$

The Inditment drawn up lies in the Scripture expressed by the opening of the book, as Rev. 20.11,12. & in it we are to observe

1. The Arraignment of the Miserable Miscreant & Damnable wretch who shall stand in his sin, & guilt, ugliness, & filth trembling. & that every one of them, not one whether wicked men or Divels, none overlookt, none omitted; none can get away from the wrath of the judge, or make an Escape, Rev. 20.12, II Cor. 5.10.

2. The Charge, or the fact itselfe for which they are arreigned & this is of all things done in the flesh, II Cor. 5.10, whether good, or bad, for

somethings they may do which are materially good. & looke how many these are so much there shall be a * * * of torment if compared with such as are both materially & formally bad; so their bad Deeds shall be called over & weighed in all their circumstances, not one Deed, or one circumstance omitted but all things as inward Corruption & Sinfull thoughts, Jer. 17.10; or Outward as words, Matt. 12.36,37, or works whether private or publick, Eccl. 12.14.

2. The Plea unto this Charge & unto it some Shall be so Selfe Condemn'd & dasht down by the dread & sparkling magesty of the Judge as that they shall not be able to speak a word, Matt. 22.25. Others will deny the fact, & put it to a further procedurall as Matt. 7.22,23, Chap. 25.24, 25.34. & then he will proceed by his own law or high Court of Justice to prove it, & bring in evidences & make it out, as Matt. 25.26, 45.

2. The Judgment given here upon, the matter being firmly made out in law the court proceed to give judgment by the $\left\{\begin{array}{l}\text{Sentence past} \\ \text{Execution there[of.]}\end{array}\right.$
The sentence is thus given, Matt. 25.41, Dep[art] from me thou accursed, into eternall flames proportiond to thy deeds prepar'd for the Divel & his Angels. [66/67]

* * * * * * on whom it is pronounced: & therefore I choose here to Consider the matter of it as it shall bee personally applied, & herein there are to be considered the $\left\{\begin{array}{l}\text{Nature} \\ \text{Duration}\end{array}\right\}$ of the thing.

1. The Nature of the Thing applied is such as that it makes the Soule compleatly miserable. & it is to be Considered as it consists in punishment $\left\{\begin{array}{l}\text{Loss} \\ \text{Sense.}\end{array}\right.$

1. In the Punishment of Loss, in this word expresst, viz, Depart from me, wherein we have something implied, which is the totall loss of every thing what ever which in this life spake any thing of happiness from God unto the now Damned whether accidentall as Estate, content, etc. or Naturall as beauty, Excellency, Strength, etc. the which the Soule rose without, but now he is to be with out according to the Sentence of the Law of God. & Something Explain'd, & this is the totall Loss of God himselfe, & all Communications of his Glory & happiness which is as much as heaven itselfe is worth unto the Saints, of which you have some touch before. & this shall be so totally Lost, as that there shall not be so much as amounts to a drop of Cold water upon the tip of ones

finger to allay the tortures of Hell, Luke 16.24,25. This then is a State where no mercy grows. O! what a loss is this? never such a loss! the Eternall Non-being of the Soule would be Chosen a thousand times over before the Sustaining of this loss! This makes way for Compleat tortures, for so long as anything of God is injoy'd so long there is Something of Wrath avoided, but the totall loss of God makes way for the Eternall tortures of Hell. & therefore this consists

2. In the Punishment of Sense, or Sensible tortures, lying in these words of the Sentence given, Into Eternall flames proportionable unto thy deeds prepared for the Divell & his Angels, in which we are to consider this punishment of Hell as it is $\begin{cases} \text{Extrinscicall} \\ \text{Intrinscicall} \end{cases}$ to the Sinner.

1. As it is Extrinscicall, it is to be considered wherein its nature lies, viz, as in the $\begin{cases} \text{Place} \\ \text{Society.} \end{cases}$

1. The Place itselfe. & let this be what it will, it must needs be an execrable place in that its the place where the Damned, & Divels are tortured for ever. If Authorities on earth prepare such dolefull Dungeons to punish evill doers in! what shall we thinke of this place. Oh this must needs be a dread full, dolefull, darksom, gloomy, dismall, & Deadly place indeed. Its Called in Scripture utter darkness, Matt. 22.12, 25.30, Hell, Ps. 9.17, Hell fire, Matt. 5.22, Wrath to come, Matt. 3.7, a Lake of fire & brimstone, as Rev. 20.13, 21.8, Everlasting Distruction, II Thess. 1.7,8, Everlasting torment, & everlasting flames, Matt. 25.41,46. Whether by this fire, or flame is intended the Pure wrath of God as some, or also materiall fire as most probable, I shall not determine, yet this is plain, it doth import the most extream tormentor which is, for nothing acts more furiously than fire upon any thing. Hence this place is the most terrible, torturing, tormenting, burning, Scalding, Enfiring, Stincking, Strangling, Stiffling, Choaking, damping Dungeon immaginable. Oh what a place is here!

2. The Society of this place are the Divel & his Angels, that is Damned Sinners, & the Damned divels. Damned Souls! oh looke on [the most] misshapen, ugly Conditioned roague on earth, & is he not a frighting spectacle, but what if thou Sawest a whole troop of Such in a most ugly gastered appearence come gaping upon thee! oh what wouldst thou do? Ay but if it were an army of Spirits, or Ghosts, what then? Ay, but Soule[s] here are Such, not a few only but a whole dungeon full, a whole Hell full of such ugly things, of roagues, Spirits, Ghosts, & Divels!

& not onely so, but here is now nothing but such! Nay & not onely so but all roaring, yelling, frying, Crying, tering, rending, froathing, fo[a]ming under the wrath of the almighty, trembling. Oh! dreadfull sight, oh hidious screech! Oh what Company is here, but this is the Society that inhabit eternall plagues. If the very appearance of a Spirit from God in a night vision unto that holy man Eliphas was so terribly terrifying as to make all his joynts to tremble, Job 4.14,15, & his hair to stand on end again; If the very appearance of a supposed Ghost upon the sea, was so tremendous as to make the very Apostles to screech out like distracted persons as frighted out of their witts, Matt. 14.26, Oh what a Sight, a terrifying Sight is here. Let this be thought on. & yet this & onely this is the Company in Hell.

2. As to the Intrinscicall Punishment of the Damn'd in Hell, & this is made by the operation of this Extrinscicall upon the Sinner, whereby the Tormenting Influences do reall[y] operate upon the Person torturing it. The Damned wretch is taken up as it were, & bound, & hurled headlong into this Lake of Fire & brimston, Matt. 25.30, & he being compleatly stript of every thing that would keep off any torture, & all the passages of reception being opened in the largest degree to let tortures in, & the instruments torturing being thus applyed, the person is as sorely wrought upon by the same, & as universally Swallowed by the Same as possibly he can be, & hell torments eate & strike as deep as can be in the
$\begin{cases} \text{Body} \\ \text{Soule.} \end{cases}$

1. In the Body, which is all over tortured. Oh! the body is all over tortured. Its Sunk down into a lake of burning fire & brimstone. It Swims in rappid Flames. If the whole Earth was all of a glowing fire Coale & the four winds of heaven were from all quarters blowing as so many bellows of a furnace upon it with all their fury to force its burning to the highest degree of intencness up & into the Center from every Side, & thou fixt in the very Centre thereof to have all this burning heat blown upon thee, & under the same kept alive by the power of God to beare this torment would not this be an unconceivable torment? but yet it would not be So much as a fleabiting compared unto the torments of Hell. Oh! the bodily tortures! as they reise upon it, which the body Sucks up as a spunge doth water. Oh! how are they drunke in at the Senses & every way.

1. The punishment received by, & working upon the Externall senses is beyond all conception. I shall indeavour [t]o do something to help our thoughts about it. Thus Consider it therefore

    1. As it is received through, & acts upon the eyes. Oh! that dreadfull firy flaming, flashing, sparkling, terrible Majesty of the Judge! how doth it send its fiery darts of terror through the very heart to behold, oh how doth it tear the very eye in pieces to looke upon? & oh those dismall & dreadfull Sight[s], those Ghostly, agasting looks of Damned Sinners, & Spirits & Divels there! Oh! who is able to immagine what torture [67/68] * * * * * * upon the sinner, as also the beholding the fury of the flames, the fiercness of the fire, & the horror of the place!

    2. As it operates upon & enters in at the eare. Oh! what pangs, & girds of torments come in this way. Oh! those Schreeches, those Cryes, those yellings, those roaring, those gusted-out Screeches, that Gnashing of Teeth of the damned there, Oh! that horrible noise & dole full Groans of Damned Divels, & burning Spirits, what eare can hear them? how will these rend & teare the very eare in their entrance! & Strike the very heart like so many bodkins; & therefore think of this. O how doth the eare prove an inlet now to hellish torments.

    3. As it operates upon, & enters by the nosthrils. Oh those smoaks, those Damps, those Choaking Damps of Hell fire, of the brimstony vapours of smoake, & all those Horrid stincks & sents, who is able to imagine what torture shall come in this way?

    4. As it operates upon, & is received by the Sense of feeling, this being the most universall Sense of all as spreading over the whole body, & runing through the Same from the inside & out, & all its doores (as I may say) set wide open to let in all torturing Influences, who is able to conceive of the tortures, that come in this way, the whole man being Swallowed up with Scalding flame in the lake that burns with fire, & brimstone, oh here comes in all sorts of torment, by whole troops on every Side. Oh, those heart quakers, those fainting turns, those Sick pangs! Oh those ashes in the joynts, pains in the bones, those Cramps, & convulsions of the joynts & Sinews. Oh those burnings, boyling & perboylings of the flesh, all rowled in flaming Coals, & bathed in burning flames! Oh! what pains are here? as if every grain of flesh was tore, & rent a sunder, as if all poysonous Creatures had tore it or were taring of it all over to pieces, as if it has filld all over with most venom Stings &

lay under the pain of the Same, which is little or nothing in comparison unto this. Oh who among us can dwell with devouring fire? who among us can dwell with everlasting burning? Isa. 33.14. Oh the tormenting torment of those flames & in the middst of all this not one drop of reliefe but all these let loose upon the Damned Soule are in the highest degree of art in tormenting. O Compleatly miserable. Compleatly miserable.

2. This Punishment as it acts upon the Internall Senses is inconceivable. O that torture that rises from the giddy distracted & * * * faculty of the whirling fancy; & the Looking Glass of the Memory? How will this receive all those Frightfull Images, or * * * of all those terrifying Sights, & hold them [a]llwayes there. & how will the Phancy always be peeping therein, & alwayes in fresh fears, & ever be Surprised with fresh afrightments? & oh how will this keep the whole man in a constant rack & always make fresh assaults upon the Soule & fill the whole with fresh flame, & the remembrance of things make a Constant Supply of Continuall Gallings of Conscience.

* * * * * * as they Enter into the Soule & oh here is the very hight of Torments! & these torments do as far Exceed those of the body as the nature of the body falls below the nature of the Soule. & whether there shall be any materiall Instrument immediatly acting upon the Essence of the Soule in Gods revenging Justice upon it, or whether the pure wrath of God shall be applyed unto it by the flames of hell in their torturing of the body, by the influence of which torture of the body, the pure wrath of God's light upon the Soule to torture it, I query not, but the Soule shall be filled with it. & all things what ever would bear of the least degree of it from the Soule being removed away, & all the intrances there into being set wide open, & the whole flood of Eternall vengeance poured out upon it, its wholy swallowed up with Such Surpassingly Exquisit torments that Surpass all degree of mans Conception.

Oh that horrid Darkness in the Judgment Called utter darkness in Scripture. Oh that madness, & Distraction that comes in this way. Thou mayst feel it.

Oh! that horrd torture of the Will, which we are forced to consider of in the Passions of the mind: & the torturing of the Affection as of Anger & Raging Wrath, oh how doth the Soule fret, & tare himselfe hereby. & of Hatred & Malice how is this as a thousand hells burning in the Soule; & of Terrour, & a Frightment which comes constantly upon the Soule as so many firy darts running through, & through the Soule. Who can imagine what these things are?

Oh, that Galling of Conscience, oh those Stobs! those stings! those gripes that it will be alwayes giving! & how will these stings be alwayes Sharpened by the Acts of Memory alwayes shewing the madness, the folly of this life, the Sin against God, against Grace & against its own Soule. & from the fancy acting in its furious way upon the same. O those gashes & strokes every one coming with Such a gird as one would thinke would make the whole person fly apieces, & the Soule to Shivers. But yet its upheld in sore wrath from dying to beare the tortures of this pure wrath of God, Mark 9.44, now all these tortures both of Soule, & Body all alway in their fresh act & in their highest degree.

But this much for the Nature of this Punishment.

2. As for the Duration of the Sentence of Punishment. & this is Eternall, Matt. 25.41,46, II Thess. 1.7,8, Isa. 33.14. Hence there is no abatment, there is not one degree less as to the matter punishing nor as to the punishment poured out upon the Damned, all is Eternall. & oh this Word Eternall, it hath a whole hell in itselfe, who can imagin what it is? Suppose the whole world from the Centre of the Earth to the utmost Circumference of the highest heavens were a Ball of the finest Paper which is, & all this Ball from the Center to the Circumference Printed with the biggest figures as thick as ever they Could be set with Ink that was ranck poyson to any that toucht it, & the Damned were to ly frying in hell but as many milions of years as the totall Sum of all those figures added contains, this would have an end & not be Eternall but when these years were expired over, & over, yet they are [68/69] as far from having their torments Ended, as they were the first moment of their entrance therein. Oh! then what are these Eternall torments. But thus much for the Execution of the Sentence. & so we have done with the day of Judgment in Seing what it is by way of Explication.

Secondly. That there shall be a day of Judgment, or the Confirmation.

1. This appeares from Scripture Testimony. [69/70]

Obedience is that part of the Christian Religion, which teacheth us that duty which wee owe unto God, whose parts are considered with respect unto their $\begin{cases} \text{Nature} \\ \text{Object.} \end{cases}$

As they respect the Nature of Obedience they are $\begin{cases} \text{Vertue \&} \\ \text{Acts of Vertue.} \end{cases}$

Vertue is an Obedientiall Habit inclining the Soul to the keeping Gods Law. [70/71]

The Acts of Vertue are that obedientiall practice flowing from vertue which are according to the Law to the honour of God.

The parts of Obedience respecting their object are
{ Religion towards God &
{ Righteousnes towards men.

Religion is obedience, immediately respecting God consisting in the duties of the first Table of the Law. & its either { Natural Worship
{ Instituted. [71/72]

* * * * * * whereby tho' there were no law leading, yet the Soule would
do it, consisting in $\begin{cases} \text{Imbracing of God} \\ \text{Waiting on God.} \end{cases}$

Our Embracing of God is our owning God to be our God as he is Good

$\begin{cases} \text{To us } \begin{cases} \text{Present by Faith} \\ \text{Future by Hope} \end{cases} \\ \text{In himselfe, by Love. [72/73]} \end{cases}$

Waiting on God is that Naturall Worship flowing from our owning of him, Whereby we {Hearken to him / Call upon him.

Calling on God is the first part of Worship consisting in the pouring out of the Soule by Confession unto God according to his Will to gain his succor. Where we are to consider the {Sorts and / Circumstances} of Prayer.

Explication

1. The thing described is a Calling on God or prayer in Greek some times calld εὐχὴν, sometimes rendered a vow, as Acts 21.23, which properly imports the Act of the desiring faculty of the Soule put forth by obliging words, but most commonly προσευχή is the word used which properly notes prayer, or the address of the Soule to another for Some thing, Rom. 9.3, Phil. 4.6, I Tim. 2.1.

2. The Description of the thing & this lies in the other Words, from

1. Its generall Nature thus, the first part of Naturall Worship. Its worship because it is a part of our religious duty done unto God. & God calls us to it in opposition unto Carnall worship, Ps. 50.15. & Sometimes all the Worship of God, as Job 21.15, Prov. 28.9, its naturall Worship & that both in respect unto the Subject praying, for it is a principall imprinted in mans Nature to pray, as appears in the most profane which are, when they are in distress to pray. Those Heathen Mariners did it, & reproved Jonah saying arise, Sleeper, what meanest thou, call upon thy God, Jonah 1.5,6. & the Athenian Heathens had an altar superscribed ἀγνώστω θεῷ, Acts 17.27, to the unknown God.

And also in respect of the Object prayed to, viz, God. For his nature being the Supream of all, in whom is all help, makes him the naturall object of prayer.

2. Its particular nature. & this lies in the rest of [the] Description layed before us from

1. Its Essentiall Act, viz, the Pouring out of the So[ul] before God, as Ps. 42.4, 62.8, Lam. 2.19, it is the pourin[g] out of the Soule, as the Will: we must have our will g[o]ing out in our request otherwise we mock God, hence prayer is the desire of the Soul, Ps. 10.17, Isa. 26.8. & our understanding also, otherwise we pray, we know not, no[r] for what. Hence I Cor. 14.15, hence we must poure o[ut] the whole Soule, Ps. 119.2. Hence prayer is Essentiall[y] in the heart that prayes right.

2. The Essentiall Property of Prayer whereby [the] heart is poured out, & this is confession, this is an Essentiall property of prayer: without which prayer ca[n] not be. & Sometimes its put for prayer itselfe, as * * * Rom. 14.11, Phil. 2.9. Now this is two fold. 1. It is [a] Confessing of what Gods Carriage is towards us * * * so it is a praysing of God, Rom. 15.9, Ps. 106.1, or 2. Wh[en] our Carriage is Godward. & So it is the Confession [of] our Provocations, as Ps. 32.5, Originall & Actuall, as Ps. 5.4,5, our State & Condition that we are on all account ready to turn aside & can do nothing as of ourselves a[s] II Cor. 3.5. & also a Confession of our Purpose, & resolutions of our heart which is implicitly a promising on the account of his grace to be as he would, & co[m]ply with his Will, Job 34.32, Ps. 51.13,14.

3. The Essentiall Manner of right Prayer. & this is thus laid down, viz, according to his Will, hence is that Matt. 6.10, & I John 5.14, & according to the rule of Faith [in] the Scripture. For this must Square all our * * * [73/74] * * * * * * Succour, as Matt. 14.31, Ps. 12.1. Now this Succour is of all sorts either for the Soule in Pardon of Sin, a Purifying from Sin, Renewing the Soule by Grace & Eternall Salvation, Ps. 51— Jas. 1.5, Or for the Body in any respect wherein it lacks Succour, Matt. 6.12, Jas. 5.15,16, this is the next end of prayer but * * * * * * ordinances, viz, Gods own glory.

The Sorts of Prayer are $\begin{cases} \text{Petition, \&} \\ \text{Thanksgiving.} \end{cases}$

Petition is a Prayer wherein the Desire is poured out before God for the removing of evill & the gaining of good things.

Explication.

1. Here is the Name of the thing described, & that is Petition, in the Hebrew it is set forth by a word that notes the Earnest desire of the Person, as שְׁאֵלָה , I Kings 2.16, Ps. 20.5, & the Greek by αἰτήματα, I John 5.15, which notes an asking, or requesting or δεήσει, as Phil. 4.6, I Tim. 2.1, which imports a begging, & Supplicating.

2. The Nature of the thing, & this lieth laid down in the rest of the Description, where you have it laid out from

    1. Its generall nature. Its a Prayer carrying up our desires before God. & herein it differs not from Thanksgiving.

    2. Its particular nature, & this is shewd as it tends to accomplish its next end, & that is by way of

1. Deploration, or a praying against what is evill, as Matt. 6.13, this you se abundantly manifested, I Kings 8, this is sometimes called an interceding against, as Rom. 1.2.

2. Imprecation, which is a calling upon God for what is good as the Presence of God, Ex. 33.15, the Favour of God, Ps. 4.6, the Salvation of God, Ps. 14.7, the Spirit of God, Luke 12.13, Grace of God, Jas. 1.5, & 4.6, the glory of God, Luke 28.42,43, & good things in this life of all sorts, Ps. 81.16.

Now Petition is Considered with respect to its $\begin{cases} \text{Subject} \\ \text{Nature} \end{cases}$ & * * *

    1. In respect unto its Subject praying & so it is $\begin{cases} \text{Private} \\ \text{Publick.} \end{cases}$

Private Prayer is that which is Carried on by persons in a Private Capacity as Closit, or Secret prayer, Matt. 6.6, thou when thou prayest enter into thy Closet, & shut thy doore, & Pray unto thy Father in Secret. & also Family Prayer, which is that praying in our familyes which God requireth. This God commendeth in Abraham, Gen. 18.19, & Joshuah resolves upon it, as Josh. 24.15, & God pronounceth woe upon those that do not, Jer. 10.25. & this Family Prayer may be considered as the prayer dayly attended on in the Family, as Acts 10.2. Or when severall families meet together in private to pray, as probably those Mal. 3.16,17, Acts 12,12.

    2. In respect unto Publick Prayer, this is that which is carried on in the Publick worship of God, as that I Kings 8, where the Minister is the mouth of the people unto God. & hence the rest are to lift up their Soules unto God in his Expressions. & hence also the Publick place is call'd an house of Prayer, As Ps. [2.]

2. Petition is considered in respect to its Nature as $\begin{cases} \text{Ordinary} \\ \text{More than Ordinary.} \end{cases}$

 1. Ordinary Petition is that which is the Prayer in the ordinary worship of God in Publick as is manifest or in Private. Now the Publick is done in the seasons of Publick worship. The Private is such as is done with respect unto rest & Labour, as Morning Prayer & evening prayer, for which there is the morning & ev'ning Sacrifices leading of us as & the practise the Saints teaching of us, as Ps. 5.3, in the morning shallt thou hear my voice. In the morning will I direct my prayer & look up, Ps. 55.17, Evening, morning, & at noon will I pray unto thee. & therefore * * * a day is as little as may be, or else Private prayer may respect our food: & so it is a praying & praising before & after meat, for this we have Christs Example, whom we are to imitate in all his imitable actions, I Pet. 2.21. Now thus he did, Matt. 14.19, & 15.36, Luke 24.30. & hence food is to be received with prayer, as I Tim. 4.4,5.

 2. More than Ordinary Petition; & this is when Fasting is added unto prayer for the removing of Evill or the gaining of Good. & it is either Private, as when Private persons set upon Fasting & Prayer alone, as David for the life of his Child, II Sam. 12.16, & that of Daniel, as Dan. 9.3—or of Private Families, as that Esther 4.16, & that Dan. 2.17,18. Or it is Publick, as when a People, or Place do it, as that Judg. 20.26, that of Ninive[h], Jonah 3, & of the Children of Captivity, Zech. 7.5, & that Isa. 58.4,5.

Thanksgiving is a Prayer, wherein the thankfull Desires of the heart are returned to God for his goodness, that he may be glorified.

1. Here is in this Description Something of the Name or thing Described & this is Thanksgivin[g,] in Greek ἐυχαριστια, which notes the right exercise of the Soule begraced, or that hath received grace at the Hand of God. Now when such a Soule is in it[s] right Exercising upon the favour received how doth it tune forth the Praise of the Lord. Yet Sometimes this word imports prayer promiscuously, as Matt. 14.36, & it is used among Authors for the Lords Supper, yet its Proper import is as is shewd. The Hebrew Express it by תודה, Ps. 50.14, & last v[erse,] which properly notes Confession as that our Praysing being but an accounting over in a Praying way unto God the Favour he hath bestowed on us. Thus much for the name.

2. Here is the Nature of the thing laid down in the other words

1. Generally its a Prayer, & herein its the Same with Petition for this, se Dan. 9.4. & indeed our things, & praises we return to God must be made prayingwise by beseeching him to accept thereof, hence is that.

2. Particularly. The Particular Nature of it is laid down

1. From its formall act, which is a returning the thankfull Desires of the heart unto God, God by his favour hath made the heart pleasant, & given it the thing it would & now its put into a thankfull frame, it falls to ring out its thankfull Desires unto God, Ps. 118 & 108.1—now this is done ordinarily either in Private in the times of private worship by returning thanks for the mercies of the night in the morning, Ps. 5.3, or of the day at the evening, as Ps. 92.2: or upon our receiving food, Ps. 22.29, Matt. 15.36, or Publickly in the Publick Worship of God, as Isa. 12 & Ps. 111.1. It is also done in any more than Ordinary as on Publick dayes of Thanksgiving as in Esthers dayes when they set apart Publick dayes of thanksgiving, as Esther 9.22.   or Privatly on Speciall occasion which God allows unto the Same.

2. From its formall Object, or Ground, & this is the Goodness of God, as Ps. 136, whether this is exprest in the works of Creation, as Ps. 19.1, or as in the former Psa[lm] or in his Providence, as Ps. 97.1—whether generally as before, or Particular unto the Sons of men, Ps. 98.4–9, & to his people in Particular, Ps. 99.2, 118. So also for Personall mercies of all Sorts consisting in

> State or riches
> Friends or relations
> Health & Strength
> Perfection in our parts
> Parentage & Posterity
> Restraining grace
> Sanctifying grace.

3. From the finall Cause of it & this is Gods glory & indeed it is in its own nature that which God is pleased to account a glorifying of him, as Ps. 50.14, & v.   to the last, its therefore the end of Petition & the work of Saints in Glory, Rev.   & glorious Angels, Isa. 6.23

The Circumstances of Prayer are either $\begin{cases} \text{Ordinarie or} \\ \text{More than Ordinarie.} \end{cases}$

1. The ordinary Circumstances of Prayer are Such whereby our Prayer is denominated from its $\begin{cases} \text{Duration} \\ \text{Pronuntiation.} \end{cases}$ As to its duration, & So

95

it is from its brevity an Ejaculation as all our salutations are, such was that in Ruth 2.4. Or Continuated, Such is the Lords prayer. As for its Pronuntiation this is either $\begin{cases} \text{Mentall} \\ \text{Vocall.} \end{cases}$ Mentall is that prayer that is put up to God in the mind without the voice, as Rom. 8.26. & it is either Ejaculatory as Probably that was, John 11.38, or Continuated, as Hannahs, I Sam. 19.10,11,12,13. [74/81]

[The Public Relations]

After the profession of our Faith was made, we were called out to give some account of the workings of the Spirit upon our hearts, that might be as a foundation for the Charitie of Gods people to act upon, in order to the inroling of us in their Soule as Suitable Matter for such a glorious structure in hand. An account of which so far as time would admit was then personally given in these Relations (here abbreviated) following, the which had, at least some, been read (& doubtless it would have been to more edification) had not the Elders & Messenger of Northampton, & Hadly Churches drove on to the Contrary.

The Account of what I had to give of the experience of God in his gracious workings to me wards that they might be given as much to edification, as might be, were reduced into the order of the Spirit in his work upon the Soule in bringing it home from Sin unto a closing with Christ. & therefore I did not go to gether up the Speciall workings onely of one season, but of what I can thro' the grace of God assert to be what I have & in some measure do injoy at present.

The Relation[13]

The work of the Spirit of God bringing a poor Sinner unto Christ consists in $\begin{cases} \text{Conviction \&} \\ \text{Repentance.} \end{cases}$

Conviction is the first work of the Spirit of God upon the Soule discovering unto it its Sin and Misery by the fall: & its help & Remedy through Grace, John 16.7,8,9, the which work as it affects the Understanding, its called illumination, as Heb. 6.4, 10.32, but as it affects the Conscience, whereby it turns its Checks upon the Will, & affections its properly called Conviction. John 8.9, Acts 18.28, I Cor. 14.24. & is a Singular spur unto Repentance.

Now in Respect unto what I have observed of this work upon mine own heart, with all humility, Soule abasement be it acknowledged to the praise of Infinite Grace, I have, & do dayly finde something of this nature. But to instance onely in such things as are pertinent to the matter in hand,

As for the first time that every any beam of this nature did break in upon me, was when I was but small: viz, upon a morning a Sister of mine while she was getting up, or getting me up, or both, fell on the giving an account of the Creation of the world by God alone, & of man especially, & of the excellent state of man by Creation, as that he was created in the image of God, was holy & righteous, & how, Eve was made of Adams Rib, & was the first woman, was Adams wife, how both were placed in paradise, the garden of Eden, a most curious place, & had liberty to eate of all the trees therein except the tree of knowledge of Good, & evill. & this God would not suffer them to eate of. But the serpent did betray them, & drew them to eate of that fruite & thereby they Sin'd against God: & God was angrey, & cast them out of the Garden of Eden, & set Angels–Cherubims, & a flaming sword turning every way to keep the tree of life. & So man was made a Sinner, & God was angrey with all men for Sin.

But, oh! this account came in upon me in such a Strang way, that I am not able to express it, but ever since I have had the notion of Sin, & its naughtiness remain, & the wrath of God on the account of the same.

An other morning (as I suppose the next) following, she began to give an account of Christ Jesus, who was the Son of God that came to save poore Sinner[s], & to bring [them] to heaven; How the Virgin Mary was overshaddowed by the holy Ghost, & was with Child, & Joseph her husband decerning it thought to have put her away privatly; but was warned by an Angel of God in a dream not to feare to take her to him because she was with Child of the Holy Ghost, & should bring forth a Son, & should call his name Jesus, for he should save his people from their Sins, that after he went up with Mary his espoused wife to Bethlehem to be taxed; where there was no room for him in the Inn, & therefore he was fain to lie in a Stable, where Mary fell in travell, & was delivered, & wrapt the babe in swaddling cloaths, & laid him in a Manger. & how there being shephards in that Country keeping watch over their flocks [by] night, an Ang[el o]f the Lord appeared unto them [telling them] that he [is] born in the City of David Christ the Lord that night; & bid them go their way & they should finde the Babe lying with his mot[her] in a Manger: & how that immediatly there was with the Angel [a] multitude of the heavenly host praysing of God, etc. whereu[p]on the shephards going to se whether it was so & found it so; further she gave an account of the wise men of the East co[m]ing to worship Christ, who inquiring where he was that [was] born King of the Jews for they had seen his Star & were come to worship him: how that Herod the King sent them away bidd[ing] them to return to him when they had found him, that he might come, & worship him also, but he intended to put Christ to dea[th.] But the wise men going out presently the Star appeared [and] led them untill it stood over the house where the babe was; they going in worshipt him, giving him gifts [of] Gold, Myrrh, Frankincense; but being warnd of God that they should not [return] to Herod they went to their own Countrey another way[;] how that Herod the King when he decerned it was wroth, & sent & slew all the Male Children in Bethlehem from two y[ears] old & under to destroy Christ. But Joseph being warned [by] An Angel, by flying into Egypt Saved the young Childs life. Thus she went on giving also an account of Christs wor[k,] his healing the sick, Casting out of people that were poss[ess]ed, Divils, his working Miracles: & yet how the Jews sought to p[ut] him to death; how Judas sold him, & betrayed him; how [the] Jew[s] crucified him, & that between two thieves, how Chri[st] Rose again, how the Angels appeared to the women giving account thereof, how that Christ appeared also, & so went u[p] to heaven, etc.: these things I well remember she spoke bu[t] cannot say she spake them in this exact order, or words: bu[t] the strange frame that I was rapt up in hereby. I know n[ot] that ever I was in * * * that high workings of Love on one [and] Greife on another, & of Anger & hatred on another, I kn[ow] not how to express it. But this I can say did abide, for ev[er] after I eyed Christ as a Saviour, the Son of God that Save[s] people from their Sins.

But alas! this Impression tho' it was great upon the aff[ecti]ons was soon over in Respect unto any Originall Sin['s test]ifying influence & [th]erefore growing up I was read[ily] laquy after the vanities of youth. But being under the vig[ilant] & watchfull Eye of my Parents, who would crop the buddi[ng] forth of Originall Sin, into any visible Sin with whols[ome] reproofs, or the Rod, I was thereby preserved from a Sin-[ful] Life. But yet the Transgression of the Sabboth, & Some degr[ee] of Disobedience to my parents, & too often the evill of ly[ing] & also inward evill, were things that did more prevai[l.] All which have had their oppositions by one reproofe or till they have been a burden unto me. For the Sabboth br[eak]ing my brethrens often reproofs & cheifly in the app[l]ication [of] Scripture, Isa. 58.13, that we ought not to attend our own w[ay] nor to finde out our own pleasure, nor speake our own [words] upon the Sabboth, as for disobedience to parents, my Mot[her] beside her sharp Correction would usualy chide, giving acount of the Stubborn Son, Deut. 21.18—& that the eye that dispise[th the] Father, & that despiseth to obey his mother the Ravens of the [valley] shall pick it out, & the young Eagles shall eat it, Prov. [30.17.]

As for Lying my mother was very severe on this acco[unt] often threttening it, & turning thus what shall be give[n] the lyer but brimston & fire, Rev. 21.8. Sharp arrows of [the] mighty with Coles of Juniper, Ps. 120.3-4, & as for the ot[her] & many more Sins I must confess I cannot say what particu[lar] means it was that discovered them unto me but this I [do] say that I have had them made ugly unto me, & so all[ways] & also I have had likewise a Cleare Sight of my undoi[ng] without Christ, & my necessity of him.

But thus much for Conviction, I come now to Repe[nta]nce. Which is * * * * * * [81/82]

Aversion is the first part of Repentance, consisting in the turning of the Soule from Sin, wherein is mannag'd the work of $\begin{cases} \text{Contrition} \\ \text{Humiliation.} \end{cases}$

Contrition is the first work of Aversion whereby the heart is broken off from Sin. This is done by the Spirit of God hammering the hard heart in conscience's F[orge,] forcing its checks for Sin so hard against the will & Affections till they recede from Sin, are unrivited from Sin, & rebound against it; & here I might have instanced in the unriviting the Affections of Love to, Hope in, & Joy on the account, of Sin; But I shall not stand there, but onely as this is carried on by the acting of the Contrary affections, viz, in the rebounding of Feare against, Anger for, & Sorrow on the account of Sin.

Now in respect unto Contrition breaking off from Sin [o]r bringing my Affections off from it, & to act against it, I dare [n]ot deny that I am wholy unacquainted therewith, & there[fo]re, in respect unto,

Feare. I am not altogether a stranger thereto; tho' I never [fe]lt such an high degree as to be terrified at the thoughts [of] Gods wrath; yet the Consideration of God as a Consuming [fir]e, of purer eyes than to behold iniquity; & that it is a [fe]arfull thing to fall into the hands of the living God: as also my [l]ife of Guilt & filth hath made me to stande in some de[gre]e of feare; & be affraid of being overtaken with Sin. So that I can [t]o grace apply that Ps. 44, Rom. 11.20.

Anger, as for this I can without presumption say that I through grace know what this means; for I know not how [to] be pleased with myselfe on the account of Sin: I have been [acq]ainted with anger on this account even unto hatred [of] Sin, & myselfe as overcome by it. & hope I can profess a [u]se of the experience of this unto a Conformity [with] those Scrip[t]ures, Ps. [37.8,] Ezek. 6.9.

Sorrow, this I must glorify Gods grace in my acknowledg[ing] an acquaintance withall, & on the bearing a direction unto duty that they could not grieve, should grieve because they could not gri[eve,] tho' it came to me, for altho' I found my heart so hard that I could not grieve, yet it had the impression of gr[ace] upon me to bring [it] to lie low on this very account. & the very thought of Sin [a]fflicted my heart with Sorrow, & so coming to

Humiliation, which is the second worke of Aversion from Sin [co]nsisting in the abasing of the Soule [unto] hell on the account [o]f its Sin & Sinfulness & judging itselfe unworthy to live, or [be] above ground, herein the Soule comes really to be out with itselfe, & to be Satisfied with nothing below an intrest in Christ, etc.

And as for this, oh that I had but more of it. Yet although [I']ll not say I am duely humbled, there is too much Selfe Love, * * * & hypocrisy within. Yet this is not without a deep [sen]se of that which is ground of Humiliation. Oh the sight of [it,] oh a lost State, oh a deceitfull heart, a vile heart, a [har]d heart, a formall heart, neglect of Christ, deadness in duty, [lov]e of vanity, & the like how did & do these Stare in my face [whe]n I have thot a Sin mortified, oh how it hath broke forth like [whe]n under a new temptation: & when I have thought to bind [my] vows unto God to its better behaviour for a time, how [dot]h it dubly attended a temptation before the time was [des]ired, whereby it worsting of me by my own ingagments: I came to se that would not do: & altho' I prayed, this nei[ther] availd; but still deadness, dulness, unspiritualness. Watch[fulne]ss would not do, heart examination oftimes ended in a [dete]station, hence an universall weriness of myselfe, disqui[etude w]ith myselfe, judging of myselfe * * * althings of myselfe [follo]wed, & I finde with the Apostle, Phil. 3.8, all things of mine [are] dung & dogs meat. & oh now how was I carried out in [pray]er after Christ, in my goings out in my comings in, etc. [t]houghts were going to heaven. I was musing every way * * * alone how to get Suitable expressions to carry up the [lov]e of my soule unto God through Christ in prayer, but my heart made its excursions, the Sons of Zerviah were [call]ed for me.[14] I thought if others did but se my heart I should [be s]hamed to se their faces. Oh! my great work, oh my hard [work,] it was, & is my heart work, Oh how have I matter of [Humi]liation, enough to make me abhor my selfe, & morn ly[ing in] dust & ashes. If I found inlargment in prayer, it was [fe]d upon, with temptations to pride, & oh the thoughts of [my] failing filld me with confusion: * * * again with indignation, as being more sensiblie abasht, & filled with inward shame of failings before men, than before God, in somuch that my own heart was a burden unto myselfe. I saw myselfe better outwardly than inwardly: & better esteemed than I deserved: my heart being such a Prison of naughtiness, & an *Akeldama*[15] of uncleaness, that I could not alow it a good thought. & thus tost up & down I have been. & what to make of this I know not. I finde too much pride in mine own heart & therefore dare not call it humiliation. The Lord assist me that I be not deceived. & oh that he would take by the hand & lead within the limits of that promise, Matt. 13.12. But this I found that by howmuch I grew the more offended with myselfe by So much the more lovely, & longed-after did Christ appear in my eye.

2. Conversion is the second part of Repentence whereby the Soule is carried to God in Christ, by $\left\{\begin{array}{l}\text{Faith \&}\\\text{Obedience.}\end{array}\right.$

Faith here is the whole Soules coming to Christ, Matt. 11.28, which consists in Faith absolutly taken whereby the Soule is united unto Christ savingly, Acts 16.31. & Its Concomitants as Love, Gal. 5.6, Hope, Rom. 5.5, Joy or delight, Phil. 4.4, that is the Graces of the Spirit of God in Faith infused Sanctifying the Affections whereby the Soule doth lay hold on Christ & holy objects.

Obedience is that work whereby the Soule is dayly carrying on the work of Repentance unto perfection, & all Duties that Christ requires, John 14.15, I Cor. 15.31.

Now as for what I have to say in this Respect

As for Faith, altho' Presumption forbids me to Say its mine, yet I dare not cast away my Confidence in obedience to that word, Heb. 10.35, & I finde it so necessary, that all obedience is to me a dead carkass good for nothing without it. Prayer is but a beating the Aire without it. & peace of Conscience I find inconsistant where it is not in exercise. & this I finde that were it not for the constant application of the Blood of Christ I should grow under the sight of my dayly failings either stupid, or distracted. & therefore I desire to come into conformity with that Mystery of Living by Faith, Rom. 4.

As for Love I can assert that I have been bound in this cord, oh the outgoing of this Affection whether inriched by the sanctifying grace of the Spirit called Love, or no, I say not, but hope it. Oh how it went breathing after Christ & longing for him, oh those inward heart panting, & musing can testify: So its working after the Grace of Christ, & wayes of Christ I can say that altho' its more Sensible at one time than at another, yet whenever I search for it it is at hand. This hath been mightily promoted in reading the history of Christs passion. & so Love to the people of God. Oh, this I have had such a sense of, that I could not bear to hear a word against them; but it was as a Quick thing in my heart that upon the entrance of a thought of such into my heart as professed godlyness in truth my heart would be Surprised with an indearing rapture toward them. & hearing them set out as such should Shine as Sparkling Diamonds in the Ring of Gods glory, oh how it did indeare me more, if it could be, to them &, oh (me thought) that I was but one of them. & so I endeavrd to be.

As for Hope: altho' when I looke upon myselfe Shame & sorrow is more in act than any thing yet I dare not but say that I have a certain expectation oft Steddying of me in the middest of fear So far as to make me subscribe to that, Lam. 3.26, its good that a man both hope, & quietly wait for the Salvation of the Lord, my vessell could never beare up in the rough Sea of temptations without this old Anchor that is fixt within the vaile.

As for Joy. I say that I never found Christ such an Austere Master as hath refused to give me any tast of the hony of Canan but he hath made me tast his good things that in some measure I can say through grace I delight to do thy will oh God. But yet in all those things I finde contrariety within greatly opposing, yet there is a Striving against the Same. & altho' I cannot say by what particular means of Grace I was brought to this experience, yet I can say some thing of all those things are with me.

As for Obedience the other part of Conversion. I have I hope set upon the work, & have found it not to be as before, for whereas the time was that I obeyed for feare of the Check of parents, I have since seen it proceed from Conscience, whereas I was wont to say a prayer I have found God to teach me to pray in prayer. Oh how hath my Soule been carryed out in prayer (I may be ashamed to * * * Son is gone back in this respect the Lord * * * * * * & God hath [to]gether made * * * [82/83] in the Ministeriall work etc. But in this respect modesty commands my Silence. The time was that I never looked within doore, but now by meditation & heart Examination I finde it a harder matter to keep Rule than the victor hath in taking a City: & as for the whereas it was a burden, since it's become delight, nay all the wayes of God have bee[n] familiar unto me, in somuch as once hearing a godly able Minister in England assert the way to heaven to be a hard way, from Matt. 7.13,14: in the use he press[ed] all to try whether they were in the way to heaven, & that from the hardness of the way I was somewhat startled thereat as thinking that surely I was not in that way because I found it no such hard work, but coming to lay down notes thereof, he laid down one from the deceits of heart, & the Sinfullness thereof. & then me thought I found hard work indeed. Oh now coming to heart I found myselfe deeply ingaged in the war. & indeed hereby I am constantly supplied with matter of Repentance in all the parts thereof. The Lord help me to carry all on to his glory.

These are some of those things that I have experienced in my Soule: & being thus called I do declare the same, I have done it in a mean manner to leave the [same] unto the judgment of Gods people whether it will hold touch in the Scales of the Sanctuary, by the judgment of Christian Charity.

This is the Order, & most of the matter, onely in some things inlarged, that was then delivered, for although I had drew it up, yet not haveing committed it verbatim, to my memory before the Elders & Messengers came, & then being something touched in my health: as also somewhat disturbed in my minde, I could not so easly fix it in my minde after. & therefore I judge some small variation in the words, & Phrases. & that something briefer. The Lord help me to live up in althings according to his will in all things.

The Relation of Lt. John Mawdsley.[16]

I must acknowledg to the praise, & glory of God, that he hath not onely given me life, & many outward mercies, but also many spirituall mercies; as many Sweet Instructions from my Parents; as also from the word, & ordinances that I lived under: So that I profited thereby, as I should, I should have brought forth much fruit. But instead of bringing forth fruit to God, I brought forth fruit to my Selfe, living a long time in

he vanities of this world, in Sins, as Pride, Worldliness, & the Lust of
he flesh my heart was lead out so strongly after, as that all Counsels, &
Reproofs would not reform me, nor make me out of love therewith. &
had God left me in this my natural state I had been miserable forever.
But herein appeared the riches of free Grace to me, not onely in sending
his son to save sinners; but also in Sending his Spirit to convince me of
my Sins, & the need I had of the Righteousness of Jesus Christ to cloath
my Naked Soule with all.

   Now the first means he used to Convince me of my need I had of an
ntrest of Christ was from a Question & Answer in a Catechize, thus.
Q. If Damnation be the reward of Sin, then is a man of all creatures most
miserable. A dog, or a toad, when they die, all their misery is ended. But
when a man dies then is the begining of his WOE.
Ans. It were so indeed, if there were no mean[s] of Deliverance. But God
hath shown his mercie in giving a Saviour to mankinde.[17] Herein was life
& death set before me. But yet the hardness of my heart & Strength of
Sin prevaild, that I was not willing to part with my Sin * * * altho' I
might have life by him. & therefore hardly believing this truth I labourd
to stifle Conviction. But God of his Infinite Grace came to stop me in
my Sin by the pains of my Parents urging that Scripture, I Chron. 28.9,
& thou Solomon my Son know thou the God of thy father, & serve
him with a perfect heart, & a willing minde,—etc. convincing of me
hereby of the danger I was in ; & that I should assuredly go to hell if [I
did] not repent truly of all my Sins, & turn from them to the living God
by faith in Jesus Christ. But still Sin was Sweet & I was not willing to part
there with. I thot I was young enough to repent & turn from Sin. & I
should do it before I should die. & so were of Conviction for a time, yet
I could not get those things so out of my minde but I was under the
influence of wr[ath,] which kept me from many Sins. Another time my
parents telling me that in a Relation of one admitted into Dorchester
Church there was this declared by the person, how that he had followed
God with Secret prayer twice aday, morning & Evening from the age of
ten years old, & had found the Comfort thereof. & so my mother told
me that it was high time for me to pr[ay] unto God, for I was more than
ten years old, & I might die bef[ore] old age, & then I should be miserable for ever, if I died in Sin. I thought it strange that I, being so young,
should pray to God, yet in Obedience to my Parents, & in fear of Gods

wrath I set upon secret prayer morning, & evening. But finding m[y
heart so hard that I could not pray to receive any such comfort
expected, I desisted again as thinking it a vain thing for me to pray to
God as yet. But now soon after there being a sore sickness in many
families whereof many young one[s] died, my parents told me, that my
turn might be next & t[hat] I should be miserable for ever & I being
exceedingly affrai[d] of death & Gods wrath, did set upon the duty of
secret prayer [a]gain. But my heart still being hard, when the hand of
God [was] removed, & I not toucht, I quickly [stopped] the same, &
labourd to st[ay] Conscience by runing into the youn[g]sters Company
with whom I grew up. After this there was great fears of the rising of
Naraganset Indians, & if they should rise their cruelties seemd grea[t] the
which fears my Parents improved upon me to stir me up to earn[est
prayer to God to secure his favour which is better than life, whereupo[n
I fell to praying again, & more earnestly than ever before. B[ut] Satan
assaulted me with more violent temptation, & worse than before, as to
make [me] to question whether there was a God, [or] no: But God help[
me by his word, & works to withstand this ass[ault.] But then Satan se[t
upon me to drive [me] from prayer again, tell[ing] me that I was young
enough; & too young to pray to God, that the[re] was few, if any So
young as I, did pray to God. Which temptation to[ok] with me so that I
quietly laid aside Secret prayer again. But [the] Lord was pleased now to
awaken me by the Ministry of the word under that Reverend Man of
God old Mr. Mather in his Exercises, viz, Gen. 12, to the 35 Chap: &
Matt. 7th to 25 Chap: in which Chapters it pleasd G[od] to bring me to
give attention unto the word preach[ed], So that in * * * one Something
was either food, or Physick unto my Soule so [the] many Sins my heart
was privie to were laid open before me. * * * he would turn to young
one to Consider their wayes & turn unto [him] or else they should be
dam'd forever. The which so came upon me that I found a reall change
wrought upon my heart. Now Sabboths [were] not such weary days to
me as before, Secret prayer Such a burd[en as] before. The word now
became Sweet & pleasant, & not such a * * * word as before. Now I
delighted to be powering out my [soul] before God. (Here now was
instances given from Severall of those [Scri]ptures which for brevity Sake
I omit onely that from Matt. 11.24 * * *) be more tolerable for Sodom
& Gomorrah in the day of Judgment for thee hearing that New England
Sinners should have their place in hell I was startled greatly, & set to
mourn afresh over [my] former Sins, Matt. 12.20, a bruised reed will he

ot break, etc.; this [was] as a refreshing unto my drooping Spirit under
he fears of he[ll.]

But when Mr. Increase Mather came out of England hearing [him]
on Matt. 5.20, Except your Rightousness exceed the Righteousness * * *
hat men might go a great way, & have in many Sweet impression of the
* * * of God & yet not enter into the Kingdom of heaven, which being
de[livered] with such great affections, that I never h[e]ard the like, I was
exceeding[ly sur]prised with fear, & so stirr'd up to more earnest prayer
o God. * * * * * * [83/84] would stand me instead. & then from Isa.
5.1, ho, everyone that is athirst come, etc. seeing that Jesus Christ was
reely tendered to me as well as to others, I have cast myselfe into his
rms & Bosome: & if I perisht I would perish there. & it pleased God
nore & more to draw out my desires, more & more to injoy god in all
is Ordinances, & so if my heart deceive me not are my desires at this
ime, that so I might injoy them in their place, which I finde a want &
need of from the Subtilty of Satan which gives me to see a want of all
neans ordaind to help me a[gain]st, & also in respect of Posterity, that
he Ordinances of God may be carried down unto them. & therefore I
proceed to ingage in this worke in this place desiring alway the prayers of
Gods people for me that I may * * * ever the Gospell of Jesus Christ &
elp for his Kingdom here in this place.

The Relation of Ensign Samuel Loomis[18]

It pleased God to bestow upon me the Instruction of Religious
Parents, who discovered unto me the bad Condition of every one by
nature, & it being a time of breaking out of evill, they thereupon took
occasion to set it upon me: the which made me Sensible that I was in
such a Condition naturally, & therefore I fell upon the means of Recovery in my private endeavors of reading & prayer by myselfe alone. After
this going to be an Apprentise to Hartford, I now [came] under the
Reverend Mr. Stones Ministry, as he was reprehending the evill of
profaning the Sabbath in the meeting, & Sporting of youth in the Evning
after it, had such an Expression as this, that the DIVELL MADE BONEFIRES
BY WAY OF REJOYCING THEREAT, which fell with such impression upon my
Spirit, as put a check unto me in respect unto such practices.

Afterwards, remooving to Farmington, under Mr. Newtons Ministry, as he was discoursing of the misery of man by nature, & of those
that sat down quietly in this State, not indeavouring to [g]et out thereof

& injoy God in his ordinances, I heard him use that, Rev. 22.15, whoever are dog[s,] & Sorcorers, & whoremongers, & Murderers, & Idolaters, & whosoever loveth & seeketh a lie, which he insisted [p]ritty much upon, & after being by friends discoursed on; & there being ever & anone on in their Relations laying down such things [as] I could not finde to be with me. So that God did so follow up my [S]oule that I was in a naturall State, that proved a burden to[o] hard [f]or me to bear, & I was not able to rest under it. & therefore in [d]istress of Soule, I was constrain'd to make my Condition [k]nown to Mr. Steel, the Ruling Elder of the Church, for Support, and [b]eing surprized with fear, that God would Surprize me with death [b]efore he had bestowed upon me that mercy of uniting me to Christ, I had some Support against the same by his pains with me.

Afterwards Mr. Newton from Isa. 55.3, incline your ear & come [un]to me, hear, & your Souls shall live, & I will make an everlasting [co]venant with you even the Sure mercies of David, had such an in[fl]uence [I] went along with him as me thought, did make me willing [to] come to attend upon Gods call. And urging Gods people to love [on]e another he laid love to Gods people as an evidence of a [c]hild of God; the which I oft putting to my heart by way of tryall, did [re]ad, that a Child of God, (altho' he was never so poore in the world,) [wa]s very dear unto me, & set very high in my heart.

Again, from Matt. 11.28,29,. Come unto me all ye that labour & [ar]e heavy laden & I will give rest, take my yoake upon you, etc., [sh]ewing what a Suitable, Excellent, & Willing Saviour Christ was [&] made Such an invitation to poor Souls as this, viz, that if any man [wo]uld now come into Jesus Christ, he would undertake that he [wo]uld have mercy at his hand, the which with his opening, & improving [of] that Promise in Matt., God was pleased to bring to home unto my [sou]le, that in admiring that God should by his Servants make such ter[ms un]to me, I could do no less than hope in his Mercy. And thus I [ca]nnot but acknowledge to the praise of God, that in the means of his [Gra]ce I have had my heart in some measure turned from the [sin]s, & vanities of this present evill world unto a desiring after God, [en]joyment of him, in duties of Obedience, in his Ordinances, & in [pri]vate Communion with him. Wherein I in attendance upon him, can [no]t but declare, that (unless my deceitfull heart beguile me) I have [co]mmonly found the quickening influences of the same in one place or another untill this day.

The Relation of Sergent Josiah Dewy[19]

The Discovery of what God hath done for my Soule to the praise of his Grace I shall endeavour to lay down as follows.

Being about 13 years old God was pleased to give me some discovery of my miserable state by nature that I might looke to him for grace. Tho' I did it weekly & unsteadily.

About my 16th year hearing Mr. Newton on that, [I Pet. 4.18], If the Righteous Scarsly be saved where shall the wicked & ungodly appear, I began to be more affected with mine own State & to be struck with fears of death & wrath. & being much perplext in myselfe fearing its approach, & my unprepard state for it, I thought if Sickness came upon me I would send for the Elders, & desire their prayers for me, hoping that the prayers of the Faith might availe me much.

In my 17th year God visited me with sore sickness & long: which did greatly exercise my thoughts. But yet I neglected my former resolutions of sending for the Elders to pray for me. & now the Counsels of parents, & Christian friends to get an Intrest in Christ took some hold upon me. But yet upon my recovery, the delights, & ralities of youth began to take much with me, but could not follow them without gripes & galls of Conscience: & was by restraining grace brought off thence. But yet I put off repentance promising to do it aftwards.

But coming under Mr. Mathers Ministry at Northampton, I met with many close convictions, that forced me to private Duties, against which Satan laid in many Excuses, as wont of time & place being a Servant. Yea I was fully convinct that there must be a great change wrought in my heart, or else I was like to be a miserable Creature.

When I was entred into a married State I saw my self now under former ingagements of attending heart-searching & repenting work, but my heart was indisposed thereto & hearing Mr. Mather on the hearts hardness assert that there was no plague like unto that, I was affrighted thereat. & soon after hearing Mr. Eliot (now of Gilford) on a lecture Sermon, was so awakend as to resolve no longer to delay but to fall to search mine own heart. But I found it hard, & difficult work to keep my heart to it. & sometimes I found that my heart would slip from the work almost as Soon as I was at it. So that I could find little rest. But after awhile God discoverd the Sin of Pride to me, which I lest Suspected. & now in a bewildred condition I knew not what to do. & advising with my Parents they directed me to Mr. Mather to whom at the length I forced an attempt, & making known to him how it was with me I desired his help & direction, who told me I was under the striving of Gods Spirit & after much Counsell, & incouragment told me I must labour to se such an evill in Sin, & Such a beauty in holiness, that if there was no Hell to punish, nor heaven to reward, I must chuse the way of Holiness, which as I mused on, I thot I never should attain unto finding my heart So in love with Sin, Yet finding a thirsting desire after Righteousness I was incouraged by that, Matt. 5[.6,] blessed are they that hunger & thirst after righteousness for they shall be filled. & as God was going on with me, he discovered unto me Sin against Light, & cheifly against Gospel Love in Gods Sending his Son to poor Sinners, which was heart melting Considerations. Afterwards, as I was alone meditating it pleased God to let a glimps of his Glory, & of the Beauty & Excellencie of Jesus Christ. & now my heart was much raised & revived hoping now I could choose the wayes of Christ for the beauty I saw therein. Then going & giving Mr. Mather an account thereof, he incouraged me as being in the way, & bed me goe home & strive to se that all I had done to be nothing. & I should finde my heart, either to sink under Discouragment, or to be stout, or to be Careless, but I could not bear the thoughts hereof as to think I was so mistaken, but durst not reject this advice. Wherefore when I was alone I found my heart sink [down] under Discouragment * * * almost overborn * * * [84/85] being thus wounded by this Physician, I being desirous to try another; & therefore making my State known to Mr. Eliot, he after many Cautions & Serious Questions gave me this advice, to wit, to labour to make deep work & to go deep, & for incouragment told me that I should have the Comfort of it: & by way of direction herein, he advised me to live much in the observing of the working of Corruptions of mine own heart, the which indeavouring after, I found through grace greatly benefficial to the Subduing this heart of mine. Hereby I found a bent of heart to sin & continuall boylings, & bublings of Corruptions in all my thoughts, words, Duties, & performances, which made me with Shame of heart to loath myselfe, & cry out, oh! wretched man that I am, who shall deliver me from this body of death? But the following words somewhat relieved me, viz, thanks be to God through Jesus Christ. Oh the swarms of iniquities that came in upon me beseeging me on every Side hereby, & now I was a shamed of mine own righteousness. I was now carried out with such an indignation against mine own heart, that many times laying hold on my breast, me thot that could I come at it I could even tare it out of my Body, & cast it a way. & now I saw I was undone, without a Saviour: & hence the price of Christ was raised in my Soul, yet I had hope in that Christ said he came to seek such as are lost. But if I should have a Saviour, oh what free Grace & mercy did this appeare, wherefore I resolved to wait upon him if it was to my dying day resolving if I perished, I would perish in away of dutie waiting at the footstoole of mercy. But a little while after this, hearing Mr. Mather upon John 6.37, all that the Father hath given me shall come unto me, & whosoever comes unto me I will in no wise Cast off, press soules to come unto Christ with earnestness: which was to believe in him, I took as the Voice of Christ to me calling me to believe on him, yet I could find no ability to me to [make] a Step towards him, & was sorely pincht at heart on this account. But hearing not long after Mr. Eliot on Ps. 119.[116], uphold me by thy word: let not [me] be ashamed of my hopes, shew what good Hopes were, I was much revived, rejoycing in hope that the Lord had sown the Seeds of grace in my heart & was much lightened of the load my heart had lain under, & the 4th day after hearing some private Christians discoursing of Free grace, & an excellent way thereby of out doing Satan by granting all that Satan could say of our sinfulness & vileness, & yet turning upon him in the Conclusion thus, & what if Christ will Save me, Satan? what is that to thee, I was greatly raised thereat. & going away into the field musing thereon, I felt a strong perswasion arise in me, of the Love of God in Christ through the riches of Grace, as made me cry out my Lord, & my God, my Saviour & my Redeemer, passing on as it were in an heavenly Rapture, & inflamed with these Considerations, on a sudden the whole face of things seeming to be changed, & I hurd me thoughts as it were these words, a Pardon, a Pardon, Christ hath purchased a Pardon. At which I was astonisht as it were to thinke of the wonderfull Free Grace of God, that ever a Pardon, & the manifestation of it Should ever be bestowed on such an unworthy Sinner, as I was. & now my heart was as it were Swallowed up with admiring & praising God, that for sometime, especially in private Duties, I could scarce thinke of any thing Else. A little while after I was strongly perswaded of mine own Salvation so that I feared not to challeng a dispute with Satan about it. But God withdrawing himselfe again, let me se my own weakness; so that I could not but think of the Psalmist saying thus I said in my Prosperity I shall never be moved, but thou hidest thy face, & I was troubled. Now the Lord Shewed me the continuall need I was in of a momentary Supply of his Grace. But now I made

some what hereof to Mr. Mather, he told me that God had carryed m[e]
through dangerous ways, & Set me on the top of the Hill: & that m[y]
worke was to watch against Temptations * * * & study the promise[s]
wherein I found * * * & cheifly in that Matt. 11.28,29, come unto me
etc. & in tha[t] Hos. 14.4, I will heale their back slidings, & I will lov[e]
them fre[ely] for mine is turned away from him. & now I began to lon[g]
aft[er] Communion with God in his Ordinances, yet having some fear[s]
forbore about halfe a yeare. & it pleased God to afflict me th[at] I kep[t]
my bed mostly a day or two, which brought me to consider what Go[d]
might aim at by it, & fearing lest it might be a neglect of Communio[n]
with God & his People I earnest sought Go[d] in the matter desiring tha[t]
he would be pleased to discover it to me by raising me up again; & i[t]
pleased God so to answer me, as that within an hour, or two, I was abl[e]
to go about my business.

So that now I was hereby so convinced of Duty that I durs[t] n[o]
longer delay: wherefore I went to the Elders, & made know[n] m[y]
desires to joyn to the Church & being joyned I may truly say I have see[n]
God here, & there, in his Ordinances & in h[is] Providences, in hi[s]
Mercies, & in Afflictions. But have gre[at] cause with shame to bewail[e]
it that I have made such poor returns for such rich benefits: that I hav[e]
done so little for him that hath done so much for me.

The Relation of Brother John Root[20]

I being under the happiness of the injoyning the Counsels &
Adm[o]nition of godly parents, who instructed me & told the dange[r]
all sons were in by Adams fall, & that I was guilty of Sin thereby; as s[o]
injoyning the Discoveries of Gods will in the light of the gospell, w[hen]
about 17 or 18 years of age, under some Conviction under Mr. Stone[s]
Ministry at Hartford, who in a sermon laying down the undo[ne] stat[e]
all persons were in by nature, shewd that if they lived & d[ied] in tha[t]
state they must lie down in Eternall Fire, which would be intollerable
which God was pleased to send so far home as to m[ake] me to Conside[r]
with myselfe that certainly I was in a bad state [&] had need labour to ge[t]
out of this state: but how to do it, I cou[ld] not tell. Yet I thought [I]
would fall to praying hard; but I [could] not tell how to pray. & bein[g]
now at Mr. Willis his house a[t] Hartford where Mr. Haynes the[n]
tabled, I desired him to de[vise] me up a form of prayer: but he denyin[g]

me tooke a bible & s[aid] there I should finde one. But with what I could find therein [I] began to Strive for private places to Pray in, & bewaile my state. This I did a while, but I began again after a while to g[row] mindless of my Condition, & so to desist from the same. But [not] long after going home to Farmington, hearing Mr. Hooker [con]demn what a sad state all men out of Christ were in, & turn[ing] to the young people, said, & you Children, & young men are [in a] lamentable state, & will not minde it. Consider, you must [die] e're long, & wither will [you] go do you think. I tell you, you mu[st] go to hell, a dreadfull place, a place of fire & brimstone (unless you repent) more over you young men that * * * Care, & time away, take down these Scriptures in your Bible, goe your way, on in Sin & forget God if you Can. Eccl. 11.9, [re]joyce oh young man in thy youth—yet know for all s[uch] things God will bring thee to judgment, II Thess. 1.8. Coming in fl[am]ing fire to take vengeance on all those that know not God nor [o]bey the Gospell of our Lord Jesus Christ, II Cor. 5.10. For we must all ap[pear] before the judgment Seat of Christ to give an account of all th[ings] done in the body according to what is done, whether good or ba[d.] Further, urging thus that if you young men will come to G[od] here is Christs Call to you, Matt. 11.28,29,30,—Isa. 55.1, E[v]ery one that thirsteth, come—at which I was thro' gra[ce] so far awakened, that I was in great Commotion of Spirits [and what] to do, I knew not, yet I fell to Seeking God thro' Christ. & w[as] very full of fears & doubts, yet I found I had a great desire to par[t with] all Sins; & to have an Intrest in Jesus Christ. In this trouble[d] & disturbed State I remain'd a long time. & then it pleased G[od to] visit me with a Sore time of Sickness, that I thought I should die [& be] found in a Naturall State, but after my Sickness * * * * * * [85/86] & desired him, & all Gods people to pray for me to God to spare my life, that I might obtain a pardon of all my Sins, Originall & Actuall: For now I was Convinced that there was no way but believing on God thro' Christ, who had laid down his life to redeem fallen man. & God was pleased so far to hear prayers as to grant me a season to Consider my State. & having recourse to Mr. Hooker for Counsell, he incouraged me to go on Seeking unto God through Christ; & to wait on Christ in his ways & means, & he hoped all things would be well, for Christ was an Alsufficient Saviour, & usually he gain'd Souls to himself gradually. Afterwards God again visiting me with Sore Sickness neer even unto Death, & sending for Mr. Hooker he prayed with me, & Counselld me: but yet fears & doubts remaind yet desiring his prayers that God would recover me & spare me if it was his will to perfect my Conversion, who was pleased to raise me up again; & after a little while I began to finde an intire love to Christ, a hatred to Sin, a thirsting after Christ, his wayes, & ordinances, & a looking for pardoning Grace, the renewing of his likeness in me by his Spirit which I had lost. & upon this Change which I found in my heart as against Sin, & Sinfull Courses unto God, Christ & his wayes, I through the Grace of God gave up myselfe to Christ, fastening on the aforesaid promises, & left myselfe with him for the mortifying of Sin, renuall of Grace, & Salvation of my soule in the wayes of his appointment. & hope I shall through free grace rest on him therein unto the end.

The Relation of Brother Isaak Phelps[21]

I being involved in a fallen State & insensible thereof tho' [g]rown to years of understanding, but sitting under a faithfull Ministry, it pleased God to startle mee by the same: & by the wakening of Conscience, through the Convictions of the Spirit therein, I was brought to consi[d]er my Condition: & being convinced that my state was not good, but miserable, being under the wrath of God, it put me upon duties, & the avoi[d]ing some Sins: & I labouring to bring my life into a Conformity unto the Law of God, & attaining something this way, thought 'myselfe [i]n a Safe Condition. & comparing myselfe with the Commands I could [n]ot charg myselfe with the breach of any, till it pleased the Lord by Mr. Warehams Labours upon the Commands, shewing the Length, breadth, & Spirituali[ty] of the Commands, the manner as well as the matter, the duty to be done, as [w]ell as the Sin forbidden. Whereby it pleased the Lord to open mine eyes & inlighten my darke minde to Se that I was guilty of the breach of the [co]mmands, & my former hopes to be but vaine. Now the Lord was pleas'd [to] lay his hand heavy upon me making me to feel the terrours of the Law. [&] meeting with many temptations to beat me off from those duties God lead me to. Yet the Lord was pleased so to help me se, as that I resolved to [k]now him, & seek him by earnest prayer, & attend upon the ministry [of] the Word by his assistance. But I found mine own Resolution many [ti]mes come to nothing: Whereby the Lord discovered to me mine own [we]akness, unability to do any thing, myselfe, all my duties & my [o]wn Righteousness to be nothing; but all were Sinfull, & pollut[ed]; & that without the Righteousness of Christ I should not be accept[ed] of him. But it pleased the Lord in hearing severall promises of [gra]ce in his word made to burdened Sinners, & especially that Matt. [11.]28, Come unto me all ye that labour, & are heavy laden, & I will [giv]e you rest. & musing that God should invite such a Sinner to come [unto] him as I was, that had neglected his Calls, & slighted his grace & Spi[rit(] many times) through his grace to worke in me some relent[ings] & brokenness of heart. & some thirsting desires after Christ, & [his] Righteousness: But I found it a very difficult thing to come to [Ch]rist, & to believe on him, & regain any power of mine own: So that [in] some measure I was, I hope, feelingly made to Cry out, Draw [near] that I may run after thee; & for the Almighty power of God to help finding my inability to help myselfe, & my unworthiness to have [help] from God. & it pleased the Lord, out of his free grace, in some mea[sure] to inable me to make my address to him, that he would shine up[on] me, & give me Repentance, & a pardon of my Sins, & to inable [me] to rest on Christ for help. And I hope he hath in some degree * * * * * * he hath graciously answered me in that he hath blessed the Ministry of the Word so to me as to in able me, to deny myselfe, & close with Christ, & Especially in hearing Mr. Wareham upon that Luke 2.10,11, (& the Angel said to them fear not; for behold I bring you good tidings of great joy which shall be to all people, for unto you is born this day in the City of David, a Saviour, Christ the Lord) shewing what good news there was to poor burdened Sinners incorraging them to come to Christ, the Lord was graciously pleased to manifest himselfe to my Soule hereby, yet I confess to my griefe that I finde a body of Death working in me, that the good I would do I do not & what I would not, that do I. But if my heart deceive me not I finde Sin a bitter thing & dare not allow myselfe in any known Sin: But do desire to injoy Christ in all his ordinances & to have Fellowship with Gods people therein.

The Relation of Brother John Ingerson[22]

I being brought by Godly Parents, who tooke great pains & Care to bring me out of a State of Nature into a State of Grace in watching over me, in keeping me from Sin, & Sabbothbreaking, in bringing me to attend the word preached, read, & in Catechising I'd little regard itt, but onely for fear of them.

The first time, to my rememberance, that God met with me was by a Sermon I heard at Darby in old England upon Ps. 15.1,2, when I was about 18 years old, whereby I was Convinct that as yet I was none that should inherit the holy Hill of Zion, but I thought I would labour to be one that Should. But this Conviction was soon over & I went on in my Sin & vanity still. & tho' I met with many Conviction that my State was bad, & was in many dangers both at sea, & land; & I saw I must Repent, & become a new Creature if ever I ment to be Saved, yet I put repentance off till afterwards. But being under Mr. Stones Ministry I was convincd that the time was come that I must not put Repentance off any longer, for the Lord had granted me the thing wherein my excuses lay & therefore I set upon Duties, & reformed in many things, & having a book of Mr. Jeremiah Burroughs I read much in it, about Faith, & Hope, & was much incouraged, till I met with an Expression thus, that if my Hopes were not such as would stand with every line of the word of God at the day of Judgment they would availe me nothing. Then being troubled I threw the book a side for a while thinking that altho' he was a good man he was too Strict, & mistaken therein.[23] & that I did believe, & that he that did believe should be saved & therefore my State was good. But coming to Northampton I heard Mr. Mather the first time upon that, that in the world ye shall have trouble, but in Christ you may & shall have peace, which incouraged me for a while. But afterwards his preaching did not please me but I thot I would keep my hopes. And the Lord visiting me with sickness that I was neer death, yet I thot I was well enough prepared for death & was not willing to hear to the Contrary: But the Lord in great mercy was pleased not to take me away in that Condition. But remaining still Confident of my good Estat, I, as I was on atime into the meadow to work, thot nothing should dash my hopes thereof. But presently the thoughts of   who murdered himselfe[24] Coming into my mind, I for a while much wondered at it. But my thots soon runing thus, What if God should leave me? then I should do so. & the temptation came so hard upon me that God would leave me, & I should certainly dy such a death; be guilty of mine own Blood, & be damned irreconcilably, that I was not able to go on to my business; but returning home, the temptation prevaild more, & more upon me, & I was filled with horrour of Conscience, the Lord did so manifest his wrath & Displeasure against me: & my Sins were like mountains ready to sink me down into Hell every moment. & not being able in the night to sleep, was forced to rise up at midnight, & Call up my Father in Law, who hearing how it was with me, & that I feared I had sinned the unpardonable Sin; & that there were no Hopes of mercy, gave me good Counsell, & prayed with me. & after having some abatement I returned home, & remain'd in that Condition: But the Lord after awile was pleased to abate the temptation, & his wrath a little. & I fell to reading & praying in Secret; being incouraged to look to Jesus Christ for mer-[86/87]cy. But Mr. Mathers Ministry was like daggers in my heart. For when I was labouring to lay hold on Christ, as I thot, by Faith, it did so rip up my State in such a way as dashed my hopes, whereby, me thot, I was one that went about to Establish mine own Righteousness, & to have something of mine own to Carry me to Christ. Wherefore I Studied upon what terms Christ was to be had, I prayed, Searched the Scriptures, & attended all duties; but could find no way to get a pardon, of Sin, & peace with God, but by Repentance of all Sin, & a Closing with Jesus Christ by Faith. I thot I was willing to part with all Sin, & would gladly be delivered from it, as seeing what a Condition it had brought me into. As for the world, I accounted it not worth regarding, so I could but get an Intrest in Christ Jesus. But how to believe I knew not. I heard many Descriptions of Faith, yet could not tell what it was, nor how to gett it. Mr. Mather being upon the work of Humiliation said be humble enough, & good enough; I thot it was the Pride of my heart, that I saw so impatient; & could not wait Gods time. I saw there was hopes of mercy for me in Jesus Christ. He came into the world to save his people from their Sins: With him the Fatherless finde Mercy; He gives gifts to Rebellious ones; the Chiefe of Sinners. He is able to Save all to the uttmost, & will by no means cast off any that come to him. & tho' I could not come to him of myselfe, yet he is able to bring me to, & keep me with, himselfe, then reading that Isa. [43.24,]thou has brought me no Sweet Cane—but hast made me to serve with thy Sins; yet I am he that blotteth out all thy Sins for my names sake. Whereupon I found myself willing, & was inabled to Cast myselfe upon the Lord Jesus Christ, to give up myselfe & all unto him; to leave my Sins, & Corruptions to him to do as he pleased. & So to leave myselfe with him, let him do, what he would with me. & if I did perish at last, yet it should be in his way, remembring Peters words, Lord to whom should we go thou hast the words of Eternall Life.

[The Foundation Day Sermon]

Eph. 2.22. In whom you are also builded (up) together,
for an Habitation of God through the Spirit.

In this Chapter we have the Apostle setting forth the duble State of all
mankinde as it falls under a double Consideration. & therefore Distributes all men into such
1. As they are either under, or without the Profession of the true God in
these Relitive terms opposed, You, & We, v. 1,3, that is you gentiles
that had not the true God & we Jews that had.
2. As they are either in a State of Wrath or a State of Favour. As they are
in a State of wrath; & thus he shews that both, those that had, & those
that had not the profession of the true God, were naturally in. & this he
shews to be a state of Sin, v. 3, a State of Death, v. 1,5, & a state of
Wrath, v. 3, the which states he doth illustrate in this Chapter in opposing of the same to a State of Favour.

As for the State of Favour, this doth not belong unto all, but unto
those alone who are brought out of the other state. For all men are either
with, or without the Profession of the true God; & all men, are either in
a State of death, or in a State of Life, yet this last belongs unto those
onely who,(whether they were before either with; or without the Profession of the true God) are brought out of a State of Nature into a State of
Grace by the grace of God, hence v. 1, you who were dead, & v. 5, we
who were dead, hath he quickned to gether.

Now this State of Favour he calls a State of Life, v. 1, 5, & doth
Illustrate it as it respects God & as it respects Gods people. & so this
state [is] that which was the Burden of the Psalm sung by the Quire of
An[gels,] those Celestiall Choristers, Luke 2.14, Glorie to God, & peace
good will towards men.

As it respects God, its a state glorifying of God, & there[fore] of
peace with God, v. 16,17.

As it respects the Saint, its a state of peace; on earth pe[ace,] hence
the partition wall is broke down, v. 14. And the Privilidge[s, that] come
in upon this state; as it is a state of peace & good wi[ll a]mong the Saints,
are treated on in this Chapter as they are [en]joyed by the Saints as they
are Considered under a $\begin{Bmatrix} \text{Politicall} \\ \text{Architectonic[al]} \end{Bmatrix}$ Consideration.

First, As they fall under a Politicall Consideration they a[re] now become Christ's Policy. And so they are considered in re[spect]

1. Unto their Matriculation into his Kingdom State. & [the] priviledges are illustrated Comparitively comparing state together, v. 12,13, ye who were without Christ ἀπηλλοτριωμένοι τῆς πολιτείας τοῦ Ἰσραήλ—a far off: are ἐγενήθητε ἐγγὺς made nigh on the priviledges come in now?

2. Unto their Infrenchisation into a City State, they are ma[de] free Denisons of the New Jerusalem, v. 19. Συμπολῖται τῶν ἁγίων they are made Fellow Citizens of the Saints. & therefore are [entitl]ed to all the Priviledges of this Corporation. Oh! what uncon[ceiv]able Immunities are these?

3. Unto their Admission into Christs Houshould State [they] are adopted heirs into Christs Family, v. 19. οἰκεῖοι τοῦ Θεοῦ, are of the household of God. O! what priviledges are here. Stand & wonder at this Change; whereby poore Sinners a[re] translated out of the Vassallage of Sin: & hell, into the commun[ion] of Israel & Kingdom of heaven; Out of the society of div[ells] to be of the Citizens of the Saints. Out of the region of the Shadd[ow of] death, into the Dominion of the Prince of Life. Out of the H[abita]tion of Dragons & Cruelties, into the corporation of the Ho[use] of God. O stand amazed at these priviledges. But thus much res[pect]ing this Politicall Consideration.

Secondly. These priviledges are to be considered as they a[re] injoyed by the Saints Considered under the * * * [87/88] * * * as these Saints are Compared to a Building. & [wh]ereby their Priviledges are illustrated from their { Substructure / Superstructure.

1. From the Substructure, or foundation upon which they are as a building raised, & laid, v. 20. & it is upon the Foundation of the Prophets, & Apostles, Jesus Christ himselfe being the Cheif Corner Stone. In this Substructure here is both a foun[d]ation Stone & a Corner Stone mentioned; not, as if these were two distincte stones: for they are not. For as Jesus Christ himselfe is the Cheife Corner Stone, so the Foundation is Jesus Christ. For other foundation can no one lay, I Cor. 3.11. But God did foretell that he would lay him to be Zion's Foundation Stone, & yet the Cheife Corner Stone too, Isa. 28.16, Behold I lay in Zion for a foundation, a stone, a tryed [s]tone, a precious Corner Stone, a sure foundation. This is the foundation then, Jesus

Christ himselfe. & he is both the foundation, & the Corner Stone, as being that Rock upon which the building is built, & that binder which holds the whole [b]uilding together. This foundation therefore is not properly the Old & New Testament, as St. Ambrose thought;[25] nor is it Peter as the Papists aver, but it is Christ Jesus, called the Foundation of the Apostles & the Prophets because they were the wise Master builders, laying this foundation, under God, I Cor. 3.10. & Because they are eminently built upon, & have an eminent [in]trest in this Foundation, Eph. 1.1. & according as things are in[v]ested in, such is the Denomination they have upon them. & in that the Apostles & Prophets did build the Church on this Foundation, therefore [it] is called the Foundation of the Prophets & the Apostles. & because they [w]ere Gods builders to lay others upon it, as I Cor. 4.15, I Pet. 2.4–5.

2. From the Superstructure, or Building raised upon this [fo]undation. Now the building raised is Considered first [ge]nerally, v. 21. On (rather than in) whom the whole building fittly [for]med together, grows into a holy Temple in the Lord. & then [pa]rticularly in the words of our text, v. 22. On whom ye also are [bui]lt together for an habitation of God thro' the Spirit. As the Temple at Jerusalem was but one, yet it had many habitations in it whereof it did Consist.[26] So the Catholick Church is but one, yet it Consists of many particular Churches, & each of these Particular Churches is as this Church at Ephesus, a Habitation of God through the Spirit.

Our text then, you se, is a Description of the Particular Church [of] Christ at Ephesus; & it doth describe it what it is,

From its Foundation upon which it is built, in this word, in [(or] rather on) whom, ye all, now who is intended in this Rela[ti]ve, you may se, v. 20. & that is Christ, who is the Antecedent of [w]hom it is spoke. & therefore Christ is the foundation of it.

From the Materiall Cause of it, couched in the word Ye, which [is] to be refered unto the persons Spoken to, & these are the Saints [at] Ephesus & faithfull in Christ, Eph. 1.1.

From the Formall Cause of it, & this is that which unites the [ma]terials into a Church State layd down in this word built up [to]gether.

From the Finall Cause of it, wherefore it is built up & is thus Expressed, viz, to be an Habitation of God. &

From the Principall Efficient Cause of it, so ordering of [the] Matter for this End. & this is laid down unto you up in this term the Spirit:

for seing all is thus acted by the Spirit, the Spi[ri]t must needs be the Principall Agent of it.

The text thus opened, the Doctrine I shall Speak to

is this that

A PARTICULAR CHURCH OF CHRIST IS BUILT UP TO BE A HABITATION OF GOD THROUGH THE SPIRIT.

[Th]at description which the spirit of God layeth down of the Par-[ticu]lar church of Christ of Ephesus demonstrating what it is from [its n]ature, is true of Every particular Church of Christ touch[ing] its nature, but you se what this is. Ergo, Now that its spoken of the particular Church of Christ at Ephesus is plain for Chap. 1.1, the Epistle is writ to the Saints & Faithfull in Christ at Ephesus. & those were suitable Matter for a Church; & you see these are the Persons still spoke to Collectively in the word "ye" in our text. & that as they had passt under the Operation of the Spirit of God in order to their Church-Incorporation, & the Spirit is the Principall Efficient Cause of a Church: & they had received the Church Informing Act of this Efficient, for they were build up together; & so are Spoke to as so formed & made among themselves an Habitation of God, thro' the Spirit, & what this is but a particular Church I know not. Nay, & Christ Speaking to his Angel here residing, calls him the Angell of the Church at Ephesus, Rev. 2.1, And as this Particular Church is called an Habitation of God So I Cor. 3.9, the Church at Corinth is Called Gods Building ($διοδομή$, from $οἶκος$ an house, & $δομή$ a building, an house building, or a raised house) & therefore God dwells in it, v. 15, so that its his dwelling place.

In speaking to this truth I shall 1. Speak to the Causes of a Particular Church;

2. Shew what it is to be an Habitation of God,

3. Consider the Emphasis of this word, through the Spirit,

4. Inquire into the Reasons why a Particular Church is an Habitation of God through the Spirit. &

5. Apply the truth with brevity.

First, as for the Causes of a Particular Church, they are $\begin{cases} \text{Externall} \\ \text{Internall.} \end{cases}$

1. The Externall Causes are onely Externall principals constituting of the thing & the ground of it but are no parts of the nature of it & these are the $\begin{cases} \text{Efficient} \\ \text{Finall.} \end{cases}$

1. The Efficient Cause of the Church is that gives forth Causative Influences from itselfe to the Constituting of it, & that $\begin{cases} \text{Principally} \\ \text{Instrumentally.} \end{cases}$

1. Principally. & so the onely principall Efficient of [it] is Gods, the undivided Trinity, hence the Church at Corinth, etc., is Gods building. All the persons in the Trinity build it. Hence they joyntly own it, & inhabit it, hereupon the House of God is the Church of the Living God, I Tim. 3.15. God the Father builds it, hence its calld Gods building, as I Cor. 3.9. God the Son builds it, hence he hath Said, on this rock I Will build my Church: God the Holy Ghost; hence its said in our text, ye are built up together through the Spirit. The Father is the Principall Efficient Cause, as the Originall of all the Efficiency by which it is built. The Son is the Principall Efficient Cause, as the Purchaser of all the Efficiency effecting of it. & the Holy Ghost is the Principall Efficient cause, as the Effuser of all the Efficiency for the Effecting of it, etc.

2. Instrumentally. Now the Instruments which God makes use in framing this building are, his Word, the Ministry of his Word & the Ministers of his word. These are the golden Pipes, convaying the holy Oyle into the Vessels of honour from the Lord of Life. These are the tooles & Artists which God makes use of in raising this building. Hence saith Paul, I as a wise Master Builder have laid the foundation, & others build thereon, I Cor. 3.10. & hence the foundation is calld the Foundation of the Apostles, & the Prophets as you heard, Eph. 2.20.

2. The Finall Cause. Now the finall Cause is that externall Cause of the thing for which the Efficient Acts. Its that which the Efficient hath in its eye & aimes at in its acting, & therefore the Actings of the Efficient are related by the End; otherwise they would never be Sufficient means in the hand of the Efficient for the attaining that which the Efficient aimes at. Now this finall Cause of a Church is thus Expressed, viz, to be an Habitation of God, εἰς κατοικητήριον, is as much as εἰς τὸ εἶναι κατοικητήριον to be an habitation of God. & as God said of the Temple on Mount Zion thus, I hath chosen Zion, he hath desired it for his Habitation, this is my rest for ever, here will I dwell, Ps. 132.13,14: So it is in this case a Church of Christ is his habitation, his rest; here he dwells if any one defile this Temple him Will God destroy, I Cor. 2.16,17. [88/89] & now the end of it is this, to be a habitation of God. The Actings of the Efficient are Archtecturiall Acts framing of it into a building. & so it is made Gods Habitation, set apart from other uses, by

himselfe for himselfe. Its therefore for his use & his alone. & therefore in our treating of his using of it, we may consider his $\begin{cases} \text{Furniture in it, \&} \\ \text{Presence in it.} \end{cases}$

1. His Furniture wherewith he adorns it & furnishes it for his Service. For Gods house is well set out. So was the Temple at Jerusalem, Heb. 9.2,3,4, 5.6: & so is his Gospel Temples, II Tim. 2.20,21. These Vessels are all Vessels of honour, vessels of dishonour, as filth are to be purg'd away. But seing the house is Gods Habitation, there must be no furniture brought into this house but what is Gods own, & hath his Marke upon it, who hath any thing to do to set any thing of his own in Gods house. But now Gods furniture consists in the $\begin{cases} \text{Utensills} \\ \text{Officers.} \end{cases}$

The Utensils or things to be used in Gods House are his houshold goods, as I may so say, & these most costly, precious, & Excellent that are brought into dayly use in his Service, & they are such as these, viz,

1. The Arke of the Covenant with all its appurtenances, as the Booke of the Law, the Mercy Seat, the Cherubims of Glory, etc. So here is the Substance of these Jesus Christ attended with his Angels, I Cor. 11.10, Eph. 3.10: these are most Choice things, & here is the Testimony of the Witness, the Oracle of God, the Holy Scripture, II Tim. 3.15.

2. The Golden Candle Sticks fild with Holy Oil giveing an heavenly flame always to inlighten the house. So here are the light in the ministry of the word, Matt. 5.16.

3. The Golden Altar, the Altar of Incense, the Incense, Censer, & fire of heaven upon the Altar; all which are found in the Gospel temple, Rev. 8.3, in the person of Christ, the Merits of Christ, the Prayers of the Saints & a holy flame of Heavenly affections Godward.

4. The golden pot with Mannah, Heb. 9.4: & the pure shewbread Table, of Gold with the Shewbread upon it, I Kings 7.48. So here in Gods house are the bread of Life, the Mannah that came down from above, John 6.50,51, Rev. 2.17. & the Table of Shew bread the Lords Table, I Cor. 10.21.

5. A Glorious Throne or Chair of state where the Lord of the house doth more especially reside, Isa. 6.1, & so here as Rev. 4.2, indeed the whole Church is this glorious throne, as may appear from Gods presence therein.

6. The Laver of Purification for all to wash in that went into the Temple, I Kings 7.38. So here stands the Bason, & Ure of Soules (as I

may say) the Blood of Christ, I John 1.7. Applied symbolically in the water of Baptizm, Eph. 5.25,26, Titus 3.5. These are some of the Utensils with which Gods house is furnisht.

The Officers in Gods house that are to use these things & to Carry on the Service of Gods house, (onely observe that some of these things are onely to be used by the stewards of Gods house but the officers) are

1. Extraordinary, as Prophets, Apostles, & Evangelists, Eph. 4.11, I Cor. 12.28, which were onely for a Season, & not to indure.

2. Ordinary, which are to indure for ever, & these are $\begin{cases} \text{Elders} \\ \text{Deacons.} \end{cases}$

Elders are such as are both teaching & Ruling as I Tim. 5.17. & these Teaching Elders are either the Teaching Elders whose peculiar worke is to hold fourth the Doctrinall part of Salvation called teaching, Rom. 12.7. Or the Pastor whose most proper work lies in Exhortation, as Rom. 12.8. & such whose special work is onely Ruling * * * * * * I Tim. 5.17. & therefore Called Government, I Cor. 12.28.

Deacons are such that are to attend the more outward Concerns of Gods House, as the Providing for the Table of the Lord, the Ministers Table & the table of the poor, hence these are the Churches Treasurer, Acts 6.

And thus in such things as these consist the furniture of Gods house.

2. His Presence in it. Now he having so furnisht it doth come & reside in it, I Cor. 3.16,17, he fills it with his glorious presence so he did the Tabernacle, Ex. 40.34, So he did the Temple, II Chron. 5.13,14: & so he doth his Gospel house, Rev. 1.12, & on. Here he meets with them & speakes to them, Ex. 25.22. Here he gives his people his blessing even life for ever more, Ps. 133.3. & hence do Gods people pant so to meet God in his house, Ps. 42.1,2. But his glory & presence here is cheifly Visible unto his people in his Own Worship & Service, wherein his Servants, & Cheifly the Stewards of his house are making use of his Utensils in his house. & so the Use of this house wherein God is especially present in it, is in his Worship in generall but to consider this in its particulars, as followeth,

1. In that light of the Ministry of the worde in which he shines forth here. For he calls this his habitation, a golden Candle Sticke, & the Ministry in it a Shining Angel, Rev. 1 last & Chap. 2.1. He uses this house as a Window of Heaven out of which he shines with heavenly light, to inlighten all men in the way to heaven. & his presence in this light appears

1. In Illumination, & Conviction, inlightening blind Mindes, & Convincing hard hearts of their Sin & Miseries. For its onely God that can effect this, I Cor. 3.6,9.

2. In Conversion, for that Sinners turn from Sin unto God, is the power of God in the Word & not of man, Rom. 1.16. Hence the instrument of this Service is nothing But God that gives blessing is all, I Cor. 3.6 to the 9 v.

3. In Edification for in that the using of this Ministry is reviving & Edifying its wholy from God.

2. In those Humble Suites that are here made to God in this house.

3. In those holy & heavenly Songs that are herein sung forth unto God.

4. In the initiating of Members into this house Baptismally in the Ordinance of Baptizme & disciplinarily in opening this golden doore unto full Communion.

5. In the Celibrating the Feast of the Lords Supper, while the king sits at the Table his Spicknard sends out its Sweet Smel, Cant. 1.12.

6. In the Ejecting of the obstinate, I Cor. 5.4. & receiving again the Penitent, II Cor. 2, for tho' some of these things are carried on & effected elsewhere yet here they are alwayes carried on.

And in Such things as these consists the Use or the End of this house. & thus we have done with the Externall Causes of it.

2. The Internall Causes of a particular Church are such as Constitute the Nature of it as $\begin{cases} \text{Matter} \\ \text{Form.} \end{cases}$

1. The Matter of a Church, & this is that of which the Church is made & Constituted, it is an Essentiall Cause of it. & this Matter is such as is holy. Holiness becometh thy house, oh Lord for ever, Ps. 93.5. Therefore the Materiall Cause is the Faithfull in Christ Jesus & Saints. Such was the matter of this Habitation of God at Ephesus as Eph. 1.1, & Such was the Matter of the Church of Christ at Corinth, I Cor. 1.1,3, II Cor. 1.1, at Phillipi, Phil. 1.1, at Colloss, Col. 1.2. It must be reall Holiness that is the Essentiall Qualification of this matter; this is the preparatory form of it, the stones of which this is built are fetcht out of the Quarry, or Stone pit of Mankind, & hewen, & Squared by the Axe of the Spirit till they are rightly pollisht & fitted for this building: & so made living stones, Eph. 21, for this Spirituall Temple, I Pet. 2.5. Onely here observe that seing the judgment under which this Matter is to pass, in the tryall of its fittness, being such as must be extended as far as the

Rules of Christian Charity concerning the worke of Grace, can reach out its hand, & this being made from [89/90] the Appearance of things, it is a fallable judgment, & hence appearing holiness with men, nothing appearing to the Contrary but Such humane infirmities, as are to be found in the best of Gods people doth sway our judgment to hope & therefore to pass the Sentence of Christian Charity Concerning the reallity of Such a Persons Holiness, & so to receive such for Saints, & fitt Matter. And that the Matter ought to be holy doth thus appear.

1. Because the Catholick Church truly so taken is holy, for the Whole building, Eph. 2.21, is the true Catholick Church, & this is to grow into a holy Temple in the Lord. Now as is the Catholick Such must be the particular; for the Catholick Church being the Genus unto the Particular, & the Species receiving its Common Nature from the Genus, the Particular Church must needs consist of holy Matter, seing the Catholick Church, its Genus is holy, hence Rom. 11.16.

2. From the State into which the Matter is brought, & every particular Stone is wrought up unto before it is laid into this building, Now this State is a State of Union or neerness unto God, Eph. 2.13, a state of Light, Eph. 5.8, of Reviving, Eph. 2.1, of Life, I Pet. 2.5, of Peace, & Reconciliation, Eph. 2.15,16, a State of Sanctification, I Cor. 1 last. & therefore of Grace. Now these things being spoke indifinitly of the whole societie, it cannot be but that they were in this State before they were associated into a Church body. & that in Peter is Expressed. & therefore it is thus.

3. From that proportion which ought to be between the Foundation, & the building. For if the foundation is Costly, the building raised thereupon must be somewhat answerable, if the foundation be holy, the superstructure must not be unholy. Now here the foundation is a Pretious Stone, & therefore the Superstructure ought to be Precious Stones. The foundation is a Pearle of great price, Matt. 13.46, & therefore the building must not be of pebbles, or paultry Stones. Nay, but God saith they shall be with fair Colours, of Agates, & Saphire, Isa. 54.12, God will have a proportion attended in his building, where the Windows are of Agats, the Gates shall be of Carbunckle & all the borders of Pretious Stones. Where one row is Saphires, an other shall be Jaspers, etc., where each Gate is Smaragdine or a Sparkling pearle, the streets are pure gold, Rev. 21.19, 20.22. God will have all things in his Building proportionably Excellent. & who can imagin that by Such Excellent allusions as these any thing inferior to the Choicest of the

Children of men are intended; & hence Saints are the Matter. Nay hence the whole building is by another Metaphor called a Golden Candle Stick, Rev. 1.12,20. & who can imagine that the Spirit of God should lay such a golden name upon a mere refuse Nature, as all Unsanctified ones are of.

4. From the Inhabitor of the House. For according to the Qualification of the Person dwelling in the House such is the Nature of the Building, Kings & Nobles do not use to build their Palaces, or Habitations of mean Materiall. It's said that Augustus Caesar having adorned Rome his Imperiall City with many Stately buildings would oft glory thus, I found the City to be of Brick, but have left a Marble City:[27] But it is him that is king of Kings & Lord of Lords that inhabits this building. This is the City of the great King, Matt. 5.35. God the Father keeps house here, I Cor. 3.16, God the Son makes these his Ivory Palaces, he walkes in the middst of the golden Candle Sticke, God the Holy Ghost Possesseth these Temples, I Cor. 3.16, & in our text. If Solomon made himselfe an ivory Throne over laid With pure gold, if Ahasuerus[28] his Palace was adorned with white, green, & blew hangings, set up with Cords of fine linnen & purple unto Silver rings & pillars of Marble, & with beds of Gold & Silver upon a pavement of red, blew, White & black Marble, Shall we think that the Throne, & the Palace, the Habitation of God him self is of base Materialls, no, no, but of the Choicest matter which is, & therefore of reall Saints.

5. From the Use & Improovment of it: For according to the Use such is the Matter to be Used. Now the Use is holy, its onely for the Worship & Service of God & you have heard in briefe some particulars of the same. Now the use being holy use this requires holy hands to carrie it on. Holy things must not be cast to dogs, nor Pearles hung in Swines Snouts. Hence you se the matter must be holy.

I might have reasoned from the necessity of being of the Catholick Invisible Church unto the right preparation of the Matter of a Particular Church from Relation that the Particular Church stands in unto Christ, as a Spouse, a Bride, a Wife, bone of his bone, flesh of his flesh, & from the Titles given unto it by Christ as fair, all Fair, Undefiled, etc., to proove it to be holy but I shall proceed no further here.

But there is an other Qualification of the Matter absolutly as a *forma preparans* of it, disposing of it for the Reception of its *formalis*

Ratio of a Church: & this is the Manifestation of this work of Sanctification, so & in Such a way as may Constrain Conscientious Charity to hope the best, & judge the best. Now this Manifestation must be therefore

1. In a life & Conversation answerable to the Rules of the Scripture, Gal. 6.16, Phil. 3.16, for sons there are who altho' in words they own Christ do yet in workes deny him, Titus 1.16. These must be noted, & not held in Communion, II Thess. 3.14: & therefore the holiness in their hearts must shine forth in their lives.

2. In the Profession, or Confession, or declaration of the same with their mouths, Rom. 10.10: with the mouth Confession is made unto Salvation. But now here comes in the pinch of the Controversy, viz, unto whom this Confession is to be made, whether unto God, or unto man, & if to man, whether to the E[l]ders onely, or to the Whole Church & when. In answer unto this, I say as for a Confession unto God that no one questions, & in the renewing of the dayly Exercise of repentance this is Carried on: But this reaches not the Matter in hand: As for a Confession holding forth some grounds to Christian Charity that the old man is put off; & the New man put on, that must be given unto the Elders of the Church. This also no man doubts of that owns the doctrine of the Gospell, for thus must persons be prepared by the Elders for Church Fellowship. All the stick then lieth here. Whether this Confession of what Experience of the workings of Gods Spirit, we have found upon our hearts, is to be made before the Church & when. Unto which I say that

> it is necessary that the Person seeking with any Church of Christ to have Communion, give an account of the workings of Gods Spirit upon his heart, either personally, or by some other, unto that Church, & the most suitablest season for it, is in an ordinary way, than when he is to be admitted into Communion.

Now this I shall endeavour to Establish by Arguments of an Inartificiall, & Artificiall Force.

Onely this one Exception I would make, viz, that in case a Member in Full Communion, that hath walked orderly all along in that State come to such a decay of his Naturall Capacity that he is not able to do any thing Considerable this way, nor to be helpt therein, & yet his godliness shines; I say, that if such a person upon the Change of his Habitation, do Change his Memberly State & put himselfe into fellowship where he dwells I do not account it Necessary to Exact a Relation from Such an one. & this being premised I proceed

1. Now the Inartificiall arguments with which I shall settle the truth of the Proposition laide down are $\begin{cases} \text{Divine} \\ \text{Humane.} \end{cases}$

    1. As for the Divine arguments these are Such Testimonies of Holy Scripture as we [90/91] finde recorded by the Spirit of God in the Old Testament & in the New.

1. In the Old Testament are Scattered up & down such testimonies as point out this truth, some in Ceremonies, & some in the substance of it, the which I shall indeavour to gather together, in part, as they hold fourth the publick Confession of Gods working upon the soule in bringing of it to himselfe, & as they hold it out to be made upon the Souls Covenanting with God & his people, i.e., when it enters into a Church State.

    1. Those that hold forth this Confession of Faith & Repentance publickly in the Ceremoniall worship are all Sin & Trespass offerings, on the head of which the Person was to lay his hand, as Lev. 1.4, 3.2,8; 13 Chap.: 4.24,29; Chap. 5.5,6,—[29] the Offring implies Faith & Repentance, on the account of his Sin; his laying his hand upon the head of the same his publick manifesting of his Sin by way of Repentance, & of his applying himselfe unto Gods appointments for his recovery in a way of Faith.

    Another of this nature is that Deut. 26.3, to the 12,[30] where you have a plain injunction laid on every man in Israel (unless Levi's tribe be Excepted) for all I say that appeare before the Lord with the Basket of First Fruits to make a Confession of their Former Misery & Gods grace in their recovery.

    2. But to Come to such Scriptures as contain this thing in the very substance of it clearly, take that Job 33.27,28.[31] He (i.e., the Penetent person) shall look upon men (אנשים humble, penetent, & mournfull men as Enosh was) & say I have Sinned & perverted what is right, & it profetted me not: (here lies the very work of repentance, & God brings him to this, you se, & to give a relation of it publickly, but he goeth on thus) he (i.e., God spoken of, v. 26)[32] hath redeemed my soul (rather than his Soule as being the words of the Penitent, & so the Hebrew word בפשי may beare & many Learned persons take it thus, viz, my soule) from death, & my life (rather than his) shall see the

The Foundation Day Sermon: "Church Records," manuscript p. 91.

light: & what is this but a Confession of the goodness & grace of God unto him, & of his own faith God ward.

Another Scripture is that Ps. 66.16,17,18,19,20, Come, & heare all ye that feare God & I will declare what he hath done for my Soule, this is the declaration of what he would do. & in this account that he gives you may observe him discovering his Experiences of Gods working upon his heart in respect unto the drawing out of his heart after him in a way of earnest prayer & prayse thus I cryed unto him with my mouth, & he was extolled with my tongue; & in respect unto his turning of him from Sin, the which he rather prooves than professes, therein shewing forth his repentance that it must needs be in respect unto the necessity thereof for his preparation; & for his being heard thus, v. 18, 19, if I regard iniquity in my heart the Lord will not heare my prayers but verily God hath heard me– & in respect unto the actings of the grace of God godward, of the account of his prayer & the grace obtained, v. 20.

To this purpose Serves Ps. 51, wherein you have a relation laid down of Gods working upon Davids heart recovering of him out of his Sin, in the Matter of Uriah.[33] But it would be tedious to lay down what is manifest of this Nature.

But I shall now pass on to such Scriptures as hold out this Confession to be made upon the soules entering into a Church State, & for this End weigh these following

Ex. 19.14: After the people were come out of Egypt they were under the Conviction of the Spirit untill they came unto Mount Sinai, & here now on the third day they were to enter into a visible Church State & therefore they were to sanctify themselves & for that end must wash all in water, the which they did. & therein, did according to the * * * * * * their Conviction of Sin, from which they were to be purged, their Repentance of Sin is held forth by their actuall washing. & their faith in the Lord, that he in their using those means that he had appointed should be really acquitted of their Sin, & accepted of God.

An other is that of Solomon, who after he had greatly Apostatized from God, & scandalized the Church of God, gives a relation of his soule Exercise in its Ecclesiasticall motions wherein he was reconciled unto the Church again, as is clear in the Whole booke of the Ecclesiastes, the which he titles *coheleth* as importing the Congregating, or in-Churching Soule, or the Soule in its betaking itselfe to the Church of God, being of the Feminine Gender.[34]

An other is that Neh. 9.2, & the seed of Israel stood separated themselves from all strangers & stood & Confessed their Sins & the Sins of their fathers: this was in order to their reentering into their Church State again formally as is plain, for upon their return with Joshua, & Zorobabel there was very little done save onely a preparation for the work; for Cyrus living not above 3 years at most as is most probable after his Decree, & his son Cambyses being a Cruell Tyrant there was so great impedments in the way that in the sixt year of Darius Hystaspis they had done little but set up the bare Fabrick of the Temple, Ezra 6.15.[35] & as these 17 years affected cheifly this, so there were about 68 more before they did any thing Considerable, viz, till the 7 yeare of Artaxerxes when Ezra came, Ezra 7.7. & altho' he came now with Such full Commision yet we Se he had not Compleated the work by far, till Nehemiah came about a duzzen yeare after him, & now the worke were Compleated soon after this worke here in this Chapter was attended as appears in the end of this 9th & the beginning of the next.

Now from these, & such places as these, in the old Testament Confession, or a Relation of the Worke of God upon the Soule is to be made, & that in order unto the Soules entering into a Church state.

Unto this as a humane testimony the manner of the jewish Church's Prosilytation of Strangers, which as a shadow will assert the same thing. But I shall not stay here, therefore as for such Testimonies as are

2. In the New Testament for this purpose. & these are such as hold forth a Publick Confession of Repentance & Faith to be made before men as

Matt. 3.6,7,8,9, Acts 19.4. John Baptist admitted none to his Baptism but those that made it. & those that would not do it were rejected. Hence the Body of the Scribes & Pharisees, tho' they came out to him, & pleaded their right from that old worn Argument we are Abrahams Seed in opposition unto this present duty, which is called fruit meet for repentance, were reprooved, v. 7,8,9, & rejected & not Baptized, Luke 7.30.

Rom. 10.10. With the mouth Confession is made unto Salvation. *Confessio et verbàlis, et realis intelligitur.* This we are Called to, Jas. 5.16, *De...confessione fratribus facta, vide Polum in locum.*[36]

I Pet. 3.15. Be ready always to give an answer to every one that askes you a reason of the hope that is in you, with meekness & feare— *Mea judicia (inquit Calvinus in locum) significat Apologiae nomen...ut*

Christiani testatum mundo facerent, se procul, ab omni impietate—[37] & if this must be made to every one, then it must be made when the Church calls for it.

Therefore to Come to such Scriptures as warrant this Relation upon the Persons entring into a Church State & I shall not stand long here, let these following suffice, viz,

Acts 2.37–41. Those that were added to the Church are such that met with the power of the spirit of God in Peters sermon as a Bodkin in their hearts, mortifying their sin, & making of them to put themselves under the Apostles advice for help, the which they attending upon in receiving it found joy. Now I say how was this known, if there was nothing of this related & upon this it is said there were added to the Church about 3000 souls. Not that the worke was finisht in that day in their personall relations & baptism, but that it was begun in that day in their Conversion.

Acts 9.26,27,28. The Church at Jerusalem would not admit Paul when he Sought to joyn to them, till he had his Conversion made out before them both in respect unto the manner of it, & the Effect of it by Barnabas. * * * * * *[91/92] By the Confession of the work of God upon the heart of Cornelius, v. 30,31,32,33, & the manifestation of Gods work on (him further no do[u]bt as well as) the rest unto Peter & the rest with him, v. 46.

Acts 19.9. The Disciples, at Ephesus, intring into a Church state, is expressed by Paul's Separating of them, & the manner how this work was carried on in order to their intering into that State, is demonstrated in the entrance of others among them, v. 18, by Confessing & shewing their deeds.[38]

I shall not stand to adde any more judging this sufficient to Confirm the truth, & thus much for Divine testimony.

Seconde, as for Humane Testimony in this matter it is drawn from the Practice of the Churches of Christ, altho' this is inferior to the former Testimony as much as humane is unto devine, yet in matters of Fact, which ought to be conformable to divine Rules Human testimony Concerning their own practice, if this practice be according to our Sense of these Scriptures will greatly Confirm our sense of these Scriptures to be the meaning of the same, Especially if we Consider that this of theirs must have some rule, & is no blamable thing. Therefore as to the

Practice of the Churches of Christ in their admitting of Members, a word or two may suffice as follows.

The first is the Practice of the Primitive church before antichrist's rise. & this was such as that their members admitted made relation of the worke of God upon their hearts, as touching their faith in Christ & Repentance of Sin; & this is looked on to be the Answer of a good Conscience spoken of in that Scripture, I Pet. 3.21. For the person Seeking Church Fellowship hath this Question propounded to him. Dost thou renounce Satan, etc? Dost thou believe in Christ Jesus? etc. To which the person answering (from a good Conscience as in the text) saith I renounce them, & I believe in Christ & the like holding forth hereby that his internall faith expressed by his externall profession is that which brings our Salvation in Baptism.[39]

Again, the Order mannaged with the *Catechumeni*, (i.e., those under Catechisticall Rudaments, which were such as were Baptized in their infancy, & such that were heathens who desired to joyn themselves to Christ & his intrest, I say the order carried on with these,) holds out a Confession of Gods work upon their hearts in order unto full Communion. For this Cathechisticall Exercise was such as they could not attend unless they gave an account of what was with them. & this was not merely with respect unto their knowledg, for after this preparation they were called *Competentes*, who yet before their Admittance to full Communion,[40] must give an account of their Faith in Christ by their practice, promise to live accordingly; & above all to learn by prayer & Fasting to beg of God a pardon of their Sins, & So were admitted by fasting, & Prayer.

Again Gregory Neocesarienis who lived about 240 years after Christ layes down five degrees to be attended in Admitting of Penitents,[41] as 1st Weeping, when the penetent stood weeping at the porch begging prayers for him: 2. Hearing, when they stood within by the *Catechumeni* to heare the word. 3. Prostration, when in a prostrate way they had further entrance. 4. Standing, or staying together with the Assembly. & 5. Communion a partaking of the Sacraments, & Can it be imagined that this graduall admition should be without an account of Gods work on their heart.

Tertullian, who lived a little before this man, speaking of those admitted upon their Baptism, hath the word, Going to the water, at that place, yea & a little before, in the Church, we take witnes that we do renounce the Divel & his pomp & Angels: & then we are thrice dipt.[42]

Now how can it with reason be thought that they used so much pains to Convert to Christ, & yet that there should be no more sign of the same yeild out of Gods reaching the heart than mearly to say I renounce the Divel. Nay but in that this is so plainly asserted we may surely Conclude that there was a further relation of Gods dealing with their Souls, which had brought them to renounce those things in their hearts & lives, & therefore to go on.

I will give one more instance in Augustin who flourisht about the end of the 4th Century or the beginning of the fifth, his words are these, which he received of Simplicianus concerning Victorinus a platonick Philosopher, whom upon his entring into the Church at Rome he baptised, viz, As the hour was come of the Profession of Faith which used to be rendered in certain Words, comitted to memory, from a high place in the Sight of the Church, of those that shall come to thy grace, he said it was offered Victorinus by the Presbyters that he might render it more secretly, as it was a Custom offered to Such who seemed to quake through Bashfulness. But he rather chose to profess his salvation in the presence of the holy assembly: For said he it was not Salvation, that he taught in Rhetorick & yet he professed it publickly. How less ought he to be affraid of thy gentle Flock, pronouncing of thy words, who did not fear in pronouncing his own words to troops of madmen. Therefore when he went up that he might make his relation, all as they knew him did whisper among themselves one unto another his name, with a whispering congratulation. But, who knew not him in that place? And it rang with a low sound in the mouth of all. Victorinus, Victorinus. Soon after they sounded fourth with joy because they saw him, & soon were silent with attention that they might heare him. He now declares the true Faith with Excellent Confidence; & they all were willing to receive him internally into their very heart.[43] Nay the Church of Rome hath Carried on the footings of this upon her thro' the depth of her Apostacy, in an Adoltrate manner untill this very day, admitting none into her Communion, but on the terms of Confession.

And some Protestant Churches[44] have revived it in their reformation unto its primitive practice, Beside New England. And unto this you may take notice of Pareus on Matt. 3.6, there are none to be received & Baptized into the Church unless by a previous Confession of his Faith, & Repentance, which Custome the Primitive Church did, & our[s] at this day doth attend, if either Jew or Turk be baptized by us.[45] & Piscator on the same place saith, that no adult Person is to be Baptized before he makes a Confession of his Sins.[46] Hence then it appears that it's no new Doctrine when persons Enter into Church Communion, to give an account of the hope that is in them.[47]

But thus much for Inartificiall Proof of this Assertion.

2. As for Artificiall Arguments proving the manifestation o. the work of Repentance & Faith upon the Soule to be a Qualificatior nextly disposing the matter of a Church to receiving the form, & that by a verball account thereof are as follow.[48]

1. It appears to be thus from the Duty the Church stands untc Christ to be Faithful in the Use of the Keyes of his Kingdom; For Christ hath hung the Keyes of Discipline at the girdle of the Church. & hence she is bound to open to whom he opens, & to shut upon whom he shuts upon, other wise the Keyes are not rightly used. But it will be impossible for her to do thus unless she may & ought to require an account of what God hath done for those that knock for admition, for she ought not tc open unless they shew their Ticket: & hence Christ chargeth her to try the spirits, I John 4.1, & Commends her for so doing, Rev. 2.2, let it not be said that this is the Worke of the Minister, the Angel of the Church & therefore it holds not out any publick Relation. For the Spirit speaks to the Church Collectively in the Angel as appears Rev. 2.7, & in order to the preparation of the worke, its peculiarly the Elders work to try, but in order to the Consummation of it, it belongs to all the society that are to give judgment[49] [92/93] in the Case & this is the Church, I Cor. 5.12. Now if she finde Christs ticket in the hand then she must open; but if there is nothing of that to be found then the doore must not be opened: for so pearls should be cast before swine. & holy things unto dogs; for ought she knows.

2. It appears from the Benefit that accrueth upon the Relating the work of God upon the Soule, & here I reason thus if it be a duty to give an account of this matter, then it is especially a duty when it will be the most Beneficiall & the most to the glory of God, this Consequence ca'not be denied with any shew of Reason. But that it is a duty is enough. & enough made out in Scripture by the practice of the Saints whom God calls on us to follow, Heb. 6.12. Therefore it onely remains that we make it out that upon entring into a Church State will be most benefici-

all, & to the Glory of God. And this will appeare *à parte* $\left\{ \begin{array}{l} Ante \\ Post \end{array} \right\}$ if I may use that distinction in the matter.

1. It will be most Beneficiall A *parte Ante*, i.e., in order to the preparation of the Soule before hand for Full-Communion: For when the Soule sees that an account of Gods working upon his Soule is of such weight as that he must make it manifest in some measure, as a Sign of his preparation for, before he be admitted into, Full-Communion how intent will it make him in observing the motions of the spirit of God upon his Soule & hating Sin.

2. It will be beneficiall A *parte Post* in respect of what Follows upon this Relation. For as it stirs up to the mortifying of Sin before it be made, so after it hath the same tendence, lest by the acting contrarily should lay the soul under the Censure of Hypocrasy. Nay & it lets the Soule fall deep into the very hearts of Gods people, as it was said of Victorinus when he had Ended his Relation, all the Church did *rapuerunt eum intró in Corsuum*, snatch him within them into their very heart. This therefore must needs be very Beneficiall & therefore now is the Season of it.

3. It will appeare from the manner of receiving such as fall under Censures for their offences: & this is by manifesting repentance for his Sin, as is apparant II Cor. 2, & if a manifestation of Repentance is necessary to Readmition, then a manifestation of Repentance is necessary to Admittance at first, because he is admitted at first on the same account: viz, his Visible intrest in Christ, unto the same Priviledges, the Seals of the Kingdom etc. & into the same state a Church State, & into the same Charity, & Love. & therefore Restauration doth bring him into the same state on the Same ground, unto the same priviledges, & into the same Charity out of which he ran by his offence after he was at first admitted, & therefore must be mannaged after the same way. & this being done by the manifestation of Repentance, it hence appears that by the manifestation of Repentance Admition is to be had, for *Quo Restauratio, ab eodem modo fit Instauratio.*

And thus I have proved that the Manifestation of the worke of Gods Spirit in order to the bringing the soule from Sin unto God held out in a Relation of the same unto the Charity of Gods people is a Qualification disposing the Soule into an immediat fittness for the receiving the *Formalis Ratio* of a Church State. & thus at last I have shew'd the Materiall Cause of a Church.

2. The Formall Cause of a Church is that which being entred into the Matter of the Church, doth give the Church its perfect Essentiall

Constitution, & makes the Church a *totum Essentiale* & raises the Materials up together to be the house of God, or the Habitation of God through the Spirit. The Materiall Cause of it lies in the Quarry or Stone-pit of humane nature, yet as it is eyed by the Principall Efficient Cause having the Eternall Love of the Decree upon it it is as so many Shining Pearles sticking in a hard & impregnable rock. But as the Instrumentall Causes Convay the Preparatory Efficiency of the Principall upon them these are broken as pearles & hewed & Squared after the Similitude of a Palace but yet are as a Company of Pearls which tho' wrought fit for use lie as a heap together in respect unto * * * * * * introduced gives them their Church Constitution & brings them into a City Frame or Temple frame from this Formall Cause therefore must needs be their Volentary Agreement, or Covenant whereby they agree to gether to walke together in the wayes of God in observance of all the Ordinances of Christ according to the Gospell: Now that this Volantary Covenant is the Constituting Differencing Principle of a Church may appear from these Arguments following.

1. That which was the Constituting Principall or the Formall Cause of the Church of Israel must neede demonstrate what is the Formall differencing Principall of any Church of Christ, because that which the formall Cause of one Church doth for that Church, the Formall Cause of another Church doth for an other Church: & therefore that which is the form of one must needs speake out what the form of another is. But now the Formall Cause of the Church of the Jews of Israel is their Covenant: hence their publick entring into this Church State is Called a Covenanting. & the act a Covenant, Ex. 19.5,6: & their turning them for their impenetency out of a Church State, or Excommunication, is called a Breaking them off from this Covenant or a breaking the Covenant as Zech. 11.10,11,14: & upon their repentance they are entred again into Church State by entring into Covenant to walk together in wayes of God as Neh. 10.28,29— Ergo.

2. That Which is the Formall Cause of a Societie (as a Society) distinguishing it from others out of Society, must needs be the Formall Cause of a Church; because a Church is a Species under this Genus, & so a Society, & therefore must have the whole nature of the Genus,[50] society in it. Onely the individuation is that which is added unto the form of the Genus whereby every Species is distinct one from an other. But now the Formall Cause of a Society is the Covenant or terms of the

Society whereby they ingage themselves to the Duties of the Societie they enter into. This is too plain to be gainsaid. Further the scripture useth Such a word as by a Metaphor implies a Covenant to import a Society, thus I Sam. 10.5, a Company of prophets חבל, a Cord of Prophets because by the laws of their Society unto which they were bound they were Combined to gether as by a Cord or band, or as the thrids of the Cord together. & so also * * * used Zech. 11.14: 10, for the Church Covenant of the Jews. & its used to set out such as were in an agreement together, Ps. 119.61. & accordingly the Greek use a word σπεῖρα, which notes a Cord also on the same account to import a troop or band of men inlisted under one Comander as John 18.3. The hebrew Express an Assembly, or Congregation by עדה , Ps. 1.5. &   מועדי synagogues, Ps. 4.8, which Come from יעד , *Condixit, Constituit*, & sometimes, to betroth as Ex. 21.8,9. & hence the Learned observe that it notes such an assembly as are at an agreement among themselves about their time, & place. & therefore surely also things & it implies a Covenant & so its applied to Dathans Company, Ps. 106.17,18. & hence there is ground to Conclude from Scripture the Formall Cause of Society is a Covenant & therefore of a Church.

3. It appears also from the Speciall Metaphors that the Spirit makes use of in Scripture pointing out this thing as they respect the entring into a Church State, as Acts 2.42, adding, or putting to the Church, which imports that it was done after the manner of men, when they are added unto any former society it is by their agreeing to the orders of the society, & therefore it is not to be questioned this was so done, Acts 5.13. Joyning, which word imports a Covenantall Joyning, and therefore is used for the Marriage Covenant, as Matt. 19.5, or as they respect the thing perfected by the introduction of the Form. & so it is Called Compacted together, & this notes joyning according to the Nature of the parts joyned & this is such as is capable Chiefly if not onely by Covenant also a Body, I Cor. 12, where the strongest union is to be found between the Members, a Building, a house, a habitation, a Temple, all which have their materiall fittly joyned & raised together binding one another, etc. & a Golden Candle Stick by all which what can less be * * * [93/94] Many other such phrases you shall find in Scripture spoken of the Church all which Artificiall Terms being, by the Law of undeniable necessity, to be expounded in that sense in which their proper Significa-tion, as they are naturally used, is most aptly represented, & found

according to the Capacity of the subject of which they are metaphorically truely applied; & therefore being Spoken of societies which can consist together of no other Joyning, Compacting, etc., by what is Covenantall, they Can represent nothing less then a mutuall Covenant.

And this was not a strange thing unto the primitive times, as testifies the answer made by the Baptized [. . . .]

Secondly. What are we to understand by this Phrase, Habitation of God.

In answer hereto I say first for the word Habitation, 2^ly the Word, viz, of God.

1. For the Word Habitation, its not to be taken Actively for the Act of God inhabitting, but passively, for the thing inhabited; & it notes these things following

1. The Lowness or littleness of the building & hence Zanchy draweth the Allusion from the Temple at Jerusalem, for as that it Consisting of many divisions, & Little Chambers was but one Temple, so the Church Catholick is but one consisting of many particulars, so saith he the Little Chambers import the particular Churches.[51]

2. That its a settled, & durable habitation, it is not a fleeting place but a place of settlement & hence *κατοικητήριον* is the word which the Seventy Interpreters make use of Commonly to render the Hebrew word מָעוֹן , which importeth a durable Habitation, by as Ps. 90.1, & the word פְּבוֹן-שֶׁבֶת , by which also a Settled Habitation is intended, as Ps. 33.14: from the place of his habitation he looked down on the inhabitants of the earth: & Ps. 107.4,7, God brought them to a City to dwell in. & Ps. 132.13,14, God Saith here of the Church the Lord hath chosen Zion, he hath desired it for his מָעוֹן , habitation: this is my rest for ever: there will I dwell, for I have desired it. Hence you se it imports a Settled habitation.

2^ly. As for the other term, viz, of God, an habitation of God. Whereby this habitation is demonstrated by the Relation it bears unto God its a habitation of God. & hereby there is implied

1. That God is the onely Author of it. Hence saith Christ, I will Build my Church, Matt.16.18. It is not Quoined by mans brain, nor of man's Framing; neither is it of a humane molding, but of a Divine. God hath sought out the matter, Squares it by his Rule, Polishes by his tooles,

raises it according to his own form that he hath framed it unto, & Rules it by his own Laws. Thus God is the Author.

2. That God is the Owner of it. Its his propertie, he is the Proprietor * * * [him]selfe, & not for another. It is not So in all things, nor in all Good things. He that is the Author of a house is not all way the Owner but it is not so here saith God this is my House.

3. That God is the Approver of it: he doth not disapproove of what he hath made but doth Greatly approves thereof. Its a piece of mans misery, that what he makes oftimes falls out not according to his minde, hence he unmakes what he hath made & makes all a new. & it may be when new made it is not pleasing to his minde, he doth not approve of it, but it is not so in this building, for in that its Gods building God approoves of it. Hence he calls it a Golden Candle Stick, etc., it all gold.

4. That God is the Improver of it. He doth not make it for anothers use but his own, & his own use is such as that he makes it the Gate of heaven, & the doore of glory. Here he opens a passage unto poor man kinde to come unto all Communion with himselfe. This is Bethel, the House of God, & therefore here stands Jacobs Ladder with the foot on earth & the Top in heaven; on which the Angels of God are descending, & ascending. & whereupon there comes down out of heaven all Grace, & blessing unto man, & goes up from earth, to heaven all seraphick praises, & Obedience as also the Separated Soules of the Saints of God upon the wings of glorious Angels. Thus God is the improver of it.

5. That God is the Defender & Protector of it. & therefore the Gates of Hell shall not prevaile against it, as Matt. 16.18,19. & hence is that Promise also Zech. 2.5.

Thirdly, what is the meaning of this Expression Where it is said, thus Thro' the Spirit, in that it is Said to be Habitation of God thro' the Spirit?

To this I say that it imports these things following

1. The (*Modus Efficiendi*) manner of Gods Efficiency in order unto it, & in it. In order to it for the building of it, his Fetching stones out of the Quarry, & Timber out of the wood, of Fallen mankinde, his hewing, polishing of them after the Similitude of a pallace, & his building them up to be a habitation of God is all by the Spirit. Hence is that John 3.5, he that shall enter into the Kingdome of God must be

born of the spirit. & so also it notes the manner of Gods Efficiency in this house in inlightening, in inlivening, in begetting, & in edifying soules herein unto Eternall life, that all is by his own Spirit. Hence the Letter kills, but the Spirit giveth life.

2. The (*Modus Habitandi*) manner of Gods presence in it, & this is by his Spirit, not in a visible but in a Spirituall way. Its true he is present in it in all his own institutions, in prayer, in the Word preached & applied in informing, Convicting, examining, perswading, directing, & Comforting, as also in Singing, & in the Sacraments of Baptism & the Lords Supper, & in the Orders, Officers, & the Discipline of this his house, but it is in a Spirituall way & therefore thro' the Spirit. & hence the whole of the worship as it is carried on by the Officers especially is called the Ministry of the Spirit.

Fourthly. But why is it So, that a Particular Church is an habitation of God through the Spirit?

Now the Reasons confirming of it are such as these following.

1. From the Causes thereof. It must needs bee Gods Habitation thro' the Spirit. For the Efficiency of it is from God thro' the Spirit; the Finall is for God by the spirit, the Materiall is Gods by the preparation of the Spirit: & the Formall Cause is introduced in obedience to God thro' the Spirit. & therefore the thing Compleated by these Causes must needs be Gods thro' the spirit.

2. From Furnishing of it, it appears to be Gods Habitation thro' the spirit. For all the Furniture of it is Gods, the Goodly gifts, & the gold of this Temple is Gods, the Chapiters, the Net work, the Pomegranates, the Bells of this Temple, the Lamps, with their kops, & bowles, the Cherubims, the garnishing of it with the tassles of gifts, with Clusters of Graces, shining like bunches of Pearles are all his. The Orders of this house, [94/95] the Rancks & Offices are his; the Discipline, the Keyes to open & shut the Doores, the Ordinances & actions mannaged here are all his & none else but himselfe can own any of these & therefore this is Gods Habitation.

3. From the Absurdity following on the Contrary, for if this is not Gods Habitation, then God hath no Politicall, Visible, Habitation on Earth: for where must it be found if not here? Not in the Catholick Visible Church, for that is onely Visible in its particulars. & if the particulars Cease, it will be a most hard taske to demonstrate its visible

existance. Not in a Universall, or Oecumenicall Counsill: for where shall we finde so much as the shallowest foot step either of such a thing, or of when it appertains to Call any Such Synod together, in all the Scripture? Not in a Classis, for that is as darke a thing to discover in the Scripture as the other unless thereby be understood, a Counsell or Synod. & then they have their rise from, & are for their matter members of Particular Churches. & therefore not in a Synod or Counsell: for these are not of a standing necessity, neither are their actions given in Authoritative as acts of Authority, binding Conscience, an other wise than the truth with the same confirmed by their Testimony binds: But Consultative by way of Advice. But if it be said God sitteth amongst the mighty & judgeth amongst the Gods, & therefore he hath his Visible Politicall Habitation in Civill Courts, I say, that this Habitation is but his Outward Court & it is Cast out also unto the gentiles. But where is his Inward Court? This is onely, or Cheifly for the mannagment of the Concerns of the Second Table. But in what Visible Court are the Concerns of the first Table mannaged, if not in a Particular Church: & therefore if this be not his Habitation thro' the spirit he must needs be without any Publick Visible Habitation on earth, but this he is not. Ergo.

Thus I have passed over at the last, the Doctrinall part of this Truth. The Application follows.

Lastly, As for the Application of this Doctrine, it is twofold, whereby I shall apply it unto the Use of the Understanding, or Judgmen[t]: & unto the Use of the Will, & Affections.

First in Applying of it I shall improove its Usefullness Upon the Understanding & Judgment by way of $\begin{cases} \text{Information} \\ \text{Reprehention.} \end{cases}$

First. By Information: Is it So that a particular Church is built up an habitation of God through the Spirit, then we may see

1. Hence what a miserable state towns & places are in while they have no Church of Christ erected & are like to be so onward. The Lord God hath not set nor is like to set his Habitation amongst them: & therefore he dwelleth not there manifestly what ever he may do in the hearts of some, yet he doth not appear a settled Inhabitant in Such a place. These are as it were Cast out at the present as the range of the Wilderness, & too oft it is manifest that wild asses have them for their

pasture. & if they are not like to have Christ raise his pavilion there they oft prove mere Cages of Unclean Birds, & Habitations of Darkness, & holds of all unclean spirits, & divels. Miserable habitations.

2. Hence it is manifest, that it is the greatest Concern of all towns, & places which is, that they enter into a Church State that Christ erect his Church amongst them. Untill this be, places are not distinct Corporations of Christs Visible Kingdom. God hath not set up house amongst them. But when they are in a Church State, God hath then set up house amongst them, he is Come to dwell publickly amongst them, his Spirit is come to actuate them, [& hence this was the very thing that Israel was] brought out of Egypt for, that the Lord God might dwell amongst them. & therefore one of the first things that they attend on when in the Wildernesse was their entrance into their Church State. & therefore it is the great Concern of towns & places to secure the Presence of God with them to get him & keep him an Habitation amongst them.

3. Hence we may se what unspeakable favor & Priviledges God allows unto those places when & where he erects his Churches. Why altho' they were habitations of Cruelty, & the ranges of Satan & his Angels before now the Case is changed, the Lord God comes & pitches his tent there, outs Satan: Sets open doores to poor Soules to come to him, so that where Satans Throne was Christ hath erected his palace. The Temple of God is with those men, the Lord God Comes & dwells amongst them, oh, here is the doore of heaven, the gate unto glory. O he makes the place of his feet glorious, & on all the glory will be a defence, he will be a glory in the middest, & a wall of fire round about. O here is priviledge indeed.

4. Hence we may se a ground of joy & praise when Christ erects his Church in any place, for then he Comes to dwell there by his Spirit. &, oh! if towns rejoyce when Noble persons come to dwell in them, because of their nobilitie & generosity, & the good deeds Expected. Oh! what ground of Joy is here when God comes to inhabit in places! Oh, how doth he herein implicitly by the Springing of his wings, scatter his nobility & generosity upon them; to relieve & feed their very Soules? to protect, & Save from the powers of darkness, & to take them & theirs to be his own for ever. O ground of joy, & Shouting! If at the laying the foundation of the Temple they cried Grace to it, Zech 4.7, how much more ground have such places where Christ erects his Church to shout out with joy saying Grace, Grace.

Secondly, By way of Reprehension, to those that are
$\begin{cases} \text{Without} \\ \text{Within} \end{cases}$ a Church State.

1. Such as are without a Church State, these have the Crown of God in this truth bending against them whether they are such as $\begin{cases} \text{Oppose} \\ \text{Neglect} \end{cases}$ it.

Such as oppose the Churches of Christ, these fight against the Almighty. The[y] do worse than Nebuchadnezzer, who set their temple of God all in red flames, & sent it into ashes. They do worse than those, Ps. 74.7,8, that had burnt up all the Synagogues of God in the Land; for they fight against the Almighty to beat him out of the world: & pul down a more spiritual Building: even the Temples of God in a more Spirituall sense, that the Lord may not dwell with men on earth, that he may have no habitation here below. Oh Woe unto their Souls: for they would have no intercourse mannaged between God & man. For there is no publick Covenanting with God but here.

Such as Neglect a Church State are under the frown of this Doctrin: for they manifest by their Negligence that they had rather be & abide in Satans Family than to be made of the household of God, as if there was better provision, better order, better society, better service, better satisfaction to be had, & better safety in Satans house than in Gods. & therefore to uphold Satans intrest tho' to the Ruin, so far as their neglect can effect of Gods house. Oh! fools & madmen! when will ye be wise? surely God will come out of his holy Habitation against you & what will you then do?

2. Those that are within, that are intred either less formally, or more formally, of those there are some that fall under the Angry aspect of God in this Doctrine as

1. Those that are not content to * * * * * * [95/96] to the Revelation of Gods will in this matter, for if this be Gods habitation, then he is the Lawgiver that laith down the Laws, & limits the Orders of the same. & all that are in it, are to be limited in their motions, & functions thereby, but now for any to stretch their line beyond these limits, as not being content with that provision of Office which he hath set up there in & therefore they must set up their Posts by Gods posts, as Prelates,

Archbishops, Archdeacons, Prebends, Vicars, Curats, Non-Residents, Proctors, Surrogates, Apparitors, Church-Wardens, Clarks, Saxstons, such like human devised stuffe, or the limitation of Office. & therefore they must Stretch the Wings of the Pastors as far as to shaddow the whole Universe, so that a steward shall not stand in this Particular house but in the Catholick, & be a Steward in any, & not in an onely house: or of allowance of means of Worship, or Service; & therefore they must have fine Garments, as Surplices, etc., Idle Prayers, as the Service booke, & New Ordinances as the Cross in Baptism, Gossops, & Kneeling in the Lords Supper, etc. Oh, this is to breake the second Command which saith thou shalt not institute unto thyselfe, etc.; & it steps into Gods throne & is as in effect to Charge him with want of Wisdom, Faithfullness, & Goodness, to order & mannage his own house. But Surely God will say to these who hath required these things at your hands, Isa. 1.12, you make the Commands of God of none effect by your traditions, Matt. 15.3.

2. Such are under the sharp Check of this Doctrin that do not keep peace in this house. What quarrell in Gods house? what a shame is this? Quarrelling Children must have the rod to still them, & yet how is this to be lamented among us? What quarrelling? what wrangling? & jangling in many Churches? as if they would fulfill the Old Proverb, throw the house out at the windows. What is it Gods house, or no? & shall not the God of Peace have peace kept in his own house? Oh! what means this smoak in the Temple? Will not the stones of the Temple agree to gather? shall they be Slipping one from an other? Will not they beare one anothers burden? Will not the Cement hold? its a sign the builden grows old & weatherbeaten, & that without new Poynting, all will tumble down. But oh! what a shame is this to all such Churches & let it be a Confounding shame. What, break peace in Gods house, where he dwells! Oh! how ill will he take it? if you bite, devoure one another have a Care you be not devoured one of another, Gal. 5.15. You are a dishonour to the house of God. You must either amende your manners in Gods house, or else you or God must out of the House, For God will not dwell in that house where the peace of God Cannot dwell.

3. Such are under the frown of God in this Doctrine, that enter or are intred into the Church in a Carnall State, this is a house of God, Soul, & darest thou enter here. O! how dreadful is this place to a Carnall heart? What dost thou here thou Carnall heart. Onely living stones are to lie in this building: what doth thy dead soule here? God dwells here by

his Spirit; but Satan dwels in thy heart? Thou bringest then an evell & an unclean Spirit into Gods habitation, & thereby goest on to bring Satan into the house of God, to give him possession of God's Palace, that he may Sit in the Temple of God as God; & that so God may be unhoused, or Cast out of his own house. Those that quarrell in it set open Doores to him, & thou bringest him in, dost thou think God will beare this? no, no, he will be avenged of thee at the last, if thou look not about thee, for thou both Comest & bringest an enemy into Gods habitation. Is a hard peble Stone suitable to be laid in that wall which is to be all of Pearls & Precious Stones? Let it be thought on.

Thus you Se who are reprehended by this doctrin. & so we have seen its usefulness improved upon the Understanding & Judgment.

The Second Sort of Improvement of this doctrine is to improve its usefullness upon the Will, & Affections by way of
{ Exhortation
{ Congratulation.

First, By way of Exhortation, Is it thus that a Particular Church is an Habitation of God through the spirit? Oh! how doth God then hereby come to worke upon our hearts, yea all our hearts to let out our affections, & to set our hearts upon a Church State. Oh! how strongly should our Affections worke towards this house? God in this Doctrine calls for all our hearts to affect this his house. & the Call is unto us according to the Relation we stand in unto it, which relation divides us all according to that 1 Cor. 5.12, in such as are in & out of it. & therefore the Call is Unto such as are { Without } this house.
{ Within }

1. Unto such as are not yet entred God cals you to stir up your hearts after a Church State for hereby you enter into his house, you hereby are made of the number of the Citizens of the Saints & of the Houshould of God. Oh therefore let your affections run unto this state & improve them so upon it as thereby to stir you up after it. Oh God saith they shall prosper that have their love here, Ps. 122.6. & now let your affections so act in your hearts towards a Church State as to Seek

1. The Promoting of the same. For this being the house of God where this is not, God hath not his publick residence. He hath not pitcht his Tabernacle: but herein the Tabernacle of God is amongst men. Therefore (my Friends) as ever you would have Gods publick presence reside with you, se that you indeavour from the heart the promoting the

Church God erects amongst you. Its true God is present in the Souls of his people, & therefore particular persons are called the Temples of the Holy Ghost, as II Cor. 6.16. & so he is present with his Soule-Sanctifying invisible presence. He is present in the Families of his Saints, hence Abraham will teach, & Command his Children, & houshold after him, etc., Gen. 18.19. And so hee is present with his Family Duty presence. But yet this is not in a publick residing way. But he is present in the Churches of his Saints, Rev. 2.1. & here he is present in his Ordinance-instituted presence, & that is as a king in the royall Throne of his Kingdome. Hence Isa. 6.1, Rev. 3.21, in this Temple is his way. Oh! then strive to promote this state. & for this end let me Suggest you with a word as a motive.

　　1. Consider what a great evill it is to hinder this presence of God; or this Habitation of God, to damnify this Habitation is a Sore, & lamentable thing. Tho' it be in the least pin of the Building for it is to Pull the house of God down about his eares (with reverence be it spoke). Nebuchadnezzars firing the Temple was less evill unto God than this injury amounts to, in that this is a living that no living temple, this is a Spirituall that an Elementary Temple. & therefore let this thought stir up to the promoting of this Habitation.

　　2. Herein are Carried on all the means of Grace allowed thee of God, for thy salvation. By means of Grace understand ordinance-instituted means. & where should these be found but in Gods Habitation? They are the furniture of his house. Thou mayest meet with some helps it may be else where, but here thou wilt find all. & the strong gales of the Spirits breathing in fresh breizes here; & therefore while thou promotest this, thou promotest these. Thereby thou will keep the door open where the Angels of God are ascending & descending. & it may be attending on thy soule. Ergo.

　　3. So long as you promote this intrest Christ is waiting on you to be gracious; But if you weary God out of his Habitation he wil be angry with your Souls & then wo, wo, wo unto your Souls. Therefore Endeavour the promoting this Habitation. [96/97]

　　2. Preparation for this Habitation. Doth God come & set up house here? & Canst thou content thyselfe without an admittance into his family? & how dost thou think thou shouldst have an entrance if thou dost not prepare for it. Oh prepare to meet thy God, Amos 4.12. Dost thou thinke Gods house hath open doores for all comers come, as come

will? without any Qualification? are any rubbish stones unpolisht fit matter for Christs Temple? why if not, then prepare thyselfe. Trim thy lamp, that thou maist have entrance. Indeed there is a two fould right or intrest in this house, viz, *Quoad* $\begin{cases} Relatione \\ Translationem. \end{cases}$

In respect unto Relation onely, & in respect unto Translation out of the power of darkness into the Kingdome of the dearly beloved Son of God. Oh this last! & nothing below this last might intrest, is that which Comprehends this due preparation for this state. O therefore stir up your selve that you may be Pretious Stones to be laid in this heavenly building, living stones in this Spirituall Temple. Repent of your Sins, reform your lives, put away the old leven, that you may become a new lump. & as a motive attend what follows.

1. Consider you are never fitt matter for this Habitation of God thro' the spirit till you be prepared matter. The New Jerusalem, that descended from heaven was prepared as a bride adorned for her husband, Rev. 21.2. This new Jerusalem is the Church, this husband is the Lord that dwels in this Habitation therefore it is not a rubbish Stone but the wrought stone that is matter for this habitation. Oh therefore prepare for it.

2. Consider that unprepared persons, if they do creep in, are fit for nothing but as Jonas in the ship, to raise tempest, & to be cast over board. O! such are like the lepros stones in the Wall, gangrenes unto the Whole, Or like Aeolus with his lancet, or Pike piercing the sides of the mountains till the storms arise. Oh! dismall works many times are made by these in Gods habitation. Oft times they proove as fire in the Thatch, & as the Bellows of Aetna to blow up all in aflame. They are fit to play the fooles part to cast about firebrands, Arrows, & death to fire Gods house, they during this estate also lose what they count off, for they gain no spirituall advantage commonly, but are oft delivered up to hardness as Ananias & Saphira, as a Curse upon their presumption. Oh therefore prepare, prepare.

3. Consider That an Entrance without a Worthiness will entaile upon thee (unless the abundant mercy of God prevent) greater wrath as in Ananias & Saphira's Case, Acts 5. Oh saith God you have known, etc., therefore will I punish you, Amos 3.2. Because Soule thou bringest, & also comest, an enemy in Gods Habitation remember the Foolish Virgins, Matt. 25, & the man without the Wedden garment, Matt. 22.12: If thou Commest in unprepared, & continuest unprepared, thou

art sure to be cast out being unprepared, into utter darkness. O think of this, & prepare.

4. Consider that this preparation consists in the Graces of the Spirit of God, hence Grace is prayed for, for the Churches, II Thess. 1.2,3, etc. & we are prest on after it. Now canst thou do without this, or Canst thou have too much of this? oh! Surely this for its own sake is worth striving for, Jude 2, thou are undon without it, oh therefore seeke after this, & so prepare.

5. Consider. Who is it that dwells in this house, why it is God himselfe: Herein that is fulfilled, Ps. 68.18, that the Lord God might dwell amongst them. God dwells in this house, the Spirit of God dwells here, it is a habitation of God thro' the Spirit, the Son of God dwels here, he was seen here, Rev. 1.13, the Angels of God are here, I Cor. 11.10, & the saints of God dwell here. & what then shall not this moove thy affections to prepare for this state? Surely it will.

6. To prepare for it is the way to have a glory [of it. The greater preparation for it, the greater] glory will be present in it, according to the preparation that thou makest for God, such will be the presence of God, in it. Oh! how glorious a presence would alwayes here appeare, if wee did but alwayes appeare here duelie prepared. For our preparation consisting in the graces of the Spirit, oh we by preparing should stir up those shining spangles of the Divine image upon our soules that they being such a presence well pleasing to God that God would in Christ give forth an answerable glory upon the same that would fill his house with glory. That we might with old Jacob say, Oh, how terrible is this place? it is nothing else but the house of God. Oh therefore prepare your Soules for this State.

3. Seek, when & not till when you are prepared, to enter into this house, as it is a fault to enter unprepared, so it is a fault when prepared not to enter. O therefore do not proceed untill prepared, but do not delay to proceed when prepared. O my friends what say you? will you be of the houshold of God or no? Will you be of the houshold of faith or no? will you be Fellow Citizens of the saints or no? Are you such as have trimmed your lamps? have your lamps any oyle in their Vessels or no? will you go out to meet the Brides groom or no? oh! then Come here. Enter your names among the living in Jerusalem. The doores of Gods house stand open unto you, have you a heart to enter or no? behold he calls thee saying turn in hither, turn in hither, why shouldst thou turn aside. & here to moove thee Consider.

1. Consider that thou hast a right in this house, for being a living Stone thou ought to lie in this Spirituall Temple.

2. Consider that thou standest in need of that provision that God makes for thee in his house, therefore being a bidden guesst come.

3. Consider that Gods house hath need of thee, what hath God been hewing, & polishing of thee for, all this while? surely it is because his house hath need of thee. If when Solomon had polisht materialls for the Temple these polisht materials had lain by, & not come into a building frame; there had been no Temple raised of polisht, & suitable matter. Living stones in this Spirituall Building lie not in it as it is of this sort here below, eternally. There is now one, & then another gathered hence as a Choice Pearle to be sett in the Ring of glory. & hence in a little time the whole building will be translated hence, Stone after Stone. & so will disappeare, if there be no addition made to it, the which that it may not disappeare, God is polishing some for it, as he is fetching some from it. & hence the building stands in need of those that are prepared for it. O you then that are prepared heare it, will you not regard this? Why if you do, then seek to Enter.

4. Consider here is the best Order which is, its a well Ordered house in all things, I Cor. 14.40. O the Order of Solomon's house was admirable, I Kings 10. But what then is the Order of Christs house? The beauty & excellency of Order adds an amazing glory to things that are excellent. Oh therefore let this quicken thee.

5. Consider here is best Service, for here is only holy service, hence here shines the beautie of holiness. Its God Service, & onely Gods service that is Carried on here. & that is onely Good Service. Oh therefore let this moove thee. [97/98]

6. O Here is the Best Society which is, if we Consider it in the lowest Consideration, you will finde thus. Why it is the household of God, Eph. 2.19, the houshold of Faith, Gal. 6.10, a Chosen people, Titus 3.5, the Elect of God, Rom. 11.7, for altho' it is a truth that there are to be found some tares in this field, some Chaffe in this floore, yet this never was made a field for the tares sake, nor a floore for the sake of the Chaffe, these have no right in it. God gives no liberty to Satans Slaves to enter into his house. Satans Servants have no right in Gods Family. No here is required Contrary Qualifications, as a Wedden garment, Matt. 22.12, Grace in the Soule, the Image of God, Rom. 8.29. O glorious Society. If the Society of a Kings family is of Nobles, & honorable ones, Matt. 11.8. What shall we then account of those that

are the Society of the Family of the King of Kings. O! how are they called in Scripture by God himselfe? why, by the most excellent things the world affords, as Stones laid with fair Colours, Saphires, Agates, Carbuncles, all the borders of pleasant Stones, Isa. 54.11,12, Stones of a Crown, Zech. 9.16, Border'd with gold, & Studded with Silver, Cant. 1.11, all fair & there is no spot, etc., oh excellent societie! Nay, but let us pass from this rank, & go on & you shall finde the very Angels of God themselves attending here, I Cor. 11.10. O glorious ones indeed! Nay but Still we may ascend higher, for here is injoyed the Company, & presence of God & Christ, & the Holy Ghost. Its Gods house, he sits here in his Throne, & judgeth right. Now the Presence of God in his throne makes heaven heaven: Oh then the presence of God in this habitation inthroned makes this house heaven upon earth. Looke here now Soule. What dost thou say to this Society? is not this a Noble, & honorable, a glorious, nay, the most Noble, Honorable, glorious, & Excellent Society which is? & what will the Consideration thereof now set thy Affections a worke to enter hereinto? oh! delay not therefore but when prepared, proceed.

7. Consider, here are highest priviledges & chiefe honour to be had in this habitation. If there are greate priviledges injoyed in great mens families, what are the Priviledges injoyed in Gods house? Surely those hold no proportion with these: Here are the Priviledges of the Children of God. Every one in it hath the priviledge of a Child & heir of the family; & as the Priviledges are great so is the Honour. It is most reall honour, upon the face of the Earth to be admitted into Gods house. What is the Honour of a Kings family? alas! it is a mock honour compared to this honour. O therefore stir up thyselfe by this Consideration to Enter here.

8. Consider, Soule that thou art called to enter here, if Prepared. Christ speakes unto thee in his language to his Spouse, Cant. 2.10,11,12, 13, arise, my Love, my fair one, & come a way. For lo! the winter (the time of thy unregeneracy) is past, the Rain (the means makeing thee to loathe thyselfe as a filthy thing have been effectual on thee) is over & gone. The Flowers (the sanctifying worke of Gods spirit) appear on the earth (in thy heart) the time of the Singing of birds (the ground of Spirituall melody) is come, the voice of the Turtle (the holy Spirit in the church) is heard in our land. The Fig tree putteth forth her green [Figs] * * * * * * Vine with its tender grape (the fruits of new obedience) give a pleasant smell, (are clearly manifested, o therefore saith Christ) arise, my Love, my Fair one, & come away. What sayst thou to this? poore Soule canst thou withstand such soul inravishing Rhetorick? Methinks it

should be like unto Sweet wine, that Causeth the lips of him that is asleep to Speak & answer. O then attend on the Call & reply to the same saying I come Lord.

Thus much for the first branch of the Exhortation which is to those that are not in a Church State.

2. Secondly. To such as are within this House. O you are the houshold of God, & yet in our text, the materials of Gods house, the materials of Gods house never appear right, but when they carry it, as the household of God. O therefore let this be upon your heart as a Call from God to behave yourselves as Gods house ought to do. You had need se to your standing for the place you Stand on is holy ground.

& therefore admit of these $\begin{cases} \text{Directions} \\ \text{Motives.} \end{cases}$

First, by way of direction attend these things

1. Study well the nature of those duties you stand in one unto an other. Take notice well of the weight that every Stone must beare, & be born with all in the whole building; if ever you thinke to abide a building of God; you will be ready to think you are overburdened one by an other, & so will be ready to Slip one from an other till the house reel or ruine unless you acquaint yourselves with those duties. You had need Carry the Candle of a Sanctified judgment in the hand of a tender Conscience in the mannaging of all duties; & especially these. For blinde Zeale, & a Sensorious Spirit will be very injurious. & so will a sluggish Conscience, & a fearefull Slavishness on the other hand, a Weake materiall will be Crusht to pieces under what the strong must beare. Strong wine must be put in new bottles. But in Case of offenses be not rash, nor high, let all be carried on with a spirit of meekness & love, both in the offended & the offender. I am affraid that such proceedings that come in the appearance of an admonition doth ofttimes inflame, more than damp the spirit, of the Offender. Christ saith tell thy brother, Matt. 18.16,17. But if the Case come to the Church remember it cometh to Christ's judgment seat & thou must behave thyselfe Reverendly. & if the judgment goeth against thee thou art not to turn judge, but to be still: thou mayest indeed in a submissive way lay down the reason of thy dissatisfaction, & so to rest, unless it be in a weighty matter & then thou mayest crave light in the Case from other Churches, tho' not judgment. O then Study well the nature of all those duties you stand in one unto

another & each unto the whole, & to every part & that according unto the relation that every member doth Stand in.

2. Have a Care of Contentions, & Divisions: you may not go together by the ears in Gods house. This is to breake the lawes in the presence of the Court, & it is a ruinating evill unto the Churches of Christ in the Country; let the Wo of others make us wary. Have a care therefore in the beginning of those things, *Principiis obsta*, etc., the begin-ing of Strife is as the letting out of water, therefore (saith the spirit) leave off Contention before it be meddled with, Prov. 17.14. Every irregular word is not to be call'd over again; this is the way to make Satan Musick upon Christs own instrument, & to place Satans tunes upon Gods Pipes. O therefore have a Care of this. The Contentions of brethren are like the barrs of a Castle, Prov. 18.19. But bear ye one anothers burdens, & So fulfill the law of Christ. And what is not meet to be born with, mannage with all meekness & let the Spirit of Christ shine fourth with a sweet behaviour. Therein lay aside wrath & sharpness, these things [oft proove like quick flashes of fire that] [98/99] meltts off the gold of the Temple, or Come like thunder Claps, that rift one stone from another. But let grace shew itselfe & not selfe, lest you appear to mannage your own, & not Christs Concerns. & meddle not in others Contests without a Cleare Call, lest thou take a dog by the eares. O therefore have a Care of Contention.

3. Be knit together in Love, this is called the bond of perfection, Col. 3.14, & the bond of peace, as Eph. 4.2,3. O strengthen this bond. Where this is firmly tied Satan is not, & so kept he cannot, he shall not enter. Persons in Church Fellowship may be Compared to a bunch of golden Arrows, & the Grace of Love to the Golden bond that binds them together. But when this bond grows slack a little he will be ready to pluck a one or other out untill the whole are in a shattered state. O therefore se that you love one another.

4. Se that you walk humbly, & closely with God, in all relations, & Duties. You will dishonour Gods Habitation, if you walk not close with God in attending the duties of your own habitation. Be much in prayer, be much watching over thine own heart. Strive to Carrie on the duties of thy Covenant with a Shine, that thou mayest have glory from the house, & bring a glory to the house. & then it will be well with thee, & the house too.

Secondly. By way of Motive to Stir you up thus to walke, beare with these things following, you cannot be too much urged here, you have deceitfull hearts, that will be apt to warpe, & Satan will assault you, you must look for it. You have no ground of any freedom from his assaults. You have neither example, nor promise of any such thing, Your priviledges will not exempt you, but rather expose you to the Same. For now you appear in the Camp of the whole world bidding battle to Satan. & what tho' you are intred & built up into Gods house, he will not be affraid to assault you therein. He is no Coward in these attempts & therefore as you have need allwayes so especially now upon your new entrance. For now he will be mostly busie. When Adam was newly placed in paradise, & did Shine there with the glorious image of God upon him, Satan was not affraid to Encounter him. But God had no sooner left off treating with him, but forth with Satan fell tampering with him, & over came him. Our Lord himselfe, soon after he was didicated to his Mediatory work by the Water of Baptism, tho' all the Perfections of grace & the Fullness of an Almighty power were in him, Satan not being danted there at, did furiously assault him. & can it be thot that he will let you go Scotfree. No, no. Therefore attend on these things following by way of motive to stir you up to your dutie in this case, the motives are of two Sorts as $\begin{cases} \text{Conviction in point of fault} \\ \text{Consolation upon your duty herein.} \end{cases}$

First here is something representing an angry aspect from him that is the lord of this house, as it fall upon you, if you fall short in your walk of the duties of this house: & that you may avoide the same let the Consideration here of stir you up, as

1. You breake your Covenant with God if you do not walk according to the Houshold of God, & is not this a dreadfull thing. O think of it, & tremble.

2. Thou wilt hereby lose the benefit of this State that thou art intred into. Now the Benefits of Gods house are great, & therefore great will be thy loss.

3. It is a Note of the leprosy in the Materialls of the building. What doth not the building su[it] th[e] end that it is raised for, oh it is greatly to be feared that the plague of * * * * * * & oh! Soule, how if thou art the piece in which this plague is? what wilt thou then do? why it is in that

piece, or stone that doth not attain unto its end, or use in the building: now where ever it is, that stone, or piece is to be ejected, if it breake out & refuse a healing. Oh! thinke of this, & be quickened.

4. Thy not walking according to thy relation will be an offence unto God in his own house, & will tend to out him thereof. God will not abide in that house where his glory doth not abide, Rev. 2.5, Jer. 7.12: & where is his glory, if it be thus that thou dost not live up unto the duties of thy relation. But thinke of this then: what hath God brought thee into his house, & will thou grieve God & drive him out of his house? Do you thus requite the Lord, oh! foolish people & unwise?

5. It presageth ruin to the building. For this is but reason, that if a building attend not its end to pluck it down again. & So will God deale with this if you walk not answerably. Oh! then let this thing stir you up to walke according to your state you are entred unto, that you may not be exposed unto such wrath.

Secondly, here is something setting the pleasant Face of that gracious & glorious One, whose house it is, before you if you walk according to the duties of Gods house unto you that have devoted yourselves. & this is sweet consolation, & therefore let it allure you.

1. This will be the way to keep Gods glorious & gracious presence in his house. For he will be with those that are with him, & oh what a Soule Filling, heart Ravishing presence is this?

2. God himselfe will then take delight in thee, & his light will shine upon thee. He will keep thee in the Secret of his Tabernacle.

3. All the sweet Consolations of Gods house shall be thine: thou shalt be abundantly satisfied with the fatness of Gods house. He shall make thee to drink of the river of his pleasures, Ps. 36.8. Are the Consolations of Gods house smal with thee. O those sweet Words! Oh, those sweet Ordinances! O, those sweet dainties. O, that sweet Countenance! O, that sweet Society! O, those sweet Duties! O, those sweet Influences that fall upon the Soule, think of the same. All the sweets of Gods house will come into thy Soule if thou walk according to thy duties therein.

4. Thou wilt hereby bring great Glory unto God. For thou wilt hereby honour him; & hereby gain Credit, & glory unto his family, that this will appear in the world glorious, thou wilt be exemplary unto others to do so; thou wilt be a means & instrument of handing down this glorious intrest of Gods house unto those that shall succeed in a

glorious way. & in all these things God is greatly glorified: oh therefore let this stir thy affections up to dutie.

Lastly. Thus will make for thee a more abundant entrance into glory itself. & are not these things sweet allurements. Oh! therefore if there be any consolation in these things from Christ Jesus thinke of these things. & lett the thoughts hereof draw out your affections to walke so in this state that you are entred into that you may be ornaments in Gods house.

& thus much for the Exhortation. [99/100]

Secondly. By way of thankfulness, is it so that a Particular Church is built up to be an habitation of God thro' the Spirit. Oh! then what ground of thankfullness is here for us? why, God has set himselfe an habitation up here. Oh how should this glad our hearts! how should it improove our Affections in the duties of thankfulness? & Methinks it calls out the affections of all here & especially yours that are entred into this habitation, unto this worke, to give hearty & syncere thanks unto God for his Goodness herein. Your Prayers, your strivings after it; your Rustlings have thro' grace prevailed. All the Wilds of the old Serpent, his Stratagims, his Temptations, which he mannaged, to the very last, to the very Treshold of the Doore to harm, & hinder this worke, are foyld, & brought to Nothing. The snare is broken the bird is fled! Oh shout for joy. Grace, Grace on this account. God hath set up his Habitation in this place, which but a little while agoe was a hold for divels, & a Cage of Dragons. Surely he hath done great things for us whereof we are glad. And truely my friends have we not occasion? Alas! if a leading man come but to dwell in a town that is going on, how glad is that town? But if he be a great man, of a good estate, oh then they are much more glad, why? he is like to be the making of the place. But yet suppose he was some Noble Person, of such a noble minde as that he should feast them, Cloath them, be familiar with them, mentain them, enrich them, Protect them, & Defend them, what should be said of such a man, how joyous would any place be upon such a persons coming to dwell amongst them. Oh, this would be a golden man indeed! But where is any such to be found? *Rara avis* indeed! Yet this happiness would be temporary; he did not come to inrich your Souls. But, lo, here is more than all this amounts to in that God hath come, & pitched his tent amongst you. There is no more comparison to be made betwixt him that hath raised

himselfe an habitation amongst you, God, the Lord God Almighty, &
such a man than there is between the glorious glory of heaven itselfe, &
the darkest dungeon the earth affords. Oh then what ground of joy, &
shouting have we! He is come, he is come to dwell among you. & hath
all felicity in his hand to bestow on you. He calls you to open the doore
of your hearts, & he will then bestow himselfe upon you. Hee opens the
doore of his house, & calls you to his royall banquets: He opens the
door of Glory & calls unto you saying come up hither, come up hither.
Oh he hath Riches, & honour, & glory, & Immortality & Eternall life
to bestow upon you, & urges them upon you. Now this is he that is
come to take up his Habitation among you. O then! with joy let us draw
water out of the Wells of Salvation. Therefore Cry out & shout thou
inhabitants of Zion, for great is the Holy One of Israell in the middest
of thee.

The Books Following contain Severall Sections
The First after an account of our Initiation Consists of 2 parts, as
{ Admitions into Church } State
{ Dismitions } Offices.

Section the First. Of Admitions
which Consists of two Chapters { Manner
{ Disciplining.

First of the Manner of Admitting.

This Sermon being then (for time being Short) in the Choise heads thereof gone over the Moderator stood up, & gave a briefe account of what was done, & propounded the Brethren to the Elders, & Messengers for their approbation unto their proceeding. If they desired further satisfaction in the Matter, or judged any thing yet further to bee attended in this Case before the Covenant was entred into, they were desired to manifest the same. If otherwise let their Silence Signify it.

Where upon nothing appearing the Moderator Called us forth to enter into Covenant, which being done in the words of the Covenant by & by recited, he pronounced us a Church of Christ orderly gathered according to the Rules of Christ in the gospell.

And demanded of the church whom they Chose to receive the right hand of Fellowship, & my selfe being desired to do it for them, Mr. Stoddard upon the desire of the other Elders, & Messengers of the Churches, gave me it in these words

I do in the Name of the Churches give you the Right hand of Fellowship.

This was not altogether approved on, but it was judged to have been most meet to have been done in the Name of Christ. But Mr. Stoddard rather Chose those words having some instance for the use thereof.

This Done, the Moderator demanded of the Church whom they Chose their officer, & into what office. Whereupon the Brethren of the Church laid my unworthy Selfe under a Call unto the Office of a Pastor unto them. Which being propounded unto my selfe for acceptance, I manifested my acceptance at the present.

Then it being demanded of the Brethren whom they pitched on to carry on the worke of Ordination, they desired the Reverend Elders to mannage the worke of Ordination for them, onely Brother Samuel Loomis they Chose to joyne in the worke of Imposition of hands. & this being manifested the worke was thus performed, the Rev. Mr. Russell,

Mr. Glover, Mr. Stoddard, Elders, & Brother Samuel Loomis laid on hands, Mr. Russell prayed before ordination, Mr. Glover Ordained, & Mr. [Sto]ddard Ended the work with Prayer. [100/101]

In the Ordination which was to this Effect (Whereas you Mr. E. T. are called by this church of Christ at Westfield into the Office of a Pastor unto them, the which Call you having manifested your acceptance of, we do here in the Name of Christ pronounce you Pastor of the Same, Etc.) the charge was almost wholly omitted.

After the whole was done Mr. Stoddard being deputed by the Elders to give the Right hand of Fellowship to me in this Office did it as before which being done Brother Loomis Set the 122 Psalm, which being sung the Assembly was dismisst with the Blessing. & so the work was accomplisht.

The Church Covenant was this following

In the sense of our own Nothingness, depending on Gods gracious supply; & in faith in his incouragements given us thereunto, We, in Obedience unto his Commands, & in imitation of his Saints, in Scripture, do here, in the presence of Almighty God, Angels, & Men, give up ourselves unto the Onely true God in Jesus Christ, to walke in his wayes with all our hearts: Bewailing so much as all those humane infirmities, which do any way hinder the Same.

And further, in awe of the same God, & dependance of the same supply of grace, we mutually oblige ourselves to walke together according to the Rules of the Gospel, in the Communion of Saints in a Particular Church Instituted State, for the Carrying on of all Gospell Ordinances, the Ministry of the Word, Sacraments, & Discipline; & also all those Mutuall Duties of Helpfulness & Subjection in the Lord one unto an other according to our places, which God requireth in his word, as means for the preventing of, or recovering from Evill, that Sin may not lie upon us but that God may dwell amongst us. Unto the performance of which Covenant So & So long as we shall remain Members of the same Society, We solemnly Oblige ourselves, Earnestly Crying in the

Name of Christ unto the Father of spirits to assist there un to. &
Subscribe our Names.

> EDWARD TAYLOR
>
> JOHN MAWDESLY
>
> SAMUEL LOOMIS
>
> JOSIAH DEWY
>
> JOHN ROOT
>
> ISAAC PHELPS
>
> JOHN INGERSON

Brother Thomas Gun being nominated for a foundation man desired to
be omitted, & was admitted the 21 the 7m without Relation, in that he
was so much decayed by age that it would be a hard thing to gather it &
he was a man of approved piety & was recomended to us by Windsor
Church.[52]

Those that are admitted, being approved, we first take them into
our Consideration in our Conference Meeting, & then the way being
Cleared they are publickly propounded in the Assembly, that if any can
give in any just ground against their Behaviour they have liberty, But if
nothing appeare, in due season they are proceeded with to admittance:
which sometimes we attend upon on a solemn day set a part partly for
that End, partly by way of preparation for the Lords Supper, & partly
for the [ca]use of Christ in [ge]nerall & other things that Emerge & then
the [person] being C[alled] out, their de[cision] made known, they if men
are desired [101/102] to give an account of some of those Experiences
of Gods works upon their hearts, the which if they thro' fearfulness, &
bashfulness, do desire the same may be read, the Church Complying to
their desires therein, the same, as also it is on the admitting of Women,
is read, the which again being acknowledged by the owner to be some of
those experiences of Gods dealing with his or her Soule, is propounded
to the Church for their judgment & that if we may proceed to admittance let their Silence Signify it.

Whereupon nothing appearing further to be done the Person is
admitted to the Covenant by the lifting up of the hands, & then the
Covenant is read unto those to be admitted according as the nature of
admittance doth admit of, & with none other alteration, the which they
Subscribing to, they are pronounced thus

We, here in Obedience unto Almighty God in Christ, receiving you, Members, into full Comunion in this Church of Christ, amongst us, & admitting you unto all Gospell Priviledges therein, according to your severall Capacities thereunto, Do promise solemnly in the Presence of God to perform unto you, as unto ourselves all those mutuall Duties of helpfullness unto which we have mutually obliged ourselves, & do   pronounce you Members of this Church of Christ orderly admitted there into.

Thus were admitted these following.

	Dni	Mo^{nth}	Day	
[16]79	10	11	1	Joseph Pomery
				Jedadiah Dewy
				David Ashley
				Elizabeth, wife of Brother Loomis
				Hannah, wife of Brother Ashley
				Ann, wife of brother Phelps
				Elizabeth, wife of E. Taylor
				Hephzibah, wife of Brother Josiah Dewy

Eliazar Weller admitted under the Watch of the Church

	9/10	01	24	These were admitted
				Samuel Root & Mary his wife
				Nathaniel Weller
				John Hanchet
				Sarah, wife of Brother Jedidiah Dewy
				Constance, the wife of Thomas Dewy

	[1]0	03	09	These admitted
				Thomas Dewy
				Mary, the wife of Samuel Taylor

		04	17	These admitted
				Mary, the wife of Thomas Root
				Hannah, the wife of Brother Joseph Pomery

	07	16	These admitted Mary, the wife of Brother John Root Dorothy, the wife of Jacob Phelps
1680	09	11	These admitted Hannah, the wife of Thomas Noble Esther, the wife of Brother John Hanchet Deliverance, the wife of Brother Nathaniel Weller
	11	20	These Received in Thomas Noble Jane, the wife of Ambrose Fowler, Sr. Mary, the wife of Walter Lee Mary, the wife of Fearnot King
1681	04	26	Samuel Loomis, Jr., admitted under the watch of the Church
	09	07	Eliazar Weller, Mary the wife of Brother Mawdsley, & Hannah, the wife of George Saxton, Jr., admitted into Full Communion
	09	24	John Ponder Hannah, the wife of Eliazar Weller & Hannah the wife of Samuel Loomis, Jr., admitted into Full Communion
1682	05	23	Katherine, the wife of George Saxton, Sr., admitted into Full Communion
	11	14	Hannah, the wife of John Sacket admitted to full Communion
1683	03	20	Ruth Smith, daughter of Brother & Sister Loomis, put herselfe under Church-watch
	4	10	Martha, the wife of Thomas * * * & Sarah, the wife of * * * came under * * * * * *

4	17	Mary, the wife of John Gun, entred under the Watch of the Church
6	12	John Noble came under the Church-Watch
7	2	David Winchel of Suffield intred into full-Communion with us
8	*	Hannah, the Wife of Jonathan Alford, admitted into full Communion

1685		
	5	26 Edward Grissill came under the Church Watch
	10	20 Nathaniel Bancroft put himselfe under the Watch of the Church, delivering & his Seed up to God & his inspection over them in this Church
	11	03 Hepzibah Boatman put herselfe under the Church Watch

1686		
	3	23 Nathaniel Phelps came under Church Watch
	9	07 Mary, wife to Nathaniel Williams, came under Church Watch
	1	13 Sarah, the wife of William Pixlie, intered into Church Fellowship, & Hannah, Daughter of Brother & Sister Noble & wife to John Goodman of Hadley did subject herselfe under the Watch of the Church

1687		
	2	09 Samuel Ashly surrendered himselfe up to God & the Watch of the Church actually
	3	29 Martha, wife of Thomas Merly, admitted into full Communion
	7	25 John Richards admitted under the Church Watch

* * * * * * * * [102/107]

08	16	Temperance, the wife of Brother Ponder, entered into Full Communion in this Church
09	13	Sarah, the wife of John Lee, subjected herselfe under the Watch of the Church

1688	01	25	Sarah, the wife of Samuel Ashly, entred into Full Communion in this church
	02	08	Mary, the wife of John Noble, entred into Full Communion here
	09	18	John & Debora Sacket entred under the Watch of the Church
1689	01	06	Abigail, wife of Samuel Fowler, admitted into Full Communion
	09	04	Hannah, wife of James Saxton, admitted into Full Communion
		18	Mary, wife of David Ashley admitted under Church watch
1690	04	29	Abigail, the wife of Samuel Bush, added into a State of Full Communion in the Church
	06	20	Benjamin Mawdesly put himselfe under Church Watch
1691	3	24	Benjamin Smith came into Full Communion
	6	02	Ruth, the wife of Benjamin Smith, received into full Communion
	9	25	Adijah Dewy put himselfe under the Church Watch
1692	5	31	Isaak Phelps, Elizabeth, wife of Thomas Hanchet, & Hannah, the wife of Joseph Saxton, came under the Church Watch
	10	28	Brother Josiah Dewy & Brother Nathaniel Weller were elected, & ordained by prayer, & imposition of hands, Deacons of the Church, in the end of a Day of fast for publick judgement set apart
1693	1	26	Steven Lee came under the Watch of the Church

9   12   Thomas Smith of Suffield entred in Full
Communion with this Church

1694   6   19   Matthew Noble & Elizabeth Church put them
selves under the Church Watch

7   9   Thomas Ingerson & John Ashley put themselves
under the Church watch

1695   12   10   Lydia * * * was received into Full Communion

11   26   Hannah Bag was receiv'd into Full Communion

12   23   Hannah, wife of Joseph Saxton, received into
full Communion

1696   3   17   Mary, daughter of Thomas Root, Settled under
the Church

4   14   Samuel Negle settled himselfe under the Watch
of the Church

8   11   Thomas Noble settled under the watch of the
Church
Samuel Bush, Jr. entered into Church fellowship

9   30   Mary, wife of Ambrose Fowler, Jr., entered
into Church Fellowship

12   07   Walter Lee entred into a State of Church
Fellowship with this Church

1697   2   11   Samuel Dewy subjected himselfe under the
Church Watch

3   09   Elizabeth, wife of Richard Church, entred
into Church fellowship

16   Mr. Ezekiel Lewis entred into Church Fellowship

| 4 | 13 | Nehemiah Loomas put himselfe under the Watch of the Church. |

& Elizabeth, wife of Thomas Noble, Jr., entred into a State of Church fellowship

---

| 5 | 4 | Mary, wife of David Ashley, Jr., received into Church fellowship |

| 8 | 17 | Sarah, wife of John Lee, entred into Church fellowship |

| 10 | 5 | Stephen [Kellog] & Lydia his Wife entred into Church fellowship |

| 1698 | 01 | 27 | Hannah Root entered into full Communion |

| 11 | 22 | Joseph Mawdsly admitted into Church Fellowship |

| 1699 | 01 | 26 | Abigail, wife of Brother Joseph Mawdsly entred into Church Fellowship |

| 4 | 4 | Thomas Noble entred into a State of Church fellowship with this church here |

| 5 | 30 | Nathaniel Bancroft entred into Church fellowship with this Church of Christ [107/108] |

| 1700 | 2 | 21 | Joseph Ashley sett[led] under Church Watc[h] |

| 9 | 06 | David Dewie entred into Church fellows[hip] |

| 9 | 24 | Luke Noble & Ma[ry], wife of John Gun, received into Ch[urch] fellowship |

| 10 | 22 | Samuel Sacket pu[t] himselfe under the Watch of the Chur[ch] |

| 1701 | 2 | 06 | Joseph Pixly put him[self] under the Watch of the Chur[ch] |

	9	30	Jonathan Ashley put himselfe under the Church Wa[tch]
	11	25	James Noble put h[im]selfe under the watch of the Church
1702	3	31	John Ingerson & Abi[gail] Lewis of Farmington * * * a Child * * * the Watch of the Church
	5	5	John Root Windsor & * * * p[ut] himselfe under the Wa[tch] of the Church
	7	13	Mary, wife of Thom[as] Smith of Suffield, [en]tred into Church fellowship with us h[ere]
	9	18	Thomas Morley en[ter]ed into a state of Churc[h] fellowship with us
	10	20	Hannah Eaglestone * * * entred Church fellowship

1703   2   4   Hannah Wife of John Saxton being in Chu[rch] fellowship with the church of Springfield, and her dismission, & re[com]mendation to us & the wife of Brother Samuel Bush were received into Church fellowship & Mary King were received in Church fellowship & Abigail, wife of Dav[id] King, was received und[er] the Watch of the Church

	8	23	Mary, the wife of Mark Noble, entred into a State of Church fellowship
	12	20	Abigail, the wife of David King, entred into a State of Church fellowship
	01	12	Eliazar Weller put himselfe under the Watch of the Church
1704	2	2	Abigail, wife of Joseph Ashley, entred into a State of Church fellowship

	3	28	John Root, the son of Thomas Root, put himselfe under the Watch of the Church
	6	11	Noah, son of John & Sarah Ashley baptized
	8	24	Jedidiah Dewy put himselfe under the Watch of the Church
1705	3	*	John Shephard, & his wife Elizabeth put themselves under the Watch of the Church
	4	17	Samuel Root the Second put himself under the Watch of the Church
	12	24	Samuel Loomas, Jr., admitted under the watch of the Church
	1	17	Esabel, wife of John Ingerson, entred into Church Fellowship
1706	1	31	Mr. Samuel Taylor put himselfe under the Watch of the Church
	12	03	William Loomas received under the watch of the Church
1707	5	10	John, son of Thomas, Root entred into a state of Full-Communion in our Church amongst us
	7	28	Samuel Loomas, Sr., entred into a state of Church Fellowship with this Church
	8	31	Lydia, wife of Nathaniel Ponders, gave up herselfe under the watch of the Church
	10	12	Agnes my Neger Se[r]vant being in Full Communion with the Church at Hadly & being recomended to this Church was received into this Church[53]
1709	3	29	Esther, wife of Charles Gantes, put herself under the watch of the Church

	5	16	Consider Madesly & his wife put themselves under the Watch of the Church
	6	20	Sarah, wife of brother David Dewy, received into Church Fellowship
1710	08	08	Rebeckah, wife of Jedidiah Dewy, Jr., received into Church Fellowship
	03	20	Sarah daughter of David & Sarah Dewy baptized
1711	4	23	Ebenezer Bush Entred under the Watch of the Church
	6	05	John Shephard & Elizabeth his Wife received into Full Communion
	7	02	Ruth, wife to brother Luke Noble, entred into full Communion
	11	20	Ebenezzar Pixly & Mary his wife entred into full Communion
	03	3	David Ashley, Jr., and Philip Loomas admitted into Full Communion
1712	1	30	Jedidiah Dewy, Jr., admitted into Church Fellowship
	3	08	Samuel Fowler, Jr., put himselfe under the Watch of the Church
	8	05	Nathaniel Bancroft & his wife entred under the Watch of the Church
	10	28	Samuel Kellog admitted into a State of Church fellowship
1713	2	05	Mary, the Widdow of Nathaniel Williams, entred into Church Fellowship
	3	24	Sarah, widdow to Samuel Root, admitted into a State of Church Fellowship

	9	15	Deborah King Entred into Church fellowship Rachel Williams put herselfe under the Watch of the Church
714	1	28	Martha, wife of John Hayns, subjected herself under the Watch of the Church
	2	18	Samuel Ashley, Jr., entred into a State of Church Fellowship
	3	16	Joshua Root put himselfe under the Church Watch
	4	20	Sarah, Wife of Joseph Root, entered into Church fellowship, i.e., full Communion with this Church [108/109]
716	5	15	Thankfull, Wife of Lt. John Phelps, entered into a State of Church fellowship in the Church
	7	02	Mary, Wife of brother Samuel Kellog, entred into a S[t]ate of Church Fellowship amongst us
	9	05	Abigail Lee entred into a State of Church amongst us
		18	Abigail, wife of Joseph * * * entered into Church Fellowship
	*	17	John Bancroft admitted under the Watch of the Church
717	4	2	Mary Hanchet entred into a State of Church fellowship
	7	15	Elizabeth, wife of Consider Mawdsly, entred into Church fellowship
718	6	02	Israel Dewy * * *
	9	08	Rebecka, the Wife of Samuel Loomas, received into full Communion
719	*	*	Hannah wife of John King entred & received under the Church Watch

	06	09	Aaron Gun received under the Watch of the Church, & his son Aaron baptized
	09	*	Stephen * * *
	*	01	Eunice daughter of John & Hannah Mawdsly Baptized
		17	Samuel Son of Daniel * * * Daughter of * * * Baptized
		24	Sarah Daughter of Joseph and Sarah Dewy baptized
1720	1	2	Moses Son of Stephen & Abigail Kelog baptized
	*	02	Stephen Kelog admitted under Church watch
	*	*	* * * the son of Isak Phelps baptized
	5	17	Elizabeth daughter of Nathaniel Bancraft Jr. & * * * baptized
	08	02	Thomas Son of Joseph Root by his Wife Sarah & Jonathan son of Philip & Rebeckah Tri[mon] bap[tized]
	12	27	Benjamin Son of Benjamin & Mary Saxton baptized

1722[54]

The Church being gathered as before is said, & Mr. Taylor
Ordained their Pastor, there was none other Teaching Officer added, &
being small, no Ruling Elder nor Deacon, Elected, onely Brother Loomis was desired to looke after the providing Wine, & Bread & to
urnish the Lords Table. & after awhile he was chosen to the Office of a
Deacon: but he not giving a ready acceptance desiring time to Consider
of itt. & at length he desired another to be joyned with him. Wherefore
he Church Chose Brother Josiah Dewy, Who desiring time to Consider
of it was so long before he would yield to accept unto Ordination, that
Brother Loomas was taken a way by death, & never ordained. Where-
ore after some ti[me] Brother Dewy desired an other to be joyned with
him in the Work & therefore the Church Chose brother Nathaniel
Weller to the Office & hence the Officers are as follo[ws] these ordained.

Elders	Ano	M	D	Deacons
1679.6.27 Mr. Edward Taylor, Pastor	1692	10	28	Josiah Dewy & Nathaniel Weller were ordaind, the first Deacons.
	1703	11	09	Samuel Root being called in the preceedin[g] summer was ordaind also Deacon
	1712	03	25	Deacon Weller & Deacon Root being taken from us by a putred fever in about a fortnights time, brother David Dewe[y] & br[o]ther Thomas Noble being Chosen by the brethren to the office of a Deacon were Ordaind Deacons the 25th 3m 1712

Ann. Dom: 1726 Octob 26
Mr. Nehemiah Bull, Pastor   [123/125]

173

[The Disciplinary Cases]

The Wisdome, Grace, & Faithfulness of Christ do manifestl
shine forth in the Particular Instituted Churches of the Saints: Wherei
may be seen not onely the Image of God in a new Edition putt forth i
Splendor again, upon the Understanding in Knowledge, upon the Wil
in Righteousness, & upon the Life, in Holiness: As also the Seals of th
NEW Covenant And New-Covenant Ordinances Dispensed; But also th
Golden Keyes of that Covenant being fitted to the Locks of thes
Churches, Matt. 16.18,19, 18.17,18, & I Cor. 5.12, 12.13, rightl
used. For Christ Considering that while his people are in this Militar
State they are not all Spirit but part flesh; & that Satan by his poysonou
darts doth oft make it ranckle & grow proud Flesh which must be eate
down by Corrosives, hath ordained the Sensures of the Church to take
down, thereby to recover the Poore Soule from his wound, & take th
Captive out of the hand of the Adversary; As also to keep the Holy Plac
Clean from being defiled by unclean ones; And that the Necessity c
things require the same, we have our experience to lay down as on
among other Evidences, Who being scarcely slipt into the Templ
Doore before the Adversary had brought us to the need of thi
Corrosive.[55]

Brother John Mawdsly's Case[56]

The Occasion of his temptation was the Land laid down for th
accommodating some of our Neighbours who having but just return'
to their own houses after the Indian war was over, before being terrifie
by that unthought of Ruine & Captivity upon poore Hatfield by
runing parcell of Indians, they were drove out from them again, & thes
rather to leave the town than to live remote again.[57] Whereupo
Authority taking it into Consideration, inacted a new Moddling of th
town, as the onely way appearing for its preservation, & set the Matte
into the hands of a Committee, viz, Major John Pynchon of Springfield
Brother John Mawdsly, who then was not come from Windsor to us bu
about to come having bought Mr. Joseph Whitings living here, &
brother Samuel Loomes. Which Committee laid out the Moddles of th
town as now it is, out of the Homelots of those neer-taking, to suppl

...eir Distressed Neighbours, allowing them by way of satisfaction two ...cres of Common Land as Convenient as they could take up, for one ...id down; & on this occasion almost four Acres of Brother Mawdsley ...omelot was improved, he before his purchase of the same, & also ...efore Authority had inacted the same, having as a full account of this ...usiness given him as the onely way appearing for the Security, & ...ttlement of the place, did fully as to appearance comply with the same ...t that also as to the matter of satisfaction if Mr. Taylor settled. But ...hen the [comm]ittee did their work being here, & appearing so cordiall ...t the case [to the] observation of all, none questioned his being satis-...ed. But as soon as we were slipt into a Church State the Cole began to ...arkle being blowed upon by the old-Madobato.[58] Whereupon he was ...eged hard by One of us, to know what would satisfy, & at last he said if ...e could gaine the Next homelot to his Wife, which was about 5 acre ...counted, of Thomas Huckplies it would do: whereupon he was pre-...ared to buy it, & Pay should be made for it by one that would take the ...Acres of the land laid out for his satisfaction by the town. The which ...as done, & now deeds were given to these seated upon the land laid ...own by him, onely his Wife would not sign them without some Con-...deration (which Refusall was upon advice to gain some small matter ...owards the Purchase of Huckplies Lot but yet nothing was gaind). ...efore this also Authority of the Generall Court approved, & Con-...rm'd the Act of the Committee, & also Enacted that Deeds should be ...iven to those placed in this New Moddle, by the first Proprietors. Upon ...he satisfaction * * * the Committee of two Acres for One, Now all ...hings rest for a while. But Provocations come ahand & the Adversary is ...ot Idle. One was about a motion made to have lane laid out into the ...outh field to make a more ready passage thither & into the Woods for ...he Neighbours, which being debated it was thought most conveniently ...o run along by Brother Mawdsly remaining End of his homelot, but ...one thought of Running it upon his land; but without it. An other was, ...t that Brother John Hanchet, who was seated on a small bit of What ...rother Mawdsley laid down, having received a Deed of Brother ...Mawdsly, & after a while going to live at Stony Brook being forced to ...ell, & Lt. Mawdsly not accepting to buy it, had sold it to another. & ...ther temptations coming upon him, the old Cole glowed & so he draws ...p this petition following to the Generall court.

To the Honorable & Much Honored Generall Court no
Assembled at Boston 27th 3m 1682

The Humble Petition of John Mawdsly of Westfield, Sheweth. Tha
whereas shortly after [the] Fight with the Indians at Hatfield, th
Honored Genera[ll] Court then made an Act for the Severall towns i
[the] colony, that lived remote, & scattered should gather neere
together in a Compact way, as judging it to be most for the good &
safety of the said Severall Pl[an]tations, & Inhabitants thereof.
Your Humble Petitioner in Obedience to your Authority & in Ap[pro
bation of your Advice, & Counsell in the said Act, did W[il]lingly la
down four Acres of his Home Lot to acc[om]modate four neighbour:
that the End promised might be obtained, & the Plantation might b
Strengthen[ed] by living neer together: And whereas the said inhabit[an
upon Satisfaction to your Petitioner tendred by the * * * have demande
& Procured Deeds for the same, [b]ut not on the behalfe, or in the nam
of your Petitioner['s] Wife, for her right therein. The Honorabl
Generall Court w[ould be] pleased to understand, that one of the sai
inhabitants na[me]ly John Hanchet,—shortly after he had possesst th
Land the said Promises hath sold away & alienated his part [of] lan
unto an other formerly settled on another of the premises, that so th
Plantation is weakened the[reby] & the End sought; & advised to is no
attended.

Now (whereas the Honored Generall Court did, in their said * *
Grant that full satisfaction should be made to your Hu[m]ble Petitione
by the said Plantation, or Inhabitants) [said] [125/126] Petitioner hat
not received above halfe of his satisfaction in respect to the Promise:
neither according to the same land sold by the said John Hanchet no
according to land next adjoyning, which your Petitioner hath Purchase
in stead thereof.

Wherefore your Humble Petitioner doth most humbly Crave, tha
the Honored Generall Court, would either grant him to have the sai
part of Land again, or the money it was sold for, in lue of the one half
of the twenty pounds, yet due for satisfaction, altho' it be not a Quarte
part of the land your Petitioner laid down for the same mentioned End
there being a high way laid out through the same which your Petitione
hath nothing for. And yet your Humble Petitioner having th
Remainder of his Land lying at the End, or near this High-Way, th

Inhabitants have a great Desire to run a further highway to his great Dammage, through the whole Lot, altho' the Town may lay out a High way, in town land as Convenient; or rather better. Wherefore your Humble Petitioner doth humbly crave you will take into Serious Consideration the Promises, & afford such reliefe as in your godly wisdom shall seem meet; & he shall dayly pray for your Peace, & Prosperity; & remain

Your Humble Servant.

At a Generall Court held at Boston the 24th 3m 1682

In answer to this Petition, the Court judgeth it meet, to refer the whole matter to the County Court of Hampshire,[59] who are hereby impowered to act therein, & settle it in such a way, as the Law in this Case doth direct, & as may remove all just grounds of Complaint from the Petitioner.

That this is a true Coppy of the Petition which is on fyle, & of the Courts Act thereupon, attests

Edward Ranson, Secr.

Whereupon we attaining to this Coppy of the Petition, etc., out of the Hampshire Court Records, read it on a Conference Day to the Church who chose then the 9th 11m 1682/3 Brother Samuel Loomis, brother David Ashly, & brother Josiah Dewy a Committee for the Church to gather up the offences therein Contained, & present them to the Church as offences, & to treat Brother Mawdsly about the same who in the beginning of winter had removed his family to Windsor; & was not with us. But being urged before this was read to the Church with the Offences therein, & to prevent a Church Process, he * * * then refused, yet on further Consideration Came up, & fell under the same before he was Called out, & tendered an acknowledgment of his Repentance, & trouble of spirit for his Failings therein. And appearing on a Conference day being the 23rd 11m 1682/3 for that End, was called out. Who began it to this Effect.

Having given Some little account as to his being under temptation about the same matter, he acknowledged he consulted with some persons that stird him up & drew up the Petition for him, about which he had much debate in his own breast, whether he should present it & did earnestly seek to God that if it was not right, he might not present it; but yet the temptation was too hard for him, & altho' at that time he had that sore streake on his leg that laid him up as a Cripple he had many thoughts in his breast about it, yet the temptation took place & he rested in his former Counsell, & went with his Petition to the Court, the which he now was Helped to light whereby he saw he had transgressed many Commands therein. & that in generall he acknowledged, & that if anyone would help him herein he should acknowledge wherein he misst it.

Whereupon being doubtfull how things would go if let alone I stept on, I took up the matter thus. In brief there appears in your petition such offences as follow, we account you have broke

1. The fift Command thereby which requireth due Honour one to an other, whereas you have chargd the town with unrighteousness in taking away your land, & allowing you but halfe satisfaction for it.

2. The Eight Command, which requireth a lawful proceeding to gain the good things of this life; The which hath not been attended on by the Petition, in that its main design is to stir up Authority to grant you the land, or the price of that land which you had given a deed of to brother Hanchet without any Consideration made to him at all.

3. The Ninth Command, which requireth truth, & truth in witness bearing. The which you have broken, in that in your Petition 1. You say you have but halfe satisfaction, (whereas you have received a Legall Satisfaction) half satisfaction according to land you have bought lying next adjoyning. 2. In that you say, that the town have a great desire to lay an other high way throu the remainder of your Lott, the which doth not appeare that they had ever any desire, & therefore not a great desire so to do. &

4. The Tenth Command which saith thou shalt not Covet, Which form of spirit herein required must needs be wanting in you, or else you could not have proceeded as you have done.

These things being the principall offences were laid before him, many others as more cunningly juggled in, in the bowels of these Complaints by the Enemy, were not mentioned unless by some generall term; the which being propounded to him, he acknowledged, that in all these particulars he had transgressed the Commands.

And being demanded whether he was sensible that he had Dishonourd God, & grieved his brethren thereby, he freely acknowledged the same.

& having Promised to meddle no more in this Matter, desiring the prayers of his brethren for him, his Case was Propounded to the Vote of the Church.[60] That if they judged brother Mawdslies acknowledgment a Gospell Satisfaction, they would manifest their acceptance of it, & the Confirming their Love to him by a lifting up of their hands, which being done the vote was declared unto him, & he urged to be more watchful for the time to come.

Brother Thomas Dewy's Case[61]

The Dewies formerly having a grant to let a saw mill upon two mile brook & the land about the pond they made grants for their incouragment when they set up their Mill, hee, Joseph Whiting, being ingaged to set up a gristmill, & finding, when he had set up one on the brook by the hill as we go to Northampton, the banks being sandy, not to hold water, agreed with them to take a fourth part in their saw mill allowing after the proportion for their Charging that they should have 3 forths in the grist Mill, & so then used it on the same Dam. & On Mr. Whitings going away in time 3 parts of the Mills came into Thomas Dewies hand. & Now the Corn Mill being Worn out, he & his brother Josiah being incouraged by work allowed them from the town to the making the Dam, & a way that was something difficult, & also hazzardous to spoile their work, by letting the water of the brook away, at the mouth of two Mile brook where they had found a Rock to found their Dam upon, they were at Charges to build a New Mill, & had set it up, & a swift mill it was. But that great Flood the summer next after in August broke a passage over their Way from the great River, almost to the Mill brook which was judged to require 30£ or 40£ in work to Make it up again. Now in this Pinch Brother Pomery, & some others had a grant to get a Saw Mill on the Brook above theirs so as it was judged it would take away two thirds of their water which proved a temptation too Hard upon Brother Thomas Dewy so that he went one morning, & cut down their Dam & hid their tooles. Of the irregularity of which fact being Convinced from a Sermon preached on this occasion on Rom. 12.19. He Confesst his Fauld, & put up this following acknowledgment which was read over & accepted on the 2d 9m 1683 by the Church, being Lords day. [126/127]

Brother Thomas Dewies Acknowledgment

In respect unto the Cutting down the Dam, & hiding the tools, I do here before God, & his people acknowledge that since I did it God hath brought me to se my irregularity, & Dishonourable proceedings therein, as a thing offensive under many Considerations, which made me grieved in my Spirit, that the Adversary should get such advantage against me, & to beg of God to pardon the evill there of. And having in point of Satisfaction for the Dammage done, agreed with the owners, [62] I desire the people of God, & especially the Church whereof I am an unworthy member, to lay by whatever Offence they may have taken hereat; & to help me with their prayers, that God may shew himselfe gracious to me herein: & for the time to come to defend me against all overbearing temptations.

Brother Pomeries Case[63]

Brother Joseph Pomery being Constable for the year 1683, had many Rates put into his hand to gether & discharge; amongst which there were two to be raised in silver by warrant from the Countrey Treasurer, & Silver being not to be had, he accepted of it in Corn Indian at 18d per bushell & Wheat, at 3s & so undertook to make it up himselfe if it fell short provided, if it Exceeded, he might have the overplus. & so the Rates were gathered. But Corn prooving low in the market he sent it not away & thereupon about March 1684/5 the Countrey Treasurers man being here, to look after Rates; he was forced to give him a Bill, to pay him about 14£ 18d in Silver the summer following. Hence there was a visible scandall, & under a bad aspect, as if he had appropriated it to his own Concern. & therefore being treated with, it appeared upon wrong disposall to debts that he should not have meddled with & what was still behinde of these silver Rates not come into his hand, & of other Rates which were not raised for the Country; but on the account of town & County use, which had been discharged by him, there were about 12£ (answering silver vallue) disposed, & still not received by him, on the towns use, & of the Rest he could give no account of: onely he said it were lost. He was cleare in his Conscience that he had never used any of it. & where it was he knew not & therefore to remove the Scandall, & to satisfy the Church on this account he made this open Acknowledgment the 31st 3m 1685.

Brother Pomery's Acknowledgment.

In respect unto the said Rates I acknowledge, that altho' I never designed any thing but the payment of the Town debts to the Countrey therewith for the which they were put into my hand: yet apprehending a liberty on the terms on which I received them, to use the same any how, provided they answered the said debt; & partly also for want of Room, having put part thereof to mine own Corn through imprudence, I have not been so distinct thereunto, as was Convenient; & so finde it too hard a thing to give so distinct an account as is desired. Wherefore altho' I have ingaged to satisfy the Countrey Treasurer, in What remains; so that the town shall not be injured thereby, in point of right, yet it hath been, & is a great trouble, & exercise unto me in that I have not manifested a greater Conscientious attendance upon the Duties I were bound, both unto the town, & Countrey respecting the same. Therefore begging of God that he would pass over all m[y] failings in this respect: & desiring you to receive this Acknowledgment in way of Satisfaction for any off[ence] in me, given hereby to you, or any other, & also to he[lp] me with your Prayers, that the Remainder of my Life m[ight] be more to the glory of God, I am

Your Brother & Unworthy Fellow Servan[t]
in the Fellowship of the Gospell Joseph Pomer[y]

Brother Joseph Pomeries Case as to the Mill matters[64]

There falling out a suite at Law between Brother Thomas Dewy, & Brother Josiah Dewy on the one pa[rt] & John Sacket, Samuel Taylor, brother Joseph Pomery, Nathaniel Williams owners of the new saw mill up stream on two mile brook, on the other part, as tou[ch]ing the streame; Which action being tryed at North[am]pton Court March 1685, & found to be the Dewys right, they had an Execution laid upon 7½ of land the upper Mill men had took up about their Mill. [The] land Executed lay on both sides of the stream; & th[ey] laid their execution upon Estate for the Rest of the Fine given them by the Court. The Land Executed w[as] delivered by the Marshall upon Value of 18 pence [per] acre which amounted to about 11ˢ 3ᵈ & returnd & Rec[ord]ed in the Cort.

Now this Execution did so rout the upper mill that altho' they had appealed to the Generall Court u[p]on their being Cast that they sought to agree, & t[he] two parties came to this Agreement following.

After the Preface it runs thus— This Present I[n]strument testifies, that in order to a Finall Isue, & Conclusion of the said Cases, & Contentions thereupon aris[ing] & for Settlement of peace amongst us, the parties ab[ove] said in respect to land appertaining, do mutually [a]gree thus to winde up the matters of Difference am[ong]st them, & oblige themselves there unto in the Cond[iti]ons following.

1. That each partie shall bear his own proper charge he hath been at in traversing the suites at Law about the same, excepting so much as the 15 Acres of land about the Upper mill amounts unto. Which the Dewies are to have on the account of their Charges allowed the[m.]

2ly That the said John Sacket, Samuel Taylor, Nathaniel Williams, & Joseph Pomery shall have liberty to improove theirs untill the beginning of October next ensuing the date h[ere]of. But then are to desist, & deliver up unto the above Dewyes all their Right & Title in their land about the said saw mill of theirs that they have taken up, not executed. & all Intrest, & Claim in the stream which they have pleaded theirs by vertue of the town Grant.

3. That the above said Thomas, & Josiah Dewy, shall remitt the 50£ given them by the Court in the Action upon the Bond, unto the parties cast therein.

4. That the said Dewyes do ingague to give to the above said John Sacket & his Partners eight dayes work [by] a hand & a teame, & six dayes with an ha[nd] more towards the Remooving their present sawm[ill] from the Present stream to some other where they shall Choose to have it set, as also to relinquish & fall free, & discharge all bonds, & Obligations that ha[ve] been before this.

Unto the faithful performance of which agreement & the [con]ditions thereof, the parties herein agreeing, & ingaging do hereunto set their hand this 21, 2ᵐ 1685.

Witnesses
Samuel Marshfield ⎫   Both parties herein agreeing actua[lly]
Thomas Noble   ⎬   appeard 29th 7ᵐ 1685, & acknowledged
Edward Neale   ⎭   the same in all & each particulars
                        joyn[tly] & severally before the
                        County Court at Springfield. [127/128]

But when October Came, it appeared that Satan had been busy with them. Brother Pomery who had first mooved in this Mill business, as to the Streame, & also as to the building the same, said he had desisted according to the Covenant, & tendered money for the land Executed; also George Saxton said the Land & stream was his, & he would uphold them in their sawing: & if his right therein was questioned they might search the Court Records. The which doing they found a Couple of Deeds of sale of this, 15 Acres of land about their mill & all appertinances thereto, the first was a Deed of sale given by Brother Pomery to William Sacket on the Consideration of 40ˢ in silver down, this was dated February the 10, 1684, at which time the Mill & Land was released from an Attachment by a Replivee, but it was supposed to be a matter of latter transacting.

The other Deed was of sale by William Sacket to George Saxton about September, probably not much after he had bought it of Brother Pomery. & both acknowledged before Capt. Benjamin Newbery at Windsor (Assistent appertaining to Hartford Colony) about September, yet probably through mistake, dated by him Acknowledged the 9th of Febr. 1685. These were brought, & put into Mr. Holyoaks hand, Clark of Springfield Court, who in Recording of them finding them to be Deeds of the same Land that he had just recorded the Former Agreement Acknowledged at Springfield, about, put a stop to his proceedings therein, & gave notice thereof.

This matter being so foul Brother Josiah Dewy drew up this paper of Charges which he laid Brother Pomery under, which Brother Pomery refusing to Fall under, were put into the Pastor of the Churchs hand to be comunicated to the Church: Who, having signified it to Brother Pomery, desiring to speake with him before the Sabbath intimating, that unless he had reason to the Contrary he would Communicate them to the Church; But Brother Pomery not attending the Pastors request nor sending reason to the Contrary, he then the eight of November 1685 Communicated it to the Church in the Audience of the whole Assembly as Follows

October 27 1685. These are to acquaint the Church that I have dealt with Brother Joseph Pomery for some great Miscarriages, in the matter of, or respecting to his last Covenant, with my brother Thomas Dewy & myselfe. & he refusing to heare, I proceed to lay before the Church, wherein I suppose he is under the breach of severall Commands, as

1. The Breach of the 8th Command in a high degree in point of Honesty, in reising on, & improoving of an Estate which is none of his own; but is alienated by him out of his hand by Covenant.

2. The Breach of the ninth Command & that in point
    1. Of Truth, in saying we have no right at their Mill.
    2. In saying that to desist sawing for an hour is sufficient to answer the Disisting mentiond in the Covenant.
    & 3. In saying the value of the land is the thing intended in the Covenant.

2^(ly) In point of Faithfulness, as 1. In the matter of Covenant Breach, & going on Contrary to Covenant agreement. 2^(ly) In notorious, & gross Hypocrisy, in pretending Peace, & a finall Isue of all Differences amongst us in that last Agreement, but going on contrary thereunto.

Josiah Dewy

This was read, & Brother Thomas Dewy, being demanded whether he went along herewith & answering Yes, the matter was thus left in the Churches hand. & Brother Pomery not being there present, the Church Ordered that he should be warned by the Church to give in his Answer to these Charges the next Conference Day; who then presenting a paper by way of Confession, which being Considered he was ordered to Resort to the Pastor, & with him to make some particular addition bringing the Confession to the matter in the Charge more plainly, & so to fit it to be propounded to the Church, the which he doing was thus prepared, & in the Audience of the Whole assembly, read to the Church upon his desiring it might be read the 13^(th) 10^(m) 1685, as follows.

Brother Pomery's Acknowledgment

In Respect unto the Charges of the Breach of the 8^(th) & 9^(th) Commands, drawn up by brother Josiah Dewy, & gone along with by Brother Thomas Dewy, against me in respect unto the Mill Matter.

I acknowledge that I am very sorry, my heart doth ake & my Repentings are very much kindled; & it grieves me very much, to thinke that ever I should say or act any thing, contrary to that last Agreement made betwixt brother Thomas, & Josiah, Dewy, on the one party, & myselfe as one on the other party. These are therefore (in way of acknowledgment of the truth of the Charges to my great sorrow of heart) humbly to crave, & beg that the Church would with an Eye of Charity looke on me; & in favour, & love Cover & pass by any failing or failings, that they, or any of them have seen in me in that matter, or any other Alienation thereof, or any thing respecting the same & that they would be dayly mindful of & Constantly helping me forward in the wayes of Truth, & Righteousness by their Fervent & Effectuall Prayers unto the Almighty God, in the Name of his Son Jesus Christ on my behalfe, that he would graciously pardon me in any thing that I have done a miss in those, or any of those matters: & that by his Grace, & good spirit he would inable me to walk more to his Glory for the time to come.

And in particular, I humbly Crave brother Thomas, & Josiah, Dewy, to forgive, & pass by all, & any thing that hath been done by me, that hath been any wayes offencive unto them: so that there may be an open heart of Love found betwixt us for the time to come according as the Rules of the Gospell requireth. & I promise to endeavour for the time to come (God assisting) to avoid all Such Temptations. So I remain

Your Brother in the Fellowship of
the Gospell.   Joseph Pomery

Which Acknowledgment (being wholy his own draught, unless some few words given him to bring it more Close to the matter, & he taking a season when the Pastor of the Church was streightened of time it was not, it may be, so meetly drawn up in some expressions as otherwise, would have been but) being read to the Church, propounded that if they tooke it satisfactory to the Rule, they would express their Readiness to forgive & pass by his Failing in this Case, & help him with their prayers by the usuall sign of lifting up their hand. The which the Church doing, It was taken, & laid before him, with a briefe exhortation to a more watchfull eye over himselfe. & so looking up to God in the Case for help & pardon he was acquitted. [128/129]

Brother David Winchells Case of Suffield[65]

Among the manifold temptations that attended poore Suffield in their disorders, Brother David Winchell being carried away so far as to utter very unworthy, & unchristian Words against their reverend

Minister Mr. Younglove at Thomas Copplies, which being taken & carried to the Worshipfull Major John Pynchon of Springfield by way of Complaint, who calling the offenders before him & finding them sadly guilty bound them over to answer their Misdemeniour before the County Court March 29 at Norhampton; whereupon the weighing the Case the ofenders were finde 5£ a piece onely in that brother Winchall fell under his fault he had twenty shillings abated. Now Brother Winchell being in Church Relation with us, & his Case upon inquiry being gaind out of the County Records he was privatly acquainted with what would be the Church Proceeding with him unless he saw meet to prevent the same by giving in an Acknowledgment of his Fault. And thereupon he on the 13th day of the 4m on Sacrament day presented this Confession following.

Brother Winchils Acknowledgment the 13th 4m 1686

To the Rev. Mr. Taylor Pastor, to gether with the Church of Christ at Westfield.

These Lines may Certify you, that whereas a Temptation over-setting me, in respect unto the Rev. Mr. Younglove, so as I unadvisedly, Rashly, & Offencively reflected against him, some of the expressions of his Sermon: therein making a bad use of them, as saying he was not the man, Isa. 51.7, & in that he said by way of Allusion to Sinners backwardness to come to God, that he that was in debt would not indure to come to the book: & that he that had on old ulcer would not indure to have it searched, I say I did unworthily retort upon himselfe. But I was Surprized with a Temptation e're I was aware, & do abhor the words I spake as very Evill, Sinfull, & Offencive, both to God, Mr. Younglove, & may justly be so to yourselves, with all their Aggravations: & do desire I may be helpt by Gods good spirit to se more of, & be more humbled for my folly herein. And wherein I fall short of what the Rule, & Duty requires, I am willing to receive light from any. And being in Covenant Relation to yourselves & sensible of matter of offence herein, I desire you would remit what e'ver is offencive therein: & that you would help me with your prayers to God that he would pardon the Same: & sanctify my present Lot, that it may be in very faithfulness &

that by his Grace I may be inabled to walke more to his Glory, I remain,
Your Brother in the Fellowship of the Gospell
David Winchill

Which Acknowledgment being in substance formerly sent as a letter (as is Superscribed) being at the time specified before, read to the Church's & ownd by him, was voted by the Church satisfactory, & so advising him to Watchfulness for the time to come & praying over the Case the Churches absolution of the offence was laid before him by way of acquittance.

[Joseph Pomery's Case]

* * * * * * having before prepared was raising their Saw Mill & at Pochassuck, & he having disguised himselfe by drink & being treated about the same made this acknowledgment in the Assembly upon the Lords day to the Church July 24, 1687.

There being a report Scattered up & down touching myselfe as that upon the day of the raising our Saw mill I should be overcome with Drinke, & I myselfe being inquired of touching the same, must acknowledge that altho' it then appeared to me under the Consideration of the Worke before us, that I had need to take something more than at other times, yet I was beguiled to take more than I dare excuse myselfe therein, or than was expedient; yea, so much as was justly scandallous to the Gospell, the which hath been a greate Exercise to my Spirit in the Consideration thereof. And altho' I should have tooke it to have been a kindness in them that were with me then, if they would on the next day, when with mee, have treated me amongst themselves, (both for my own sake & that the Gospell of Christ might not have been reproached thereby) & so have kept it Secret: yet understanding that its made publick to the Reproach of Religion, & the Relation I stande in; & that my Failing herein is so Circumstanced that nothing less than an open acknowledgment of my Repentance, seems to answer that Relative duty I stand in; nor to cleare the Church, & Intrest of Christ from Reproach,

nor to gain your Christian Charity towards mee in this Case, I do here openly declare my Sorrow on this account; & earnest beg your Prayers to God for mee, that he would shew me mercy & grant me Strength against all such Temptations for the time to come. I Remain
Your Sorrowfull, & Unworthy Brother in the
Fellowship of the Gospell   Joseph Pomery

Which Confession being voted Satisfactory, & he laid under an Exhortation to true Repentance & Watchfulness for the time to come he was absolved: & so concluding with Prayer the Assembly was dismissed.[66]

Sister Abigail Bush[67] being Charged by her Brother John Lee, For calling him in derision John Walter, & his Wife Mrs. Sarah Lee, for saying of her Father Walter Lee, in anger, she would give a piece of eight which was all the money she had to send him out of the Land, & upon his being about to Marry again, that he married not for Love. And that he was as hot as a Skunk, & the woman as hot as a Bitch. She was treated with about the same: & readily acknowledged all, unless that about her father, the which she altogether denied that ever She said so of him; or remembered any thing of it. And her brothers proofe failing him in those particulars, we proceeded & took her Confession of her repentance & read it the 18 2ᵐ 1697 as follows

As for the things whereof my brother hath Charged me, I acknowledge as far as I remember that I did call him John Walter, yet not thinking thereby to reflect upon my Father at all, but as having heard others so call him. And I [129/130] * * * * * * I calld his Wife, Mrs. Sarah Lee, in foolishness. For which I am grieved, & sorry in my heart for my Sin therein.
And as for that which argues my undutifull Expressions about my father, as that I would give money to Send him out of the Countrey, etc., I remember it not. But the other expression, of him, as that he married not for Love, & of that said of my mother too much unchristian here to be mention'd, I acknowledge with griefe & Sorrow of heart, that I have sinfully offended therein: & desire to beare the sense thereof with sorrow of Heart before God for pardon thereof. And wherein I have offended either my Parents, or Brother, or others, or this Church I desire they would overlooke it, & pass it by: & help me with their

Prayers to God, that he would be gracious unto mee, pardon, the same, & enable mee for the time to Come to walke more uprightly, & as becometh the Gospell of Christ, the Which I hope he will enable mee to attain unto.

This Confession being voted satisfactory, a briefe exhortation was laid upon her to watchfulness, & to be very tender of Parentall honour She was acquitted, & the whole was Concluded with a briefe Prayer.

Suffield Concerns[68]

The Address of Severall Members of severall Churches that were inhabitants of Suffield dated 1st of the 10m 1697
To the Rev. Mr. Edward Taylor, & the Church of Christ at Westfield.
Rev. & Beloved in the Lord.
Altho' it hath pleased the Lord so favourably to Smile upon us, & to Crown our endeavours with success, As far, as that we may haply now say, wee are Supplied at present with an able, hopefull, & promising young gentleman, laboring amongst us in the worke of the Ministry: yet notwithstanding there is a Circumstance between him, & us, lies as a bar in the way to obstruct our Embodying together, & settling him in office over us, at present. Now the greate Impediment, or obstruction in our way, is a Difference in judgment. We have declared to him, & now declare to your selves, that according to the Platform of Church Discipline, agreed on by the Synod; & the generall Practice of the Churches, we can, & should freely, & heartily close with him & settle him in office amongst us as to matter of judgment which motion of ours the Rev. Mr. Benjamin Ruggles seems not to comply withall, but hath declared that his Principalls are presbyterian principalls: & desires to gather a presbyterian Church: & to bee settled a presbyterian Minister. Now this being a new way to us, contrary to what we have been taught & Practiced hitherto; we think it not meet, or safe to ingage herein, without the Counsill of & advice of the Godly wise about us: & accordingly we whose names are under written, do now make our application to your selves, to gether with the Elders & brethren of other churches adjacent, to give us advice in this weighty, & momentous Concern.
Rev. & Beloved; we would not in the least cast any reflection upon the Reverend Mr. Ruggles, tho' of a Contrary perswasion to ourselves.

Yet we who are the present Actors upon the Stage, & being now to lay a Foundation & that not onely for ourselves, but for posterity, we look upon it to be our Duty to act very warily herein: & to endeavour to lay such a foundation as that not onely we may have Comfort in it, while we live, but that our Children also, & such as shall survive us, may have the benefit, of what we now do, when we shall go off the stage, & be actors here no more.

The Question which we do now State, & present to your view & syncerely desire a Candid Resolution of is this: Circumstances between the Rev. Mr. Ruggles & ourselves being as have been expresst, & we being desirous, if it might be with a spirit of Love, & Unity to settle him amongst us

How far we may Comply with Mr. Ruggles his desires, without Sin, & breach of Rule? & if in case wee may not Comply, then what is our next work to do?

And we beseech the Lord, who is the onely wise Counselour & who is wonderfull in Counsill, so to direct, & Counsill yourselves, as that you may be able by your grave, & sage Counsill to set us in such a Good way, as that there may be no jarring, Discord, or Scism amongst us: but on the Contrary, that we may sweetly, & harmoniously agree, Cordially, & Heartily close with each other: that we may be of one Heart, & one way to serve the Lord: that being knit together in Love, & setting to with one sholder the work of God amongst us, may be carried on with facility: & the House of God built without the noise of Hammers. & in fine, our hearts desire to God is, that what is now acted & done in this affair, may be that which may most promote, & advance the Honour, & intrest of Christ: Conduce to the Comfort, & benefit of ourselves whilst we live, & of our Children, & Successours, when our hoary Heads shall be laid in the Dust.

Dated	Your servants in the Cause of Christ	
Suffield	Anthony Austin, Sr.	Victory Sikes
December	John Pengilly	Jonathan Taylor
the 1st 1697	David Winchill	Samuel Rent
	John Hanchett	Nathaniel Harmer

A Reply to this Address given by our Church.

To our Brethren of Suffield Members in Church-fellowship, in Severall Churches of Christ in the Countrey, Grace, Mercy, & Peace be multiplied.

We have read, & Consider'd your address made unto us: & are sorry to finde you so Constrain'd to Apostasy from the Practice of the Churches of Christ in the Country, by Mr. Ruggles, to a new practice, upon the terms of his settlement with you. & do desire him that is Mighty in Counsill to give you counsill in this Case. And so far as we may in any measure be instrumentall thereof, we propounde to you what we judge to be from him with us, as follows.

1. For your first enquiry, we say we shall pass it over & refer you to our answer given to the other.

2. As for the other Enquiry, thus, If we may not be advised to the terms given us, then what may be our next worke to doe?

1. We Cannot advise you to come up to Such terms. For the Considerations of the Beginnings of New-England & of Church Discipline here admitt of Such Circumstances, that were we not so Cleare, whether the Congregationall, or Presbyterian practice was most Evangelicall, & of Christ, we could not easily advise against the Same. For when we look on those Worthy, & Renowned men of God, that laid the Foundation here, Men, who for Naturall Abilities of Choicest Endowments, who for Acquired Accomplishments of Depth of Learning; who for Supernaturall Qualifications of Sanctifying Grace, inferiour to few in the learned part of the World: & also for the persecution that they sustain'd for the Discipline of Christ in his Churches under Prelacy in their Native Countrey; & that they, & their Children after them, might enjoy Church-Fellowship, & the Communion of Saints in a way purely Evangellicall, & Christ therein, left Father, & Mother, Brethren, & Sisters, [130/131] Friends, & Relations, Homes, & Lands, to follow Christ in a Wilderness. And as the Result of much reading both Ancient, & Modern Authors, much Dispute amongst themselves, much in Searching after the minde of God in the Scriptures, & much in Prayer to God for his Guidence; & also Standing cleare from all byassing Temptations one

way or other, We say, that these men should be left of God herein, to lead all into Errour, & Falshood, we cannot easily be brought to believe. And further upon the begining of our present practice, the Able & Godly Authority of the Countrey, after a time of experiencing the practice of this Way, Calling a Synod to give in a Moddle of Church Discipline from the Scriptures: & having that drawn up, which is professt, & practiced by these Churches ever since (& since hath been envigorated by Synod upon Synod) did Confirm & Establish the same to be attended on by Gods people here, the Practice whereof, God hath been pleased graciously to own for sixty years & more, in giving Such a blessing here upon in Such a Signall way, as is beyond all instances in all Humane History that ever we have read, or heard of, in all the World. So that wee cannot but account all Counsill to any such practice; that should turn upon them herein, as left of God, Rash, Unwarrantable, & Sinfull.

2^{ly} That as you have laid Mr. Ruggles under a Call; upon the same supposition which we take to bee that all the world in a settled way of the Gospell proceed upon (viz, that the Minister calld, will go on in his Practice according to the Order of the Churches in the Countrey) so now our advice is, that you do more explicitly renew your address unto him, that he would go on with you according to the Establisht order of the Churches of Christ in the Countrey.

3. In Case he accepts not on these terms, we account it unreasonable for any mans-sake, to advise you to withdraw from the churches of Christ here, in their establisht order from their beginning. You are to attend the Footsteps of the Flock, Cant. 1.8, & we judge it your Duty under this Case to Continue your Relation each unto the Church whereunto he belongs, as a member, unless by reason of Distance, any of you see meet to remoove the same to any Church neere, walking in Gospell order.

4. Our further advice, & Exhortation to you is, that you take all speciall heed, & more especially under your present Circumstances to hold forth an Holy, Humble, Christlike spirit of Practicall Piety in the Sight of all: that if any should reflect against you in this you may have their very Consciences rise up against themselves on your defence, as mentainers of the First Love, Piety, & Order of these Churches, from which they are the Leaders into Apostacy, Decay, & into the Subversion of the same. Now desiring that you may be carrying on the truth in Love,

Eph. 4.15, & increasing in Christ the Head in all-things, we recommend you to his Grace, & remain

Your Brethren, & Friends in the
Fellowship of the Gospell in the

⎧ Sent the ⎫
⎨ 3ᵈ 1ᵐ ⎬ Church of Christ at Westfield as
⎩ 1697/8 ⎭ attests Edward Taylor Pastor of
the Same.

12 of 9ᵇᵉʳ 1700

Deacon Josiah Dewy, & his Wife had their Dismissions to carry on & to joyn to the Church that was upon gathering in a place about eight miles on Hartford Side Norwich, called at present Lebanon. And also it was at this time determined to call brother Joseph Pomery, & his Wife members in Church fellowship with us, to give satisfaction for their going a way from us & so abiding, contrary to the Duties of their Covenant without liberty from the Church or any desiring of the same. & answerably a letter was writ & sentt to them dated 15.9.1700.[69]

The Members in Church State, at Suffield pertaining to Severall Churches in other places, seeing Mr. Ruggles like to lead them in other paths than what the Orders of the Churchs of Christ in the Countrey had walkt in, made the matter some what difficult as to its procedure, in so much, that in a town meeting the town voted or agreed to advise in this Case with the County Court sitting in Springfield March   who advised them according to Law to ta[ke] the advice of Neighbouring Elders in the Case the which they did & wrote to us as follows.

To the Rev. Mr. Edward Taylor Pastor
of the Church of Christ in Westfield

Rev. Sir:

After all due satisfactions to yourselfe & yours, these may acquaint you, that at a Legall town Meeting of the Inhabitants of Suffield held Mar. 23, 1698 it was there unanimously agreed on, & Voted according to the advice of the Court to invite the Rev. Mr. Stoddard, yourselfe, Mr. Williams, Mr. Brewer (who were nominated by the Court) & to adde to them the Rev. Mr. Mather of Windsor, to come upon the place in some convenient time, as the town shall after agree on, to advise the Rev. Mr. Ruggles, & ourselves respecting our present Circumstances, in order to his settlement amongst us in the Worke of the Ministry, according as the Law directts: It was also agreed to invite those Rev. Elders upon the place (on said account) the last tuesday of this instantt April. And therefore it is our desire that you will please to grant us your presence upon this account at that time.

Suffield	Signd by	Thomas Roming
Apr. 11 1698		Thomas Huxly
		John Mighil, Sr.
	In the name of	Thomas Coply
	the inhabitants	Joseph Harma[r]
		Selectmen

These things disturbed Mr. Ruggles, who in that he could not hinder the towns proceeding to attend the Courts advice, labour'd to interrupt it by writing in the name of some to the same Elders to come to gather to the place to gather a Church & to ordain him [131/132] amongst them their officer upon the same day, viz, the last tuesday of Aprill, the Coppy of which letter to us was as follows,

To the Rev. Mr. Edward Taylor, Pastor
& to the Church of Christ in Westfield.

Grace, Mercy, & Peace be multiplied in our Lord Jesus. These may signify unto yourselves, that we by the Grace of God, having some sense of the want, & desiring the benefitts, priviledges, & advantages of Gods house: & having made our address to the Honored Court, in the last sessions, for their approbation, & encouragment for our proceeding, to bring ourselves into a more orderly, & politicall Church form: & being favorably answer'd according to the intent of our Petition; We thought it good, as to give you timely, & mature Notice of it, so to desire your Candide Concurrance with us, & approbation of our proceedings, & therefore it is our Desire, & request, that you would please to grant us the presence of the Rev. Elder, & the Messengers of your Church, at Suffield on the last tuesday of this Aprill instant, in order to the Settling of a Church, & Ordination of Mr. Benjamin Ruggles amongst us: Not

further to adde, save onely our earnest entreaties to you all, to address the throne of Grace with your supplications on our behalfe, that the God of all grace will please to direct us, in this greate affair so to mannage & demean ourselves, as may conduce to the glory of God, & to the advancement of the Cause of Christ, & to our mutuall Edification building up, & establishment, in the Service of our Redeemer, & in the most Holy faith of our Lord Jesus Christ.
Yours in the Lord.

6th April
A.D. 1698 }

Benjamin Ruggles.

In the Name, & by the Desire of those that are desirous, then to be gatherd into, & Settled in, a Church State.

This strange, & Factious letter caused greate displeasure. The Pastor of this Church tooke no notice of it, resolving to attend at the place upon the day in the matter of the towns letter according to the advice of the Court, to make peace, but when the day came not being well in health did not go. Mr. Stoddard, & Mr. William, not of Hatfield (who was wrote to) but of Dearfield, went to the place, & some others: & made a shift to remoove some difficulties, that was laid in the way against some of disorderly walking, & so bringing to some little better agreement amongst themselves brought Mr. Ruggles to promise that his proceeding with them in order to admissions should be by a bringing, whom he admitted to make a Profession of their Faith, & to admit by the major Vote of the Brethren. & so they layd by the ordination & Church Gathering till the last Wednsday in May following: & that the Elders & Churches sentt to should then appeare to assist in the Worke. But none other letters should be sent to them. Whereupon some scrupled saying then there was no Call.

Brother David Winchill, brother John Hanchett, & his Wife, & Brother Thomas Smith all inhabitants of Suffield being members in Fulcommunion amongst us desired not their Recommendations to the Work from us but onely their liberty, which if they saw meet not to use, their state might abide firm with us. David Winchill, & Thomas Smith made use of it, & proceeded with them. John Hanchet & his Wife, did not use itt.

The day coming, Mr. Stoddard, the Williams, Mr. Chauncy of Hadly, & Mr. Brewer with some brethren of their Churches appeared, & Carried on the Work: those Members of ours & Springfield Church had their liberties to proceed. The Members belonging to the Bay Churches as Ipswitch, Rowly, etc., & one of Windsor Church in fulcommunion had no dismissions, Recomendation, etc., yet were not withstanding urged, & proceeded, & covenanted here, to greate offence of severall. This was the first instance in these parts, if not in the whole Countrey, of Members in express Covenant Relation with other Churches that were torn away without Dismission or liberty. [132/133]

1699

Brother Samuel Bushes Acknowledgment of the account of his telling Colonall Pynchon, who on his wedden Contrack asked him whether he had the Clarks Certificate, answerd, that he had one but he had lost it, Made 22 3ᵐ 1699.[70]

Whereas, I understand, that my answer upon my Wedden day to Colonall Pynchon, who askt me whether I had the Clarks Certificate, & I thro' ignorance & inconsiderateness, not thinking it to be any other than a note to certify that I was published according to Law; & being hurryed in the morning before I went to Springfield, till I thought the Clark was gone from home about his business, it was moved that a note from an other person to intimate this matter of publishment was attended according to Law, might serve, I went with another to certify the thing, not designing but to pay the Clark what was his due. & upon such a bottom standing, I answerd to the Question; that I had one, but I had lost it. But the matter since being looked into; I am Convinced that I have Sin'd & done evill in so saying: & desire to beare the sense thereof upon my heart before God & desire also that the Offence hereof may be passed over by the Church and by any other offended thereat. & that they would help me with their prayers to be more watchfull for the time to Come.

This Confession being read in the assembly was accepted by the Church, & voted. & So a briefe advice was given him to Watchfulness, & chiefly to se that the beginning of matters be laid right, for if not commonly temptations afterwards will be ready to rush over things not warrantable but evill & so he was dismisst.

Pochassuck Matters occasiond by the Petition following.[71]

We whose names are underwritten being sensible of the greate necessity of having an Highway laid out from Westfield town to the upper end of Pochassuck Meadow, & we have requested the Select men to lay us out a way there, which they have refused to do, which layes us under a necessity of petitioning up to the Sessions for reliefe in this case.　　　　Wherefore we the Subscribers of this Petition, do humbly request of this Honored Court, that they would be pleased to order, & state us out a way.　　　　That we must have a way to our houses, & lands, that so we may pass freely without any molestation, & without being accounted transgressors, is such a notorious truth: that nobody will deny it: & to produce reason for it, we shall count labour lost.　　　　But the main end of this our Petition is, that we may have an Order from this Court, for an Highway to be continued, where it has been ever since it was a town & there men doe quietly, & peaceably injoyed it ever since we had any occasion that way; till of late we have been interrupted. & therefore we your Humble Petitioners request a Continuation of said way, which we trust your Honors will readily comply with, considering these reasons.

The first Consideration that we shall moove to your honors is the Antiquity of this way that we petition for. For it has been a way time out of minde. The English improove it ever since it was a town. & the Indians before that: time out of minde: which by the Laws of England (as your honors well know) it ought, & would be a high way for all that have occasion to use it. Besides some presidents may be produced of High way[s] that have been laid out upon the like circumstan[ce] besides this many highwayes in this Land are onely by antiquity.

A second thing that we shall moove to your honours [is] the great inconveniency of having a way at any ot[her] place for either we must go over other mens l[and] or else we must go a greate way about. & if we m[ay] be permitted to go over other mens lands, it is a Co[nsi]derable way about, & chargeable to make a way [and] if we must go round about its a further way. [Be]sides the cost, of making a way there [will] be Considerable which burden will be too heavy f[or] us to undergo. There-

fore we request of your Hon[ours] the high way may be continued wher‹
we ha[ve] been wanted to go: & that your Honours would be pleas[ed
to Consider our Case, & Speedily order us a way f[or] our Case i‹
difficult. For now we cannot pers[ue] the work of our Calling, nor dc
these Civill Duties [which] are required of us, nor attend the publich
wors[hip] of God without being counted trespassers. Which [con]sider‹
ing these things, we hope your Honours will gran[t] our request, & sc
we leave our Case, praying Go[d that] he would be pleased to direct you
in this & all ca[ses] that come before you—
We take leave to Subscribe ourselves your Honours Hum[ble
Petitioners

Isaak Phelps
Nathaniel Weller
Nathaniel Bancroft
Jedidia Dewy
Matthew Noble
James Noble
John Shephard

David Ashly
Richard Church
Samuel Bush
John Sacket
Adijah Dewy
Hezekiah Phelps
Thomas Brown
John Phelps

Received in Court of Sessions at Northampton Decemb. 3. 1701
attest John Pynchon Cl[erk][72] a true Coppy of the Originall upor
file.

This Scrible nonsensicall, tautologicall & illogicall writ by Pomery
the Lawyer fu[ll][73] of Falshoods & Untruths from the first to the [last] of
it, where for a close they are brought i[n] as so circumstanced under ar
impossibili[ty] to go about the Concerns of their Private i[m]ploymen‹
or the Publick worship of God wit[h]out being counted Trespassors. &
yet but two, or three of the Petitioners were dwel[ling] at Pochassuck, &
concernd in the way desire[d] & in that the select men here sought to
a[re] also Petitioners, etc., did create no smal[l] stir in the Church, for the
four first men[ti]on'd being in Church fellowship did inconsideratly
some at least, set their hands to itt, being willing to have a way settled for
the[ir] Neighbours at Pochassuck & their own goi[ng] thither, in that
there was none but what was made by occasionall, & Cattles going i[n
to the Woods while all things lay in commo[n] since used, save onely
part of it, viz, on th[e] side the river hath been by the town laid out [as] a

way for the town Use. But after some deb[ate] about it, they acknowledged their Errou[rs] in point of truth, & desired the Church to [ad]mit
the same & to help them with their pray[ers] the which was passt under
the Vote of the Church [as] Acceptable. & so all were thro' grace took.
[133/134]

1704

The Following Coppies were sent to
the ministers of this County & read
by mee this 24 day of 10^m in the
whole assembly after the publick
worship was over, in order unto
the visits here urged upon.[74]

To the Rev. Solomon Stoddard, Pastor
of the Church of Christ at Northamton
to be Communicated to the Association

Deare Brethren   { Cambridge
                                                     { Nov. 6. 1704

The Ministers, who sometimes met at Cambridge, have thought it
proper to entertain you with certain proposalls, agreed a while a goe by a
much greater Convocation at Boston. The Coppy of which proposalls
here enclosed will sufficiently give you to understand the intentions of
them: & we have all possible reason to believe your good affections for
Such intentions.

Its well known, that the Pastors who have taken the pains, personally to visit their flocks; & suitably, prudently, & faithfully address all
persons in them upon the greate Concerns of their Everlasting Happiness, have had an Unknown success attending their Holy Labours.
Chrysostom, Austin, etc., an encouraging example, for Such labours, in
after Ages. All the publick Sermons in the days of Calvin did not more
good at Geneva, than the private Visits, which the Severall Ministers of
the Citie by joynt Consent, made unto the severall Families under their
Charge. Both Englands have seen greate instances of Diligence, &

Advantage in their discharge of the Evangellicall Ministry. But that the Pastors of our Churches may the more Comfortably enjoy the assistance of one an other, which doubtless all finde more than a little needfull for them, under the Difficulties which in their Ministry they often meet withall, you are very sensible how usefull their well formed Associations may be unto them. The most early times of New England propounded them, & practiced them: our Churches did betime feell the benefit of them; & it is to be hoped, that where such Associations have been already formed, they will be lively mentaind, & preserved: & usefully Carried on; & that where they are not yet formed the Lord will stir up his servants to Consider what they shall do that they may not incur the inconveniency of him that is alone.

But there is one thing more that hath been greatly desired, & never yet so fully attain'd unto, viz, that the severall Associations of Ministers may Uphold some Communion & Correspondency with one an other; & that they would freely Communicate unto each others by Letters that whatever they may apprehend a watchfull regard unto the greate Intrest of Religion among us may call to be Considered.

It is with Speciall respect unto this Design, that the Ministers of the Association sometimes meeting in Cambridge do now make this assay; & having laid these things before you, do heartily recommend, you & all your Studies to serve him unto the blessing of the Lord.

They do it by the hand of
Sirs, Yours .
Samuel Willard, Moderator

To the Reverend
to bee Communicated
Boston 1^d 4^m 1704

To serve the Greate intention of Religion which is lamentably decaying in the Countrey, it is proposed

1. That the Pastors of the Churches do personally Discourse with the Young people in their flocks & with all possible prudence, & goodness endeavour to win their Consent to the Covenant of Grace in all the glorious articles of it.
2. That unto this purpose the Pastors do take up the labourious, but

Engaging practice of making their personall visits unto all the families that belong unto their Congregations.

3. That the Pastors Communicate to their people in this way of proceeding as far as they can publickly, & solemnly to Recognize the Covenant of God, & to come unto such a degree of the Church State, as they shall be made willing to take their station in; but not to leave off till they shall be qualified for, & perswaded to Communion with the Church in all Speciall Ordinances.

4. That for such as have submitted to the Government of Christ in any of his Churches, no Pastors of any other Churches any way go to shelter them under their wing from the Discipline of those from whom they have not been fairly recommended.

5. That they who have not actually Recognized their subjection unto the Discipline of Christ in his Church, yet should, either upon their Obstinate refusall of such a subjection, or their falling into other Scandalls, be faithfully treated with proper Admonitions, About the Method, & Manner of managing of which Admonitions, the Pastors with their severall Churches, will be left to the exercise their own Discretion.

6. It is desired, & intended, if the Lord please, that at the Generall Convention of the Ministers there may be given in, by each of the Pastors present, an account of their proceedings, & success in that Holy work undertaking, which hath been proposed: that so the Lord may have the Glory of his Grace & that the Condition of Religion in the Countrey may be the better known, & served among us.

7. As a subservancy to these greate & Good intentions it is proposed, that the Associations of the Ministers in the severall parts of the Countrey, may bee strengthened, & that the severall Associations may by letters hold more free Communications with one another.

Voted & Unanimously Consented unto.[75]

Touching our Brethren Steven Kellog & Sergant Joseph Mawdsly,[76] who, did somewhat boggle at our Church fasts which in the wintertime wee had attended once a month ever since we were in a Church State, except those few years that we had a monthly lectures up, & at length they wholy desisted & pleade against as unlawfull being stated fasts. Whereupon on the 27th of March 1710, the last Fast that winter Brother

Kellog being there, & Sergnt Mawdsly the day before setting forth upon a journey to the Bay I enquired of Brother Kellog the reason why [134/135] they withdrew from the Duty of Fasting & Prayer with the Church? His reply was in effect thus, He was not cleare touching the Lawfullness of the stating of them. For stated fasts were held unlawull by the Consociation of the Elders in the Bay.[77] It was replied that I had Evidenced on these words Sanctify a Fast, Call a Solemn assembly, that God required his People to set dayes a partt for Fasting & prayer: & I had given instances in the Practice of Gods people as the Church in Babylon, for 70 years together keeping monthly Fasts, & of the Fasting of the Pharace twice in the week instanced in by our Saviour who onely instanced in what was commendable in him, & Christs not finding fault in that matter though he found fault with the Pharisees Pride, was a manifest approving of the fixt fast, twice a week: & also of Annas the Prophetess, her Fasting day & night for a long time, Luke 2.37, Luke 18.12,14: & told him that if he now saw meet to acknowledge his Errour & promise reformation he might make his peace with the Church. He said he saw it not this way or to the same Effect. & he would come unto me & shew me the booke. I told him that if he did not do what I offerd him, I layed them under the Charge of Breaking of Covenant with God & the Church. For in the Church Covenant he had Solemnly promised to walk with this Church of Christ in obedience upon all Gospell Ordinances & here was the Gospell Ordinance of Fasting & Prayer that he had withdrawn from, the Winter before this I think he was but twice at it. & this winter not once but now (which he ownd afterwards that he came not to it as to a Fast) & so I orderd him & Brother Mawdsly to appeare before the Church the next Conference day which was 12th 2m 1710.

In this Interim they came to mee & brought a book & I read the Matter & told them that the Book in that matter was very Authodox, & I easely went along with them. For they spoke against stated Fasting that were fixt to be kept in the Season Stated, when it came every yeare, & so yearly for ever. Our monthly fasts were no such things, but were Occasionall fasts, occasion'd by the Circumstances of Divine Providence, & according to the Fasts of Gods people in Scripture, & the practice of the Churches in New England. But all I could say was no light to them, & they concluded that the Church would not Judg as I did. I replied, that if so, I would suspend them, & rebuke the Church. Then they desired time to take Counsill: I told them that I stood in no need of Councill as to my proceeding: & they would have time enough to take Councill when we had done our Duty. They replied that perhaps they might receive light & give satisfaction. Whereupon I granted time. They desired me to direct them to whom to go: I told them to go to whom they pleased & at length they went to Mr. Stoddard, & desired me to write their case to him, & accordingly I did[78] & they received Conviction from him, that our fasts were not Stated Fasts but Occasionall & with much adoe was brought to Confess their Errour, which on the next day being Conference day I ordered them to appeare 11^d 2^m duly owned, as follows.

That they not being so clear as to our Monthly fasts, were not so easy under them, but meeting with that book of the Confederacy Elders before laying down that Stated fasts were unlawfull, & they knowing no other Fasts Stated, but our monthly fasts, took our monthly fasts to be Stated fasts, but having now received light in the matter they saw that they had erred, & desired the Church to pass by the Offence thereof & to help them against the same by their prayers, & they promised by the assistance of divine Grace to endeavour to attend upon the same for the time to come. Which Confession being ownd by them was voted satisfactory & so with a briefe Exhortation they were acquitted.

Rebecca Ashlys Case who being with child by Fornication after she was recovered of her lying in gave in this Confession to the Church which was took in writing 4th 4^m 1707[79]

Where as to my greate sorrow, publick shame & greate Sin I have been Carryed away by overbearing temptation to the transgressing God's law that saith, thou shalt not Comit Adultery, in severall acts with John Mawdsly. & hereby have indeed given Gods people just ground to be offended with me, & to turn me out of the hearts & respect of Gods people whose Charity I have wounded by my Sin, as well as my own Soule. Wherefore in Sorrow of heart, & sense of so greate a sin & Evill against God & my own Soule, as Whoredom is: the greate Trouble & griefe that I have hereby overwhelmed my dear & tender parents & other relations with, the greate dishonour to God herein & other Considerations that come upon me of an Heart burdening Nature, I say in the sense & sorrow of heart hereupon, I spread before the Church & people of God this my Confession & acknowledgment, earnestly desiring them to Compassionate mee in this Sorrowfull Condition that I have rusht myselfe into; that altho' they may be rejecting of mee, as an increaser of the Sinners & sorrows of the place, yet to pitty me & my poor Soul, to pardon my Sin & to help mee by their prayers to God for a true Sight of my sin, & that I may obtain a Pardon thereof from God. & oh! that I might be assisted by his Grace to true Repentance of this & all other Sins, & that I may obtain strength for the time to come to be more watchfull & to live as becomes the Gospell of Christ which I desire to do & promise by the Assistance of grace to endeavour after.

Your Servant Rebecca Ashly

This being read & propounded to the Church was accepted.

Sister Abigail Bush, her Case[80]

Brother Walter Lee complaining of his Daughter Abigail Bush as touching her Carriag as being unworthy he according to advice, took Goodman Taylor & Sergeant Nathaniel Phelps to go with him to treate her, who went the 4 of the 2ᵐ 1712 & demanded satisfaction of her for her bad carriage to her Father, telling him that she would shutt up his door if Sarah (her brother Johns Widow) came to live [135/136] with him there, or he took her to live there with him, asserting that the house stood in her hand: Claiming part of his homelot where his house stands to bee hers. And the Persons, viz, Goodman Taylor & Sergeant Phelps testify, that she refused to give him any Satisfaction, but said that it was her land: & that the Whole Lot (i.e., an acre & half) was hers, adding also that she never had had a farthing for what she had done for her father, since her own mother died nor since this last womans' death but that her Father had run up & down the town exclaiming against & slandering of her; & that is all she had for her pains. She being in the Garden when they came Sergeant Phelps told her what they came about & desired her to go in with them into the house that they might discourse about it. She said she was about her business, & would not go in with them: They told her that her Father was dissatisfied with her & they came to have her give him Satisfaction. She replied that she had done him no wrong & would give him no Satisfaction. These men also said that Widow Loomas & Hannah, John Flowers Wife & others heard the same. Whereupon she was Cited to appeare the next Conference which was April 8ᵗʰ where she appeared & being calld out the

natter was read to the church & she was calld to answer who acknowledged all & that she had offended in so doing, in a decent humble
manner desiring the Church to pass by her offence. & help her with
their prayers that God might pardon her sin & inable her against the
same endeavoring for the time to come to avoide the same.

The Church considering the Same set her a time of triall for two
months space in which time no thing appearing of unworthy carriage she
was calld out upon the 31 of June & the same matter read again before
the Church which she acknowledged & desired as before & so the
Church accepting the same absolved her.

Brother Stephen Kellogs Case[81]

Being at the raising a Barn where the weather being warm & much
Cider brought & after at Joseph Pixlies drinking with others, it was
reported that he was overtaken with drinke, but itt not being proved, he
being sensible that many were offended, stood up according to advice,
upon our Conference day, in the meeting of 17 4ᵐ 1712 & spake to this
effect. That he was sensible that he was a poor sinfull Creature apt to
offend in many things to his greate griefe, & if any had observed any
offence in him, he earnestly desired that they would pardon the same, &
help him with their prayers, & he hoped that God would inable him to
walke with a greater watchfulness over himselfe for the time to Come, or
in words to the same effect, which was acceptable to the Church & so all
things was an end.

Abiel Williams Case, she being ensnared by Young John Sacket[82]
& overcome to Comitt Fornication with him & was thereby got with
Child & after she had recoverd her lying in Gave in this Confession
Following, in the assembly upon the Lords day the 29 4ᵐ 1712.

I being left by God to be overborn by a temptation carried on upon
me by John Sacket the younger, to the breaking of the Seventh Comand,
a greate & scandalous sin, to the dishonour of God, & therefore to the
offending of Gods people, especially the Church of God, which is a
greate exercise to my Soule, & therefore I am desirous to be reconciled
both to God & his people, especially to the Church: that as they have
seen my fall they also might have a sight of the sorrow of my heart on
this account. Oh the sorrow of my heart is such in that I have thus Sind

against God, it wounds my Soule. Its with me first & last. The publick shame is greate, but oh! the Dishonour of God is greater: the thoughts hereof, how heavy are they upon mee on this account? I earnestly beg that you would pardon me as to the offence that I have hereby given you: & that you would receive me into your Charity which I have wounded, & that you would help me with your prayers unto God for mee that he would pardon my sin & pour out his spirit upon mee. & bring mee up to himselfe in Christ & for the time to Come that he would Secure mee from overbearing temptations & enable me to resist all the assaults of the Adversary. That I might walk Humbly & without offence & come to an Holie Closing with all Gods Rules both in the inward & outward man: & that I might have true & saving repentance, all my dayes, not onely of this Sin but also of all other Sins; & that I may have true Gospell Faith in Christ. All which by the help of God I shall, & hope to, be syncerely Endeavouring after & so I remain Your Sorrowfull Servant.

Abiel Williams

This Confession tooke from her own mouth 31 3ᵐ 1712 & now read & ownd by her, was with her case propounded to the Church who accepted of it & so she was absolved & then presst on to a watchfulness over herselfe & a humble walking with God.

Brother Stephen Kellogs Case. Hee being Complained against as being disordered by drinking & the report being all over the town, I enquired into the Same. Brother Samuel Bush asserted that Samuel Loomas said at his house to this Effect, that he was much disquieted, or disordered by drink (as he judged For he saw him not drink) yet he could not well get out of his Chair & yet was Oft shifting up & down; that his Speech was disordered, & some expressions were such as he took his reason to be disordered. The same matter did John Bancroft assert & said Daniel Bag could say as much & also young John Gun. Brother John Shephard asserted that he judged he had drunk too much, that he was much disordered thereby, his Speech was so much, it was offencive or to that effect. Nehemiah Loomas at whose house he was late at night, being sought to Speake what he observed, would not testify any thing, yet would not clear him but said his brother William could say more than he, but yet he said that he was very talkative or Words to the same import. But I proceeded no further.

Wherefore I sent for Brother Kellog & discoursed him about the matter. He in the upshot, gave in this Confession to the Church upon the 11th of March 1712/13.

I having been treated touching a matter of Offence in mee, as having drunk Cider or Other matters to offence, & that there hath been given in severall Testimonies to Convict of the same (tho' none of them to charge me as being drunke, as I am informed) & being sensible that I have taken more than is meet & that others, I perceive, did observe it in me, & thereby were offended: which matter is unto mee hearty sorrow, & griefe, I doe indeed fall under the same: & with griefe of heart bewaile it: bewailing that I should give offence thereby, to God, & his people, scandalize Religion, & bring reproach to myselfe, & mine own name, & also wound the Charity of Gods people. It is a hard thing, & burdensus griefe to my Soule. [136/137]

That therefore, as you have seen mine offence, So I Spreade before you the sorrow of my heart for the same. I do here acknowledge that its very grievous to me to think on it & do beg that you would pass by all the Offenciveness that my falls have produced in you & still allow mee your Charity, & help me with your prayers to God for me, that he would keep me from all Offence, for the time to come: & I shall endeavour by the Grace of God to walke more watchfully, & Warily.

Upon the reading of this & his owning of it, it was propounded to the Church who accepted of it & voted for his absolution: whereupon he was acquitted & laid under a short Exhortation & so restored.

Brother Benjamin Smiths case as follows.[83]

When Colonall Partridge, Justice Partridg Judge of the Probates of Will, & other persons in Concern in this matter, Mr. Pynchon, Clerk of the court of Probate & Mr. Pomery the Queens Attorney, etc., were at Westfield to settle Estates & Wills about May 1712,[84] Lawyer Pomery going home with Brother Benjamin Smith to his house drew up I suppose upon his advice a letter to the Court at Northampton tending to desire the Court touching Walter Lee of Westfield to seclude him from Law, or to put him under Guardians as being old & very fickle, or not ftt to mannage his Conserns, (I have not the Petition by mee) but it was

writ in the name of Certain inhabitants of Westfield to be subscribed b[
them. Brother Benjamin Smith brought it to me to Subscribe it. I wa[
surprized, when I saw it considering it an unrighteous thing, & not to b[
supported, judging it to be a seeking to put him out of the Law or unde[
Guardians, etc., & refused to Subscribe it. He desired me to draw up[
petition * * * as not being any room to seeke any thing to help th[
matter, he doubted * * * that the Court could do anything to restrai[
Walter Lee from disposing of his Estate, unless they did some way o[
other debar him of the law which I could not see nor did I desire. Bu[
Benjamin [Smith] still urged me to take it into Consideration & to d[
what I could, which I complied with & wrote up this Petition following

To her Majesties court of the Generall Sessions of the Peac[
held at Northampton, the first Tuesday in March 1711/12[
All Health.

We whose names are underwritten being earnestly desired t[
present to your Consideration our true Concluding thoughts touchin[
our Neighbour Walter Lee. That if there be any influence of any benef[
in the matter, proceeding from your hands that may be beneficiall t[
prevent future Difficulties & unrighteousness, your Wisdom ma[
appear calld upon a good & rationall ground we comply so far with th[
Desires laid upon us.
   ˙ He having many years past Covenanted with his Eldest Son, Joh[
Lee, & therein cast himselfe upon him as to his mentainance both fo[
himselfe, & Wife, during their Live[s], & in way of recompens[
bargain'd, & made over by Deed confirm'd according to Law all his i[
lands & goods, etc., Moveables, & other. Which business proove[
greatly offencive to his other Children w[ith] us here, whose unworth[
Carriage of them towa[rds] him their father, etc., was a reason wh[
they put him not into their provision for him (Who yet would not hav[
accepted of him upon any other ter[ms).] They taking advantage of hi[
weakness, feeble[ness] & decays of old age, to prevail with him to mak[
ov[er] by Deed his Land, & Goods unto them & himselfe to re[ly] upo[
their provision, telling him that John hath no[t] fulfilld his agreement[
Wherefore observing the Decays of Age upon him to a greate measur[
of Childishne[ss,] Feebleness & Changeableness, according as he i[
pl[eas]ed or Displeased; & his proneness to relieve * * * person tha[
strike in with his humor, & the weakness of his Understanding, we can[

account him competent to make any legall Convayance of any estate away by Covenant in case it was not under a fa[ir]er consideration. Some judge that he had need have [the] Eye of some Honest person over him to see that he is Comfortably provided for, & not whedled into inconveniences nor unwarrantable Covenantall Alienation to his own Sorrow. These things we present to y[our] prudent Consideration, that if you see any thing [by] your hands, beneficiall in this Case it may be thankfully received. & Subscribe ourselves your Honors Humble Servants.

A Coppy from the Originall on ⎱ Edward Taylor
file, Test John Pynchon Cler. ⎰ Nathaniel Phelps
                                    Samuel Taylor
                                    David Dewy

Now upon this Covenant made by Walter (after the Death of his first Wife) he went to his S[on] Johns to live, & took his provision with him whi[ch] was a part of a Barrell of pork * * * & I[ndi]an Corn, & he observing that John had not any Fresh meate, but his family lived upon his porke, seeing when his own was gone he should have n[o] meate to live upon, he therefore judging John had not kept his agreement with him went to his Son & Daughter, Bush & was with them about 5 months they say, until he was married to his second wi[fe] & then he lived upon his own provision, & John d[o]ing onely his greate worke, & he Complain[ed] greatly against John & so he lived mentaining himselfe & the 2ᵈ & 3ᵈ Wife untill they were dead & now his Son John being dead & his third wife being dead he wanted some body to looke to him & resolutely refused to go to Johns Widow saying th[at] her daughter, one of them, told him to his face that he w[as] not worth the Droppings of his nose, & so desired daughter Bush to look after him, & she could not refuse to relieve her father, & was with her about el[ev]en Weeks, & then being offended went to live with his Sons Widow, & would not make any satisfa[ct]ion to his Son Bush for what he had done for h[im.] His son Bush seing all by Covenant made over to [John] & his Heirs after their Father was dead expected that if he did not gain satisfaction while his Fath[er] lived, he could not come at anything after h[is] Death, laid him under a Warrant & sued him f[or] his debt. But was None suted by reason that the Con[sta]ble had not made an account of his summoning him to appeare. Whereupon Smith improved by [the] Widow & heirs had got Lawyer Pomery their attorney who when urged to let fall the Non Sute, & to jo[in] issue he refused, giving this reason, that he had oth[er] matter to non sute the Case, saying if Walter Lee was not a Man in Law, but was put under Guardi[an] by the Court at Northampton as desired by Mrs. Lee & others, in a petition by them sent to the Co[urt.] [137/138] & so the poore [Bush] Suffering a non sute was fain to beare the Charges of his own Attourney, of the Entring his Action, & of Smiths attorney, & of 20ˢ that Smith brought of Charges for himselfe etc., & the Old man openly declared to be no man in Law & this effected by my Petition above cited. & so I was made to desire, & petition that of the Court which was the very thing that I opposed & to avoid the same refused to subscribe to Pomerie petition tending to that end. Whereupon I was much offended, & Concluded that my draught was abused & knowing that that Petition was Carried to the Court by Brother Benjamin Smith who knew that I refused to Subscribe Pomeries draught as judging that the design therein tended to move the Court to put Walter Lee Some way or other out of Law & that he knew that I held so dewing unrighteous, & also that I accounted that that Court had not power sufficient to put a man out of the Law, I accounted that I ought not to let such abuse alone & not to looke into the Case. & on a day he Coming to my house, Brother John Root being present, I treated him about it as abusing me in producing Goodman Lee to be laid under Guardians by the letter that I wrote & he knew that I would never have wrote it if I had thought it should have been made to serve Such a Design. He denied that he had done it but asserted my letter had done it, & many unhandsom things then being vended, I forbade him the appearing to the Lords Table till he had manifested his repentance for such abuse. & the next Conference I brought it to the Church. Some Swaying amongst them Winkled about it but he being not present two of the brethren were orderd to Cite him to appeare the next Conference to answer to this Case.

Before which time I having wrote a letter to Colonall Patrick (or Partridge) intimating how my Letter was wrong took by the Court & made to serve a Contrary design than that that it was wrote upon, & another to the Court clearing my * * * as being no way designing any such thing as should put Walter Lee out of the Law, to the dammageing of such as had laid out any Credit upon him which by his present State as out of Law they could not now come at, in these Words.

Westfield 2ᵈ 3ᵐ 1712/13 To the Honored Court, held at
Northampton the 3ᵈ of March 1712/13.

Whereas Benjamin Smith Senior, now living in Springfield bounds,
soon after the Honorable Colonall Partridg went from our town last
summer, about May, brought a note drawn up as he said by Lawyer
Pomery to the Court of Session—to be held at Northampton soe desiring them to put Walter Lee out of our town (in effect) under Guardians
as incompetent to mannage himself, (or to that purpose, so far as my
memory serves me in this Case,) desiring me to subscribe & set my hand
to it, my Spirit rose up in me against all such unrighteousness. & I told
him that I knew no man could say, as that note, or to that effect.
& refused to do it. & my reasons for refusing to Subscribe it are such
as these.

1. Its a false Witness & a breach of the 9ᵗʰ Command. 2. The man is
Compos mentis, tho' a weake man & no man can honestly deny it. 3. He is
of Sufficient Capacity now to Carry on the Concerns of his Calling
answerable to his former carrying out of the same, greate worke onely
excepted, & if his wife was alive, he would be beholding to none of them
for his tables. 4ˡʸ Its a very unrighteous thing to seek to make such a man
an * * * or shut out of the law his birth priviledge having deserved by no
disorderly behaviour so to be treated; & in case he should be excluded
the benefit of the Law, I suppose it will follow, then in case he should
transgress the Law by murder, Theft, etc., he is not within the Penalty of
it. I can see no reason, but to debar men of their righteous dues, why any
man should desire he should be excluded & made uncapable of Law. On
these Considerations I refused to set my hand to the note drew up.
& in that he prevailed with me to draw up the [one] I did, it was onely
to desire that (if you had power Sufficient (which I told Smith,) I did not
thinke you had such power) to prevent his selling his land, & the
appurtinances thereof, nor for that he had not Capacity.

About a weeke before this to the Court I had wrote One to
Colonall Partridg, viz, this following,

Honored Colonall, after my humble Service to your honour I make
bold to trouble you with a few lines touching old good man Lee of our
town. For hearing that at the last Court at Northampton, Lawyer

Pomery appearing against good man Bush his Honest Case that was then Non Suted, said that Goodman Lee was not a man in Law being put under Guardians (or to that effect) & mention'd my name Countenancing the same. Which makes mee suspect that the Court is abused & that by such as effected it, by abusing a note that I with some others sent to the Court, being urged there unto by Ben. Smith. For when your Honour & some other went from our town last, Goodman Smith soon after brought to me a note drew up (as he said by Lawyer Pomery to the Honoured Court desiring in Effect that Walter Lee might bee put under Guardians, or rather out of the Law as I now apprehend for at this Copying this matter I have not the note by mee) as being so decayed that he was not competent to mannage himselfe (or to that end) & desired me to subscribe it. I rejected it & knew no man could say so, & judged it a very unrighteous thing. For tho' the man is not able to mannage strong worke as Plowing, Carting, etc., yet when his land is plow'd he plants, Woods, hills, & gathers his Corn: Reaps his Winter grain, pulls his Flax, makes his hay, buys what things he needs, of Merchants, Shoemakers, Taylors, & payes them, is rated in the town, & payes his dues. But he being over fickle, & of low intellects: & having made a Covenant with his son John last yeare deceased, Wherein he made over all that he had of Lands: & all his moveables, that he should die possesst of upon the Condition of his Honourable mentainance both of himselfe, & wife so long as they live, he complain'd of John as not having fulfilld his Covenant nor mentain'd him, he was inclined to breake the Covenant & sell his lands which could not be without greate unrighteousness for John, tho' he was in severall things faulty, yet he did for him what he stood in need of & carried on his plowing, mowing, Carting, & found him wood for 14 or 15 years. Which things being by me considered, I yielded to [138/139] good man Smith's Desire to do what I did showing in that he was so fickle, & under the decayes of old age & so thereby his Passion, & fickleness advance. I judged him not capable to alienate his land & desired that he might be prevented & you had power to do it, that you would do it. & I told good man Smith I could not se how you could do it unless you put him under Guardian & that I never could count him in such a State as required Guardians. But I fear mine ignorance hath been dishonestly interpreted to bring about unrighteous Designs. I can't but present this to your Honor & if there be need to the honoured Court, that you may see how the Court is abused; & if by anything of my writing, glossed on to effect the thing, I am abused too. I

desired nothing but that he * * * he not alienate his land & good man Smith knew this was all that I desired & judge him of as good a Capacity to look after himself. Still, as to his understanding, as he was no * * * agoe (Pardon my blottings) its * * * thing * * * make an innocent man of sound mind uncapable of Law because he is weake & Unstable.
Sir Yours Honors Humble Servant.   Edward Taylor

Touching these matters, & others, they were wrote before I had gain'd a sight of the letter sent subscribed by myselfe & others to the Court & I had forgot the speciall terms used in the letter it being a twelve month * * * before we had any debate about it, & so many after writing about it to the Colonall & to the Court. & in the treating Smith in the Matter I used such terms as Lawyer Pomery, & Smith now use about it, Pomery asserting in Open Court that good man Lee was not a man in Law being put under guardians, & that upon the desires of Mr. Taylor & others & put under Guardians. Hence in my letters I used the terms put under guardians, but I meant further consideration. I * * * Partridge that term Guardian was not the matter of my refusing to Subscribe lawyer Pomeries draught when Smith brought it to be Subscribed by mee, but I judged that it tended to put Lee out of the Law & that I wrote as desiring the Court that if they Could, that they would prevent Walter Lees Alienating his land, I since having a Coppy of the letter I finde the same to be onely an intimation of Walter Lees Circumstances, not desiring, nor advising any thing, but onely intimating that if there was a change in their * * * that might prevent future difficulties, it might be gratefully received being exerted.

These two letters of mine, Colonall Partridge had inclosed in a letter of his, & had sent again back to me which I could not english the meaning of. But he being kin to Smith it was after manifest to me by his letters to me that Smith had determind Councill & that the person that he, by his wreskless tongue had made him, his side man.

When that the Day of our Conference being come Smith appearing was calld out, & the query propounded, Why he had sought & effected Walter Lee's * * * & hereby to be put under guardians, &, as was judged, to be put out of Law?

His Answer was, that he desired that the Letters that Colonall Patrick had sent to me might be read. I told him that they were nothing to the purpose, & bad him answer to the Question * * * answer to the Question: He desired that they might be read: I told him that they would not, & urged him to answer to the Case & not to make the matter worse, or to that effect.

When he saw he could not gain the reading of the letters (I had them not with mee neither did I imagin to see such arrogancy in any as to demand the reading of letters sent in private to mee, but I suppose that he had been with Colonall Partridge, & had desired to see them & the Colonall had told him hee had sent them in a reply in the matter to me), he turn'd away & being halfe turnd spoke with a voice something low & if my ears deceived me not said, I will not, but when this came around none would own that they heard him, & being turnd round with his face upon mee & with haughtiness demanded thus, Sir, What should a man thinke of such an one that sends letters to several persons defaiming of him & would not let them be Seen? I gave no answer. Hence he renewed his Charge saying what shall One think of such a man (or person) that sends letters to Several persons defaiming of him & would not let them be seen? I replied that you may think as you please. And now seing his behaviour I attempted to put the Church to the voting.

But Ensign Kellog, as I think, or Captain Phelps, said that the Matter was not proved. I replied to the Captain, that as to his seeking the matter & carrying the letter to the Court was too manifest to be denied. He that is the first moover in a matter & Carries it thro' all intermediate * * * to the last Cause * * * to the producing of the Effect must needs be the Cause of the effect, & that Ben. Smith had done this thing was manifest. Capt. Phelps had the face to say that I had denyed that heretofor, I denied that ever I denied it, i.e., or a right sense. Capt. Mawdsly said yea, that was so, But it was not prooved that Brother Lee was put under Guardians, or out of the Law. I instanced that I had proofe that Lawyer Pomery asserted it in the open court. Hee replyed that that was not any proofe. For Lawyers oft say in their pleadings, [what was] not. Then I said that we must have a Sight of the Court Act: Smith said that he would * * * one, I said, that it was not free, that he should be Charged therewith. He said that he would spend [one hundred pounds] but he would cleare his name with me thereat. But with all he desired to have more time allowd him; I asked him how much, what untill next Conference in a month or so. He haughtily replied in a month or two or etc. But I seing his provocation order'd him to appeare at the next Conference, & so dismissed the people.

Smith now steps out & desires the Church to stay, some being gone * * * body of them moving, & he said, that he was sorry if he had offended them & much more & * * * he talked * * * Taylor. & as I think now he said if they were offended with him he * * * * * * [139/140] desired them to tell him, & what it was? This did Subtilly that he might say that the Church had nothing against him. The Church held their peace. But I am not Certain whether he spake this last clause at this time or at some other. But he also shewd greate unhandsomness in his whole mannaging of himselfe.

The next meeting which was that day forthnight, having gaind a Coppy of the Court act, it was so dark, that it did not appeare whether he was put under Guardians, or no but therein was particularly orderd Sergeant Nathaniel Phelps, & David King to have an Eye over him, etc. Whereupon Lawyer Pomery in the open Court asserted that Walter Lee was not a man in Law, being put under Guardians, & so could not be sued. I seing it a difficult thing to bee made out that he was put under Guardians or out of Law, let that fall, & retracted that matter, & Calld him to an account for his behaviour in the former treating. He asked me wherein, I answered in severall things, as 1. For Disobedience unto the Authority of Christ in the Church. Who being Calld out to answer the Query (before mentioned[)] answerd not but in the turning about said, if my ear deceived me not, you would not; this he denied (he utter'd with a lowering his voice) & others either understood it not or would not speake, however he never answered to it & so went against that Command, Heb. 13.17. 2ly For Provoking turning aside to impenitent things desiring that the Letters Colonall Patridg had sent mee might be read. 3ly For the provoking Reflecting upon me as writing defaming letters of you, saying haughtily What should one think of such a man that wrote letters to persons defaming of you, & would not let them be read, both of which matters were false. 4. For assuming false Speaking upon your Pastor in saying he was urged by you to write the letter to the Court, which in its preface saith, thus we being earnestly desired do so & so. 5. For your threatoning what you will do, you will spend 100£ to Cleare your name. 6. For your thrusting yourselfe into the Officers work: & taking his Work away from him in determining of & propounding matters to the Church: these were the Chief matters of offence in him at that time. He denied his detaining of & propounding to the Church, saying he did not do so, he remembred no such thing saying that he did not so. At length Brother Samuel Bush said you did say so, & gave him his words. Then he said he was Sorry for it. I asked him whether he was heartily Sorry for it. He smartly replied, that I had nothing to do with his Heart. I said but I had, for if he was not heartily sorry for it, his Sorrow was no satisfaction. & now I propounded his Case to the vote of the Church both negatively & affirmatively, & the Church voted not at all, neither ways. I was now offended with the Church, & told them if they would vote neither for nor against him, they would constrain me unto New Methods moving either to call a Councell or Suspende the Administration of the Lords Supper which I perceived afterwards was offencive, they telling me that I said I would suspend the Church. I told them if I said so which I did not remember or intend, that I should not administer the Lords Supper to them & turning to Smith I Commanded Smith in the Name & by the Authority of Christ to repent of his Sin, & I thinke I did also of that which he knew of privatly Comitted against me, & to manifest his Repentance that the Church might receive him into their Charity, telling him, that this was not an Ecclessicall Admonition; but a ministeriall admonition. He began to flutter as if I tooke too much upon me. I told him that I would mentain it, I would not come to him to teach me my office work.

But now about Smith having a Coppy of the Court touching Brother Lee & seing me in the Garden, came to the fence & shew'd it me, & withall told me that hee was offended with me ever since he was sick some years ago when he sent for me & I treated him so then. Now when I went to him I found him very sick of a raging fever more likely to die than Live, & his life & Conversation had never been so even but almost all that had to deal with him were never over forward to take his word more, some would call him knave, some a lyar, some a Cheater, & I know not of one instance wherein he paid according to agreement, would riggle so as that men were oft fain to yield of their right unless they sued him & he was too talkative & Subtill for them in Law.[85] Now I being Calld to him I applied myself to him as I was used to do to sick persons, to looke over his life past to see what was amiss therein & so renew Repentance & so to go humbly to Christ by Faith. He began to brisk up as toucht to the Quick & urged me to tell him wherein he had faild: & was offended, & kept this upon his Spirit rankling till now & saith he had been offended with me ever since, & told me that he thought he shold never be reconciled to me again. I said that if God tooke him once to do he would quickly pull that out. & in that he manifested an implacable frame of Spirit I forbade him ever to approach to the Lords table till he had repented of this, & this is the matter mentiond between him & me.

But in the Close of the day we fixed upon tuesday following in the afternoon [140/141] for the brethren to come together to mannage this matter, & Smith being a restless spirited man he frequently was with them & had gaind some not to act which was against their express Church covenant & others he had gaind to his side so that Old Captain Phelps never spake a word to my remembrance, but on his Side. Deacon Noble openly opposed me & in a faithlesse matter which he afterwards Confesst to me: & thus his false tongue having wheadled away the brethren to himselfe, was the reason why Smith was so turbulent. Now I found Smith, by his threatoning, & knowing his proneness to law & seeing his provocations so great I was something jelous that I might have the matter that was between him & me fisht out to my dammage in law. Wherefore, I betooke myselfe to Authority & deliver'd it in writing first to Colonall Partridge who made no right improvement of it. But at length the brethren came with Smith from Samuel Bushes which I have ground to suppose to be Smiths counsill house & being Called out he tenders a Confession such as it were, viz, I confess that in severall things I spake unneedlessly; & that my Carriage was not as it ought, & I am sorry for it, & I humble pray the Church to forgive me & I hope for the time to Come to take better heed to my wayes. This was writ so that I could not read it, but Smith coming to my house before the next Conference, I desired to see it & I then tooke a Coppy of it & drew up another thus, for In respect to my Carriage & Expressions then as offencive (some whereof are given me in writing) I herein declare in the presence of the Church, that I am heartily sorry for the same: & desire that God would help me & pardon the same, & that the Church would forgive me all offenciveness in the same & help me with their prayers.

This I read to him, & tenderd him. He would not take itt, nor accept it. & so he stood till the next Conference, & then being calld out, he still insisted upon the first Confession. I replied that it was not so much of a Gospell Confession as Simon Magus his nor as Pharaohs.[86] & now I propounded his carriage to the vote both negatively & affirmatively, if they judged that he had not offended signify it by the lifting up of their hands. I propounded itt then that if they judged him to have offended to signify it by their silence & there was not one appeared to vote him a Non-Offender, nor one that appeared not to judge him an Offender.

Brother Bancraft desired time to be granted which was granted to the next Conference, then after the Questions Answerd, I calld him out,

& demanded his Confession. But he stuck where he was before. Where-upon I laid him under a Church Admonition which did so nettle the old Captain Phelps that he could hardly tarry till prayer was done & being done out he went shucking as he went. I follow'd him, & put forth my hand to him. He said that he was Caught but Smith was such an one that nobody cared for him & yet he endeavoured to bear him out in treading down the Authority of Christ in the Church. & Smith I sup-pose had held them in hand that his Cousin Colonall Partridge & Mr. Stoddard & other elders would dissert & be against me. Mr. Stoddard did not do well letting Smith see that he accounted Smiths Confession sufficient & wrote to me to accept it. & Mr. Woodbridge of Springfield was beguild by him also greatly & held a communion with the Church by letters & not by mee. Which when I came to see it I was offended with him. Smith was at mee now for a Councill. I told him, that they might take Councill that needed it, I knew the Rule of my proceedings: I asked him whom he would Choose for a Councill. He said Mr. Stoddard, Mr. Woodbridge & Mr. Brewer. I told him noe, I would have no such Councill. They had judged the Case before they had heard it. But if he would Choose Mr. Stoddard & Mr. Williams of Hatfield, I would have brother Woodbridge & Cousin Buckingham. He liked not them. I told him that they were the Ancientst Elders upon the River. He offerd mee to meet Mr. Brewer & Mr. Woodbridge at his house. I told him I would: & so on the 21 of July or thereabouts which being come together Smith I have ground to think, having bygotted Mr. Brewer, Mr. Brewer rashly began to blame me, & Censure me for meddling in the matter. I inti-mated that I was slandered in the Face of the Country & made the petitioner to the court that they would make brother Lee to be no man in Law & to be put under guardians. For so Lawyer Pomery openly asserted that Walter Lee was no man in Law being put under Guardians upon the desire & advice of Mr. Taylor & others which was an unrighteous thing in itselfe & Contrary to my desires. He * * * both [141/142] reasons warranted one to cleare my own name from desiring or advising to an unrighteous thing, indeed the Contrary to the putting Lee not of Law was the reason why I could not put my hand to Lawyer Pomeries draught. Religion also requires itt. We are to inquire into sin upon suspicion, Deut. 13, & not to suffer Sin if wee Can hinder it. It was Jobs Honour that he searched out the Cause that he knew not, Job 29.16. The elders in the Bay do in their answers to Certain Questions assert that elders are to inquire into the Carriages of the Church.[87] Its the work of the Elders to looke into the manners of the people. Why else are they calld ἐπισκόπους, Overseers, Acts 20.28. But still this man persisted in his folly. & I began to be offended, & told him, that I came not there to be blaim'd without Conviction. I would not thus faile in the End of my coming, for illiterate persons to say as he did it was less strange. But for him that had learned the Arts & rules of reason to talke so, I would not thus go on but if we could do any thing to help in this Case & end the Difference I was here to labour at that. He said that good man Smith must Confess his Fault. I told him that I came about that but if they could bring him to itt, that he might give in a gospell Confession I was ready to accept it. & So Mr. Brewer drew up one I could nott accept it & then he drew up this which still in severall things were not pleasing, yet I accepted it which was this

Whereas there have been of late some things wherein in some late discourse with Mr. Taylor I have been found justly offensive, I doe here freely & Willingly offer for the satisfaction of any so offended that in the aforesaid discourse which I finde Cause to reflect upon myselfe that I am guilty of many rash, hasty, & unadviced Words & expressions: & that I had not that regard to him in my discourse as the 5th Command doth require. For which I am heartily sorry, & earnestly desire forgiveness, both of God, him, & all that may be offended thereat: & hope I shall watch myselfe better for the time to come & promise by Gods help so to do.

Benjamin Smith

This Confession did not please me though I accepted of it. For it mentions not anything of what nature the discourse was of as if it was onely an occasional discourse. Whereas it was a Church processed discourse & in that it seems to make the Matter particularly mine, whereas the Church was offended & had voted him an offender, & had laid him under a Church Admonition. & in that it onely mentions & slenderly onely a failing in Some regard unto the fifth Command, when it was a trampling underfoot the Authority of Christ in the Church. Yet I acepted tho' the worst of all was this that I can't see sufficient reason to thinke that it flow'd from Evangelicall Repentance.

But some time before this, after Smith was laid under the Churches admonition, hee offers to obtain the Lords Supper in the West Church at Springfield. Mr. Woodbridg writes to me about it advising me to receive Smiths acknowledgment for he was informed by reliable persons, that when the Church came to ackt they would * * * me for tho' they would no speake in my presence yet they spoke freely to Smith & he desires to know how Smith stood with us. I wrote to him that the Church had voted him an offender, & he was under the Churches admonition & that he could not regularly administer the Lords Supper to him. Smith still makes a fresh attempt upon Mr. Woodbridg, & Mr. Woodbridg writes a letter to the Church inquiring after the same matter of the brethren which were stilled by him & the Church & sends it open subscribed with about * * * of his people not s[u]bscribing it to the officer to be Communicated to the Church. Smith gathers the brethren of the Church together at Samuel Bushes & delivers it to them wherein the same inquiries about Smiths State are propounded to them for their speedy Answer & I suppose Smith had told them of my Letter. The two Captains come late I thinke on the frighday night to me & show me the Letter subscribed. I was offended thereat, that my testimony was not credited by Mr. Woodbridge, & that he offer'd as if designing to do mischief to write to our Church & not by the Officer, & to send his Letter sanballats like open, & the Captains Consulting with me I read a Coppy of the letter that I sent, & told them that they deserved not an answer, yet I would have them Carry it Civilly. This letter of Mr. Woodbridge, I suppose came to them not on the frighday night but on the Saturday. For Mr. Woodbridge when I came to him told me that hee received a letter from them the frighday night before he wrote them, subscribed by, he thought, all the Brethren of the Church but he had given Mr. Brewer both the letters, & he would not deliver the letter sent on the frighday night but onely that which was in answer to what the Captains s[h]ew'd mee on the Saturday late I thinke. & in this Answer they write that they had tooke a vote & were Satisfied with their Brother Smith. Now the Captains were earnest with me to Call the Church together to Consult about it quickly, I would have had it let alone till the Nex Conference, & so Captain Mawdsly. But Capt. Phelps was earnest for the meeting to be upon tuesday following & accordingly I on the Sabbath after the Worship was past, I desired the brethren to Come to my house on Tuseday, in the after noon as I take it, & when they were come I began to reproove them for their Dealing thus fallaciously, so that Mr. Woodbridge in his letter tells me that they would not act when they were putt to it: & that they spake freely with Smith tho' they would not appeare when I was with them: & I began in the matter. And Capt.

Phelps stood up & said he was satisfied [with] Smith; all the rest folowed him their leader. And I being amazed hereat told them to this effect or in these words, that I was not, [142/143] & therefore as he was aid regularly under a pastorall & also a Church Admonition so he was ike to abide untill he manifested his Gospell Repentance.

Touching Mr. Woodbridge's letter, my memory is not so clear as hat I can give so cleare an account as is desired but if I mistake not he old me that before that even, the night before it he received a letter ubscribed with he thought, the hande of all the Brethren of the Church. But the last gave an account that the Church had taken a Vote & was Satisfied with the man.

But these things I understood not till I met with Mr. Woodbridge & Mr. Brewer at Smiths where Mr. Woodbridge was ingenious & tolld me the matter but Mr. Brewer (as an Abettor of Smith) seemed to be lumb, & would not let me have a Sight of the letter firse sent, he having t. But yet he wrote Smiths Confession & drew it up, as much in favour of Smith as could be & I am sorry that I accepted it without a more particular acknowledgment of his offences, & of his offending the Church which had voted (*nemine Contradicente*) that he had offended.

Now the Sabbath after we had met at Smiths being the 26 of July in the Evening Capt. Phelps & Capt. Mawdsly Coming to my house, I gave them an account of what Smith was brought to, & I had accepted of if the Church accepted it. They seemed to be pleased therewith & well they might for they had openly declared, and disorderly, themselves satisfied. I told them that I designd to finish it with the Church upon the next Conference, & then to set apart a day of Humbling ourselves before God for our Failings in this managing of Smith's Case. For there had been greate failings, & if the Church would not Comply therewith then I was resolved to have a Councill to direct us in this Case. But I told them withall that I was resolved to speake plainly to the Church & lay the failings of the Church before the Church but in our address to God I designed not to propound particulars but leave such as went upon prayer to proceed in their Confessions, & Petitions as God should assist, in a Generall way. They approoved of the Same.

July 26 being our Conference, the Conference being Ended, I detaind the Church, & recited what was to be done, Brother Smith having given in a Confession of his failings, it was to be read & Voted. Captain Phelps replied, that they had received satisfaction or done it already. I told him that what they had done I knew not or to that effect, but what they had done was no Church Act. He lay under a Church Admonition regularly administerd, & if they would not regularly receive his Confession, he must abide so far, as he was under the Admonition This prickt the Old man. So I proceeded & Smith having before Captiously demanded his recommendations, & for his absenting from the Worship on Severall Lords dayes pleaded that he attended Where he ought to attend I having read the Confession, & put it to the Church vote together with his dismission.

These they readily voted. Smith not being here, I could not make a personall Application of it. But he when I saw him accepted not of the Dismission: & therefore the next Conference I declared that hee was not free to accept of his dismission[88] & so he was restored to his Standing & laid under a brief exhortation to an humble walking & to true repentance of his Sin that God might not be dishonored nor himself troubled, etc.

Then I turnd to the Brethren & bespake them thus: Your Actings have been very grievous, irregular & greatly wounded mee. I take the same to be greatly disorderly.
1. You have acted matters belonging to the Church Officer, & so excluded him from his Worke.
2. You have acted with an offending person under Church process & tooke him away from the process that he was under.
3. You have profest you have received Satisfaction, which if true it was taken by you in private for such offences as were Censured by you in the face of the Church openly to be offences.
4. You have herein given a bad example to others to rise up against their officers judgment, that tends to bring in all disorder & confusion in matters of Church Discipline. These things, & many others of the like nature very grievous I can do no less than testify against, entreating & * * * to consider of the same [and] never be weadled away for the future into such behaviours.

Then I offered them either to Call a Councill to direct us about these things; or to set apart a day for Humiliation to Humble our Souls with fasting & Prayer before God to pardon us of all our failing in these things & not designing that these things would bee the particular matters of our Confessions & prayers, butt onely in a Generall way. Captain Phelps now Carried it very perversely, asserting that I on the Evening to the Lords day told them, viz, Him, & Captain Mawdsly that I would not mention these things, that I would not meddle with them: I replied that I

aid I would set things before the Church & deale plainly with them but
would not lay things down as the particular matter to be in Speciall
spread before God in prayer. He denied the same, and Captain Mawdsly
went on to say that he understood with him, I told them that I could not
help their understanding if they understood it not. For I told them plain
enought. & if upon their enquiry into the Matter of the Confessions
Ensign Kellog rose up & said that he could not Comply with it on these
erms propounded for he was not faulty therein. I replied that then he
was cleare (& yet this man told me himselfe that Smith in the beginning
of his matters had been with him & prevailed with him not to act) but
out he went into the porch. But Brother Bancraft, rose up & desired me
o propound the Fast to the Church. He doubted not but the Church
would vote the fast & let the Captain, & others do as they pleased. I
propounded the Fast. All voted save these three souldiers but when
Capt. Mawdsly saw that he was left he fell in, & the Ensign being called
n he buggled a while, & so Complyed. But Capt. [143/144] Phelps
never complied to either but intred upon a discourse very unbeseeming
o him & said that they had done but what I desired them in Smiths
Case for I gave them leave to treat him. If this had been so as he said yet
hereby it could not be that I gave them leave to meet together in distinct
meeting & plot with him against the matters in him offencive & to draw
up letters to other Elders & Churches against me, & the Satisfaction
required of him for the same. & further this desire of mine was after the
Church had regularly voted him an offender. For When I refused to read
his Papper that he gave me to read of his Confession, & had read it the
next Conference, not to take a vote upon it, but had drawn up an other
adding the matter of his Confession unto Certain things given him in
writing, tendering the same unto him, & hee refusing those, I put it to
the Church vote touching his offences, which when the Church had
voted him an Offender, Brother Bancraft desired time for him, for he
said that he was in a falling way, then I desired the brethren to treate him
to bring him into a better Confesson. & no such thing as they had acted
as to take a Vote that they were Satisfied with him as they had openly
wrote that they had to Mr. Woodbridge, & to Mr. Brewer subscribed
with most of their names. This desire of mine being before he was laid
under the Church Admonition. The Capt. denied it to be before it. I
evidenced it thus, that it was upon Smiths bringing me the paper that
you brought him to, & that you Capt. told me that Smith wrote & he
would have had you to have wrote, but refused saying that I would

know your hand. For I desired you not to labour with him to bring him to a better Confession, till the Church upon my refusing to set thi to vote, & he refusing any other, was voted an offender. For then Brother Bancraft desired time for him & failing, & then I desired you to bring him to a better Confession & not to do as you have done & thi was before the public Admonition. This the Captain had denied til Severall brethren Confirmed it to be so, then he had nothing to say on this debate. I told him that he did not do well & I said the Church had another leader besides me to rule them. & having occasion to use tha Hebrew 13.17, to submit yourselves to them that have the rule over you He in hast turned thus & he said also, Not as Lords over God's Heretage I demanded Wherein had I been as a lord over Gods Heretage?[89] Were such? He said, no, that he did not say so, but yet he said that I did tha which belonged to the Church. The Bay Ministers, said that Suspensior belonged to the Church. I said that the Bay Ministers did not say so. For they say that it belongs to the Elders to suspend by Authority before the Case can be heard by the Church. He said that the Bay Ministers say tha three things Elders may not Doe, viz, They can't Elect Officers, they Can't Admit Members, & they can't Suspend.[90] I said it is not so. For i they Can't suspende, then they are bound to administer the Lord Supper, to whomsoever the brethren will have them Administer it & this will make the Elders the Church Slaves to Administer the Lord Supper, & Baptism to all to whom they please, which will wholy den the Elders to have any Office Judgment at all. Indeed the Elders alone o themselves can't Elect Officers, Admit Members, nor Excommunicat offenders. But they Can suspende.[91] He replied, What power is in the Church. I said When the Rulers bring matters to the Church to have their judgment given in Such things they have a power or right o judging, but such things as are not comitted to the Church by the Elder where there are Elders, the Church (i.e., the Fraternity) have nothing to do at all in ordinary Cases. Then he said there was no power in the Church. I said that that followd not, What all, or none at all. Wha Consequent is this? But however this is more than can give a clear Scripture for. And you do not well to be thus troublesome. Who said how do I faile the Rule I replied that you carry yourselfe very uncomly & not as you ought to do & that I was sensible that there was som other leader in the Church than I: he bad me prove it. I told him wha Mr. Woodbridge told me that he & Mr. Brewer had received two letter from them subscribed by them & the last he judged by all the Brethrer

>f the Church, & by him as the foreman. He bad Mr. Woodbridge
>rove it. I told him that if there was need, I doubted not but Mr.
Woodbridge could proove itt by your own hand.

And so I told him I knew my office & would not come unto him to
earn my duty, & at the length appointing without him A Fast to humble
>urselves before God & beg pardon for our Failing which was on [Aug. 2],
preached upon Matt. 13.3, Repent for the Kingdom of Heaven is at
>and, In which words I held out, that Repentance was a principall foun-
lation Grace upon which the Kingdom of Heaven was built. On the
>abbath day after I appointed the Lords Supper.⁹² & so ended this
>uarrellsome matter.

Now the Greate Encouragement to Smith in this his Evil Case
>eems to me to be Colonall Partridge, his Kinsman, & Mr. Stoddard, Mr.
3rewer, & Mr. Woodbridge & for my reason hereof are certain Letters
>hat I shall here set down.

1. From Colonall Partridge

>mith having gaind mee to draw up that Letter to the Court before
ranscribed, & the Court then seing it drew up an order touching
>oodman Lee * * * order that put Goodman Lee under Guardians & so
>e then not a man in Law & that upon the Desires or the Advice of Mr.
Taylor [144/145] etc., which was not onely unjust in itselfe but Untrue
>lso. For Mr. Taylor never advised nor desired any such thing as is
>nanifest in the letter above to the Court. But being thus made the
Author of what I judge very unjust I judgd that I was bound to clear
>nyselfe from being the Author of any such unrightousness & therefore
> wrote one letter to the Colonall & another to the Court to rem[ov]e
>nyselfe from being any desirous of any such things but the Contrary.
The letters may be read above. These Letters it seems displeased the
>olonall: for what I know not: unless it was because the putting Good-
>nan Lee (as Lawyer Pomery asserted in the Court to be) was put out of
>he Law & [I] called it an unrighteous thing * * * to be upon my letter
>vhich hereby is denied to be it so desirous, or advising any such thing.
>o that the unrighteousness of the same must needs fall upon the Courts
>alse Sense given of the letter as sent. And Deacon Noble, & William
>mith being with the Colonall perhaps to se what hee said, he reads my

letter to them with greate offence & put as I suppose Smiths sense upon it as being a defaming him so much as when Smith was Calld out upon the Article touching, desired letters, he Confidently affirmd that I had writ to his defamation & produces Deacon Noble & his son William Deacon Noble stands up & said that he heard Colonall Partridge reade i & asserted that I reflected upon Smith in it; I denied it, & desired him to give in What. He could not tell what. & I said that I reflected on none & I was offended with him for such witness, & yet he could not tell wherein I had done so * * * not all my Deacon to rise up thus against me. Afterwards Deacon Noble being in my study with me I read him the letter deliberately. & asked him wherein was there any reflection or what wa a miss? He said, no there was none, there was none. But Colonall Partridge, he, his wife & son were offended, & had blinded him, or to that effect, but now he saw no reflection nor untruth in it. But Smith lay at him so hard that he could not put him off for he threatoned to constrain him if he would not speake.

Now I come to Colonall Partridge's letter, I design onely to write out but one yet the others were *ejusdem farinae.*

Reverend, & honored Sir.   Hatfield, July 9. 171:

After my humble Service presented to yourself, Mrs. Taylor, & al yours, I am much concerned relating to the Difference between Benjamin Smith, & yourselfe, & that it should have an Evill Influence in your Society, & Neighbourhood. He hath been with me, showing him selfe desirous to prosecute his dissatisfaction at law, saying he hath been with Mr. Stoddard, & others of the reverend Ministers who have wrote to yourselfe in his behalfe: & also the greatest part of your Church hath declared themselves satisfied in what he Offers to acknowledges & hath done it, & yet yourselfe holds him off; & he cannot enjoy the priviledge of Church Communion in all the Ordinances. Also that yourselfe without any voice of the Church hath Suspended him from the Ordinances & hence of yourselfe as aforesaid have declared him under an Admonition. If this be true, I humbly propose as I understand

1. The first Matter of offence that yourselfe received from the said Benjamin Smith hath been of a long standing & the late matter of offences was management referring to Father Lee & his Estate, in both which, I humbly query whether the Rule hath been attended, Matt 18.15,16,17. I humbly propose whether any member can be under Suspension before the said rule be attended, & there Dispenced by the

ders & Major part of the Church: or be of No validity. Now as to the
rst. Your Paper enclosed shews it was of long Continuance, & of some
ords, it may be, not suitable; & not so taken notice of as to be
roceeded with according to the foresaid rule. & he since of a long time
dmitted into Communion in all the Ordinances. Therefore too late to
oject now unless of an higher nature, etc.

As to the 2^d I humbly think things are misunderstood. I humbly
onceive what the Court did, was onely leaving Father Lee to the Care
' John Lee, not to Guardenship: neither could the Court do it. Guar-
enship belonging onely by Law to the Judge of Probate. & I believe no
ich thing hath been done by mee, nor will it appeare so to bee. Neither
n I see the procedure in it according to the foresaid rule.

Therefore I humbly entreate that this matter may be Consider'd by
ourselfe, & that you would please to accept of his acknowledgment, &
ing the matter to an issue at home rather than to the Law, or a
ounsill of Ministers. But if one of these must be, please to Call a
ounsill as aforesaid, & no. I believe as the Case is Circumstanced
efore, it will be whenever it comes, very hard work to vindicate the
roceedings aforesaid to be according to Rule, which may much disturb
ourselfe in your old age & attain no end but a leven in the Spirits of
rethren: a wrong to your Ministry, & needless disputes to run such
iviall offences to such an Height as greater offences & of an higher
iture cannot be mannaged as by one party in a Church onely being
ore than any of our Presbyterian Ministers have acquired to them-
lves; & if they did, I humbly conceive it more than the rule allows. I
ay God guide in this matter to a Comfortable issue. I am your humble
ervant.   Samuel Partridge

This letter (& others that I transcribe nott) of the Colonalls is full
' mistakes & of offences in his spirit that he hath received from his
nsman Benjamin Smith, whose case he espoused, & was a back to him
aking him bold & impudent. Unto which I made him this return.

Much Honour'd Colonall.
fter my Humble Service presented to your Honour & to Madam
artridge & to all yours I give you hearty thanks for your kinde letter, &
our thoughts therein. As for the attempts made by Benjamin Smith in
rder to Civill Law, I conclud that if he could lay hold on any thing that
ould bear an action against me he would, that made mee to address

myselfe to your honor as to Authority in that note I put in your hand[93] i
case I should have occasion to instance of his implacable Spirit, who ha
held a prejudice against me so many years, for that wherein I did one
my duty & office of Charitie to his Soule. I knew not but that I migl
intimate to Some the particular offence in him of a private nature th:
might gain it of mee for his Satisfaction & so it might come forth to m
dammage unless I had the defence of Authority on my side. This offenc
was not any thing [145/146] Contain in the Admonition that I lai
him under, for it never hath been mentiond to the Church: but is one
the thing mention'd in the bottom of the note wherein his offences we
given him in writing, saying, these are the matters offencive besides wh:
is between you & mee, I know not but when I urg'd him in admonisl
ing him to repent, intimate also that between himselfe & me which h
knew. Now Sir, the Common Prayer will not admit a person to th
Lords Supper, if I mistake nott, that bears ill will to his brother. I ha
nothing of offence upon my spirit against him for his seeming to k
offended at my advice, & never thought that hee had bore me ill will o
that account.

As for his taking a Course of Law I know not any thing wherein
have offended the Civill Law.

As for the Last matter occasioned by old goodman Lees Case,
shall lay down the matter faithfully as follows. When Smith, had wit
much adoe, prevailed with mee to write to the Court touching goodma
Lee, I refusing altogether any thing that might put the man out of th
Law as he well knows, I proceeded as your Honour knows. But unde
standing that at the Court held at Northampton that Lawyer Pomer
asserted that Goodman Lee was not a man in Law, & that my letter, etc
did desire the Court to that effect, I accounted myselfe greatly abuse
thereby, & presumed that B. Smith had done it. Where upon March 3
1713/14[94] he coming to my house I treated him about it, asking him t
this effect, asking him, why he had caused goodman Lee to be put und
Guardian? He answered roundly that he did it not but I did it: my lette
had done it. Hence angry words passt on both sides: & then I forbad h
approach to the Lords Table, till he had given me Satisfaction. He mad
a light matter of it saying, he would not trouble me, or words to th:
effect. The next Conference I committed the Case to the Church & tw
of the Brethren were ordered to cite him to appear (& this was befor
we had any Sacrament) the next Conference. He appearing, I, when th
exercise was over, I calld him out & demanded of him thus, seeing h

228

d sought & effected Brother Lee, a brother of the Church to be put
der Guardians, & so as was supposed outt of the Law, we required
m to give a Reason of his so doing? His reply was this in the very first
ace, thus, I desire you to read the letters that Colonall Partridge hath
nt to you; & this in a provoking way. I replied that they were not to
is matter, & wished him not to make his Case worse, but to answer to
e matter. & if any brethren desired to see them if they would come to
y study, they should see them. He still insisted on the letters & seeing
could not gain them, for I had them not with me, he turns himself in
s provoking, & unhandsom way lookt on me, saying, Pray Sir what
ould wee thinke of the man that writes letters up & down to persons
faming of him, & will not let them be seen? I think I made no answer.
e saith again, pray Sir what should one think, or I thinke of such a man
writes letters to persons defaming of him, & will not let them be seen?
no answer to the Question could be gained from him. This was the
st thing offencive, his not answering to the Question & his provoking
uestions & Carriage. Its a breach of the fifth Command in point of
onour & disobedience to that word, Heb. 13.17, & of that I Thess.
11,12,13. Its a dispit done to Christ, Matt. 28, *ult.*, Luke 12.16. I did
ot use any of these Scriptures yet that might provok him. This his
arriage is utterly destructive to all Discipline in Christs house.

2. We come to the letters sent to the Court. & I said that I being
ged by him wrote as I did. He wholy denied itt, that he urged mee. I
ld him that when I refused to set my hand to Lawyer Pomeries letter,
desired me to write, I refused. He entreated me again. I told him that
could not, there was no room for me to write: I knew not what the
ourt could do in the Case unless they should put him out of Law
hich I thought was not righteous, or Words to this effect: then he
ayed me to take it into Consideration & do what I could, then I
elded. This he will not account urging. But reading the letter itselfe
rit to the Court it came thus, We whose names are underwritten being
rnestly desired, etc., he would not own this to be urging.

3. I seing no answer or reason could bee gained, I attempted to put
e matter to the vote, & then he desired time, to Consider of it. I askd
m, how much? till the next Conference, or a month? He replied, a
onth, two months, or a year, or words to that purpose.

4. Seing nothing could be gaind, I propounded it to the Vote. Some
id that the Matter was not proved. I replied that he was the first
oving Cause, & had carried the letter to the Court & moved them to

do it, & they had done it. Their reply was, thus, it did not appeare th[?]
goodman Lee was put under Guardians or out of Law. I said that Lawy[?]
Pomery asserted it in the open court. They said that Lawyers in pleadi[?]
used to say many things that were not so, then I said that wee must ha[?]
a Sight of the Court act. Smith, said that he would procure one, I sa[?]
that I was not willing that he should be charged therewith. He for m[?]
kindness said that he would spend 100£ but he would cleare his nam[?]
& then the meeting breaking up he was desired to be at the ne[?]
Conference. He said that he knew not whether he should.

The next meeting that he came to, I having received your honou[?]
Letter, & seing it was difficult to determine whether the Court had p[?]
the man out of Law, & not knowing how the Lawyers would interpr[?]
it, I was doubtful in the Case, & being desirous to put the favorable[?]
Sense on it I retracted the matter; if the Church saw meet & if broth[?]
Lee was not outlawd [146/147] But as for Smiths Carriage I could n[?]
let that pass, it being so offencive, & so I instanced in the things alread[?]
mentioned, his Carriage was so offencive & provoking that itt was n[?]
to be born. & now upon his Carriage, I attempted to put itt to vote, as[?]
thinke. But the Church would not vote neither wayes. Then I spake t[?]
them to this effect, that if they would not act one way nor other the[?]
would constrain me to new methods, i.e., not to administer the Lor[?]
Supper to them or a Counsill or make a Separation. This last I utterl[?]
could not beare & one of the other I could avoid, etc. Smith desire[?]
that he might have his Charges given in in writing, the which I gave hi[?]
in writing in as easy terms as I could well express them which I suppo[?]
your Honour hath seen. & now the meeting breaking up Smith steps u[?]
& detains them, as having some thing to say to them, whereupon son[?]
being gone out and others standing made an halt & he bespeaks the[?]
thus, that if hee had offended any of them or the reverend Mr. Taylor [?]
was sorry for it, etc., & then all departed. I considering that this w[?]
onely a wily thing in him & that the matter might be of a bad Cons[?]
quence, put this in as a matter of offence among his offences which we[?]
not given in till the next Conference, as his Steping in & assuming of t[?]
Officer's office. The next meeting being come we fell upon the matter, [?]
he seems to deny his meddling with the Officers work in detaining of t[?]
Church & propounding to them saying I did not, did I? But Broth[?]
Samuel Bush said you did & Gave him his Words. He then said, I a[?]

Sorry for it, I said unto him, are you heartily Sorry. He roundly said, You have nothing to do with my heart. I said but I have. Hee again in ɔo[a]st said, you cannot see my heart. I said, no but I have to do with it for all thatt. Then he gave in a long schoole to prove his Offences, no ɔffences, I saw the tenure of it & gave it him again, telling him we expected his repentance & needed not any plea against the same as not Sinfull. But to hasten, seing nothing answering the Gospell, & the Church backward to their Duty, I designing to put an end to the matter & trouble the Church no more therewith, I laid him under a Pastorall Admonition, & told him that it was not a Church but a Ministeriall admonition. This toucht him to the quick. Hee told me that I had nothing to do so. I told him, that I would not come to learn my work of him. Now the brethren desired that we might meet on an after noon in the week following to Consider the Case, it was on Wednsday come Sevenight following in the after noon, the day being come, & meetting still with opposition to repentance, I propounded the matter to the Church Vote that if they judged Brother Smith had offended in this Case they would signify it by their Silence. Every person lifted up his hand: I propounded it in the negative first, & not a person lifted up his hand or opposed. Now Smith presents me with a bit of paper & in it was writ what I could not read, I gave it him to read, he had much ado to read it tho' his own writing, & he Calld it a Confession, & would have me propound it to the Church to vote, I refused to do it. Capt. Phelps, Smiths advocate, asked me what Course they must take, if I would not read their Cases & put matters to vote. I told him, they might desire a neighbor Church to inquire into the reason of our proceeding, or call a Councill.

Before the next Conference Br. Smith came to mee. I desired him to lett me see his Confession. He shewed it to me & read it, I pend it outt, & itt was thus. I acknowledge that in severall things I spake unadvisedly & my Carriage was not as it might & I am Sorry for it, & humbly desire the Church that they would forgive me & I hope to Carry it better for the time to come. This I should have had to have Considered on before now. I tooke my pen & wrote itt thus. In respect to my Carriage, & Expressions then, as offencive some of which are given me in writing, I confess in the presence of the Church that I am heartily Sorry for the Same, & desire that God would pardon mee & help me: & desire the

Church to forgive all offencivness therein, & help me with their prayers. I read it to him: he would not accept of it. I desired him to take it & Consider of it but he would not.

The next meeting Smith appearing was calld out; he began to plead his case as before, I told him that if he would make a Gospell Confession, which we expected wee were ready to accept it. He desired his acknowledgment might be propounded to the Church. I told him I could not propound to the Church what I approved not of nor would vote for, & I took & read that which I had wrote & he would not accept of that. I told him that his was not so much answering a Gospell Confession as Pharao's or Simon Magus his. Then I proceeded upon the Church Vote. Captain Phelps rose up, & Opposed, & said, that it was not Voted. I said it was. He said not by any Sign. Brother Kellog, & Captain Mawdsly said but it was, the Negative thus, that if any was not offended, let such lift up their hands & not an hand was lifted up: & the affirmative was Voted by their Silence: & none spake against it. Then I laid him under the Admonition of the Church. This is a true account of our process with him, which was laid upon his Offencive behaviour in his being treated, & his impenitancy in the Case.

But your Honour accounts my not propounding his desires to the Church contrary to the Congregationall way, yea, to run higher than Presbyterianism in laying him under a Pastorall Admonition. To which I replied that this is a mistake. No Congregationall Divine that ever I saw ever asserted that the ruling Officers work was to bring what ever the humors of Sinners would have brought to the Church. Christ did not erect an Office to bring the perverse humours of Sinners into the Church, this would be strang to his Wisdom: & would set the Churches all on aflame. Nay the Platform gives the Minister his Ministeriall Judgment: Hence he is to judge of all things belonging to his Office: & accordingly he is to act. The Church hath nothing to do in such things as belong to his Office. He is not to aske the Brethren leave whether he shall perform his Office or no, & the Ministers in the Bay in their printed Questions Cases give the Elders a negative Voice unto all the Brethren.[95]

2. Touching Suspension, they in the same place say, that the Pastor of the Church may authoritatively suspend. He is not to be imposed on to administer the Lords Supper to impenitant Visible Sinners whom the brethren will not eject nor cast out or judge guilty.[96]

3. Concerning Pastorall Admonition distinct from Ecclesiasticall. I had it from Mr. Urian Oaks his own Mouth, that the Pastor hath power

to Charge & Command. And Brother Woodbridge having had Captain W. under a Ministerial Admonition, he was offended, & bringing Mr. Hooker to brother Woodbridge, who hearing the Case, turnd on Capt. W. saying, What offended, at a Ministeriall Admonition? rebuking of him therein. [147/148] & in that he would not allow of Ministeriall Admonition, It is particular enjoyned the Ministers of the Gospell to Charge, I Tim. 3.1,3, & Chap. 5.20, they are Charged to rebuke & Reprove, II Tim. 4.21, & to warn them that are unruly, I Thess. 5.14, they are described to be over the rest, & to admonish them, I Thess. 5.12, & they are commanded to do it with all Authority, Titus 3, *ult.* Hence it is a ministeriall duty to admonish. I think its not an easy taske for any one to give a clear proof of any Ecclesiasticall Admonition in Scripture wherein the vote of the Church was taken in order thereunto, not that I deny an Ecclesiasticall Admonition so managed. As for a Councill, I never was against it or refused it, but I thinke its a tempting God to call a Councill in clear things. But I thinke, that [not] every turbulent person under Church Process, should bee humourd upon their desires by calling a Councill or that Churches should be at Charges of a Councill upon the Humours of such as are offencive. I told Smith often that if he lacked Councill hee might Call one & I would appeare to mentain our proceeding. I also told the Church that if they were desirous of a Councill, I would propound it to the Church. But I never saw any desire of any Councill: but I would not burden them therewith unless they desired it.

This letter I wrote to the Colonall but after considering the length of it I abridged the matter & send onely the Epitimy of it to him.

But here the Colonall tells me that Smith had been with Mr. Stoddard & other ministers that had agreed to write on his account; True, Mr. Stoddard, Mr. Woodbridge, & Mr. Brewer of Springfield as well as the Colonall had harkend to Smiths Story offending that rule that saith, I Tim. 5.19, Against an Elder receive not an accusation unless in the presence, ἐπὶ δύο ἢ τριῶν, or by two or three witnesses, & in judging the matter thus heard they suite that Description, Prov. 18.13, He that answers a matter before he hears it its a folly & shame to him. Indeed Mr. Stoddard wrote a note to me advising to accept of Smith's Confession but I could not Comply with it. But Smith I Supposed was flushed upon this; but Mr. Stoddard Orewent what he did in so doing. Mr.

233

Brewer & Mr. John Woodbridge dealt worse for they never wrote to me but wrote what Smith effected in them unto the brethren of the Church, by Smith who gathered Capt. Phelps, a Soure & prejudices old man & some others, with whom they held a Correspondency that was very shamefully unwarrantable. Onely Mr. John Woodbridge pastor of the Church on the West side of the River at Springfield wrote a letter unto me to enquire on Br. S[mith] his account to desire to know how he stood with us, he desired to partake with them in the Lords Supper the following Lords day, whether they might admit him regularly, for they heard that he was under offence in the Church. I wrote to him an account that they could not regularly admit him for he was under both a Pastoral, & also an Ecclesiasticall Admonition. & on the Fr[i]gday in the same Weeke Mr. John Woodbridge & the brethren of the Church write this following letter to the Church at Westfield & send it open, sand-ballat like,

> The West Church of Springfield to the Church of Christ at Westfield Sendeth greeting
>
> We being met together, Goodman Smith renews his desire of partaking with us in the ordinance of the Lords Supper. We understand that there is a difference between yours, & him. We are loath to do any irregular action that might be Offencive to you, therefore desire you to give us intimation if it be so: & if it be not healed to make it up with as much Speed as may be with Convenience & with as much tenderness as the rule of the Gospell will allow of seing the Case is Circumstanced as it is. Not else but that we are your brethrens in the Faith & Fellowship of the Gospell.
>
>
>
> John Woodbridge, Joseph Elis, Joseph Bodnatha, John Bag, Charles Fory, Isaak Frost, John Petty, Nathaniel Morgan, Thomas Barbar Benjamin Stebbin.
>
>

This letter was not dated but was brought the first day of July & then Smith gathered together most of our Brethren & delivered it to them. I knowing nothing of it, it was a little too gross for them to give answer to it. I perceived that they knew not what to do: & they brought it to me & shewd it. I stranged it thinking John Woodbridge would never have come nigh such an Ugly thing, but Conjecturing that some hedd-strong blades amongst them did drive on the matter so hard that he was Constrained to prevent difficulty amongst them but he told me, no, it was an oversight in them not to bee justified. Our Captains that brought it to mee would have had me to have returnd them an answer. I denied it, & told them that they deserved no answer. My answer to the same query was not Credible with them. Yet thinking some heady brains had drove it on I yielded that they should make some return thereof & they that they might have some thing to say, Captain Phelps the Master of Miss rule, & of Smiths acknowledgment mentioned before takes a vote of some of the brethren there & forces by frowning words them that refused, to accept of Smiths owning it. & so they Vote that Smith was accepted amongst them by vote. But this give him not Welcom I think amongst them. I knew none of these things untill afterwards.

And now as for this letter as to the matter of it, it is not without offence as implying that we held him to harder terms than the Gospell required, whereas he would never manifest any repentance of his Sin. But these backshardend him in his Sin. If in the Classicall rule, Classes undermine class & uphold offenders thus, all will run into the like Confusion. For its manifest that this pervers fellow being restless in his perversness prevailed with our easy brethren, & gaining the Old Sour Captain to be his proctor improoved his Cousen Partridge & the deceived ministers as his backtelling them that both Magestrates & Ministers would leave me & so led them in the dirt.

But Colonall Partridge in his letter pleads that his Cousins Offence was triviall & of a low Nature. Yet if so it being a Visible Sin it requires Visible repentance answering the Gospell that a Church in her releasing the offence, may have faith to believe that Christ would justify the Same in heaven as it is, Matt. 16.19, & 18.18. But his Sin was greate in its own nature. 1. It was rebellion in its own nature against the Majesty of Christ, & this is said to be as the Sin of Witchcraft, I Sam. 15.23, & Stubborn-ness is Idolatry. 2. It is the letter of it a treading underfoot that Scripture that saith keep thee far from an Evill Matter, Ex. 23.7, Confess your Sins, one to an other, Jas. 5.16, & that Heb. 13.17, etc. 3. His Carriage therefore was an abuse of Christ in his own house, & a turning of him out of doors. 4. It was utterly destructive unto any Gospell Discipline in the Church, etc.

At length he being uneasy under these admonitions, & debard from Church Communion he came to a little higher Confession of his

Sin & so was absolved. But not without my Sorrow & the Church keeping a day of Fasting & prayer to beg pardon of their failings herein we came to a [148/149] settlment & peace.

Brother Ensign Stephen Kellogs Case.

Some time in this Spring 1714 When Ebenezar Millar of Northampton was about buying fatted Oxen, He & Brother Kellog & others 4 or 5 of them at John Shephards when he was trading about John Shephards Oxen, they had there 2 or 3 pots of Cider amongst them & going thence to Samuel Ashlys they had a pot or 2 there. & there Ensign Kellog fell Vomitting, & some said or took him to be drunk. He neither was asserted to reeke, Stagger or to be discomposed in his reason, but he accounted it to be from the Quesiness of his Stomach. Hence he is Complaind of to Authority as drunke, & Daniel Bag & John Shephard give upon oath before Colonall Pynchon that they judged him to be drunk or overgone with drinke. Hence

He was Complained on to me with other times as being overgone at Windsor. Which we enquired into by Capt. Mawdsly & Deacon David Ashly, & they could not finde any Such thing but the persons instanc'd in cleared him, onely they observed that he talked something briskly. I sent for him & discoursed him & was Satisfied about that of his at Windsor, but that at our town he Confessed the thing denying that he was drunke, but owning the fact as not justifiable, & desired me to draw up a Confession for him in these words or Words to the same Effect.

Where as there hath been a Complaint put in against me as offending in point of drinke & that Unto Vomitting whereof there hath been Conviction given in to Colonall Pynchon, I do acknowledg the same with griefe of heart, altho' I did not then nor do I now account my vomitting to be from the Excess of What I drank but from a ill disposition of my Stomach that oft provokes me to vomiting when I have tooke nothing. Yet probably had I seen a person under the like Circumstances I should have given him the like testimony. But yet being heartily grieved hereupon, I confess I have not been so wary as I should have been considering the experience that I have of the Crasy State of my Stomach. Wherefore not justifying my selfe in the matter I ly low before God, & desire that the Church & all that have been offended hereat, to pass by all the Offence that they have taken up & to help me with their prayers to God that what ever evill there was therein, he would pardon the same & helpe me by his Grace to watch over myselfe better & to walk for the time to come more inoffencively, the which I promise by the Grace of God to endeavour after.

This Confession was not Satisfactory. Whereupon a time was set for approbation & indeed he was not a drunkard nor did fall on ordinarys, but unwariness was his fault when with others he might take more than was to be justified, whereby his tongue was used more than at other times but the time set being sooner than was usualy, no disorder found, his Confession was accepted by almost all of the brethren, tho' some upon what ground they would not act I know not.[97] Too much will & unworthiness was in it I fear. This was October 9, 1714.

Sister Abigail Dewies Case[98]

There fell in an unhapp difference between Thomas Dewy, & John Ingerson. Dewy had as it was said 120 or more hens young & Old, which he kept giving them Corn such as came to his street door in the Street which many of them infested John Ingersons house, garden, Barn, & Barly sowed by his barn when in the Ears, etc. & Ingerson spake to Dewie about his hens to keep them away, but met with provoking language for a remedy. So that Goody Ingerson wrong or brake the neck of an hen that sat in her Garden & after seing no reformation she killd some of their Chickens that infested them in their house, flying up & down that troubled them to turn them out of their house, & if the doore was open in they would come again, that Ingerson was fain to be their Hentender. So that they had no other way left but to kill them & so Carry'd them home: & one time when Goody Ingerson had Carried Some home Dewey's girle ran after her as she was going home & emptied a Chamber pot of Chamber Lee upon her head. & another time goody Ingerson sent her little girle with a Chicken or two more that he being infested with had killd & when the girl was returned almost to her fathers door Dewies girle ran after her hawling her back again, & Dewies wife stood in her own doore with a Cord in her hand shaking it, saying to her girle, bring her, bring her. & Justice Parson being in the town, Dewy fetched a Warrant for John Ingerson to bring him before him for killing his hens & frighted Ingerson so that he being a fearfull man & not so Crafty as the other agreed with Dewy to beare the Charges & also to give him 3ᵈ apiece for all the Chickens that he had killd & Dewy had eaten. But Dewies Wife being called before the Justice & by him demanded whether she said to her girle that halled Ingersons girle back bring her bring her she said No to the Question as attested Benjamin Mawdsly, Thomas Mawdsly, Young Benjamin Mawdsley, Ensign Stephen Kellog, Jonathan Fowler, Luke Noble at first but afterwards they had gaind him to fall back, Hanford Old & they had prevailed also with him to doubt, John Ingerson & his Wife, Hannah Alvard, Widow Hannah Loomas. Capt. Phelps said he took it that she denied to the Question & so did the Captains Wife. These I treated & had them all assert the same & they said that Samuel Sergeant Phelps, Nathaniel Phelps of Northampton, then here & Jonathan Sacket could testify the Same. But she denighed that she denied this to the Justice. This matter being brought to me, I went first to justice Parsons, & asked him whether he could say anything to it whether she denied it when he asked her whether she bad her girle bring her. He said he remembered nothing of it. But Capt. Mawdsly said Yes Sir there was something said, for if you remember, she sat at the end of the table & desired that she might be calld out & examined, & you called her out & asked her whether she said bring her, & she was about to deny it & Luke Noble said, Abigail, its a vain thing for you to deny it for I heard you say bring her.

I seing the woman deny absolutely that she denied the matter to the Justice, I was affraid of Difficulties unless I could prevaile with the wom[an] to suspect her me[mo]ry & therefore the day before our Conference [149/150] I went to her, & her Sister Ashley being with her in her house, I desired her to go a part for I had something to say to her. & we went into the other room. I told her that there was laid in a Complaint against her for denying to Justice Parsons that she said to the Girle bring her: She said, she did not deny it. I told her I discerned it would be proved that she did denie it she said then she would fall under the Proof, I told her then it must be put upon proofe & that would make a great Stir & when proved, she must fall. & it would be easier to do it now by Suspecting her memory. She said that she well rememberd. I said I would have her suspect her memory, which She might very well do: & if she did not suspect her memory when it was proved the

Censures would go on for it would be unreasonable to believe her deniall against 6 or more positive assertions. She said there were more would testify that she did not deny it. I told her that they were negatives & could never be accepted against affirmatives: beside it would set altogether by the ears & therefore I advised her to suspect her memory & prevent all this stir & evill. & now it was as I thinke that she said that she thought it was the best so to do, or words to this purpose. Then I told her that I had had a many ugly things in my hand that had kept us off a great while from the Lords Supper[99] & I would fain finish them to morrow & so this of hers, she said she thought she should not be there, for she was not Well. I told her that if she could own what I should propound to the Church, I knew not but it might be accepted if she was not well & so could not be there. & then I repeated what I would say & asked her whether she could own the Same. She complied. I repeated it again & said I will not promise you to use the very same words: my memory will not Serve me but I will promise you to use the same as much as I can, & I will use nothing but what shall be words the same or to the same Sense. & so she complied therewith.

The next day the fifth as I take it of October after Brother Kellogs Case was ended I declared Sister Dewies Case thus, There being a Complaint laid in against Sister Abigail Dewy for denying to Justice Parsons that she said to her girle that halled John Ingersons girle back, bring her, & discerning Sufficient proof to be had, of the same, I was afraid of hard things unless I could prevaile with Sister Dewy to suspect her memory, & she thinking when she had heard me, that It was the best so to do. Then I told her that I would willingly finish the matter tomorrow she said she was not well she thought she would not be there, I told her I knew not but it might be accepted if she could own what I am now about to relate she Complied, & it was thus, That she was sorry for the matters that had fallen out & tho' she had no hand in the abuse that goody Ingerson met with from the girle in empting the Chamber Lees upon her, yet she was sorry that she did not more Severely treat the girle for it. & as for her denying that she said to her girle bring her before the Justice tho' she doth not remember, that she did deny it yet understanding that so many do say that I did, I do indeed suspect my memory that it may fail me in the matter & therefore I desire that all that are offended with me on that account, would lay all offence thereat by & help me with their prayer, & I hope I shall & promise to endeavour to walke by the Grace of God more warily for the time to Come.

When I had uttered these words her husband stood up & impudently denied them. I asked him what he denied, he said, that his wife suspected her memory, I told him that he was not there. He said that she told him she did not suspect her memory. I told him to this effect that she complied with me so to do & I repeated the matter two or three times to her & she Complied with my proposition, thinking it the best, but she would fall under the Witnesses. So the matter was delayed till the next Conference Octob. 19. Witnesses were brought that asserted that they heard her say no to the Question. His father another soare person denied the Witnesses indeed, I did not call them out to own their witness; but did not put the matter to vote but deferrd it till the next Conference, & this I suppose he aimd at that he might now have time to pervert if possible the Witnesses. & so he implied himself as I am informed by severall of them & when argument would not prevaile with them he endeavoured to effect it by ill Will & offence that he used wherein I had offended one, but going to one that he heaved to make him retract found him so resolute that he told him that he would Confirm his testimony by Oath before any authority. This I Suppose knocked him down. So that she Novemb. 1. Came with her Husband & gave me this Confession following.

Sister Abigail Dewies Confession

Whereas there hath been Sorrowful things about the matter of my answer to Justice Parsons, as if I had denied to him that I said to my maide Servant bring her, viz, good man Ingersons girle, I do not remember that I denied it. But perceiving that severall persons tooke it that I did deny the matter & have been offended, yet I am ready to doubt whether my memory fails me not, possibly it may, & therefore I desire that all that tooke it that I did deny it, & have received offence upon the same, would lay by all offenciveness, & accept me into their Charity, & help me with their prayers to God that he would pardon what ever offence there may be therein, & I hope by the assistance of grace that I shall endeavour to walk more warily for the time to come.

Thus I calld out Sister Dewy & read it November 2ᵈ to the Church & she owned it & so I propounded it, both negatively & affirmatively, & none opposed it but all except Capt. Mawdsly accepted it. & so she was absolved.

Brother Ensigns Kellogs Confession took & accepted the 2 day of December 1720[100]

This May having been so many times sadly & brought out on the account of Drink * * * him about February in the year 1718/19 Debuke a butcher of Boston being come to buy Fat ware, & he being with him had taken too much which being prooved upon him by brother John Root, Sr., & John Bancraft, & the Church being very hardly brought to acts of Charity as to accept of his Confession I advised him to forbare to appeare at the Lords Table until he give a due testimony against his sin: & partly for a triall of his behaviour in which time going with a Neighbour into the Westcountry to buy Wool * * * it very well till he came at Suffield & * * * [150/151] the Ordinary for a drau[g]ht of Rum, he took so much as did disorder him which heareing of [I] treated him about it, & he fell under it with sorrow, & had not Confidence to put himselfe upon the Churches judgment till now: & being urged upon it he was on the 20ᵗʰ of 10ᵐ 1720 becalled he appeared & manifested his repentance by the Following Confession,

About February come two years I being at John Phelpeses house, when Debuke a Boston Butcher was chaffering about Fat ware, & Cider being somewhat plentifully used, & the same coming oft to mee, I was, as is testified against me disguised therewith, & to my hearty sorrow tooke too much, to my wounding, & to the offence of others that have given in testimony of the same: the Which testimony I fall down under, & I hope God hath made mee truely sensible of the Evill thereof: & I am not able to give you an account of the sore sorrow of heart that I have sustand on the account thereof. & that I might not offend any of my Christian Brethren by any appearances at the Lords Table before I had manifested my Sorrow & Repentance for the same, I did being advised thereto, for beare to approach to that holy Ordinance all this time. But now being called out to do it I readily appeare to do the same in the bitterness & anguish of my Soule applying myself to my present Confession intreating you all to lay all your offences aside, & to accept of me again into your Charity & to help mee with your prayers unto God that he would pardon my Sin, & not leave me to myselfe, nor to any over bearing temptation either to the same offence or to any other. I hope that God hath given me a true Sight of my Sin herein: & I further promise by the grace of God so to endeavour after a greater Watchfulness over myselfe for the future that I offend not herein as in any other way Who am

Your Sorrowful Brother in the
Fellowship of the Gospell.

This Confession made with suitable behaviour was put to the breathren, that if any had any reason to refuse acceptance I desired the same to manifest the same. & none made any objection & so propounded it to the Church that if they accepted of the Confession & granted the request they would Signify it by the Usuall Sign of lifting up of the hand & Severall hands * * * & none opposing, he was pronounced to be reconciled & the readiness of the Church to forgive him & so being laid under an exhortation to a greater Watchfulness over himselfe against all offences, chiefly against failling in drink he was absolved.

The Publick Records of the Church of Christ at Westfield, of all unto whom the holy Ordinance of Baptism hath been administred therein, from the beginning.[101]

ANNO DOMNI 1679

Moneth the 6th day 31
Ebenezar, the Son of Josiah, Dewy baptized
Mary, the Daughter of Samuel Loomis baptised

The Seventh Moneth
7 day, Joseph, & Mary, Children of John, Ingerson, baptized

The Eight Moneth
19th day, Deliverance, the daughter of Nathaniel Willer baptized

The Ninth Moneth
3rd day, Josiah, the son of Isaak, Phelps was Baptized

The Eleventh Moneth
4th day, Hannah the Daughter of Joseph, Pomery, Baptized
11th day (Samuel, the 5th 10^m 1680) David, John Hannah, the Children
    of David Ashly Baptized
        Item, Sarah, Jedediah, & Daniel the Children of
        Jedediah, Dewy were Baptized
        Item, Eliazur, & Hannah Children of Eliazur Weller
        were Baptized

The First Moneth
24   Samuel Root admitted into the Church into full Communion, was baptized

Anno Dni 1680

The Second Moneth
4th day, Hester, & John, the Children of John Hanchet were baptized

11th day (Thomas, Adijah 5th 10^m) Samuel, James, Mary Hannah, & Elizabeth, the Children of Thomas Dewy, Baptized

3 day, Elizabeth, the Daughter of Eliazur Weller Baptized

The fourth Moneth

6^{day} Mary, the daughter of Samuel & Mary Taylor, Baptized

27^{day} Samuel, the Son of Thomas, & Mary, Root Baptized

Abigael, the daughter of John & Ann Root Baptized

The 9th Moneth

7^{day} Dorothy, & Hannah, the Children of Jacob & Dorothy, Phelps, were Baptized

The 10th Moneth

5^{day} Comfort, the Son of Lt. John & Mary Mawdsly baptized

These are the Children in the Power of t[hei]r parent[s] * * * of this Church who [were ent]red i[n]to a Church State here.

Samuel, & James the Sons of Mr. Edward Taylor
Benjamin, Joseph, Mary, Consider, & John
Children of Lt. John Mawdsly
Ruth, Sarah, Johannah, Benjamin, Nehemiah, William &
Phillip Children of Ensign Samuel Loomis
Hephzibah, Josiah, John, Sarah, Nathaniel,
Children of Sarg. Josiah Dewy
Mary, Sarah, John, Samuel, & Hannah the Children of John Root
Isaak, John, Hannah, & Hizeaiah, Children of Isaak [Phelps][102]

M.   D.   The Eleventh Moneth

11   09   Hannah, the Daughter of Joseph & Hannah Pom[ery,] Baptized.

11	20	Mary the Wife of Fearnot King Baptized	
		John, Samuel, Ambrose, & Elizabeth,	under
		Children of A[m]brose, & Jane Fowler baptized	watch of
		& aComing Stephen, & Hannah, Children of	the
		Walter & Mary Lee baptized, they also	church
		committing themselves	

12   20   Abigail, the Daughter of Thomas, & Constance Dewy, bap[tized]

           Elizabeth, the Daughter of Thomas & Mary Root, baptized

Ano Dni 1681

·2   03 Israel, the Son of Jacob, & Dorothy Phelps, baptiz[ed]
     24 Mary, & Elizabeth, the daughters of Fearnot & Mary King were
         baptized

3   01 Abigail, the daughter of David, & Hannah Ash[ley] & Joseph, the
         son of Samuel & Mary Tay[l]or, were baptiz[ed]

      8 Hannah, the wife of & John the son of, James Saxton * * *
         the said Hannah, baptized

     15 Jonathan, the Son of John, & [Mary] Ingerson baptiz[ed]

4   19 Abigail, Nathaniel & Elizabeth, children of Walter, & Mary Lee
         baptized

     26 Samuel, the Son of Samuel Loomis Jr. & Hann[ah] his wife baptized

5   03 Thomas, the Son of Jedediah, & Sarah Dewy, Baptized

         ⎰ Samuel, the son of John Hanchet & Esther his wife;
     10 ⎱ Charles, the son of George Saxton Jr. & Mary his
           wif[e,] were baptized

     31 Antony the Son of William, & Sarah Pixly baptiz[ed]

6   07 Abigail daughter of Mr. Edward, & Elizabeth Taylor baptized[103]

8   16 Daniel, the son of Isaac by his Wife Anne Phelps, bapt[ized]
         [243/244]

*   25 Susannah, Mary, Elizabeth, Nathaniel, & John, the Children of
         John & Patience Ponder baptized

[10] 12 Elizabeth, the daughter of Joseph & Hannah Pomery, baptized
[10] 19 Abigail the daughter of Fearenot & Mary King baptized

         Thomas, the son of John & Patience Ponder Baptized

1682

[02]   16   { Joseph, & Experience }   the twins of Josiah, & Hephzibah Dewy, Baptized

John, the son of William by his Wife Randall baptized on her right as being under the Watch of the Northampton Church

03   Joshua, the son of John by his wife Mary Root Baptized

10   Nathaniel, the son of George Saxton, Jr., by his wife Hannah Saxton baptized

[1]1   07   Rebeckah, daughter of Thomas & Hannah Nobel, baptized

14   Benjamin & Joseph, sons of George Saxton Sr. & Catherine baptized

[12]   04   Mary, the daughter of David & Hannah Ashly baptized

11   Elizabeth, daughter of Samuel, & Mary Taylor, baptized

1683

01   25   John, the Son of John & Abigael Mun, under the Watch of Springfield Church, baptized

02   22   James, the son of Samuel Loomis, Jr. & Hannah his wife, baptized

[03]   13   Nathaniel, Son of Nathaniel & Abigail Gailer of Windsor, under the Watch of Windsor * * *

20   William the Son of Benjamin, & Ruth Smith baptized

[04]   10   Martha the wife, & Martha the daughter of Thomas by the said Martha Mawrly: & also Sarah the daughter of Daniel & Sarah Saxton were baptized

17   Mary, the Wife of John Gun, entred under the Church Watch, had her children, Thomas & John Baptized

[05]   29   Sarah the Daughter of Thomas & Mary Root baptized

[06]   12   Abigail the daughter of John & Abigail Noble were baptized

[09] 25 Joseph the son of Mr. Younglove member of Hadly Church, &
          Hannah the dauter of Timothy Haile member in full Communion
          of the Church of Windsor were baptized

[10] 02 David the son of David Winchell baptized
      22 Hannah the daughter of James & Hannah Saxton baptized

  *   18 James the son of Thomas by his wife Constance Dewy, baptized

  *   06 Abigail daughter of Joseph, & Hannah Pomery baptized

[11] 13 Benjamin the son of Jacob & Dorothy Phelps baptized

[12] 03 My Daughter Bathshuah, by my wife Mrs. Elizabeth Taylor, was
          baptized

[1] 02 Martha daughter of John & Patience Ponder baptized

  1   09 Samuel the son of Samuel & Abigail Fowler, baptized
      23 Mary daughter of Mr. Daniel Denton member of Springfield
          Church baptized

1684

  3   4 Experience, daughter of Fearnot, & Mary King, baptized

  *   * Joseph the son of Jedediah, & Sarah Dewy baptized

  *   * Hannah the daughter of John, & Esther Hanchet baptized

  *   22 Sarah, daughter of Peter Brown member of the Church at
          Windsor, & Abigail daughter of William by his wife [Mary]
          Randall, under the watch of Northampton Church baptized

  5   20 Elizabeth, Daughter of Samuel & Mary Taylor baptized

  7   14 Thomas, the Son of Thomas, & Mary Morly baptized

  8   12 Abigail, daughter of Nathaniel, & Abigail Galer member under
          the watch of Windsor Church baptized
      19 Noah son of Isaak & Ann Phelps baptized

 12   08 My daughter, Elizabeth, by my wife Mrs. Elizabeth Taylor,
          & Ruth, daughter to Benjamin, & Ruth, Smith were baptized

      22 John, son to John & Mary Noble, was baptized

1   01 Debora the Daughter of Fearnot & Mary King baptized

     15 Mercy the Daughter of John & Mary Root baptized

1685

2   12 Mary daughter of John & Mary Gun, baptized

3   31 Rebecka daughter of David & Hannah Ashly baptized

5   19 Bathsua daughter of John, & Ester Hanchet; likewise Mary daughter of David, & Elizabeth Winchel were baptized

     26 Edward Son of Edward & Abigail Grissill was baptized

7   06 James, the Son of James & Hannah Saxton; & Mary the daughter of Walter & Mary Lee baptized

     13 Joseph son of Joseph & Hannah Pomery, baptized

8   25 Jonathan, son to Samuel & Abigail Fowler, baptized

9   22 Elizabeth the daughter of John, & Mary Mawdsly baptized

10 06 Timothy Son to Thomas by his wife Mary Root, baptized

     20 Elizabeth daughter of Nathaniel, & Hannah Bancraft, baptized

11 10 Lydia daughter of Joseph & Hepzebah Bodman was baptized

1   21 Hannah daughter of Jedediah & Sarah Dewy baptized

1686

3   23 Thomas the Son of Nathaniel & Eunice Phelps baptized

4   04 Mary Daughter of Mr. Edward by his wife Mrs. Elizabeth Taylor baptized

     09 Israel son of Thomas & Constance Dewy baptized

6   01 Sarah daughter of John & Patience Ponder baptized

     08 Joseph son to Jacob & Dorothy Phelps baptized

	15	Stephens, son of John & Mary Noble baptized
8	10	Thomas son of Samuel & Hannah Looms baptized
	31	Mary daughter of Thomas & Martha Morly baptized
9	07	Medad the son of Joseph & Hannah Pomery; as also Mary, Abiel, & Rebecka children of Nathanial & Mary Williams baptized
	28	Hannah Daughter of William & [Mary] Randall baptized [244/245]
10	19	Mindewell Daughter of Josiah & Hephzibah Dewy baptized
11	16	Phebe Daughter of James & Hannah Saxton baptized
12	20	Benjamin, son of Benjamin & Ruth Smith baptized
1	06	Mercy Daughter of Samuel & Mary Taylor baptized
	13	John Son of John & Hannah Goodman baptized

1687

1	27	Daniel son of John & Mary Gun & Nathaniel & Jonathan children of Nathaniel & Eunice Phelps baptized
2	03	Mary daughter of Samuel & Sarah Ashly baptized
4	12	Ebenezar son of Isaac & Ann Phelps: Also Mehetabel Daughter of John, & Ester Hanchet baptized
7	02	Ebenezar son of Fearnot by Mary King baptized
	25	Ebenezar son of Samuel Bush, a member under the Watch of Sudbury Church, baptized
8	02	Elizabeth the Daughter of Nathaniel & Mary Williams baptized
	09	John, the son of John & Abigail Richards baptized
9	06	Abigail daughter of Samuel & Abigail Fowler baptized
	13	John the son of John & Sarah Lee was baptized
12	19	Hezekiah my son by my wife Mrs. Elizabeth Taylor was baptized

1688

3   20   John son of John & Deborah Sacket baptized, Deborah being a member under the care of Windsor Church.

4   03   Edward son of Nathaniel, & Hannah Bancraft baptized

    24   Joseph son of Thomas & Mary Root baptized

5   01   Jedediah Son of David Winchel; also John son of Joseph & Hannah Pomery baptized

8   14   Eunice daughter of Nathaniel & Eunice Phelps, baptized

9   04   Samuel son of Samuel & Sara Ashly baptized

10   09   Jedadiah son of Jacob & Dorothy Phelps baptized

11   13   Abigail daughter of John & Abigail Richards baptized

12   10   Elizabeth Daughter of James & Sarah Saxton, baptized

1   03   Mary daughter of Jededias & Sarah Dewy baptized

1689

2   21   Elizabeth, daughter of William & [Mary] Randall baptized

4   23   Elizabeth of John & Mary Noble baptized

5   21   Samuel son of Benjamin & Ruth Smith baptized

8   20   Sarah daughter of Samuel & Mary Taylor baptized

9   14   John son of Nathaniel & Mary Williams baptized

10   15   Elizabeth daughter of John & Sarah Lee baptized

11   26   Abel son of Thomas & Martha Morly baptized

12   23   Mary daughter of Samuel & Abigail, Fowler baptized

[1690]

5   27   Joseph the son of William & Hannah Sacket baptized

6	17	Thomas son of Benjamin, & Mary Mawdesly baptized
7	21	Thomas the son of David & Mary Ashly baptize[d]
9	15	Ebenezer, son of John & Esther Hancet bap[tized]
	22	Abigail the daughter of John, & Deborah Sacket baptized
12	15	John son of Fearnot & Mary King baptized
	22	Sarah the daughter of Joseph and Hannah Pomery Baptized
1	15	Mercy daughter to John & Mary Gun baptized

1691

6	2	Jedediah son of David Winchel baptiz[ed]
7	6	Nathaniel Son of Nathaniel & Mary Williams baptized
8	4	Daniel the son of Samuel & Sarah Ashly baptize[d]
9	1	Thomas son of John & Abigail Richards: & Lois daughter of Nathaniel & Eunice Phelps were baptized.
11	17	Mercie, daughter of John & Mercy Fowler baptized
	31	Hannah daughter of Samuel & Hannah Loomis baptized
12	21	Elizabeth the daughter of Benjamin & Ruth Smith baptized

1692

2	10	James son of Jedediah & Sarah Dewy baptized
	24	Sarah daughter of John & Sarah Lee baptized
3	29	Benjamin son of Benjamin, & Mary Mawdsley baptized
5	10	Child of Hollowday of Suffield bapti[zed]
	31	Hannah the wife & Hannah the daughter of Joseph Saxton baptized
6	21	Hannah Daughter of William & Hanna Sacket baptized
	28	Hannah daughter of Samuel & Mary Taylor baptized

8   16   Mary daughter of John & Mary Noble baptized

23   Sarah daughter of Samuel & Hannah Bliss belonging to Springfield Church bap[tized]

30   Jonathan son of Jonathan Burt (under the watch of Springfield Church bap[tized]

10   04   Thomas, Samuel, Elizabeth, Hannah, Mary & Sarah, children of Thomas, & Elizabeth Hanchet baptized

11   01   David son of David & Mary Ashly baptize[d]

29   Isaac son of Isaac & Mary Phelps baptiz[ed]   [245/246]

1693

1   26   Thomas son of Stephen & Elizabeth Lee baptized

2   16   Ruth daughter of Mr. Edward Taylor by his Wife Mrs. Ruth Taylor baptized[104]

6   20   Daniel son of John & Deborah Sacket baptized

27   Samue[l] son of David Winchell, & Abraham son of John & Mercy Fowler baptized

7   17   Sarah daughter of Samuel, & Sarah Ashly, & Abigail daughter of Nathaniel & Mary Williams baptized

8   01   Adijah son of Adijah, and Sarah Dewy baptized

29   Hannah daughter of Samuel & Abigail Fowler baptized

9   12   Mary, Daughter of Thomas Smith of Suffield baptized

1694

2   22   Hannah Daughter of Joseph and Hannah Pomery baptized

3   20   Deliverance daughter of Samuel, & Hannah Loomas baptized

6   19   Joseph, & Hezekiah children of Matthew & Hannah Noble & also Hannah & John, children of Richard & Elizabeth Church, baptized

7	02	Aaron son to John & Mary Gun baptized
	09	Thomas son of Thomas & Sarah Ingerson, & Sarah daughter of John, & Sarah Ashlie, baptiz'd
	16	Jemima daughter of Benjamin & Mary Mawdsly were baptized the 26 of the former month viz 6ᵐ
	16	Ruth daughter of Ambrose & Mary Fowler: & Rebecka daughter of William & Hannah Sacket, baptizd
8	07	Joseph, Son of Joseph & Hannah Saxton baptized
	28	Rachel Daughter of Benjamin & Ruth Smith, & Abigail Daughter of John & Sarah Lee, baptized
9	18	Abigail daughter of Jedediah & Sarah Dewy baptized
12	17	Moses son of Thomas & Sarah Ingerson baptized
1	03	Rachel Daughter to Richard & Elizabeth Church baptized
	10	Joseph son of Samuel, & Mary Taylor baptized
	17	Mary daughter of David & Mary Ashly baptized

1695

1	31	Naomi my daughter by my Wife Mrs. Ruth Taylor baptized
3	12	Samuel son of Stephen & Elizabeth Lee baptized
4	9	Sarah Daughter of Thomas Smith of Suffield baptized
	30	Deliverance daughter of John & Esther Hanchet baptized
6	17	Mercy daughter of John & Mercy Fowler baptized
9	17	Mercie the daughter of Thomas, & Martha Morlie baptized
10	22	Hannah daughter of John & Sarah Ashly baptized
	29	Mercy daughter of James & Hannah Saxton baptized
11	12	Deliverance daughter of Thomas & Elizabeth Hanchet baptized
	19	Esther daughter of Samuel, & Abigail Fowler baptized

26 David son of John & Mary Noble, & Hannah daughter of Daniel & Hannah Bag baptized

12 02 Aaron son of Isaac, & Mary Phelps baptized

1 16 Rachel daughter of Samuel & Sarah Ashly baptized

1 23 Sarah daughter of Adijah, & Sarah Dewy, baptized

1696

3 17 Mary the Daughter of Thomas Root by his first wife baptized

4 14 Samuel Neale subjecting himselfe under the Watch of the Church was baptized

5 5 Jemima daughter of John & Abigail Richards was baptized

12 My daughter Ann born the 7th day of my Wife Mrs. Ruth Taylor; and also David son of John & Deborah Sacket were baptized

26 Joshua son to Samuel & Hannah Loomas baptized

8 11 Thomas Son of Thomas & Elizabeth Noble baptized

9 1 James son of Richard & Elizabeth Church was baptized

12 7 Mindewell daughter of Joseph & Hannah Saxton baptized

1 14 Mary daughter of Ambrose & Mary Fowler baptized

21 Jonathan Son of William & Hannah Sacket baptized

1697

2 4 Mindewell daughter of Joseph & Hannah Saxton baptized

11 Sarah daughter of Samuel, & Sarah Dewy baptized

4 6 Miriam daughter of Thomas & Sarah Ingerson was baptized

5 5 Johannah daughter of Thomas, & Mary Smith of Suffield baptized

25 Thankful daughter of Thomas by his Wife Sarah Root baptized [246/247]

7 26 Jacob, son of Samuel, & Sarah Ashly Baptized

8   04 Jonathan son of Benjamin, & Ruth Smith: & John son of John & Sarah Ashly were baptized

9   07 Hannah daughter of John and Mary Noble baptized
        14 ·Isaak son of John & Mercy Fowler baptized

10   5 Stephen the son of Stephen & Lydia Cellog baptized

11   30 Lydia Daughter of Stephen & Lydia Cellege

12   27 Daniel son of Daniel & Hannah Bag baptized

        Elizabeth, daughter of Samuel & Marie Ashly baptized

1698

4   5 Sarah daughter of Samuel & Abigail Fowler baptized

7   18 Matthew, son to Matthew, & Hannah Noble baptized

8   16 Caleb Son of Caleb, & Elizabeth Root of Farmington baptized

        30 Benjamin, Son of John, & Deborah Sacket baptized

9   27 Susannah daughter of Joseph, & Johannah Smith of Farmington baptized

10   04 Nehemiah Son of Nehemiah, & Thankfull Loomas baptized

        11 Joseph son of Richard & Elizabeth Church baptized

11   22 Abigail Daughter of Joseph & Abigail Mawdsly & Esther Daughter of Adijah, & Sarah Dewy baptized

12   29 Job son of Thomas, & Elizabeth Noble baptized

1   05 Sarah daughter of Thomas, & Lydia Pixly baptized

1699

3   15 Elizabeth, daughter of Samuel & Sarah Dewy baptized

        22 John Son of Thomas, & Martha Mawdsly baptized

6   06 Nehemiah son of John, & Sarah Lee baptized

20 Mehetable my daughter by my Wife Mrs. Ruth Taylor baptized, being a week old

8 01 David son of Thomas & Sarah Ingerson baptized

12 11 Johannah daughter of Samuel & Sarah Ashlie baptized

01 24 Abner the son of Joseph, & Abigail Mawdsly & Noah son of Mark Noble baptized

1700

2 21 James Son of Joseph, & Abigail Ashly baptized

3 05 Jonathan, son of Thomas & Elizabeth Noble Baptized

05 21 Samuel son of Samuel, & Mary Bush baptized

28 Patience, & Thankfull tw[i]ns of John, & Mercy Fowler baptized

8 06 Moses, Son of John, & Sarah Ashley baptized

13 Samuel Son of Ambrose, & Mary Fowler bapt[ized]

20 Moses son of Stephen, & Lydia Kellog baptized

9 10 Ebenezar son of Daniel & Hannah Bag baptized

24 Solomon Son of Matthew & Hannah Noble baptized

10 01 Luke son to Luke & Hannah Noble a[nd] Daniel son of Joseph & Hannah Saxton baptized

10 15 Jonathan son of Richard, & Elizabeth Church baptized

22 William son of Samuel & Elizabeth Sacket baptized

29 Job son of Benjamin, & Ruth Smith bapti[zed]

11 05 Isabel daughter of Samuel, & Abigail Fowler baptized

11 12 Abigail daughter of David & Mary Ashly baptized, 12th of 11m

1701

2 06 Jonah son of Joseph & Abigail Pixly baptized

3 04 Ezekiel, son to Samuel & Sarah Ashly, Abigael Daughter of Nehemiah, & Thankfull Loomas baptized

7 14 Mary daughter of Adijah & Sarah Dewy baptized

8 19 Hannah daughter of Samuel & Sarah Dewie baptized

9 02 Jacob son of John, & Mercy Fowler baptized

23 Thankfull daughter of Joseph & Johanna Smith of Farmington, & Deborah daughter of John & Deborah Sacket baptized

30 Abigail daughter of Jonathan & Abigail Phelps baptized

10 14 Keziah, daughter of Nathaniel & Mary Williams baptized

28 Mary daughter of Mark & Mary Noble baptized

11 25 Daniel son of James & Ruth Noble baptized

12 22 Azariah son of Benjamin, & Mary Mawdsly baptized

1702

1 29 Ebenezar son of Thomas & Martha Morly & Ebenezar son of John & Sarah Ashly baptized

2 05 Kezia My daughter by my wife Mrs. Ruth Taylor baptized [247/248]

* * * * * *

2 12 Benjamin son of Isaak & Mary Mecham of Enfield baptized

19 Johannah daughter of John & Sarah Lee baptized

31 Abigail daughter of Nathaniel & Abigail Lewis of Farmington & Isabel daughter of John & Isabel Ingerson baptized

4 14 Thomas, son of Caleb & Elizabeth Root of Farmington baptized

5 05 Sarah daughter of John, & Sarah Root, Rachel daughter of Daniel & Hannah Bag, & Marie daughter of Samuel, & Marie Bush baptized

8 04 Abigail, daughter of Joseph & Abigail Ashlie, baptized

   25 William son of John & Marie Noble

9 01 Seth Son of Thomas, & Elizabeth Noble baptized

   15 Sarah, daughter of Joseph, & Abigail Mawdslie baptized

   29 Samuel son of Richard & Elizabeth Church baptized

10 13 James son of James & Anne Saxton baptized

   27 Abigail daughter of Stephen & Lydia Kellog baptized

11 03 Aaron son of Samuel & Sarah Ashly baptized

12 07 Samuel Son of Luke & Hannah Noble baptized

   14 Elisha son of Matthew & Hannah Noble baptized

   30 Elizabeth daughter of Samuel & Elizabeth Sacket baptized

1 07 Joseph son of Joseph & Abigail Pixlie baptized

   14 Eleonar daughter of Thomas & Sarah Ingerson baptized

1703

2 4 Gideon son of Thomas & Hannah Gun baptized

   11 David son of David & Abigail King baptized

   18 Samuel son of Samuel & Sarah Dewy baptized

5 18 Charles son of David & Sarah Dewy, & Joseph son of Ambrose & Mary Fowler baptized

6 15 Mary daughter of Benjamin & Ruth Smith baptized

   22 Nathaniel son of Nehemiah & Thankfull Loomas baptized

7 19 Mehetabel daughter of John & Mercy Fowler baptized

   26 Israel son of Thomas, & Elizabeth Noble baptized

8 10 Moses son of David, & Marie Ashly baptized

11	09	Naomi daughter of Nathaniel & Mary Williams baptized
	30	Abigail Daughter of Adijah & Sarah Dewie baptized
12	27	Isaak son of John & Mehetabel Sacket baptized
1	12	Abigail daughter of Eliazar & Abigail Weller baptized

1704

2	23	Margarit daughter of John & Mary Noble baptized
3	28	Elisha the son of John & [Mary] Root baptized
5	02	Elizabeth daughter of Samuel & Abigail Fowler, baptized
	09	Abigail daughter of Mark & Mary Noble baptized
6	06	Azariah son of Jonathan & Abigail Ashly baptized
8	01	Samue[l] son of John, & Sarah Lee baptized
	15	Nathaniel son of Nathaniel & Abigail Lewis of Farmington baptized
	22	Rebeckah daughter of Jedidiah & Rebeckah Dewie baptized
4	11	Noah son of John & Sarah Ashly baptized 11 of the 4m
8	29	Ezekiel son of Joseph & Hannah Saxton baptized
9	26	Elizabeth daughter of Samuel & Elizabeth Sacket baptized
10	10	Jane daughter of James & Catherine Noble baptized
	17	Daniel son of Steven & Lydia Kellog, & Katherine daughter of James & Anne Saxton baptized
12	04	Ann daughter of Daniel, & Hannah Bag baptized
	11	David, son of Joseph & Abigail Mawsly, & Naomi Daughter of Joseph & Abigail Ashly baptized
	25	Thankfull daughter of David & Abigail King baptized

1705

2   01   Jashet son of Samuel & Mary Bush & Elizabeth Daughter of Richard & Elizabeth Church baptized [248/249]

3   29   John Shephard & Elizabeth his wife & Jonathan their Child, & Abigail daughter of Joseph & Abigail Pixlie

4   17   Abigail daughter of Samuel and Abigail Bush baptized

     24   Jonathan son of Samuel & Mary Root baptized

5   29   Moses son of Thomas & Hannah Gun baptized

7   02   Jonathan son of Eliazar and Mary Weller baptized

8   21   Obediah, son of Matthew and Hannah Noble baptized

9   18   John son of John & [Mary] Root baptized

11   06   Elizabeth daughter of Thomas & Elizabeth Noble baptized

12   03   Roger son of John, & Sarah Ashly baptized

     10   Margaret daughter of Jedidiah and Rebeckah Dewy baptized

     24   Rebecca daughter of Samuel & Rebecca Loomas baptized

1   03   Mabell daughter of John & Mary Nobel, & Mindwell daughter of Ambrose & Ruth Fowler baptized

1706

1   31   Ezra son of John & Mehatabel Sacket & Rachel daughter of Nehemiah & Thankfull Loomas were baptized

4   02   Mary daughter of Samuel and Mary Root baptized

5   21   Abraham son of Benjamin Dibble of Simsbury baptized

6   04   Deliverance daughter of Samuel, & Sarah Dewy baptized

     18   Noah son of Thomas, & Lydia Pixly, & Bithia daughter of Adijah & Sarah Dewy baptized

7   08   Ebenezar son of John & Mercy Fowler baptized

22 Nathaniel son of David & Sarah Dewy baptized

8 28 Elisha son of Nathaniel Lewis & Abigail his Wife: and Elizabeth daughter of Caleb & Elizabeth Root both of Farmington baptized

9 04 Esther Daughter of Joseph Smith & Johannah his Wife, of Farmington baptized

24 John son of John & Elizabeth Shephard & Moses son of David & Abigail King baptized

10 08 Hannah daughter of David & Mary Ashly baptized

22 John the son of Mark & Mary Noble baptized

29 Orpah daughter of Nathaniel & Mary Williams baptized

11 12 James son of James & Cathar[ine] Noble baptized

2 02 Martha & Joshua Children of W[il]liam & Martha Loomas baptized

16 Philip son of Philip & [Hannah] Loo[m]as baptize[d]

1707

2 13 Martha daughter of Jonathan & Abigail Ashly baptized

4 15 Moses son of Joseph & Abigail Pixly baptized

5 20 Ephram, son of Steven, & Lydia Kellog baptized

27 Elizabeth daughter of John & [Mary] Root baptized

6 24 Samuel son of Samuel & Rebeckah Loomas Ra[ch]el Daughter of Samuel & Marie Bush; & Margaret Daughter of John, & Sarah Lee Baptize[d]

7 21 Abigail Daughter of Daniel, & Hannah Bag baptized

28 Mary daughter of Joseph, and Abigail Mawdsly baptized

8 05 Hannah Daughter of Matthew & Hannah Noble baptized

12 29 Mary daughter of Eliazar & Mary Weller baptized

1 7 Zerviah, daughter of Jedidiah & Rebeckah Dewy baptized

1708

2   11   My son Eldad Taylor & L[y]dia Daughter of Jonathan & Sarah Ashly baptized[105]

     25   Thomas son of Thomas & Abigail Dewy baptized

3   23   Abigail Daughter of Samuel & Sarah Ashley baptized

4   13   Jonathan son of Samuel and Sarah Dewy baptized

5   13   Lois daughter of Thomas & Elizabeth Noble baptized

     08   Reuben son of Thomas & Hannah Gun baptized

8   17   Jacob Son of David & Sarah Dewy; & Joel son of Philip & [Hannah] Loomas Baptized

     31   Joshua son of Nathaniel and Lydia Ponder baptized

10   19   Step[h]en son of David & Abigail King baptized

11   29   Ruth the Daughter to Luke & Ruth Noble baptized

12   12   David & Noah twins of Ambrose & Ruth Fowler & Ann daughter of Josiah & Elizabeth Phelps of Colchester baptize[d] [249/250]

1   6   David of James, & Catherine Noble Baptized

1   13   Esther Daughter of Samuel & Rebeccah Loomas baptized

1709

2   3   Ann Daughter of Adijah & Sarah Dewy & Abigail Daughter of Nathaniel & Abigail Phelps, baptized

3   06   Mary daughter of Samuel & Mary Bush baptized

     29   Elizabeth Daughter of Charles & Martha Coats baptized

7   25   Margaret daughter of Eliazur & Mary Weller baptized

8   16   Joseph Son of Samuel & Sarah Ashly Baptized

     23   John son of Joseph, & Abigail Pixly baptized

     30   Marcy daughter of Steven & Lydia Kellog Baptized

9	27	Ezekiel son of John & Elizabeth Shephard Baptized
10	04	John son of John & Mary Ashly Baptized
	18	John son of John Hanchet of Stony Brook baptized
11	08	Miriam Daughter of Mark, & Mary Noble baptized
	15	Hannah daughter of Joseph & Abigail Mawdsly baptized
	22	Ruth Daughter of Daniel, & Hannah Bag baptized

1710

2	2	Moses son of Luke & Ruth Noble & Sara daughter of Jedidiah & Rebeckah Dewy baptized
	9	Elizabeth daughter of Philip & Hannah Loomas baptized
	23	Daniel son of John & Mary Root & Abigail daughter of Thomas & Abigail Dewy baptized
	30	Margaret daughter of Samuel & Mary Root baptized
3	07	Thankfull daughter of Nehemiah Loomas baptized
	21	Benoni Son of Samuel Sacket dead, & Elizabeth Sacket baptized
4	4	Charles son of Charles & Esther Coats baptized
	11	Esther daughter of Matthew and Hannah Noble baptized
5	*	Lydia daughter of Jonathan & Abigail Ashly Baptized
	*	Rhode daughter of Consider & Elizabeth Mawdesly baptized
5	08	Anne d[a]ughter of William & Martha Loomas baptized
8	15	Israel son of David, & Mary Ashly baptized
	22	Nathaniel Son of Eliazur & Mary [Weller] Baptized
9	12	Nathaniel son of Nathaniel & Abigail Phelps baptized
	26	Rebecca daughter of Samuel & Rebecca Loomas baptized
12	4	Benjamin son of David & Abigail King baptized

1711

3　6　Abigail Daughter of Philip & Hannah Loomas baptized

5　1　Lydia Daughter of Ebenezar & Miriam Bush baptized

3　20　Sarah daughter of David & [Sarah] Dewie baptized, being forgot is recorded out of its place

6　19　Israel son of Consider & Elizabeth Mawdsly Baptized

7　19　Sarah daughter of Samuel & Mary Bush baptized

　　26　Abigail daughter of Nathaniel & Lydia Ponder baptized

8　07　Ebenezar son of Thomas & Elizabeth Noble baptized

9　11　Aaron the son of Luke & Ruth Noble Baptized

　　18　Preserved the son of John & Mary Ashly Baptized

11　6　Edward son of Charle[s] & Esther Coats baptized

　　20　Jonathan Son of Joseph & Abigail Pixly baptized

12　17　Noah son of Stephen & Lydia Kellog, & David son of John & Mary Root baptized

1　9　Israel son of Thomas & Abigail Dewy baptized

1712

2　6　Nathaniel son of Nathaniel & Hannah Eggleston baptized

　　20　Eliakim Son of John & Mehetable Sacket baptized

3　03　Samuel son of Samuel & Mercy Fowler baptized

4　01　Jacob son of Hansford Old baptized

　　15　Rhoda Daughter of Jedidiah & Rebecca Dewy baptized [250/251]

7　7　William son of William & Martha Loomas baptized

8　19　Isaak son of Consider & Mary Mawdsly baptized

9　02　Margaret daughter of Daniel & Hannah Bag baptized

　　16　Jonathan the son of Jonathan and Abigail Ashly baptized

10   28   George son of George & Hannah Phelps under the care of Spring-
         field Church baptized

12   15   Elizabeth daughter of John & Elizabeth Shephard baptiz'd

     22   Mabell daughter of Samuel & Rebeccah Loomas baptized

1713

2   12   Mary daughter of Philip & Hannah Loomas baptized

3   24   Noah son of Mark & Mary Noble baptized

4   07   Ebenezar son of Ebenezar & Miriam Bush baptized

7   13   Mabel daughter of Enock & Mercy Buck held under the Watch
         of Weathersfield Church baptized

8   18   David & Ebenezar twins of Eliazer & Mary Weller baptized

9   08   Samuel son of John & Mary Root baptized

     15   Desire daughter of Nathaniel & [Elizabeth] Bancraft baptized

10   13   Esther daughter of Nathaniel & Esther Gun baptized

11   10   Steven son of Charles & Esther Coates baptized

     24   Thomas son of Thomas & Elizabeth Hanchet baptized

     31   Beulah daughter of Joseph And Abigail Sacket baptized

1   21   Elijah son of Ebenezer & Mary Pixly Baptized

1714

1   28   David son of Joseph & Abigail Pixly, Daniel, & Elizabeth twins of
         Consider & Elizabeth Mawdsly, Samuel & John, Children of John
         & Martha wife of the said John Haines, & Abigail the daughter of
         Samuel & Martha Root Baptized

2   11   Sylas son of Steven & Lydia Kellog: & Jedidiah son of Jedidiah &
         Rebeccah Dewy Baptized

3	09	Steven son of John & Elizabeth Root Baptized
03	16	Mercy daughter of Joshua & [Margaret] Root baptized
	30	Sarah Daughter of Israel & [Sarah] Dewy baptized
04	06	David Handford & Elizabeth * * *, Thankfull daughter of Thomas & Elizabeth Noble, & Margaret daughter of * * * & Hannah Mawdsley baptized
	20	David son of Samuel & Marcy Fowler b[aptized]
6	29	Aaron son of David & Abigail King [baptized]
8	03	Miriam Daughter of Nathaniel & L[ydia] Ponder Baptized
	10	Joseph son of Joseph Sarah D[ewy] baptized
9	07	Sarah Daughter of Daniel & Hannah [Bag] baptized
	14	James son of William & Martha Loomas [baptized]
11	09	Moses, the Son of Adijah, & Sarah D[ewy] baptized
	16	David Son of Deliverance, & De[borah] Church baptized
	23	Asa son of Luke & Ruth Noble Baptiz[ed]
12	13	Benjamin son of Jonathan & Abigail Ashly ba[ptized]
	20	David son of Samuel & Rebecka L[oomas] baptized
1	13	Mary daughter of John Sacket & Mehetable his wife, baptized
	20	Lydia Daughter [of] John & Mary R[oot] baptized

1715

01	03	Jerusha daughter of Philip & Hannah Loomas baptized
	17	Sarah daughter of John & Elizabeth Shephard baptized
03	21	Joshuah the son of Joshua & Margret [Root] Baptized
04	18	Obediah son of Samuel & Ma[ry Bush] & Jerusha daughter of Samuel & Rebeckah Dewy baptized
	25	Hannah daughter of Thomas & [Abi]gail Dewy baptized

6   27   Joseph, son of Joseph & Sarah [Dewy] baptized

7   11   Rachel daughter of Captain [Joseph] & Abigail Mawdsly bapt[ized]

8   30   Elizabeth daughter of Th[omas] & Elizabeth Hanchet bapt[ized]

9   10   Josiah son of Samuel & Ma[ry] Kellog baptized

11   11   Martha Daughter of John & Martha Hains baptized

11   29   Abigail daughter of C[harles] & Esther Coats baptized

12   05   Huldah daughter of E[bene]zar & Miriam Bush b[aptized]

12   Lydia Daughter of Consider & [Elizabeth] Mawdsley baptized
[251/252]

1716

* * * son of Joseph & Abigail Sachet

Constance daughter of Israel & Sarah Dewy baptized

Sarah daughter of Joseph & Sarah Dewy baptized

Rheda the Daughter of Matthew & Hannah Noble baptized

Martin son of Jedidijah & Rebecca Dewy baptized

Jonathan son of Thomas & Sarah Ingerson baptized

Daniel, & Esther Children of George Granger of Suffield, being
under the Watch of Springfield first Church, baptized

Caleb son of Handford & Elizabeth Olds under the Care of Springfield Church, Baptized

Moses son of Ensign Stephen, & Lydia Kellog baptized

Anna daughter of Deacon Thomas & Elizabeth Noble baptized

Debora daughter of Deliverance & Debora Church baptized

Solomon son of John & Mary Root baptized

Thankfull Daughter of William & Martha Loomas, & Margret
daughter of Joshua & Margaret Root baptized

George son of David & Abigail King baptized

Joseph son of Joseph & Abigail Mawdsly, baptized

* * * the Daughter of Nathaniel & Elizabeth Bancraft baptized

David son of Daniel & Hannah Bag baptized

Samuel son of Samuel & Mary Root, & Naomi daughter of Luke & Ruth Noble baptized

Anne daughter of John & Hannah Bancraft baptized

1717

Azzubah, daughter of Daniel & Esther Gun baptized

Ebenezer son of Jonathan & Abigail Ashly baptized
Joseph Sayler put himself under Church Watch & was baptized, & his son Joseph & his Wife

Bethesda daughter of Samuel & Mercy Root baptized
* * * son of Philip & [Hannah] Loomas baptized

4	16	Moses son of John & [Eliza]beth Root baptized, & Jonathan Son of * * * Philips * * * Trimmon baptized
6	18	Dinah daughter of Nathaniel & Lydia Ponder baptized
8	13	Ann daughter of John & Hannah Mawdsly baptized
	20	Thomas Son of Joseph & Mary Root, & Ruth Daughter of Consider & Elizabeth Mawdsly Baptized
9	10	Samuel son of Samuel & Mary Kellog baptized
11	26	David son of John & Elizabeth Shephard was baptized
12	09	Abigail Daughter of Thomas & Elizabeth Hanchet baptized

1718

1	26	Hannah daughter of [Jedediah &] Rebecka Dewy baptized, this was out of its place which is 1717/18

2   06   Job son of Joseph Mawdsly, & Abigail his wife Baptized

2   13   Jonathan son of Joseph Layer & Hannah, was baptized

3   18   Daniel son of Samuel & Mary Bush baptized

3   25   Hazel & Mabell—Twins of Samuel & Rebecca Dewy, & Lydia daughter of Joseph & Sarah Dewy baptized

4   1   Isaak, son of Hanford & Elizabeth Old baptized also Daniel son of Thomas & Sarah Dewy baptized

4   15   Naomi daughter of John & Mary Root baptized

          George the son of Benjamin &   Saxton Baptized

6   3   Edward son of John & Hannah Bancraft baptized

8   5   Joseph son of Joseph & Abigail Noble & Eldad & Hasuel twins of David & Abigail King baptized

        19   John the Son of Philip & Rebecka Trimon, & Moses Son of John & Thankfull Phelps baptized

9   2   Mercy daughter of Samuel & Rebecka Loomas baptized

9   16   Zecharias the son of Ebenezar & Miriam Bush, & Hannah the Daughter of Joshua & Margaret Root Baptized

9   23   Ezekiel the son of Nathaniel & Abigail Lewis of Farmington baptized

11   22   Jonathan the son of Benjamin and Martha Loomas baptized

1   04   Israel son of Israel & Sarah Dewy baptized [252/253]

1719

1   12   Mary daughter of John and Hannah King baptized

3   3   Aaron son of Ensign Stephen & Lydia Kellog baptized

04   7   Abigail daughter of Joseph & Abigail Sacket baptized

       14   James Dewy put himself under the Watch of the Church

5   5   Stephen son of James & Elizabeth Dewy baptized

5   26   Margarit daughter of Philip & Hannah Loomas baptized

*   15   Thomas son of Nathaniel & Lydia Loomas baptized

7   13   Anne daughter of Deliverance & Deborah Church baptized

8   4   Sarah daughter of Thomas & Abigail Hanchet baptized

10   13   Benjamin son of Consider & Elizabeth Mawdsly; & Aaron son of Aaron & Esther Gunn were baptized

      27   Margaret daughter of Charles & Esther Coates baptized

11   13   Mary Daughter of Daniel & Hesther Gun baptized

1720

02   3   Moses son of Stephen & Abigail Kellog baptized

02   17   Anne daughter of John & Hannah Bancraft baptized

4   *   Steven son of Joseph & Mary Root baptized

4   *   Thomas son of Moses & Katherine Ingerson baptized

5   *   Mary daughter of Jededia & Rebeckah Dewy baptized

8   *   Eli son of Joseph & Abigail Noble Baptized

10   4   Aaron son of Joseph & Sarah Root baptized

11   *   Moses son of Samuel & Rebecka Loomas baptized

11   28   Sarah daughter of Thomas & Sarah Ingerson baptized

12   12   Hannah daughter of John & Hannah King baptized

2   15   Hezekiah son of William, & Martha Loomas baptized

1721

2   15   Aaron son of Israel & Sarah Dewy baptized

4   17   Eli son of * * *

*   *   Jonathan son of Deacon Thomas, & Elizabeth Noble baptized

5	5	David son of Samuel & Mary Kellog baptized
5	12	Erastas son of Joseph & Abigail * * * Baptized
5	30	Hannah daughter of Joseph & Ann Seger baptized
07	14	Thankfull Daughter of John & Thankfull Phelps baptized
08	06	Elizabeth daughter of James & Elizabeth Dewy baptized
08	22	Stephen son of Stephen & Abigail Kellog, & Ann daughter of Aaron & Esther Gun baptized
12	09	Thomas Son of Thomas & Abigail Dewy bapitzed

* * * * *

1	29	Martin son of Samuel, & Mary Root, David son of Ebenezar & Miriam Gun, & Elizabeth daughter of Jonathan & Constance Fowler baptized
2	10	James son of John, & Mary Root Baptized
2	18	Mercy daughter of Consider & Elizabeth Mawdsly baptized
*	*	Moses son of Deliverance, & Debera Church baptized

1722

2	*	Ruth Daughter of Joshuah, & [Margaret] Root baptized Kezebriall son of William & Martha Loomas baptized
3	25	Abel son of Edward & Martha Old baptized
03	13	Gideon son of David & Abigail King baptized
05	5	Sarah daughter of Josiah & Elizabeth Phelps baptized
06	5	Samuel son of Samuel (who now put him self under the Watch of the Church) & Johannah * * * Mercy Daughter of Samuel & Mercy Fowler baptized
06	19	Samuel son of Luke & Ruth Noble Baptized
07	14	Sarah daughter of John & Hannah Mawdsly baptized
09	11	Abigail daughter to Ebenezar & Lydia King
*	*	Sarah daughter of Jonathan King baptized

10   22   Johannah daughter of Matthew Noble * * * was baptized

11   5   Sarah daughter of Lt. * * * baptized * * * then subjecting herself
           under the Watch of the Church

12   11   Joseph son of Philip & Rebecca Trimon baptized

1723

2   23   Aaron son of Nathaniel & Lydia Ponder baptized & Jemmima
           daughter of * * * & Thankfull Ponder baptized

      30   Preserved son of Joseph & Abigail Noble baptized

3   29   Mercy * * * of Nathaniel & * * * [253/254]
*   *   Josiah son of Stephen & Lydia Kellog & Mercy daughter of
           Thomas & Elizabeth Hanchet Baptized

*   7   Sarah daughter of David Ashly Jr. & his Wife subjecting themselves
           under the Watch of the Church * * * [baptize]d & Thomas Noble
           Jr. also subjecting himselfe under the church watch & his Child
           Sarah

*   *   Mary & David * * * under the Watch of the Church * * *
           Mary baptized

*   27   Abigail the Daughter of William & Abigail Clark Baptized

*   23   Miriam daughter of Thomas &   Ingerson was baptized

*   12   John Lee having subjected himself under the Watch of the Church
           had his son John baptized & Ephraim Stiles likewaise having
           subjected himselfe under the Watch of the Church had his Child
           * * * baptized

*   *   * * * the son of Josiah & Elizabeth * * * baptized

*   *   Experience the daughter of Josiah & Margret Root baptized

1724

* * * * * *

*   *   Mary daughter of Deliverance & Debrah Church baptized

*   2   Prudence daughter of Burt & Sara Temple baptized

*   *   Samuel son to Samuel & Mary Hanchet, & Noah son of Joseph
&. Sarah Dewy baptized

*   4   * * *

      7   John son of Aaron & Esther Gun baptized

*   25   August the month * * * son of John & Mary Root baptized

1725

*   3   Hannah Daughter of James & Elizabeth Dewy baptized

      6   Rebecka daughter of Isaak Stiles this day * * * under the Church
Watch & his wife   baptized

*   [2]3 Martin son of Daniel & Thankfull Ashly baptized the 23 of August

*   7   Clark son of Joseph & Abigail Pixly baptized

*   *   Hannah daughter of Luke Noble Jr. now received under the Church
Watch & Hannah his wife baptized

*   *   Anne daughter of Luke Noble Jr. & * * * baptized

*   *   Jonah son of John & Mary Lee, Benjamin son of Philip & Rebecca
Trimmon, & Thomas son of Thomas &   Noble baptized

*   *   Seth son of John Sacket Jr. & Sarah, baptized

*   *   Isak son of * * * Hannah baptized

*   *   * * * day of the 27 Johannah daughter of * * * Ingerson baptized

*   * Mary daughter of John, & Elizabeth Shephard baptized this 20th of June 1725

*   * 25 of July 1725 David Dewy subjected himself under the Watch of the Church & his Child David was baptized

* * * * * *

7m 4 day of September was John son of Ebenezer King baptized

17 Oliver, son of David & Mary Ashly baptized

Consider son of Matthew & Hannah Noble baptized the 17 day of October 1725

December, 27 Abigail Daughter of Charles Dewy (he now putting himself under the Watch of the Church) by his wife Abigail Dewy, was baptized

1726

Sarah daughter of * * * John Phelps baptized the eight of February

Section 2ᵈ   Dismissions[106]

Section the Second touching Dismission

Dismission is an Ecclesiasticall proceeding with Such of the Members in Particular Covenant together, as are hereby emembrated, or discharged & put out of the membership of the Society of the particular Church. And this is done by $\begin{cases} \text{Dismission \&} \\ \text{Excommunication.} \end{cases}$

1. Touching Dismission

Dismission properly so Calld is Such an act of the Church whereby her members enjoy that liberty purchased them by Christ, & doth evidently evince the Clamor to be a Sclander that is cast against particular Churches, as Pound wherein the Disciples of Christ are Penfolded, or imprisoned. For hereby when her members remoove their habitation so far from the Society as renders it impossible, or very difficult unto them, to perform the Duties of their Membership, to the Societie; or otherwise on due Consideration desire to joyn to some other Society, She in tender love to them granteth them their desires, with a recommending of them to Such orthodox Churches of Christ as shall be meet for them to joyn with & easy to perform Covenant Duties mutually.

And in case the Members so remooved at such a distance as is inconvenient, or impossible for mutuall duties to be attended according to Covenant, do neglect to seeke their Dismission & the Church after greate patience exercised towards them findes a perseverance therein, & no satisfactory reason for it, she may & ought to send them a Dismission with an advising & urging them to walk in the Orders of the Gospell & joyn to Such orthodox Churches wherein mutuall duties may be attended.

Such hath been the practice of this Church from its beginning as Occasion hath offerd. & therefore

Sister Hannah Saxton, wife of George Saxton Jr. was upon his remooving his Family to Gemaica on long Island Recommended to the Church of Christ at Gemaica, with this Consideration that in case she met with disappointing difficulties, she should return us the account & reason of her non entrance, that we might know our duty.

Deacon Josiah Dewy, & Hephzibah his wife both of this Church remooving to a new Place Called Lebanon about eight miles west of Norwich, sending for their Dismissions Were Recomended unto the Work of Christ to be erected into a Church State there, the 12th day of 9br 1700. And now Brother & Sister Pomery Members in Church fellowship with us having departed from us without acquainting the Church were sent to, to give a reason that might be satisfactory for their so doing & Continuing without seeking for their dismissions in a letter dated 15th 9br 1700. But no answer being made thereupon, the Church proceeded to vote their dismission, & send it after them, which they did. & sent it in the letter following

Brother, & Sister Pomery,

You having withdrawn yourselves from us, in a way not ordinary: & we having wrote, desiring you either to take your Dismissions from us, or to return unto us; & now in a years time since the Same having heard nothing at all from you, cannot but beare it as a greate grievance knowing, that hereby, your Covenant with us thus doth solemnly made, doth wholy faile as to the end thereof. And therefore we after severall years patience thus exercised, in that you having cessated all Covenant Duties amongst us by your absence, & Distance from us, are necessitated to, & have also voted your Covenant nulld, & to send you your Dismissions from us, that you may settle yourselves in some orderly Church of Christ where you shall see Convenient to your abode. & shall hereafter account you to have Cessated your membership amongst us. & so pressing you upon the entering where Covenant Duties may be attended, we do testify unto you our ceasing to account you any members of our Church.

Edward Taylor Pastor of &
by Order of the Church.

The Church at Suffield being about to be founded, & three of our Church Members being inhabitants there, desired of our Church their Recommendation unto that work when the time of its proceeding came.

But we seing their proceeding like to be not according to the Order of the Churches in the Country, could not do that. Yet, we readily left them to their liberty, to do as they saw Duty lay upon them in that matter. And Brother David Winchell, & brother Thomas Smith entred with those other that then entred into Covenant. & so their liberty granted was their Dismission. Brother John Hanchet, and his Wife, used it not. & so still remain members with us.

Mr. Ezekiel Lewis being a Member of our Church & being settled at Boston, desired his Dismission from us to the South Church in Boston, the which was voted & sent him thus.

> To the Reverend Mr. Samuel Willard, & Mr. Ebenezer Pemberton Teaching Elders, to the Brethren, & South Church in Boston, Grace, Mercy, & Peace be multiplied.

Whereas Mr. Ezekiel Lewis, a Member in the Ecclesiasticall Fellowship of the Gospell amongst us in this place, being by the good hand of God called to have his Residence amongst you, hath desired his Dismission, & Recommendation of him to your Fellowship in the Gospell. We readily, & heartily grant him his Desire, & recommend him to your Special Fellowship: Desiring you to receive him, as becometh the Saints [of the] Churches of Christ: & desiring the Special bl[es]sings of his grace to be poured out upon y[ou] in all things: but especially in all your ho[ly] Administrations to the everlasting benefit o[f your] Souls, to the Advancing of the intrests of his kin[g]dom, & to his own glory, We remain your br[eth]ren in the Fellowship of the Gospell.

| { Westfield } | Edward Taylor by Order |
| { 24th 7ber 1703 } | & on the behalfe, of the Church. |

Sister Noble Widdow of Brother Thomas Noble, being Married again to Mr. [Medad] Pomery of Northampton, & settled with him there, was, upon desire, Dismissed, & [re]commended unto the Church of Christ at [No]rthampton about the End of April 1705, by our Church.

13 8m 1707: Sister Elizabeth Church, her husband re[m]oving from Westfield to Colechester, desiring her [dis]mission & the Recomenda-

tion to the Church at Co[le]chester, had her desire, & was dismissed by us & [re]comended to that Church. [307/308]

1710. 12ᵈ 2ᵐ Sister Mary King, desiring her Dismission to the Church at Windsor, had it sent her by the Church.

1710 Aboutt time of the Spring Sister Mary Noble desiring her Dismission from our Church to the Church of Christ at Darby had itt sent her.

1710 Brother John Hanchett & his Wife desiring their dismissions to the Church at Suffield, had it granted & del[i]verd as also Sister Smith the Wife of Thomas Smith of Suffield being crasie could sildom attend here on the ordinances we sent her dismission together with recomendation to the Church at Suffield about August.

Deacon Nathaniel Weller & Deacon Samuel Root being taken a way in a bout a forthnight time by a Putrid Fever Brother Thomas Noble & Brother David Dewy were Chosen by the Church to the office of a deacon & were settlen in that Office by Ordination the 25 day of May 1712.

13.11ᵐ ⎫   Reverend Sir, together with your Church
1714 ⎭   Graces Mercy & Peace in Christ be multiplied

Benjamin Smith, a member in Full Communion & Covenant State with this Church at Westfield having some time this last spring, desired of me his Dismission I propounded his desire to the Church, who granted the same, and complied, that when he came for it to me I should write him his Dismission from our Church to what Orthodox Church of Christ he should desire to be dismisst (For I remembred not that he mentioned any Church to which he desired to go & settle with). But he never came for his Dismission & attended not his Covenanted duties in our Church never Since: but we presume that he hath attended the Sabbath worship with you. Which neglect of his Covenanted Worship etc., with this our Church, being judged insufferable, I propounded his Case to our Church upon our last Conference Tuesday the 11, the 11ᵐ 1714, & tooke the Vote of the Church, who voted his dismission to your Church, & that I should write the same to you. Accordingly I here declare, that they have dismissed [h]im to your society. Who desire the Lord to be with him, & with you in all Your Sacred Administra[t]ions especially, Who remains

Your Humble Servant & the Unworthy Pastor of this Church.

P A R T T W O

Related Sermons

[The Revised Foundation Day Sermon]

A Particular Church is Gods House[1]

Eph. 2. 22. In whom you also are builded (up) together for an habitation of God thro' the spirit.

n this Chapter we have the Apostle setting forth the double state of Mankinde as it falls under a Double Consideration: & therefore distributes all men into Such as are

1. Either under, or Without the Profession of the True God, in these Relative terms opposed, viz, YOU, & WEE, v. 1, 3. i.e., You Gentiles that had not, & We Jews that had the True God. Or

2. Such as were either in a State of Wrath, or a state of Favour. As they are in a State of Wrath, the which he shews, that both those that had not, & those that had the Profession of the true God were naturally in. & this he shews to be a State of Sin, v. 3, a State of Death, v. 1, a State of Wrath, v. 3. The which States he doth illustrate in this Chapter, opposing the same to a State of Favour.

As for the State of Favour. This doth not belong unto all: but unto those alone that are brought out of the other State. For tho' all men are either With, or without the Profession of the True God & so either in a State of Death, or in a State of Life; Yet this last belongs unto those only, who (whether they were before either With, or Without the Profession of the true God) are brought out of a State of Nature, into a State of

Grace by the Grace of God. And hence he saith v. 1 You Who were dead, & v. 5. We, who were dead, hath he Quickened together.

Now this State of Favour, he calls the State of Life v. 1.5. & doth illustrate it as it respects $\begin{cases} \text{God } \& \\ \text{The People of God.} \end{cases}$

As it Respects God its a God Glorifying State. & therefore it is a State of Peace with God, v. 16,17: As it Respects the Saints, it is a State of Peace, On Earth Peace. So that this State is that which was the Burden of the Angelicall Song sung by those Celestiall Choristers, Luke 2.14, Glory to God in the highest; On Earth Peace & Goodwill towards, or among men.[2] Peace on Earth. Hence the Partition Wall is broken down, v. 14.

Now the Priviledges, that come in upon this State as it is a state of Peace, & Goodwill among the Saints, are treated on in this Chapter as they are injoyed by the Saints. & as Considered under a $\begin{cases} \text{Politicall } \& \\ \text{Architectonicall} \end{cases}$ Consideration.

First. As they fall under a Politicall Consideration they are now become Christs Policy. & so they are Considered in respect

1. Unto their Matriculation into his Kingdom State. & so their Priviledges are illustrated Comparatively comparing State, & State, [1/2] together, v. 12, 13. Ye who were without Christ, ἀπηλλοτριωμένοι τῆς πολιτείας τοῦ Ἰσραήλ—a far off, are ἐγενήθητε ἐγγύς, etc., made nigh, etc. Oh! what Priviledges come in now?

2. Unto their Infrenchilation into a City State. They are made Free Denisons of the New Jerusalem v. 19, Συμπολῖται τῶν ἀγίων, Fellow Citizens with the Saints. And therefore are adopted to all the Priviledges of this Corporation. Oh! what Unconceivable Immunities are these?

3. Unto their Admission into Christs Houshold state. They are Adopted Heirs into Christs Family v. 19, Οἰκεῖοι τοῦ θεοῦ, the Houshold People of God. Oh! What Priviledges are here? Oh! stand & wonder at this Change. Hereby poor sinners are translated out of the Vassallage of Sin & Hell, into the Common Wealth of Israel, & Kingdom of Heaven: out of the Society of Divells to be the Fellow Citizen of the Saints: out of the Region of the Shaddow of Death, into the Dominion of the Prince of Life: out of the Habitation of Dragons, & Cruelties, into the Corporation of the Houshold of God. Oh! stand amazed at these Priviledges. But thus much respecting this Politicall Consideration.

Secondly. These Priviledges are to be considered as they are injoyed by the Saints under an Architectonicall Consideration, i.e., as those saints are compared to a building. & thus their Priviledges are illustrated from their $\left\{\begin{array}{l}\text{Substructure \&}\\ \text{Superstructure.}\end{array}\right\}$

1. From the Substructure, or Foundation upon which they are as a building, raised, & laid, as v. 20. Its the foundation of the Prophets, & Apostles, Jesus Christ himselfe being the Chiefe CornerStone. In this Substructure here is both a Foundation Stone, & a Corner Stone mentioned, not as if these were two Stones distinct: for they are not. For as Jesus Christ himselfe is the Chiefe Corner Stone so also the Foundation Stone is Jesus Christ himselfe. For other Foundation can no man lay, I Cor. 3.11. But God hath told us that he hath laid him to be Zions Foundation Stone, & yet a Chiefe Corner Stone too, Isa. 28.16, saying behold I lay in Zion for a Foundation, a Stone, a tried Stone, a Pretious Corner Stone, a Sure Foundation. Jesus Christ then is this Foundation; Yea he is both the Foundation & the Corner Stone as being that Rock upon which the Building is built, & the Binder that holdeth the Whole building together. This Foundation is not therefore properly said to be the Old, & New Testament, as St. Ambrose thought[3] nor is it Peter as the Papists aver: but it is Christ Jesus called the Foundation of the Prophets, & Apostles because they were the Wise [2/3] Master Builders under God laying this Foundation, as I Cor. 3.10. & because they are eminently built upon, & have an eminent Intrest in this Foundation, Eph. 1.1. And according as things are intrested in, Such is the Denomination they have As the God of Abraham because God is Abraham's God, Gen. 17. 1, etc. So also in that the Prophets & Apostles did build the Church on this Foundation, its therefore called the Foundation of the Prophets, & Apostles. They were Gods builders to build others up upon it, as I Cor. 4.15, I Pet. 2.4,5.

2. From the Superstructure, or Building Raised upon this Foundation. Now the Building raised is considered

1. Generally, v. 21. In (or rather to attend the Metaphor On) when the whole Building fitly framed together, grows into an holy Temple in the Lord. & then

2. Particularly v. 22, in the words of our Text. On whom ye also are built (up) together for an Habitation of God thro' the Spirit. As

Solomons Temple was but one, yet it had many Habitacles in it of which it did Consist. So the Catholick Church is indeed but one, yet it hath many Particulars of which it doth Consist Saith Zanchy.[4] Now Each of these Particular Churches, is, as this Church at Ephesus, an Habitation of God through the Spirit. Our Text then you se is a Description of a Particular Church of Christ. & Doth describe it what it is from

1. Its Foundation on which it is built, in this Word, In (or rather *on*) Whom. Now who is intended by this Relative Whom, you may see v. 20. & its Christ himselfe. For he is the Antecedent whereto it is to be referd, wherewith it agrees, whereof it is Spoken, & that is the Foundation.

2. Its Materiall Cause of which it Consists, this is couched in the Word You, which are the Persons spoken to, & set out to be the Saints, & Faithfull in Christ at Ephesus, Eph. 1.1.

3. Its Formall Cause Constituting of it, & uniting the Materialls into a Church State, & this lies in the Word Built up together.

4. Its Finall Cause Wherefore its built up, thus expresst, To be an Habitation of God, i.e., to be Gods Dwelling place.

5. Its Principall Efficient Cause So ordering of the Matter for this End. & this is expresst thus Thro' the Spirit. For seing all is thus acted by the Spirit, & the Spirit must needs be the Principall Agent.

The text thus Analysed, the Doctrine I shall speake to is this.

Doct. A PARTICULAR CHURCH OF CHRIST IS BUILT UP AN HABITATION OF GOD THRO' THE SPIRIT. [3/4]

That Description which the Spirit of God layes down of the Particular Church of Christ at Ephesus, demonstrating what it is, from its nature, is true of every particular Church of Christ touching its nature. But you see what this is. Ergo

Now that its spoken of the Particular Church of Christ at Ephesus is plain, for the Epistle is writ to the Saints & Faithfull in Christ at Ephesus Chap. 1.1, & these were suitable Matter for a Church. & you see these are the Persons still spoken to collectively in the word "You" in our Text, & that as they had passed under the Operation of the Spirit of God in order to their Church Incorporation & the Spirit is the Principall Efficient Cause of a Church. And they had received the Church-enforming Act of this efficient; for they were built up together, & are Spoken to as so formed, & made among themselves an Habitation of

God thro' the Spirit. And what this is but a particular Church, I know not. Nay, & Christ speaking to his Angell here residing calls him the Angell of the Church at Ephesus, Rev. 2.1. And as this Particular Church is called an Habitation of God, so the Church at Corinth is called Gods building, I Cor. 3.9, οἰκοδομή from ὅικος, an House, & δομὴ, an Edifice, an house-building, or a raised House, & therefore God dwelles in it, v. 15. So that its his dwelling place.

In Speaking to this Truth I shall

1. Speake to the Causes of a Particular Church.
2. Shew what it is to be an Habitation of God.
3. Consider the Emphasis of this Word, Thro' the Spirit.
4. Inquire into the Reasons why a Particular Church is an Habitation of God thro' the Spirit.
5. Apply the Truth with brevity.

First. As for the Causes of a Particular Church; & they are
$\begin{cases} \text{Externall} \\ \text{Internall.} \end{cases}$

First. The Externall Causes are onely Externall Principalls constituting, or raising up the thing, & laying down the End of the thing; but are no parts of the nature thereof. And these are the $\begin{cases} \text{Efficient,} \\ \text{Finall.} \end{cases}$

1. The Efficent Cause of the Church is that, which gives forth Causative influences to the Constituting of it, & that $\begin{cases} \text{Principally} \\ \text{Instrumentally.} \end{cases}$

1. Principally. And so the onely Principall Efficient is God, the undivided Trinity. Hence the Church at Corinth is Gods Building etc. All the Persons in the Trinity Build it: Hence they joyntly own it, & inhabit it. Hereupon the House of God is the Church of the Living God, I Tim. 3.15. God the Father builds it. Hence calld Gods Building, I Cor. 3.9. God the Son builds it, & hence, said he, on this rock will I build my Church, Matt. 16.16. God the Holy Ghost builds it. Hence in the text Built up together an habitation of God thro' the Spirit. The Father is the Principall Efficient Cause as the Originall of all the Efficiency by which it is built. The Son is the Principall Efficient cause, as the Purchaser of all the Efficiency effecting of it: & the Holy Ghost is the Principall Efficient Cause, as the Effuser of all the Efficiency for the Effecting there [4/5] of, etc.

2. Instrumentally. Now the Instruments that God makes use of in framing this building are this Word, the Ministry of his Word, & his Ministers thereof. These are the golden Pipes convaying the Holy Oyle into the vessells of Honour, from the Fountain of Grace, & Life. These are the Tooles & Artists which God imployes in building himselfe an House. Hence saith Paul, I as a wise Master builder have laid the Foundation, & others build thereon, I Cor. 3.10. And hence the Foundation is calld the Foundation of the Apostles & Prophets, as you heard, Eph. 2.20.

2. The Finall Cause. Now the Finall Cause is that externall Cause of the thing for which the Efficient acts: its that which the Efficient hath in its eye, & doth aime at in its acting: & therefore the actings of the Efficient are regulated by the End. Otherwise they would never be sufficient means in the hand of the Efficient for the attaining that which the Efficient aims at. Now this Finall Cause of a Church is thus expressed viz to be an Habitation of God. εἰς κατοικητήριον is as much as εἰς τὸ εἶναι κατοικητήριον to be an habitation of God. & as God said of the Temple upon mount Zion, Ps. 132.13,14, the Lord hath chosen Zion, he hath desired it for his Habitation; this is my rest forever; here will I dwell, for I have desired it. So it is here a Church of Christ, is his Habitation, his rest, here he will dwell. If any one defile the Temple of God him will God destroy, I Cor. 3.16,17. Now in that the Finall Cause is to be an Habitation of God, the Acting of the Efficient is as an Architect framing it into a Building, that so it may become Gods Habitation, set apart by himselfe for himselfe from all other Uses to his own. Its therefore for his Use, & his alone. And here we may Consider his
$\left\{\begin{array}{l}\text{Furnishing of it}\\ \text{Presence in it.}\end{array}\right.$

1. His Furnishing of it. For this is a Subordinate End thereof, viz, to stow up his Treasures in it which are the Furniture of it; & hereby he both adorns it, & fits it for his Service. For Gods House is Well set out. This is a Greate house wherein are Vessells of Gold, & Silver, of Wood also, & of Clay, of Honour & also of Dishonour, II Tim. 2.20. The Temple at Jerusalem while it was Gods Habitation was richly furnisht, Heb. 9.2,3,4,5,6, & so is Gods Gospell Temple, the Vessells of Dishonour are to be purged away, II Tim. 2.21. So that its onely to be stowed with Vessells of Honour. The House being Gods own, there must be nothing brought in it but what is Gods own, & hath his Marke upon it. Who hath any thing to do to Furnish Gods house with his own paultry

Ware? God will have nothing strange to him brought into his house, Ezek. 44.9. This ware doth not Suite the End of Gods house which is for his own Furniture consisting in Glorious $\begin{cases} \text{Utensills} \\ \text{Officers.} \end{cases}$

1. Utensills: & these are his Household Goods as I may stile them, & are most Costly, Pretious, & Excellent. & are of dayly Use in his house, & house hould Service. The which are these [5/6]

1. The Arke of Covenant Wherein the Holy Records, & all its appertinances are kept, & also the monument of Divine Miracles, viz, the Book of the Law, the Pot of Mannah, Aarons Rod that Bore Almonds. Over it the Mercy Seate, & Cherubims of Glory hovering over the same, etc. So here is the substance of all these, The Lord Jesus Christ, Rev. 1.13—Chap. 21. The true Arke of the Covenant having the Covenant laid up in him, & the Law of God; the Golden Pot of Mannah itselfe, & the Mannah in it. The true Propitiatory or Mercy Seate, I John 2.2, attended on with his Glorious Angells, I Cor. 11.10, Eph. 3.10. The Testimony of Witness, the Oracles of God are laid up here, II Tim. 3.15.

2. The Golden Candle Stick filld with the Holy Oyle giving an heavenly flame to enlighten the house. So here is the light, hence it is Called a golden Candle Stick filld with flaming angells to give an holy shine alwayes, as Rev. 1.20, Matt. 5.16.

3. The Golden Altar, or Altar of Incense, the Insense, Censor, & Fire that came from Heaven upon the Altar, All which are the furniture of the Gospell Temple, Rev. 3. In the Person, & Merits of Christ, the Prayers of the Saints, & the holy flame of Heavenly affection.

4. The Hidden Mannah, the Pure shew bread Table of God with shew-bread on it, Heb. 9.4. So here in Gods house is the Hidden Mannah that came down from above, Rev. 2.17, John 6.50,51. The Lords Table being the Table of Shew bread Table indeed, I Cor. 10.21, & so the Bread of life.

5. The Laver of Purification for all to wash in that enter into the Temple, I Kings 7.38. Here stands the Basen & Ure of our Souls the Blood of Christ to wash in, I John 1.7, applied symbolically in the Water of Baptism, Eph. 5.25,26, Titus 3.5.

6. The Glorious Throne or Chaire of State, where the Lord of the House doth more especially reside, as Isa. 6.1. So here the Whole Church is as it Were Christs Throne. And thus we have as it were some of the Utensills, or Furniture of this House.

2. The Officers in Gods House that are to use these things, & to carry on the Service of the House therewith, (yet some of these things are to be used onely by the Stewards of the House) I say the Officers are

1. Extraordinary, as Prophets, Apostles, & Evangelists, Eph. 4.11, I Cor. 12.28, which were onely for a Season, & not Successive, nor perpetuall.

2. Ordinary, which are to endure for ever, & these are $\begin{cases} \text{Elders} \\ \text{Deacons.} \end{cases}$

Elders are both Teaching & Ruling, as I Tim. 5.17. The Teaching Elders are either Such whose peculiar Worke is to hold forth the Doctrine of Godliness, & therefore are calld to attend teaching, Rom. 12.7, as the Teacher: or whose more proper worke lieth in Exhortation & hence is pressed to this Work, Rom. 12.8, as the Pastor. The Ruling Elders are Such whose Speciall Worke is such as the mannaging the Rule of Discipline, in preparing, matter to be comitted to the judgment of the House, & in Moderating, ruling, & going before them therein, & hence called [6/7] Governments, I Cor. 12.28. That which is Comon to both the Teaching Elders is Preaching the Word & Administring the Seals to the House.

Deacons are Such that are to attende the More Externall Concerns of Gods House, being the Treasurers of the Church to provide for the Table of the Lord, the Ministers Table, & the Table of the Poore, as Acts 6.

Now in such things as these Consists the Furniture of Gods House.

2. His Presence in it. He having so furnisht it, doth come, & reside in it, I Cor. 3.16,17. He fills it with his Glorious presence. So he did the Tabernacle, Ex. 40.35. So he did the Temple, II Chron. 5.13,14: & so he did his Gospell House, Rev. 1.12, & on. On this mount Zion he commands his blessing even life for ever more, as Ps. 133.3. And hence it is that the soule doth so pant after Gods presence in his house, Ps. 42.1,2. But his Glory, & Presence here is Chiefly visible here unto his people in his own worship, & Service wherein his Servants, & Chiefly the stewards of his house are making use of his own Utensills in his house. And so the Use of his house wherein he is especially present in it in Generall lies in his Worship, the which let us Consider in Some Speciall Particulars as follow

1. In that Light of the Ministry of the Word, wherein he here shines forth. For he calls this his Habitation, a golden Candlestick: & the

Ministry in it as the Shining of an Angell, Rev. 1, *ult.*, Chap. 2.1, etc. He uses this House as the Window of Heaven, out of which he shineth with Heavenly light to Enlighten all men in the way to heaven. And his presence in this Light appeares

1. In illumination & Conviction, inlightening blinde mindes, & Convincing hard hearts of their sins, & Miseries. For God onely can effect this, I Cor. 3.6,7.

2. In Conversion. For that sinners turn from Sin unto God its the Power of God in the Word, & not of man, Rom. 1.16, II Cor. 4.7. Hence the Instruments of this Service are nothing, but God that gives the blessing is all, I Cor. 3.5—

3. In Edification. For in that the Use of this Ministry is Reviving, & Edifying, its wholy from God, I Cor. 3.6,7.

2. In those Humble Suites that are made to God in his House.

3. In those Holy, & Heavenly Songs that are here sung to God.

4. In the Celebrating of the Feasts of the Lord at the Lords Table. While the king sits at the Table my spicknard sends forth the smell thereof, Cant. 1.12.

5. In the Initiating Members into this House. Baptisimally in the Ordinance of Baptism: & Disciplinarily, in opening the golden Door to full Communion.

6. In Ejecting Impenitent Sinners, I Cor. 5.4, & receiving again the Penitent, II Cor. 2.7,8, Matt. 16.19. & altho' some of these things may be Carried on else where, Yet this house is Raised to Carry on these things in, & in these & the like things Consist the Use & End of this House: & Gods Dwelling in it. Thus for the Externall Causes.

Secondly. The Internall Causes of a Particular Church are such as in the Constituting of it, Enter into the Essence of it & are the Parts thereof as $\left\{ \begin{array}{l} \text{Matter} \\ \text{Form.} \end{array} \right\}$ [7/8]

First. The Matter of a Church, Now the Matter is that of which the Church is made & Constituted: its an Essential Cause of it. And this Matter is Holie. Holiness becomes thy House, oh Lord, for Ever, Ps. 93.5. Therefore the Materiall Cause of it that it is made of must be Holy. It must be reall, visible Holiness that is the Essentiall Qualification of the Matter for this building. This is the *Forma Praeparans* of it. The Matter simply considered are Stones fetcht out of the Quarry, or Stone Pit of Mankinde, & thence Rifted up, hewen, & Squared by the Stone axe of the Spirit, till they are rightly fitted & Polisht for this Building; & so passt under the Preparatory form, Quickening of them, Eph. 2.1,5. Hence they are Living Stones for this Spirituall Building, I Pet. 2.5, & so implanted into Christ Jesus hence are faithfull in Christ Jesus, Eph. 2.1, & saints as the Matter of the Church at Ephesus were, as also at Corinth, I Cor. 1.1,3, II Cor. 1.1, at Philippi, Phil. 1.2, at Colloss, Col. 1.2: etc. & surely the Spirit of God doth not Stile these Saints that he had not Sanctified, or that their Relation to the Church, or Churchhood required not to be really Holy as an Essential Qualification preparitory to their State.

Onely here observe, that seing the judgment under which this matter is to pass in the triall of its fitness, being to be such as must be extended as far as the Rules of Christian Charity Concerning this fitness, can reach out the hand, & being made by the appearance of things, it is a fallible judgment. And hence appearing Holiness with men, nothing appearing to the Contrary, but such humane infirmities that are to be found in the best of Gods people, doth Sway our judgment to hope, & therefore to pass the Sentence of Christian Charity concerning, the Reality of Such a Persons Holiness, & so to receive such for Saints, & fit Matter. And now that the Matter ought to be really visibly Holy, that Gods Habitation is made of, may further appear I shall endeavour to do these two things, prove its $\begin{cases} \text{Reality} \\ \text{Visibility.} \end{cases}$

1. The first *Forma Praeparans* of the Matter is Reall Holiness. & besides the Scriptures already Quoted take these arguments

1. Because the Catholick Church truely so taken is Holy. For the Whole building, Eph. 2.21, is the true Catholick Church, which grows into an Holy Temple in the Lord. Now as is the Catholick, such must be the Particular. For the Catholick being as the Genus to the Particular, & the Species receiving its Common nature from the Genus, the Particular must needs consist of Holy Matter seing the Catholick Church its Genus is Holy. Hence Rom. 11.16.

2. From the state into which the Matter is brought, & every particular stone is wrought up unto, before it is laid into this building. Now this state is a State of Union, or neerness unto God, Eph. 2.13, a State of Light, Chap. 5.8, of Life or revivall, Eph. 2.1, I Pet. 2.5, of Peace, & Reconciliation, Eph. 2.15,16, of Sanctification, I Cor. 1.1, *ult.* & therefore of Grace. Now these things being spoke indifinitly of the whole society, it cannot [8/9] be but they were in this state, before they were

associated into a Church Body: & this is express[ed] in Peter, I Pet. 2.5. & therefore it is thus,

3. From the Proportion that ought to be between the Foundation, & the superstructure. For if the Foundation be costly, the superstructure raised thereupon, must be some thing answerable. If the foundation be Holy, the superstructure must not be unholy. Now here the foundation is a Pretious Stone, Isa. 28.16, & therefore the Superstructure ought to be of pretious Stones. The foundation is a Pearle of Greate price: Matt. 13, therefore the Building must not be of pebbles, or paultry Stones. Nay but God saith that they shall be with fair Colours, of Agates, & Saphires, Isa. 54.12. God will have a proportion attended in his Building. Where the Windows are of Agates, the Gates shall be of Carbuncles, & all the borders of Pretious Stones. Where one row is Saphires, another shall be Jaspers, etc. Where each Gate is Smaragdine, or a Sparkling Pearle, the streets are all pure gold, Rev. 21.19,20,21. God will have all things in his Building proportionably Excellent. And who can imagine that by Such excellent allusions as these, any things inferiour to the Choicest of the Children of men are intended: & hence Saints are the Matter. Nay, hence by another Metaphor the whole Building is called a Golden Candle Stick, Rev. 1.12,20, etc. & who can imagine that the Spirit of God should lay Such a Golden name upon such a Refuse Nature as all unsanctified Ones are?

4. From the Possessour of it. For according to the Qualification of the Person dwelling in the House, Such uses to be the Nature of the building. Kings, & Nobles do not use to build their Palaces, or Habitations of Mean Materialls. Solomon Built the Throne of his Kingdom of ivory & overlaid it with pure Gold, II Chron. 9.17. Augustus Caesar is said to adorn Rome his Imperiall City with many Stately Buildings, & to say of it, *Urbem reperi lateritiam, refin quam Marmoream*, I found the City to be of brick but shall leave it Marble.[5] But now its the King of Kings that is to inhabit this House. This is the City of the Greate king, Matt. 5.25, God the Father keeps house here, I Cor. 3.16, God the Son makes this his ivory Palace, Ps. 45.8. He is that most glorious Person walking in the middest of the Golden Candlestick, Rev. 1.12—God the Holy Ghost Possesseth these Temples, I Cor. 3.16, & in the text; If Solomon made himselfe a throne of Ivory overlaid with gold: If Ahasuerus[6] his Palace was adorned with white Green & blew Hanging, set upon with cords of fine linen, & purple unto Silver rings, & Pillars of Marble, & with Beds

of Gold, & Silver upon a Pavement of Red, Blew, White, & Black Marble: if Augustus Caeser had his Marble City to reside in, Shall we think the Throne, the Palaces, the Habitation, the Royall city of God himselfe is of base Materialls? No, No: but of the Choicest materialls which is, and therefore Reall Holiness is the Qualification thereof.

5. From the Use, & Improvement of it. For according to the use such is the Matter to be used. Now the Use is an Holy Use; its onely for the worship, & service of God. & you have in briefe had some particulars of the same. Now the use being Holy calls for holy hands to Carry it on, Holy things are [9/10] not to be cast to Dogs, nor pearls hung in Swines Snouts, Matt. 7.6. Now then to instance here, its use is this, God useth it to dwell in it, its Gods Habitation.[7] But God dwells not in an unholy house, if any defile his house him will God destroy, I Cor. 3.17. God will not let unholy ones come nigh him, Isa. 1.16,17,18, Hab. 1.13, Ps. 94.20. So God useth it as a store house of all Grace: He Stows up all the Grace of his Spirit in it tho' he gives grace to fit for it to such as are not at the present of it, yet all his Sanctifying Graces are bestowed on it, & Stowed up in it, Ps. 45.13, Ezek. 16.10—she is the Receptacle of Divine Grace. But no unsanctified person is such: its impossible for a person unsanctified to be a Storehouse of Sanctifying Grace. & there is no piece of this building discharged from this Use; so its used as a golden Candlestick to hold out Holy & heavenly light. Hence called a golden Candlestick. But its impossible for an unholy person so abiding to receive this light, Eph. 5.14, & therefore he cannot hold it out; hence not be of this Candlestick. So God useth this House as his Court of Judgment. He hath a kingdom upon Earth, & laws to rule his Subjects by, Matt. 3.3, Heb. 1.8. He Gives the keyes of his kingdom unto his Church, Matt. 16.19, John 20.23. The Church therefore is the Subject Recipient of all Ecclesiasticall Laws, & in it God keeps his Court of Judgment; she is Gods Court, Gods high Court of Justice in Spirituall things. Hence she is blamed, if she neglects her Worke of judging, I Cor. 5.12, & Calld to it by God, v. 13, so Chap. 14.29. But now no unholy person can be a Competent Judge in Gods House. God never Committs a Spirituall Case to a Carnall judge, se I Cor. 2.14. Nothing less than true Holiness can Qualify a Person to judge Spirituall Cases. Hence the Matter of a Church must be really holy.

But to give some few other arguments unto this Truth as an Amantissa to what hath been Spoken to I suppose will not be a transgression, & therefore that the Matter of a Particular Church is to be Really Holy may thus appeare

1. From the Relation the Church stands in unto Christ as its Owner, & Builder. Its the Church of God, Acts 20.28, Christs Church, Eph. 5.27, its the Bride the lambs Wife, Rev. 21, he calls it his Spouse, his Undefiled. Hence it stands in such a Relation to him, as no unsanctified person can stand in. No such Relation can be constituted in an unholy Heart. Christ hath a reall title to every Stone in his Temple, & a reall Propriety in every Stick of Timber in his Building. Satan cannot say, this Piece of timber in Christs house is mine, or this stone in his Temple is mine, no, no, avant, Satan: Its all Christs. Christ will not build his house of thy Materialls. But all are Satans that are unholy: So long as the soule is unholy it is Satans, its a Child of wrath, Eph. 2.2,3, Rom. 6.16. Hence not matter for Christs House, in that Condition. [10/11]

2. From the Provision that God makes for his Family it must needs be that all in the House be really Holy. For such as are not really Holy have no right to it, nor appetite after it, nor Power to eate thereof, nor Concoctive faculty to digest the same into nutriment. And I shall shew what this Provision that God makes is, Now the Provision that God mentains his Family withall is wholly Spirituall. The meate is Spirituall meate, & the Drinke is spirituall Drinke, I Cor. 10.2,3, Milke for Babes, & Childrens bread, Matt. 15.26, it is the Hidden Mannah, Rev. 2.17, the Living Bread, or Bread of Life, John 6.48–51. It is Holy food, its not Spirituall onely in that its food to nourish the soule that is a Spirit. For in some Sense Morality or Humane Learning may do this. But in that it is Holy food that nourisheth the New man in the Soule, so that the Soule makes its increase hereby according to God, Eph. 2.21, Col. 2.19, it grows in Grace, II Pet. 3.18, it feeds upon the Lord Jesus Christ in the Word & in the Sacraments, John 6.53, 54–63, I Cor. 10.24. & hence the inward man grows Strong by this Nourishment, II Cor. 4.16, Eph. 3.16, Col. 1.11. This is the food then its Spirituall, Holy, Christ fed upon Savingly, & his Graces influenced thereby. But now this Provision is above the Capacity of any unholy person. No Man in a State of Sin can feed upon this food, such an one hath no right to it, its Childrens bread that must not be cast before dogs, Matt. 15.26, nor must Dogs be set with Children at the Table. They have no appetite to it, they have lost the relish of Spirituall things, Rom. 8.5, τὰ τῆς σαρκος φρονοῦσιν, they relish the things of the flesh, but not the things of the Spirit, that are

after the Flesh. They have no power to receive this food, I Cor. 2.4, they Cannot feed upon the Bread of Life for their Life, for if they could they should live for ever: but this is impossible for one in his unholy state. If it was possible (which it is not) for such to feed on this Provision, yet he could not Concoct it into Nourishment, it would be lost unto him, & not nourish him, it would pine & starve him. He wants a Concoctive faculty for this food. What then should Such do in Christs house? God will have none in his house, that Cannot eate at his Table, that cannot live upon his food, nor feed upon his Provision; but when the Soule is Sanctified, & truely Holy, Oh then it is Hungry, & thirsty after this Food, Matt. 5.6, Cant. 2.5. Hence the Matter of the House must be truely Holy.

Obj: This is a μετάθεσις εἰς ἄλλο κενὸν to run from the Matter in hand for that respected the Matter of the Building the House Consisted of: & not the Qualification of the Family Dwelling in the House.

Sol: 1. The Matter of the Building Constitutive, & the Members of the Family in our Case are one & the same: & therefore their Qualifications the Same.

2. The Spirit of God in Eph. 2.19. Hath the respect to the Members of the family, & yet runs to an instance respecting the Matter of the Building in our [11/12] Text. Therefore pertinent to the Matter in Hand.

3. From the necessity of the Ejecting such out of this House that appeare visibly unholy. For if the Visibly unholy are to be outed, than such as are not really Holy are not matter for it. For the Reason why the Visibly Unholy are to be outed is because they now appeare to be unholy & not holy or not fit matter, for there is no medium between being Holy, & Unholy, to be morall is no medium. He that is onely morall is Unholy, hence the morall Vertues of the Heathens are called by Divines *Splendida Peccats*, Shining Sins, & hence this makes but a tinckling Cymball, I Cor. 13.1, Paul durst not be found in it for a world, Phil. 3.9. In this Case all Faith below Sanctifying is not Profitable, I Cor. 13.2. & there is no Faith but Justifying that is Sanctifying. If a leprose Stone is not to abide in the building, it is not to be laid in the Building, that that is not fit matter to ly in it, is not fit matter to be laid in it, That that is to be outed was never fit to be inlaide, the reason why it is to be outed now is because it appeares it never was matter fit to be laid in, &

you can never produce any one instance of any person onely morall that was accepted in this Worke in all the Word of God. But now the Visibly unholy are to be outed, I Cor. 5.2,3,4,5,6,7,13. The Old Leaven must be purged away, the Leprose Stone must be plucked out of the Building, Lev. 14.40. Thus then you Se true Holiness fits the Matter for this building.

Obj: But here you having asserted that this Matter must be really Holy what shall we thinke then of the Children of the Church in their Unconverted State? are they no members? Then why have they Baptism & are under the Discipline of the Church? If they be Members, are they not the Matter of the Church? Is there a Difference between the Members & the Matters of a Church? If none, then Satans materialls are Matter of Gods Temple. Members in his Family that cannot feed on the Provision Christ allows, & ought to be outed? What say you to this?

Sol: 1. These are matter in Polishing, but not as yet polished.

2. The Matter of this House is to be Considered as to its

{ Extern Relation
{ Intern Form.

1. As to its Externall Relation, so there are Materialls belonging to & Vessells of Dishonour, in, this House, II Tim. 2.22. They having onely a Relation to it, are in truth of it, i.e., the House claims them to be hers & they claim her to be theirs tho' as yet they are dead in sins, & Children of Wrath, & of Satan. But

2. As to its Internall Form. So the Materialls are onely living Stones, such as are truely Holy. & in this sense are our arguments to be taken. None but such as are truely Holy are to be tenented & joynted into this Building; tho' the other being born in, they belong to the family, & are not to be outed for none appearance of Holiness, yet they are not to be laid in as Matter fit for the Essentiall form of the Building 12/13] till they are truely Holy as to the judgment of Charity. The Essentiall, & Internall form of this House, that Which Cements & Compacts the Whole together requires true Holiness in the Matter recipient of this form: & untill this form be introduced the matter tho' it may be matter related to the Church it is not matter informed, *Actu exercito* with the form of the Church, & therefore not Compleate matter of a Church. They are matter in Hewing, or at best onely Hewen, but not matter laid into the building. The Relation to the Building is of two sorts. It may be of Parentall Dedication as the Infant Seed of Covenanters, as Ezek. 10.1, II Chron. 20.13. So did Hannah dedicate Samuel,

I Sam. 1. Or of Personall Combination, Neh. 9 *ult.*, 10.28. The first is an accidentall Relation of the Matter to the House, & requires not, but obliges to internall Holiness. But herein lies not the Formall Cause of a Church. & therefore this is incomplete Matter. The latter is that wherein the Formall Cause of a Church Consist, & therein lies the right unto Full Communion & all Ecclesiastick previlidges onely they are injoyed according as persons are Capable thereof. This last requires true Holiness in the Matter of it Qualifying & preparing of it to the Reception of the form, as hath been made out by the Arguments laid down. & thus much for the removing this Objection. & now by this time you may se it evinced that Reall Holiness is requisit for the fitting the Matter for a Church State, & so I shall pass to the next thing.

2. There is another thing requisit unto the *Forma Praeparans* of the Materiall Cause of a Church, & this is the Visibility of this Qualification of reall Holiness: It must not onely be Reall Holiness But Reall Visible Holiness. For *De occultis non judicet Ecclesia*, For the Visible Church hath not to do with invisible matters any further than they are Visible. Therefore the Matter is to manifest this Holiness of it, & this Visibility thereof doth further as a *Forma Praeparans*, dispose it to the Reception of the *Ratio Formalis* of the Church & in such a way as doth Constrain Conscientious Charity to hope the Best, & judge the Best. &
this is done in a Regular $\begin{cases} \text{Conversation} \\ \text{Confession.} \end{cases}$

First. Reall Holiness is made Visible by a Holy & Regular Life, & Conversation. God calls for this. Shew me thy faith by thy Workes, Jas 2.18. Let your light so shine before men that they may Se your good works & Glorify your Father that is in Heaven, Matt. 5.16, I Pet. 2.12 This is a living up to the Rule, Gal. 6.16, Phil. 3.16. This is to manifest your selves to every ones Conscience in the Sight of God, II Cor. 4.2 Pure Religion, & undefiled brings forth the Practice of Piety, Jas. 1.27 Whereas some there are do profess in Words that in Workes do deny God, Titus 1.16: Such a mans Religion is vain. This then is one way whereby Holiness must be made visible. [13/14]

Secondly. Reall Holiness is made Visible by an Holy, & Regular Confession of the same. With the Heart man believes unto Righteousness, & with the Mouth Confession is made unto Salvation, Rom 10.20. But now here comes in the pinch of the Question, viz, Unto whom this Confession is to be made; Whether unto God? or unto Man

And if to man, whether to the Elders of the Church onely, or to the Whole Church? And When?

In answere whereto I say, As for Confession unto God, no man Questions, as in Prayer, & the dayly exercise of Repentance, this is carried on. But this reacheth not the matter in hand. But as for a Confession, or Relation of Some experiences of Gods gracious Working upon the hearts, by the means of Grace, holding forth some grounds for Christian Charity to judge the old man is put off, & the new man put on, I suppose none will deny but it is to be given to the Elders of the Church, whose worke it is to attend on Soule Cases, Heb. 13.17, & to prepare them & their Concerns to be propounded to the Church in order to Churchfellowship. The Stickle then of the Question is brought into this narrow { Whether this is to be made to the Church / When it is to be made to the Church.

1. Whether this Confession is to be made to the Church or no?

Sol: It is necessary that the person seeking Church Fellowship with any Church of Christ, give an account of Some of his experiences that he hath had of the Workings of Gods Spirit upon his heart either in his own person or by Some other acquainted therewith.

This I shall endeavour to settle, onely take this limitation, that I intend not as to single Acts of Communion, such as when the Members of one Church do partake of the Seales in another Church by vertue of the Communion which one Church holdeth with another: but of a State of Church Fellowship as when a Person enters into a Church State. And also, in Case a Member in Fullcommunion in one Church, that having walked orderly therein all a long, fall under such decay of his naturall abilities, that he cannot give any account Considerable, or distinct, nor easily can be helped in this Case, altho' his piety otherwise shines, I say such an one Changing his Habitation, & desirous to change his Church Relation, & enter into Fellowship with the Church where he dwells, it is not needfull to exact a Relation from such an one. & yet the Church so agreeing may admit him upon his Dismission & Recomendation from the Church he belonged to, Rom. 16.1,2. These things premised I proceed to prove this Confession of Gods Worke ought to be given to the Church that Communion is sought with: & this I shall do by two sorts of Arguments { Inartificiall / Artificiall.

First. By Inartificiall Arguments. For in this Case they are the most forcible, as laying down matter of Duty, & matter of Fact; & these are both $\begin{cases} \text{Divine} \\ \text{Humane.} \end{cases}$ [14/15]

First Divine Arguments for it. & these are such Portions of Holy Scriptures as shew that this work must be & was as prove that it was required as a Duty, & was attended as a matter of fact of the $\begin{cases} \text{Old} \\ \text{New} \end{cases}$ Law.[8]

1. That it was Required, Something there is in the Ceremonious Law will evince this by these Scriptures. All those texts that require the Person to lay his Hand on the Head of his Sin offering, & Trespass offering, as Lev. 14.3, 23.13, So Chap. 4.19, 5.56, require this Confession. His bringing his offering implies faith, & Repentance on the account of his Sin. & that in truth for else all is in vain as theirs, Isa 1.11,12,13. Their laying their hand on the Head of the Offering implieth their[9] Open confessing of their Sin in way of Repentance, & of their applying themselves unto the Way of Divine appointment for a Remedy

Again, take that for this End, Deut. 26.3–12. Where you have a plain injunction laid on every man in Israel (unless some of Levi be excepted) that appeare before the Lord with a Basket of Summer fruits to make[10] Confession of their former Misery, & Gods grace in their Recovery.

So that Job 33.27,28.[11] He (i.e., the Penetent Person) shall looke upon men, (אנשׁים Humble, mournfull men as Enosh was) & say I have Sinned, & perverted what is right, & it profitted me not, (Here lieth the very worke of Repentance, & God brings him to this you see, & to give a Relation of it publickly, but he goeth on thus) He (i.e., God spoken of v. 26) hath redemed[12] My Soule (rather than his Soul as being the words of the Penetent, & so the Hebrew Word נפשׁי may beare, & many learned persons take it thus, my Soul) from Death, & my (rather than his) Life shall Se the Light. And what is this but a Confession openly made of his Repentance of Sin, & of Gods Goodness to him, & of his Faith Godward.

Secondly that it was done,

To this purpose Serves Ps. 51 which is a Relation given by David of Gods working him up to Repentance, & Recovering him out of his Sin in the Matter of Uriah,[13] which he gave to the Chief Musician to publish to the Church.

Again Ps. 66.16,17,18,19,20. Come & heare all ye that feare God & I will declare what he hath done for my Soule. This is a Declaration of what he would, or was about to, do: & then he gives you an account of his Experiences of Gods working upon his heart in drawing out his heart after him in earnest prayer, & Praise, saying, I cryed unto him with my mouth, & he was extolled with my Tongue. & also in respect to his Conversion the which he rather prooves than Professeth, thereby shewing his Repentance implicitly also, as a thing necessary to his being heard saying If I regard iniquity in my heart the Lord will not heare me: but verily God hath heard me, & also as touching the actings of his Grace Godward with respect to the actings of Gods grace towards him, as, Blessed be God that hath not turned away my Prayer, nor his mercy from me. [15/16]

An other is that of Solomon, who after he had greatly apostatized from God, & Scandallized the Church of God gives a Relation of his Soul Exercise in its ecclesiasticall motions wherein he gives satisfaction in a way of Reconciliation to God & his Church again as is cleare in the whole book of the Ecclesiastes; which he stiles *Choheleth*, as importing the congregating or Enchurching Soul, or the Soule in its betaking itselfe to the Church of God, being used in the Feminine Gender.[14]

2. So in the New Testament you may have many Scriptures for this End. Some holding it out to be a Duty, as Rom. 10.10. With the mouth Confession is made unto Salvation. What Confession is this I pray? Surely its such a Relation of the Dealings of God with the Soul in bringing of it up unto himselfe from Sin as Salvation is the finall upshot of the same, its an account of those Impressions upon the heart as accompany Salvation. Such an one Paul oft made, Acts 22.3–22.

Some account that text, Jas. 5.16, Confess your Sins one to another to hold out a Confession of Offences, & Profession of Repentance that the Church may pray powerfully on the account of the Sins made known to her, as Grotius.[15]

So we may fitly improove this in I Pet. 3.15. Be ye alwayes ready to give an answer to every man that askes you a reason of the Hope that is in you. For saith Calvin,[16] the sum is thus much that we ought to have the Confession of our Faith in readiness, that we may bring it forth as oft as there is need. & after again saith hee, the same answer or Apology notes in my judgment that Christians should testify to the World that they are far off from all impiety. Now if this must be done to the World then much more to the Church of God with which the Soul seekes Communion. Oh Saith Augustine, *Dic hominibus quid es, dic Deo quid esses*. Tract. in 1 Epist. Joha: 1, 9. Tell men What thou art: tell God What thou art. This shews a Confession should be.[17]

But as touching Matter of Fact se these texts. John Baptists Converts Did this, Matt. 3.6. Paul did it again, & again, Acts 22.6–22, & Chap. 26.13 — & if he did it to Enemies shall it be thought he did it not to the Church: nay he did it to the Church too, & Barnabas for him, Acts 9.26,27. And Timothy is said to have Confessed a good Confession before many witnesses, I Tim. 6.12. But se more of this nature in the next head.

Thus you have something holding out this confession that it should be & was by Divine Testimony. & if we may tread in the foot steps of the flock (the which we are called to, Cant. 1.8) we shall finde abundance of Examples of this nature. What are the Psalms but almost wholy full hereof, as also other Scriptures. But I shall stop here, & as for humane Testimony, as also Artificiall Arguments for the Proofe hereof, they will fall in with the other heads, & there I reserve that both heads may be evidenced therewith at once; & therefore [16/17]

Secondly. That this Confession is to be made upon a Persons entering into a Church State, i.e., into a Full, & compleate State, I shall endeavour to evince by Authority $\begin{cases} \text{Divine} \\ \text{Humane.} \end{cases}$

First. By Divine Authority, or Testimony fetched out of the Word & for this End take these following Scriptures.

1. That seems to Shaddow out as much as this, which required the Children of Israel, Ex. 19.14, in order to their Entering into a Visible Church State at mount Sinai to Sanctify themselves, by Washing in Water, & then on the third day to appeare to enter into the Church Covenant. Now God had laid them under Conviction of their Sin before, & now he calls them to attend upon this Ordinance which in the very design of it speaketh forth an open acknowledgment of it, & a repentance thereof & true Faith in order to their being acquitted therefrom. For their Washing in water, was according to the Dispensation of Grace that the Church was then under a publick manifestation of their Conviction of Sin, Repentance, & Faith. & this God requires before their Covenanting.

2. Another is that concerning the Basket of summer Fruits, Deut. 26.2 to v. 11, which being to be done every yeare, could be an injunction

nely taking place upon the Person that was *Sui juris*, & not on such as vas under Coverbarn, as they say. & being thus it follows that when hey came into a Complete State they were to attend this Ordinance with the Basket of the first fruits. And whatever typicall nature there nay be found in this ordinance, its cleare there is a Confession of the soules sensibleness of Gods Gracious Dealing with his people in generall n bringing them out of the typicall State of misery, into the Typicall state of Grace & Favour, & to enjoy the Typicall Dispensation of the Church State. & this being done personally it is to be done in syncerity, & so holds forth the Souls sense of his former misery, & of his present avour. As this was Chiefly that which was required during the Churches being under the Churches Typicall Dispensation. For then as to the Visibility of holiness God chiefly calld to the Conformity unto the Ceremoniall Type or Rite, & hence we se in this ordinance something of Confession made in order to a perfect State, & without this none came to be in a Complete State.

3. That is a more cleare instance in this Case, Neh. 9.2. They had apostatized from the true God, & God Cast them out of his house, Jer. 12.15. He wrote them a Bill of Divorce & put them away, Jer. 3.8, brake down their Church State, Isa. 5.5,6. But shall it be so forever? Yea if they repent not. But if they repent, turn, & acknowledge their sin, then God will bring them unto Zion, Jer. 3.13,14. And now here you have the History of the thing done. They were humbled & repented, & God brings them back again. And now being returned, their Church State was not perfected, they had been tinckling about 3 years, (the time Cyrus [17/18] lived after the Decree he put forth for this end) in preparing for the Work. & then Cambyses his Son being a Cruill Tyrant great impediments lay in their way. So that in the sixt year of Darius, probable, Histaspis, they had done little but set up the bare fabrick of the Temple, Ezra 6.15, in Seventeen years time. And 68 more were rowled over their heads before they did any thing Considerable till the Seventh of Artaxerxes, when Ezra came, Ezra 7.7. And altho' he came now with such full Commission, yet we se he had not compleated the worke by far, till Nehemiah Came about a dozzen years after that.[18] And now they complete their Church State, & therefore now in the text read The seede of Israel separated themselves from all Strangers, & stood, & Confessed their Sins, & the Sins of their Fathers. & so perfect their work by Confederation, Neh. 10.28,29.

This may suffice as to old Testament hints of the matter.

But to come to the New Testament. Here we shall finde the thing more cleare, & therefore

1. Take that of Johns, Matt. 3.6,7,8,9. John Baptist admitted none to his Baptism but Such as made a Confession of their Sins shewing their Repentance therein. Hence the main body of the Pharisees were rejected, tho' they pleaded a right thereto upon the old, & oreworn argument, We are Abrahams Seed, in opposition to the present Dutie of Repentance, & Confession, which is Called fruite meet for Repentance & so they were not baptized, Luke 7.30. Now if John would not admit to baptism such as were in Covenant without Confession of their Sins. Then surely it holds good that it is to be made in order to a Church State. And hence some greate Expositers looke on that Good Confession that Paul asserts that Timothy made before many Witnesses, I Tim 6.12, was not in the Preaching of the Word as some will but a Relation made at his Baptism, when he was received into the Church. And altho ὁμολογία the Word read Profession, or Confession, in this place, is used also for a Sermon, yet in this place, where no mention is made of any preaching, or any Single Sermon, but an Instance is Set before him of this Good, ὁμολογίαν, v. 13, which is onely the Relation that Christ gave touching himselfe, & his work before Pontius Pilat, it seems most likely to import some Speciall Relation or account that hee gave to the Church of his hope & of Gods gracious dealing with him, upon his admittance into Church fellowship.

2. Those threethousands that were added to the Church at Jerusalem gave a Relation of their Conversion by Peters Sermon, Acts 2.37–41. For tho' its onely said they were pricked at the Heart, yet thereby is intended the whole worke of God upon the Soule. & this as to the Convincing Efficacy thereof working true Repentance mortifying their Sins, this is cleare in their seeking for Reliefe in this Case. But if it be said that an account of the worke of Grace upon the Soule was above the worke of a day.

True. So it is. And so it can hardly be thought that it was not above the [18/19] work of one day, especially that piece of the day that remained after Peters Sermon, which began not till nine a Clock in the forenoon Called the third hour of the day, v. 15. The Spirit of God therefore recordeth not the manner of the Churches order in receiving onely he hints thus much that they showed the reason of the Churches Charity in receiving & the Dating that upon the Day wherein this was wrought, viz, the day of Peters Sermon. & by that Sermon there were added those three thousand to the Church vertually, but not formally till the *Modus Ecclesiae* the Ecclesiastick Order was attended fully. & on the same day there was formally added these to the Church. For the text shews first the Worke received upon their heart to be declared which was done distinctly one by one untill the 3000 were arrived at. Secondly, the Effect hereof in their Syncere seeking advice, & taking of it, 3ly Much Exhortation was given with the advice. 4ly Their manifest joyous receiving of the Word, 5. Their Baptismall Transactions, 6. Their Covenantall ingagueing to the Church. And these things were above the Worke of a day, unless we should grant them to be as Expeditious as were the Spaniards that drave the Poore Indians in flocks or Whole Companys to be Baptized.

Hence probably their Covenanting with the Church was in the same day.

3. The Church at Jerusalem would not admit Paul, when he sought to joyn with them, till they had a Relation of his Conversion made to them, both as to the Manner, & the Effect thereof by Barnabas, Acts 9.26,27,28. If it be said they was affraid of him because he had persecuted them, True so they might well. But this respects not the Relation. For it is cleare that he gave an account of his Discipleship before, & of his endeavour to satisfy the Church in this matter: else the Church could not be said as it is said, viz, they did not believe he was a Disciple, i.e., a Convertt. & the reason of it is their feare of the truth of the matter, so that they admitted him not; they wanted therefore some Witness to Confirm what Paul had affirmed. & therefore Barnabas takes Paul, & declares his Case, & asserts it, & now he is received. Hence a Confession is made.

4. The Foundation of the Church at Cesaria was begun by the Relation of the work of Gods grace on the Heart of Cornelius, & on the rest was the worke of God manifested extraordinarily unto Peter & those with him, Acts 10.30,31,32,33, & 46.

5. The Disciples at Ephesus had their Entrance into a Church State intimated to us by Pauls Separating them, Acts 19.9. And the Manner how this worke was Carried on in order to their Entring into this State is hinted to us in the Adition of others, v. 16, which was by Confessing & Shewing their Deed.[19] Now we have no reason to thinke that the additions attended one Method, & the foundations an other; for the Reason is the same to all. & hence we Se Confessions finde footing in the Word. And thus much shall suffice touching scripture Testimony in this Case. [19/20]

Secondly. Humane Testimony evidencing the same, & for this I shall produce such as these following. For altho' this testimony be as far inferior unto the former even as much as Humane is to Divine, Yet in matters of Fact that are to be Conformable to a Divine Rule, Humane Testimony touching the Practice of Gods Church which runs Conformable to our Sense given of these Scriptures (& Chiefly considering that this practice must have some Rule, & is no blameable thing,) is no weake manner of arguing; but doth greatly confirm the meaning we have laid down of the same. And as to the Practice of the Church of Christ touching their Admitting Members a Word or two may suffice.

1. Therefore it will not be impertinent to Consider something of the Manner how the Church of the Jews mannaged their Admission of their Proselytes. & this as a Shaddow will teach us something in this Case. The Person to be admitted first was Washed in water, which implicitly was an acknowledgment of his Sins, & Repentance. Then Circumcised, wherein he Covenanted, & then presented his Offering. See Weems *Synagogue*.[20]

The Standing Practice of the Church of Christ from the Apostles dayes, & on in the Primitive Church before the Antichristian Smoke rose out of the Bottomless Pit, & darkened the sun, & the Aire of the Gospell. Now this was such as that in order to the Admittance of a Person into Church State he manifested the Worke of God upon his heart as touching his Repentance of sin, & Faith in Christ. This, you have had a taste already began in the Apostles days & is looked on by the Learned to be the Answer of a Good Conscience mentioned I Pet. 3.21. The intent of which is looked on by many[21] to be thus much, that when the Person to be admitted, & baptized, was calld forth, there were such Questions as these propounded, Dost thou renounce Satan? He answerd I renounce him, Dost thou believe in Christ? He replied I believe. And this is calld ἐπερώτημα συνειδήσεως ἀγαθῆς εἰς Θεόν the Answer, the Evidence, the Declaration (as the word notes, being a Court term) or stipulation of a good Conscience towards God, & shews the internall faith expresst by the outward Profession. And Tertullian calls it the Answer of Salvation, as that I Tim. 6.12, Confession, the Testification of Faith, & Cyprian, the Interrogation of Baptism.[22] Now as for persons grown, being then admitted into a Church State the text seems by this one word, the Answer of a Good Conscience, to intend the whole Relation of Gods worke upon their heart. & not the bare answer to the Questions thus propounded, which was more no doubt than that answer [20/21] alone, as will further appeare in other instances. & if this be the intent of the place, as is thought. Then it holds out that in the Apostles dayes there were relations given of Gods worke upon the soule in order to Admittance into a Church State, tho' as to the form of Renunciation whereby the Persons to be baptized renounced Sin, the World, the Divell, & his Works, & covenanted with God, the Father, Son, & Holy Ghost that they would acknowledge him to be God, believe in him & obey his word, there is no mention express (saith the *Magdeburgencian Centuriators*)[23] Yet the Confession itselfe that they to be baptized must hold out, & the Effects of Baptism comprise such things as Peter seemeth there to looke unto when, I Pet. 3, he calls Baptism the ἐπερώτημα of a Good Conscience towards God. Thus we have then some thing of this matter here so I shall give some other testimonies touching the Same. This may suffice touching the Practice of the first Century from Christ's birth.

Also for the Practice in the Second Century. Now the Practice had made a term grown almost peculiar to this Work as Carried on upon Admissions at their Baptisms, & Absolutions, of Penetents. For the Relations they made calld in Greek ἐξομολογέω, & so the word *Exhomologesis* the Latine Writers oft kept intending the account, made upon Admissions, & Absolution, of their Repentance & faith as the ground for the Churches Charity to act upon. This being premised I now shall proceed to instance for the Second Century.

Let an instance out of Justine Martyre who lived under Adrian, & wrote an Apology on the behalfe of Christians to the Emperors Adrian & Antonius Pius about the year of Christ 137, the first. & thus saith, How are we dedicated to God, when regenerated by Christ, we will now shew that we seem not to dissemble any thing troublesomely. As many as being perswaded believe these things which we teach are true, & promise to live accordingly, above all things they learn by prayer, & fasting to beg of God pardon for their former Sins. We joyning Prayer & fasting together, they are led thence by us to the Water of Baptism. Thus He.[24]

Victor who lived in this Century in case of necessity he leaves it at liberty to baptize any coming of a gentile—so he give [21/22] a Relation of his Christian Beliefe. But it is observed that the exact manner of their ecclesiasticall proceeding in this Century in order unto Baptism, & so unto Church fellowship was not left with any Diligence upon writing. And hence there is not so cleare accounts to be found of their first Entrance as there is of their Restoration after they had openly fell into

Scandalous Sins. & here I shall cite an instance or two out of Irenous who flowrished about the year 180 & was contemporary with Victor. He saith that there was a Certain Beautifull Woman, wife of a Certain Deacon in Asia defiled both in body & minde by an heretick calld Mark & followed him, who after being by great pains converted by the Brethren, spent all her time in Confession, lamenting & bewailing her Sin. & writing of Certain seduced Women of Rhodes saith they made this Confession in publick. And this at length became a matter converted by the Roman Bishops into Auricular Confessions, & Satisfactions, say the Magdeburgensians Cent. 2.C.6.P.112.[25]

Further this will more abunduntly appeare to be attended on, if we consider the Method they all attended with their *Catechumeni*, or such as were under Catechisticall instruction preparing for a full State as the Children of the Church, & such of the Heathen as inclined to receive the Gospell. Where its observed that when the *Catechumeni* were ripe for Baptism they were then upon their suing for it Called *Competentes*, or persons Competent thereof. & when they were admitted to the Sacrament they were Stiled Believers or Christians. So the *Catechumeni* grew up next to be *Competentes*, & the *Competentes* to be *Fideles*, Se Mr. Nortons answer against Apolonius, p. 6,7.[26] & Can this be attaind unto, & no account of their Faith & Repentance given. Who can imagine it? But of these things we shall have a Cleare account in the Next Century, & therefore to come to the practice of the third Century runing take an Instance.

1. Out of Tertullian who flowerisht in the beginning of this Century, about 230 years after Christ at Rome sometimes & at Carthage where he was born & bred, hee shews us thus much, He that comes to be baptized must attend prayer often, Fasting, be upon his Knees, & watch, with the Confession of all his faults. Hence say the Centuriators, the Faith of Adult persons was for a certain time before they were baptized tried, & they put upon the very same exercise of Repentance & Confession, as clearly appears from the rites of Baptizing which Tertullian wrote in the book stiled *Corona Militis*.[27]

2. So Origen hints, who was a famous writer at Alexandria in Egypt, saying when we come to be baptized we give a Confession of God the Father, Son, & Holy Ghost renouncing all other Gods, & Lords. Yet we confessing this become not the Lords Portion unless we Love the Lord our God with all our Heart & with all our Soule, & cleave to him with all our might.[28] [22/23]

3. Further take another cleare instance out of the same Origen you may have it in his Second Homily on the thirty seventh, but in our Bible the 38 Psalm, 11 verse. He that Confesseth to God on the account of his Sins, & grieveth in Soul while he repents—saith thus, laying open what things he is like to Sustain, who betakes himselfe to Repentance, & Reformation, how his Friends & neighbours leave him, & stand afar off because he turns himselfe to give a Relation of his Sins, & Sorrow. He therefore saith: My friends, & my neighbour approached against me & rose up. Understand, I have a Faithfull Person, but yet weake who may even be overcome by some Sin: & therefore howling for his faults, & every way seeking a Cure of his Wound, & a Recovery; tho' he is prevented, & slips, yet willing to prepare his medicine, & his Salvation, If then such an one mindfull of his fault Confesseth the things he hath Committed & by humane blushing sets light by Such as up braid, & note or Scorn him that makes the Confession—that he will not cover nor hide his spot, but shall declare his fault: yet will not be a whited Sepulcher, that Seems beautifull before men,—but within full of all filthiness, and dead mens bones. If there be then any so faithfull as that he is guilty of something within himselfe let him come out in the middest & charge himselfe, & Such as feare not Gods Judgment to come, hearing these things—begin to detest him whom before they admired, & recoile from his friendship that will not hid his Fault. He then saith consequently of them, who maketh the Relation, i.e., a Confession, My Friends, & my neighbours drew neer & Stood up against mee. And a leafe further in in the same sermon directing the Soul to whom in this case he should go Saith Onely looke diligently about thee to whom thou ought to confess thy sins, first try the Physician to whom thou ought to shew the Cause of thy mallody, that he know how to be weak with the weake, that if he at length, who hath formerly shown himself both learned, & Compassionate shall say any thing, if he give thee any Counsill, do it, follow it. If he understand, & foresee thy sickness such as ought to be brought out in the assembly of the whole Church, & Cured, whence probably others may be edified, this is to be procured by much deliberation & the advice full skilfull of that Physician.

But in case the person neglect this counsill he bespeakes him thus. Thou slightest the judgment of God, & dispisest the Church admonishing thee, thou fearest not to communicate with the body of Christ [23/24] coming to the Lords Supper, as if thou wast clean, & pure, as if there was nothing unworthy in thee, & thou thinkest to avoid the judgment of God in all these things. Thou rememberest not that that is writ, that for this cause many are weake, sick, & fallen asleep among you. Why are many Weake? Because they judge not themselves, nor examine themselves, nor understand what it is to approach to such & so excellent Sacraments, or to Communicate with the Church, they suffer the same that feverish persons are wont to suffer when they presume upon healthy persons food, bringing ruine upon themselves.[29] Here its cleare that this *Exhomologesis* or Relation is manifestly treated of as a known practice in the Church at Alexandria mannaged without the least questioning of it, in order to a Church State, & Church Fellowship, as being carried on by one whose friends & Familiars do set against it, & when they cannot hinder it, do scorn & upbraid, yea & become despisers of him that makes it.

4. Take an instance out of Gregory Neocesariensis who was Origen's Scholar & heare him speaking in this Case: it Chiefly respects Penetents & he layeth down five degrees to be attended in order to their admittance as

1. Weeping, when the Penitent stood weeping at the door begging their prayers.

2. Hearing, when he Stood by the *Catechumeni* within the door to heare the Word.

3. Prostration, when he in an humble way had further entrance.

4. Standing, when he tarried standing with the Assembly.

5. Communion, when he partooke of the Sacraments with the Church,[30] and can any man imagine such a proceeding to be, & yet the Church never have an account of Gods dealing with his heart?

5. The last instance in this Hundred of years is that of the Church at Rome in their admitting Philip the first Christian Emperour in the World being then the Roman Emperour unto whom Origen sent an Epistle. Yet such was the practice of this Church that she would not receive into her Society the Emperour of the World till he had given an account of his Repentance & Faith. Heare the Words of Eusebius who saith of him thus, He being a Christian, & desirous to be a Partaker, and be joynd with the multitude in the Prayers of the Church on the last day of Easter vigills; but could not be admitted till he had first rendred an account of his Faith, & coupled himselfe with them which for their Sins were examined, & placed in the room of penitents; & except he should do this he could not be admitted, therefore he being in many things faulty, willingly obeyed, & declared by his Works, his religious,

& syncere minde towards God.[31] Let these instances suffice for this Century.

But I shall now come to the fourth Century, & see their practice in their Admissions how it was now, & you may see this was by giving an account of their Hope & here take this one instance out of Jerom that saith, the sinner did put on sackcloath, stood until the day of Pascha in the ranck of Penitents, did publickly confess his Sins; the Bishop, Elders & all the people weeping in the meantime.[32] And Sozomen saith in the Roman Church was an open place for Penitents where they stood sad & as mourning.[33] Surely then they made relations. [24/25]

But to come to the fifth Century, in the begining of which Augustine, that famous Light of the Church of Christ at Hippo in Affrica flowerished & still shines with glory in all the Christian world for his famous Workes, & piety. & here from him you shall have one instance for all of the Church of Romes Admission, of one Victorinus a Platonick Philosopher. It is thus related from Simplicianus by him, That it fell out at the time of Confessing which used to be rendred from an high place in the sight of the Church at Rome in certain Words committed also to memory by such as came to his grace, he (i.e., Simplicianus) said it was offerd Victorinus by the Elders, that he might render it more secretly, as it was used to be offerd to some that thro' bashfacedness seemed to quake. But he chose rather to profess his salvation in the Sight of the Holy assembly. For (said he) it was not salvation which he taught in Rhetorick, & yet he professed it publickly. How much less ought he to be affraid of thy gentle flock in pronouncing thy Word, who was not afraid of Companies of mad men, in pronouncing his own words? When therefore he went up to make his Relation, all, that they might know him, buzzed his name one to another, with a whispering Congratulation. But who knew not him that is there? And it was sounded with a low Sound thro' the mouths of all, Victorinus, Victorinus: They soon sounded with joy. Soon were silent to attend that they might hear him. He then declared the true Faith with excellent Hope. & they all were willing to hall him into their very heart within, & rapt him in with Love & joy.[34] Who sees not here the thing pleaded for, before our Eyes?

But I shall pass ore any further instances thus accounting this enough to satisfy any one touching the Practice of the Primitive times. Yet as to this matter I cannot well omit the sense of Theophylact, who lived in darker & more Degenerate times of the Church, that he gives on Peters Confession. For saith he,

Peter Confessed him (i.e., Jesus) to be the son of God, saith Christ that this Confession shall be the foundation of Believers. Therefore every man that shall build the House of Faith, is to lay the same Confession down for its foundation. For tho' we build up a thousand vertues & have not the Right Confession, our Foundation, we build upon the Flesh.[35]

Nay who can't track the footsteps of this Confession, thro' the whole time of the Antichristian Apostasy, as they have metamorpozed it into Auricular Confession. & hence its onely to be reformed, but not rejected, the which other protestant Churches beside New England have don it, as Pareus saith, None are to be received & baptized in to the Church but by a Previous Confession of faith & Repentance according to the Custom of the primitive Church, & ours at present, if either Turk or [25/26] Jew is to be baptized.[36] & Piscator saith so too, viz: That Baptism is not to be administrated to any grown person unless first he shall make a Confession of his Sins.[37]

The Churches of Bohemia in the Confession put forth at Geneva 1581, affirm the Baptized must endeavour when they are grown up, & desire to partake of the Lords Supper, that they may be able to make a Confession of their Faith with their own mouth & of their own accord, & to renew their Sanctification whereby they were Consecrated to the Lord.[38]

And the famous Mr. Rutterford requireth such a Profession as may notify to the Church that there is Saving Faith, & that they be invisible saints, that desire to joyn themselves to any visible Congregation.[39]

And for Conclusion of this head take the answer of Socrates to Eudemon, that had perswaded Nectarius Bishop of Constantinople to lay aside Confessions & permit none to take them, & to lay open the Holy mysteries of the Gospell to the liberty of any that would, to partake thereof, Oh, saith he, thy advice, Oh Priest, whether it shall availe the Church or no God knoweth; yet I plainly se that thou hast ministered occasion, that one may not reprehend an others vice, neither observe the advice of Paul; Have nothing to do with the unfruitfull works of Darkness; but rather rebuke them.[40]

These things being put together do clearly evince by Humane Testimony, that Relations of our Faith, & Repentance are to be laid before the Church in order to Admission or Church Fellowship. Thus far by Inartificiall pleas.

Secondly. Artificiall Arguments. Now I shall endeavour to settle it as a truth to be attended in order to Church Fellowship, that an account of some of those experiences of Gods dealings with the Soul in bringing it to faith & Repentance, is to be made before the Church. And for this end take these Arguments that follow.

1. It appears from the Duty the Church stands in unto Christ to be Faithfull in the Use of the Keyes of his Kingdom. For Christ hath hung the Keyes of Discipline upon the Girdle of the Church. Hence she is bound to open to whom He opens, & to shut upon whom he shuts upon: Otherwise the Keyes are not rightly used. But it will be impossible for her to do thus unless she may, & ought to require an account of what God hath done for those that knock for Admission at her doore: for she ought not to open unless they shew their Ticket.[41] And hence Christ Chargeth her to try the Spirits, as John 4.1,[42] & commends her for so doing, Rev. 2.2. Let it not be said, that this is the work of the Minister, the Angell of the Church. For the Spirit speaketh unto the Churches (Rev. 2.7) collectively in the [26/27] Angell. In order to the Preparation of the Worke, its peculiarly the Elders Worke to try. But in order to the Consummation thereof it belongs to all the society that are to give a judgment in the Case; & this is the Church, as I Cor. 5.12. Now if she finde Christs Ticket in the hand then she must open: But if there be nothing of that to be found then the Doore must not be opened.[43] For so pearls should be cast before swine, & holy things unto dogs, for ought she knows. Hence a Relation is requisit.

2. It will appeare from the Benefit that accrews upon this Relation of the Worke of God upon the Soule. And here I reason thus, If it be ever a duty to give an account of Gods working the heart to himselfe, then it is especially a duty at that time when it will be most beneficiall, & most to the glory of God. This consequent cannot be denied with any show of Reason.[44]

But that it is a Dutie is enough, & enough made out in Scripture, by the practice of the Saints, whom God calls us to follow, Heb. 6.12. If it should be no duty to make known the Worke of Grace upon the Soule, then Gods work may be Conceald: & his Grace be hid in the heart, & there smoothered up; & no man ever know how sweet it is, or how bitter sin feels unto the soul & David presumed, & acted arrogantly when he said The judgments of the Lord are sweeter to his taste than the

Hony or the Hony Comb, Ps. 19.10, 119.103. So that Gods worke on the soule is wholy of a Private Concern: & not beneficiall to others, no more than mere morallity. But the Contrary is true, our Light is to shine every way, that others may see, & glorify God, Matt. 5.16. & the tongue of the just is as Choice Silver, Prov. 10.20, nay a tree of life, Chap. 15.4: & may it be dropping out other things; & yet nothing of its own Experiences of Gods goodness, & grace to it? Who can imagine any such thing? Well we take it then to be granted that it is a Duty to declare our experiences of Gods dealing with us. But then to assume, I say, to give an account of Gods Dealings with us, in bringing us out of a State of Sin to himselfe in order to an Admission into a Church State, will be then most beneficiall, & make most to the Glorie of God. & this will appeare (if I may use these terms here) A *Parte* $\begin{cases} Ante \\ Poste. \end{cases}$

1. It will be most beneficiall unto the soule giving of it, A *parte Ante*, i.e., in order to its preparation for Full-Communion, which all will grant, to be a thing to be prepared for. For when the Soul Sees that an account of its experiences of Gods working upon it is to be given by it in some measure as a Sign of his preparation for, before it be admitted into a State of Full-Communion, how intent will it make him in observing the Motions of Gods Spirit upon him: & its own answer thereto in hungering after Christ & his Wayes, & in hating of, & getting away from Sin? And this will be to the Glory of God.

2. It will be most beneficiall *A-Parte-Post*, as to what follows. For as to what went before it, it was beneficiall for the mortification of Sin; so as to what follows, it will tend thereto lest by the Contrary doing it should fall under the Censure of Hypocrisy, & so scandalize the Church. Nay, It lets the Soul fall deep into the heart of Gods people, as it was with Victorinus hereby *Rapierunt eum intus intra Cor*, the people Snatched him into their very heart within them. It gives them light [27/28] to Enlighten them in their Judgement which now the Church is to pass upon the Person: it will be beneficiall now in order to the Peace, & Comfort of the Consciences of Gods people that Voted Such into the Church: For they have not done it without manifest ground for their Charity to act on: & so their Conscience will speake for them in time to

Come. It will be most to preserve the Church pure, & clear from Scandall when she requires an account of Gods working on the Soule, before she receive any one whereas the Contrary would neither tend to preserve her in purity, nor from reproach. Hence now it makes most for Gods glory; & our & the Churches Benefit: hence now to be made.

3. It will appear from the Manner of Restauration of Such as fall under the Censures of the Church for their offences. For *Restauratio fit eodem modo quo Instauratio.* It being nothing else but a Setting of him right again in that Condition out of which he was Cast for his Impenitence, viz, a Visible intrest in Christ, the Visible priviledges of his house, the Visible Seales of his Kingdom, a Visible Standing in his Church, a Visible Share in the Charity of his people. He for his visible impenetency is cast out of these things by the Censures of the Church. And Restauration doth bring him into the visible possession of these things again. He had a visible possession of these things granted him by Admission: but by the Censures he was Ejected these things again. And by Restauration doth invest him with these again. Now if it bring him into the same Condition, surely it is to be Carried on in the Same manner. What reason to the Contrary? Why should there be a Different way to his Readmission, to that which was attended on at his first Admission? Why should the Charity of Gods people require more now to founde its judgment on than before? Why should the terms of a Visible Interest in Christ, in the Priviledges of his house, in the Seals of his Kingdom, in a standing within the Walls of Jerusalem, etc., be harder to an offending brother once in Covenant, than to one that never was within? Surely its hard to resolve. Nay, & still its more hard, if we Consider that Restauration is nothing but the bringing the thing restored back into as desirable & Commendable a state as it was in at its first erection. What is the reparing of a thing but the bringing of it as neer to its first beauty & excellency as it can be? Instance in what you will. And so in this Case the Soule is Repaired again by being brought to its first spirituall Excellency. Hence Rev. 2.5. Do thy first Works. And this Restauration is made by holding out the repentance of Sin, this is the offenders hearing, Matt. 18.15, & grieving, II Cor. 2.6,7,8. & its called for by the name Repentance. If then Readmission is upon visible Repentance it then follows that Admission at first, was, & must be upon no lower terms than Visible

Repentance. & thus from the manner of Restauration in case of offence we See the Manner of Admission at first must be by an account of Faith & Repentance laid before the Church.

But before I pass from this matter I shall adde as follows an other argument or two,[45] & remove some objections as Paper & packthrid to what hath been weighed out upon this matter already & therefore to proceede [28/29]

4. It appears from the judgment to be passt by the Church upon those she admitts into a Full State that the time when she is to have this Relation made is upon her Admission, & the Argument runs thus. The time when an account of Gods Working the Soule to Faith & Repentance is then to be laid before the Church when the Church is to pass a judgment upon the Soule touching its fitness for a State of Full Communion in the Church. I suppose none will deny this Proposition, unless they will not grant the Supposition it is founded upon, which is this that the Church hath power of judgment so to judge. And this again, I suppose will be granted by all: For every Distinct Society of men have a power essentiall to itselfe as such Sufficient in its right exercise for its own preservation. Whether Family, or Companies of Freemen in a Citie, or Cities or Corporations. And if so, why shall not a Church Society have a power flowing from its Essence Sufficient in its right exercise, for its own preservation? Is the most free Society most lame, & insufficient for its own preservation? Surely no. Then she must be invested with a power of judging to judge the fitness of Such for Admission that she admitts to be of her. For without this power she can neither receive nor refuse any. But whosoever will may & whosoever will not may not when he will, be of her. But this is most absurd & Contrary to the Keyes of Binding, & Loosing, Matt. 16.19, John 20.23. And indeed Contrary to all men. For all grant the Church power of judging, even such as differ about the Confederation of the Church. Well then I take it for granted that it is a truth, that the Church is to judge whom is fit for a state of Full-Communion, & to be a member of her. & therefore an account of the Souls experience of Gods treating of it is at that time to be laid before the Church when the Church is to pass this judgment. The Reason is because if it be not at that time, it is not any thing that falls under the judgment of the Church: the souls fitness

for Membership, & a Full State is not *res judicanda* & the Church is not to meddle therewith. But if this be right then, I demand what is the matter about which the Church is to exercise this Power of judgment? Nothing less than Gods working Faith, & Repentance upon the heart can fit the Soule for a Full State of Churchhood, as hath been already proved; & therefore the Church is to have the evidence thereof as that which is necessary to her giving judgment.

But now the Church is to pass a judgment upon the Soule touching its fitness for a State of Full-Communion in the Church at that time when the soul is received into this state, my reason is this, because the Churches receiving, or Admission is an act of judgment. She judges whether [29/30] she is calld of God to receive him, whether he ought to be received, whether God would have her receive him, whether God hath received him & acts accordingly. Hence a Relation of Gods worke upon the Soul is now to belaid before the Church. The matter to be judged must be heard; no judgment can be passt of an unknown Case. Mans law, John 7.51, doth not, & much more Gods, judge any one before it heare & know the Case. Nay Christ would not judge a Case unheard who saith as I heare I judge, John 5.30. Hence the Case is now to be heard. If now she must judge, now she must heare.

Obj: Let the Life, & Conversation Speake. This is Obvious to all.

Sol: So let it; & let it be heard too, Jas. 1.26, 27, Chap 2.16,17,18. For a Profession, & Faith without it are vain, & deade. Yet this is not of itselfe enough. For

1. This simply taken would open the Church doore & let even Socrates, & Cato in as suitable matter of the Church.

2. This taken with a profession in generall makes any paultery stuff, be it never so rotten under the barke, fit matter of Christs Church; its allone as to say Christs Church is made of whited sepulchers, or rotten wood painted, & guilded over, but this Christ cries out upon, as Matt. 23.25,26,27,28.

3. In the mouth of two or three witnesses shall every word be established that is passed under a judgment sentence, Deut. 17.6, Matt. 18.16, II Cor. 13.1. The life is one & but one, & let it speake. And the Mouth is another, & must give in its testimony of the work in the heart that is saving. For its a Confession unto Salvation that it makes, Rom.

10.10. And therefore the Confession must be of the Saving worke. Hence when evidence is given by both these of the Souls fitness for Church-Fellowship & Full-Communion, the case is ripe for the Churches judgment, & she is to give her judgment then & not till then thereupon.

Obj: Tho' this may be granted in order to the Admission of Heathens Converted that are out of a Church State, yet its not the same with such as are the Ofspring of Christians, & in a Church state already by their Birth, & Baptism.

Sol: 1. By way of Concession, it is to be granted, their Case is not altogether the same. For the One was dedicated to God in his Parentall Covenant, the other not; the one is under the visible Covenant & Baptism, the other not; the one within the visible pale of the Covenant, & under the Watch of the Church, the other not. & yet also the other is (may be) in reall Covenant with & Union Saving unto Christ whereas the one is not. So that the Case is not the same, yet

2. By way of Negation, the Difference will not argue a different manner of Admission into a Full State: that the one should be under a Call, the other under none, to give a Relation of Gods work [30/31] upon his Soule in order to his entrance into a Compleate State For these reasons following

1. The State of both before Conversion is naturally one & the same & both stood in equall need of the same worke of the Spirit to prepare, & fit for Full Communion, as being both in a Fallen state, & in a State of wrath, Eph. 2.2,3. Hence

2. The Covenant Relation of the One onely obligeth to seeke for & doth imply a necessity of, and yet infuse not the Qualifications befitting for a Full State: & therefore if he hath these Qualifications, he hath them from the same hand that the other had them from: both from free grace. Both under an absolute necessity to persue them; the one under a Covenantall necessity also.

3. The Parentall Covenant of the One cannot alter the manner of the Full State Admission: For then the Condition of the Covenant would not be the same to all. For the one should be admitted upon Covenantall Dedication, & the other upon nothing less than Supernaturall & Spirituall qualifications converting the Soule as to the judgment of Charity. Now this never was intended by God, nor in the Covenant of the Parents, that their Children should have a right to all Ordinances without Conversion. But the Childs right to all Ordinances lieth upon

the same foundation as its parents did, viz, Personall Qualifications inhearing. & hence his Admission must be in the same way as his Parents were, viz, by manifesting the same.

4. The manner of Admission to a Compleate State is the same to all. For the state itselfe, the Author, & Object of the state, the Qualifications fitting for the State, the Exercise of the state, & the Benefit as to its nature, are all the same to all. & hence the manner of Admittance thereinto must needs be the same to all.

Obj: The End is not the Same. For to the Converted it is an Ordinance of Confirmation; but to the Unconverted, of Conversion. & therefore the manner of Admission is not the Same.

Sol: The Consequent may be denied. For the manner may be supposed to be suitable to the state of the unconverted. For if it was suited (as indeed it is) to the state of the Converted, it would be above the state of the unconverted; yet if it be suited to the state of the Unconverted, its not above the Capacity of the Converted. But

The Major is utterly false in that it asserts it to be an Ordinance instituted for the Conversion of the Unconverted. For it is not Ordaind to Convert. For it contains in it a *Contradiction in Adjecto*; to say a Compleate state, & yet an unconverted state is a Contradiction; & a Church State in an unconverted state is not compleate but *κατίστατaι*; in a lean sense. There is nothing that [31/32] is transacted in a Full State that is a *Proprium Quarto modo* of that state that ever was instituted by Christ to be a Converting ordinance Simply Considered. Those things that are thus proper to a Full State are the $\begin{cases} \text{Supper} \\ \text{Censures} \end{cases}$ for the Dispensation of the word is not such a *proprium*. For tho' the Officer be Seated in the Church, yet the influences of the Word are extended to all Auditors, according as God shall See meet. And as for some other Church transactions, as Votings, so also Sending officers & Messengers as a Call shall be allowed there unto, I judge none will account these ordinances of a Converting nature. & the like may be said touching some other matters. So that there is nothing peculiarly proper to a Full-State can be imagined a Converting Ordinance unless perhaps the $\begin{cases} \text{Lords Supper} \\ \text{Church Censures} \end{cases}$ be: therefore touching these.

First. That the Lords Supper is no Converting Ordinance, as to the Partaking thereof in Eating, & Drinking, (for the seeing, and hearing the same administred is & ought to be common to all, as please to tarry, as well as the word is) will appear from these Arguments $\left\{\begin{array}{l}\text{Artificial}\\\text{Inartificiall.}\end{array}\right\}$

    1. As for arguments Artificiall, that according to the Rules of art, are gathered out of the Frame, & Artifice of the thing itselfe, such are these few, in stead of many, following.

1. *Ab Antecedentibus absolutiò necessariis.* It appeares that the Receiving of the Lords Supper is no converting Ordinance from the absolutely necessary Anticedent preparatory thereunto. For altho' there is a Commendable preparation to be attended on in order to the attendence upon the Word preached yet its not so absolutly necessary to the Benefit thereof, nor is it of the same sort with what is required in order to the Lords Supper. Its not so necessary. For altho' upon the want of Preparation for an Ordinance, the Soul may go without the benefit thereof, & doth indeed sin therein, yet God never requires that the unconverted soul should prepare itselfe Evangelically for Communion with him in any ordinance save onely for the Convincing it of its miserable Condition that so it might finde the want it stands in of freè Grace in Christ & so Seeke for it, for such preparation that is evangelicall, lies in the souls stirring up in him of the Graces of the spirit suitable for the Ordinance to be attended on. But these he hath not, nor doth God require that he hath them, before he hath received [32/33] them. But as to the Lords Supper he requires that there should be an Evangelicall Preparation as absolutly necessary not onely to the Benefits thereof but also to the Escaping the guilt of the blood of Christ, & sore judgments, I Cor. 11.27–29. Now this Preparation lies in three things *Antecedaneous* to the Lords Supper as

    1. Baptism. This must precede the Lords Supper. Now its a hard matter to prove that Ever any Person that was *sui juris*, i.e., at his own Dispose were baptized either by John Baptist, or the Apostles, that did not first hold out signs of Saving Conversion. For tho' Christ order'd it to be administred upon Discipleship, which implies a Receiving of the Doctrine, an Entrance into the schoole & an Attendance upon the Schoole Discipline, & so it properly goeth along with the Doctrine of the Covenant, as Matt. 29.19,20. Yet it is most hard to prove that ever it was administred to any that did not appear really Converted. For when persons were brought thus to receive the Doctrine of the Gospell, they sildom fell short of the Grace of the Gospell. Hence the New Birth is stiled a being born of the spirit & of Water, John 3.5. The Water in baptism as the sign, & seale, & of the spirit as the ground & Cause of

Regeneration, so its called the Washing of Regeneration, & the Renewall of the Holy Ghost, Titus 3.5, because frequently upon baptism the
Emblem, & seale of Regeneration Extraordinary, & ordinary gifts of the
Holy Ghost brake forth visibly, Matt. 3.6, Acts 8.36,37. So 10.44,45,
46,47,48. So the Laver of Water by the Word whereby it is sanctified &
Cleansed, Eph. 5.26. And it is said to Save by the Answer of a Good
Conscience towards God, I Pet. 3.21. And hence the Primitive Christians
administered it to grown persons onely when they, holding forth Qualifications fit for Full Communion, were received into the Church. Now
seing the Lords Supper is never to be administred before Baptism, &
Baptism to such as are (*absolute foris*) no way related to the Church, was
rarely if ever administred without visible Holiness, its cleare that the
Lords Supper is no Converting Ordinance.

    2. A full State of Churchhood. This is another Antecedent abso-
lutely necessary to the Lords Supper. Tho' scripture instances abound of
Baptism before a Church state, yet there is not one instance that ever the
Lords Supper was administrd but in a Church society, & to such onely
in a Full state, I Cor. 11.18,22, Acts 2.41,42, so 20.7. A Particular
Church is in greate measure erected for the administring this Ordinance
unto. But now such as are in a full State [33/34] are Visibly Holy: or
thus such as are to be admitted into a Full state, are to be Visibly Holy.
None but such are to be admitted into this state. These, & onely these
are born upon the High Priests Breast Plate before, & in the Holy of
Holies.[46] The Stones in the breast Plate were each one Pretious, & they
were the Emblem of the Church Visible on Earth, which is to consist of,
onely, the most pretious, Jer. 15.19. But this hath been already proved,
that the Matter of a Visible Church is to be Visibly Holy. The Temple of
the Lord is Holy, I Cor. 3.17. It is to be really Holy, or not really Holy.
But shall not Gods house be really Holy? Who dare assert this? How
Contrary to the scripture is this? se Ps. 93.5, Zech. 14.20,21, I Cor. 1.2,
Chap. 3.17, Eph. 2.21, etc. The Spirit of God calls such, as are fit matter
for a Church state that is Compleat, τελείοις, I Cor. 2.6, such as are
Perfect. & so the Primitive Christians called such as they received into
Full Communion, the *Perfecti*, such as are perfect, And what sound
minde can imagine, the soule Unconverted to be Complete, or Perfect?
Well, hence it doth appeare, on all accounts, that the Unconverted are
not fit matter for Full Communion, or for a Church state compleate. &
seing this state must be entred into, before the Lords Supper be received,
it must needs be, that the Lords Supper is no Converting ordinance. For

that cannot be an Ordinance of Conversion, that follows such duties, that require Conversion in order to the injoyment thereof. But such is the Lords Supper. Ergo, its no Converting Ordinance.

3. Selfe Examination. This is another necessary Antecedent, Preparitory to the Lords Supper, I Cor. 11.28. Let a man examine himselfe, & so let him Eate, etc. This is a Duty that must be attended upon by the Soule that is in the next Capacity unto the Lords Supper, that hath nothing to do but to come, & receive in order to the Church; for it is a Duty urged on every one in the Church. Therefore it doth not ly in opposition unto a satisfaction, that is to be given in a way of Entrance into a Church State, the which the Church at Ephesus practized, Rev. 2.2,3, & was commended thereupon, & we are all Called unto, I John 4.1. But its put in opposition unto an unworthy approach, by such as are Visibly Worthy. And therefore we may Consider herein the
{ Duty required
{ Object of the Duty.

1. The Duty here required, & this is Self Examination. Let a man Examine himselfe, δοκιμαζέτω, let a man Examine, try thro'ly, way himselfe in the ballance of a right judgment: The Duty [34/35] here required is Such as being rightly attended is more than a bare Triall. For the Word is oft used to approve, as Rom. 2.19, I Cor. 16.3. Now then as it is so used oft, So Dr. Lightfoot, Dr. Hamon,[47] etc., do take it in this place & so to do, is to pass or carry on all those works, & Duties upon his own Soul, as render it to be unto its own Conscience in the Sight of God, the Δόκιμος approved, mentioned I Cor. 11.19. Indeed the Work here called for, to be carried on by a person upon his own Soul, is that whereby he is indeed constituted an approved person, it makes him an approved person, both in his own Conscience, & in the sight of God. And nothing less than such a Duty, can be conceived to be the Duty, that the Holy Ghost would call for, & direct to, when he comes to Correct such as failed in order to their Speciall Communion, that they appeared to hold with God. But a bare triall, or examination onely discovers, & makes the Faulty person ἀδόκιμος disapproved in his own Conscience before God. Therefore the Duty here called for, is such, as makes the soul, the Δόκιμος approved in his own Conscience before God: & by Consequence before all men.

2. The Object of this Duty. Or the thing the Soule is to carry this Duty upon. & this is Himself. Let a man examine, approve himself or make Himselfe approved, ἑαυτόν, Himselfe. He must lay out all his

work upon himselfe, that he may make himselfe approved of by himselfe, he must render Himselfe approved to himselfe, & to God, & to the Church, nay to every mans Conscience, II Cor. 4.2, must render himselfe proofe proofe. So that a mans Selfe is the Object of this worke of Probation, or Approbation as to his $\begin{Bmatrix} \text{Soule} \\ \text{Body.} \end{Bmatrix}$

First As to his Soul. This is the most noble part of a man: & therefore this must be proved approved, as to its Faculties & their Qualifications. & here to instance

1. The Understanding. This is an object of this Duty, & must pass under the Triall. For he that hath no spirituall Discerning Eye in his understanding, is not prepared for the Lords Supper, I Cor. 11.29. Its not a morall Light that will Serve in this Case. It must be an approved Light unto a mans Conscience in the sight of God touching this matter: & nothing less than a light letting Christ into the soule savingly, & inlightening the soule to a Saving Closing with Christ, will render the Understanding *approved* in this Case to a mans conscience in the Sight of God. Conscience will not approve without the approbation of the Holy Ghost. The Holy Ghost will not approve [35/36] without a saving light be in the Understanding: So that the Understanding can, & doth savingly, & sanctifyingly see the nature, & Use of the Lords Supper. For till then, it falls under the guilt of the Lords blood as is avered by the Text, v. 29. Hence nothing less than a sanctifying Light is the Qualification of the Understanding in this Case rendring of it approved for the Lords Supper in the Court of Conscience before God.

2. The Will. This is an other object upon which this Approbative Probation is to be laid. This is the best, or Worst Faculty of the soule, its the Uniting Faculty whereby sin, or Grace is ours in a most proper sense. And therefore we are to call this to the touch, to se whether it is rendred approved, by the inbeing of approvable Qualifications. For nothing less will render it approved. It will be ἀδόκιμον, disapproved, if any other than such Qualifications be seated in it, or in union with it. And nothing less than sanctifying Qualifications will render it approved in Conscience before God. And here I shall onely mention these

1. Evangelicall Repentance. This is that Qualification of the Will that Disunites it from Sin; that is the sin mortifying thing in the Soul that breakes the Covenant with Hell, & makes the league & agreement with Death not to stand: & here Come in those gracious Qualifications, as are seated in the Disaffecting Affections, as a Dislike to Sin, & Selfe as

sinfull, Griefe, Anger, Hatred, & Loathing, because of sin these things God calls for, Rom. 12.9, Jas. 5.1,2, Ezek. 6.9, etc. And till the soul mortifies Sin thus by the spirit, Rom. 8.13. The Court of Conscience cannot pronounce the Will δόκιμον, approved in the sight of God.

2. Saving Faith. This is the Qualification of the Will that Unites it to Christ, that plants it into him, that convayes all saving influences into the soul from Christ, Eph. 4.13,16. & that doth Evangelize its Repentance, & bring in all Sanctifying Graces upon the Uniting affections, so that it hath the Grace of Love, Feare, Reverence, Joy, etc. This is the hand to take, the Mouth to eate, & drinke Christ in the Lords Supper Without which the Soul, tho' it receive the Lords Supper, it receives not the Lord in the Supper. & then it receives but the sign of the Deliverer, & so hath no deliverance from the Curse. An Historical Faith will not unite the Will to Christ; tho' it doth the Assent to the truth of the History. And Conscience, unless it erre, cannot approve the Will unless it be savingly united to Christ. Now then together up this, it is cleare, the Will must be Savingly Converted, before it can be approved of by Conscience in the sight of God. And hence the Soule is to be Converted before it can be approved of by itselfe in the sight of God for the Lords Supper.

So here, the Affections, yea & the Judgment, & Conscience itselfe are the Objects, that must pass under this Approbative Probation, in order to the [36/37] Lords Supper. Whether they are of a Right Quality, rightly qualified for this Ordinance, & rightly improving these Qualifications that so they under this *Dockimization* may be found to be *Dockimai*, Approved. But I shall run my thread out too long thus, if I should draw it out, as I might, before I winde it up. Let this therefore suffice, as touching the soule, as the Object of the Duty here put upon, in order to the Lords Supper. And here we se nothing less than a Saving Work upon the soul as the suitable Qualification of it, whereby it answers to the Duty to be passed upon it, in the Call upon us, put forth in this Command, δόκιμα ζέτω, let a man prove himselfe or pass himselfe under an Approbative Probation.

Secondly. The Body, i.e., the Outward man, as to its Actions, the life, & Conversation. This is the Object of this triall also. For both to go into this ἑαυτόν Himselfe. Now the Outward man must be looked into, to see whether it is δόκιμος, approved, which if it be, then it must be adorned with Qualifications, according to the Will of God, John 14.14,15. If not it is not approved of. If it be not fruitfull in the fruits of

New Obedience, or if its sins are not Repented of. But if these be: & its behaviours are good fruits flowing from a good principle, then the Verdict Conscience gives in, is this, that in the Examination the Person is approved, but if otherwise he is not approved, but Reprobated, not fit nor worthy for the Lords Supper.

And thus we Se by this Preparatory Work of Selfe Examination, that nothing less than saving Conversion, is a sufficient preparation for the Lords Supper. Ergo, the Lords Supper, no Converting Ordinance.

Obj: But the word δοκιμαζέτω, examine, doth import Onely a trying, viz, whether we believe, in a more generall way, the Truth of the Gospell, & Discern & understand, that Christ, & his Death is Signified by the Lords Supper, & that we live not in open sins.

Sol: 1. This is a dry, Jejune, hungry, sapless Sense of the Text, & is a Clipping the Wings of the spirit of God therein, not requiring unto a most holy Ordinance of most intimate Communion with God, Holy Qualifications inhering, as necessary.

2. The word implies more than this, where we are put upon the same duty, by the same word, tho' not in order to any solemn Ordinance preparation, but as it respects our own Spirituall Consolation, & Salvation, II Cor. 13.5. Here the word is put in opposition to being Reprobats.

3. The Objection is as much as to say, that the spirit of God Convincing of the abuse of the Lords Supper, & giving Direction how to attain the End, & benefit thereof, doth yet give such direction, & require onely such duty, as doth not bring the Soul to the benefit thereof, unless the benefit thereof, can be had without an intrest in Christ. For [37/38] the Examination onely of Faith in the Doctrine of Christ, & of Doctrinal knowledge, & of a Negative fitness in life, is such as if there be no more doth not Carry in it any Saving intrest at all. And if this is all, that wee are called unto by the Holy Ghost, then this must be sufficient to the attainment of the End, & Benefit of the Sacrament. For it cannot be supposed that the Holy Ghost should blaim such, as failled in this ordinance, & attained not to the End, & Benefit thereof, & yet should call, & direct unto a Dutie in order to the same, that should be insufficient to the attaining the same, & yet its so, unless the End, & Benefit, can be attaind unto without an intrest in Christ. But surely, if there be any saving benefit in the Lords Supper, it cannot be had, but as a fruit of Union unto Christ. So that this sense of the Objection Cannot be the meaning of the spirit of God in the place, but the former. Now then to gether up this argument,

Seing that Ordinance, whose absolutely necessary Antecedents preparatory to it, are such as imply Conversion, is no Converting Ordinance. And seing the Lords Supper appears to be such an Ordinance,
It is hence cleare, that the Lords Supper is no Converting Ordinance.
And thus much for the first Argument.

2. *A Collatione Canae Dni inediis Regenerantibus*. It will appear that the
Lords Supper is no Converting Ordinance, by Considering it with the
means ordain'd of God, for Conversion. & here I argue thus
> That, which bears no suitable Proportion unto the Ordinances or-
> dained for Converting souls to God, is no Converting Ordinance.
> But, the Lords Supper bears no Suitable Proportion to such
> Ordinances.
> Ergo, the Lords Supper is no Converting Ordinance.

The Major there is no shew of Reason to Question. For Ordinances
instituted to be means of Conversion, are of one & the same peculiar
Property, & nature in that speciall respect.

The Minor is the matter of controversy. & so to be ratified, which
is thus done by an Induction of Particulars thus
> That ordinance that the Unconverted are not under duty to attend
> on, that is not of Equall extent with, that hath no Promise nor
> Evidence of, nor manner of Operation according to, a Converting
> Ordinance, is no Converting Ordinance; it bears no Proportion
> with a Converting Ordinance, Ergo it is none.

For these things are the Properties of a Converting Ordinance.

1. Its an Ordinance Extended unto the Unconverted, a unconverted, such is the Property of the Word & Prayer, etc., Mark 16.15,
Preach the Gospell to every Creature, Acts 26.17,18, Matt. 5.44. The
Object to be Converted must be layd under the Operation of the Means
of Con-[38/39]verting. & therefore the means of Conversion must be
extended to the Persons to be Converted, be they never so vile, &
wicked, never so heathenish, & barbarous, they are not to be debard
from it, denied of it, but be urged to it. For it is to worke upon them,
Hos. 6.4,5. Converting means work not after the manner of Witchery
that their Operation should reach such person Sits not under them
visibly. Nay but Faith comes by hearing, Rom. 10.17. Therefore the
means of Conversion must be extended to the Unconverted.

2. The Unconverted are under Duty to attend these means seing God sends them to them, they are under a Duty to heare, & therefore the spirit of God speakes thus to all, Let him that hath an Eare to heare heare, Rev. 27.11,17, etc.; & threatens the neglecter, Prov. 1.24,25,26, so Chap. 28.9. If they attend not they greatly Sin.

3. Converting means have Gracious Promises going along with them to incourage, yea, & threatonings too, to rouse up poor sinners in an unconverted State to attend on them, & to approve themselves to God, as thus Heare, & your Souls shall live, as Isa. 55.1,2,3, Prov. 1.23,24,25. This is an other property of a Converting Ordinance.

4. There are Cleare Evidences that Converting Ordinances do convert. The Spirit of God hath attested this to be a truth. Faith comes by hearing, Rom. 10.17. It pleaseth God to Save by the foolishness of Preaching, I Cor. 1.21, so Rom. 1.16.

5. Converting Ordinances work in a way of inlightening the minde to Se Sin, & its wretchedness by sin, Acts 26.18, Eph. 5.14, & to se Christ Jesus, & the Excellency of Christ, & Grace, II Cor. 4.4,5,6, So by Convincing the Soul of its sin, & Misery, John 16.8,9, Acts 2.36,37 & so bringing of them to Repentance, & Faith upon Pastors preaching, Acts. 10.34—It is replied that God granted to the Gentiles Repentance unto life, Chap. 11.18. & faith comes by hearing, Rom. 10.17. And thus doth any Converting means bring a person to Conversion. Now then that Ordinance that hath not these five things bears no suitable Proportion unto Converting Ordinances.

But the Lords Supper hath none of these Adjuncts attending upon it. For

1. It never was held forth to unconverted persons, as such to bring them out of this state. It never was heard to be administred to heathens. But, if it be of a Converting nature surely those that have the most need of Conversion, as Infidells, & Atheists, have greate wrong done them, in that Such an Eminent means of their Conversion is denied them. & so also are such as are Excommunicated for Visible Impenitency in sin. For if it be Converting, all unconverted are wronged by the Church crying out *Procul hinc, Procul hinc* [39/40] *este Prophani*. But who dare lay such a Charge in against the spouse of Christ? How will it redound to Christs Dishonour?

2. The Unconverted are not under any Duty to attende it in this state. God calls them first to Repent, & believe, Matt. 4.17, in order to

their entrance into the Kingdom of God. Now have we any instance of any unconverted person Wellcome at this Table, but the Contrary, as him that wanted the Wedden Garment, Matt. 22.12, seems to hold out, & the sore guilt that lights on the Unworthy, I Cor. 11.27,29. & the impossibility of one in Communion with sin, & Infidelity to be in Fellowship with Christ, & the Temple of God, II Cor. 6.14,15,16.

3. There is no Promise of Conversion annexed to this Ordinance to incourage the Unconverted while so, to approach, nor threatoning in case they do not come while unconverted. There are Promises indeed & threatonings indeed in case they abide unfit to come: but none on the account of their not coming in an unconverted state. Simply Let any such be produced, if there be any.

4. There is not the least hint in the Scripture that ever any one was Converted in receiving the Lords Supper. But we instead of bringing the receiver from his Unworthiness (& all Unworthiness is of the same generall nature with unconvertedness, viz, sinfull) do finde it brings divine judgments upon him for his unworthiness, I Cor. 11.29,30—

5. The manner of the Operation of the Lords Supper influences the Recever in, is not as a Converting Ordinance doth. It doth not influence nor operate upon the Soule by inlightening it, & Convicting it of Sin, & Misery, of Grace & Christ, nor by Repentance, & Convayance of the Habit of Faith. But by stirring up the memory to act upon Christ, to excite Faith in Christ a Crucified Saviour & of Thankfulness to God & joy for what Christ hath accomplisht for the soule: & it draws out to the most intimate application, & living on Christ. This is cleare. & tho' Repentance is to be excited by the seing, & hearing the Preparation of the Elements, that is but occasionall: & all may attend the same that please, but from the Essentiall act of Participation, there is no such manner of operation carried on upon the Soul. And hence we say it acts not as a Converting Ordinance. Hence then all being put together, it comes to thus much, that the Lords Supper bears no Suitable proportion unto a Converting Ordinance. & therefore the Lords Supper is no Converting Ordinance.

Thus for the Second Argument may be sufficient.

3. A *necessitate Fidei Salvificae ad recte participandum*. I argue [40/41] from the necessity of Saving Faith to a right partaking, that this Ordinance is no Converting Ordinance. & the Frame runs this

That ordinance unto whose right participation as to its benefit, Saving Faith is Absolutly necessary, is no Converting Ordinance.

None will deny this, For Saving Faith, & Conversion, *mutuò se ponunt ac tollunt*, go hand in hand together.

But to the right Participation in the Lords Supper, Saving Faith is absolutly necessary. The Which is thus made out

1. The Lords Supper requires in the Receiver the neerest, & closest receiving, & applying, of Christ Crucified, which is; & that in the most open, & Visibly way. For it calls him to take & eate, & drinke the Elements, & the things therein Signified, which is the closest application that can be.

2. The Lords Supper, rightly received, Communicates Spiritu[al] & Saving nourishment unto the New Man. Its not for the food of the Body. Oh! saith Christ in this respect, have you not houses to eate & to drinke in? I Cor. 11.22.

3. The Soule in its receiving doth profess these things: & therefore that he doth make the most close, & neerest application of Christ unto its Soule: for what more close, & neer application of any thing; more intimate & vitall, or more nourishing, and strengthening, can there be, than of that which is taken, & eaten; as the sacramentall Elements are?

4. Hence the Lord doth require, that the Receiver have & have in Exercise a Spirituall Recipient instrument, & power. For nothing can be received without these. And also a Spirituall Concoctive power & Faculty that Spirituall nourishment may be made, & received, by the Food received; For nothing can nourish, where these are wanting.

Now nothing less than a Saving Faith can perform these Offices. An Historicall Faith cannot make this most close, & intimate Application of Christ to the Soule, nor Communicate Spirituall, & Saving nurisment to the Soul, nor Constitute the spirituall Concoctive Faculty, & power to make the bread of Life nutritive to the New Man. For then Carnall Persons can do this: for they have such a faith: nay such a Faith is in Divells, Jas. 2.17,18,19,20, no, nor to the Soule where the New Man is not. Absurdities enough will follow upon this. Where Saving faith is not there is onely a Receiving the Elements of Bread, & Wine. Doth God require onely the Bread, & Wine to be Received? Doth he not require the thing Signified thereby to be Received, viz, Christ, & the Benefits of the

New Covenant? Can these be received with out Union to Christ Or can Union be constituted without saving Faith? What then is [41/42] required in this Take, Eate, Take, Drinke? What? onely the use of the Elements? & not the thing Signified? Nay, Christ saith, have you not houses to eate, & to drink in? Or Despise you the Church of Christ? But what is there then required our Receiving, applying, & feeding on Christ to our Spirituall nourishment of the New Man? & what? neither an hand to receive, nor a faculty to Concoct, nor the New man to nourish in the Soul? Or can these be where Saving Faith is not? What absurdities are these? Is it onely a Faith that God calls for that will not answer the End of his calling for it, viz, to receive & live upon Christ savingly? The just shall live by Faith? What then is it that the soule doth that receives without saving Faith, but ly unto God in that his receiving is a profession of his answering Gods call, when he saith, Take Eate, Take, Drinke? Doth God make it a Duty of any to do that, wherein he cannot but lie in the presence of God? If no, then a Saving Faith, being onely that that answers the Call, is absolutely necessary to a right receiving of the Lords Supper.

Obj: God requires persons tho' in a State of Sin to Pray, & to heare & Obey him. Yet their prayers, hearing & obedience are sin, Prov. 15.8, 21.4.
Sol: 1. These are naturall, & not instituted worship: & the reason is not the same touching naturall, & instituted worship. Naturall worship is that duty to God flowing to God from the Essence of our nature. & yet the accidentall Evill Cleaving to nature prevents their being pleasing to God. But instituted Worship is founded upon a New Covenant account; & calls for New Covenant Qualifications.
2. Where the Worship is such as holds forth a New Covenant Fitness God never makes it the immediate duty of a Person unfit thereto, to attend thereon; For he never layes a person under a necessity of Sinning. For so sin could not be sin. Hence to gether up this argument.

Seing by what hath been said its cleare that Saving Faith is absolutly necessary to the Right Partaking of the Lords Supper.
And Seing that Ordinance unto which Saving Faith is absolutely necessary to the right partaking thereof, is no converting Ordinance.
Its Cleare that the Lords Supper is no Converting Ordinance.
Thus much for the third Argument.

4. *A natura Rei.* The Arguments issuing out of the Nature of the Lords Supper deny it to be of a Converting Nature. And their languague runs thus

The Seale of Confirmation & growth lying in Speciall intimate Communion with God, is no Converting Ordinance.

The reason is this, because this Seale Ever presupposeth, the thing, to be confirmed that it is. If it be said that Baptism is such a Seale, I say not so, it never was looked on so to be. There ever hath been this Difference [42/43] held in the Church of Christ between Baptism, & the Lords Supper that Baptism is a Seale of Initiation, the Lords Supper of Confirmation. Hence called implicitly thus Confirm your Love to such an one, II Cor. 2.8, i.e., absolve him, & Admit him to the Lords Supper. Whereas Baptism is stiled the λουτροῦ παλιγγενεσίας, και ἀνακαινώσεως πνεύματος ἁγίου, Titus 3.5, The Laver of Regeneration & the Renewall of the Holy Ghost. For altho' there is a Confirming of Some thing in every Seale, & so in Baptism, yet it is rather on the Souls part a Ratifying, & Visible Confirming his part of the Covenant he enters into with Christ. For a Visible Covenant requires a Visible Seale before it is visibly compleat, & herein both parties do perfect the Covenant, & that as to their mutuall attendence upon each part. But the Case is otherwise touching the Confirmation in the Lords Supper as you shall se by & by. So that this being said I suppose this Major Proposition will be granted, Therefore to go on.

The Lords Supper is in its nature Such a Seal of Confirmation, as it doth thus appeare.

1. Its a Seal of Confirmat[ion.] For if it be a Seale it is either a Seal of Confirmation, or of In[itiation.] But its not a Seale of Initiation for it is not Coext[ended] * * * with the Word so that all that receive the Doctrine of the Gos[pell] * * * [p]artakers thereof: The Commission runs not, go teach * * * Christ, but teach, & baptize, as Matt. 28.19, Mark 16.16. It * * * those first things as Baptism is, Eph., Heb. 6.1,2. N[or] * * * was; That which is administred as a Seale in the last place * * * Administrations, is not an Initiatory, but a Confirmatory S[ea]le. It is added as a Confirmation to all other things, as

1. Its a Confirmation of the souls Visible growth up in the Covenant, for it being administred in the last place, & unto Such onely in a full state, God thro' the Churches Charity in this ordinance, Confirmed to the Soule, visiblie confirms its Visible growth up in his Covenant.

2. Its a Visible Confirmation of their Right in the Covenant Promises, & Blood of the Covenant. For this being in its own nature a visible Sign of Christ Crucified, as the Bread of Christs Body broken, & the Wine, of Christs blood shed, & that as it is applied, & fed upon by Faith; it becomes not onely a Seale, but also a means of Confirmation visibly, of a right in the blood & Promises of the Covenant.

3. Its a Confirmation of the Acceptance, & Love of God unto the Soule. For in the Souls acceptance hereto by the Church, God shews it that favour, as visibly to confirm his Love hereby. For the Church is to receive onely such as he receives, Rom. 14.1,3.

4. Its an intimate Communion with God. The Soul in this Ordinance holds a most familiar Communion with God & Christ, I Cor. 10.16, John 1.3. Its the Lords Table, I Cor. 10.21, the Lords Supper, I Cor. 11.20. Now if so then its the Lords [43/44] Feast. & so δεῖπνον, Supper, I Cor. 11.20, is used, John 12.2, & this is made for familiar friends. Here now Christ the Son, & God the Father, & the Holy Ghost are more eminently at the Table Welcoming his Guesst. Here the Soule in the Visible Signs doth feed on Christ. So that it is in the kinde of it, a kinde of Visible Communion with the Invisible Trinity. So that now you see the Minor made out, that the Lords Supper is in its very nature instituted to be a Seale of our Confirmation, & Growth: & a most intimate Communion with God. & seing such an Ordinance is no Converting Ordinance, the Lords Supper hence appears to be no Converting Ordinance.

Thus much for the Fourth Argument.

5. *Ab Effectis indignae Participationis.* I reason it no Converting ordinance from the Effects of Unworthy Receiving, thus

> That Ordinance, whose unworthy attendence, makes guilty of the Body, & Blood of Christ, & bring[s] Sore judgments is no Converting Ordinance.

Suà vi stat ista. This Proposition will stand upon its own legs. For tho' not to attain to the End of any Ordinance is Sin: & as such as in a Conclusion heaps the Soule under the Blood of the Covenant & hath its hardning Influence of abuse of * * * so of judgment in the End. Yet if it be a Converting ordin[ance] * * * more grace, than to Charge the Soule directly * * * Blood, etc., upon its not right attendance. May, * * * inflict judgment upon such as faile Sin[full] * * * inflicted judgments upon the usting Israelites. * * * was in their mouths the Wrath of God was upon them, etc., Ps. 78.30,32. But as to the ministry of his Word he doth not use to be so hasty. But he exerciseth Patience, & Long-Suffering to lead to Repentance, Rom. 2.4. The guilt of Christ's blood in the neglect of a Converting Ordinance is not direct: but reflect. & not a Covenant Guilt but a Covenant neglect, or rather the neglect of the Covenant, as to the Coming into it. Now God useth to beare long on such account, because he treats them under Such means in Order to their Conversion. But as for such as peculiarly speake forth singular Communion with God in Christ, & a coming up to the Full Call of the Covenant, now no wonder, if sore judgments be inflicted, if persons carry themselves unworthily.

But now the Unworthy attendance upon the Lords Supper, makes guilty of the Body, & Blood of Christ, & brings sore judgments. Ergo,

That it layes the Soule under such guilt, se I Cor. 11.27,29. That it bringeth under sore judgment is plain, I Cor. 11.29, as First it tends to harden the soul in Sin, & introduce Spirituall Hardness. For when a Carnall Person hath attaind to a Full state, & the Highest attainments in Gods house of Visible Fellowship, how ready is the heart to beat off all calls to the un-[44/45]converted, all Convictions, & Exhortations. & to say, I am in a full state, & Conformity of the Gospell. And also to lay hold of the Consolation of the Gospell, & the Promises, & to say, these belong to a Full State in Gods House, & such is my state, & therefore these are mine. Such a plea did they use, Matt. 7.22, Luke 13.26. We have eaten, & drunk in thy presence, they seem to beare themselves against Christ's sentence he laid them under, as if it was not right, because they had Eaten, & drunk in his presence. Much more then will they do it here against his calls, & Censures in the means of Grace, as if they were not the persons spoken to, or Concerned therein, for their state implieth an higher attainment. Hence the Lords Supper tends to harden the unconverted: i.e., Unworthy partaking hardens, & this is the Sorest Judgment.

Secondly, It bring Calamities & sorrows, Judgments consisting in Sicknesses, & Death, I Cor. 11.30. For this Cause, what Cause? Unworthy Partaking of the Lords Supper. For this Cause many are sickly among you, & many sleep. So that now it is cleare, that unworthy partaking of the Lords Supper makes Guilty of the Body, & Blood of Christ, & brings Sore judgment. Ergo, Its no Converting Ordinance.

Thus much for the Fift Argument.

6. *Ab Absurdis*. I conclude from the many Absurdities that unavoidably follow hereupon, that the sacrament of the Lords Supper is no Converting Ordinance. For its sure that that which is the Will of God carrieth no Absurdities with it. If therefore there are Absurdities unavoidably follow the asserting the Lords Supper to be a Converting Ordinance, then the Lords Supper is no Converting Ordinance. But here are many Absurdities follow upon this Assertion, as these & such like

1. That a person in a state of Sin Visibly, should have the Visible seale of a state of Growth in Christ; in a State of Wrath & Damnation should be esteemed according to God worthy of the seale of the Covenant of Grace, & salvation. *Proh. Dolor.* ῥήσσει.[48]

2. That a person in a State of Sin, can worthily partake of the Lords Supper: For if he partakes unworthily, he is guilty of the Body, & Blood of the Lord: & eates & drinks Damnation to himselfe. But a Person in a state of sin can not Partake Worthily. For he cannot Examine himselfe, for this is to pass a judgment on Spirituall things which he cannot do, I Cor. 2.14, δοκιμξέτω, try *fac seipsum probatum, viz Sibi, Deo, et Ecclesiae.* This is above his power. & if he cannot do this he cannot partake worthily, if he can do this, still he is not Converted.

3. That a Person in a State of Sin either can receive both sign, & the thing signified: or may warrantably receive the sign without the thing signified; & that the bare Sign, or the receiving the bare Sign is Converting. [45/46]

4. That Saving Faith, & Repentance are not of absolute necessity unto the attaining the Benefit of the Lords Supper.

5. That a Converting Ordinance is not to be administred to all that stand in need of Conversion. For it is not to be dispensed to Pagan, & Flagitiously Wicked Persons by the Consent of all.

6. That Unconverted Persons do receive sometimes greater Benefit from the Lords Supper, than a Child of God is capable to Receive. For such are brought by it to a Saving Union to Christ, & into a state of Grace, the which the Converted having already cannot receive from it. So that it doth the Sinner more good than the Saint.

7. That Faith sometimes comes by eating, & drinking, & not alwayes by hearing. & so the Apostle was not right in saying that Faith comes by hearing.

8. That Saving Faith gives no more right to a Visible seat in Christs Visible House, & a place at Christs Visible Table on Earth than Civility doth. Or that Christ hath no form in his Schoole peculiar for those that

are taught savingly of God, but what he sets such upon, that having learnd no Saving lesson in his schoole.

Well then, seing these & such Absurdities as these unavoidably follow the tenet, that the Lords Supper is a Converting Ordinance, it is clear to us that the Lords Supper is no Converting Ordinance.

And thus by these Six Arguments Artificially gathered out of the Fabrick of the Matter is it made out to be no Converting Means.

2. Arguments may be laid down of an Inartificiall Stamp to evince the Same truth, & here I shall cite some Testimonies as

1. Divine. But here note that during the times of the Pen men of Holy Scripture, seing none giving themselves up to God in a Church state, but Such as unto the judgment of Charity, were Visibly in a Converted state, Acts 5.13, we must produce by inference our Testimonies because they had no occasion given to write of the matter directly. & therefore take these

1. Holy things are not to be cast to Dogs, Matt. 7.6, so Chap. 15.26. Dogs are persons in a State of Sin: The Syrophenician Woman was put among them, till her faith did shine, Matt. 15.26,27,28. These Holy things intended, are not to be taken for Converting Ordinances. For then the word, & the Convictions of the word are not to be held out to them: but they are, Mark 16.15, II Tim. 3.16, 4.1,2,3, Titus 1.9,10,11,12. It therefore remains to be Understood of the Chiefe Mysteries of the Gospell.[49] And as hence duty stands incumbant upon us, it chiefly calls us not to administer the Lords Supper to such. These Holy things that Dogs may not partake of, are not ordaind to convert Dogs then.

2. The Old Leaven is to be purged out, I Cor. 5.7. What is that old leaven, but impenitent, & visibly non-converted ones. Now if old [46/47] Leaven is to be purged out, the Purging out is rather the Converting, ordinance. But the Lords Supper that he is removed from never was ordained for his Conversion, for then he should not be purged from it.

2. Humane Testimonies. Now here you may note the Greate Care Gods Faithfull ones Have used to keep Unconverted Persons from this Ordinance: which is a Cleare demonstration that they held it no Converting means of Grace. And take some instances touching this matter

$\begin{cases} \text{Before the Rise of} \\ \text{After the Recovery from} \end{cases}$ Antichrist.

1. Before the Rise of Antichrist, heare the Witness of the Church given in this matter by some famous Lights that shown forth in their dayes.

Here I shall give an instance first out of Origen showing the greate care they took to see that those they admitted were brought wholly up to God, saith he, Christians when they have tried the Souls of their Auditors, having conference with them privatly, after they appear to have Covenanted sufficiently to desire more uprightly to live for the time to come, do then at length admit them into Fellowship. But yet they hold apart from the rank of such as they lately had received, Such as have not yet received the token of their perfect Purification. And there is among them an other certain Appointment, that every one should carry it according to his power to desire nothing, But what things were seemingly for Christians; among whom Some certain persons are appointed, to search into the life of such as come to them, & to observe diligently how they be have themselves. So that Such as live badly they separate from the Church Fellowship: but such as are not such they receive with all their Soul, & do no doubt make better dayly. Thus he.[50] Surely such a behaviour cannot stand with the apprehension of a Church state, or the Lords Supper a means of Conversion.

Take another out of Origen wiping off Celsus his reproach calling Christians Worms Crawling together in some dirty Corner, he saith, among Philosophers there are many adulterous: but saith he these Evills are in no Christian, if thou search who properly is a Christian; & if it chance that the same things are found to be in some of us, yet not in such as are received unto our Table (or Cession) & that convene to gether to pray, seing that they were such are excluded from them of this sort are excluded. We therefore are not Worms crawling together.[51]

Take another instance out of Chrysostom, who in his 83 Homily upon the 26 of Matthew saith thus of Christ, it was not enough for him to be made man, & to be scourged with Whips, but he brings us into one mass with himselfe, nor doth he thus make us his own body by faith onely, but in very deed. Wherefore ought he not then to be more pure that partakes of this sacrifice? What sun beams should not that hand exceed that [47/48] handles this Crown? That Mouth, that is filled with the fire of the Spirit? That Tongue, that is died in this wonderfull blood? Let it come into thy minde with what honour thou art honourd; What a Table thou enjoyest. For we are fed with that which the Angells tremble at in beholding, nor are they able to look on it without amaizment for the glory which thence reboundeth: & we are brought into the Same mass with him, being one Body & one Flesh of Christ.[52] And again in his Notes on the First to the Ephesians saith thus, After the Mysteries are over thou mayst approach, but while they are Celebrating withdraw, for it is no more lawfull for thee to be here than for one of the *Catechumeni*. Also touching Penitents thus, thou hearest the Cryer standing & saying, as many as are yet to repent, abstain ye; also, if thou art of the Penitents thou oughtst not to partake. For as much (he saith again) as none that are not initiated may be present, so neither may the initiated, if they be polluted.[53] Surely then he tooke not the Lords Supper to be a Converting Ordinance.

The like we may gather from Augustine who speaking to the *Catechumeni* saith, let them pass over the Red Sea (that is be baptized) & eate Manna, (that is the Body & Blood of Christ) that as they have believed in the name of Christ, so Christ may betrust himselfe with them.[54]

And tho' Augustine was very large in administring the Lords Supper, yet he constantly cried out that the Unworthy eat & drunke judgment to themselves. So that it doth appeare that He tooke it not for a Converting Ordinance, for then the Unworthy would not have eaten judgment.[55]

Hence from the Restraint of the *Cathechumeni* from this Ordinance there came in use a Distinction of the *Missa Catechumenorum*, & *Missa Fidelium* & also there was at the time of the Lords Supper this Proclaimation, Holy things for holy Ones, which was as much as to say If any one be not Holy let him not approach.[56]

By all these things it appeares that the Primitive Christians did not account the Lords Supper a Converting Ordinance.

2. After the Recovery from Antichrist. Now here you may take notice that its the Doctrine of Antichrist to assert the Lords Supper a Converting Ordinance, against which Protestant Divines in generall make opposition. The Papists Positively assert the Lords Supper gives Grace to convert Sinners. The Bull that Pope Leo the tenth sent roaring out against what he counted Errours of Pestiferous Poison in Luther brings [48/49] in this in the first place that he charges him with, That he affirms it to be an old Errour to say, that the Sacraments of the New Testament do give Grace to them (*Qui non ponunt obicem*) that hinder it not.

Whereunto Luther in his reply answers from Rom. 14, Whatsoever is not of Faith is Sin saith he, that the Sacraments of the New Law can give no Grace to unbelievers, for as much as the Sin of infidelity is the greatest Obstacle. Its plain that Luther intends that they cannot be accounted instrumentall Causes in their own nature. And Mr. Fox in his Marginall note, the Obstacle letting Sacraments to give Grace is the actuall purpose of sining, say the Papists. The onely obstacle letting sacraments to give Grace, is unbeliefe, Saith Luther. But the truth is that sacraments neither with Obstacle, nor without obstacle, do give Grace to the Believers, or Unbelievers; but onely signify Grace given by Christ, Saith Mr. Fox. Se *Acts & Monuments*, Vol: 2, p. 643.[57]

And you have Ames replying in this matter against Bellarmine (mentaining that Error of theirs that the sacraments give Grace) in his *Bellarminus Enervatus*, Tom. 3, *Cap.* 5.[58] Se also Mr. Gillespy against the Erastians in his *Aarons Rod blossoming*, Reciting the Protestants in Generall against the Papist in this matter, & then he confirms by 20 Argument[s] the Lords Supper to be no Converting Ordinance, Book 3. Cap. 12 & 13.[59] But I will proceed no further here. Thus it then appears that the Lords Supper according to the judgment both of Former, & Later Divines, is no Converting Ordinance. & this may suffice touching it.

2. The Censures. Now its true these belong to a Church State, & may indeed become a means of Conversion, Jas. 5.19,20. For as private admonition, etc., may do this: so also may Ecclesiastick do: But yet the Censures never were Instituted properly to Convert a Sinner from a State of Sin unto God. For what reason will not disdain such a Conclusion as this as holds that a Person unfit visibly, for Visible Church Fellowship should be received in that he may therein be laid Under the Censures of the Church as means of Conversion, whereby unless he come up to a Visible Fitness he is sure to be Cast out again. Nay, the truth is, that because the Censures have some peculiar Opposition in them against Sin, to bring to repentance of visible Sins, & an awe in them to bestrain from sin, they are to be extended further than a Full State reacheth, & to reach to all that are given up to God in the Church, & so stand related to, & are Under the Watchfull Eye, & prayers of the Church, as Ps. 144.12. But they are Specially ordaind for

1. The Reclaiming a Brother by Repentance from Particular sins that are Visible, & Provable, Matt. 18.15,16, Gal. 6.1,2, Luke 17.3,4.

2. The Securing the Church from Scandall. That there may be not reproach cast on nor infection found in, the Church nor cast on God & his cause, I Cor. 3.17, Chap. 5.1,2–7, Chap. 11.22, II Cor. 6.

3. That the Bond of Charity may be kept firm among them in this state, Matt. 18.15,16,17. So that it is not a Converting Ordinance prop-

erly so taken. Hence then Seing neither the Lords Supper, nor Church Censures are Converting Ordinances properly, its Cleare that a Church state is [49/50] not ordaind for Converting such as are compleatly in it to God, i.e., that is a Full State of Church hood is not ordaind for the Conversion of Such as are in it. & thus I having cleared the Argument of this Objection I return to it, & say Seing the End & Benefit of a state of Full Communion is the same to all, all are to Enter into it the Same Way. & hence by a Relation of the Work of God on their hearts. But let this Suffice for this Argument.

5. I argue it from the Duty that Every Person to be admitted standeth in, fully to satisfy the Charity of the Church, & on this account it will appeare that in order to his Admission, there ought to be a Relation made of Some of those experiences he hath had of Gods worke upon his Soul. & here the Argument runs thus.

Every one to be admitted ought in order thereto to attend the best course, he is calld to, to Satisfy the Charity of the Church.

I am ready to think that this Proposition hath such a fair looks that none Can find fault with it. For a Church state is such, as all are to be knit together in love, Col. 2.2, to exercise true love one to another, Heb. 10.24, I Pet. 1.22, to be shewing forth the Effects of Love in bearing one With an other, Eph. 4.2. Covering one another's infirmities in love, I Pet. 4.8, helping one another out of Sin by Love, Gal. 6.1, Edifying one another in Love, nay, & holding the Unity of the Spirit in the bond of Peace, Eph. 4.3,16, which Cannot be done without Love. Hence, Such as are to be admitted are to take the best course they are Called to to bed themselves in the very Love of the Church: & hence they ought to Satisfy the Churches Charity.

But the giving an account of the Worke of God upon his heart being calld to it, is one of the best Courses he can take thereto.

What Course better can be imagined? Fix upon any Way what ever, & se whether there is any thing therein comparable to this for that end, in case his Life be answerable. For herein he shews his Christian humility Condiscending to Satisfy the Charity of all his Observations of Gods comming in one Means of Grace, & in an other upon his heart, & his own Spirits Working under the same, herein he openly avouches the Efficacy of the Spirit of God in the Ordinances, evidences the truth of Gods Word upon his own Experiences, & gives an open testimony of what he finds: & so doth visibly give forth the Glory due to the means of Divine Grace, & the Honour & praise to God on this account: He shews how God Convicted & drew him: how he struggled under the same & yet was overcome, & carried Captive, Submitted himselfe, & Followed him, threw down his Weapons, & had his heart set out on Christ. Oh! this must needs let him into the Very hearts of Gods people. If to tell many pritty stories, will lay a man in the heart of such as love Such tales, How much more will this lay a person in the very heart of [50/51] the People of God Whose joy, & delight is to se the Workings of Gods spirit upon the hearts of the Children of men. & fitting them for the Holy things of God. And hence it appeares that such as are to be admitted are to give an account of their Experiencing Gods Working upon their hearts, in order thereto.

      6. I argue this Relation at the time of Admittance, from the Duty that every one is under to Keepe the Church free, & clear of Scandall, & here the Argument encounters the Case thus.

      Every one is to attend the best means to keep the Church free from Scandall, & Reproach.

      I am Confident thou canst not be a Christian if thou denist this. The Church is the most excellent Fabrick that ever was raised, its built of most Choice Matter, Fair Colord Stones, Pleasant Stones, Pretious Stones, Saphires, Agates, Carbunkles, Isa. 54.11,12. Living Stones built up a Spirituall House, an Holy Temple, an Habitation of God thro' the spirit, I Pet. 2.5, Eph. 2.21,22. Raised upon the best foundation, the Foundation of the Prophets, Apostles, & Jesus Christ, who is the Chief Corner Stone, Eph. 2.20. It is the most transendently Excellent society that ever was & that as for Costliness, more pretious then all the World being purchased by the blood of Christ, I Pet. 1.19, of the Son, the Onely begotten Son & dearly beloved Son of God, Heb. 1.2,3, I John 2.1,2, which is by the Holy Ghost Stiled the Blood of God, Acts 20.28. For Accomplishments & Qualifications, as the Graces, the Sanctifying Graces of the Holy Ghost, as Cant. 4.9,10—to the Enravishing the Heart of Christ, Rev. 21.1,2—as to Possession, & Enjoyment, the Houshold of Faith, Gal. 6.10, the City of the Saints, the Houshold of God, Eph. 2.19. As to Patrimony, or Birthright Heirs of the Promises, Eph. 2.12,13, Heirs of God, & Coheirs with Christ, Rom. 8.15,16,17. Whose is the kingdom of Glory, Luke 12.32. As to Relation, the Spouse of Christ, II Cor. 11.2. The Body of Christ & that Corporation whereof he is the head, Eph. 1.22,23. & as to Attendents, which have the Holy

Angells of God their Guard & Waiting Men, Heb. 1.14, Ps. 34.7. & as to the Rule of their carriage, viz, the Will, & Law of God, Isa. 8.20, Matt. 6.10. Now such an House as this, is to be kept clean & pure, such a Society as this is to be kept free from all reproach, & scandall by all means, I Cor. 3.17, 10.32. For if this be reproached or a scandall lie on it, it will be a stumbling block in the Way to it. & a dishonour to the Owner of it.

But now one of the best means to keep this clear from scandall & reproach, is for all to give a Relation of Gods Work on their hearts in order to their Admittence.

The Censures after are to scoure it of scandall, & Reproach. But if there be Admissions without any Relations, the Church doth not so much as heare the Person she judges fit for such an Excellent state speake for his own heart, nor shew any thing how that stands. & then can it be possible for her to escape Reproach? Can she clear herselfe of scandall, & never see that those she receives, are Cleare from the same in heart? [51/52] Can it be supposed to be no Scandall, or Reproach to be voide of Holy-ness in heart? Or to be of an Uncircumcised heart? God reproacheth such, Jer. 9.25,26. Doth the Church Profess Holiness,& to be of a Circumcised heart? And will it not appeare a Reproach & scandall to be the Contrary? Is it not a Reproach, & Scandall to profess one thing, & to be another? Or to take no care, or to use not suitable means, to se that she be, as she professeth? And are suitable means attended in this Case, & yet the person never heard to speake a word of Gods Working upon his own heart? Who can tell what God hath done for the heart, if the Person speake not? Surely then the Church doth not do its duty to keep itselfe from Reproach & scandall, that Admitts whom she never hears to speake for themselves. But when they have held out an account of What they have met with, she hath now to judge, whether it is sufficient to let in Christ, & now she can go no further. So that this appears to be one Chiefe means to keep the Church from scandall, & Reproach & therefore the Conclusion follows naturally, that Every one is to give an account of his Experiences at his Admittance into a Full state of Church Fellowship.

Thus I have laid down something Evincing, that a Publick Relation of Gods Working upon the heart is an other thing necessary, in order to the Visibility of holiness, as *Forma Praeparans* of the Matter putting it into the next Capacity of its receiving the Formall Cause of Church-hood compleate. & thus I have done with the proof of the Matter.

But here are Still some piddling objections that some disaffected Spirits cast out, as bolts shot against the Case, which I shall endeavour to Obviate thus

Obj: 1. To Fix these Relations upon the time of Admissions, is without all Warrant, & therefore a Superstitious thing.

Sol: 1. Fix what way you will to be attended on in order to Admission (for there is a necessity of some way), it may be said more rationally to be without all scripture Ground, & so Superstitious, for there is not so much as a foot step of any other way found in Scripture.

2. I doubt the Objector will not stand to it, that every thing to bee attended upon in the Church on necessity, that we have not cleare Scripture for, & yet is Constantly attended on, is Superstitious. For then what would the meeting twice upon the Lords Day, Praying before, & after sermon, Singing of Psalms before alwayes, & sometimes after sermon, Baptizing Infants, & on the Lords Day, & in the After noon after sermon the bringing Water in a Basen, etc.? Would not these things be superstitious by the same Rule?

3. By that time these Arguments are considered well, it will bee cleare whether these Relations be without Scripture Warrant, or whether any other practice can produce the like Warrant. Wherefore let this be [52/53] attended, till some other way of Admissions is made cleare out from scripture to be the way of God than this.

Obj: 2. Protestant Divines have all along struck down Confessions, in their opposition to Papists, as superstitious. If evill in them, are they good with us?

Sol: 1. They have so done, & done well in so doing; for their Confessions are not what we plead for. Theirs being a Confession of all the sins that ever a man commits once in the yeare at least in the eare of a Mass Priest, in private, that he may give him a Pardon, & is such a thing Warrantable?

2. What is Auricular Confession of a mans sin in the Priests eare, to a Relation of Gods Working upon the heart by his spirit in the means of Grace, laid before the Church, as matter for their Charity to act on, in order to their receiving him into their Society.

3. Protestants that Opposed this Papish Confession, yet ever retained Confessions, & the Manifestation of Repentance publickly before the Church, for such sins as they accounted scandalous, when visible, as their Practice at this Day Evinceth. *Ecce homo.*

Obj: 3. But these Relations Discourage many good Christians from seeking Full Communion. & some are against them, & will not come in rather than to be brought to such terms.

Sol: 1. If this was Good arguing, then we might bring Gods Laws to mans Will, & make them Suite every man: or as a Taylor doth the Cloath, Cut out of the Piece a garment that he fits to the back of his Customer. Such Commands as are too Streat, wreath them, as on the Tyrants iron Bed.[60] Such as are too wide, or large, Cut them shorter. But is this good doings. Because men like not Relations, some thro' timerousness, some thro' Pride of heart, therefore they are not the ways of God: or if Gods Wayes, they are not to be attended on. What Divinity is this?

2. This rather shews it to be the Way of God, because the hearts of men are so much against it. For mans heart is utterly out with Gods Wayes, Rom. 8.7.

3. Who soever these Good Christians are I know not, but this I know full Well, that if in truth they be Good Christians, yet the objecter doth design to draw a plea in, over the back of their goodness for non-Converted persons admission to the Lords Table, as to a Converting Ordinance. Which is a Popish Doctrine. But yet its no Sign of a Persons goodness to be so fixed upon his Own notion, as to pluck up the Warrantable practice of a Church to let him in: as if he Saw more than all the Church, & therefore never seekes satisfaction, or Will receive none.

4. If these be in truth Good Christians, yet they are not Good enough for Full Communion: For they are so humorsom, that they are not like either to receive benefit from, nor be beneficiall to, the Fellowship. For if their notion doth not take place, nothing will please. Hence more fit to bee out than In. But I will detain you no longer. Thus much for the Materiall Cause of a Church, viz, It is Visibly Holy Matter that is in the next Capacity [53/54] to the Reception of the *Ratio Formalis* of a Church State.[61]

2. The *Ratio Formalis*, or Formall Cause of a Church, & this is that which being entred into the Matter of the Church, doth give the Church its perfect Essentiall Constitution: it makes the Church a *Totum Essentiale*, & raises the Materialls up to be the House of God; or the Habitation of God thro' the Spirit. The Materiall Cause lies in the Quarry of Humane Nature; yet, as it is eyed by the Principall Efficient Cause, having the Eternall Love of the Decree upon it, it lies as so many shining

343

Pearls, sticking in an hard, & impregnable Rock. But as the Instrumentall Causes convay the Preparatory Efficiency of the Principall upon them, they are broken off, as Pearls hewen & squared, yea, & Polisht after the similitude of a Palace: But yet are as a Company of Pearls which tho' fitted for royall Service, lie Scattered up & down, Sparkling among other Stones; or at best, but as an heap of Stones laid together ready for the building, & to be raised into an Holy Temple. But the Formall Cause once introduced, gives them this Church Constitution: and brings them into a City frame, or an Holy Habitation. This Formall Cause therefore must needs be their Voluntary Agreement or Covenant, whereby they agree to walke together in the Wayes of God, in Observance of all the Ordinances of Christ, according to the Gospell. Now that this Voluntary Covenant, is the Constituting Differenceing Principle of a Church, may appear from these Arguments $\begin{cases} \text{Artificiall} \\ \text{Inartificiall.} \end{cases}$

First, Artificiall Arguments setting fast this matter, might be many. I shall produce some few, & they are drawn out

1. *Ab Ecclesiae Naturâ*, from the Common Nature, or Genus of a Church, & this is this, it is a Society of Men. & hence the Argument faces the Case thus

That which is the Formall Cause of a Society, as a Society, is the formall Cause of a Church.

This I doubt not but all Reason will close with. For the Generall nature of a Church is a Society. & a Church is a Species contain'd under this Genus. And there is nothing more in the Species,[62] than in its Genus, save onely its individuating Difference, that differences Species from Species, as the *Proprium Quarto Modo* of every Species. Hence that which distinguisheth a society, as a Society, from all that are not of the Society, must needs be the *Proprium quarto modo* of Every Society, as a society. & hence the Form, or the formall Property thereof. None can deny a Church to be a Society. It must therefore have the *Ratio formalis* of a Society.

But now the Formall Cause of a Society, is the peculiar Covenant Terms of the Society, whereby they are ingagued to the Duties of the Society entred into.

This is too full of Reason to be rationally Opposed. For none are any [54/55] society: or associated, that come not up to the terms of the society. To say the Contrary, is to say, & unsay, or to say that that

Unassociates a Society, & makes a Society, & no society all one, laying a Society Waste, as carrying in it *Contradictio in Adjecto*. Further scripture will evidence that Combinations or Covenants are the formall Reason of the Societies As for instance. The Hebrews call a Company חבל a Cord, as I Sam. 10.5, A company (חבל , a Cord) of Prophets, & the Greeks σπεῖρα, a Cord, i.e., a Company inlisted under one Captain, fitly answering our English term Band, John 18.3, Acts 10.1. & this Constitutive Cause Forming the One into a society of Prophets, & the other of Soldiers was their Combination, & Covenant binding them to the Duties of the societies, as a bond, or Cord. And so its also used for this Ecclesiastick bond or Covenant, Zech. 11.14,15, as also such as were in an agreement together, Ps. 119.66,חבלי רשעים, which the Greeke render by another word Signifying a Cord, as οχοινία ἁμαρτατῶν, bands of the Wicked, i.e., the Wicked Company Combined together. So the Hebrews also called an Assembly, or a Congregation that came to worship God by עדה , Ps. 1.5, & פרעדי a Congregation, Num. 16.2, from יעד Condixit, Constituit: & sometimes *Desponsavit*, to betroth, as Ex. 21.9, who hath יעד betrothed her, & to betroth is to Covenant. & hence the Learned observe that it notes such a Congregation, as are at an agreement among themselves about time, & place, & then surely all of the matter, of their assembling. Hence a Covenant appears to be implied in all these words, which yet some speake less than a Society, & chiefly an assembly. So that now if I winde up the Result of that which is spoken, it appeares, that the Formall Cause of a Society lies in a Voluntary Covenant about the Duties of the Society, Ergo, the Form of a Church is such a Covenant. Thus much from the Generall Nature.

2. *Ab Exempla*. I argue from the Example of the Church of Israel of old, & the Argument hence ariseth thus,

That which was the Formall Constituting Principall, of the Church of Israel of old, is the Formall Cause of Every Church of Christ.

The Reason is manifest: For that which is of the same nature must needs have the Same form, For the Form is Essentiall to the Nature, & the Nature is according as the Form. But a Church of Christ is of the same in all ages. Hence Christs Church of old was of the Same Nature of old, as his Church is now. & therefore it must be that the Same Formall Cause that Constituted the Nature of his Church then, must be the Form Constituting Cause now. For the form of one Church doth the same thing for one Church, & onely the Same, as the Form of an other doth for an other. And therefore finde out but the Form of one, & you have found out the form of Every One.

But now, The Formall Cause of the Church of Israel of old was their Covenant. Hence their transacting the Matter was their Covenanting, & the Event was the Covenant, Deut. 29.1. Moses made a Covenant with the Children of Israel; & their Unchurching of them is calld a breaking this Covenant, [55/56] as Zech. 11.10, 11.14, & a breaking off, Rom. 11.17. And on the Contrary when they were matter by repentance prepared for a Church state they were Reinchurched by their Covenanting together to walke with God in his Laws of Churchhood, Neh. 10.28,29— Ergo, A Church Covenant is the Formall Cause of a Church.

3. *Ab Eximiis Scripturarum Metaphoris.*[63] The Formall Cause of any Church is drawn out of those Scripture Metaphors looking this way. For it is but Rhetoricall Atheism to say scripture similitudes are *Ad Pompam*, & not *ad Pugnam*. Wherefore I argue from this place thus,

That which answers Scripture Metaphors touching the Formall Cause of a Church, is the Formall Cause of a Church.

This I judge none can deny that admit the scripture to be of God. But the Church Covenant answers Scripture Metaphors thus. Ergo

This will appear by searching into these Metaphors with respect the $\begin{cases} Totum \\ Forma. \end{cases}$

1. Such as Respect the *Totum*, or the Whole Church, & these are many. Some few whereof I shall instance in, respecting

1. Things Artificiall. And thus a Church is called a Building, I Cor. 3.9, an House, I Tim. 3.15, and Habitation, Eph. 2.21, a Temple, v. 20, a golden Candle stick, Rev. 1.12, *ult.*, Chap. 2: Now here I Enquire What are the Formall Causes of all these Artificiall things? Surely none can imagine any thing else but their Uniting bonds, or their joyning together, which Constitutes, and forms each of them into its particular nature by uniting the separate parts together. But then if a Church is thus stiled, it is because God would teach us something hereby. And if he would teach us any thing by these Metaphors, then there must be some Analogy, & suitableness in the Metaphors to the thing given us by these Metaphors.

And therefore that which is most pertinent in them to their being, & end, must be granted to be in the thing designed by them. Now then as they Cannot be without their parts be joyned, & Combined together which Combination is their form; so they hold out that in a Church, which is the meaning of them, there must be such a Combination together of its parts, that answers this their joyning & What is this Combination, but a Covenant. For nothing else sets the parts together Visibly, but a Visible Covenant.

2. Things Morall. And thus a Church is Stilled an Houshold, Gal. 6.10, & a Family, Eph. 3.15. Now how is an houshold, or Family Constituted but by a Voluntary agreement, & Covenant. Others out of this Covenant are not of this household: When any are admitted as members of it, it is by Covenanting, as Servants, & Tablers. As for Children, they are members of it, by vertue of their Parents Marriage Covenant, which is the foundation of the Family. Yet when they come to enjoy any Distinct Authority in the Family, it is by agreement, with their Parents: as in the Marriage of the Heir, the rest when ripe, begin New Families by Marriage. And hence [56/57] this Covenant which is the Very formall Cause of a Family argues that a Church being Gods Family must be constituted by a Mutuall, or Voluntary Covenant as its formall Cause.

3. Things Naturall. And so the Church is likend to an Olive tree grafted, Rom. 11.[17–20], & unto the Naturall body, I Cor. 12.12–27. Now wherein consists the form of the Olive tree but in the Uniting together of its parts: & as grafted but in the joyning of the Graff with the Stock? And Wherein consists the form of the Naturall Body; but in the Uniting of its members together in their places? And what answers this Uniting the members of the Body of Man or of the Olive tree, in the Body, or Olive tree, the Church, but the Uniting the members together in such a way, as they are Capable of, & as is proper to the same: & this is in a Covenant way. Hence a Church Covenant is the Visible Formall Cause of a Church. Thus much appeares from these Metaphors representing the *Totum*, or Whole Particular Church.

2. Such as respect the *Forma*. There are some Metaphors the spirit of God useth in this Case to intimate unto us the Form itselfe of any Church visible. & that it is a Mutuall, & Voluntary Covenant to attend the Concerns of a Church. And these are borrowed from the Terms of

1. Art, more generall as Adding as Acts 2.41,47, προσετέθησαν, the Lord put to the Church: now here was this Addition, or Apposition

made to the Church, surely in such a way as was Proper to, & Usuall with men: & this is by an agreeing unto the terms of the Society, so a Servant is added to his Master, Matt. 20.1,2 so a Souldier to his Company under his Captain. So then here Again, more Speciall, as Joyning, Acts 5.13, *κολλᾶσθαι*. Its a Metaphor borrow'd from Artists that joyn things artificially together with Glew & the spirit of God borrows it to import the Marriage Covenant, as Matt. 19.5, Mark 10.7. And for the Church Covenant, Here & also Acts 9.26.

2. Nature. The Spirit borrows some terms of Nature, to intimate this unto us by, as Eph. 2.21, *οἰκοδομὴ συναρμολογουμένη*, fittly framed together: or better expresst, Chap. 4.16, fittly joyned together, it properly imports such a joyning, & Compacting to gether, as is that of the joynts by its nerves, or Sinews. & altho' this imports the Union the Soul stands in unto Christ, & the spirits Uniting one member by these Nerves to an other: yet, as a Visible body it implies the Nerves of that body as such joyning each Member to its place in the Body. And what doth this import but Such a manifest joyning of every member to this body or Church as another is joyned to that, or the other. & what can this be but a Covenant. Now then its cleare that a Church Covenant suites the very design of scripture Metaphors. & therefore this is the Form of a Church.

4. *Ab Effectis*. There appear the Effects of the Form of a Church flowing from the Covenant, as prove a Church Covenant the Form of a Church. And hence the Argument defends the truth thus.

> That is the Formall Cause of a Church, from which the formall Effects flow. But the Formall Effects flow from the Covenant Ecclesiastick, Ergo,
> The Church Covenant is the Formall Cause of a Church. [57/58]

The Major no reason can deny. Formall Effects being such as are the Proper Effects of the Form.

The Minor is thus made Currant, by two instances.

1. The Covenant makes the Church Compleate, & perfect. Its the Property of the Form to inform all the Matter. Hence the Matter of a Church is brought into a Church State by the Form of the Church entring into it. The matter is not Related to, but onely prepared for the Church State, till the form be introduced: but when the form is intro-

duced, then the matter is put into a Compleat state of Church-hood. Now all this is done by the Church Covenant. Ergo its the Form.

2. The Exercise of Church Censures flows from this Covenant. The Exercise of Church Power is an Effect flowing from the Formall Cause of a Church. For the Form is the *Pomcipium Operandi*. Actions flow from the Form, for if the form be destroyed actions cease. But now the Exercise of Church Power flows from the Church Covenant both $\begin{cases} \text{Subjective} \\ \text{Objective.} \end{cases}$

1. Subjective. In respect of the subject in which it is seated, & by which it is Exerted. For altho' the Lord hath limited it, so that not all in Covenant may exert it, as I Tim. 2.12. Yet none may exert it but such as are in the Covenant. & these must, & are blamed in case of neglect, I Cor. 5.2, 4.7,13. No man out of Covenant can, or hath any Call, to exercise Church Power.

2. Objective. In respect of the Object about which this power is exercised, & this is Onely such as are in Covenant. For such as are not in Covenant cannot be touched by the Church. The utmost of its extent is but to put out of the Church Such as answer not the End of Church-Fellowship, & of this power: & it can go no further. But if a Person be not in Covenant he cannot be outed: nor Commanded to attend upon the Church: Every man is born a free man: & no man can take a way this freedom by any right, & Command his attendance. He must oblige himselfe to that society first, that shall exercise authority Over him. Its not in this case as in Civill Authority. Christ saith it shall not be So here.

Hence there must be a Voluntary Subjection, or Covenant before Ecclesiasticall Authority can reach, or be Exercised. & thus it appears that the Formall Effects of a Church flow from its Covenant. And thus we se a Covenant the Formall Cause of a Church.

But let this suffice touching Artificiall Arguments.

Second. Inartificiall Arguments for this End follow. I need not Produce Such as the Scripture allows, they having been touched on already. I shall therefore produce a testimony or two touching the Practice of the Primitive times out of a Doctor or two that then wrote, shewing that Persons were then admitted into Church State by their Covenanting with the Church as follow

And take that in the first place before cited out of Justine [58/59] Martyre who lived in the next Century to the Apostles. He speaking of the Baptized whom were Admitted when baptized saith   Take an other more pregnant out of Origen that lived in the next Century to Justine Martyre. Christians, saith he, when they have had a triall of the Souls of Auditors, by Conference held with them in private, after they appeare to have sufficiently covenanted that they will live more righteously for the time to come, admit them into Fellowship.[64] Thus he.

Take one more out of the Booke of the Ecclesiasticall Hierarchy which tho' it goes under the name of Dionysius the Areopagite is deemed to be pend about the fourth Century. In this Booke the Authour treating of the rites observed in Baptism saith thus

Then the Whole Sacred Church being Called together to assist, & Celebrate the Persons salvation, & to give thanks to Divine Goodness the Minister at first sings with the Whole order of the Church, a Certain Hymn, that is contained in the sacred Scriptures. Then he comes to the man that's there present, & askes him wherefore he came? Who, after according to his love to God, he hath from what things were delivered by him that received him, accused his being without God, his ignorance of the true Good, & Emptiness of the Action of a Godly life, & desired that he may obtain that God (*Quasi sequestro*) & those things that belong to him, he then explains to him the perfect Cause whereby he is to approach to God, who is perfect, & intire: And a Divine Life, & Conversation being explaind to him he further inquires of him Whether he determineth to live So? On whose head when he hath promised the same he laieth his hand. & the sign being given, he bids the Priest to write down fairly the Names of the Person & his surety, etc.[65] But these instances of this nature may Suffice in this Case, to evince a Church-Covenant.

> Obj: But what make these Instances for, as touching the Church Covenant? These indeed proove that persons in their Admission, Covenant to live Holily. & this is altogether needfull. But what is this to a Church Covenant?

Ans: The Church-Covenant is such wherein persons promise in the presence of God, & his people to endeavour to live up to God in attending those Lawes of Obedience & Orders that God hath instituted, & enjoyn'd. Now God having instituted & injoyn'd a particular Church state, & Order [59/60] He that Covenants to attend on the Laws of

God, being Called thereto by any Church, doth Covenant with that Church to do it: That onely is capable of treating of him in Case of transgression. They onely are the Witnesses of the Covenant, they therefore are onely Capable to convict: & Censure him. & therefore his Covenant either fixes him in that Church, or in no Church: if in no Church, then he is no Church member & then a Church may admit persons into Covenant to attend on the Rules of Obedience, & orders & Institutions of God, & yet not incorporate him into a Church State, nor make him any Church member, or to be in Covenant with any Church, but such Conclusions are absurd. Wherefore when the Primitive Churches did thus Covenant, as in the Instances, they ever ingaged them, therein to walk in a Church State accordingly among them. But in the instances given, We Se the former in Express terms: & therefore the other follows.

Further so far as we have light in this Case we assert that in the Primitive times Members stood distinctly related to some Particular Church: so that Each Church knew its members, & the subjects of Discipline otherwise there could be no admission, nor Excommunication: otherwise there could be no appropriation by admission, nor any possibility of Excommunication. For Excommunication is the passing of a juditiall sentence Exterminating of an impenitant member, but none can be Exterminated that is not within the Limits, or term of the Church: none can be judged by the Church that is not known to be within, I Cor. 5.12. Hence in the Primitive times, Churches by this Covenant entred in at their Admission, did incorporate into their own body the Admitted: & Constitute Membership, & mutuall *propriety* in one an other. Hence these instances make to the matter in hand.

Further. Admission, & a Promise is manifestly found here. & on these terms we may lay down such Conclusions, as these.

1. That the Primitive Churches knew their own members. Admission was of Such as were known, at least known thereby.

2. That no man could make himselfe a member against the Churches Will: nor could the Church make a person a member whether he will or no. This would be absurd indeed.

3. Hence Admission being the Constituting Cause of Membership, doth necessarily require a mutuall Consent between the Person admitted, & the Church admitting: the Admitted Consents to the terms of the Admitters. And this Consent is a Covenant, the which they enter into one with another.

4. This Consent must be manifest. For the Admission is an open, & manifest Admission. If the Consent be not manifest, & open, then the Church did admit without it for that which was not manifest, was as if it was not to the Church admitting & then no Consent necessary. & then the Church might, tho' there was a non manifested discent admitt & so any not opposing. But if the Consent be manifest & open, then

5. Hence there was a Church Covenant attended in the Primitive times [60/61] in the Admission of Members & in the Promise that they then made.

And thus I have done with the Formall Cause of a Church Consisting of a Church Covenant. & thus far of the Internall Causes Constituting a Particular Church.

Secondly. What is the meaning of this Phrase, Habitation of God in our text, & Doctrine?

In answer hereto, I say, I shall Consider the Word $\begin{cases} 1.\ \text{Habitation} \\ 2.\ \text{Of God.} \end{cases}$

1. For the Word Habitation: it's not to be taken actively, for the Act of God inhabiting, or dwelling in it; But passively, for the thing inhabited, viz, this House, a particular Church; & touching it therein is intimated to us thus much.

1. The lowness or littleness of the Building. Hence Zanchy draws the Allusion from the Temple at Jerusalem. For as it Consisting of many divisions, & little Chambers, was but one Temple. So the Church Catholick is but one Consisting of many particulars. For saith he, the Little Chambers import particular Churches.[66]

2. That its a Settled, & durable Habitation. Its not a fleeting place: but a place of Settlement. Hence κατοικατήριον is the word which the Seventy Interpreters commonly use to render the Hebrew word מָעוֹן, which notes a Durable Habitation, as Ps. 90.1; & the Word פמכון-שבתו , Ps. 33.14, which also imports a Settled Habitation. He looked down from the place of his Habitation. & Ps. 107.47. He brought them to a City to dwell in: also Ps. 132.13,14. He saith of the Church The Lord hath Chosen Zion; he hath desired it for his מָעוֹן , Habitation forever. This is my rest for ever; here will I dwell for I have desired it. & thus you se it note a Settled habitation. So that tho' it notes a little yet a lasting Habitation.

2. As for the other term, importing the Proprietor of it, viz, of God. It sets forth the Relation it stands in to God; its the Habitation of God & hereby is implied

1. That God is the onely author of it. The Lord hath founded Zion, Isa. 14.32, Ps.102.16. & Saith, I will build my Church, Matt. 16.18. Its not Coined by mans brain: nor is it of mans Framing, nor of a Humane shape, but of a Divine mould. God hath sought out the Matter: squares it by his Rule, Polishes it by his tooles, raises it in his own Form, that he hath framed it unto: & he rules it by his own Laws. Hence God is the sole Author.

2. That God onely is the Owner of it. He is the Proprietor, it is his propriety. He hath made it for himselfe, & not for another. He saith of it. I will build My Church. So saith he, this is my rest for ever, Ps. 102.14. It is not so in all things, nor in all good things. One man, sometimes, may be the Author of a thing & an other may be the Proprietor, or owner. But it is not so here. God is both the Author, & the Owner of his Church. [61/62]

3. That God is the Approover of it. He doth not disapproove of his own Deed but greatly approoves thereof. Its a piece of mans misery, that what he makes oft times prooves not pleasing to his minde. Hence he oft unmakes what he makes, & makes all anew: & yet may be when new made it prooves not pleasing nor still doth he approove of it. But it is not so with this Building. For in that its Gods Building God approoves it. Hence he calls it a golden Candle Stick. Its all Gold. Se Ps. 87.2.

4. That God is the Improover of it. He makes it not for anothers Use, but for his own. Hence he uses it to display his Glory in, Ps. 102.16. Hence Ps. 87.3, Glorious things are Spoken of thee, O! City of God. Here he sets ope the Gates of Heaven; this he makes the Doore of Glory. Here is the open passage for mankinde to enjoy all Communion with himselfe. This is Bethel the House of God, here stands the true Jacobs Ladder with the top reaching into heaven, & the foot on the earth, on which the Angells of God are ascending, & descending: & on which comes down all Grace, & Blessing out of Heaven to man: & thereupon go all Seraphic praises, & Obediences from men on Earth to God in heaven: yea, & the Souls of the Saints of God attended on with the Convoy of Glorious Angells: wafting of them thither with their Seraphick Wings. God himselfe dwells herein, as you may se, Ps. 132.13,14, its his

rest for ever. Christ walkes in the middest of the Golden Candlestick, Rev. 1.12—Here he Commands his Blessing even life for ever more, Ps. 133.3. Hence God is the Improover of it.

5. That God is the Defender, & Protector of it. Therefore the Gates of Hell shall not prevaile against it, Matt. 16.18,19, & hence is that Promise, Zech. 2.5, Isa. 4, *ult.*

Thirdly. What is the meaning of this Expression in the Verse, Thro' the Spirit, an Habitation of God thro' the Spirit?

Ans: To this I say, it imports these things following

1. The (*Modus Efficiendi*) or manner of Gods Efficiency in Order to it, & in it. In Order to it for the building of it. His fetching stones out of the Quarry, & Timber out of the Wood of Fallen mankinde, his hewing, Polishing of them after the Similitude of a Palace, his building them up to be an Habitation of God, are all effected by the Spirit. Hence John 3.5, he that shall enter into the Kingdom of God, must be born of the Spirit. So again, it notes the manner of Gods Efficiency in it, as in his Inlightening, Inlivening, Regenerating, & Edifying Souls herein unto Eternall life, that all is the Effect of his own Spirit. Hence the Letter kills, & the Spirit gives Life.

2. The *Modus Habitandi*, or manner of Gods presence in it. & this is by his Spirit, not in a Visible but in a Spirituall way. Its true He is present in it, in all his own Institutions, in Prayer, in the Word Preached, Applied, in Information, Conviction, Examination, Persuasion, Direction, Consolation: So also in Singing, in the Sacraments of Baptism, & the Lords Supper: Yea, in the Orders, Officers, & the Discipline of [62/63] this his House. But it is in a Spirituall manner: & therefore thro' the Spirit. Hence the Whole of Divine Worship as Carried on by the Officers especially, is called, II Cor. 3.8, the ministration of the Spirit. & thus we Se the Speciall Emphasis of this Phrase, viz, thro' or by the Spirit.

Fourthly. But why is a Particular Church an Habitation of God thro' the Spirit? What reasons are there to evidence it?

Ans: the Reasons Evidencing it that I shall name are these following, viz,

1. From the Causes thereof. It must needs be Gods Habitation thro' the Spirit, For the Efficiency of it is from God thro' the Spirit: the Finall

Cause is for God by the Spirit. The Materiall is Gods by the Preparation of the Spirit: & the Formall Cause is introduced in obedience to God, thro' the Spirit: & therefore the thing Compleated by these Causes must needs be Gods thro' Spirit.

2. From the Furnishing of it, it appears to be Gods Habitation thro' the Spirit. For all the Furniture of it is Gods. The Goodlie Gift, & the Gold of this Temple is Gods. The Pillars, the Chapiters, the Net Workes, the Pomegranates, the Bells of this Temple, the Lamps with their knops, & Bowls, the Cherubims, the garnishing of it with the Tasles of Divine Gifts, with Clusters of Choicest Graces, shining like bunches of Pearles, are all his by the Speciall efficiency of the Spirit. The Orders of this house, the Ranks, the Officers are his, the Discipline, the Keyes to open, & shut the Doores; the Ordinances, & actions mannaged here, by his Spirit, are all his: & none else but himselfe can own any of these: & yet these are the Spirits furniture hung up here by the Spirit. & hence this is Gods Habitation thro' the Spirit.

3. From the Absurdity following on the Contrary. For if this is not Gods habitation thro' the Spirit, then God hath no Politicall Visible Ecclesiasticall Habitation on Earth. Where can it be found if not here? Not in the Catholick Visible Church, for that is onely Visible in its Particulars: & if the Particulars Cease it will be an hard task to demonstrate its visible Existence. Not in an Œcumenicall, or Universall Counsill. For where shall we finde so much as the Shallowest footsteps of Such a thing in all the Scripture? or of whom it appertains to call any Such Synod together? Not in a Classis; for that is as darke a thing to discover in the Scripture as the other; unless thereby be understood onely a Counsill, or Synod & then they have their rise from, & are as touching their Matter, the Members of Particular Churches: & therefore not in a Synod, or Counsill, for these are not of Standing necessity: neither are their Actions given out (Authoritative) as of Divine Authority, binding Conscience, any otherwise than the truth confirmed by their testimony bindes: But Consultative by way of Advice. But if it be said, God sits among the mighty, & judges among the Gods, therefore hath a Visible Politicall Habitation in Civill Courts, [63/64] I say that this Habitation is but in the Outward Court, & this is cast out unto the Gentiles. But where is his Inward Court. The former is onely or Chiefly for the mannaging the Concerns of the Second Table. But in what Visible Court are the Concerns of the first Table mannaged, if not in a Particular Church? And hence if this be not his Habitation thro' the

Spirit, he must needs be without any Politicall Visible Ecclesiasticall Habitation on Earth. But thus he is not, Ps. 132.13,14. Ergo.

Thus have I done with the Doctrinall Part of this truth.

Lastly. As for the Application of this Doctrine, it shall be twofold, wherein I shall apply it unto the $\begin{cases} \text{Understanding, \& judgment} \\ \text{Will, \& Affections.} \end{cases}$

First, I shall endeavour to apply its usefulness unto the understanding, \& Judgment in a Use of $\begin{cases} \text{Information} \\ \text{Reprehension.} \end{cases}$

First. By way of Information. Is it so that a Particular Church is built up an Habitation of God thro' the Spirit? Then this Doctrin may be usefull to inform our Understanding, \& judgment by the Light it sends forth to us in Severall particulars as follow

1. Hence see in what a miserable state towns, \& places are while they have no Church of Christ erected, or like to be erected in them. The Lord God hath not erected nor is like to erect himselfe among them an Habitation: \& hence he dwells not there openly. What ever he doth in the hearts of Some, yet he doth not appear a Settled Inhabitent in Such places. They are at the present as the range of Wilderness: \& too oft it is manifest that wild asses have them for their Pastures. And if they have not Christ at all going about to raise his Pavilion among them, they oft proove Cages full of uncleane birds: Habitations of Darkness, Holds of all Unclean Spirits, \& Divells. Miserable Habitations.

2. Hence its manifest that its the greatest Concern that towns are concernd in, that they entertain a Church State, that Christ erect his Church among them. Untill this be Places are not Corporations of Christs Visible Kingdom. God hath not set up house among them, till they are in a Church State, but then he comes to keep house amongst them, he come to dwell publickly there. Oh! happy place, that hath the Lord dwelling among them! Here is the best Neighbor \& therefore the best neighbourhood; This is a fruite of Christs asociation, \& receiving gifts for men, that the Lord God may dwell among them, Ps. 68.18, the Spirit of God comes to keep Court among them \& to actuate them; \& hence this was the Very thing that Israel was brought out of Egypt for: that the Lord God might dwell among them. Hence one of the first things that they attended on in the wilderness was their incorporating into a Visible Church State. So that it hence appears, that it is the greate Concern of towns to secure the Presence of God with them in his Settled Habitation.

3. Hence see what Unspeakable favour God layes outt on towns, &
places, when, & wherein, he erects, & mentains his Churches. [64/65]
Why? Altho' they were Habitations of Crueltie, Places of Dragons & the
Rangers of the Divell, & his Angells before; now the Case is Changed.
The Lord God Comes, & pitches his tent there: outs Satan: sets open a
doore to poore Souls to come to him. So that where Satans Throne was,
Christs Palace is erected. The Temple of God is with these men. The
Lord God comes, & dwells among them. Oh! here is the Doore of
Glory! the Gate of Heaven! Oh! how doth he make the place of his Feet
Glorious? & on all the Glory will be a defence? He'le now be a glory in
the middst thereof: & a Wall of Fire round about. Oh! here is an Happy
Priviledge! Happy are the People that are in such a Case.

4. Hence See What ground of joy, & praise towns have, when Christ
comes to erect himselfe a Church amongst them. Then he Comes to
dwell there by his Spirit: & this is matter of joy & praise. If towns
rejoyce when Noble Persons come to dwell in them, because of their
Nobility, & Generosity: & because of the Good Deeds expected of them.
What ground of joy then have towns when God comes, & sets up
house among them? makes himselfe an Inhabitant, nay an Householder
among them? How doth he by the spreading of his Wings over them,
spartle his nobility, & scatter his Generousity upon them? How doth he
in the Sprindging of his bounty over them, Relieve, & feed their very
Souls? Protect, & Save them from the Powers of Darkness? & take
them, & theirs for his own for ever? Oh! what ground of joy, & Shouting? Hence at the laying of the Foundation of the Temple the People
shouted for joy, Ezra 3.12, & when the Top Stone was laid, brake out in
shouting Grace, Grace, Zech. 4.7. Oh! what ground of Shouting for joy,
& Singing of the Tunes of Praise, yea, Glory to our God when Christ
comes and erects his temple in towns & place? This is ground of shouting out, Grace, Grace indeed.

Secondly. By way of Reprehension, Convincing Severall Persons of
Faultiness in this respect: & these some $\left\{\begin{array}{l}\text{Without}\\\text{Within}\end{array}\right\}$ the Church.

First. Some there are Out of a Church State, & carry it so, as that
this Doctrine Strikes the Frown of God hard upon them. Whether they
are such as $\left\{\begin{array}{l}\text{Oppose}\\\text{Neglect}\end{array}\right\}$ it.

Such as Oppose the Churches of Christ. These fight against the Almighty: they do worse than Nebuchadnezzer, who turnd the Temple of God all into red Flames, & brought it to ashes. Nay worse than those, Ps. 94.7,8, that had burnt up all the Synogogues of God in the Land. For they fight against the Almighty to beat him out of his own house, nay out of the World: they strive to pull down his House, the Temples of God in a more Spirituall Sense, to destroy these Spirituall Buildings, that the Lord may not dwell among them, that he may have no Habitation here below. Woe to their Souls! they would [65/66] have no intercourse between God, & Man; for there is no publick covenanting with God but here.

Such as Neglect a Church State are also under the Frown of this Doctrin for they manifest by their negligence, that they had rather be, & abide in Satans Family, than to be of the Houshold of God, as if there were better Provision, better Order, better Society, better satisfaction to be had, & better Safety, in Satans house, than in Gods. And therefore they will rather uphold Satans intrest; tho' so far as their neglect can effect, to the ruin of Gods House, by neglecting God. Oh! Fools! & Madmen! When will ye be Wise? Surely God will come out of his Holy Habitation against you: & what will you then do?

2. Some there are In a Church-State, that are Entred either less Formally, or more Formally; & yet fall under the angry aspect of God in this Doctrine, as

1. Such as are not Content with the Provision of, nor their Station in it, which is according to the revelation of Gods will in this matter. For if this be Gods Habitation, then he is the Lawgiver that layes down the Laws, the limits, & the Orders of the same: & all that are in it are bound, & to be limited in their Motions, & Functions thereby: but now for any to Stretch their line beyond these limits, as not being Content with that Provision of Officers that he hath set up therein: & therefore they must set up their Posts by Gods Posts, as Prelates, Archbishops, Archdeacons, Prebends, Vicars, Curats, Non-Residents, Proctors, Surrogates, Apparators, Church-Wardens, Clarks, Saxtons, & Such like humane devised Stuff: or the Limitation of Office; & therefore they must Stretch the Wings of the Pastor, etc., as far to Shaddow over the Whole Universe: So that the Steward stands not in this Particular House, but in the Catholick Church: & be a Steward in any, & not in one onely house, or of allowance of means of Worship, & Service: & therefore they must have fine Garments, Surplices, Idle Prayers, etc., as

the Service Book, or New Ordinances, as the Cross in Baptism, & Gossops: & kneeling in the Lords Supper: & Marrying to be an Ecclesiasticall Worke to Celebrate. This things are Such as are both against the Second Comand, that saith thou shalt not institute to thyselfe, etc., & also to Step into Gods Throne, & not to permit him to rule in his own house, not his Laws to be Sufficient for his own house: & it is in effect to charge him with the Want of Wisdom, Faithfulness, & Goodness to order, & mannage his own house: & therefore they are, by their tampering, introducing by their own invention the brats of their own brains in his house: & fill it with their own trumpery. But surely God will Say to these as he did to those, Isa. 1.12. Who hath required these things at your hand. You make the Commands of God of none effect by your tradition, Matt. 15.3. Shall not God nor his Laws rule in his own house? Shall the meanest man living have an absolute power to carry on the Orders of his own house, if they be not inconsistent with the Laws of the CommonWealth? And yet shall God be denied the rule of his own house by his own laws? Shall mans inventions be set up in Gods house as the laws thereof? Will you grant to the meanest housholder what you will not grant to God? Oh! this makes God aweary of his house; & of your being in it. & to say to you, if you were better than [66/67] you be. What hath my beloved to do in my house? Jer. 11.15. Oh! then those that this offend fall under Conviction in this respect, in that they are not Content with Gods Provisions in his own Habitation.

2. Such are under the Sharp Check of this Doctrine, that keep not peace in Gods House. What Quarrell in Gods House? What a Shame is this? Quarrelling Children must have the rod to still them. Is not this a thing to be lamented of in Gods House? And yet, oh! What quarrelling? What Wrangling? What jangling in many Churches? as if they would fulfill the old proverb: Fling the House out at the Windows. What is it Gods Habitation, or no? Or is the God of peace not the God of it? or is he gone out of his own house? Or is the greatest honour in Gods house to have it Charm with a Contentious Spirit? Is Quarrelling the Sweetest musick in Gods House? Oh! Shame? What means then this Smoake in the Temple? Do not the Stones in Gods building agree together? Will they be Slipping one from another? Will not the Covenant Cement hold them fast one to another? Will they not beare one anothers burdens, that so they might fulfill the Laws of Christ? When its thus its a Sign the building grows old, & weatherbeaten: & that it lacks new Pointing without which all is in hazzard of ruin.[67] But oh! what a Shame is this to

all Such Churches? Is this a Sign that these are Gods Habitations by or thro' the Spirit? What then is it but to break the Peace in Gods own House? yea & the peace of it too: How ill will he take it? If you bite, & devour one another, take heed you be not devoured one of another, Gal. 5.15. You are a dishonour to the House of God. You must either mend your manners, in Gods house: or else either you, or God must out of the House. For God will not dwell in that house where the peace of God cannot Dwell.

3. Such are under the frown of this Doctrine that enter into a Church state in a State of Sin. Art thou Such an one, harke Soule! this is the House of God, Soul, & darest thou in a state of Sin enter in it? Oh! how dreadfull is this place? What makes it so? Oh! Sayth Jacob, its no other but the house of God, Gen 28. What then dost thou here, thou Carnall Heart? Onely living Stones are Suitable matter for this Spirituall building, I Pet. 2.5. What dost thou then here dead in trespasses & sins? God dwells here by his Spirit: But Satan dwells in thy heart. Thou bringst then an Evill, & Unclean Spirit into Gods Habitation. Oh thou hereby bringest Satan into Gods Temple. Thou possessest him of Gods house: that he may sit in the Temple of God, as God: & that so God may be unhoused, & Cast out of his own house. Those that quarrell in it set open doores to him, & thou bringest him in. Dost thou thinke God will beare this at thy hand? Nay surely he will be avenged on thee at the last if thou repent not. Is an hard pebble fit to be laid in that Wall which is to be made all of Pearls, & pretious Stones? Oh! then thou art to be Convicted of Sin, that Crowdest into the Church in a state of Sin.

Thus you se how this Doctrine lets in light to the Understanding & judgment to Convict Severall Persons both out of & also in a Church State. & So I have done with reflecting its Usefulness upon the Understanding [67/68] & Judgment.

Secondly. I come now to improove this Doctrine upon the Will, & Affections, as its Excellence poures out allurements to attract them to the Duties incumbent respecting this truth & this is done in a way of $\left\{\begin{array}{l}\text{Exhortation}\\\text{Congratulation.}\end{array}\right.$

First. By way of Exhortation. Is it thus that a Particular Church is an Habitation of God thro' the Spirit? How then doth God come herein to worke upon our hearts, yea upon us all to let out our Affections after, & to set our hearts upon a Church State? Oh! how Strongly Should our

Affections worke towards the house of God? God in this Doctrine calls for all our hearts to affect his house. And the Call comes upon us according to the Relation we Stand in unto it. Which Relation divides us all according to that, I Cor. 5.12. Into Such as are Within, & Such as are Without it. & therefore the Call is to Exhort as Such are $\left\{\begin{array}{l}1.\ \text{Without} \\ 2.\ \text{Within}\end{array}\right\}$ this House.

First. To you that are not as yet Entred. God Calls you to stir up yourselves to Stir up your hearts after a Church State. Oh! an Entrance into this State is an Entrance into Gods House. Hereby you shall be made Fellow Citizens of the Saints, & of the Houshold of God. Therefore let your affections run into this State. Improove them so upon itt, as to Stir you up after it. God Saith they shall prosper that love it, Ps. 122.6. Oh! therefore Set your affections so to work upon the Church of God as to Seek after these things.

1. Seeke to promote the Same. A Particular Church being the House of God, where this is not, God hath no publick Residence, hath no open house: He keeps no house there, nor hath pitched his Tabernacle there. Herein the Tabernacle of God is with men. Therefore my friends, as ever you would have Gods publick Presence reside with you: as ever you would have God keepe open house among you, se that you endeavour from the heart the Promoting gods Church that he erects amongst you. Its true God is present in the hearts of his People: & therefore particular Persons probably are called the Temple of the Holy Ghost, II Cor. 6.16. & so also he is present with his Soule Sanctifying invisible presence. He is also present in the Familys of his Saints. Abraham will teach & Command his Children, & houshold after him, Gen. 18.19. So he is present with his Family Duty Presence. But yet this is not in a publick residing way mannaging the matters of his visible kingdom. But he is present in the Churches of his Saints thus. Here he is present in his Ordinance-instituted presence, Rev. 1.12—Chap 2.1. & this is as a king in the Royall throne of his Kingdom, Isa. 6.1. In this Temple is his way. Strive then to promote this House, & the State of this House, Rev. 3.21. For this end let me present you with a Word of Motive.

1. Consider what a greate evill it is to hinder this Presence of God or this his Habitation. To damnify this Habitation is a sad & sorrowfull thing; tho' in the least Pin of the building: for it tends to pluck [68/69] the House of God down, to turn Christ out of doores. And Nebuchadnezzers firing the temple, did less injury unto God than this

evill amounts to. For this is a Living that not living Temple. This is a Spirituall, that an Elementary Temple. Oh then on this Consideration, be stir'd up to promote this Habitation.

2. Herein are Carried on all the means of Grace allowd thee of God for thy Salvation. By means of Grace understand Ordinance-instituted means. And where are these to be found but in Gods Habitation? They are the Furniture of his House. Thou mayst, it may be, meet with Some helps also else where: but here thou with all. The Strong Gales of the Spirit come here in fresh breizes, While therefore thou promotest this, thou promotests these. Hereby thou wilt keep the doore open, where the Angels of God are ascending, & descending; & perhaps attending upon thy Soule.

3. So long as you promote this Intrest Christ is waiting on you to be gracious. But if you Weary God out of his house he will be angry with your Souls: & then Woe, Woe, Woe to your Soules. Oh therefore endeavour to promote this Habitation.

2. Prepare for this House. Doth God come, & set up house here? & canst thou Content thyselfe while out of this house? Art thou well enough out of Gods Family? But how canst thou thinke to obtain admission without preparation? Doth Christ set open doores for all Comers? If so then his house can't be desirable. If not, then prepare to meet thy God here, Amos 4.12. Are there required no Qualifications preparatory for Gods Habitation? Are any rubbish, Unpollisht Stones fit matter for Christs Temple? If not, then, prepare thyselfe: trim thy Lamp, that thou mayest have an Entrance. Indeed there is a twofold right or Intrest in this Habitation, viz, Quoad $\begin{cases} Relationem \\ Translationem. \end{cases}$

One is that of Relation onely, as Such as are Committed to the Watch, & Care of this house to train up for Christ, the other is that of Translation out of the power of Darkness into the Kingdom of his dear Son, Col. 1.13. Oh! this last, & nothing below this last is that right wherein this due preparation consists. Oh therefore Stir up yourselves, strive that you may be pretious Stones to be laid in this Heavenly Building, Living stones, in this Spirituall Temple. Repent of Sin, Reform your Lives: put a way the old Leaven that you may be a New Lump. Oh! Se that you be Sanctified Matter for this Sacred Temple. & to stir you up to this Exhortation accept of these motives.

1. Consider you are never fit matter for this Habitation till you are prepared matter. The New Jerusalem that came down out of Heaven was

prepared as a Bride adorned for her Husband, Rev. 21.2. This New Jerusalem is the Church; this Husband is that Glorious one her Lord that dwells in this Habitation. Therefore this Habitation is built not of Rubbish Stone, but of Wrought Stones. Oh! therefore prepare.

2. Consider that unprepared persons, if they do creep in are fit for nothing, but as Jonas in the ship to raise Tempests, & to be Cast o're-bord. Oh! such are like the leprous stones in the Walls gangrening the Whole, or as to Aeolus with his speer piercing the Sides of the mountains till Storms a-[69/70]rise. Dismall worke many times are made by such in Gods House. Oh! they oft proove as fire in the thatch; or as the Bellows of Aetna that blow up all into a flame. They are fit onely to play the fools part to fling about Firebrands, Arrows, & Death in this Habitation. And during their Unfitness for it they lose what they pretent to account of: for they gain no Spirituall advantages as a fruite of their admission: but oft are given up to hardness of heart, as Ananias, & Saphira; as a Curse upon their Presumption. Oh then Prepare, Prepare.

3. Consider, that an Entrance without a Worthiness will Entaile upon thee greater Wrath, which will unavoidably overtake thee unless abundant mercy Cut off the Entaile. Se Ananias & Saphira's Case, Acts 5. Oh! Saith God, you have I known therefore will I punish you, Amos 3.2. For thou both bringest, & comest an Enemy into Gods Habitation. Remember the foolish Virgins, Matt. 25, & the man without the Wedden garment, Chap. 22.12. If thou comest in unprepared & Continuest so, thou art sure to be cast out into utter darkness. Oh! therefore thinke of this, & Prepare.

4. Consider that this preparation lies in the Graces of the Spirit of God. Hence Grace is prayed for; for the Church: II Thess. 1.2, & 3.18, & we are prest on after it. Now canst thou do without Grace? Or canst thou have too much of it? Oh! this is Worth Striving for on its own account, Jude 2. Thou art undone without. Oh then seek for it & so prepare.

5. Consider who it is that dwells in this House. Why? its God himselfe. Here in that is fulfilld, Ps. 68.18, that the Lord God might dwell amongst them. God dwells in this house: the Spirit of God dwells here. It is an Habitation of God thro' the spirit. The Son of God dwells here. Here is his Walk, Rev. 1.12—Chap. 2.1. The Angells of God are here, I Cor. 11.10, & the Saints of God dwell here. What then? Wilt thou rush into this House unprepared? What run into the presence of the King Eternall, & of the King of Kings: the King of Glory; & also of the

Nobles, & peers of heaven, & in a slovenly way? What not prepare for admission, & Entrance into this royall Family, the Houshold of God? Dost thou not care to honour this Family? If thou hast any affection to this Habitation then Prepare thyselfe, Strive for thy Beautifull Garment that thou mayest be prepared for it.

6. To prepare for it is the way to have the Glory of it. The greater preparation for it, the greater glory will be present in it, according to the preparation thou makest for God, such will be the presence of God thou will meet with in it. Oh! what a glorious presence of God would alwayes here appeare, if we did but alwayes here appeare duely prepared. Our preparations lying in the graces of the Spirit, if we by preparing did both Store up, & Stir up these shining Spangles of the Divine Image in us, they being such God glorifying Beames would be answered with an answerable Glory whereby this house would be filled with Glory. So that we [70/71] might with old Jacob, say, Oh! how Terrible is this place? It is nothing else but the House of God. Oh! therefore if this glory hath any influence upon thee let this Come so upon thee to moove thee to Prepare, & so prepare for a Church State.

3. Seek when, & not till when you are prepared to enter into this house. As it is a fault to enter unprepared; so it is a fault, when prepared, not to Enter. As therefore this Doctrine calls us not to Enter till prepared; so it exhorts when prepared not to delay to enter. Oh! my Friends, what say you, will you be of the Household of Faith? will you be of the Houshold of God, or no? Will you be Fellow Citizens of the Saints? Are you such as have trimmed your Lamps? Have your Lamps any oyle in their Vessells, or no? Will you go out to meet the bridegroom, or no? What say you hereto? Oh! then heare the Call of this Doctrine: Come Come, Enter your names among the Living in Jerusalem. Will you Subscribe with your hands unto the Lord? Behold, the Gates of Zion are open unto you. The Doores of Gods house invite your Entrance. Will you bless the Entry of Gods Habitation: shall the place of his Feet bring its blessing upon you! Oh then Seek Admission here. Behold God calls thee wilt thou attend. He saith turn in hither, turn in hither: Why then shouldst Sleep without the Gates of Jerusalem. Therefore admit of these few Suggestions to Stir thee up to this Exhortation.

1. Consider, that thou hast aright to Enter: thou being a living stone oughtst to lie in this Spirituall Building. Thou feet should Stand within the Walls of Jerusalem. Oh therefore Come, & Well come.

2. Consider, that thou Standest in need of the Provision that God hath made in his house: & now thou art a bidden Guess, Come.

3. Consider that Gods House hath need of thee. What hath God been hewing, & polishing of thee all this While for? Surely it is because his house hath need of thee. If when Solomon had pollisht the Materialls for the Temple these pollisht materialls had not been layen in the Temple but had layen by, there had been no Temple raised of Polisht & suitable Matter, Living Stones in this Spirituall Temple ly not in it, as it is of this Sort here below, eternally. There is now one, & then an other gathered hence, as a Choice Pearle to be set in the King of glory. And hence in a little time the Whole building will be translated hence Stone after Stone. & so will disappeare if there be no addition to it. The which that it may not disappeare, God is pollishing others for it, while he is fetching Some from it. And hence the building stands in need of those that are prepared for it to Supply the places of those that God takes from. Oh! then heare it you that are prepared for it, shall the Building want you, & be reeling, & you stand & looke on & not Care for it. Can you let it fall? If not, then seek an Entrance, the Lord hath need of you.

4. Consider, that here is the best order which is. Its a Well ordered House in all things, I Chron. 14.40. The Order of Solomons house was ad-[71/72]mirable, I Kings 10: But what then is the Order of Christs House? The Beauty, & Excellency of Order adds an amazing Glory to things that are Excellent. Let this then Quicken thy motions.

5. Considere that here is the best Service. Here is onely Holy Service. Here shines the beauty of Holiness. Its Gods Service, & onely Gods Service, that is carried on here. & this is onely good Service. Let this then moove thee to Seek an Entrance.

6. Here is the best Society which is. Consider it in the lowest Consideration, & you will finde it thus, what then an othere considerations? Why? Its the Houshold of God, Eph. 2.19, its the Houshold of Faith, Gal. 6.10. Its a Chosen people, Titus 3.5, the Elect of God, Rom. 11.7. For altho' it is a truth, that there are to be found some tares in this Field: some Chaffe in this Floore: yet this was never made a field for the tares Sake, nor a floore for the Chaffe's Sake. These have no right in it. God gives no liberty to Satans Slaves to enter in to this house. Satans Servants have no right in Gods Family. No, here are required Contrary Qualifications, as a Wedden Garment, Grace in the Soule, Matt. 22.12. The Image of God in the Work of Sanctifying Gifts, Rom. 8.29. Oh! glorious

Society! If the Society in a Kings Family consists of Nobles, & Honourable ones, Matt. 11.8, what doth the Society in the Family of the Kings of Kings Consist of? What titles are there given to them by God himself in Scripture? Why? Such as are borrowed from the most Excellent things the world affords us: as, Stones laid with fair Colours: Agats, Carbuncles, Borders laid with pleasant Stones, Isa. 54.11,12, Stones of a Crown, Zech. 9.16, Bordered with Gold, & Studded with Silver, Cant 1.11. All Fair: & no Spot, Cant. [4.7]. Oh! Excellent Society! Nay! but let us pass to something else, you shall finde the Angels of God attending here, I Cor. 11.10, & yet to ascend higher. Here is injoyed the Fellowship, & Society of God himselfe, & of Christ, yea, & of the Holy Ghost. Truely our Fellowship is with the Father, & With his Son Jesus Christ, I John 1.3. Its Gods own house, he Sits here in his Throne, & judges right: Now the Presence of God in his Throne makes heaven heaven. Oh! then the Presence of God in this house inthroned, makes this house heaven upon Earth. Looke here now, Soule, What dost thou say to this Society? Is not this a Noble, Glorious, & Honourable, nay most Glorious, Honourable, Noble, & Excellent Society which is? And shall not the Consideration hereof so influence thy affections as to raise in thee Strong desires to be made a member of this Society? Why? If they do, then seeke for Admission into God's house. Knock at the doore that it may open to thee. For God is within indeed.

7. Consider that here are the Highest Priviledges: the Chief honour is to be had in this Habitation. If greate Priviledges are injoyed in Greate mens Houses what are those injoyed in Gods Family? Surely those hold no proportion with these. Here are the Priviledges of the Children of God: every one in it hath the Priviledge of a Child, & Heir in the House. & as the Priviledges are greate so is the Honour in it. Its the most reall honour upon the face of the Earth to be admitted into Gods house. The honour of a Kings house is a mock honour to this. Seek this then. [72/73]

8. Consider, that thou are calld to Enter, if prepared. Christ speakes to thee in his Speech to his Spouse, Cant. 2.10,11,12,13. Arise, my Love, my Fair one, & come away: For, lo, the Winter is past, the rain is over, & gone, the Flowers appear on the Earth: the time of the Singing of Birds is Come; the Voice of the Turtle is heard in our land: the Figtree puts forth her green Figs: the Vine with its tender Grapes gives a pleasant Smell. Arise my Love, my Fair One, & come away. What saist thou to this poore Soule? Canst thou withstand such Soule inravishing Rhetorick? Methinks it should be like Sweet Wine, that goes down pleasantly,

that causes the lips of them that are a Sleep to Speake, & say, Behold, I come, Lord.

Well then let these & such like motives as these stir you up to seek Admission into the Church. & thus much for the first branch of the Exhortation, which is laid upon those that are Without.

Secondly. This Doctrine brings an Exhortation upon you that are Within, & the Compleate Members of this Family. Shall I speake the Case as it is? heare then: For itts a greate Word that I am Speaking & yet not I but the Lord. You are the Household of God, You are both the Materialls of Gods house: & the Members in it: Now the Materialls of Gods house never appeare in Suitable Colours, but when they carry it as the Houshold of God. Therefore let this bring a Call from God into your very Souls to exhort you to behave yourselves as the houshold of God. Shew forth in your Lives that you are an habitation of God thro' the Spirit. Your Standing is upon holy Ground, Se to the Place of your standing. Walk worthy of the Family you are Come into, lest you dis-honour the house of God. & for this End admit of a few $\left\{\begin{array}{l}\text{Directions} \\ \text{Motives.}\end{array}\right.$

First. By way of Direction I shall present you with these Considerations following.

1. Study well the Nature of those Duties that you stand in one to an other, take notice well of the Weight that every stone must beare, & be born with as it is in the building, as ever you think to abide a Building of God. For unless you Consider well these Duties, you will be ready to thinke each burdened by another, & so to Slip one from another in many Cases. Nay almost in all wherein the Case comes pinching upon you. You had need have the handle of a Sound judgment in the hand of a tender Conscience in the mannaging of all Duties, & especially of such as these & how should this be had without knowledge of them. A Blinde Zeale & a Censorious Spirit, will be very injurious: so will a Sluggish Conscience: & a Slavish Feare, on the other hand, a weake Matter will be Crusht to pieces under the burden that the strong must beare. Strong wine must be put in Strong bottles. But in Case Offences be not rash, nor high, all ought to be treated with gentleness: a spirit of meekness & Love is honourable, in all Cases, both in the Offended, & offender. Christ saith, tell him between him, & thee, Matt. 18.16,17. But if the Case come to the Church, remember it Comes before Christs judgment Seate. & thou must behave thyselfe reverendly. If the judgment comes against

thee, thou art not to turn judge, but to be Still. Thou mayst indeed in [73/74] a Submissive way lay down the Reason of thy Dissatisfaction: & then rest, unless it be in weighty matter: & then thou mayest crave light in the Case, from other Churches, tho' not judgment. Wherefore study well the nature of those duties you stande in one to an other, & each unto the Whole, & to every part.

2. Have a Care of Contentions, & Division. You may not go together by the Eares in Gods House. This is Shamefull: it is to brake the Laws of the King in his own Court, & is a ruinating evill to Gods house where ever it is. Let others evills make us wary. Have a care in the beginning *Principiis obsta.* The Begining of Strife is as the letting in of great Waters, therefore (saith God) leave off Contention before it be meddled with, Prov. 17.14. Every irregular Word is not to be Calld over again; this would make Satan Musick upon Christs Instrument & play his tunes on Gods pipes. Oh! have a Care here. The Contentions of Brethren are as the Bars of a Castle, Prov. 18.19. But beare you one anothers Burdens, & so fulfill the Law of Christ. Yet what is not meet to be born with, mannage with all meekness: & let the Spirit of Christ shine forth in all Sweet behaviour therein. Lay aside Wrath & Sharpness: these things oft proove as quick flashes of fire that melt of the Gold of the Temple; or that break out like thunder Clapps that rift one Stone from another. But let Grace, & not Selfe, shew itselfe, lest you appeare to mannage your own, & not Christs Will. Meddle not in others Contest without a Cleare call, lest thou seem like him that takes a Dog by the Eares, Prov. 26.17. Oh! then have a Care of Contention.

3. Be knit together in Love. This is Calld the Bond of Perfection, Col. 3.14, & the Bond of Peace, Eph. 4.2,3. Strengthen this Bond. Where the Truelove Knot is fast tied Satan is not, & so kept, he cannot enter. Persons in Church-Fellowship may be Compared to a Bunch of Golden Arrows: & the Grace of Love the Golden bond binding them all together. But if this Bonde slack, unty, or break, Satan will Easily pluck out one from another; nay they will be shattering, & falling of themselves one from another, untill the Bundle be destroyed. God threaton'd to remoove the Golden Candlestick at Ephesus When the Bond of Love grew Slack, Rev. 2.5. Oh! therefore Strengthen the Bond of Love.

4. Walke Humbly, & Closely with God, in all Relations, & Duties. You will Dishonour Gods Habitation, if you walke not Closely with God in the Duties of your own Habitation. Be much in Prayer, Watch greatly over thine own heart. Strive that the Duties of thy Covenant may

Carry a Shine thro' thy Whole life, & Conversation, that thou mayst bring a Glory to Gods House, be a Glory in Gods house, & be made Glorious with the Glory of Gods House. & then it will be Well with thee, & the House too. Thus much touching the Directions.

Secondly. Some Motives to force upon this Exhortations may be of use here. You can't be too urgently treated; you have deceitfull hearts, apt to warp aside, & Satan will assault you: look for it. You [74/75] have no ground to Expect any Exemption from him: no Example, no Promise. Your Church Priviledges will rather Expose than Exempt you from Satans assaults: as being apparently in the Camp in the Sight of all the World, bidding battell to Satan & all his Hosts. What tho' you are Entred, & built up into God's house, this is one of Christs Garrisons, & Castles fortified against Satan: & he will be Storming it: & assaulting you in Gods own house. He is no Coward. And as you have alwayes need to play the man, so now especially upon your first Entrance, for now he will be mostly busy. When Adam in the Glorious Shine of Gods Image upon him, was first placed in Paradise Satans fingers itched to be at him, & he soon assaulted him. God had no Sooner departed from him, but Satan set upon him, & over set him. Our Lord himselfe soon after he was Consecrated to his Mediatory Work by the Water of Baptism, tho' all the Perfections of Grace, & the Fulness of an Almighty Power were in him, Satan was not danted there at, but fell furiously upon him. & Can it be imagined that he will not Cast a dart at you: or that you should go Scot free? Nay, Nay. You have ground to Expect his Encounter: se to it therefore. & accept of these Motives to force the Exhortation upon you. & they shall be laid down before you by way of

{ Conviction in point of Fault,
{ Consolation in attending Duty.

First. Here is something representing an Angry aspect from him that is the Lord of house, as it falls upon you if you fall Short in your Walke of the Duties of this house. And that you may avoide the Same let the Convictions of these Arguments upon the Supposition of failure supply the place of motives to urge you to Behave yourselves according to the Duties of Gods house.

1. You Breake Covenant with God wherein you walke not according to the Laws of the house of God. It is no less than Covenant Breach With God, & his people. & is not this dreadfull: oh then have a Care of this: & therefore See to your behaviours.

2. Thou wilt hereby lose the Benefit of this House in greate measure, that thou art Entred into. Now the Benefits of the House of God are greate: & therefore greate will by thy loss if thou look not to it. Oh! then Walke according to the Houshold of God.

3. Its a note of the Leprosy in the Materialls of the House. What doth not the Building Serve the End it was raised for? Oh! its greatly to be feared then, that the Plague of Leprosy, & Rottenness is in the Stones or Timber of the House! & how if thou art the piece in which the Plague is? What wilt thou then do? It is in that Piece, or Stone that doth not attain its End, or Use in the Building. Now where ever it is, the Stone or Piece wherein it is, it is to be ejected, if the Plague breake out & refuse an healing. Oh think of this then, & be quickened to duty. [75/76]

4. Thy not walking according to thy Relation will be an offence to God in his own house. And will tend to out him thereof. God will not abide in that house, where his Glory doth not abide, Rev. 2.5, Jer. 17.12, & where is his glory if it be thus, that thou livest not answerable to thy Relation in it. What hath God brought thee into his house, & wilt thou grieve him in it, & drive him out of it? Dare you thus requite the Lord? Oh foolish people, & unwise! Wherefore Se to thy behaviour.

5. It presages ruine to the Building. For this is but reason, that if a Building attend not its End, to pluck it down again. So will God deale with this house, if it answer not its End, Rev. 2.5, & if you walk not up answerably to the State of the House you answer not the End of it: & then you Se the Conclusion. Oh! then be stir'd up to live up to your high Relation; & to honour Gods House by living up to the Laws & orders thereof. Thus much of this sort of motives.

Secondly. There are Somethings setting the Pleasant face of that Gracious, & Glorious One, whose house it is, before you that walke according to the laws of this House to inflame you to keep up to an holy walking answerable to the Nature & authour of this House. & the motives of this Sort take as follow.

1. This answers the End of Gods house. You are the House of God for this End. God raiseth up himselfe an house, & Comes, & dwells in it to hold forth the Beauty of Holiness therein, & thereby, Ps. 110.3, & 50.2; so 27.4, 48.1,2. & hence its calld a golden Candlestick to hold forth the flaming light of Holiness, & on this account God will delight to abide in his House, & will rejoyce in't. If therefore thou findest any delight to delight God Walke up to the Excellent nature of this House.

2. This will be the way to keep Gods Glorious, & Gracious Presence in it. For he will be with those that are with him. & how is his Gracious, & Glorious presence in his Church, but in this glorious shine of the Graces of his Church Exercised? hence Glorious things are Spoken of it, Ps. 87.3. Oh! what an heart Ravishing thing is this? strive therefore to live so as it may be thus.

3. God Himselfe will then take delight in thee, when thou art a glory in his House. His light will shine upon thee when thy walk is delightfull to him in his house. Shall not this allure thee.

4. All the Sweet Consolations of Gods house shall be thine when thy behaviours answer the Dignity of Gods house. Thou shalt be abundantly Satisfied with the fatness of Gods House: & he shall make thee to drink of the river of his pleasures, Ps. 36.8. Are the Consolations of Gods House Small unto thee? God keeps a Noble House, a Rich Table. Oh those Sweet Words! Oh, those Sweet Ordinances! Oh, those Sweet Heart ravishing Dainties of Gods House! Oh, that Sweet Countenance therein shining! Oh! that Sweet Service! Oh that Choice Society! Oh! those heart inflaming Influances, that the Soule meets with here. Oh! thinke of these, for all the Sweets of Gods House [76/77] are thine if thou behave thyselfe aright herein.

5. Thou wilt hereby bring Greate Glory to God. Thou wilt hereby Honour him; & gain Credit, & glory to his Family: hereby Gods house will appear Glorious in the World. Thou wilt become examplary in so living to others to draw them to do the like. Hereby thou wilt be an Instrument handing down gloriously, this glorious intrest of Gods House to Such as shall Succeed: & God will account himselfe greatly glorified in all those things. Now thou professesst thy selfe to be bound up in, & for the Glory of God. & therefore let these things allure thee to Holiness.

6. This will make for thee a more abundant Entrance into Glory itselfe, II Pet. 10.11. Now are not these things Sweet allurements to draw thee to live answerably to the House of God of which thou art a member. Oh! then if there be any Consolation to be had in these things, let the Influences thereof inflame your hearts & affections to walke answerable to the Nobility, & Glory of the House of God, that you have inrowled your names in.

Hitherto by way of Exhortation.

Secondly. By Way of Congratulation or Thanksgiving. Is it so that a Particular Church is built up an Habitation of God thro' the Spirit: then what ground of Thankfulness for us in this Place in that God hath Erected a Particular Church here? Why? God hath raised himselfe an Habitation among us. Oh! how should this Glad our hearts? How should it ingage our Souls, & improove our Affections in the Duties of thanksgiving? Methinks it calls out the Affections of all here; & especially yours unto this Worke, that are entrd into this Habitation. Oh! therefore fall upon it. Strive to give hearty & Syncere thanks to God for this Grace, & Goodness of his herein. Your Prayers, your striving after it, your Wrastling for it, have thro' Grace prevailed. All the Wiles, & stratagims of the Old Serpent, & his Temptations, which he mannaged to the very last, yea, to the very Threashold of the Doore, to harm, & hinder the raising of God an house amongst you, are foiled, broken, & brought to nothing. The Snare is broken, the Bird is fled. Oh! shout for joy, Grace, Grace unto it. God hath Set up his own Habitation here, even in this place, which was, but a little while agoe, a Cage of all hurtfull & unclean Birds, a Den of Dragons, an hold of Divell; & an haunt of all foul Spirits. But now it is made an Habitation of God thro' the Spirit. Surely the Lord hath done Great things for us, whereof we are glad. Truely my Friends, have we not Occasion of Praise? Alas! if a leading man do but come to a place to dwell, at a town in its begining, how Glad is that town? But if he be a Nobleman, & of such a Noble minde, as that he should Feast them, Cloath them, be Familiar with them & mentain them, Enrich, & Protect them, what should be the Esteem of such an one? How joyous would any place be upon his Coming to dwell among them? Oh! this would be a Golden man indeed. But where [77/78] is any Such to be found? He is *Rara avis* indeed! Yet this Happiness would be but temporary: it would be no Soule inriching thing. But loe, here is tenthousand times twice told more than all this. The Eternall God is Come, & hath pitched his tent, & raised his Temple among you. There is no more Comparison to be made between God the Lord God Almighty, that hath raised himselfe an house among you, & such a person as is here instanced in, than there is between the Glorious Glory of Heaven itselfe, and the darkest dungeon underground. Oh! then what ground of joy & Shouting have we? He is Come, he is Come to dwell among us: & hath all felicity in his hand to bestow upon us, if we do not grieve him in his own house. He calls you all to open the doore of your hearts, & he will Come, & banquet therein with you: Hee opens the doore of his House & calls you to his royall Banquet that he hath prepared. He opens the Golden doore of Glory, & calls you, saying, Come up hither! Come up hither. He hath Riches, Honour & Glory, & Eternall Life to bestow upon you: & urges them upon you: Now this is he that is Come & hath set up his Habitation among you. This is the Highest Honour & the brightest Glory, the Noblest Family, & the most royall Palace that is under the Cope of Heaven: & the next indeed to that which is Eternall, in the Heavens. Oh then, Ps. 47.6, Sing praise to God, Sing praise, Sing praise to our King, sing praise. With joy let us draw Water out of the Wells of Salvation. Nay Cry out & shout, oh thou Inhabitants of Zion, for greate is the Holy One of Israel in the middest of thee, Isa. 12, *ult.*

[The First Disciplinary Sermon]

Westfield } Matt. 18.17. If he shall neglect to
2 10ᵐ 1713 } heare them tell it to the Church.
& if he neglect to heare the
Church let him be to thee as an
Heathen man, & a Publican.⁶⁸

Our Lord Christ is a king, he was Born a king, & as such
was he sought for by the Wisemen of the East, Matt. 2. He
was acknowledged such by the people, Matt. 21, Luke 19.3.
He was treated as such by Pilute & unto him he acknowl-
edgd himselfe to be such, John 18.37. & as such he was Crucified. His
title was writ thus Jesus of Nazareth King of the Jews.

A King is a Relative term. Its Correlate is a kingdom. A King without a Kingdom is *Vox et praeteria nihil*, an Empty Sound in the Aire. A
Kingdom is a Politicall Body Consisting of a Supreme Soverngn Politicall Head, & of a Politicall Body under that head regulated by a Body of
Laws mentaind by that head. Laws imply a need that the kingdom stands
in of the same, by way of Direction of the Lives of the people & by
way of restraint from what is offencive. This Law then as given forth
Supposes a possibility in the people, one & every one, of going Contrary
thereunto & hence also arises a necessity of officers to inspect the peoples
lives to see whether they come up to this Law, or Whether they transgress the same. & if they transgress it, they must be reduced to it again,
or else in vain is the Law; if they must be reduced unto it, then there

375

must be force used, & Constraint upon the transgressour, & hereupon, that transgression must be prooved upon the Transgressour: & for the well hearing & determining the Case, there is a necessity that not onely officers but also Courts be erected, thro'out the Kingdom to heare & determine the same. & if the transgressour will obstinately persevere in his transgression, to Cut him off from the body, by Execution, imprisonment, or Banishment, as Ezek. 7.26. And so in a Spirituall Sense & Ecclesiasticall is it with Christs [1/2] Kingdom. Christ is the Supreme & Mysticall Head. His Church is his mysticall Body, Col. 1.18. In this his Kingdom, he hath his Laws to be attended. His subjects are liable to offend his Law, if they had had no neede of his Law they never should have had it given them & now it is given them they are liable to offende against it. Hence this Kingdom of Christ hath need of Courts & officers to looke unto the Subjects, that they having the Laws of the Kingdom of our Lord to live up unto & these Laws they being prone to transgress, & so to be a dishonour to the Kingdom & to its King & so to miss of the Benefits & designs of these Laws & eternall glory: Hence Christ their king hath Erected Courts in his Kingdom, & Officers to Carry on his Concerns in these Courts, i.e., to read & explain the Laws of his Kingdom; to looke after offenders, to hear the Complaints of his subjects, to Summon up the offenders to try the Cases between them & also the cases between offenders & their king that if possible such as offende may be reduced from their trespasses, or if impenitency in sin be not overcome, the impenitant according to the Laws of the Kingdom may be cut off from the City of the Lord, Ps. 101, ult., or expelld the Kingdom.

My Text is a Direction in such Cases as are offencive, how to proceed therein, in bringing of them to the Court; & it Consists of two Suppositions & their Conclusions.

1. The First is in order to the Entrance of the Action, & its Triall, thus, if he (i.e., the person trespassing) if he neglect to heare them, them mentiond in the former verses, Christ is very tender of the peace of his Churches, the Court of triall: its pitty that they should be courts of Common pleas, where every brazen face & graceless heart is starting up to pervert the Law of the Case, & to darken the truth, & so to befog the Court, by Coulouring over a bad Case, & darkning a Cleare case, as is too frequent in Courts of pleas, & so to bring in false judgment, & hence Christ will not admit a Case here entrance till necessity force it, & therefore in tenderness also to the reputation of the offending brother or

Sisters name he will [2/3] not admit its entrance till the offender be first treated in private alone in Case the trespass be an offence not open in the face of the world as wee say. & if this Secret treating is ineffectuall, then a second must be made & witnesses produced. Hence saith Christ take with thee one or two that in the mouth of two or three Witnesses every word may be established, i.e., made out: now here will be evidences for thee that thou hast labour'd to Convince him. & now the Supposition in our text comes in, if he neglect to heare them, παρακούσῃ, heare them not right, amiss, or is angry, or gives no sign of Repentance for his trespass, no reformation, no good is gain'd by this proceeding & thou having sufficient evidence to evidence all to be true to the Church, & thus he neglect all dealings hither to, then tell it to the Church, this is the Conclusion upon this supposition: the matter is now ripe for the Church, now let an Entrance be made unto the Case. Oh! the Patience of Christ to an offending Disciple! oh! the Pains he is at to bring him off from his Sin & Reduce him! & oh! the Obstinace & impenicy of Sinners how will they expose their good names, Reputations & esteems to open Shame before they will turn from their Sins? how will they withstand all means of Grace, teare Christs seamless Coate a pieces, & Cast fire into the temple, & raise an hellish dust and smoke in Gods house to darken the way of Sion, & to Smoother & Choake such withall as Come thither before they will fall down under their faults & Confess their Sins! But now to the Court it is to be brought. & hence I lay down this Doctrine

Doct. That when Church members falling into Sin & withstand all Secret
& private treating to bring them off from the same by Repentance
then their Case is to be Committed, or brought, to the Church, tell
it to the Church. [3/4]
Qu: 1. What is the Church here in this place to which the Case is to
be brought?
Ans: In generall the Church in this place is the Speciall seat of judgment unto whom Christ hath given a speciall Right & Authority to judge
the case referrd unto it. To deny this would be in effect to assert that
Christ orders the matter to be laid before Such to be issued that have no
right or power to meddle with it. But who dare imagine or assert any
such thing? But now this being undeniably true there will of necessity
follow such things as these. 1. That this Church must be a Society or
Court of judicature. Matters to bee judg'd not by voluntary Reference,

as in arbitration, but by Constraint forcing the Delinquent whether he will or no to an issue, are brought to a Court, or as a Court. A single justice acts as a Court but such a person is never Styled as in our text a Church or an assembly. Hence Church here is a Corporation of people & no Single person, or Sort of persons of that societie. 2. This Church must be such a Society unto which the Offender is bound & obliged as a member, & must attend its Citation & demands in some way of God. & this is done by Covenanting. We read of persons being added to the Church, Acts 2.41, & of joyning, Chap. 13, Which Could be no otherwise done but by their free & Voluntary Consent to the terms required of all belonging to the Society, which is a giving up of themselves to them, as II Cor. 5.8, & this is a promise or Covenant. This gives a right unto the Church to deale with all its members in an Ecclesiasticall way. Nothing else doth it. Township Cohabitation, or Parochiall limitation, neither of them can Constitute any Ecclesiasticall membership. For if they could, then a Civill Constitution would be Sufficient to Constitute a Spirituall Corporation. But this it cannot. For the *Constitans*, & *Constitutum* are both of the same Common Nature. But some adde therefore to these a Constantall evidence upon the Same publick worship must go with the Cohabitation. But suppose this be granted, yet the former pro-[4/5]position lies as a Stumbling blocke in the way that breakes its legs & throws it head long down. Hearing is a matter to which the Convenience of Cohabitation serves, & it makes no membership of the church but onely of the town. & town members, & Church members are *species distinctae*. And further a Constant attendance upon the publick worship in the place can't give Cohabitation to Constitute Church membership for then persons will be Church members whether Churches will admit them or noe. And it may be enquired what is this Constant attendance upon the publick worship in the place? is it to attend it for a month, two months, or a yeare Constantly in the place where the person dwells? Many Merchants, & Gentlemen come about their Concerns to London, Boston, or other places, & dwell there so long, may be in one parish, & constantly there. Are they now hereby made Church members of the Societies where they attend & dwell? or if they dwell in one Parish & attende in another? or as in Boston that is not distributed into parishes & they attende some times in one place, Some times in another place. I enquire of which Church is it that these are Church members of? Surely no man can define. Further as this shews absurdity enough to block up this new crotchett, yet there is still more against it. For its wholy inconsistant with Admissions, & Dismissions. For the Persons coming to places of but for a month, or two, etc., destroyes his Church state of membership in that place whence he comes from, whether he & that Church will or noe, & becomes a member of that Church where he dwells whether it or he will or no. Nay in one word for all, I say, that Such a Notion is utterly inconsistant with Church Discipline. For the Inhabitants of London, yea & of Boston too, are many of them notoriously Prophane, Adulterors, Drunkards, Theeves, Murderers, Oppressors, Cursed Swearers, Liars, Cruell Unmercifull Witches, Dealers with Divells, & some, Excommunicates, etc. & the Civill Majestrate Comands, as he ought [5/6] to doe, all his subjects to attend the publick Worship of God either where he lives, or else where, & tho' no Conscience concern puts them upon the same, yet to escape the fine upon noneattendance they attende usually for Convenience Sake, Where they dwell; & so are as Complete Members as any by this attendance, tho' Excommunicated or never so vile. Onely if the Minister is indeed Conscientious, he if he knows that they are vile & Wicked, or Excommunicated, he will not administer the Lords Supper to them. So that to assert cohabitation with a Constant attendance upon the publick worship makes a Church member is to unchurch all Gospell Churches in the World & therefore this can't do it, But voluntary Covenanting doth it. The Brotherhood here in our text is not Constituted by naturall Generation, as that between Children descending from the same Parents, as the Children of Israel: but by Society Constitution, as members of the same Spirituall Society, as all Church Members are: & this is done no other way, but by a mutuall Obliging themselves to walke together, as Such, in attending upon the Rules & Duties belonging to Such. & hence every member of Such a Society, or Church of Christians doth properly belong to that particular Society, & Church into which he is thus incorporated: & that Church & that alone hath a rightfull Power, & Authority, to Call up such as offende, & to heare & determine such offences as are Committed by any of her members. But thus much in Generall. I come on therefore

2. More Particularly. & hence my answer is $\begin{cases} \text{1. Negative} \\ \text{2. Affirmative.} \end{cases}$

1. Negative. & here I shall show what Church is not intended by our Saviour. For the Word Church is variously taken that is used in our text & in the Scripture. Sometimes it is used for a Concourse of people flockt together any how, as Acts 19, *ult.*: he dismisst the Assembly, so v.

32, that riot & rable that was in a tumultuous way got together, or it may be used for people brought together in a more orderly way in the monthly sessions, or *Commitiis proumeiae.* Hence ἐκκλεσια being variously used I say [6/7] Hence by Church here ἐκκλεσια Christ designed not

1. Any Civill Court of Pleas. He goes not about to take the worke of the Civill Majestrate out of his hand, as to direct his Disciples how to prosecute one another at the Civill Law when they trespass one against another; but to direct them to Convince one another of their offences if they sin that they may be brought to repent of their Sins. Christs eye was not upon distributive Righteousness fining persons for their offences: But upon Evangelicall Righteousness bringing his Disciples off from sin by Repentance & new obedience. Hence the Church here to which the Offence is to be brought is not the Civill Court nor

2. Is it the Jewish Church whether its Concerns are Considered as mannaged in their lesser Assemblies as in their Synagogues, wherein its manifest that they did Carry on some sort of judicature, as Matt. 10.17, Acts 9.1,2, John 9.23,24. But these acts of theirs in the Synagoges seem to be but the Execution of what was Committed unto them by the greate Councill of Elders Called the Sanedrin as the Parish priests execute in their Churches the Excommunications that are sent them from the Bishops, or Archdeacons Court if I am not mistaken, as I thinke I am not: And as for the matters of the Sanhedrin, it is Cleare, that matters offencive whether morall or Ceremoniall belonged to the Tabernacle, & after to the Temple where the Confessions were to be made over the head of their Atonement offerings, Lev. 4. Hence Ecclesiasticall Cases tho' they might be prepared yet could not be taken up in their Synagogues but at their Temple, when it was standing: & now its altogether unreasonable to thinke that Christ should refer their offences to be issued by them for they were enemies to Christ & his Disciples. Hence he should hereby give his utter enemies occasion to blaspheme his Cause & intrest as not sufficient to end its own Difficulties, nor heale its own maladies, that his people were so Contentious that there was no Cure amongst them to be had for their own sins & Quarrells, nay & yet more these Courts would persecute them to death as Christs disciples. Christ should hereby deliver his Sheep up to Wolves, & put his Lambs [7/8] into the mouths of Lions to devour them if he should send them with their offences to be issued in the Jewish Consistories. You se how they flew upon Paul when he attempted to purify himselfe after the manner

of the Jewish Ceremonies, Acts 25.27,28. Nay still Learned men do not Stick to affirm that the Jewish Sanhedrin is never calld ἐκκλεσια, Church in the Scripture, at least in the New Testament: & yet its to be considerd that the order of bringing a matter offencive to the Jews Sanhedrin is not observed to be as is here required as that it is first debated in secret then private before it be brought to the Church.

Obj: If it be said, there was no need of a New instituted Church, Gods institution of the church of Israel was sufficient as an example & the Gospell Church State being according there to would be a Compleate Church sufficient of itselfe to answer all the Ends of Churchood, & if Christ therefore had not used terms familiarly known in his time, his present disciples would not have known what he had ment, and hence doubtless the word church was familiarly given to the greate Assembly of the Elders without doubt, & this was the church undoubtedly intended by Christ.

Sol: This plea makes no proof of the matter. & is not sufficient to beare down those greate absurdities that must be borne down before it will permit the Jewish Church to be the church that Christ intended. But here are further matters still to appeare against this Quibble. For
1. In that its said that Christ used terms well known as to what they imported else his Disciples could not tell what he intended thereby, is no proofe that Christ by Church in our text intended the Jewish Church or Sanhedrin, nor that the word church was not familiarly known to his disciples there present. Doubtless tho' the word is not frequently used in the New Testament during our Saviours Conversing in the Flesh, yet it was or might be familiarly used to signify an assembly met together of a Religious Concern & about religious Worship. & this they could not but know that Christ intended Such a Flock when he said on this rock will I build my Church, Matt. 16. & further our text considered with the Context opens itselfe & shews that Christ intended a Society authorized to Carry on a sacred & Ecclesiasticall Judicature.
2. This Objection will wholy exclude all New Institutions from the Gospell. For no old terms will suite new institutions being suted to express things of another nature. & if they then be used, they will bely the New insti-[8/9]tutions: For the old Titles being fitted to express such ordinances to which they were first applied express the Nature of those Ordinances. When those Ordinances cease & New ones are instituted, they have a New Stamp put upon them differing from the Former, as in the Ordinances of Baptism, the Lords Supper Seals, so Church. Now the

terms peculiar to the old Testament Seales, or to the Sanhedrin, unto these they would onely in some Sense agree & would sende us to the things Signified by circumcision, Passover, the Sanhedrin, etc., to know what these Gospell Ordinances are, which would not agree in many things to the same. I shall instance in the Jews Sanhedrin supposing as Some, that it is the Church intended in the text & hence is an Example to the Gospell Church. I say it no way suites or squares with a Gospell Church. For

1. It was principally a Civil Court & such as the present Parliaments of England are Consisting most of Civill persons & a Consistory of Ecclesiasticall Men. So did the Sanhedrin; it Consisted of 66 Elders or Seniors of the Eleven tribes & onely four of Levi's tribe & the High Priest was very sildom any member of them. Hence as the Parliment determines in Civill Cases that inferiour Courts cannot issue, & also Secures the Sacred Rites, & matters of Religion against such as would ruin the sacred Concerns. So did the Sanhedrin. But what have Gospell Churches to do in any such matters? Or how do they Consist of an Over mattching number of Principall Seniors Chose out of all the body of the State or Kingdom? 2. The Sanhedrin was to Sit in Jerusalem that principall City, & had nothing to do with either morall, or Ceremoniall trespasses as Sin that makes the Soul unclean for Church fellowship, that ever I yet have understood of, for this belongd onely to the Sacred officers & was attended at the door of the Tabernacle, Lev. 4.4. But the work of the Sanhedrin is to punish the Offender. Now what hath any Gospell Church to do with the inflicting any Corporall punishment on any? & truely tho' the Sanhedrin did meddle with some great matters belonging to the synagogues, yet multitudes of Church [9/10] Cases there are that never can be brought from all parts of the Kingdom to it. If Christ then by Church in our text intended a Church of the same Form or shape it must be one single society chose out of a Realm or State divided into twelve parts out of which eleven of them being in a Civill State & the twelfth in an Ecclesiasticall State & fewer out of the Ecclesiasticall part than out of any of the other of the eleven parts, & they must sit in the principall place of the Realm, to judge all weighty Cases, both Civil & Sacred brought to it, & punish the offenders with Corporall punishment even unto death if the Case require it. Can this be the nature of a Gospell Church? or was there ever such an Ecclesiasticall Society in the World? except the Man of Sin? which doth not yet paralel it as to its Constitution. Nay Christ stiles the Sanhedrin, as is very probable, Matt.

5.22, συνεδρίῳ (Sion which word its judged by learned men is derived from the term Sanhedrin) Councill: & by the spirit of God called γερουσιαν, Senate, Acts 5.21, & πρεσβυτέριον, englesht Acts 23.5, all the state of the Elders. & may well be englished the whole Presbytery. So that we have no need to think that Christ in our text calld the Sanhedrin *Ecclesia*, Church. So that by these & such like reasons as these its easy to Conclude that by Church in our text we are not to thinke that Christ intended the Church of the Jews, or their Sanhedrin.

3. By Church here in our text, we are not to thinke is intended the Church Catholick, or the Whole Body of Christians upon the Earth living at the same time. So the term Church is sometimes used in Scripture, as I Cor. 12.28. For church so taken, tho' it Contains all the intred people of God & the mysticall Body of Christ & his Elect admitted on Earth that Contemporate, yet this Church Can't be this subject of Discipline or the Court of Ecclesiasticall judicature, but onely in its particular parts & Societies of Particular Churches. Suspende all particular Churches in the world, & the Catholick is onely an intrest, & no kingdom or Seate of Judicature. It hath no Courts in it.

4. Church in our text is no Nationall, or Provinciall so-[10/11]ciety, nor Metropolitan, or Dioscessan Church. Such Churchs had no being & were utterly impossible to have any Being before Whole Nations Received the Gospell of God & his Grace or whole Provinces, & therefore Could not be the Spirituall Courts of Christs Kingdom. & untill they had a being the Disciples of Christs in case they sin'd against one another, or against God, & could not take up the offence privately, had no way laid down unto them to deale to issue their Contentions. For the Church could not act before it had an Essence. *Operari sequitur esse. & non Entis nulla suratt praediatae.* And there were no such Churches as Nationall, Provinciall, Metropolitan, or Dioscaesan in the Scripture. The Spirit of God writes not to such Churches, but unto the Churches in Nations, & Provinces, as to the Churches of Judea, Gal. 1.22, Churches of Asia, I Cor. 16.19, Rev. 1.11. The worde is in the plurall Number when it notes the Societies of Christians seated in distinct Lands or Nations & so also when it imports them as seated in distinct Provinces as the Churches, (in the plurall & not Church in the singular number) of Galatia, Gal. 1.2. But when the term is given to a Society of Christians dwelling in a City, its mostly uttered in the Singular, & not in the plurall number, as the Church that was at or in Jerusalem, Acts 8.1, Chap. 11.22, the Church at Corinth, I Cor. 1.1, so the Church of Ephesus,

Smyrna, etc., Rev. 2.1,8,12,18, Chap. 21.7,14: etc. Now then there were no such Churches as Provincial, Nationall, etc., in the Apostles dayes, they could not be the Church in our text that had now the Authority of a Court of judicature in its hand to judge of Controversies & to put the obstinate into a visible state of Heathens & publicans. And indeed this Church was at the present a Church Capable to judge such Cases, & you see it presently after Christs death put forth acts of judging, as Acts 2.47. Hence these after named Churches are merely Humane Devises, having no being in Divine institutions. & all their power is a mere humane Donation, & not of Christ. Christ sends not his Disciples to these Churches.

5. Church in our text is not a Classicall Church. There [is] [11/12] no possibility at the present for any Classis. For a Classis consists of the Elders, & messengers of Severall Churches in Consociation together, conveaned together as a Spirituall Court to carry on matters of Ecclesiasticall Discipline. Now as a prudentiall Business, in a way of help unto the Churches of Christ & Strengthening one anothers hands in all hard matters, by Advice, Counsill, & light unto them these are of greate use, & are to bee highly esteemed. But as to any right, Power, or Authority to judge & exercise Discipline, Church Discipline, it hath none at all, unless it be the Church in our text to which Christ sends the Offenders with their Offences to be judgd & determined, saying when other means faile to the prosecutor tell it to the Church. But now I say that a Classis is not the Church in the Text. For. 1. It was impossible that there should be a Classis now in being, there being onely One Gospell Church in Being & hence there could not be any Convention of the Elders & Messengers of Churches. 2. If by Church in our text is intended Classis then Christ would not have any Church Discipline carryed on till such a Classis was in Being. But as we se the Contrary carried on, about 50 days after Christ was Crucified, Acts 21.47, yea & before in the Case of Matthias, his call & Election in the room of Judas, Acts 1. So indeed it cannot be granted to thinke that Christ should not provide means to reduce his Sining disciples, but should let them ly obstinately in Sin to their own hardening & to the Scandall of his Cause & intrest, till a Classis was Convened & formed is very hard to receive. Further its also hard to thinke that Christ should intende a Classis by the word Church: & give not the least intimation that is, that he intended not such a Society that the Word Church is in all the New Testiment is by the Spirit of God, made most peculiarly proper unto. 3ly. I am ready to question whether

there ever was such a Society in the world as that is Calld a Classis untill within some few hundreds of years, when the reformation from Antichristian Errours began & had made some proficiency. And then a necessity Constrain'd the Reformers to fix on some way of Discipline, England made use of the way, that they founde [12 / 13] as Serviceable in the present Case. Some others fixt upon the meeting of the Ministers that could well meet together to determine upon Church matters, & some others upon other wayes. & this of Classes consisting of Elders & Messengers of Churches in Consociation had been a most prudentiall way, had it not been dubd with a *Jus Divinum*, & made it to Stande in such a station as robs the Gospell Churches of that right & Authority that Christ hath envested them with & made them the proper subjects of. But seing the Classis is of such a late date, it is impossible that it should be the Church in our text to which the offences are to be brought. We read of Councills, & Synods, which are for giving light, but nothing of Classes.

6. Church in our text is not the Presbytery, or ruling officers of the Church. For altho' no Church Can impose upon them or intermeddle in any thing peculiar to their office. They can't constrain them to Administer the Seals to such as they judge not the Qualified subject of nor restrain them from a Pastorall, or Ministeriall admonition of obstinate or open offenders, I Tim. 5.19,20 & II Tim. 4.2, Titus 2, *ult.*, nor hinder them from suspending offenders from the Lords Supper. Yet these are not the Church. Our Lord doth not onely direct his speech in our text to his disciples in generall, but Eminently to his Apostles & saith to them if So & So, tell it to the Church. Tho' they were Extraordinary Elders & officers of the Church, yet they are not the Church, but onely part of the Church.

7. By Church Christ intends not the Fraternity onely tho' the power of judging doth ly in the hands of the Fraternity with their Ruling officers, yet they alone are not the Church. They are but part. & the Sorority is as really part of the Church & have as reall a Conscientious Concern in Church Concerns & Discipline as the fraternity tho' they may not meddle in judging, it not being permitted to them as well as some other Matters, but thus as to the Negative part.

2. As to the Affirmative part of the Answer. I say, that by Church here we are to understand a Gospell [13 / 14] instituted Particular Society of believers in Covenant together to attende upon all Gospell ordinances of Divin worship & Discipline. That it is to Carry on Gospell discipline

Can't be denied for Christ orders Offences to be brought to this Church saying tell the Church. & so about seven weeks after Christs Crucifixion 3000 were received into their Society, Acts 2.41, & *ult.* These were acts of Church Discipline: So also it is for the Celebration of all Divine Ordinances of Worship as the Ministry of the Word, Sacraments, & prayer, Acts 2.41,42. They Continued in Breaking of Bread, Prayer, & in the Apostles doctrin, Acts 2.41,42, etc. This Church Contain the Whole Body of Believers associated, Theophylact styles it ἐπὶ τῶν τυς ἐκκλεσια προέδρων, the Confessions of the Church.[69] The whole body upon their seats. Such was the Church of Corinth that was urged to its judicature & blaimd for their slowness to this work & urged upon it, I Cor. 5.11,12. & their Censure is said to be a punishment (ἐπιτιμια, a Censure) inflicted by many, & the same working repentance was to be removed by many, II Cor. 2.7.—And the members of this Society were Confederated one with another, either expressly, or implicitly. For it is a distinct Society & the Members of it are the proper members of it & of no other Society. They Can claim the Relation to it & the priviledges of it, & its injustice in it to deny them the same. & so they stande in no such respect to any other Church nor any other Church to them. This hath power to Call them to an account, to Command their Attendance, & to judge their Cases, I Cor. 5.5,6,12. & to absolve them upon repentance, to Suspende & eject them out of their Society, if they abide obstinate. And this Church can't summon up, or etc., any that are not members of it, it may as warrantable Cite before it persons in another Contrey to appear before it, as persons at the next doore, that are not members of it. Now this membership to this Church & not to any other must be made some way. Every person is born free & belongs no more to one Church than to another. Civill Constitutions contening ma-[14/15]ny Countries into townships Can't make a member of a town a member of the Church in the Place. Church Membership making, lies without the Sphere of the Civill Orbe. Divine Institutions Constitute not any one a Member of this or that church, tho' Divine Operation in the heart makes the Soule a member of the Mysticall Body of Christ, yet God leaves the person to his own Choise to Choose what Church he will joyn himselfe unto. Now when he joyns to any he must come up to the Orders, & Conditions required by the Church to membership & subject himselfe thereto, or else he is no more a member of that Church than of another: & so of none. Now this Consenting, & Complying with these terms is a Covenanting. The good man of the

House that went out to hire laborers agreed with them, συμφωνήσας, agreed with them, that is he Covenanted with them. They both concluded in one voice & that was a Covenant. If a man come to be a member of any Corporation, he comes up to the terms of membership; to be a member of a town, he Complies to the terms thereof, or to be a member of a Family, he comes up to the laws & Orders of the Family, nay if a Company go about any undertaking they Confederate together, & so are bound one to another. & shall Churches of Christ not Covenant together, to Carry on Gods Church Concerns? shall Churches be the loosest Societies which are? Surely its most unreasonable so to Conclude. Hence they are Confederate Societies.

Now touching this Particular Church some Considerations are to be had as to the Materialls, & the manner of its building. As to the Materialls they are to be the Choicest Sort of men Not spiritually dead but living Stones, Eph. 1.1,5, I Pet. 2.5, Pretious Stones, Isa. 54.11,12, Precious Sons of Zion. For the Building must be an Habitation of God, Eph. 2, *ult.* I Cor. 3. Hence they must be the pure in heart & clean in hands. Celsus slandering the Societies & churches of Christians is answerd thus by Origen [15/16] in his third book against Celsus. Christians when they have tried the mindes of their Auditors having had discourse with them alone, after they have signified sufficiently that they appeare to desire or Will to live more rightly, then at length they admit them into their Society. Then they separate otherwise men from the ranke of others whom they lately had introduced who have not received the badge of perfect purgation. And there are some other things with them that every one should prefer according to his power & to will no thing but what appeares meet for Christians, among whom othersome are appointed who inquire into the lives of Such as come to them & make diligent search how they behave themselves. Hence then such as live evilly they Separate from their Church fellowship, but receive with all their heart such as are not of that sort & undoubtedly do bring them to be better day by day. Thus he according as Merlin, gives it. Mr. Rous in his *Mella Patrum* a little varies in his relating it, but nothing as to the matter here in our hand, etc.[70] Justin Martyre who flourisht about 130 years after Christ goes on to the same effect saying in his *Apology for Christians* to the Emperor Antony the Pious, saying we being perswaded by reason & the word have departed from them, i. e., Demons & adhere to that alone unbegotten God by the Son himselfe, we formerly rejoyced in filthy adulteries, but now we imbrace Chastity, we did use magick

Arts but now we Consecrate & dedicate ourselves to God, we did amble after rich possessions & Glory, but now we hold what we have in Common & Communicate with Certain poor people. & our heavenly father rather will have repentance than punishment. And such as are found not to live as Christ hath taught—are not Christians altho' they profess with the tongue the Doctrine of Christ. Such are onely Christians in name & we desire that they were punisht by you, (our Magistrates). But such as are perswaded & believe the things to be true which were deliver'd by us & receive them to live accordingly by their own & with fasting & prayer to beg of God remission of their former sins & so with us are taught to fast & pray together with us are had by us there, where there is water & therewith are regenerated as we were. For in the Name of the Parent of allthings, & of our Saviour, Jesus Christ & the Holy Ghost they are washt in water, And wee according to such elevation bring the believer now, & he being joynd to them which are [16/17] called the brethren thither where they are gathered to prayers in Common & Supplications both for themselves & for him now illuminated & all others of all nations, to be performd with an earnest minde that we may be worthy & fit who by the truth acknowledg'd may also by works themselves be found good and officious, of the affairs & keepers of the things committed to us & that we may be Saved with eternall Salvation. When prayers are ended we Salute ourSelves by turns with mutuall kisses. Then is brought to him that presides over the brethren, bread, & a Cup of Wine & Water, which being took he offers praise & glory to the Father of all things thro' the name of the Son, & the Holy Ghost & largely executes the Celebration of the Eucharist according as he hath dignified us with these his gifts: & when he hath ended prayers & thanksgiving all the people present with Joyfull approbation Cry out saying Amen. After this those that are calld the deacon, i.e., ministers, distribute it to everyone present that they may partake of it in which the thanks are acted, viz, the Bread & Wine, & Water & Carry of it to them absent. This *Aliment* is calld by us the Eucharist; which it is lawfull for none to partake of but such as believe our Doctrine to bee true, & are washed in the Lavor of Regeneration for the remission of sins, & Regeneration, & that lives as Christ hath taught.[71]

I will give one more instance & this out of Tertullian who flourisht about 196 years after Christ. He saith in his *Apoligy against the Gentiles*, Now he saith I will declare the affairs of the Christian Religion, that ye might shew good things as well as refuse bad, we are a Body concerning the Conscience of Religion, & the Unity of Discipline, & of the Covenant of Hope. We come into an assembly & Congregation that praying to God we might as it were surround him with our hand lift up in prayers. This force is gratefull to God. & we pray for the Emperours & their * * * , for the State of the World, for the peace of affairs & the delaying of the End. We are gatherd together for the Commemoration of divine scriptures. If the Condition of the present times force us to admonish anything or to acknowledge itt. And we certainly nourish the Faith with holy voices, we are erect in Hope, & fix our Confidence: & Corroborate Discipline with nothing less than the inculcations of the Comands: & also we attend Exhortations, Castigations, & divine Discipline & Judgment with great weight, by some, as in Gods sight which [17/18] is a Choice foregoing judgment of the future judgment & last day: if anyone so offend that he should be banisht from the Communion of & of the Assembly all their Commerce.

And herein Certain approved Elders do rate obtaining this Honour, not by price, but by Witness: for no offices of God are gaind by price, altho' there is a kinde of Chest not for ordinary Sums, that is gatherd as if of bought Religion, yet & a small pittance any that will puts therein when he if he any time Can or upon a monthly day. For none is compelld but offer freely. This is a *depositum* of Piety. For the things given are not to be spent in pampering, or putting men in unthankfull Gluttoniny: but to feed the Needy, & interring them, & upon Children, Infants & Orphans, etc.[72]

I will mention no more; these are the accounts given of particular Churches or Gospell assemblies, & they were in the next age following the Apostles. For Justin Martyre lived in the next age & was the Famous Pastor of the Church at Rome. & Clement that lived with the Apostles as is thought to be Him mentioned, Phil. 4.2, Wrote to such a Church as these wee speak on, viz, his Epistle to the Church at Corinth.[73]

Now in these accounts we may see plainly these things:
1. The matter Constitutive of these Churches, for here we see they were the most Choice of people Whose hearts & lives were strictly tried & lookt into: & if they were founde addicted to any Sin they were not received into Fellowship. Tertullian hardly admitted them to Come into the Assembly. Some set them at the Doore onely. But if they were judgd gracious upon the tryall, they hugd them in their hearts.
2. The Manner how these Qualified persons were made members, & here are two things observable. 1. They make manifest to the Church

their fitness for it. They pass under a Strict triall, this they tender themselves unto & render a Reason of their Hope as is a duty, I Pet. 3.15. So did Paul, so did them at Ephesus, Acts 19.18,19. & this Course did the Church at Ephesus attend in their admissions, Rev. 2.4, & so also the Church at Jerusalem, Acts 9.26,27. & John Baptist expected it of such as he admitted to his baptism, Matt. 3.6,7,8. & so we see these members went in the same path they were in & so were presented to the Church. Here they past that search of a good Conscience, as I Pet. 3.21, & shewd the same being presented as such [18/19] by the Elders that tried them; which trial is calld συνειδήσεως ἀγαθῆς ἐπερώτημα, the interrogation or enquiry of a good Conscience towards God. There is a twofold Search is to be made, the One by Every person upon his own Soule to see whether he can finde a good Conscience in his breast pleading for him before God, as they Eph. 1.11. & also the enquiry made by the Elders that tried him; & the result of this enquiry finding a good conscience pleading for him before God in Christ is to be laid before the Church by his own mouth, as they did Acts 19.18. & David offers himselfe to do, Ps. 66.16. Or by the Elders that searched it out as Barnabas did for Saul, Acts 9.26. And its altogether unreasonable to thinke Seing a Church is a Society of Spirituall Lovers that are knit together in their Souls by Love & are calld to truthe & in Love, Eph. [4.15] & that if any one falls into Sin which as a kankering rust will eate a Sunder the golden Chain of Love, is not to be permitted to stand a member in this Society unless he manifest unto it his repentance of his sin as Credibly true Repentance, that they should admitt Sinners, as all are by nature & also by practice before Conversion, without an open manifestation of Repentance. For Where repentance is not there is an impenitantt, & Where it is not manifested there is manifest impenitancy of it being sought for, is refused to be evidenced. For a recovery out of Sin by repentance is but the restoring the offender into that state by shewing his repentance, that he was brought into, in his admission & therefore it being the method whereby he is set right as he was in his admission, it is the way that is to be taken in admission. For Such actions that bring lapsed persons into a right State from their falls are actions of the same sort as those were of whereby they were set in the state with the Church out of which their falls cast them. Renewalls are onely a putting of things, or persons in the same State, as nigh as may be, that they were in when at first they were all new, And Hence the same worke as made at first a member accepted into membership, will when he falls, renew him again into acceptableness as before. & seing manifest repentance doth this, manifest grace or repentance is requisit to entrance [19/20] into Church fellowship. It seems altogether unreasonable to imagine, that the most Noble, Royall, I Pet. 12.5, & Celestiall Society in the World, wherein the Angells of God attende as Observers, I Cor. 11, & Servitors should not be Concerned in the qualifications of her members in that the Highest & holiest Qualifications under Heaven are absolutely necessary as to their natures, unto this State, & nothing less than such Qualifications are Sufficient; & in respect unto the highest Degrees of these qualifications, the Highest are not too high for it. Where as no Society of men on Earth to which appertains any beneficiall Priviledges but have an inspection in the admission of persons into their Qualifications, whether they are fit for their Society or noe. Nay they are Commanded to try the Spirits, I John 4.1, & in the primitive Churches it was done, as at their Baptisms when they were admitted as we see out of Justine & others. And indeed they when tried by Church Officers their state was laid before the whole Church assembly. Origen saith upon Ps. 38, if thou forseest thy sickness is such as ought to be spread forth in the Assembly of the Whole Church to be healed, & perhaps others thereby Edified let a Skillfull Physician be procured.[74] And in the Church of Rome they had a place on purpose Erected where to the whole Church had the state of persons to be admitted did give an account of their Faith. Se Augustin in his eight book, *De Civitate Dei*.[75] And indeed Seing Christ in our text hath made this Church the Seate of Judgment, the *Res Judicandae* are to be laid before it for a determination, for they are Relat & must go together. Hence Christ saith tell it to the Church. & the Qualifications fitting persons for this Society belongs to her as matters to be determined on by her. She may not set open doores for all to enter. The judging in the Church at Corinth was performed by the whole body Capable of putting forth an act of judicature: & the rest had their personall judgment given in their own hearts for the Church is as Tertullian hath it, *Corpus de Conscientis*, Religion is & must judge of her own Members, as well such as are to be made so as such as are so.[76] If these within are to be tried by her & cut off if they repent not of their errours which when Evidenced, then she is to judge whether they be to be let in before they be let in & made members of her Body. But we see the last & the reason is as good for the first. If an impenitent person visible may not abide in her: he may not be let in by her. Hence the Signs of repentance [20/21] must be laid before her. For She must hear if she must judge. She is a Spirituall Court of Aire & Terminer.

2. It hence also appears that he must be Covenanted with the Church whereof he is a member. For if there is to be such a strict triall made into the heart & behaviour of the person that seeks Church Fellowship, as these Authours hold out, it is because this person is not to Stand in as remote a respect as others from it, but is seeking a Speciall Relation to, Propriety in, & Priviledges of this Church, above what he hath with any other, or can have with any in the loose state that he stands in or that any other Stands in while not a member & that the Church is to have a greater Propriety in, & Power over, & Confers more Priviledges upon him than on any that enters not into her Communion. For unworthy walking in such as are not of her Society can't be calld up before her by any Authority in her hand: nor can any so standing from her membership demand any divine ordinance at her hand. Now this relation that is Constituted between this Person, & this Church, whereby they have Mutuall interest, mutuall Propriety, & mutuall priviledges going on one in another, etc., must be Constituted by some mutuall acting between them too: Now all Relation & the Intrest, Propriety & Priviledges thence flowing (naturall Relation onely excepted) unless it be violent as that between an Conqueror & his Vassalls, which is tyrannicall is Constituted by Confederation. Such is the Relation between man, & Wife, Master & Servant, Buyer & Seller. By Relation I intend such as is between Man & Man, & not any Logicall Relation. & Such whose Correlates are *ejusdem generis*, & not between a person & his Performances: nor such bare Relations as is of no power or intrest with, speaking of that tho' the correlats have either over the other. However Every Society hath laws & Priviledges belonging to it, & every member of any Society must consent to the Laws of the Society, & if not the society laws will Cut off his membership. Now all such Societies require a Consent to the [21/22] same. Who will take any man into his house that will not Submit to the Orders of his House. & shall a Church take in any that will not Submit to the Orders of the church: if such werein they are to be put out by the order that Christ hath given in our text. & can it be then thought that Christ doth authorize her taking in such as will not Consent to these orders? We finde in Scripture that such as the Church received joyned, Acts 5.13. How are persons joynd together but by promises, & Consenting one with another: And here unto take

Tertullions word for it speaking of the Churches that the Apostles gatherd, I therefore say, that we with these, & not alone now Apostolicall but amongst *all which to these are Confederated* as to the Society of the Sacrament, use these Compendiums when we graple against Hereticks touching the faith of the Gospell: Thus He in *lib. 4., Adversus Marcionen.*[77] And I suppose this is the reason why Cyprian saith, that Christ hath commanded the Covenants of Charity be preserved incorrupt & inviolated, Cypr: *de verritate Ecclesiae.*[78]

But before I go any further this Church being now perfectly essentialed: Consisting in right Matter rightly formed before I come to its Workes may be Considered as it is thus Erected & so it is $\left\{ \begin{array}{l} \text{Inorganick} \\ \text{Organick.} \end{array} \right\}$

1. As it is Inorganick. So it hath its Standing of Right Matter, rightly formed, But it hath no Organs or Instruments whereby to attain its End & reason of its Churchood. Yet it hath a power & Authority Committed to it by which it may put out acts to attain its end. Hence it is not to continue in this state no longer than necessity constrains. Hence it must be granted upon necessity to Choose some Suitable brother to propounde matters unto it that do occur during its present state, as suppose persons appeare desirous to joyn to it, he may take an account of their Qualifications & propound them to the Church & take the Churches Vote in the Case & declare it to the Admitting or non-admitting of them. He may do the like in case a member offende, & may proceed to Censure by reproof, or also to [22/23] Absolution. Cyprian is Cleare in this case, Saying if any be exercised in any inconveniency, or in Danger of Sickness; our presence with any Elder present (i.e., pastor) not being expected, that is present or there be no Elder found & his departure begin to urge, they may make the Confession of their offense with the Deacon also, & bonds imposed on them, upon their repentance they may approach unto the lord in peace; so hee.[79]

Further upon the same reason, this brother may Call the Church together, consult about immergent affairs with them & with other Church Elders, etc., may propounde persons to the Church vacant of officers, for officers, may address the Churches desire to Persons Suitable for Church office as Elders, etc., & bring them to the Church to preach, that the Church may taste their Gifts, may take the minde of the Church & spread it before them, May as occasion requires upon advice & Consent of the Church Write letters to the Elders of other Churches with their Churches to Convene with this Church as a Councill, or to

assist & help in advise about, & in Ordination of their Elders, etc.
Necessity Constrains this matter: For this state of Churchood as Inor-
ganick is not to be Continued in any longer than unavoidableness
Constrains.

2. Organick. Now an Organick Church is such as is furnisht with
all Offices, that Christ hath instituted to accomplish the End of
Churchood. & here note, that I speake of a Church that hath all instituted
officers fill'd up now. But yet such a Church is Organick tho' it may
have onely sufficient officers in it to attend the End of Churchood tho' it
may not have all in it that are divinely instituted as when its Condition
can't obtain it. Many Churches are too Small & low to have both
Pastors, & Teachers, to have both Teaching & Ruling Elders, both
Deacons & Deaconesses; & yet have Officers sufficient for their state.
Now these are also Organick as well as those that have all in them. Now
these Organs or Officers are such as attend the $\left\{ \begin{matrix} \text{Spirituall} \\ \text{Secular} \end{matrix} \right\}$ Concerns
of the Church.

1. First. The Spirituall. & these are called Elders, I Tim. 9.19 [23/24]
17.19, πρεσβύτερον in its proper & Strict Sense it imports an ancient
person, one touching τέλος, the end of his life, or an Ambassador which
used to be grave Solid, Worthy men in years. & its brought by the Spirit
of God to import a Church Officer under Christ imployed as his
Ambassadors to his Churches to Dispense his Oracles to them, II Cor.
5.20. We are Ambassadors of God for Christ, πρεσβεύομεν, we carry
on the office of ambassadors of God for Christ's sake, & beseech you
to be reconciled. From this word, πρεσβύτερος, they are englisht in
the Scripture Elders. & sometimes they are Called Priests tho' usually
another word is so englisht, & they are also Called presbyters, & it
intends the Same as Bishops or Pastors of Particular Churches. And their
Office in Preaching the Word authoritatively, in Exhorting, in admonishing & Rebuking offenders that are obstinate with all Authority &
Command. Either as the Pastors or Teachers or Doctors of the Churches
in which any Member is that is obstinate in his sin, & that both Ministe-
rially in the executing his teaching office, I Tim. 5.20: or in his Ruling
Work as Governing the Church. Hence are those Calls, II Tim. 4.2,3,
Titus 1.2 ult., or as the Church her instrument in carrying on of the
Discipline of the Church. & here he is to apply the Censures of the
Church upon the offender in case of Obstinacy by Admonition &

Excommunication. This Work Diotrephes abused usurping it to him-selfe, III John v. 9,10.

These Elders have their particular judgment that the body of the Church may not meddle with. For they come in the Name & Authority of Christ to Speake & teach, etc., & Administer the Sacraments. & also Discipline, they may suspend any offender, by vertue of their office power upon warrantable grounds: tho' the Church do faile in doing their Duty & when the Case is before the Church the Church pleade want of light to Convince the matter to be Sin, & so refuse to vote the matter an offence yet these Elders may warrantably exercise their own office judg-ment & rebuke the offender & admonish him by vertue of his own office power & suspend him from acting in, or receiving the Lords Supper with the Church till he manifest his repentance. & if the brethren would absolve him, or do, it will not availe: but in so doing they rebell against Christs Authority in the Rulers. & in Case the brethren should so act against their officers, their officers, (I mean Pastors & Teachers,) their power is Sufficient for their non administring the Lords Supper to them; to Some, or to all, if all be in this insurrec-tion, till they repent. Childrens bread must not be given to dogs, Matt. 14.[80] The brethren can't constrain them to administer the Lords Supper to whom they please, nor to put what they will to the [24/25]Church vote, neither may the Church propound, no not by the Ruling Elder any thing to the Church without the leave or against the judgment of these Elders ordinarily. Cases more than ordinarilie will warrant Some actions at some times that are not ordinarily to be meddled with, in such cases, other Elders & Churches are to be Consulted with & desired to inquire into the matters, or they may Call a Councill to help & give light in the case. For these Elders having their own office judgment, which is a talent not to be laid up in a napkin, are to use the Same: & if they judge a matter not meet to be brought to the Church, or the matter when brought to the Church, not rightly judged they may warrantably refuse to propound it to the Church, or to the vote of the Church; or if being overborn or thro' mistaking any Circumstance, he doth put the Case to the vote, & the vote doth either Cleare the guilty, or Condemn the Innocent, either thro' ignorance, or Envy, he may warrantably refuse to Declare, or pronounce any such sentence. For his office judgment Can't be imposed upon. His power lies in his office, & his execution of it is to be according to his judgment. If the Case be a matter of morall evill & so

Sin full, if it be not a matter of prejudice, but of Conscience, & be obstinantly mentaind against cleare Evidence it is to be brought to the Church: tell it to the Church saith Christ. Such matters the Churches of old Censured: & the Officers that are rulers have their own judgment that the Brotherhood can't take away nor hinder the Exercise of & their office power & right of judging will warrant them in their right use of it, & it is a power above both the Whole Church who are Called to be obedient to it, Heb. 13.17, & above any part or member of it, & so above the Ruling Elders, who are onely helps in government Chiefly, & not hindrances, I Cor. 12.28. These Elders are to teach all in the Church their duty & so also the Ruling Elders theirs. They are the highest Authority that Christ hath in the Church. If they Erre a Councill may be called, or other Churches may be desired to enquire into the Case. But the members of the Body can neither Call them to an account nor hinder their actings.

Its folly to say, that they are in some Churches men of too weake judgement to Carry on the Work for this will not deny them their power & right belonging to their Office, but will shew the weakness of their judgment that calld them to their office.

2. The Ruling Elders & their work is peculiarly about Discipline & ruling not the other Elders: but the Body. [25/26]

But here before we leave this its meet to Consider what power or right of judging that is resident in the Body of the Church Organick distinct from that in the Rulers, or Governours of it. For this Sort of Rulers are Called ἡγουμένοις, as Heb. 13.17, i.e., Governours, & πρεσβυτέρου, I Tim. 5.19. Rulers such as Stand in higher place & office than the rest. And their work is to lead, go before, & rule the rest, to let their Light shine before others, Matt. 10.15,16, to teach, Convince, Exhord, admonish, reproove, to Charge, rebuke & that with all long suffering & Doctrine, II Tim. 4.23, Titus 1 & 2 last. And as to matters offencive to receive Complaints to weigh them to see that they are proved, to labour to Convict the offender, to moderate between the parties at variance, & if possible to take up the Case between them; if not to use his own judgment whether its fit to be brought to the Church, whether its a Case of Conscience in the Complainer, or of Prejudise in which Case I am ready to thinke it ought not to be brought to the Church unless the Facts be an Evident Sin & not by way of Consequence, or farfetcht Circumstances. For Christs Court here is a Court of Conscience & not of revenge, a means to bring to repentance, & not to serve Sin. & also to judge whether its so Circumstanced as its like to have a fair issue in the Church, whether its right for the Church & the Church ready for it: or whether it is not like to be as a fireball in the Church to Set the Church all on afire. In which Cases & the like he is to use his own judgment for all things are to be done for Edification & not for Destruction, II Cor. 13.7,8. & judging it fit for the Church & the Church fitt for it he is to deliver it to the Church, shew its Evill, make it Cleare to be so & so, & to excite the Church to their duty & to give a right judgment in the Case for Christ as they are bound to be faithfull & shall answer it at Christs bar. & at length to take the Vote or Sufferage of the Brethren: If its manifest that their vote is not right, or that they are Equally divided both as to the affirmative & negative parts, they are divided he may put in his own vote or hold it back as he sees it is right. But if he sees it is rather over voted on the wrong side either to the dammage of the innocent, or the acquitting the guilty, he may inquire into the reason of their So voting: & if he see it is unrighteous, or is like to set a fire in the Church, & if the Church be obstinate & will not be reduced by reason to a righter issue he may refuse to declare the vote: & also may withhold the Administration of the Lords Supper till they reforme. [26/27] His office judgment will warrant him in so doing. Nothing can warrant him in acting amiss against his Office judgment. When the vote is taken & his office judgment is approving of it he is to declare it. If it be in matters of Admission of members, he is to declare that the Church hath received them: & so take a promise of their attending upon the Duties of a member of this Church admitted unto a full State of Fellowship with them, & that he will attend upon the ordin[an]ces of the Gospell, the Sacraments, Ministry of the Word, & Discipline & a Subjection according to his place to all mutuall duties amongst the members thereof to keep from or recover out of Sin, to the glory of God, etc. But if the vote be taken in matters of offence, and is for his clearing & rightly, he is to declare him acquitted with some brief Counsill & exhortation. If it be such as is against the person, it binds, & here when its a right vote its the Elders duty to declare it ordinarily, with some serious and weighty word of reproof in away of Exhortation, or church Admonition & if still obstinancy abides after due time of triall allowed, the Church vote being took touching his obstinancy or impenitancy its the Work of the Rulers to pass the sentence of Excommunication upon him, & so to deliver him up to Satan, I Cor. 5.4,5, I Tim. 1, *ult.* & this must be done with all Authority sharpness & Comand, Titus

1.13, 2 *ult.* & yet in a way of greate Sorrow upon the Spirit, its Called a lamenting Such, II Cor. 2.1,2,3, Calld making sorrowful. & a bewailing, II Cor. 12.21.

But having made all right there belongs to the teaching Elders onely the Administration of the word, Baptism & the Lords Supper. There also belongs unto the Elders the Ordination of officers orderly Called to their office by the Church, & as to the work of ordination Touching the Call & acceptance they are to inquire into the same & seing the Call declared by the Church in the presence (if nothing constrain the Contrary) they are to lay it before the person calld & take his acceptance thereof which done they are to proceed to the imposition of hands with prayer, & then the hands not removed, to declare him having received the Call to be seated in Such an office in that Church, & so with some enforcing motive answerable to the nature of his office to press him to a faithfull discharge of the same, which if Elders & Chiefly teaching Elders, there is to be given the Right hand of Fellowship, & as to the Ordination of Teaching Elders, it usually [27/28] was Carried on in the ages succeeding the Apostles. Hence Cyprian in Epistle 55 to Cornelius saith thus, Moreover (for I speake being provoked, I speake grieving, I speake being constraind) that when a bishop was to be set in the place of one that was dead, when he was chose by the Suffrage of all the people in peace, when in persecution he was protected by the help of God, when joyned to all our Collegues faithfully approved four years by his people in his Office, etc., when such, by Certain desperate & wretched men that stand with out the Church, seem to be opposed, let such appeare that oppose.[81]

So he also speaks of himselfe, saying To that which Certain Fellow Elders as Donatus, Fortunatus, Novatus & Goedcia by himself alone wrote me, I could not write again. For I determined from the begining of my Office to do nothing by my own private opinion without the Counsell, & without the Consent of my people.[82] And yet more in Epistle 68, hee with others, viz, Caecelius, Primus, Polycarpus, etc., it must be diligently observed, & held that touching the Divine & Apostolical tradition which is held by us & almost by all the provinces that for the right Celebration of Ordinations, that, the next bishops of the Same province convene to that people for whom the Ruler is to bee ordaind, & the Bishope in the presence of the people, those who exactly know the life of every one & that hath an inspection into everyones actings.

Thus saith he it was done with us at the Ordination of our Collegue Sabinus, that by the suffrage of all the Brotherhood, & the judgment of the Bishops brott together present that wrote to us of him, his Office was laid on him; & hands: & he was put in the place of Bacilidis.[83]

And so the famous Synod of Nicea decreed that if it could be a Bishop should be ordaind by all the Bishops of the province. But if this was hard to be done, he should have three at least to do it.[84] [28/29]

The *jus Ecclesiasticum* or power of the Church being essentially of Different sorts & seated in Differing subjects is when rightly acted mixtt together & makes a Sweet harmony, now the Spouse is terrible as an army with Banners, Cant. 6.10, yea now the whole description in the Verse doth clearly shine forth upon Her. She looks forth as the morning, fair as the Moon clear as the Sun, terrible as an army with Banners. But there oft is found darkning fogs that cloud her glory thro' the pride & perversness of some less Conscious either of their duty or the Churches Beauty & Gods glory & oft by a wrong understanding of this Right or Power. For the Right of Ruler is purely & solely that which the Elders are invested with & the Brethren have nothing to do in it. The *jus judicii* is both in the Elders & Brethrens hand & the Brethren cannot act any thing of it untill the *Res judicandae* or matters to be judg'd are brought to them by their Ruling officer or officers. They may no more meddle therewith than the Jury meddle with matters to be judged that the judge & officers of the Court never Commit to them. So to do would be rebellion against the King; & thrusting the Magistrates & Judge off of the Bench: & it would be so in the Brethren in Case that they should take & judge any Case in the Church that the Ruling officer Commits not unto them. Hence its not amiss here to Consider in what things this Right in the hands of one & of the other lies to be exercised with, & here

1. The Right of Rule in the hand of the Rulers. Now this is extensive as far as their Office judgment is to be extended. For tho' it is not a *Jus Regnandi*, it is a *jus Regutandi*, which cannot be without a right to judge. 1. Of What Doctrine is fit to be held out & improoved, 2. When & to whom the Sacraments are to be administred. 3. of Reproving & Admonishing authoritatively, 4[ly] of suspending from the Lords Table, 5. Of Charging the whole body to keep to the rules of Christ, 6. Of taking an account of persons fitness for Church Fellowship, & of the offenders whether their Cases are ripe for the Church judging, either for Convic-

tion, or Absolution, 7. of Calling the Church together, & Propounding matters to the Church. 8. of Ordaining Church Officers Elected: & Excommunicating the obstinate, Condemned; & absolving the penetent, & that officially [29/30] performed. Yet note that I have mentiond Such things as peculiarly fall upon the Teaching Elders: & Severall of them do not ly within the limits of the Ruling Elders office; & some of them also may & ought to be performed *Ex Charitate* out of Brotherly Love one to another as our text implies.

But yet there are Some things that the Ruling officers Cannot doe, viz, no Such acts as are the act of a mixt nature put fourth by the whole body regularly acting. These are Such as neither part alone can put forth. For unless they are put forth by the whole they are no Church acts, as for instance 1. The Rulers cannot receive any person into the Church alone, this Would be to take away all from the Church that belongs to it & is to be exercised by the Brethren, 2. The Ruling Elders Cannot Absolve an offending Brother alone. 3. The Ruling Elders can't Cast any out of the Church alone. Such belong to the whole body. *Quod pertinet ad Censures, debet ab omnibus tracturi.* 4. They Cannot set or ordain officers in the Church without the Church: Each part in these things have a right of acting.

2. The Body of the Church can not put forth by the Brethren, much less can the Brethren, who in most Churches are the smaller number, I say they can't put forth a Church act alone in an organick Church. No act in an organick Church can be without or against the minde of the Ruling Officers ordinarily. Hence their Convening without them, if to act any thing Contrary to their mindes is faction, or disorder if not rebellion: for them to propounde matters to the Church, i.e., to themselves & take a vote as if they were a Church is not warrantable. Its to invade the officers work & to Cast Christs power & Authority out of his own house for such to rise up against officers for the offender whose Case is proved before their eyes to be Sinfull & to declare they are Satisfied with him when he stands before their faces, vindicating his offences as no offences & hath never held out any what of repentance but in a few words that no way express the Case, but a little Sorrow for nobody knows what & this of their own drawing up complying with him, & when he will not admit the offencive matter to be mention'd, etc., is for the brethren to breake Covenant with God & the Church to rise up against Christs officers his authority in them, & to turn them out of their Office, & to Carry the offender on in his im-[30/31]penetency. & so to make the

offenders Sin their own; & hinder such as thus, & this act expose themselves to the wrath of God in so doing & God will judge for the Same.[85]

But such things as these following ought to be Committed to the body of the Church, & when by the officers they are brought to the Church for their Judgment & Consent they are bounde to act & their Suffrage or vote is to be given for or against:

1. In admitting of members: For they that are admitted are made all of one Body & to feed at one Spirituall table & to carry on one & the Same intrest of Christ they are all bounde to see that Such as are admitted by them be persons of the Same Spirit, I John 4.1, Rev. 2.2,20, & accordingly we se the ages succeeding the Apostles Conscientiously seeing into the State & Condition of those that they admitted into their Societies. Hence as you have heard Origen, Christians as much as in them lies examine the minds of their hearers.[86] But this will more appear in the next head, dealing with offenders.

2. For triall of Offenders. These Christ in our text orders them to the Church. & Cyprian saith, When with peace granted to us all by the Lord we begin to return to the church, viz, out from persecution, Every offence shall bee examined, you being present & judging. & those were the brethren.[87] They, [(] that had in time of Persecution fallen) do return dayly & knock at the Church doore: we (saith he) anxiously weighing & soliscitously examining whom ought to be admitted again, & received into the Church. For some there are whose Crimes resist them so that brethren do obstinately & frequently refuse, that they can't be received at all, to the Scandall of many whom for the faith are not so to be chastised as that the sound & whole should be destroyed. Nor if that pastor is not profitable or advised, that mixeth the Diseased & Contageous Sheep with the flock, that is tainted with the distemper of the bad abiding with them. And a little after this he adds, saying, I can hardly perswade or wrest the people that they will permit such to be admitted. And their griefe is so much more juste because one & another, I did thro' my easiness receive the people refusing & gainsaying, who after grew worse than they were before.[88] [31/32]

3. The censures to be given upon the Case both of binding & loosing if this be not matter belonging to the Church, Christ would not order the offence to be brought to the Church And the Church is *nomen multitudinis*, & can't intende onely a part of the Church as the Elders onely: but the *totum Societas*. & the triall is nothing unless the Conclusion be given in, & the Conclusion given in, is the Censure of the Case given in upon a

Suffrage taken wherein the Case is discovered to be found Sinfull & a fault, & so an admonition to be given: & if persevered in an Excommunication is to be passed upon the Same. And if the Conclusion of the triall is Such as goes upon the Case as not Sinfull or offencive, then there is a loosing the person looked on as an offender, or if after Censured or Excommunicated, he repents & makes his *Exhomologesis*, i.e., Confession, which being brought to the Church & the Brethrens a vote is given in that its satisfactory he is released & loosed again.

4. The Producing & Electing of officers & causing them to be Ordained. But here it is to be noted that all Church Acts being of a mixt nature there are required to the same, the acting both of the Rulers & the Ruled. Hence in the acts of Discipline it belongs to the Rulers to propounde the Matter to the Church to take the Votes or Suffrages of the Brethren & to apply the Censures, to the persons whose Case is Condemned by an Authoritative Reproofe, or admonition; or by the laying of the Censure of Excommunication upon the Offender. So did Paul, I Tim. 1, *ult.* & so comanded Timothy, I Tim. 5.14, & Titus, Chap. 3, *ult.* So here culing over & settling them & ordaining officers in their offices, by the Prayers & laying on of the hands of the Elders, so was Timothy ordaind, I Tim. 4.14. & Cyprian is cleare, here touching this. The Ordination of Priests (Elders) ought not to be but by the Conscience of the people assisting, that Crimes of bad men may be detected, & the deserts of the good may be declared & the Ordination may be just & * * * fittly which hath been tried by the Suffrage & judgment of all.[89] [32/33]

5. The Church hath a right & legall Authority to depose their Unworthy officers for their evills either in life or in Doctrin. For the argument will run from the less to the greater, if they have power to withdraw from a brother that walks disorderly, then much more from a disorderly officer. For disorderly walking in an officer is a greater offence in a Church officer than in a brother or sister, & that by so much, by how much the Officer is in a higher place in the Church, than a Comon member. But they are Called to withdraw from a disorderly Brother, II Thess. 3.6. Further its cleare upon that trite maxim, *crisis est Constituere ejusdem est destituere*. There where the right of Constituting lies, there lies the right of making Destitute the Same. Now the Church hath power or right to Electt & Call as appeares in the Calling of Deacons, Acts 6.3,4,5. Now the argument here will run from this Choice of Deacons, to the Choice of other Officers. The reason is the same for

Both. & so also as to deposing or Ejecting out of the relation. If they can put out of their Fellowship an obstinate offender, in membership only, then much more an obstinate offending officer. He that hath right to do the less may also do the greater. & this the Ages Succeeding the Apostles attended. Hence Cyprian is plain saying, the Common People obeying Gods Commands & fearing God ought to Separate themselves from a Sinner that is set over them, & not to mix themselves with the Sacrifices of Sacriligious Priest. Seing they have the greatest power of Choosing the Worthy & of refusing Unworthy Priests. So hee.[90] & hereby its cleare that thus it was in his Day. But this power, or right must be warily & regularly be used. For if all the ruling Officers are Scandalous, there must be some other of the Church delegated in it, by whom it must act, & most orderly in this Case, is to bee with the advice & assistance of neighbour Elders. The Case not being ordinary necessity Warrants to such proceedings that are not warrantable in Ordinary Cases. Thus Much touching the Church. [33/34]

Secondly What is intended by this injunction of Christ Saying, Tell it to the Church?

Sol: It may be Considered here whether it is an Injunction Commanding or onely a bare Direction, shewing us in such Cases, & this being Considered, I shall answere the Enquiry therefore

1. First touching the nature of this Proposition, Tell it to the Church. Whether it be a Comanded Duty, or a Bare Direction, in which Consideration, it is to be known of what sort the Offence is of. If the Offence be of the Nature of a Morall Evill, which the offender is fallen into, & he is treated according to the former order given in the Former verses then the offender abiding obstinate under his Sin, the spirituall Leprosy is upon him: Hee must either be Cured or shut out of the camp, Eph. 5.8. Now he that doth not endeavour his Cure Consents with him in his Evill to let it alone, & to let the leper lodge in the Camp which is to defile the whole & to bring a Slander upon the Church as if it was an hiding place for impenetent Sinners, yet pretending itselfe to be a Society of visible Saints, & that the Church either fails the Duty which She professes, or else Christ is defective in his institutions not having given her any Rulers or Authority sufficient to keep herselfe Clean or to purge her house all which are false therefore in respect to such sinners of her Society this proposition is both an Injunction & a Direction too. But if the matter of offence is a matter of humane weakness onely, which the best of the

saints of God using their best watchfulness against are liable to & oft are surprized into, these ought to be Covered over with love: its enough in such Cases to testify against them in saying they are not right & shewing a Dislike against the same: Christ did but so unto his sleepy Disciples, Matt. 26, who faild in the very matter that he set them about. But where the offence is of a scandalous nature & must be purged, as Drunkeness, Uncleanness, Oppressing Unrighteousness, Sclander, Lying, Abusive Striking, Cursing, Swearing, Stealing, Sabbath breaking, Heresy, etc., this Maxim is both an Injunction requiring, & a direction shewing how the Case is to be brought to the Church. And these things Con-[34/35]sidered, I shall shew the way in which the matter is to bee brought to the Church. For these words do not onely require the matter, that can't be taken up other wayes, to be brought to the Court, to be Authoritatively determined by the Church but the manner how it is to be done. Now the Direction implicitly contain in it, as a Command in such Cases, is, that the matter is to be brought to the Church according to the Orders of Gods House. For Christs Kingdom is well ordered in all things. This David glories in, II Sam. 23.5. & hence Christ saith, I Cor. 14, *ult.*, Let all things be done decently, & in order. Hence

1. Every one may not Start up & pop his grievences oute to the Church himselfe alone. So doing is not according to Order, & if anyone be so voide of good manners, in Gods Court, & impudently brazenfaced the Church ought not to meddle therewith. Christ hath Ordained Rulers for the bringing matters to the Church: If any one bring any Case to the Church & not by them he presumes against Christs Authority in the Church & turns his Officers out of their office that Christ hath put them into. & so to do is audacious presumption: & tends to utter Confusion, & makes her a Court to satisfy the malice of wicked designs, to execute upon the Object of their malice, their revenge in bringing the same out to Open Shame, & not to true repentance. & yet here is frequently pleaded Conscience to bring the offender off from Sin by Repentance, when indeed it is manifestly cleare, that its nothing but ill will moves the prosecutor, acting upon a design to bring the person under visible shame. Hence
2. The Offence is to be brought to the Church by the Rulers of the Church. All Elders are Rulers, but if there be such an Elder whose office is onely Ruling it properly belongs to him to bring it to the Church. But men [not] suitably qualified for the Office of Ruling, & to put persons

unfit for it, experience doth proove them to do more hurt than good. There are very few Churches with us now that have any such officer, but in such Churches that have such, the Offences are to be delivered to the Elders that are teachers, For Rule is in their hand also: & they are to bring it to the Church, if they judge it fit to be brought to the Church: For they have their par-[35/36]ticular office judgment, which is to be exercised about all things that belong to their Office. Otherwise the Officer is not required by God to act in his office according to his judgment but the judgment that he must act by lies in an other mans breast, neither are his office exercise to him any matter belonging to his own Conscience, because he is not to exercise any of his own judgment thereabout. Hence on this point denying Elders their Office judgment Church Officers are made most like blinde Biardin a mill passing his rounde not by the guidance of his own Eyes, but by the Eyes of his driver.[91] & so every perverse spirit bringing to them must be a warrant to them to bring the same to the Church. But there is no such thing of Confusion, & mischief in Christs house. Hence the Elders the Rulers in Christs house must have their Office judgment upon the matters brought to the Church, whether they are fit to bee brought to the Church, or not under the present Circumstances either of the Matter, or of the Church, as 1. In case the matter offencive is more Humane infirmities which are founde in the Best of Gods Saints, & so belong not to Church Censures, & to lay the person being not able to be Convicted that such things ought to be brought to give Ecclesiasticall satisfaction, cant be Charged with obstinacy in not doing it, & hence the Case must fall now, or the person Censured for such a matter as will not beare the Censures. So 2^ly, In case its manifest that its managed not to bring the offender to Repentance, nor to Cleare the Church from Scandall, but in a way of ill will & Malice under the pretence of Conscience, for in such Cases the Design of Christs Rule is not attended, but the Design of Satan to cast dirt upon a Child of God, & that by Christs Rule by making a pretense to his rule the reason of such things that are transgressions against Christ, 3. When the matter produced as offencive is a matter that in a prudent Conjecture is such as will hazzard the peace of the Church: But if the Matters are such as a Conscientious Elder Can't in Conscience bring to the Church & yet scandalous, it will be his Wisdom to advise with other Elders about them: & if possible, take them up another way. & if the offence be morall Sin & Evidenced & yet under appearance of being mischievous in the Church, he had better [36/37] in my judgment

Suspend the Offender from the Lords Table by his Pastorall, or Office power till the church is under better Circumstances to try his Case. He hath Evidence Convictive of the fact upon the Offender why he ought not to approach the Ordinance, unrepented of. His Office power will warrant him in Suspending of him, & his prudence in not bringing Such an hazzardous Case to the Church in her sickly state will pleade for him as a piece of good Wisdom. Now these things or such like matters being warily Considered, being out of the way, the Officer is to spread the Case before the Church.

1. Query. How if the Church will not admit it. Probablie there may be reason under due Circumstances to reject some Cases. Yet these very sildom if ever have fallen out. But if the Church hath not good reason so to do she sins against Christ in denying a Speciall means of grace to his Disciples. But if she so do & the offence is made out to the Rulers the Pastor or Teacher may & ought to deny such the seale unless he give a manifestation of his Repentance of his Sin. For it is not in the power of the Church or Members to impose upon the Rulers or constrain them to exercise office acts upon any person whom they judge, as officers, not to be the Subjects recipient of such acts.

Query. But what should the person do that brings the Complaint to the Church in Case the Church admits it not, or judges not aright? Or in case the Elders will not bring it to the Church?

Sol: 1. Such may if they please Call a Councill in the Case. 2. or they may Complain to other neighbour Churches & desire them to search into their Case & advise them in the same Cases what is their Duties. Thus either they may do.

Thirdly. Why is it thus that such offences that Can't be taken up in Secret nor privately are to be brought to the Church?

Sol: 1. Because Christ doth give forth Laws by which his Kingdom is to be Regulated. No Kingdom can be regulated or govern'd without laws, Christs kingdom is the best kingdom which is. Hence it must be ennobled by the best Laws which is. & if these Laws be transgressed, & these transgressions can't be issued in Secret, there must be some Courts erected to determine Such Cases or else Such offences are not inj-[37/38]urious to the Laws & Welfare & entrest of the kingdom. But to imagine the transgression of any Law to be no injury to that Law, nor intrest of the Kingdom is implicitly to mentain that Such Laws are not suted to the welfare or benefit of the Kingdom, & that they are not just or Good, & better broken than kept. But no man that owns Christ to be Lord can the least admit of any such Conclusion touching the Lawe of Christs Kingdom. Shall the true Melchizedeck, the King of Righteousness not give his subjects suitable & Righteous Laws? or that the Laws of his Kingdom are not good for his Kingdom, nor righteous? But if his Laws are Suitable, good, & Righteous, they are to be mentaind & looked after that if they be transgresst the transgressours are to be punished according to the Law. Thinke of this. Hence Courts are erected in Kingdoms to keep transgressours down, & so it is in Christs Kingdom. Christ hath erected particular Churches as his Visible Courts to try the Cases of his people that are visibly offencive before & Can not be issued in a more secret or private way & these are particular Churches as is manifest in our text. Tell itt to the Church: Ergo.

2. Because Christ hath accomplisht the Particular Church with whatever is necessary to determine all such offences. He hath given it the Keys of his Kingdom, Matt. 16.19. I will give unto thee the Keyes of the Kingdom of Heaven, etc. If it be said that this authority was given to Peter onely, I say that there is no reason so to thinke, for then when Peter died, he carried the Keys along with him & so all power of the Keyes was buried in his grave, & there remain'd untill Pope Gregory found them in Peter's grave & so the Pope pleads that all the Power of the Keys is in their hands ever since. But indeed Peter received them as personating the Church: & hence the power is by Christ given to the Church, therefore Christ in our Text orders the Case to be brought to the Church. & makes a promise to the Disciples to give them this power of Binding & loosing, Matt. 18.18,19, John 20.23, & blaims the Church of Corinth for not exercising of it, I Cor. 5.5,12. He hath Sett rulers here to judge, I Cor. 12.28. We finde Church Rulers Carrying on the rule onely in particular Churches in the Scripture & nowhere Else. Hence it is that matters of Sin in Christs Kingdom when they can't be any other wayes issued must be brought to particular Churches to be determined, or else must be let alone in his [38/39] Kingdom. But Sinners are not to be let alone in his Kingdom. Christs Scepter is a Scepter of Righteousness, as Heb. 1.8,9, he loves Righteousness & hates wickedness. Therefore God anointed him, Ps. 45.7,8. & hence the unrighteous shall not inherit the Kingdom of Heaven, I Cor. 6.8,9. & God forbids his to eate

with such, I Cor. 5.11, & to have no Communion with the works of Darkness, Eph. 5.11. & therefore Particular Churches are referr'd to. The matter is to be brought to them.

3. Because All those Duties wherein the Speciall authority of Christ is exerted are peculiarly put forth in particular Churches. Now there where is Seated & exercised all Authoritative Exercise that Christ hath ordered to be Carried on, thither the offences of his people, that Can not elsewhere be issued, are to be brought, to be determined. For the Determination of such Cases is an act of Power, & Authority. For when the offender, or offended, are either of them so pervers, as that they will admit of no terms of Reconciliation in a peaceable way in private, they Carry for the most part their own pervers spirits with the matter Committed to the Church: & therefore if the Determination that the Church gives in upon the Case, be against them they would still be as before & will not heare the Church, as is the Case supposed in our text. & hence saith Christ let him be to thee as an Hethen man: etc., let the Church determine it. Here is the Authority of Christ in this determination.

But now all Authoritative Acts of an Ecclesiasticall nature are such as are to be Carried on in particular Churches, such as are to carry on such acts are Seated in particular Churches as Authoritative Preaching, Authoritative Exhortations, Authoritative Reproofes, Admissions, Admonitions, & Excommunications, & Absolutions, Acts 20.28. They are all carried on by the Rulers of the Church & these are nowhere to be found but as they are the officers of Particular Churches. Loosen this pin & you will Confirm the proceedings unto Reproofs, Admonitions & Excommunications of Dioscessans, Metropolitans, if not Abbotts, & Popes to be of Divine Authority. Say not that the Apostles did Carry on all these Authoritative action & Exercises, & yet were not seated in any Particular Churches. For tho' they were examplary in the manner of their doing yet they were not in their Offices for they & Evangelists were extraordinary officers [39/40] & as such Christ invested them with extraordinary power so that they had more than an Ecclesiasticall Authority, they were to gather the Evangelicall Churches & teach them their duties, & go before them in all workes, & ordain their Pastors, & teachers: not waiting for their Call to them but to Call them to their worke of ordaining of their Officers. But if this office of Apostlship, or of Evangelists had been necessary to have Continued, there should not have been ordered such Officers as should be fixt & settled in particular Churches as we Se not onely our particular officers at this day, but so upwards ever Since the Deaths of the Apostles & Evangelists. Yea, & such so seated in their particular Cure by the Apostles, as Acts 14.22, Eph. 20.17,28, & Titus 1.5, & Rev. 2–3 Chaps.

If it be said, that the Extraordinary, & Ordinary Officers are seated in the same Church, I Cor. 12.31, & this was the Catholick Church & not any Particular Church: for the Apostles, etc., were not fixt in any particular Church, & hence, Ordinary officers standing in the Catholick Church doth not prove that in that their worke is Authoritative, that the Particular Church have seated in them all Authoritative Worke.

Ans: 1. That which is Called Catholick Church, or Church Militant is styled Church not properly but onely *Secundum quid*, & in some Consideration, viz, as Collectively Considered united in one & the intrest & Profession, but as such they can never perform any Church Exercise, all Ecclesiasticall Duties of this Body of Men ever scattered up & down & all over the world & can never come together are Carried on in particular Churches. Deny all particular Churches, & there Can't be found any Ecclesiasticall duty Carried on in the world. Hence

2. Tho' the Extraordinary & Ordinary Officers are seated in the same Church, yet not in the same way & manner. For the Apostles were seated & sent out by Christ as seated in his intrest before any particular Gospell Church was gathered, to Call & gather & Constitute Gospell Churches & hence received their Call, Office, & Authoritie from Christ immediatly. & not from any Particular Church. Hence their Office Can't be limited objectively. & their Authority is answerable to their Office. & so they could exercise their Office Authoritatively in any Particular [40/41] Church. But the Case is quite otherwise with Ordinary Officers. For the Particular Churches are before them, they are Called, & put into their Offices by particular Churches & are seated in that Particular Church that Calls them for the extent of their Office can't be beyond their Call, neither can they exercise their Office over such that are not of that particular Body that subjected themselves under him in their Call. & seing these particular Churches are all of the same nature; they are each distinct one from another, & have no power one over another; but Stand of an Equall height endow'd with Equall Priviledges one as another, one Call of an officer for itselfe, can't be a Call upon its officer for an other Church. & hence Particular Churches have a particular propriety in their own particular Officers, & their particular officers in them. & hence the spirit of God styles each Particular Officer according to his particular right & propriety mutuall between them as the Angell

of the Church at Ephesus, & the Angell of the Church at Smyrna, etc., Rev. 2. So a Servant of the Church at Cyncrea, Rom. 16.1. Now every Particular Church being a Part of the Catholick Church, he that is seated in the Particular Church is seated in the Catholick. & hence the Extraordinary Officers & the Ordinary officers are seated in the Same Catholick Church but not in the same manner of way. For the Extraordinary were imediatly sent out by Christ to Carry on the intrest of the Gospell among all people, which intrest as it is received is onely calld the Church Catachrestically & in some Sense. & the Ordinary officers are seated in the same intrest calld the Catholick Church catechrestically. I say they are seated therein *mediurle Ecclesia particulari*. Hence this matter being thus I return & affirm that there is no Ecclesiasticall Authority from Christ since the Apostles dayes ever exercised but in particular Churchs. But in particular Organick Churches is exercised all Ecclesiasticall Authority under Christ, as the Preaching the word as at Jerusalem, Acts 2. Admission into Church Fellowship, v. 40,41, Administring the Lords Supper, v. 41,46, Acts 20.7, so at Corinth, II Cor. 11, so admonition, II Thess. 3.5, Excommunication, I Cor. 5.5,12, & absolving the penetent, II Cor. 2. [41/42] So that all Ecclesiasticall Authority being exercised in a particular Church it must needs be that a Particular Church is the seate also of Church Censures & this alone. & hence such offences as Can't be taken up in private according to the rules of the Gospell, are to be brought to the Gospell Church to which the offender belongs to be determined by it.

4. Because all the means of Grace ordain'd to bring Gods children to repentance & reformation of what is amiss in them are not carried on upon them till they are brought to answer for their offences manifested before the Church in which they have a particular right as members. For the judging & Censures of the Church are speciall means of Grace to be carried on in that Society of Church fellowship to which they belong. & Christ requires that all the means of Grace that he hath ordain'd to bring his people from their visible falls be made use of to reclaim them, nothing must be held back. Now the Censures of the Church are ordaind for this end, as well as the Calls of the word. The rod & Reproofe give wisdom, Prov. 29.15. If you be with out this Chastening as well as that of affliction, Heb. 12.6, where of all (erring Children) are partakers, then are you bastards & not sons. Hence Christ in our text ordains this Course to fetch back his erring Sheep upon the mountain, as it & its Context is manifest, & it was the means of Grace that did

reduce & bring to repentance that person on whom it was laid, II Cor. 2.6,7. But now upon this matter it is cleare that the Offence must be brought to the church. For *de non auditie non judicat Ecclesiae.* Hence saith Christ, tell it to the Church.

USE 1. For Information. Seing this is so that Church members that offend, & Cant be reconciled in private are to be brought to the Church to be judged, then

1. We may hence se that the Best Societies of People under Heaven have Some persons among them that are very sinfull & perverse, that are a Scandall unto the Societies & Churches whereof they are members. Of all Societies in the whole world, that society is the best where in is to be found no fault but all Excellent things, & hence the Church triumphant is the most Excellent Society which is, for there is no Spot in it, but all [42/43] glorious, Eph. 15.27, out shining the Sun in the firmament, Matt. 13.43, & the nextt is the Church Militant who yet hath spots in her, Cant. 6.4,10. The moon hath Spots. The best Societies of the Militant Church oft if not always have some transgressing the Laws of the Kingdom. Hence the King of this kingdom hath laws peculiarly put forth to deale with Such. Here are laws most excellent of which Some are to reduce them if it can be in private by repentance which if these effect not the matter, they must be prosecuted in Courts he hath erected to issue the matter, either by bringing them to repentance, or if that is not effected, to remove them out of the Society, as in our text & Context is Cleare. Now in vain is there a provision of Laws made touching Such concerns as are impossible ever to be. Hence some there are that are visible transgressours in the Best Societies on Earth. The tares are among the Wheate in the field till the Harvest, Matt. 13. Some seed fell upon the High Way, & some on rocks, some among thorns as well as some on good ground. There was a Cursed Serpent in paradise, a Cursed Cain in Adams Church, a Cursed Ham in Noahs arch, a Corah & his Companies in the Church in the Wilderness, a Judas in Christs flock, the Nicholaitan Crew in the Church at Ephesus & Some blaphemous in the Church at Smyrna, some Balaamites & Nicholaitans in the Church at Pergamus, some Jezabel & idolatrous in the Church at Thytria, a Spirituall Death prevailing among them at Sardus, some of the Synagogue of Satan & lyars heaving upon the Church at Philadelphia, & a Company of Neuters Lukewarm bosters in the Church at Laodicea, Rev. 2, & 3 Chapters. In the Church at Rome many Carnall, & many

Legalists, in the Church at Corinth some Lascivious, some Sensualists, in the Churches at Galatia, some given to Jewdaism, & Hypocrisy, in the Church at Philippi, some of Concision, & Belly Gods in the church at Colloss, some time servers & Philosophy mongers. & in the church at Thessalonica some workings of the man of Sin & the Mystery of iniquity. & the Churches tho' after they were increased yet they waxed more Corrupt from the Apostles days & more superstitious. So that there is no societies but what have Some frequently that sin against the laws of the societies & So in the Churches of Christ we see Christ lay in against such either to reform or reject them [43/44] either to better them or banish them, either to bring them to repentance for their Sin, or to expell them for their impenitancy in Sin.

2. Hence we See that the Churches of Christ are not to Consist of Impenitant but of Penitant sinners, if sin appear in their Members they are to be treated with privatly to bring them to repentance of that Sin: for in their admission they manifested their repentance, or else they could not be admitted. John Baptist would not baptise but upon the Confession of sins, Matt. 3.4,5,6,7. The kingdom of Heaven is founded upon Repentance, Matt. 3.2, & Chap. 4.17. Repent for the Kingdom of Heaven is at hand. The Concerns of this Kingdom in the Visible application of them are founded upon visible repentance. Its a foundation Grace of this Kingdom, Heb. 6.11, it calls for repentance of all them it admits: & if when they are admitted sin that is not Such as if merely of Humane Infirmities, but of the nature of morall Evill, they are to be treated with, to bring them to a sight of their sin to repentance but if this be not attain'd thereby, the matter is to be laid before the Church. & if so, then the Church is not to permit such in their Society unless they repent, for if they heare not the Church, they are to be reputed as Heathens & publicans, i.e., put out of Church Fellowship. The Churches of Christ therefore are not to beare with visible impenitants in her bowells. They will be as gangrenes in the body, *abundare morbida totus grex insititur*, saith Origen, One Scald sheep infects the whole flock.[92] If a person in the society abides in impenitancy but for one Single Sin, he is not to be permitted to abide in the Fellowship of the Church, can it be imagined by any sounde reason, that persons may be admitted into the Fellowship of the Church in a State of impenitancy, or with out manifest Repentance. John Baptist would [not] admit such without manifesting of it by fruits evidencing it, their pleading Covenant right as Abrahams Seed was not sufficient in his judgment, Matt. 3.7,8,9. All that are

admitted into Church fellowship are admitted *sub forma Penetentium,* under the form of Penitents, & therefore it must be manifested to rationall Charity. For repentance is not a fruite of nature, but Gospell grace, which if it be not in the Soule the person that is admitted today may manifest that he [44/45] hath it not to morrow, by falling into some manifest transgression, which he refusing to manifest his repentance of may be brought to the Church forthwith, for he may still shew impenitency & so for the want of the same may Soon be Cast out again. & thus we See what Church work doing & undoing follows in case impenitant persons, as such, as not evidencing their repentance be admitted into Church fellowship; surely such as are not to be permitted, when in, are not to be admitted when out. Now repentance being a gospell Sanctifying Grace if it be requisite to Church fellowship, then sanctifying Grace is absolutely necessary to Church membership, for the duties of Church fellowship require it; the Brethren are admitted by the same to be members of Christs Spirituall Courts; & they will oft proove respecters of persons & unfaithfull upon his bench if the true feare of God be not in their hearts. They are [not] to Sitt at Christs spirituall banquet & at the Lords table without it, this will not be attended Honourably, without the Wedden Garment, true Grace, Matt. 22.12, nor can they eate of the Heavenly Mannah, Angells food Without a Spirituall appetite. & this is none of Nature's procuring, I Cor. 2.14. Its the Work of true faith, Rom. 1.16.

3. Hence we may see that Every Gospell Church is the Gospel seate of all matters of Ecclesiasticall Discipline. Where Christ orders the matters to be issued, there he hath given power & Authority to issue & determine the matters. & this you see is the Church. He would not send the offended with the offender that will not comply with the offended to the Church if the Church had no power to issue the Cases that he orders to be brought to her. He would not order the person that hears not the Church to be accounted as an Heathen or a Publican, if there was any appeale to be allowed to any Superiour Court, or if the Church had not full power & Authority given her by Christ to issue the matter. So that we see hence that the Church is the Sole determiner of matters of Discipline belonging to herselfe. Here is nothing further to be done after the Church hath given in her Conclusion, & the offender hears it not, but that he is to be held as an Heathen man & a publican. Hence the [45/46] Gospell Church is the Seate, & onely Court to heare & to determine all Controversies that fall in belonging to the Discipline due

to her members. None but she hath the authority to Call up, & judge her members ecclesiastically, or with an Ecclesiasticall judgment. Christ sends them to none other Court therefore she alone decides the Case. If light be wanting she must Seeke it, but the issuing the matter lieth in her hands. Councills are onely to give light, & to be helpfull; but as to any judiciall sentence Christ hath not given them any warrant to pass any such act upon any one. They may advise & perswade to what is right: but Christ doth not warrant them to judge any ecclesiastically.

4. Hence we See that a greate weight lies upon particular Churches, & Christ takes it for granted that they will issue the Controversies of Discipline aright: there are very many matters of Discipline that belong to the Church as Admission of Members, Calling, Electing & Ordaining Officers, hearing & judging of offenders, Condemning & Ejecting the obstinate, Absolving & acquitting the Innocent & Penetent. If Christ did not expect faithfullness in his Churches in these matters, he would never have sent the offender to have his Case issued in & by his Churches. Righteous judgment in Civill Courts he expects: but if in the place of judgment, either Civill, or Ecclesiasticall, wickedness is there, & in the place of righteousness, iniquity be there its bad. (Oh! saith Solomon upon this observation) I said in my heart God shall judge both the righteous & the wicked for there is a time there for every purpose, & for every worke, Eccl. 3.16,17. God will be avenged upon such dealing. But if Christ did not expect all righteous dealings both in admitting & in determining matters, it would not be according to justice in Christ to send Cases to be tried to the Church, nor could it be a righteous thing to so order the offender, in case he accept not of the Conclusion made, to have no other where to bring his matter; but is to be accounted for an Heathen, & a Publican. The very ordering the Case to be brought to the Church, & much more that he is to be accounted an Heathen & a publican that neglect the Churches Conclusion, do strongly suppose that the Church hath [46/47] Authority to act & issue her own Cases of Discipline & that She will act it righteously.

5. Hence see that Case, determined aright by a Church, that are properly her own work, are to be acquiest in: You are to sitt down with the Righteous sentence that the Church makes of the Case. In your differences about offences, you are seeking Righteous Conclusions about the nature of the offence if it be an evill either essentially, or Circumstantially, i.e., a transgression or sin, in its own nature as being against Some rule of Gods word, or by reason of some Circumstance & so is to be

repented of, the offended he judges it is, & so would have its author to manifest his repentance of it. & if it be not repented of, it is a justifying of Sin, & he that refuses to repent of it either saith its not Sin: or that all Sin is not to be repented of, & so rejects the Call of the Gospell, & grows harden'd in Sin. But saith he it is not Sin & so not to be repented of. For to repent of what is not Sin is to make myselfe a sinner, & that to be Sin which is a righteous thing, neither of which I can do but in so doing I abuse my own Conscience, & the Rule. This plea is oft made Craftily by perverse persons Concluding that proofe of its Sinfulness will be hardly made, & so they harden themselves in sin, tho' sometimes its a righteous plea of a Child of God. Hence the Enquiry is made to finde out what is right in the Case, & so its brought to the Church to determine, the Church upon Search into the matter, gives in the Conclusion. Suppose against the authour & declares that he hath sind, & that Rightly the offender ought to accept of the Conclusion & repent. Suppose the Conclusion comes to cleare the person offending, that he hath not offended the rule as to any Evidence thereof, the prosecutor is to be Satisfied, till better evidence appear For the Church is the last, nay the onely Court, of Christ to hear & determine. Its an unrighteous thing not to sit down with this righteous sentence. He that heares not acts like an Heathen, & is to be so esteemd; He charges Christs Court [47/48] with unjustice, & this is an High Charge & greatly offencive to Christ. & its unreasonable in any ordinarie Case to be unquiet unless a Councill be calld upon the matter, & perhaps the sentence of a Councill will be as uneasy to the offender as the Conclusion of the Church. If Christ sends you to this Court & none other: but determines you to be unto others as an Heathen & a publican, if you heare not her issue of the Case You are bound to accept of the issue she brings, or she must put you out of her Fellowship as Heathens & Publicans are.

6. Hence se that the Churches of Christ are to be well versed & studious of the Laws of Christ's house & to be tender Conscienced, that they may not erre in judgment. A Court that is to heare & determine, are not to be ignorant of the law: they must judg Righteous judgment, Ps. 72.1,2, the prayer is thus, give the King thy judgment, oh God! & thy righteousness unto the Kings Son: He shall judge thy people with righteousness & thy poore with judgment. It is said of Jerusalem, Isa. 1.21, that it was full of judgment, Righteousness lodged in it. Righteous judgment must abide here. Here our king the Melchizedeck King of Righteousness sits & in this his Throne judging right, Ps. 82.1, you must

therefore study his Laws, that you may be accomplisht to give righteous judgment in all Cases that are brought to the Court: You can not do this unless you be acquainted with his Laws & your Conclusion is matter of great Consequence, it will wrong Christs disciples & Court too to give an unjust conclusion.

USE 2. By Way of Conviction to all Churches upon severall Failings in this matter. There is great sin oft appears in members, yea in the body of the Fraternity, & in the Whole Body, whereby Christ is dishonoured, & his Churches sclandered thro' the perversness of Some humorsom persons they can't see, as its presented, & their blindness must be the light of the whole, or there will be greate Clamors, if not Convulsions in the Body, & Such are ready by their perversness [48/49] & shamelessness to rise up against the Elders & oppose them. If the Rulers miss it, they may be discourst in private, or help may be gaind of other Elders being desired to enquire into the matter, or by a Councill but audacious dealing & rising up against them yea, and plotting with the Offender whose case is laid before the Church, as matters offencive & so prooved, is great rebellion against Christ & his Authority, let these persons be never so greate, aged or of Civill Authority. & Christ will be offended hereat, & often powres out Divine judgments for such abuse of his Grace & Authority.

The Failings or male administration may bee supposed to bee in order to $\begin{cases} \text{Admissions} \\ \text{Persons admitted.} \end{cases}$

First. As to admission of Members into their Societie: or of Persons into office. Here is required the acting of the Church by the Suffrage of the Fraternity & often times now about Satan is very busy: for if he can prevaile to disorderly proceeding he damnifies the Charity that should prevaile in the Society: & brings a Scandall upon the Church. The Church ought to be very wary, & Conscientiously diligent in this matter. It is the bringing in, or Shutting out persons of Christs house. To keep out such as ought to be admitted, or to receive such as ought to be kept out, is greate evill in the sight of God, to refuse such as Christ hath received, or to receive such as Christ refuses, is a great unfaithfulness in the Church: & an abuse of Christs Authority in her hands. To receive such as do not heare the Church is to receive such, as if they were in, were to be turned out by our text. & such are all impenitent persons.

And such as are received of the Fraternity, are made hereby members of Christs Ecclesiasticall Court of judgment to judge offenders. & how can Such that are impenitant, judge impenetence? that are ignorant of spirituall things? I Cor. 2.14. Or be faithfull in this matter to Christ, when they are unfaithfull touching judging [49/50] of their own Souls. Hypocrites in heart such as crowd themselves in by hand & Shoulders, & never know what repentance is, can't be expected to judge right touching others. & yet Some there are are ready to thrust open doores to let all in, or all that rowle not with the Sow in the mire of all vice. These make the gates of Zion so wide that whole herds of Swine may come rushing in to the Holy place & regard not that of Christ, Matt. 3.12, that he will throughly purg his floore. But still there is also failing on the other hand, when persons are so penuriously Severe either by a misguided Zeale, or thro' prejudice & illwill oppose Such where there is no grounde to oppose. These make the Doores of Gods house as small as the Eye of the Needle, & can hardly be entred by Gods Children. Some uncharitable members are so humorsom, that altho' there are sufficient demonstrations of Repentance & the Feare of God, yet rumblings create difficulties, that are dishonourable to the intrest of the Church: Discouraging to Humble penetants, displeasing unto Christ & damnifying to His Visible Intrest, & such things as these may be the Circumstances of a Church either in admitting persons in to Church Fellowship, or in Electing of Officers.

2. Secondly. Matters may be matters of Reproofe in dealing with such as are admitted: Members may & oft do offend. & here offences oft are many, as disorderly walking of members. Some there often appeare that they are Enemies to the Cross of Christ as those Phil. 3.18,19, whose end is destruction, whose God is their Bellies, whose glory is in their Shame, who minde Earthly things. Those make Church worke & Church faults. Some looke not after them, as that Church that Sufferd the Woman Jezabel to Seduce Gods Children, Rev. 2.20. Some either too little, some not enough, some are too rigid; & in all there is fault. Not to act in such Cases is to faile the Covenant with God & the Church as the Church of Thyatira; to do too little; as the Churches of Affrica, who had their members that apostatised in time of per-[50/51]secution, whom they advised to repent: but would hardly be perswaded ever to receive them again into their Communion. Against which errour Cyprian did greatly labour as is manifest by his Epistles. On the other hand some are so remiss that they do not bring Such as fall into manifest

Sin, that they bring them not up to the rule: nay tho' their Sin is evidenced in the face of the Church, are ready either not to act & so to breake their Covenant with God & the Church: or to Complot with the offender upon terms below the rule, & accept of such Confessions of sin as falls short of Repentance, which Compared with Pharaohs, Ex. 10.16, who said, I have Sinned against the Lord your God & against you. Now therefore forgive I pray thee my Sin, onely this once & entreate the Lord your God that he may take a way from me, this Death also. & also with Simon Magus, his Acts 8.24, who said pray ye to the Lord for me that none of these things may come upon me, I say, these Pagan Confessions will appear far more like Gospell repentance, than what some of Church members give in as matters of Confessions when cleare proofe is made of their Sins, & yet they perversly will drive without feare, or shame the acceptance of such sorry matter, as if such Straind words were Gospell Repentance, & that Christ had promised to loose in Heaven Such as a Church should loose on Earth upon Saying such words. God will judge such judges. Still here is another fault in this matter in my judgment, & it seems to me universall, viz, over hasty acceptance of Confessions given in, as soon as a Confession is given in & read, if it is accepted the person is presently absolved, which frequently tends to harden the Offender, before he is absolved & received I thinke it would be better to do as they in primitive times did, take time to try whether the person walkes penetantly or no before he is acquitted. This hastiness [51/52] in this matter, tho' where there is Shining forth & Humbel Frame of spirit under the Sense of his Sin, & Sinking under it, it is justifiable, Yet where the person carries it haughtily proudly, & yields no further than he is drove by force of argument to Confess, there can hardly be any Conscience Convicted that there is any repentance of any Sin. For its the property of true repentance to keep a Sense of Sin so upon the soule that Causes the soule to ly very low in its selfe, & judge that it can never ly low enough.

So some times there may be too great severity, persons may be too hardly dealt with all. The person offending may be much broken for his Sin, & ly very low & humble under the sense thereof, So that the Church can't tell in what they can bring him higher; & yet hold off from the Duty of absolving him, but keep him under Such a hard hand as is greatly Distressing. This was the dealing of the Church of Corinth with that Sorrowfull & penitant person that you read of in II Cor. 2. He was almost swallowed up with sorrow. This indeed is to be over much righteous, i.e., to require more than the Rule requires, & than Christ Calls for, & hence an errour to be reproved.

So again such a Church is in a grievous Fault who, when the Case offencive is laid before them & evidenced, & they are Calld to act, the brethren let the Case fall & will not act neither pro, nor Contra; this is not consistant to the Covenant duty which is to Carry on Duty of Discipline against visible offenders. But may be here is Worse Still: here is a plotting with the Offender, & taking his Case, plead, & mentain, some surly, or Humorsom, or Soure rises up & pleads his Case & partly by Soureness, & partly by perversness over powers the rest of the brethren, & for that end have meeting set & come together, & perhaps the offender by his guilefull tongue hath jugled & wimbled in Severall one or more ministers of other Churches to humor him too far in the matter that never heare the Case but from the offenders lips, whom he now presents as deserting the ruler of the Church & that will not be as he is, when they are calld to heare & help in the Case & [52/53] thus He gathers the brethren into unwarrantable & Disorderly Coventicles & with one or two soure & Masterly persons on his side over powers the rest that are in their Age, parts & abilities & sway in their places in fervour to Comply with them against the proceedings of their Rulers, & to cloake the whole with a shew do receive an acknowledgment of him that he shall say he is sorry for nobody knows what, which no way answering the rule requiring repentance, & when the Ruler of the Church can't with a Safe Conscience propounde it to the Church for their Concurrance, they rise up in a disorderly way one by one after a bold face hath said he is Satisfied, & so it runs through whole, & thus they rise up & run Christs authority out of doors, that is in the hand of his officers, & the End of Churchood as to Church-discipline, yea & is distructive to all Church Discipline, a few Factious, humorsom, Soure persons will receive in, keep in, & impose thereby, upon the Pastor of the Church whom they please, & so prevent a Conscientious Pastor or Teacher from his office as to any Discipline or from Administering the Lords Supper unless he will do as they please which thing is so Contrary to their Covenentall duty, that it will wounde the Conscience of any Godly Pastor, to administer the Lords Supper to any Such brethren. So that all such brethren that thus Conspire with the Offender, Whose Case is brought & prooved before the Church, I see not how they can be admitted to the Sacrament before they acknowledg their Sin. Such a brotherhood deserve the Censures of the Church. For they put their teaching officers either to do that that they Cannot answer for before Christ; or else to desist their Office & leave the Church. Such things therefore make Sport for the powers of Darkness: & Sorrows among the Children of God. God will be offended & avenge himselfe of the quarrell of his Covenantt. Shall such a Brotherhood be Christs tribunall upon Earth, that he sends his offending disciples to to be judged at. Nay he will spew such Churches out of his mouth [53/54] Except they repent & reform, Rev. 2.5, & Chap. 3.15,16.

USE 3ᵈ For Caution, & Exhortation, is a particular Church the Seate to which an offending Church member thereof not brought to repentance by private treating is to be brought to have the matter issued? Then let this be

1. A Caution & Call to all to have a Care. 1. Not to stumble at the sins of Church Members. These are grounds of Lamentation, but woe to such as Stumble here at. There's no man on Earth is Secured from Sin, Jas. 3.3. We all very much offend. This World is a Sinfull, therefore a sinning place. & there is no man on Earth but hath his Spots, Deut. 32, & he that looks for church members to be as bright as the Holy Angells shall looke till his eyes Ach before he finde such nor a Church on Earth wherein Satan hath no intrest. Indeed these blots, & blurs are Shamefull, & occasion the falls of many: & hinder many persons Charity; & open many foule mouths to bespatter Gods Heretage with durty revilings: yea & lower the Endeavours of many from labouring after Sanctifying Grace & lower their thoughts of Church Members & of Churchood. But oh! have a Care of these things. Let not the Faults of Church members nor the Failings of Churchs in their Duties be such impregnable Rocks in the Fluctuating & turbulant sea of this unquiet world at which & against which you dash, stave to pieces, & Shipwrack your Stately Vessel as it is Sayling to the Holy Land calld, Luke 16.22, τὸν κόλπον Ἀβραάυ, Abrahams Bay, in which he landed safely. But if you bee by these rocks shipwrackt & swallowd up in these waves you are Surely Cast away & will never touch nor come at that glorious Land of Promise. Have a care therefore of these rocks & bewaile them: & look better to yourselves & Strive to be better persons & enter better members into a Church state.

2. Let it Caution, & Call upon all Church members to see better to themselves than what such are of whom our text speakes. 1. Have a Care that thou do not Sin. Go away & Sin not, Watch against Sin. Sin is the

Costliest thing in the world: & its intollerable in Church members. Gods Churches tho' there are many sinners in them, they are not to beare [54/55] with Sinners, I Cor. 5.11, Eph. 5.6,7,11. Art thou a member of that Society that is erected by Christ against Sin & dost thou not watch against Sin, dost thou daringly go on in provoking language, & Carriage? In Cheating & Guile, in Covetousness, & oppression, in Equivocation & falsifying, in Excess of Drinking, & abusing the good Creature in unrighteous dealings, & have a Care of Stubbornness? In such offences as call for Christian treatment, Reproofe, & repentance hereupon? & doste stand off from the rule & refusest to acknowledge thy offence? Wilt thou? darest thou Vindicate thy action as no Sin? Art thou grown to such impudency, & boldness? dost feare no Colours? Wilt thou not be smitten by the Righteous, nor accept it as a kindness? doth this pretious oyle or ointment breake thy Head? Wilt thou abide Stubborn under this brotherly usage? shall thy Crime & trespass with thy Stiffness be brought to be judged by the Church? and what now wilt thou in the face of the Church of Christ lift up thy brazzen face? Darest thou put all upon proofe & is there a Circumstance wanting of proofe which if it was prooved would not proove the nature of the thing to be Sinfull, but onely more Sinfull: for the thing itself is Sinfull, & as such its brought to the Church to be judged? & darest thou harden thy brow to plead from that nonprooved Circumstance a *non peccari*, that thou hath done nothing amiss, & so hardenest thy heart against the Call of God to Repentance? Alas! alas! what pitty is this? Shall a church member thus stand out without fear in his Sin? Shall a visible professed member of Christ, thus appeare a member of the Divell? & so Constrain the Church to deliver him up to Satan as an impeninant hardned sinner? Oh! then let every Church member have a Care of themselves that they sin not. & if thro' ignorance, inadvertancy, passion, or temtation they are overtaken & fall into sin, Se that you stand not in it but repent, accept of the brotherly precious oyle that will not hurt your head; but heale your soules. Repent, Confess & give glory to God. Beat nott away from you your brothers help much less the Churches call upon you to repentt.

2. Let its Caution the Church to be wary that they abuse not the place that they stand in under Christ. You see that Christ hath made you his spirituall Court, & refers the Cases of [55/56] his Children that belong to you, if they can't be taken up in a private way, unto you to issue the Cases there is then a greate trust committed unto you: the Eminent Concerns of his Kingdom are devolved into your hands. Se then that

you mannage all aright. The body of the society Consists of various sorts of persons, some have nothing to do in passing of judgment tho' they are to be satisfied in their own Spirits touching their fellow members. As the Sorority, or sisters. Oh! have you a Care of yourselves: be not too remiss on the one hand as if you were not Concern'd in this matter: nor be ye too Censorious, as if you were judges, keep you within the duties of your place.

2ly: Another sort are such to whom belong the right of judging matters regularly Committed to them which ordinarily is done by Rulers of the Church in the Society of the whole Church. Oh! have a Care to your duty you abuse when you step out of your bounds, & wickedly act when you intermeddle with the Officers or Rulers worke. They as Rulers, & Governours of the house of God, have their Office judgment to pass upon all things that are brought to the Church, whether matters fit or fit at such a time to be brought to the Church: Christ never instituted a Church to be troubled with, nor officers, to bring to the Church, the quarrells, the Envy & malice of envious persons to his Churches to set them all on a fire, or if they bring the offences of their brethren or sisters to you, you are not to Conspire with the offender against your Rulers, nor one with an other against the offender when he manifests repentance. If therefore you receive matters not given you by your Rulers or judge matters regularly brought to you, without or against your Rulers, you thrust Christs rule & authority a way from you. & trample it under your feet, you rise up against the Rulers whom Christ Charges you to obey, I Thess. 5, Heb. 13.19. You thrust Christ out of his own house. You Can't act a Church act without your Church rulers, if they be seatted amongst you. Your right lies onely in judging matters brought to you by *them* & that too must be with them & not without or against them While you have them. The Elders & Teaching officers are to Teach, Admonish, Reprove, Administer the Sacraments, Prayer, & Carry On of rule over you, in leading you & acting with you in all discipline. See [56/57] therefore that you keep within your own Sphere & attende upon the Duty that belongs to you. Your duty is nothing of Rule. All that ever is laid out to you by the Lord Christ is matters to be tried by the Church when regularly brought to you. You sin against Christ if you accept of anything that is not brought to you by your Ruling officers, nor Mannaged among you by them, in case they are not removed from you. Your work is such as lies in judging & is Called the Power or Right of judging such as are $\begin{cases} \text{To be admitted members by you} \\ \text{Offenders impenetent among you.} \end{cases}$

None that ever have wrote juditiously Ever hath pleaded any more save onely when you want officers in which Case I Urge you, not to be Heady, nor factious but advise with the Godly & learned Elders of Neighbour Churches. & so proceed. Depend nott upon your own judgment in Such a Case. Its above you to judge the fitness of a man for the House of God. But Some thing of his unfitness you may bee aware of. If he be vain, & trifling not Serious, & Pious, you may observe. Choose not such an one. But when you see a pious disposition, & an answerable Conversation with an Answerable Commendation by the Godly, Orthodox ministry let your Call be laid on Such. Butt as to your Admissions be not too remiss. You are to have no fellowship with the unfruitfull worke of Darkness. Such as go on in such wayes you may not Eate with, I Cor. 5.11. Such as do not give forth evidences of their repentance if they were in were to be put out as such as heare not this Church, as in our text & therefore not to be received in, therefore be not too remiss or careless, not heeding who they be that you admit; & on the other hand be not too rigid Censorious, & Curious & not admit such as shew forth the gracious actings of Soul & an answerable life & Conversation; this is to reject those that Christ hath received. So as to Matters offencive be not over Curious, yet See that there are proofs of the Fault, & observe the Spirit of the Offender, if he fall down, & manifest Godly sorrow, & a penetent spirit be ready to forgive, riggle not here: But if he manifest an unsuitable spirit, pleads against his con-[57/58]fession & will not move any further than constraint is upon him; all that he doth is hardly any owning his case to be Sinfull, be Slow here. If you can't finde his Confession, such as you can judge Christ accepts or that its such that Christ allows not of in Heaven, have a care what you do. Give him time to evidence his amendment in this matter. Yet observe the judgment of your officer that leads you: he may see further in the spirit of the Offender, & into the nature of the Offence than you & never act to absolve or acquit the offender, or to account his offence nothing when you See the Ruler if he be the Pastor of the Church judges otherwise. For you are bounde to be lead by him, Rev. 13.17. If your Elders can't evidence the Sin or innocency of the Case to you, Seek further light by a Councill. But you can't impose upon your Elders, one thing or other against their judgment. Hence be very wary in these Cases.

& if the Offender will not come up to the Rule nor heare the Church Christ saith let him be as an Hethen & as a Publican, & so to move here to consider here: & to move to this Consider.

1. That Christ having made the Church his tribunall, & you the Fraternity the members of the same to issue the Cases, with your Rulers, it is greate unfaithfulness in you to your trust, if you act unrighteously, or against your Rulers. & it is not ordinary where you may not act as they. Hence you

2. You bring the guilt of much Sin upon the Church in your issuing the matter not right as the guilt of abusing your trust, you make yourselves guilty of the offenders offence, you interpretively Charge your Elders with unrighteous judging that Case as sinfull, when you declare it to be otherwise, you bring a Scandall upon the Church as judging a miss. You breake Christs Law in not doing justice, you incourage Sinners in their Sins & impenetency & give occasions to the Enemy of the Churches to revile them & say the rude mob if they be Concernd in judging will never be ruled by their Elders, but will beare Sway right or wrong: these things are awfull.

3. Christ will not beare long with such Churches. If a prince see his Magistrates on the bench draw aside & Consult with the faulty persons that the justice of his Laws will fine & punish, to take their part, plead their Cases, & set them at liberty to the dammage of the righteous prosecuter he will turn upon such Courts & turn the members off of that Bench & punish them. So will Christ do to his. I am affraid Gods judgment will light upon this Church on this accountt. He hath dealt so with Churches better than you, as the case in Churches Rev. 3.5, & the 3.15,16. Oh then repent & beware. [58/59]

[The Second Disciplinary Sermon]

Westfield ⎱
31 11ᵐ 1713⎰ Matt. 18:18. Verily I say unto you What so ever yee shall bind on Earth, Shall be bound in Heaven & what so ever yee shall loose on earth, shall be loosed in Heaven.

In the former verse we have Christ ordering that the Offence of an Obstinate offending Brother, (& by the like reason of an offending sister) be brought to the Church whereof such offenders are members, in Church fellowship. & the Conclusion, & issue that the Church makes of itt, & yet upon the Supposition, of the offenders nott regarding the same, a Speciall order given touching Such offenders, that they should be reputed as Heathens & Publicans. Why shoulde offended so hold them but because the Church by Casting them out of her Fellowship, hath put them into such a State in manifold Considerations as Heathens & Publicans are in, viz, *Extranaei Faedoris*. But now so to doe is hard worke. These offenders often set up their Brissles at the same, affections in some working & soureness in others clay. & stubbornness oft in the offender googling & cookling yea, threating & being wrath hereat, make to Carry on this piece of service for Christ: So that the Church is ready oft times to fall into Convultion fits aboute it. Hence Christ to Stir up to this Worke doth lay in the words of our text, which is a gracious Promise to incourage his Church to this worke, touching which we may Consider

1. Some thing taken for granded as a matter implied in the Promise, & that upon which the promise is made, viz, That the Church will determine & issue the matter aright that is Committed as an offence, for her to judge. For it can not be that he should promise to ratify & Confirm what shee doth if she doth not judge righteously. For it can not be that Jesus Christ the Righteous, I John 2.1, Should promise to ratifie an unrighteous determining of a Faultt.

2. The Verse itself laid upon this Foundation, in which is

1. The Manner in which the promise is made, & this is given us in the word, Verily I say unto you. Some looke upon it to be an Oath of Confirmation: but its certainly a strong asseveration confirming the matter asserted. [59/60]

2. The Matter thus asserted 1. An Express promise upon this righteous determining the matter, thus What ever Ye shall binde on Earth shall be bound in Heaven: & Whatever yee shall loose on Earth, shall be loosed in Heaven: & there is in this promise a Severe threatening in case the determination is not given in aright, that is rightly according as it is evidenced to bee. In which words we are to Consider Who it is that is spoken unto in these words. Christ was speaking of the Church in the Former verse but he Speakes not to the Church, but in this verse he directs his speech directly to the second person in the plurall number saying yee. Now who are these yee?

Sol: In generall these are the Persons that binde & Loose, & therefore they are members of the Church with her Officers if the Church be Organick. For you see the binding & Loosing, in the Former Verse is the Work of the Church, who sets down the sentence which not being attended, the Offender is to be held as an Heathen man & a Publican. The Offender can't get out of this bonde when in it but by the loosing of it by the Church, & therefore she binds & looses & hence she is the person designed by this yee. If it be said, but how is it made out that Christ by the term yee, seing its the second person, & not the third that would import the Church, that Christ directs his Speech unto saying, Whatever Ye shall binde or Loose: It rather is thought that he spake to some others by, as to the Apostles, for Peter & so doubtless others of the Apostles, were here as appeares in the following verses. To this I say,

1. The speech of Christ is directly spoken unto the offended person & the one or two that he tooke with him to treate the Offender, who

426

abiding obstinate in his offence are also offended & these are Severall & may rightly be Spoke to in the plurall number & calld Yee. & these were in a brotherly relation one unto another & that in the Church to which or in which they were all members. & these are the persons immediatly Spoken to, who binde the obstinate in bringing of it unto the Church in the first place in that they bring it to the Church, as the first agents: & in the Churches binding of the offender in Condemning his Sin, & answerably as to loosing. & these being in Church fellowship the whole Church is spoken to in these part being used for the [60/61] whole. For the Offender & the Offended must be both be members of the Church & in its Communion, that hath the offence to trie, & issue, for if otherwise it can't be that this offender proved guilty Can be outed the Communion by the Church whereof he is not in Comunion. Hence the Speech being directly made unto the offended who is orderd to take one or two more in case of obstinacy, & if the same still appears, to tell it to the Church, it must needs be that if the Church doth not release but binds, that they binde. & hence Theophylact saith on the text, not onely the Priests loose those things that are loosed, but we also that are injured, whatever we binde or loose even those things are bound or loosed; But these now being directly Spoken to them that are members offended are the persons that not onely first by themselves, but joyntly with & in the Church do binde & loos, so that by a Synecdoche the Church is Spoke to as the Persons binding & loosing.[93] And Augustin argues strongly that in Peters binding & loosing the Church bindes & looses. Hence he saith in the 51 Tractate on John the 12, that Peter, Matt. 16.24, signifies the Body of the Good, the body of the Church, yea the body of the Church yet in the good—So that what ever thou (saith Christ) shall binde on Earth shall be bound in heaven, etc., if this be spoke to Peter onely, the Church doth not bind or loose. But if this binding & loosing on Earth be done in the Church, because when the Church excommunicates, the Excomunicated is bound in Heaven. When he is released by the Church, the reconciled is loosed in Heaven, then Peter when he received the Keys, seing this was done in the Church, he signifies the Holy Church.[94] From what is here asserted, you see that one person according to Austin may be Spoken to & the whole Church designd by Christ in the matter that he spake.

2. Suppose by the Word Yee in the text is intended the Apostles they then are not spoke to as Apostles, for the Apostolicall [61/62] Office being onely personall, & temporary, it Ceased in the Ceasing of the

Apostles who were the onely persons invested with it. But this Binding
& loosing on Earth doth not Cease with the Apostles; it Continues in
the Church & is to Continue to the End of the world. & is to be exerted
as occasion calls for it: Hence is that call, I Cor. 5, *ult.*, Titus 3.10. But
they are spoken to first as disciples as you see, Matt. 18.1, John
20.20,23. & as Ministers of the Gospell: & as such they were the matter
& officers of the Particular & of that first Particular Gospell Church in
the New Testament, & so as such this Binding & loosing belongs to all
such successively to the End of the World, that is, to the Disciples of the
Brotherhood, & the Ministers seated in all Particular Gospell Churches
in the world. A *quaterius ad omnes valet.* Hence this binding, & loosing is
that which is done by the Disciples, & Officers (i.e., Ruling officers of
the Churches of Christ) i.e., the Disciples & Officers of Particular Gospell Churches. For these disciples to whom the promise is made have it
made to them as Disciples Simply & absolutely Considered, or else as
Considered Embodied into a Society to carry on the orders of Christ in
the Gospell Administration. Now it can not be with any sue of Reason,
that they as single Disciples, they should have such Authority to binde,
or loose at their pleasure & that Confirmd to them with such a promise,
that Christ will mentain it in Heaven to be right. Nay further if they as
Disciples can doe it alone, then its no Church Act; nor hath the offended
brother any need to bring the offence to the Church in Case the brother
be Obstinate. & so this Sense would make that institution of no force,
nor use, say not that the Ruling Elder or Elders are officers and they do
it by vertue of their office. For there is noe Church Officer that is not an
officer of a particular Church. He that is put out of his Office in a
particular Church is noe Church Officer. Those that talke of an Officer
first & last in the Catholick Intrest, calld the Catholick Church, make an
officer without the Object of his Office exercise, for the Exercise of his
office is Confined unto a particular Church. His Call must be before his
Office: none can call him to a Church Office but a particular Church.
Hence he can't be calld to any Catholick intrest of the Gospell. Hence no
Catholick Officer, the Officer is made so by the Call. Hence no binding
[62/63] or loosing but in a particular Church. There is no Catholick
Officer Since the Apostles, but such as are fixed officers in a particular
Church. If an Officer & not fixt in Some particular Church, then there
may be an officer of the Church, Seated in no Church & this will bring
in none Residents, & so Jesuits, Monks, Friars, & what not may

become Church Officers. & hence also officers may be without any Cure, yea & that all his Dayes, & such officers may never put forth an office act all their lives; as probable it is with the Pope & his Cardinalls. So that its a vain thing that Christ sets the Offended about when he saith, tell it to the Church, & if he heares not them let him be unto thee an Heathen & a publican. For the binding & Loosing is no Church act, but the Acts of such as indeed are styled Disciples, & Officers not Enchurched, or in any Church Society: but are Certain *individuums vagrant* & its such as never come together that may do it. But this is so absurde, that there is neither Scripture nor Reason for it. But in an Organick Church the Disciples are inchurched, in to members of the Body & Organs or Instruments that are to Carry on the Duty of the whole body. & hence our text is spoke unto the whole as to the matter of the Church in Generall as Disciples, & being Consider'd as a body incorporate are both the members & Officers of the Church, & acting in their Encorporated Society receive & judge the Offence of that member of her Corporation that is brought to her to bee judged, & the Judgment they give of the Case is that of the Church which the Offender is to heare, the which being neglected, he is to be accounted as an heathen & as a Publican.

Secondly. What are we to understand by this right Binding & Loosing, which Christ here promises shall be Confirmed & Ratified in Heaven?

Sol: This Binding & Loosing is to be Considered in respect to its
{ Object
{ Subject putting it forth.

1. Its Object, or that which is bound, & this primarily & this is the Matter offencive that is broughtt to the Church & is Called trespass, v. 16. If thy brother trespass, ἁμαρτήσῃ, Sin this of what nature or sort ὅσου in our Whatsoever. & Hence its rendered, John 20.23, Sin, & then in a secondary [63/64] the persons offending, ἁμαρτωλός, as some assert. For though they are not primarily judged, yet the sin being found in their hands, they are judged the offenders, I Cor. 5, *ult.*, for he that Sins is a sinner, & the right judging of this as the matter offencive, judges the person offending an offender, & if so this is a right binding on Earth, & Christ will mentain this to be right in heaven. & if the offender persevere, & doth not Evidence his repentance thereof unto the Church, he goes on in impenetancy & so the Church Ejects him for the same &

Casts him out of her Corporation or Society for the same, & Clears herselfe from being an hiding place or a den of Sinners. And this binding Christ promises to make it pass & be approved on in Heaven.

2. As for this Loosing on earth, it is such as that upon the triall of the Case, the Evidences, & Circumstances being given in, it appears not to be Sin, or evill, or if such yet the person whose fault it is, hath manifested himself greatly Sorrowfull, & as to Christian Charity truely penetent & humble upon the account thereof, so that the Church remits & pardons the Same. This is that right Loosing on Earth that Christ promises shall be justified in Heaven.

Secondly, as to the subject binding or loosing, & this is to be Considered as it is Ecclesiasticall, Officiall, & Personall.

1. Ecclesiasticall. And so it is the Church herselfe to which the Offender doth belong, as a member of her Society. & thus the matter is Carried on by the Whole, II Cor. 2, by the tacit compliance of the Sorority, & the sufferages of the Fraternity, & the Leading, Voting with, taking & applying the Voting of the Fraternity unto the Offender. This is therefore done by the Whole Church, or the Majority which is this & such Cases, is to be accounted the Whole Church.

2. The Officiall or Pastorall Binding or Loosing. This is a Pastorall, or a Teaching Elders Duty. & it is distinct from the Ecclesiasticall, which is done by the body of the Church. I am sorry that Our Congregationall Divines say so little of itt, For it is oft on this Silence that the Body of the Church, whose liberty & right of judging of Cases & persons regularly tendered to their judgment is defended by that lubricous & darke word Power of judgment, the most of the Body not seeing how power being in them can be withstood by others are ready when some soure & subtill person amongst them [64/65] not liking the matter in hande, or striving to beare out the Offender from the Censures of the Church, that these fetters of Christ upon the legs of his Soule, is ready to raise a faction in the Church, boldly & impudently claiming the Power of Binding & Loosing to be the Peculiar Priviledge of the Church, & so they may determine the Case, whether the Ruling officers will or noe. Whereas in an Organick Church there can be no Church act ordinarily without the Ruling Elder or officer be in it, & so make a faction in the Church, as it was once in our Church. I brought a turbulent & unhandsome living member of our Church out to the Church by way of enquiry after a matter of Sclander cast upon myselfe by the lawyer Pomery in the County Court at Northamton asserting a person there sued on an action

of Debt, that he was not a man in Law being put under Guardians upon the Desire or Advice of myselfe & Certain others of our Neighbours, which matter I utterly refused & accounted an unrighteous thing in it-selfe. & when this man brought a letter drew up as he said by the lawyer tending to desire the Court to do what I judg'd tended to put the poor man out of Law & desired me to subscribe it, I refused, but he prevaild with me to write some thing which I did but nothing to that matter, but onely thus much that if they could do any thing that might prevent the person from alienating his land & State it might be gratefuly accepted, not desiring any thing. This person I told that I judgd the Court Could not do & to put him out of Law I accounted it unlawfull, but he took my writing, carried it to the Lawyer & with him to the Court, who so far acted in the Case that the Lawyer in the Open Court asserted that the man sued was not a man in Law but was put under guardians, & that upon my desire or advice. I calld him out to give a reason of his So doing. He rose up with Contempt, would not answer to the enquiry, but scornfuly & provokingly carried it in the face of the Church fixing falshoods & slanders upon me & would not answer to the Case. Where upon I let the former matter fall: & Calld him to give Satisfaction for his Contempt & treading underfoot the Authority [65/66] of Christ in the Church & drew five or Six Articles against him. He being turbulend Spirited man, & wordy goes privately to the brethren & overtalks them & they not coming to me. And there being an old soure stiff man in the Church who was not pleased in the matter & by reason of age & some more Craftiness of headpiece than many carried on almost all things in the town, set himself to clog the Case, & if he did anything it was by way of staving the matter off. When I saw the Offender after severall meetings pleading his Case & coming to no Confession I propounded him to the Church to vote both affirmatively, & Negatively, the Church that is the brethren would act in neither. I was offended, & rebuked the Church, telling them if that they would neither Act for nor against the Offender, they would Constrain me to new Methods, & I should be Constraind to Call a Councill in the Case. Or suspend them from the Lords Supper, i.e., suspend the administration of the Lords Supper to them. And after the offender saying that he was sorry for one particular article that I drew which he denied till it was proved upon him, & then I asked whether he was heartie in it, he answer'd Snappishly, that I had nothing to do with his heart. I told him I had to do with his heart. But seing that Church would not act, I betook myselfe to the Offender thus,

I here in the name & Magisty of Christ Commande you to repent of these your Sins & great Evills & to manifest your Repentance to the Church in due time that you may have them to forgive you, & this I Charge you to do upon your perill as you shall answer it at the day of Jesus Christ, or to this Effect, Saying, this I do lay upon you, not as a Church Admonition but as Ministeriall Admonition. This touched their Choller, viz, His, & his second the old soure blade. He told me I had nothing to do to treate him so. I told him I would not come to him to be taught what was my office. Now the old Captain desired that the Church might Set apart a time on purpose to handle the Case. It was done. & the day being come the Offender & the Old Captain & severall meet together before they come to my house. I knew not what about but at length they Came. We fall upon the Worke. And I propound the Offender to the Church Vote, they all vote [66/67] him an offender *nomine excepto*. He then gave in a paper in which was writ something that I could not read & I gave him to read that gave it to me, he stumbled itt out, & the Old Captain Calld it a Confession, & would have me put it to the Church to vote. I told him no I would not, there was nothing in it Confesst. I could not take that for repentance. & I knew my office well enough & I would not be imposed upon by any. I ought to have had it to have Considered it. Some desired mee to give the Offender time. He was falling. I told him that I was free to & desired him to Consider it till the next Conference, & desired them to endeavour to bring him to a better Confession, for I thought that they Could do more with him than I could. The Old Captain who had factiously drawn with the offender the brethren to send letters to Mr. Woodbridg & Mr. Brewer the two ministers of the two Churches at Springfield, who by that the Offenders Collaguing tongue shamefully run themselves aground, which when I understood it, I began & intended to reprove the Church, the old Captain was ready to bandy the matter & bad me prove it, I told him of the letters that they had sent & so & so, he told me that I had given them leave to treatte Smith but now at the Conference Smith was Calld out after the Exercise was over & I then laid him under the Church Admonition. The which did so nettle the old Captain that he could hardly tarry till all was over, & then he crowded out & went on a pace shugging his Shoulders, I followed him & bad him give me his hand, he gave it saying that he was Caught, meaning in that as I suppose he did not order his paper, that he counted a Confession, to be given to be voted not till a vote had passt in the Church that he had offended, that being first gained & I not putting his paper to vote Smith lay under the vote as an offender. He further Said Smith was such a man that nobody, he meant that he had carried so badly that nobody loved him. & this was the man that he strove to beare off from the Censures of the Church. But having gaind a sorry Confession tho' better than the former I read it & the Church accepted it, & so I reproving the Church [67/68] for their acting as they had done, & their underhand dealing with me in this matter, & writing as a Church to other Elders & unworthily I was ashamed to see or that others should see it & I was resolved either to call a Councill upon the Case, or else that I would have a mutuall forgiveness one of another & by keeping a day of Humbling ourselves before God by fasting and prayer to beg forgivness of our offences. I was resolved if this was refused to have the help of a Councill. The Old & young Captains & the Ensign oposed both, but I fixtt upon fasting & prayer. The Captains opposed this, but the Ensign said that hee was not faulty in the matter & went away. & the Captains opposed being I Suppose egregiously faulty. But a brother of the Church wisely urged me to put the Fasting & praying to the vote of the Church: he doubted not but the Church would comply with it: the which they did gladly, all except the Captains & the Ensign. But when the Young Captain saw that the brethren had left him & the old Captain, then he Complied, & they Calling the Ensign in, who tarried in the poarch, he complied: I then turnd upon the old Captain for his Compliance & he refused, & acted very ugly. But we went on with the day. He was at the fast & I preacht a Sermon of repentance upon Matt. 4.17. Now this was in great measure from the want of Light in many touching the Power of Binding & Loosing officially. The Perversness of the offender & of the Old Sour Captain asserting that the Power lay in the Church. For the old man did not Stick in the Church in effect to deny the Rulers power, asking me in a disdaining way what the power of the Church was if the Rulers Could do so & so. I told him the power of the Church lay in giving their judgment upon those Cases that were regularly committed to the Church by their rulers. But now that there is this Binding & Loosing officiall is cleare for they are described to admonish, I Thess. 5.12, & they are charged to reproove & rebuke, II Tim. 4.2, & 5.20, to reprove Sharply as occassion requires, Titus 1.13, & with all Authority & Comand, ἐπιταγῆς, Chap. 2.13.

3. There is Personall Binding & Loosing too: Every particular person is to do it for himselfe. For unless every person doth in particular binde or

loose the offence for himselfe he can't doe it in the Church as a Mem-[68/69]ber of the Church in the vote of the Church, nor can any in their privatte treating of the Offender, as v. 16 requires, either binde or loose the offence, either forgive the person, tho' he heare the Case at the mouth of the offended brother, nor binde in Case he hears not, & bring it to the Church unless he hath warrant from Christ so to doe. & if he have warrant so to doe, then what he doth in this Case a right shall be so Confirm'd in Heaven. Hence Origen & Augustin, if I mistake not, and Theophylact, do mentain a personall forgivness here required upon the Offenders falling under the Conviction of his Sin : & this is Called for in other Scriptures, as in Matt. 6.15, unless ye forgive others their Sins your heavenly father will not forgive you your trespasses, Eph. 4.32. Now all these Bindings, & Loosings whether Personall, Officiall or Ecclesiasticall if rightly done Christ will ratify the same in Heaven: & that according to the promise laid down thereto in our Text, tho' this promise doth mainly respect the Ecclesiasticall Binding & Loosing.

Thirdly. Why shall this Binding & Loosing rightly performed be Confirmed & Ratified in Heaven?

Sol: 1. This promise of Binding & Loosing in Heaven, whatever is rightly Bounde & Loosed by the Church, etc., on Earth. First is to Strengthen & encourage his Churches & people to the Same to do it, & to do itt as it ought to be done. When God put his people upon Dutie, he layes in some thing of Promise either expresst or implied to stir them up & encourage them to their dutie. When he gave his Church the ten Commands at mount Sinai, he excites them to the Same, saying I am the Lord thy God that brought thee out of the Land of Egyptt, out of the House of Bondage, Ex. 20.1,2. So Isa. 1.19,20. If ye be Willing & obedient, ye shall eate the Good of the land. But if the worke be hard to be Carried on that he setts them about, he laies down answerable Encouragements, greate incouragements to greate worke. When thou Walkest thro' the waters I will be with thee & thro' the Rivers they shall not over flow thee: when thou walkest thro' the Fire thou shalt not be burnt, neither shall the Flaims kindle upon thee, Isa. 43.1,2, etc. I will be a wall of Fire rounde about thee, & the Glory in the middst of thee, Zech. 2.5. I will be with you to the End of the World, Matt. 28, *ult.*, etc. But now the Binding & Loosing in our text is a very harde worke, this binding is a laying them in Chains, a putting them into the Stocks, & into little Ease, itt goes against mens Will. & work that is hard made

Moses so shift the worke off from his own Shoulders. & at length to refuse it saying, Ex. 4, send by the hand of whom thou wilt send yea & in his executing of it, they are ready to Stone him to death, as Ex. 17.4: & they Charg him with slaying the people of the Lord, as in Num. 16.4,1, much more when they are touched about [69/70] their Sins now the Offender will sly in the Face of him that touches here. Its a proverb, Touch a galled Horse & hee Will Kicke. Meddle with mens Sins & they will be ready to fly in your Face. When God did but coast upon this shoare Cain was ready to fly in Gods Face, saying am I my brothers keeper, Gen. 4. This made Jeremiah so much sorrow that he was ready to resolve to meddle no more in this work, Jer. 20.9. But God fired him outt of this purpose. This Made Elias flee out of the Land to mount Horeb for his life, I Kings 19.2—this made Ezekiel Sit astonisht at Tel: Abud Certain days & dumb till God roused him up by telling him that he would require the sinner's blood at his hand that died in his sins, if he did not warn him to repent, Ezek. 3.15,16,17,18. On this account Amos is Commanded to flee into the land of Judah & not to prophesy any more at Bethel, Chap. 7.12,13,14. This made Pashur Smite Jeremiah on the mouth because he foretold the ruin of the Cities of the land for their sins, Chap. 19.13,14,15, Chap. 20.1. Yea they seek his Life, & Cast him into the Dungeon & tell the King that he ought not to live, for he conspired against the intrest of the King & the City, Chap. 38. This infired Jeroboham against the Prophet that proclaimed Gods Judgment against his Bethel Sins, that he ordered the Prophet to be apprehended, I Kings 13.2,3,4. This enflamed Uzziah against the Priest that withstood his Sin of Entring into the Temple, II Chron. 27.18,19. Yea & a better man than these put the Prophet Anani in prison on this account, II Chron. 16.7–11. Yea this cost John Baptist his head, Matt. 14. Hence its hard work that lies in dealing with the sins of sinners. Oh! to Cast an oare in this durty & muddy Channell will make the mudd & durt to rise; touch a Serpent & he will bite you if he Can. & on this account such whose worke lies in this roade will finde greate difficulty to Carry it on, & be ready to desist with Jeremy & say it is hard worke. But now to strengthen his Churches & Servants to Carry on this so hard a Service of his, he promises that their binding & Loosing aright shall be Confirmed in Heaven. & this Promise doth mightily strengthen their hands, & Encourage them in their Worke. For here in they see that Christ is resolute & will have the Worke be carried on: & hereby they see a

Command implicitly on them to Carry it on, & aright. & this will adde strength to them in it. & hereby they see that Christ will stande by them in it & mentain & Confirm their right doing of it in Heaven.

2. Because this binding & Loosing is a Choice means of Grace in his Churches administerd in that it will be Confirmd in heaven. & here I argue thus, that is a Choice means of Grace on Earth that [70/71] shall be ratified in Heaven. Christ will mentain nothing done on earth, in Heaven, but what is Good & right & on Earth was a means of grace. How ever this is don on Earth as a Choice means of Grace, & in that Christ promises to Confirm the Same in Heaven, it is a manifest evidence that it is a Choice means of Grace. For altho' all things done aright on Earth shall be vindicated in Heaven. Yet all things done aright on Earth have not a particular promise that they shall be so done in Heaven as this binding, & Loosing hath. & further that it is a Choice means of Grace as appears 1. in respect of the Church that Carries it on for it makes Grace to shine forth in the members of the Church, every one shining in their right performance of his duty to reclaim an offending member by repentance, neither over doing by too much rigiddness, nor underdoing by too remissness. & also it tendes as an excellent means to provoke the members to keep a strict watch over themselves that they fall not into Sin, nor defile their garments: & if they be Surprized into Sin, that they stande not in Sin; but that they repent lest they be laid in those bonds with which they shall then be fetterd in Heaven. But that they recover themselves out of the Snare of Satan by Repentance & such a Release as shall to their Glory be foiled & Ratified by Christ in the High Court of Heaven. & yet further, it will make to the Glory of the Churches & of Christ. For by the attending aright upon this Binding, & Loosing, that shall be mentaind & ratified in Heaven, it will manifestly evidence that there shall not be one visible impenitent Sinner tollerated in Christs Churches on Earth, nor an visible penetant Soule excluded the Churches of Christ. & that which tends wholy to this must needs be a Choice means of Grace. And 2. It must needs be own'd a Choice means of Grace to bring back by repentance the Soule in Church fellowship, that is overtaken with a fault. Such often we finde by wofull experience to reject Secret treatings & private too, yea & will not regard the Churches sentence neither: but Continue impenitent in Sin, proved on them, till they be outed the Church, but now the Consideration that all these bonds hung on them by the Church & Children of God, will be Confirmed in Heaven, & if they repent & be released here, this Loosing

shall be Confirmed in Heaven will mightily Constrain to repentance &
on this account Christ hath promised to binde or loose in [71/72]
Heaven as the Church on earth doth rightly binde or loose on earth.
Now Christ hath instituted all the means of Grace that are to be
Celebrated in divine Ordinances, to be administred to such of his
Visible Saints as rise up so high in visible Standing as to have the
Enjoyment of Full-Communion with his Churches in all Church
Ordinances. He will denie them none of those means of Graces that may
& in their nature are fitted to bring them off from Sin & tto true
repentance. For if any of those be withheld, that person is not in full-
Communion in the Church. Christ is Faithfull, & will as occasion calls
allow all to these. & therefore if they fall into manifest Sin, they shall be
treated to bring them to Repentance. & if they under all means used for
this end abide impenitant, & obdurate, the last is a rejecting of them,
Titus 2.10, a Casting of them out of the Society of Church Fellowship,
I Cor. 5.12. This is the last: & Christ promising to ratify in Heaven this
when rightly done, gives it further strength of influence upon the Soule
to bring the sinner to repentance & promising to loose what the Church
rightly looses, doth ope a doore of incouragementt, & allurement to
draw to repentance as a matter very acceptable in Heaven. Hence it is that
Christ promises to binde & Loose in Heaven what is rightly bound &
loosed on Earth.

USE 1. By way of Inference that will informe us in & about Such
    truths of Christ as these following
1. First. Se hence that there frequently are Founde matters in the
members of Christs Churches that are to be Condemned. Christ here
saith what so ever ye binde on Earth shall be Bound in Heaven. There
are not onely sins visibly perpetrated by Church members but perversly
adhered unto. For the Churches of Christ are not to punish their
members offending with pecuniary fines, as they do in the Bishops
Courts wrongly Calld Spirituall, & so to release them setting them in a
right State, when they have payed their fine, & this upon the beare
presentment & Single word of the Apparitor, untill they offend again by
nonobserving of their Canons, many of which are nothing of an Evill
nature, etc. & then another bit of silver will be Satisfaction Sufficient.
But its not so in Christs way. The offender is to be bound till he repent &
his Sin is to bee Condemn'd if Sin, if not it is not to be Condemned but
[72/73] Then the person is not bound, but if he be stubborn & his fact

Sinfull being Condemned he is bound by the Church till he repent &
manifest the same, & then he is Loosed. & hence there is matters
frequently founde in the Churches of Christ to be bound & Loosed.
Christ otherwise would not say as he doth in our Text.

2. Hence see that Gods Church, & people have Sufficient Authority
from Christ to binde & Loose sins, & offences as occassions do
requires. Now if this Binding or Loosing was a thing that Christ did not
approve of, or that his Church & people had not his Warrant for the
performance of, tho' he liked the thing itselfe & would stande by the
same when done by such that he gave power to do it, yet he would never
incourage any to do itt, by an promise to ratify the Same & to mentain it
in heaven, as done by them, in that they had no power from him to do it.
& therefore it would be presumption & usurpation in Such as Should
do it thus. The Kings righteous Laws are such, that he determines shall
bee Equally carried on among his Subjects: & he erects Courts, &
orders what magistrates & Judges as he judges meet to hold such Courts:
& their just determining those actions that they give in he promises shall
Stand. But if any other persons whom he hath not appointed to be the
Person that should keep this Courtt, should take upon themselves to be
a Court & as such should summons offenders appearing & should
condemn the unrighteous, tho' the sentence should be right, yet the king
would Certainly punish the judge & the Magistrates, that should so do,
as userpers & rebells. They could lay no claim to the Kings promises to
ratify their sentance. But those judges & Magistrates that he hath
order'd to keep such Courts he will stand by their righteous sentences.
So here Christ hath given his promise to his Church & people that what
ever they binde on Earth shall be bound in Heaven, & whatever they
Loose on Earth shall be loosed in heaven. & hence its a Sufficient
Evidence that they have sufficient Authority from Christ to Binde &
Loose righteously, as matters are Evidenced. [73/74] It is true they must
do it righteously. & then Heaven will own it.

3. Hence see that Gods Churches & people are bounde to be very
impartiall & Exact in their trying & issuing the Offences & the
judgment that they pass upon the Cases brought unto them. They ought
to keep themselves from all respect of persons in these matters. God
requires the Civill Court to have no respect of Persons in judgment, Lev.
19.15, Deut. 1.17, 16.19, and he also requires the Same at the hand of
his Churches & people & both in Admission & in matters of
offences. Here is binding & Loosing: you must do both aright & then

Christ tells you, that the Case shall be so done in Heaven. But if you do not do the matter righteously, God will require at your hand, he will not Confirm an unrighteous Case because you judg it righteous. But if you faile thro' neglect of duty & Carelessness, God will require it at your hand, much more if pride & passion, Will & Humor, Respect of Persons or Disrespect, if bribery, or guggled aside with the Offender, or you are drawn aside & Complot with the Same, you will not judge right in the matter. But God that hath told you that he will binde & loose in Heaven what you binde & loose on Earth hath laid this before you to Stir you up to judge so as he will Confirm your Sentence. For if you do not do your worke a right he will call you to answer it in Heaven, why you do not do that which is right? & much more in that you have not been Stird up by this promise of his to Confirm the righteous determining in these Cases. Oh! therefore you must be impertiall in the judging here. And hence you ought to be Studious & Conscientious in the matter, not to binde where you ought to loose, nor to loose where you ought to binde.

4. Hence see that such whose Cases are brought to the Church for triall ought not to Cloude a bad Case nor to pleade it to be no offence, neither ought any brother pleade or Colour any such Case that is to be tried. Its a Shame that any should so doe. He that Clouds over his offence & maketh that to ware a Good face which is a bad thing doth but paste over his Sin by impenitency till the day of judgment, & then itt can't be hid; then it shall have its mask pulld off: & the Case now shall be laid in eternall [74/75] Bonds. There will be no opportunity allowd thee to take them off by repentance. If thou beguilest the Church or thy Brother that they do not determine the Case as it is, but loose what is to be bounde, Christ then will binde what the Church Looses: & thou by Cheating the Church dost but baffle an ordinance of the means of Grace that should urge thee upon repentance. & so double thy sin, harden thine own heart, please the powers of darkness & so come forth under heavier Chains bound at the day of judgment to ever lasting Condemnation: & he that pleads that offence no offence, by Some Circumstance alleviating it, or that may darken it, thou dost thereby involve thyselfe in the offence, & make it thine own, dost darken the matter that it appears nott so bad, nay scarcely appears bad at all & so handest in a wrong judgment about it, hardenest the offender, that the proper end of Discipline is not attained unto, viz, the Repentance & reformation of an offender, & a Clearing the Church of a Scandall. &

this will be heavy upon thee, & upon the offender; if not upon the Church that Suffers herselfe so to be imposed upon by thy Craftiness. For if the Church hereby looses what indeed should be bound on Earth, Christ will binde what thou loosest & that in heaven Eternally.

5. Hence see what a Fearfull state such are in whose Cases are here rightly bound upon Earth, & what Comfort this truth brings unto those that do rightly binde them. Oh! their Determination shall stand & be stood to & vindicated in Heaven. This thing declares that such are in a dreadfull Condition whose offences are thus issued if they regard not the Same. Alas! such set themselves against all the Ordinances of Grace ordaind by Christ to be used in applying the sinners Sin manifestly upon him, to be repented of. Hence such Condemn the Church & people of God, in their righteous judging on earth: Such set themselves against the Warrant that Christ hath given them that judge, as if it was vacate by their judging, [75/76] as if Christs Churches & people by judging aright, had lost their right of judging. But yet these offenders thus opposing the Binding of the Church can't get this clause cansell'd or raced out of their Commission by all their riggling, that what ever ye binde on Earth shall be bound in Heaven. Hence this will be refreshment in the very heart of Gods people that have bounde the offence as it is evidenced to bee. & it is as Cutting a bodking or saw in the heart of the obdurate offender. For he hereby rises up against God against Christ against the saints & Angells in Heaven, & against Heaven & the Kingdom of Heaven this Eternall kingdom in which this matter rightly determined on Earth shall be confirmed & ratified in Heaven. Thus affronts all these by thy obduracy & impenitancy in thy sin: & these are all against thee. The word is ratified in Heaven that hath Commissionated the Church & people of God to binde thy Sin evidenced by promising them that the same shall be bound in Heaven. So that such as oppose this righteous judgment is in a bad, most dreadfull and fearefull Condition. Who shall then Stand before the son of man that are such? As this binding on Earth rightly performed will be a most refreshing thing to the Soul of the Church of God that doth upon the thoughts that Christ will ratify it in Heaven: so on the Contrary it will bee a most dreadfull thing for the stubborn & obstinate, that regards not this binding on Earth but to grinde his malice & revenge upon, when he sees that God hath promise to fasten the knot of this bonde & binde it over again & that with an Everlasting tye in Heaven.

USE 2. Is this a truth that Christ hath promised to binde & Loose in
  Heaven Such as his Church & people bind, & Loose aright on
  Earth then this truth doth rebuke such as

1. First Pretende to Binde & to lose on Earth & Yet do not do it a right.
The Pope pretents to binde & loose according as persons Carry it to
him, & not according [76/77] to God nor his Word: but God will at the
last unty most of these his bonds & binde himselfe Eternally down in
the same, Rev. 18.6,7,8. This string of Beads shall be broken to pieces; it
hath neither any right to this worke, neither is it hereby done at all
aright. So there are other that come a little negher to the right of doing,
but yet what they do is not at all done a right. Such as binde in iron
Chains & loose by Silver keyes, as your spirituall Courts falsly so called.
Will Christ pull these thongs in Heaven that such do bind the Disciples
of Christ on Earth with? Or loose those bonds of Wickedness, that they
have let slip for silver bits? Nay, Nay, these make the Ordinances of this
nature, but picklocks to empty the Cabbinets of Worldly Jewells. Christ
will in heaven say to these, Who hath required this at your hands?

But it comes more directly with rebuke unto the Churches of Christ
which do not judge aright the offences that they have a right to judge
when brought to them aright, that give their verdict, or rather their
Maldict not aright: they binde where they should loose, & loose what
they should binde & not thro' mistake & against their will or from the
difficulty of the Case, but thro' respect or disrespect of persons thro'
favour or affection, or thro' prejudice, or ill will or friendship or
Relation, or by plotting with or being drawn aside with the offenders
tongue, or Frighted from the right: Oh! let such persons or Churches
know that Christ is offended with them: & he will not binde nor loose in
Heaven what they so binde or loose on Earth, but will take down their
binding & loosing on Earth to be an offence to him & heaven: & he will
interpret it a putting a trick upon him as if by his promise to binde or
loose in Heaven he had bounde himselfe to Confirm their abusing of
him on Earth. Nay, nay, but he will make all such evill binding &
loosing the Cords of their iniquity that he will binde them in to their
Smart, & may be to their Eternall ruin. Do you thus deale with the Lord
oh foolish people & unwise? He will one time or other, make you smart
for it. Nay yet this is such a way as Christ will not beare with. If it be in a
single person God will require it [77/78] at his hand, if it be in the
Brotherhood onely they rise upon disobedience to the Authority, &

Kingly office of Christ in his Church. & it tends to all Confusion, & Conspirusy against the Rulers of the Church & to Chase their Pastors & Teachers that are truely Godly, who can't be Compelld to administer the Lords Supper to manifest impenitent sinners, or to release such as ought to be bounde, or to binde Such as ought to be released for in so doing they do that which they in their hearts can't judge that Christ will binde or loose such in Heaven as they do on Earth and then Christ require it at their hands. Nay, they will not know how to administer the Lords Supper to Such a brotherhood, who are thus making insurrection against their Rulers, by their binding or loosing whom the brethren, presume to binde or loose. & so by this faction the Teaching Elders shall either be necessitated to binde or loose, where they can't judge Christ will or to act against their own Consciences in administring the Lords Supper to such or to let the Ordinance fall, & not be administered, or to go away from such a society. & hence Such actes, deservedly fall under Severe rebuke.

Secondly. This Doctrine brings all such under a sharp rebuke that are rightly bound by the Church. How many bonds & heavy chains are hung upon the legs of thy soule, that thou canst never Shake nor brake off again but by repentance? & dost thou not heare Christ telling thee, that he will binde the same in Heaven? Dost thou think that Christ tells thee an untruth? or saith it, & will not do it? That he presumes & saith matters at adventure, on a sudden, or in a passion? & so misseth the truth or that he is a man that either lies, or will repent hereafter, & that it shall not be as he saith? Darest thou harbor such a Supposition that Christ the Son of God, the onely wonderfull, & inconceivable person in the world is ignorant, rash, passionate, & a false Speaker, if not a lyar? Shall truth itselfe be untrue? Darest thou stand upon such a point, & lay thy salvation upon it? Doth the salvation of all the Elect of God depend upon such a ticklish point, that is possible to be false? Or will it do thee any hurt to repent of sin, or of that which is attested to be sin by all that [78/79] heare it. Hence private treating & Secret touching the offence is nott regarded: no repentance is moved & so the first person binds & cannott pardon thee; nor the 2, or 3 in the Second treating, can'tt pardon nor forgive thee: & so they lay thee in bonds & Condemn thee & then thy fault is brought to the Church & she hears it, & sees it Evidenced against thee, & Condemns it & so binds thee. & thou neglects still, hearest not, & Christ now orderst thee to be held as an Heathen, & a publican & Still thou beatest back repentance & abidest in all these bonds, & all the Churches of Christ that walk in the order of the Gospell hearing of it, they binde thee, ratifying what is done in denying thee Communion with them. And Christ tells thee that whom she binds on Earth shall be bounde in Heaven. & for thy encouragement to Repent saith, whom she looses on Earth shall be loosed in Heaven. Oh! hardness of Heart in Sin! darest thou thus run abreast against the word of Christ? Must his Word be false, if thou hast grounde to stand upon impenitence? What saist thou? What thou thinkest to get the herdstall off of thy head, or bit out of thy jaws, by concluding that the Church & people of God have not judged a right; & therefore their Sentence will not be ratified in Heaven.

But how if it be? Art thou so Censorious as to Condemn them all? But what is the matter their Sentence is putting thee upon? Is it Repentance: & is not this always a duty? Is there nothing of thy Case to bee Condemn'd or are the Testimonies altogether false Witnesses, that Call thee to repent? Can'st thou not justify the sentence upon the testimony, tho' thou knowest the matter false? But is it so false, that there is nothing amiss in this Case of thine to be repented of? that thou holdest off from repentance? Be it so yet surely thou oughtst to Shew a penetent frame of Spirit under the sense of thy Case so Circumstanced, as that thou canst not avoid a just sentence condemning thy Case? Matters are [79/80] sildom, or never so Circumstanced: But if the Case is in its essence otherwise than the sentence, yet the soul may justify the Sentence, & shew true Repentance under the Circumstances that render it to be a visible true sentence, & so as such it shall be Confirmd in heaven. & thou condemnd for opposing repentance on this account.

USE 3. For Exhortation. Is it thus that this right Binding or Loosing shall be ratified in Heaven, then let this truth Stir up all the Churches & people of God to a right proceeding in this matter. Be not too harsh & rigid, nor too remiss or heedless in this matter.

Consider you bind or loose for Eternity, as the Painter replied when asked why he was so long about his work said *Pingo Eternitati*, I paint for Eternity. So here you binde or loose for Eternity. Therefore se that you do it exactly that your doing be not Condemned. Christ stands by you & records in heaven, your judging, Whether it be a sentence of Condemnation, or a sentence of remission. If you do it right, he will Condemn what you Condemn: if not a right, he will release, what you Condemn. & Condemn you, for the Condemning what you ought to

release, & your releasing, what you ought to Condemn. Oh! therefore
you ought to looke about you in this matter. But the Call of this Doctrine
falls into two Branches; it Comes upon the Agents, & also on the Objects.
1. The Agents: viz, such as Binde or Loose, whether single persons, or
Church Societies. Oh! See you that you do not this matter Carelessly.
You may not refuse the worke Christ Calls you to it; He saith, that if thy
brother sin against thee, much more, if he sin against God, go & tell
him between him & thee alone, ἔλεγξον αὐτὸν, Convince him by
arguing with him: thou shalt not suffer sin to be upon thy brother: but
Shalt in any wise reproove him, Lev. 19.17. It is a blot unto him: it is a
blemish & disgrace to the Church. Therefore Convict him but be not
too sharp lest he be provoked & then the reproofe for one sin frequently procures [80/81] another, & an other sin. Hasty words stir up
strife, Prov. 15.1, a soft tongue breaketh the bones, Prov. 25.15, be not
too sharp reproofe is to be administered with all long-suffering,
μακροθύμως, it is in effect with gentleness, it imports a drawing out of
the θυμός or irrascible seate which is the will or anger to a greate length
before it stirs. Crossness enough too oft is founde; the offender is
frequently offended with him that goes to pull him out of the mire. So
that a man that hath experienced this worke, had rather go with Jonas to
Tarsish, than to tell such persons of their Sins. & if Conscience to the
Rule did not oblige them, they would never meddle here. For it oft
prooves, as the meddling with a Wasps nest. & hence wisdom & mild-
ness is greatly required in this matter. But here is the thing that will
support you: you may not leave it off nor refuse itt: & you must not be
Censorious, nor too rigid but yet, if it be brought to the Church, & the
offender is perverse & arrogant, there may & ought to be used sharpness, Titus 1.13. Yet not so, but where there is falling & signs of Repentance, you must loose the Same; & forgive. But if on the other hand there
is impenitency & hardness then you must binde & Christ will stand by
you & tells you that heaven shall binde such. And now looke you to it,
for the last means of Grace to Constrain an Impenitant Sinner to repentance is in your hand, in greate part of it therefore Se to it, that the
sinners blood in impenitancy fall not on your heads, Ezek. 3.15,16,17,18,
do your worke whether binding or Loosing; & that a right & it shall be
ratified in Heaven. & this is that which may stir you up to your duty &
to do it aright.

2. The Call Comes upon the Objects of this Duty, & these are
both such as are to be admitted into Church society, & such as are

offenders in it. Oh, se that you come up to your Duty. You that are to have your Case tried in order to your entrance, all are not to be admitted, or permitted in to the Kings Palace. He hath his Life Guardes to prevent such as are not to enter. So hath Christ Jesus the King of saints. He hath his, Cant. 3.7,8. Behold his bed which is Solomons, threescore valient men are about it, of the valient of Israel. Each one hold swords being expert in war, every man hath his sword up on his thigh because of fear in the night: None impenitent [81/82] person may enter here. Such as if in, appearing as they are, are to be Cast out, are not to be admitted if out till they evidence themselves not to be such as are to be cast out, if in. But all impenitent persons if in, & appear such are to be Cast out. They heare not the Church, Matt. 18.18, hence are to be as Heathens & Publicans. And on this account you are under duty to Satisfy the Church touching your Faith and Repentance; those that John Baptist admitted to his baptism did bothe these, Matt. 3.5,6. & * * * such as did not come up to do this he rejected with Severe rebuke, v. 7,8,9. This they did that began the Church at Ephesus, Acts 12.18,19. & this was done for Paul himselfe before he could have Communion with the Church at Jerusalem, Acts 9.27. & the Church demanding this as the ἐπερώτημα of a good Conscience, I Pet. 3.21. They are bounde to do it by that Call, I Pet. 3.15: Thus also the primitive Churches did require when at baptism they admitted persons members. Hence baptism is styled, Titus 3.5, to be a means of Salvation, διὰ λουτροῦ παλιγγενεσίας καὶ ἀναχαινώσεως πνεύματος ἁγίου the washing of Regeneration & the Renovation of the Holy Ghost.

2. You that are members admitted into the Communion of the Church that are apprehended offending. Are you surprized by a temptation into Sin. Oh! then repent repent, God bestows upon thee such a Choice means of Grace it may be, upon thee, as by a friend, a Brother, or sister in fellow membership with thee to Come & tell thee of it to move thee, & finde thee, to repent. These rebukes are faithfull, better than the flatterings of an enemy. Gods Children under the actings of a gracious spirit esteem them as precious ointment, Ps. 141.5. Do not thou Swell, grow not proude herat, fall down & shew a penitant frame of sensibleness of thy Sin. If thou dost not thus thou hardenst thyselfe against the Grace, & Call of Repentance, & art bound by thy brother & so brought to the Church & this being prooved, you are like to be bound there untill you repent manifestly. & both these bindings will Stand Confirm'd in Heaven: & is not this a dreadfull Case then. Nay but if you

repent & manifest it, you shall be loosed both here & in Heaven too: & you avoide much sin & impenitancy & a great disturbance that other wise you will raise in the Church. & so be in the way of duty. & will not this be most Comfortable.

Oh then

Repent, Repent of your falls.

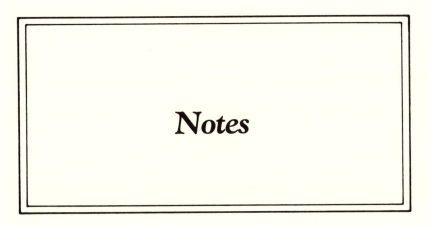

Notes

Notes: "Church Records"

[1]The first four leaves of the CR were badly worn before the pages were placed in linen sheets when the volume was rebound in 1929. Sections of this material were transcribed by Louis M. Dewey (*Westfield Times and News-Letter*, 56 [13 May 1896], 2) and John H. Lockwood (*Westfield and Its Historic Influences* [Springfield, Mass.: Press of Springfield Printing and Binding Co., 1922], I, 107-12). We have adopted their readings for lacunae in the manuscript; such material is bracketed and italicized.

[2]Taylor is apparently inaccurate here. The town record books indicate that Holyoke was not contacted until after a town meeting in August of 1668, and that he left some time before the last of October of the same year. The first reference to Fiske occurs in a meeting of 24 September 1668 (see "Grants of Land at Worronoco: 1658-1725," the meetings of these dates).

[3]Taylor's account of these events is in *The Diary of Edward Taylor*, ed. Francis Murphy (Springfield, Mass.: Connecticut Valley Historical Museum, 1964), pp. 38-40.

[4]Taylor refers here to the material he assembled in "Heads" in the "Book" (see Mignon, "Another Taylor Manuscript at Yale," *Yale University Library Gazette*, 41 [October 1966], 72-73).

[5]Lockwood provides a relatively complete summary of Westfield's experiences during these skirmishes, I, 100-253.

[6]What Taylor means by this cryptic reference is not clear; even from the most generous point of view, however, his postponement of the organization of the church suggests that he was not particularly eager to commit himself to the "Clonian Rusticity" of Westfield. He did not leave Cambridge under the most auspicious circumstances: the "whispering, back-biting tongues" of the Cambridge gossips, as he says, made him "much desirous to go from Cambridge" (*Diary*, p. 38). Granting the complete sincerity in his "treating" the spiritual problems of Elizabeth Steadman, the woodman's wife, the talk was enough to cause him to consider giving up his place at commencement. And though the "Fellows" advised him to accept the Westfield "call"—to "respect the Colledge good"—Taylor does not seem to have been very impressed by the prospect of life in a frontier settlement.

The account in the CR glosses over the fact that nearly four years passed between the time he arrived and the beginning of Philip's War. During this period, members of the community urged Taylor to initiate the procedures for gathering the church; and when he declined, George Phelps, Joseph Whiting, and Samuel Loomis, as representatives of the Town, exchanged a series of letters (copied by Taylor in his "Commonplace Book") with the Northampton Church, for the "incouraging of Mr. Taylor amongst us unto the Comfortable Carrying o[n of] that greate worke before us...." The first letter was written in July of 1673; apparently no reply was received, and the second letter was sent a week later. The committee for the Town urges the Northampton Church to help them in their "Weak Condition" by allowing another Northampton member to settle in Westfield. The reply suggests that Taylor has no valid reason for further delay:

N. H. 29 July 73

Beloved Brethren & Friends,

We have received yours bearing date the 9th of this instant, & cannot but approv of your thoughtfulness about Coalition into a Church State, & the setting up of the Ordinances of the Church in your Plantations....

We have, we hope in the feare of God, pondered your motion, & weighed what answer the Lord calls us to return thereto.—We have considered your Condition, & tho' we pretend not to any decisive power to put an issue to that Question, whether you have such necessity of help as is spoken of? yet so far as concerns us to pass a judgment thereon in order to our Answer to your motion, we do deem that you are already furnisht with a Compitancy of men for the Comfortable beginning of Ecclesiasticall work; you may compare with some other places who have comfortable proceeded therein; so that we cannot understand any such cause of feare that the work will miscarrie in your hands: neither is this our judgment alone, but the judgment of those to whom you committed the Care of giving direction in your proceeding. & perhaps others who are standers by, may be more competent judges in this case than yourselves. Moses himselfe tho' filled of God to judge the whole people of Israel was mistaken in judging of himself.... We have a promise of Gods presence in his worke whi[ch] will abundantly supply all defects, Jer. 1.6,7,8.

We have also considered our own Condition in what capacity we are to gratifie your desires, & truely when we compare the Smallness of our number & Strength with the weig[ht] of the work that lies upon our shoulders, it forbids us to entertain any thought that that way its an heavy burden unto us that we cannot carry on the work of Christ among ourselves with more beauty & strength than we do.... When you have considered our Condition with an impartiall eye, we hope you cannot censure us for retaining what help God hath given.

...These things considered, with much more that might be alledged, we do concur, that the Lord does not call us to grant your requests; & do desire that you would forbare any further motion to us in this kinde. This answer being the result of our deliberate thoughts.

. . . You alledge that the granting your motion would be an encouragement to Mr. Taylor; you shall we hope finde us forward as much as in us lies to encourage him, yet are confident when our answer is weighed our denial will be no discouragement unto him; we are perswaded Mr. Taylor has more wisdom, moderation, & love to ourselves, than to be contented with nothing but what will be so prejudiciall unto us.

. . . The Lord Strengthen your heart to go on undantedly in his work: & despise not the day of smal things: the Lord has been wont by Small beginnings to carry on his greate worke in the world. . . . You have the Command of God (which you express yourselves sensible of) we may say then . . . , Go forth in the Strength of Gods call, & he will be with you. Thus we take leave & committing you to the guidance of the Lord, we rest

Your Loving Brethren $\left\{ \begin{array}{l} \text{Sol: Stoddard} \\ \text{John Strong} \end{array} \right\}$ in the name of the Church.

The citation of the passage from Jeremiah seems not totally gratuitous: "Ah, Lord God! behold, I cannot speak: for I am a child. But the Lord said unto me, Say not I am a child: for thou shalt go to all that I shall send thee, and whatsoever I command thee thou shalt speak."

Their request to "forbare any further motion to us in this kinde" was not heeded by the Westfield men. On 21 August they renewed their requests for assistance, answering point by point the refusal of the Northampton Church. Near the end of the letter they comment:

You desire your Answer may lay no Bar in the way of our Proceedings. We assure you, that if our aime be not accomplished, that if it lay not a bar in the way of, yet it will put such a demur unto, our proceedings, that we know not when we shall get on: for Mr. Taylor is utterly averse to any Coalition into a Church State without further encouragment, & where to have it, if not of you, we know not: wherefore we earnestly desire you to consider our Condition.

Taylor records no answer to this letter.

By the following summer, Taylor had "Changed [his] Condition, & entred into a married State . . . ," and planned, as he says, to organize the church the next summer. But Philip's War intervened, and the proposed organization was again delayed. After the war, however, two more years elapsed before the church was gathered, even though the Westfield group had sought and received authorization from the General Court in the summer of 1678.

It is difficult to account for the protracted delays, and Taylor's demonstrable unwillingness to commit himself to Westfield, and, perhaps, to the ministry itself. Nine years, during which time the sacraments could not be administered, seems like an inordinately long time, particularly in relation to Taylor's later concern with the strict observance of the Lord's Supper.

[7]"J.F." is Taylor's father-in-law, James Fitch.

[8]Cf. the similar, but considerably briefer, headings in the "Book":

The Application of Redemption considered $\left\{\begin{array}{l}\text{Absolutely}\\\text{Relatively.}\end{array}\right.$

Absolutly its nature lies in $\left\{\begin{array}{l}\text{Union to}\\\text{Communion with}\end{array}\right\}$ Christ.

1. Union is wrought by Effectual Calling.

[9]John Calvin, "*Commentariis in Epistolam Romanis,*" *Commentarii in omnes Pauli Apostoli epistolas* (Geneva, 1580), p. 28.

[10]In a marginal note, partially trimmed away, Taylor refers to Cicero's *De Officiis* (*Liber Primus*, XI). The passage is a reference to the oath of allegiance (*sacramento*) which Cato's son swore before he began his service under General Popilius: "*Sed cum amore pugnandi in exercitu remansisset, Cato ad Popilium scripsit, ut, si eum patitur in exercitu remanere, secundo eum abliget militiae sacramento, quia priore amisso jure cum hostibus pugnare non poterat.*" Taylor's marginal note reads: "*Sacramento* to Serve * * * *apud suet.* & hence is that [of C]ato to Pampilius who had * * * his Son from his service * * * who yet went a long with * * *." Taylor had a copy of *De Officiis* in his library; it was used as a textbook when he was at Harvard (see Johnson, *PW*, p. 215, Item 129).

[11]Taylor here apparently refers to *Disputationum theologicarum miscellanearum pars prima* (Geneva, 1652), written by Friedrich Spanheim, the Elder, a professor of theology at the University of Leyden. Taylor owned a copy of the work (see Johnson, *PW*, p. 207, Item 35), which was also known as "Disputationum Syntagma." We have been unable to locate the specific passage Taylor refers to.

[12]This material on the "Day of Judgment" has been previously published in *American Literature*, 42 (January 1972), 525–47.

[13]Taylor's "Relation" has been previously edited by Donald E. Stanford, *American Literature*, 35 (January 1964), 467–73. For a discussion of the "Relation," see Daniel B. Shea, Jr., *Spiritual Autobiography in Early America* (Princeton: Princeton University Press, 1968), pp. 92–100. Shea's judgment seems to us to be quite accurate: "Of surviving spiritual autobiographies by the more eminent Puritans, Edward Taylor's is the most regular, the least interesting on its own merits, a narrative which is unusually successful in suppressing evidence of the character and personality of its author..." (p. 92).

[14]Cf. II Sam. 2.18ff.

[15]A transliteration of an Aramaic term, Ἀχελδαμά is literally a "field of blood." The reference is to the field which Judas purchased with the silver "reward of iniquity" (see Acts 1.19).

[16]John Mawdsley (also spelled Maudsley, Mosely) was born in Dorchester, Massachusetts, in 1640. The "old Mr. Mather" he refers to is Richard, the minister of the Dorchester Church from its organization in 1636 until his death in 1669. His son Increase "came out of England" in the fall of 1661; Mawdsley apparently heard him preach during the time Increase stayed with his father in Dorchester.

The Mawdsley family was associated with the Deweys in Dorchester, where the families seem to have been involved—as they were in Westfield—in milling. The Deweys moved to Windsor, Connecticut, in 1641; shortly after

Mawdsley moved to Windsor in 1664, the Dewey brothers, Thomas, Jr., Josiah, and Jedidiah moved to Northampton and established a mill there. The Deweys then settled in Westfield shortly before the town was organized in 1669, and Mawdsley was again associated with them in mill work, though he returned to Windsor in the early 1680s, where he owned the mill and several large tracts of land. (For information relating to Westfield settlers, we are indebted to Louis M. Dewey's eight-volume typescript, "Genealogical Notes," in the Westfield Athenaeum.)

[17]We have been unable to locate this exact source, though it is similar to question and answer series in a number of early catechisms. It is also possible that the source is Richard Mather's *Catechism* (Cambridge, 1650), of which there is no extant copy.

[18]With Taylor and John Ingerson, Loomis is one of the three foundation men not native born. His father, a woolen draper from Braintree, Essex, brought the family to Windsor, Connecticut, in 1638, when Samuel was five years old. His apprenticeship in Hartford brought him under Samuel Stone's ministry, also a native of Essex, and—as Loomis experiences—committed to the observance of "exact Sabbaths."

The Reverend Roger Newton's ministry at Farmington was a troubled one, and Loomis was not admitted to the Farmington Church until 1661, four years after Newton had been dismissed. When Loomis moved to Westfield in the spring of 1674, he was appointed ensign of the foot company, and was active in preparation for the Indian troubles. Though never ordained, he was elected deacon of the Church, and was selected as the layman to participate in the laying on of hands at Taylor's ordination.

[19]There is no record of Josiah Dewey's residence in Farmington, though he must have spent some time there before Newton was dismissed. Dewey moved to Northampton in 1660, when he was nineteen; Eleazer, son of Richard Mather, had organized the Northampton Church two years earlier. Josiah was admitted before Mather's death in 1669, and retained his membership there until the Westfield Church was organized ten years later, though he had moved to Westfield in 1668.

As a carpenter, his work took him to a number of areas; he was first granted land in Westfield, for example, as payment for building the minister's house. And it was probably on one of his trips that he heard the Reverend Joseph Eliot, John Eliot's second son, pastor of the Church at Guilford. With his brothers in Westfield, he became a fairly influential man, serving as selectman for a number of years, farming, milling, and acting as Westfield's builder. In December of 1692, with Nathaniel Weller, he was ordained deacon of the Church. Four years later he moved with his large family to the then pioneer settlement in Lebanon, Connecticut, and received his dismission from the Westfield Church in November 1700.

[20]John Root, one of the original grantees of Westfield, came from Farmington, Connecticut, several years before the town was organized. He must have spent some time in Hartford, perhaps as an apprentice, where he came under Stone's ministry. The Haynes he refers to is probably Joseph, son of the

governor, and Hooker's successor; the "Willis" he refers to is more than likely one of the family of George Wyllys, the grandfather of Taylor's second wife, Ruth Wyllys. Root came to Westfield in 1666; he acted as commissary officer during the Indian disturbances. He lived only eight years after the Church was organized.

[21] The Phelps family came to Westfield from Windsor, a year or so before the town was organized; George, Isaak's father, was one of the original petitioners for land. The family had come from England to Dorchester at the same time as the Mawdsley and Dewey families, moving to Windsor and then Westfield as had the Mawdsleys and Deweys.

Isaak, about Taylor's age, was quite a prominent man and large landowner in Westfield. He was selectman for twenty-four years, town clerk for nine, town treasurer for over twenty, and for a number of years the town's schoolmaster. His conversion dates from his earlier years in Windsor, under the ministry of the Reverend John Wareham, who was noted—so Cotton Mather says—for "those deadly pangs of *melancholy*" which occasionally kept him from partaking of the Lord's Supper, though he administered it to his congregation. In later years, Taylor and Phelps were often at odds, but their disagreements seem to have been the result of two strong-willed men, leaders in the secular and spiritual affairs of the town, adhering rather stubbornly to opposing but validly held principles.

[22] Little is known about John Ingerson (spelled "Ingersol" in the Town and Court Records). The reference in his Relation to "Darby in old England" is the only information known about him before he settled in Hartford in 1650. His name does not appear in the authorization from the General Court nor in the letters of invitation to the visiting Elders and Messengers. He seems to have been selected rather late as a foundation man, in place of the ailing Thomas Gun. Dewey and Ingerson were the two foundation men from the North-ampton Church; when asked for more help in the exchange of letters in 1674, the Northampton leaders replied that they had already supplied more than their share.

Ingerson had moved to Westfield some time in the middle seventies; he is listed as one of the selectmen in 1676. Apart from the striking account of his conversion, and a few offices he held in the town, little else is known about him. He lived only four years after the church was organized.

[23] Ingerson apparently refers to Jeremiah Burroughs' *Gospel-Revelation in Three Treatises* (London, 1660), to one of several similar passages, such as the following: ". . . Bee willing to examine your hopes, to lay them to the rule of the Scripture, and that very narrowly; And if you find your hopes cannot stand with the Word, then resolve thus with yourselves, the work is yet to bee done, the very laying of the foundation of that great work, of the saving of my soul, it is to begin" (p. 327). See also pp. 330–31. Taylor owned Burroughs' commentary on Hosea (cf. Johnson, Item 47).

[24] A blank space is left in the text; there is no indication of the person Ingerson is referring to.

²⁵This comment appears in Ambrose's discussion of Peter's confession, *"De Incarnationis Dominicae Sacramento,"* *Omnia Opera* (Basil, 1527), II, 234.

²⁶The annotation Taylor cites here in the left margin is largely trimmed away. The reference is Hieronymi Zanchii, *"Commentarios in Epistolas Apostolicas,"* *Operum Theologicorum* (Geneva, 1619): ". . . *sicut erat unum tantum templum Salomonis, multa autem habet* κατοικητήρια, *habitacula, è quibus constabat sic catholicam Ecclesiam, unam quidem esse, sed multas habere particulares, è quibus constat . . .*" (VI, 74). Johnson lists two references to Zanchy in the inventory of Taylor's library (see Items 16 and 75); neither entry is specific enough to indicate which titles or editions Taylor may have owned.

²⁷See below, RS, note 5.

²⁸Probably the Persian King Xerxes I (486–465 B.C.); cf. Esther 1.6.

²⁹Taylor notes here in the left-hand margin, "Arthur Jackson on the place." Vol. 3 of Jackson's *Works* is listed in the inventory of Taylor's library (see Johnson, *PW,* Item 189). This reference, however, is to Vol. I, *A Help for the Understanding of the Holy Scripture, Containing certain short notes upon the five books of Moses . . .* (Cambridge, 1643), p. 274, specifically to the commentary on Leviticus 1.4, laying down the necessity for public confession in the process of being cleansed from sin.

These Scriptures, excepting Chap. 13, all refer to the command to the penitent to "lay his hand upon the head of his offering"; Leviticus 13, and 14 as well, deals specifically with the ceremonial rituals required for the cleansing of the leper. Taylor is inordinately fascinated with the leprosy-sin identification, and with the minutiae of the Hebrew ceremonial offerings for the purification of the leper-sinner:

> . . . I finde myselfe defild:
> Issues & Leprosies all ore mee streame. . . .
> My seate, Bed, saddle, spittle too's uncleane.
> My Issue Running Leprosy doth Spread:
> My upper Lip is Coverd: not my Head. (Med. 27, Series II)

See Karen Rowe's discussion of this Meditation and the passages in Leviticus 13 and 14, in *American Literature,* 40 (November 1968), 370-74.

³⁰The marginal note refers to "Mr. Cotton in the way of the Congregationall Churches cleared." In Chap. V, "Of the fruits of Congregationall discipline," Cotton presents a brief series of comments on the purity of the primitive churches, attributing their success to the vigilance with which they screened applicants. In this context, Cotton stresses the need for public confession: ". . . Their exact strictnesse in examing and trying their *Catechumeni,* before they received them into *Ecclesians Fidelium,* brought forth this savory and spirituall fruit, the purity of Churches. . . . And as their strict examination received their members pure; so their strict censure kept them pure" (*The Way of Congregational Churches Cleared* [London, 1647], p.100).

³¹Taylor refers here in the margin to Jackson and "Hutchison" on Job 33. 27, 28. Jackson's comments appear in Vol. 3 of the *Works, Annotations Upon . . . The Book of Job, the Psalmes, the Proverbs, Ecclesiastes, and the Song of Solomon*

(London, 1658), listed in Taylor's library (see Johnson, Item 189). In his discussion of these passages, Jackson insists, as Taylor notes, that public confession is necessary for coming to God: "[These verses] contain the sick mans Confession of Gods dealing with him; to wit, that being recovered he looks upon others with pity, and out of a desire of their conversion should acknowledge how he had sinned, and did thereby bring Gods hand upon him, and how upon his repentance God shewed him mercy again" (p. 248). The second reference is to George Hutcheson, *An Exposition of the Book of Job* (London, 1669). He comments on the passage much to the same effect as Jackson: "So these Verses will contain the last effect of all this proceeding betwixt God and the afflicted man; Namely, the recovered mans confession and acknowledgement (to the honour of God and edification of others) both of his sin v. 27 and of Gods goodness towards him. . . . I take this to be the right reading of v. 27. That the afflicted man shall confess his miscarriage, before others" (pp. 485–86).

[32]The marginal note here reads "Pol. Synop: in loc," a reference to Matthew Poole, *Synopsis Criticorum*, 5 vols. (Amsterdam, 1669–1676), a copy of which Taylor owned (see Johnson, Item 187; we cite from the London edition of 1669-1676). This reference is to the "*Commentatorum in Jobum*," II, col. 356.

[33]Taylor cites in the margin the following comment from Poole's *Synopsis*, "*Commentatorum in Ecclesiasten*," II: ". . .*David. . .post conversionem poenitentiam suam publicè professus est, Psalm* 51" (col.1813).

[34]Taylor refers again in the margin to the "*Commentatorum in Ecclesiasten*": " חלהלת *Haec vox consilium ejus in hoc Libro scribendo explicat, nempe ut sceleratam vitam abjuraret, & resipscentiam profiteretur, ac reconciliationem, cum Deo & Ecclesia*" (col. 1815).

[35]A rather characteristic Taylor annotation. His point is that the Jews, upon their return from Captivity, reaffirmed their commitment to Yahweh, demonstrating, in Taylor's view, the need for public confession of sin for restoration, and hence the necessity of public confession upon the initial admittance into church fellowship. But the two marginal notes ("read Jackson" and "Dr. Owen Ercit 15 before his on Heb., p. 194") refer to attempts to determine the chronology of the reconstruction of the Temple.

In his *Annotations upon. . .Joshua, Judges, the two Books of Samuel, Kings and Chronicles; and the Books of Ezra, Nehemiah, and Esther* (Cambridge, 1646), Jackson argues that the reconstruction of the Temple was more than likely begun under the reign of Darius, the son of Hystaspes, rather than Darius, the son of Cyrus (II, 749). John Owen, *Exercitations on the Epistle to the Hebrews* (London, 1668), in his computation of the chronology of the book of Daniel, urges the higher probability of the work beginning under the reign of Darius, the son of Cyrus. In either case—and this seems to be Taylor's reason for citing Owen—". . .the people had done little more than built the *bare fabrick*, all things as to the true order of the Worship of god remaining in great confusion, and the civil state utterly neglected" (I, 193-94). Taylor owned several of Owen's works (see Johnson, Items 33, 34, 45, 60, 70).

³⁶Both citations are from Poole. The first from the *"Commentatorum in Epistolam ad Romanos,"* IV, pt. 2, col. 232; the second from the *"Commentatorum in Epistolam Jacobi,"* IV, pt. 2, col. 1476.

³⁷Calvin, *"Commentariis in I Petri,"* p. 29. In the margin, to the right of this citation, is an illegible Latin note, largely trimmed away. We have been unable to decipher any of it.

³⁸The left-hand marginal note is a reference to Grotius on Acts 19.18, as cited in Poole, *"Commentatorum in Acta Apostolorum,"* IV, pt. 1: *"Annunciabant delicta sua . . . Graeci h. l.* Δεῖ πύντα, etc. *(Fidelem omnem oportet confiteri peccata sua,* etc.)" (col. 1560).

³⁹Taylor here bases these statements about the practice of the early church on citations from Tertullian and Cyprian, as quoted by Poole, *"Comentatorum in I Epistolam Petri,"* IV, pt. 2, col. 1525. The marginal annotation is only partially legible; the statement is probably *". . . fidem internam exteriori professione, dum quis baptizatur, expressam, id esse quod in baptismate nos salvos facit."*

⁴⁰Taylor cites here in the margin Justin Martyr's comments on catechetical instruction in the early church, and identifies the source of his citation as John Norton, *Responsio ad totam quaestionum syllogen a clarissimo viro Domino Guilielmo Apollonio propositam* (London, 1648), pp. 5-6. Taylor owned a copy of Norton (Johnson, *PW*, Item 119).

⁴¹There is no marginal reference here to Gregory, but see below, the second version of this sermon, note 30.

⁴²Taylor notes here in the margin, "Tertul: Coron: Militis: Cap. 3." This citation, and the same one in the second version of the sermon (see below, note 27) is taken from the *Centuriae Magdeburgensis,* 7 vols., ed. Matthias Flacius (Basil, 1559-1574).

⁴³This long passage, quoted in the right-hand margin, is paraphrased from Augustine's *Confessions;* Taylor identifies the source as "Dr. Owen on the spirit, p. 310, out of Augustin: Confess bk 3 [actually bk. 8]." One would expect Taylor to cite from his own edition of Augustine; the citations in the "Manuscript Book" indicate his possession of substantial sections of Augustine's work before the church was organized. But this citation, as he notes, is from Owen's Πνευματολογια: *or, a Discourse Concerning the Holy Spirit* (London, 1674), pp. 310-11.

⁴⁴Taylor refers here in the margin to the *"Bohemica Confessione"* from *Harmonia Confessionum Fidei, Orthodoxarum, & Reformatarum Ecclesiarum . . .* (Geneva, 1581): *". . . Baptisato . . . ubi adoleverint . . . quo deinceps quando communione Coenae Domini uti expetunt, fidem suam, ore proprio suáque sponte profiteri, & sanctificationem suam, qua Domino consecrati, sunt, renovare possint"* (pp. 93-94).

[45]Pareus' commentaries on Matthew and Hosea were in Taylor's library (*PW*, Items 26 and 29). This reference is to *In S. Matthaei Evangelium Commentarius* (Oxford, 1631), p. 94.

[46]Johan Piscatore, *Analysis Logica Evangelli Secundum Matthaeum* . . ., 3d ed. (*Herbumae Nassoviorum*, 1606): "*Baptismus nulli adulto conferendus est, nisi prius ediderit confessionem peccatorum* . . ." (p. 65).

[47]Taylor adds the following marginal comments:

Nay Mr. Ruterford 1. 2 p. 196, requires such a confession, as may testify to the Church that there is saving truth, & that they be invisible Saints that desire to joyn themselves to any visible Congregation.

Mr. Hooker par. 3. p. 5. of *Church Disc.* saith, he must ever give some reason of his hope in the face of the Congregation, & when admitted, ingage himselfe to walke with them in the covenant of the Church according to any of the rules of the gospel that either are or can be made known unto him.

The reference to "Mr. Ruterford" is to Samuel Rutherford's *The Due right of Presbyteries or, a Peacable Plea for the Government of the Church of Scotland* (London, 1644), who insists that ". . . profession is a condition required in the right receivers of the Seales in an Ecclesiasticall way; but faith giveth the right to these seales. . ." (p.194). Rutherford also insists in *The Covenant of Life Opened: Or, a Treatise of the Covenant of Grace* (Edinburgh, 1654) that a confession of saving faith is necessary: "he that beleeveth both really, savingly, and also professedly and visibly, is saved" (p. 85).

The reference to Thomas Hooker, *A Survey of the Summe of Church-Discipline* (London, 1648), is, with one or two minor changes, a direct quote of the material in pt. 3, Chap. I, p. 5.

[48]These terms, "artificial" and "inartificial," are references to Ramistic dichotomies. Artificial arguments "demonstrate themselves from the facts to any observer at any time." But not all facts are available to all men, for past historical events exist beyond man's direct comprehension. Hence inartificial arguments are those which "must be taken on trust, on testimony." By artificial arguments, then, a man "may see by himself"; through the inartificial "he may see by another man's eye" (cf. Perry Miller, *The New England Mind: The Seventeenth Century* [Cambridge: Harvard University Press, 1967], pp. 129ff.).

[49]Taylor cites here in the right-hand margin Calvin's comments on I John 4.1: "*Publicum examen ad communem Ecclesiae consesum & πολιτείαν spectat*" ("*Commentariis in Johannis Apostoli Epistola*," p. 61).

[50]A marginal note here, largely trimmed away, seems to be a statement of the distinction between the Genus and Species.

[51]See above, note 26.

[52]Gun was one of the original foundation men authorized by the General Court; because of ill health, John Ingerson was selected to take his place.

[53]For a discussion of the extent of slave-holding in Western Massachusetts, see Henry Morris, "Slavery in the Connecticut Valley," *Papers and Proceedings of the Connecticut Valley Historical Society, 1876–1881*, 1 (1881), 207–17.

[54]Beginning with the entries at the end of 1722, the handwriting is illegible. There are only four entries between 1722 and 1726, all in Taylor's hand; the first notation in Nehemiah Bull's script is for 11 December 1726. Manuscript p. 110 is blank; the record of admissions continues in the handwriting of subsequent ministers through manuscript pp. 111–22. Taylor's script begins again on manuscript p. 123.

The negotiations for a successor to Taylor, as recorded in the "Town Records, 1696–1762, City of Westfield," were quite protracted and not always amicable. Taylor suffered a severe illness in December of 1720 (see "Edward Taylor's Valedictory Poems," *Early American Literature*, 7 [Spring 1972], 38–63). A year after his illness, Deacon Thomas Noble and a selectman were appointed by the Town to "discourse with Mr. Taylor concerning giveing a minister a call." At the same meeting (9 January 1721/22), and before Taylor was contacted, the Town also voted to "send for Mr. Brown at Newhaven to come up & carey on the work of the ministrey with us three or four months in order to a settlement." Nothing came of the overture to Mr. Brown, and a year later (8 April 1723) Isaac Stiles was engaged to "atend the school for the year insewing & to assist Mr. Taylor in the ministery in order to a setlement amongst us." On 20 August of the same year, the first of a number of disputes in town meetings occurred; the Town "voted to Give Mr. Isack Stiles one Hundred pounds a year as a setled yearly salerey when he shall undertake the whole work of the ministrey upon him. . . ." The sum granted to Stiles was 20 £ more than Taylor had ever received; because of this, and perhaps other reasons as well (Taylor had partially recovered by this time), "sundrey persons Disented against all things that were acted at the aforesaid meeting," and insisted that their names be entered into the record. Stiles' response to their offer suggests he was aware that the attempts to replace Taylor were not agreeable to a fairly large number of people: "Gentlemen, upon mature Deliberation & Good Advice I have Thought fit & advisable to accept your call at present with this proviso that there arise no sufitient Discoragment which if there should I shall then look upon my sellf free from any obligation to you." By the late fall of 1724, however, Stiles had apparently decided not to become involved in the Town's problems; there is no further mention of him in the "Records." (Stiles married Kezia, Taylor's youngest daughter, on 1 June 1725.)

The Town began negotiating with the new schoolmaster, Bull, in the fall of 1724, at first simply to help Taylor with the preaching. But in a meeting of 20 August 1725, when "it was proposed to the Town whether or no they Did not want a minister beside Mr. Taylor, it was voated in the afirmative," with no dissenting votes recorded. Bull seemed to have wanted more money than the Town was willing to pay; six months later (23 February 1725/26) the Town voted to urge Bull to "accept on reasonable terms." And in a 3 March meeting, they voted to give Bull fifty acres on condition that he accept the call, 100 £ in labor towards building him a house, and 140 £ in "Money towards a Settlement if he Settles with us in the Ministry." Even these inducements were apparently not enough, and funds were voted (26 September 1726) for the entertainment of several interim ministers. Bull, however, was finally ordained on 26 October

1726, and Taylor, according to Bull's account (Lockwood, I, 320ff.), was present at the ordination, assisting in the laying on of hands. Bull's account of these negotiations in the "Church Records" is phrased in less mercenary terms than the entries in the "Town Records."

On the other hand, the Town was not always as careful about paying the minister as it might have been. The "Records" indicate that Taylor's salary was often in arrears, that the Constable was authorized to serve warrants on those who had not paid (meeting of 22 December 1696, for example), and that, particularly in his last years, Taylor was not paid at all. (For an account of the suit his son Eldad filed against the Town, see below, note 66.) Bull perhaps had just grounds for his caution.

[55]In his study, *Delinquent Saints*, Oberholzer provides a general view, based on a large number of Massachusetts church records, of the types, numbers, and disposition of cases which were adjudicated in specific churches. He discusses briefly some of the items in the Westfield records, as we note in reference to individual cases; generally, however, he focuses on cases after Taylor's tenure. He does not provide transcriptions of these accounts.

[56]The point at issue in Mawdsley's case is the relative value of town lots and the common land. Mrs. Mawdsley's reasoning seems to be that if they had been paid for the improved town lot which they had given up, they could have bought "Huckplies Lot" adjacent to their town lot. To further complicate the matter, a portion of the town lot given up had been sold by John Hanchet, and the Mawdsleys felt that they should have received at least some of the sale price (cf. Lockwood, I, 186ff.; Oberholzer, *Delinquent Saints*, pp. 206-08).

[57]Cf. Lockwood, I. 220ff.

[58]Apparently a localism for "Satan"; Lockwood (I, 187) transcribes the word as "Adversary."

[59]For an analysis of the judicial structure of early Massachusetts, see George Lee Haskins, *Law and Authority in Early Massachusetts* (Hamden, Conn.: Archon Books, 1968); the specific structure and development of the Hampshire County Court system are discussed in Joseph H. Smith's fine introduction to his edition of John Pynchon's journal of the cases of the County Court of Hampshire, *Colonial Justice in Western Massachusetts (1639-1702): The Pynchon Court Record* (Cambridge: Harvard University Press, 1961).

[60]Mawdsley's promise to "meddle no more in this Matter" seems to have been kept; there is only one entry related to this case in the court records, "A Book of Records of the Acts of the Country Courts holden at Springfield & Northampton in the County of Hampshire, 1677-1728":

> Lt. John Maudsley of Westfield presenting a Petition to the General Court held at Boston, May 24, 1682 respecting some part of his homelot by him Layd downe for the accommodating of some Neighbours there...the said General Court did Refer the whole matter to the consideration of the Countie Court in Hampshire, & did Impower them to Act therein & to settle the said busyness as the Law Directs in such case, & as might remove al grounds of just Complaint from said Peti-

tioner, this County Court therefore takeing into Consideration the said matter, did respite the whole Case to be Issued at the next Court at Northampton, where the Inhabitants of said Westfield might appeare to alleadge what they have with them so to doe; & in the meane time Lt. William Clarke & Capt. Aaron Cooke of Northampton were desired & appointed by this court as a Comittee to goe upon the Place, & to view the same & to give the best information they shall find to give to the said Court At a Countie Courte holden at Springfield Sept. 25, 1682:

John Pyncheon   Magistrates
Peter Tilton
Lt. William Clarke
Capt. Aaron Cooke Associates
Lt. Philip Smith (1,60)

[61]Thomas Dewey, older brother of Josiah (one of the foundation men) and Jedidiah, was the messenger who brought Taylor to Westfield from Cambridge (*Diary*, pp. 38–39). One of the original grantees of Westfield, in addition to being a partner with his brothers in the corn mill, he was the owner of the public house, farmer, and an influential man in town affairs.

This is the first of several litigations—two of which appear in the "Church Records"—involving the Deweys and rival mill operators. The brothers had established the first mill with Joseph Whiting in 1672. That mill "being worn out," the Town authorized Thomas Dewey and John Mawdsley to build a new mill: "At a Town meting Desember 17, 1680 there is Granted to Lt. Maudlsy, Thomas Dewey, Sargent [Josiah] Dewey liberty to sete a griste mil and a sawmile at the mouth to t[w]o mile brook; and so long as thay maintayn a griste mille the towne grants them liberty to improufe the low land this side the brook" ("Miscellaneous Records, 1675–1695, City of Westfield," n.p.). This mill was damaged during that "great Flood. . .in August" (perhaps referred to in the title of Taylor's poem "Upon the Sweeping Flood Aug: 13.14. 1683"). The Deweys were apparently slow in repairing the damage, and the rival mill operators (see below, "Brother Joseph Pomeries Case as to the Mill Matters") began to build a dam which would divert the water the Deweys needed for their mill. And, being tempted, as Taylor says, Thomas Dewey "went one morning, & cut down their Dam & hid their tooles."

[62]What satisfaction Dewey made is not clear; for when Pomery and his partners took Dewey to court, Dewey was ordered to pay only six shillings in court costs:

Joseph Pumery, Samuel Taylor, Nathaniel Williams, Stephen Lee & Samuel Phelps Plaintiffes, Thomas Dewey Sr. Defendant in an action of the Case for unjustly cutting downe a dam upon two mile Brooke in the town bounds of Westfield, which dam was erected according to grant of the town of Westfield, & for felloneously takeing, & for a considerable time concealing & carrying away or hideing of their tooles, al which unjust actions of the said Dewey hath proved very prejudiciall & greatly to the damage of the aforesaid Pumery & the Rest of the Owners, & to the value of forty pounds according to attachment entry money 20£.

In the action depending in Corte wherin Joseph Pumery...& Thomas Dewey defendant for cutting down of the dam, the testimonys & evidences in the Case being procured & read in Corte & transferred to the Jury, they find for the Defendant Costs of Corte as per bill six shillings allowed of in Corte. ("A Book of Records," I, 90)

[63]Joseph Pomery, the youngest son of Eltweed, was born in Windsor, Connecticut, in June 1652. He was the younger brother of Medad Pomery of Northampton, deacon of the church there, merchant, town officer, and Associate Justice of the County Court. Joseph moved with his father to Northampton in 1672; when his father died the next year, Joseph moved to Westfield. He lived there until 1694, moving then to Lebanon, Connecticut (at the same time Josiah Dewey and his family moved), and finally to Colchester about the turn of the century.

Joseph seems to have been a somewhat erratic person; on the other hand, this case does not seem to have "shocked" the village of Westfield, as Oberholzer asserts (p. 191). There is no mention of the matter in the "Town Records," and only one entry of a court action which might be possibly related: in March of 1684 one Daniel Saxton sued Pomery for an "Action of Debt to the some of six pound" and Pomery was ordered by the Court to pay. But Pomery was not the only town constable who had difficulty in collecting tax rates, or misjudged the relative market value of "country pay" (see the *Pynchon Court Record*, p. 318, for a similar case).

[64]Although there are several fairly long entries in the "Court Records" (I, 88ff.), the stages in the litigation are not exactly clear. The Deweys apparently filed an action in the County Court against the rival mill operators, and the court ruled in the Deweys' favor. The judgment does not seem to have been enforced at first, for the defendants filed an appeal, although during the time of appeal the defendants were enjoined against using their mill. When they ignored the restraining order, the Deweys brought an additional suit, which was also decided in their favor. In the interim, however, Pomery had apparently sold the land on which the mill was built to George Saxton, also formerly of Windsor and one of the original grantees in Westfield.

From the evidence available, it appears that the dispute was finally settled by the action of the Church, according to the original agreement signed in November of 1685 at the County Court in Springfield. Pomery's confession is dated in December of that year, and there is no further entry in the "Court Records" which would indicate some other disposition was made.

[65]John Younglove, probably from Ipswich, preached first at Brookfield for a year or two, with no more success than he later had at Suffield. Before he moved to Suffield to organize the church, he had taught at Hadley for six or seven years. Whatever his failings, he stayed in Suffield for only a year or two, and was advised by the Court to cease preaching. Younglove (and his wife as well) seems to have irritated a number of people during his short stay; in

addition to this case against Winchell, Younglove's wife Sarah brought action in the County Court against Mary Pengilly for "Publishing making uttering or spreading False reports tending to the defamation" of her character (see the *Pynchon Court Record*, p. 374).

[66]For nearly a decade there are no disciplinary cases recorded; there is no evidence of a hiatus in the manuscript. Taylor seems to have enjoyed a period of relative quiet in his own congregation, although it is during this period that he apparently threatened to leave Westfield. The problem seems to have originated in the difficulties in collecting his salary. In December of 1692, the Town voted to give Taylor his usual salary of 80 £, but desired him to "abate 10 pound thereof." At a town meeting in December 1696, "Isaac Phelps, Samuell Root and Jedediah Dewey were chosen and appointed to view the rates past that were made for Mr. Talers maintanens and take an acount of what is yet unpaid." The following year Taylor again received 80 £, but the pay, as was customary, was "country pay"—staples for the family, corn, cloth, and so on. And something seems to have been amiss in the supplies paid in, for the Town appointed a Committee to "cause to rectifying any thing in the said provisions." The next year, 1698, the Town Constable was again charged with collecting Taylor's rate.

Finally, in January 1698/99, Taylor was given the choice between "provision pay" and money; the entry, quite unlike the earlier notations regarding Taylor's salary, suggests that he threatened to leave unless the Town became more careful in meeting its financial obligations: "It was. . . voted that the town doe desire Mr. Taylor's continuance and setlment amongst us in the work of the ministry and for his incorigment do ingage to alow him eighty pounds anualy in provision pay at the prices wee formerlly use to pay or in money so long as he continues with us in the work of the ministry" ("Town Records," 30 January 1698/9). But the problems did not end with this agreement.

In November of 1730, six months after Taylor's death, his son Eldad filed a complaint in Inferiour Court against the Town "for their neglect of fullfilling their obligation to his father with Respect to his salerey or maintainaince." A brief, in the handwriting of Isaac Stiles, apparently filed in support of Eldad's complaint, evidences the Town's carelessness in regard to Taylor's salary—and Taylor's threat in 1698 to leave Westfield.

> The Town of Westfie[ld] did note June 31—1698/9 to allow mr. Taylor annually £80 so that it is clear that his years service began Annually June 31. The £80 Rat[e] which was Committed To William Loomis March 1725/6 was the last £80 Rate which was made for mr. Taylor which was the whole of it due the 31 of June—1725/6 some time before the Rate was made[.] Now the time of mr. Taylors Heirs ask Pay of the Town of Westfield is 3 years 4 months, & 24 dayes— one year and almost a Month of which time mr. Taylor Carried on the work of the ministry in Publick for the last sermon mr. Taylor Preached was some time the Latter end of feb. 1726/7.
>
> How the Town of Westfield can justify themselves that they have done their Duty: looks very strange to me for if we should allow the £60

granted in feb: 1726 to go toward the following [year] yet there remains above £20 Due for the time mr. Taylor carried on the work of the ministry in Publick——

Now why mr. Taylor should have no support from the Town after he was disabled from preaching in my opinion cant be justified for * * * as mr. Taylor stood in the relation of minister to that People they were under both natural & moral obligations to support him—their neglecting of him as they did was not only unnatural but in my opinion very evil and sinfull.

There is a clause in the Agreement which the town of Westfield makes great Improovement off: as a salve for their neglects (viz, so long as he continues with us in the work of the ministry[).]

1. The Agreement was made in the year 1698/9 a little better than 30 years ago at which time mr. Taylor had a design of leaving the Town as I have heard him and also some of Westfie[l]d say—[S]o it seems to be Implied in the Introduction of agreemen[t] or vote; which is as follows (It was unanimously voted that the Town does desire mr. Taylors Continuance and settlement amongst us in the work of the ministry:) therefore that Clause in the vote (so long as he continues with us in the work of the ministry[)] needs be lookt upon by an Impartial eye, to be in opposition to his leaving of them and goeing to some other place: or his quiting the ministry there; and was * * * the least reference to his being disabled from preaching——

2. An other thing I would offer is that the Agreement in a strick sense does not cut mr. Taylor off from a following; for so long as mr. Taylor Carried on any one Part of the ministerial wor[k] he Continued with them in the ministry. Now Praying for the people in private Counselling Exhorting and Reprooveing in private these and such like are parts of the ministerial work which mr. Taylor was capable off * * * desisted from preaching and * * * the [Town] of Westfield have charity to beleve. [1/2] That he was constant and faithful in it; those who did belong to his family do say that many persons come to him for the resolving of their doubt, for counsel and direction in the conserns of their souls after his last confinement to his house—and if so he continued in the work of the ministry—and according to the vote should have been supported——

[If] mr. Taylor had been unfruittful, and it had been any fault of hissen that he did not preach any longer then there had been Reason for withholding maintenance from him; but he was fruittfull and did to his utmost for the good of that people—I remember when the Committe apointed for seeking after Another minister (to help mr. Taylor) Came to the ministers of this lower Part of the Countrey; being upon some special occasion Convend at Westfie[l]d—speaking upon this * * * the Committe generally said that they had no desire nor the least design of Cuting mr. Taylor short of his following * * * had been a faithfull servant of it: * * *

Finally if it should be Concluded that the Town Agreement Expires with
mr. Taylors last sermon then I would Appeal—

1. To the law of God—God made bountifull provisions for his ministers under the Law—those who at a certain Age were to cease from
   their Publick Labours they would not cut short of their maintenance
   from the people[. D]oubtless Gods will in this matter (as to main-
   tence) is the same under the gospel—this seems to be plain from the
   Apostles Argument in the I Cor. 9.9: it is written in the Law of Moses
   thou shalt not muzle the mouth of the ox that treadeth out the corn;
   doth god take care for oxen: and from v. 14 * * * even so hath the
   lord ordained Etc: have the apostle argued from the maintenance of
   ministry under the gospel from the provisions which God made for
   the same under the law—from whence I argue that if those under the
   law were to be maintained; when by Reason of age; were to cease from
   the Publick ministry—
   Then it is the will of God that those under the gospel who through
   Age are Incapacitated for the publick ministry should have their maintenance notwithstanding Continued[.] Where else was the force of the
   apostles argument——
2. I would Appeal to Humane laws—our laws have made very good
   provisions in such cases—for where Agreements between Ministers
   and People happen to be Expired—those who set in the seat of Justice
   are Impowered and Required to take care that Justice be Duely Executed which is what we ["we" is cancelled in the manuscript] the Heirs
   of the Reverend mr. Taylor do Humbly Pray for.

This sort of problem was not restricted only to Westfield, however; in
1697, for example, Stoddard, whose annual salary was 100£, offered to take
80£ if Northampton would pay in money rather than provision (see Perry
Miller, "Solomon Stoddard, 1643-1729," *Harvard Theological Review*, 34
[October 1941], 277-320).

[67]Abigail Bush was the eighth and last child of Walter Lee, one of Westfield's earliest settlers, and one of the most interesting reprobates (see below,
note 83). Abigail's comments refer to her father's forthcoming nuptials; in his
late sixties Walter married Hepzibah, widow of Caleb Pomery of Northampton.
Samuel Bush, Abigail's husband, moved from Suffield to Springfield in 1686;
his first wife Mary died the next year, shortly after they had moved to Westfield. A carpenter, he married Abigail Lee in 1690. (Oberholzer discusses this
case in the context of "Domestic and Marital Relations," pp. 123ff. He is
mistaken in several particulars.)

[68]Sections of this material, and Taylor's involvement in the "Suffield Concerns," are cited and analyzed in Donald E. Stanford, "Edward Taylor Versus
the 'Young Cockerill' Benjamin Ruggles: A Hitherto Unpublished Episode

from the Annals of Early New England Church History," *New England Quarterly*, 44 (September 1971), 459–68. Taylor's eulogy to those "Worthy, & Renowned men of God, that laid the Foundation here" is one of the clearest statements of his reverence for orthodoxy, and a moving one as well. It is also the source of his anger at Stoddard in this particular situation: when one disregards such practices as requiring letters of "Dismission," not to say the requirement of a Public Relation, New England's apostasy has indeed been sanctioned by Stoddard's actions. Taylor's "involvement" seems to have had some effect, however; the Church in Suffield, as Stanford notes, was apparently organized and conducted according to Congregational principles.

[69]Taylor's irritation at Stoddard and the other Elders for permitting members to be admitted without Dismission may account for this brief entry relating to the Deweys and Pomerys. These incidents occur more than two years later and both letters are also recorded in the section on Dismissions. By entering the notation here Taylor seems to be saying that the Church in Westfield would not be a party to such slackness.

[70]This is apparently the same Samuel Bush who married Abigail Lee in 1690, although nine years seems like a rather long time before his transgression was discovered. There is no mention of this incident in any of the court records.

[71]We have found no reference to this petition in any of the court records. The laying out of highways, however, seems to have caused more litigation than almost any other matter.

[72]In December of 1697, "Mr. John Pynchon the 3d," grandson of the Colonel, was appointed Register of Deeds, in addition to his duties as Clerk of the Court. He married Taylor's daughter Bathshuah in 1702.

[73]This reference is not to Joseph Pomery (who had moved to Colchester from Lebanon earlier in the year), but to his cousin, Ebenezer of Northampton, one of Medad's eleven children (see below, "Brother Benjamin Smiths Case").

[74]For the context of these letters, which preceded "The Proposals of 1705," see *The Creeds and Platforms of Congregationalism*, pp. 465ff. The attempts of the more conservative ministers to establish "Consociations" would have been welcome to Taylor; he may have felt, however, and particularly in light of Stoddard's innovations and his recent experiences with the Suffield affair, that the proposals were too little and too late, which indeed they were.

[75]This phrase also occurs at the end of the ministers' circular letter; it may not refer to any action of the Westfield Church.

[76]Stephen Kellog did not come to Westfield until the late 1690s; he had been a weaver at Hadley, and continued that trade in Westfield. Joseph Mawdsley, son of John the foundation man, was born in Windsor shortly before his father moved to Westfield. Like his father, he was a miller. Both men had joined the Church in 1697/98; both were of a completely different generation than Taylor's. They must have been as puzzled by Taylor's rather opaque explanation of the differences between Stated and Occasional Fasts as he was by their challenge of his authority.

[77]The passages at issue here are more than likely two sections of the propositions drawn up in the second meeting of the Reforming Synod of 1679.

The first is in Chap. XXIII, "Of Religious Worship, and of the Sabbath-Day": "Solemn humiliations, with fastings and thanksgiving upon special occasions, are, in their several times and seasons, to be used in an holy and religious manner." The second occurs in the question and answer sequence of the "Propositions":

...No *time* is to be made *holy* to the Lord, but what is made holy by the Lord; and if there be no *institution* of God, the great Lord of time, for a *stated time*, to be made *holy* to himself, 'tis a *superstition* in any man to make it so.

...Solemn *humiliations* and *thanksgivings* are moral duties to be observed *pro causis et temporibus*. And the Direction of Divine Providence in laying before us fresh *occasions* of them, is to be regarded; which cannot be done if they be made perpetual.

...He [St. Paul] suffers not us to sacrifice our Christian liberty unto humane impositions of stated holy days upon us, nor a private person to impose it upon himself. (Mather, *Magnalia*, II, 200, 260-61)

[78]Taylor copied the following letter into his "Commonplace Book"; Stoddard's reply, if he made a written one, is not included:

When Sergeantt Mawdsly & Stephen Kellog, wholy left off the Duty of Fasting & Prayer with the Church in our Monethly Fast, & being treated with in order to Conviction which had no effect I told them that, they must be brought to the Church Censures, they desired me to write their Case to Mr. Stoddard which at length I yielded to & wrote as Follows.

Reverend Sir

We have a Case of Difficulty fallen in amongst us by two of our brethren in Church fellowship, viz, Serg. Mawdsly & Stephen Kellog.

It hath been our practice ever since we were in Church-fellowship, to turn every other Conference into a Fast on the Occasion of the Circumstances of the times, in the Winter Season: Save onely some few years, wherein we had a monthly Lecture, the which Lectures proving an Occasion of greate disorder & Sin in the town, & no preventing the Same appearing I let the Lectures Fall: & returned as before to Fasts. Now these two brethren, seemd nott pleased in the matter, at Such time as in the begining of winter we set them up again. But the winter, before this, I think one of them was but Once, & the other but twice at them, which gave me occasion to reprove the neglect thereof in my Fast Sermons: But they were not there to fall under the same.

Last winter returning to our Fasts again they have wholy absented: onely Lt. Kellog coming to the last (which he saith not as to a fast) & Sergeant Mawdsly setting forward to the Bay, the Day before. I in the end of the day enquired of Brother Kellog, Why So, [126/127] & told him it could not be born. & orderd them to appeare the next Conference, laying in the Charge of Breach of Covenant with God & the Church, wherein they obliged themselves to walk according to the Rules of the Gospell, in the Communion of Saints, in a Church instituted State with this particular Church of Christ in attendence upon all Gospell Ordinances, etc. & here is a gospell Ordinance of Fasting & prayer withdrew from.

Yesterday in the Evening they came to mee but admitted no argument that I could present them with as light to them. Whereupon I told them, that I must go on to the Censures of the Church with them. They intimated so much, that I conjectur'd that they thought the Church would not proceed. I told them that I should then Suspend them. Then they desired time to Consult. I told them that I wanted not light as to my duty. In short, they desired me to write their case to you & I complied to trouble you thus. I can't convict them that our Fasts are Occassionall & not Stated & they like not in that they are not in the publick Meeting house but in a private house. If you can prevaile with them to acknowledg their Failings in this matter & promise Reformation it will be a means of peace otherwise we are like to have trouble.

For as their practice is a breach of Covenant so it is intollerable, & a greate infamy to any Church to have Such in their Communion as be down, & withdraw from Fasting & Prayer with the Church. Such a practicall part of Piety. Let us have your Prayers. & so I am

Westfield   Your Servant: Edw. Taylor
6: 2ᵐ 1710

[79]This case is listed out of order; it occurred three years before the previous case. Nothing in the condition of the manuscript would account for this interruption. Taylor may have decided to enter this account after the recent problems with Mawdsley over the monthly fasts, suggesting that perhaps not all cases which came before the Church were entered in the "Record."

Rebecca Ashley, daughter of David and Hannah Ashley, was twenty-two at the time of this confession; she married Samuel Dewey in the spring of 1714. Their first child, Miriam, was born in May of 1713. It is possible, however, that the woman is Rachel (not Rebecca as Taylor records), the daughter of Samuel and Sarah Ashley. Rachel was about thirteen years old at this time; she married Samuel Kellogg when she was in her early thirties. John "Madsley" is the grandson of the foundation man; in 1714 he married a young woman called Hannah.

The court record of this case suggests that Taylor may be in error, and that it is Rachel, not Rebecca, who is involved:

Att a Court of General Sessions of the Peace Holden at Springfield, May 20, 1707

Rachel Ashly of Westfield singlewoman appearing in Court and acknowledging that she had been Guilty of the Sin of Fornication And that she had Lately been Delivd of a Femaile Bastard Child, and Charging John Mawdsely of Westfield upon oath to be the Father of Said Child

—The Said John Madsley also appearing in Court Denyd the Fact and putting Himself upon the Case was Commitd to the Jury who Returnd their verdict upon oath that the said Madsley is Guilty, the Court upon Consideration thereof order the said John Madsley and Rachel Ashly to pay as a fine to Her Majestie the Sum of Fifty Shillings Each and Costs. And also order the said Madsley to Pay to the Said Rachel Ashly for and Towards the Maintenance of said Child the Sum of Two Shillings per Week and that During the pleasure of this Court. And that he enter into Recognizance the sum of fifty pounds for the performance thereof, Accordingly the said John Madsley acknowledge himself before this Court to be indebted to the said Rachel Ashly In the Sum of Fifty pounds to be well & truly Paid to the said Rachel Ashly In Case he Shall fail of truly Performing the said order of this Court. ("Copy of a Portion of Court Records," p. 1)

In this connection, cf. Med. 75, Series II, dated three days before this confession, especially stanza 7:

> Both grac'd together, & disgrac'd. Sad Case
> What now becomes of Gods Electing Love?
> This now doth raise the Miracle apace,
> Christ doth step in, & Graces Art improove.
> He kills the Leprosy that taints the Walls:
> And Sanctifies the house before it falls.

[80]This is the same Abigail who had previously been disciplined for saying that her father was as "hot as a skunk." Goodman Taylor is Samuel Taylor, the local blacksmith.

[81]This is the first of three such citations that Stephen Kellog of the "fasting" case is disciplined for. The last—and the last recorded disciplinary case—occurs two years before his death in 1722.

[82]The principals in this case did not marry. Abigail Williams, who was nineteen at the time of this incident, married Thomas Dewey, son of Adijah, the next summer. They latter settled in Suffield. John Sackett, the grandson of one of the first Westfield settlers, married Sarah Mackerany and remained in Westfield.

In the September session of the County Court, two months after the action of the Church, both appeared:

> John Sackett 3rd and Abiel Williams both of Westfield in the County of Hamshr appearing in Court and Confessing that they have Committed the Sin of Fornication Together Order'd that they Pay as a fine to her Majestie the Sum of Forty Shillings Each and Cost and the Said Abiel Williams Declaring upon oath that She had lately been Deliv'd of a Bastard Child begotton on her body by the Said Sackett (he being Presst not Denying the Same) This Court Therefore Further order that the Said John Sackett Pay to the Said Abiel Williams the Sum of Two Shillings Six Pence per Week During the Pleasure of this Court, and that he find Sureties for the Performance thereof (and also to Indemnifie and Save Harmless the Said Town of Westfield from all Charges for the mainte-

nance) Accordingly the Said John Sackett with John Sackett Jr. of Said Westfield appeard In Court and acknowledg'd themselves to be joyntly and Severally Indebted to the Said Abiel Williams in the Sum of Forty Pounds to be well and Truly Paid to the Said Abiel Williams in Case the Said John Sacket Tertius Shall fail of Performing the order aforesaid of Paying to her the Said Sum of two Shillings and Six Pence a week as aforesaid and oblig'd themselves to Indemnifie and Save Harmless the Said Town of Westfield free from Charge for the Maintenance of Said Child. ("Copy of a Portion of Court Records," pp. 45–46)

[83]The sequence of events in this case is not always clear, although Taylor goes over most of the incidents at least three times, twice here, and a third time in the second of the two disciplinary sermons justifying his actions. In addition, the first and most detailed account (manuscript pp. 137–45) is nearly illegible. The handwriting suggests that Taylor wrote in haste, if not in anger, and we are not as confident of the accuracy of our transcription as we would like to be.

Walter Lee had a long history of brushes with the law. In March of 1659 he was ordered by the Court to return Edward Elmer's hog, and fined six £ for damages, apparently to the hog. Lee moved from Northampton to Westfield in the early 1660s; in the first entry in the court records (28 March 1665) relating to Westfield—still called Woronocco—Lee was cited by the Court because he "very seldome" came to "God's ordinances on the Lords day, he not having been at the meeting at Springfield from Feb. 8th to this tyme, and very seldome the rest of the winter past." He was also admonished by the Court, and bound over "upon suspicion of killing a steere" of one of the local settlers, for which he was convicted and fined 50 shillings and 3 £ 4 shillings Court costs. In 1666 Cornelius Merry, a Northampton Irishman, was fined for calling Lee a "rogue, dog, rogue and thiefe." The next year Lee was cited for profaning the sabbath by thrashing corn, insulting one Isaac Sheldon by calling him a "member of old nick and a member of the Divell," and for his contemptuous remarks in "Saying he thought he might as well beleeve his boy (when he Said Springfield Commissioners threatned him with the Stocks and promised him Some new clothes) as the Said Commissioners in declaring what his boy Said against him." The next year he was sued for debt, and complained against for illegally impounding Ambrose Fowler's cattle.

He worked in Westfield as a stone mason, building Taylor's chimney, among others and seems to have been a farmer of sorts. He managed to stay out of trouble in the seventies (though the Indians burned his barn during Philip's War) and was successfully sued for debt in the eighties only twice. He was finally admitted to the Westfield Church in his early sixties, three weeks before the death of his first wife, 29 February 1696. His second marriage in 1700, to Hepzibah, widow of Caleb Pomery of Northampton, precipitated his youngest daughter's disparaging remarks. (Cf. Louis M. Dewey, "Ancient Westfield," *Westfield Times and News-Letter*, 42 [18 May 1892], 2, and Smith, *The Pynchon Court Record*, pp. 116, 120, 239, 319, 321.)

After his first wife's death, Walter had lived with his son John, and in 1699, deeded his whole estate to him. When his son died in 1711, he lived variously with his son-in-law Samuel Bush and John's widow and family. (Taylor says that during this period he married for the third time, though there is no other record of it.) The attempt to have Walter declared senile and put under the guardianship of the court seems to have begun when Samuel Bush filed suit to force Walter to pay for his maintenance. Had Walter disposed of ("alienated") his land to pay Bush, John's heirs, who could not receive the inheritance until after Walter's death, might have lost much of what they felt was rightly theirs.

In any case, Bush apparently filed suit sometime in the summer or fall of 1711, although the case was not decided until December of 1712. When the Court authorities were in Westfield that spring (Taylor gives the date as May of the following year) to settle estates and probate wills, John's widow engaged lawyer Pomery to represent her. Ebenezer Pomery, son of Medad, and nephew of Joseph of the "mill matters," was Sheriff of Hampshire County, and "His Majesties Counsel" for the district. Two months earlier, however, Taylor and several other church members had sent the petition (p. 208) to the Court. Pomery's strategy—aided by the petition—in answering complaints filed against Walter, and helping John's widow and her son John retain the inheritance, was to have Walter placed under guardianship so that he could not be held responsible for the debts he incurred. And he used Taylor's petition to further these ends:

> Whereas This Sessions [4 March 1711/12] are Informed by a Rvd. Mr. Taylor and Several of the Principal Inhabitants in Westfield Respecting the Condition of Walter Lee of Westfield who is now by Reason of Old Age much Impar'd in his Understanding and not Capable to Manage his Estate and Said Walter Lee when he was of Sound mind & a Disposing memory Conveyed his Estate to his Son John, Who is now Dead, for the Maintenance of his Father, Now his Grandson, John Lee to whom the Lands descend is Willing to take the Care of his Said Grand Faither, Ordered by this Court that the Said John Lee Grandson to the Said Walter Lee take the Care of his Grand Father with the assistance of Serg. Nathaniel Phelps & David King Neighbours to the Said Lee, and that the Said John Lee have the Use of the whole Estate both Real and Personals for the End aforesaid, and that the Said Walter is Concluded by this Court and Declared to be Uncapable of Conveying any of his Estate Either Real or Personal. ("Copy of a Portion of Court Records," p. 42)

At the time, Taylor seems not to have been aware that his petition was so used, though it is not clear from this account that it was by Taylor's petition alone that the Court acted. But when Bush's suit came before the Court, it was dismissed:

> Samuel Bush of Westfield in the County of Hampshire, Carpenter Plaintiff vs. Walter Lee of Said Westfield Defendant. In a plea of Debt Due by book from the Defendant to the plaintiff to the Sum of nine Pounds Eight Shillings in money which the Defendant Neglects to Pay to the Plaintiff. The Plaintiff and Defendant appeared in Court. The Defendant Pleads the writt ought to abate there being no Sumons left with the Defendant. It is

Considered by the Court that the writt shall abate and that the Defendant shall Recover against the Plaintiff Cost of Court Taxed at one pound Eleven Shillings. ("Inferiour Court of Common Pleas Holden at Northampton 2 Dec. 1712," p. 46)

It was, of course, Pomery's responsibility, as sheriff of Hampshire, to see that the principals in the case received summonses.

By this time Taylor must have been told that his petition had been in part responsible for Lee being placed under guardianship; and in the last of February, 1712/13, he wrote the first letter to Samuel Partridge, and one to the Court on 3 March. It was natural for Taylor to address the letter to Partridge; he had been the senior of three magistrates who had ruled on Lee's competency and had heard the suit brought by Bush. Partridge was one of Hadley's most important citizens; his second wife was the daughter of Seaborn Cotton. He was colonel of the regiment for the Hampshire area, attorney, clerk of writs, and rose from Clerk of the Courts in 1684 to Associate Justice in 1695. After Pynchon's death he was the senior Justice of the Hampshire Sessions.

At about this time Taylor had his first meeting with Benjamin Smith (though Taylor later says this first interchange occurred in 1713/14, a full year after the case had been closed; see below, p. 228). Smith was Partridge's nephew. William Partridge married Mary Smith, a daughter of Joseph Smith of Hartford; William and Mary had two children, Samuel and Mary. Mary Partridge then married John Smith, apparently no direct relation to the Hartford Smiths. When his only sister's husband died in 1676, Samuel Partridge became guardian of the children, and was appointed by the Court as one of two executors of the estate. Benjamin, the youngest son, received lands in "Coniticat in the township of Weathersfield." He married Ruth Loomis, daughter of the foundation man, sometime before 1683; they both joined the Westfield Church in 1691. A year after this disciplinary case, Smith was dismissed to the West Springfield Church; several years later he was granted a license as an "Inholder Taverner and Common victualler," which was renewed each year until his death in 1737.

Partridge had apparently shown Taylor's letters to his nephew, and particularly the one in which Taylor comments on his spiritual as well as medicinal "treating" of Smith. These comments (see below, note 93) prompted Smith's accusation that Taylor had been "defaming" him. Some time before the next conference day two weeks later, Taylor received the letter from Partridge (the one he could not "English") attempting to explain the legal status of Walter Lee. Though the exact dates are not clear, Taylor must has suspended Smith about the middle of April. While he did not suspend the Church for not acting when the case was first propounded to them, he apparently did not administer the Supper during the period between their first refusal to act and the end of the case, some seventeen weeks later. Meditation 113, for example, is dated 12 April 1713; the next Meditation is not dated until 9 August 1713, the day Taylor says he administered the Lord's Supper after being "off a great while."

In the meantime, Smith had consulted with Stoddard, and had requested permission of the West Springfield Church to take Communion there. The Reverend John Woodbridge wrote to the Westfield brethren; Smith delivered the leter to Isaac Phelps (see below, p. 234) about the first of July. Some of the members, apparently pressured by Phelps, agreed that Smith's original confession, rejected by Taylor, was acceptable, and, without Taylor's knowledge, so informed the West Springfield Church. Then, on 19 July, Partridge wrote to Taylor, urging him to accept Smith's confession; his reference to Taylor's apparent "presbyterian" leanings must have particularly irritated him. And the reference to Taylor's "old age" probably did not help matters either.

On 21 July, Taylor met with Woodbridge and the Reverend Daniel Brewer, minister of the Springfield Church, at Smith's house. After what appears to have been a fairly acrimonious session, Taylor reluctantly agreed to accept the confession Brewer wrote out at that meeting. And so on Sunday, 26 July, the confession was finally read, Smith's case propounded to the Church for their vote. The brethren accepted Smith's confession, Taylor lectured the congregation on their failings, and, after some debate with Isaac Phelps, a fast day for 2 August was agreed upon. The next Lord's Day, 9 August, after an interval of seventeen weeks, Taylor appointed the Lord's Supper, and "so ended this Quarrellsome matter," except, of course, for the two disciplinary sermons, preached about five months later.

There is no direct reference to these events in the "Town Records"; it is clear, though, that Taylor's later reluctance to move to the new meeting house is in part explained by his distaste for Colonel Partridge. The Town argued for about three years, trying to decide where the new building should be located. Finally, in desperation, Partridge was authorized to make the "Desition of the same matter," and the Town agreed to accept his judgment. Taylor, however, was not so obliging.

[84]This is the first of several dates which do not seem to be accurate. This visit more than likely occurred the year before. Taylor says that he sent the petition (dated in March 1711/12) after the members of the court were in Westfield.

[85]We find few references to Smith in the various court records. In one case, John Sacket lodged a complaint against him, but the record does not make clear on what grounds; and when they were called to appear, both parties had apparently agreed to settle out of court. In a second entry, Fearnot King of Westfield complained that Smith had kept some cloth he was supposed to weave and deliver to King. Smith apparently refused to deliver the material until King had paid for it, and the Court voided the suit against him (*Pynchon Court Record*, pp. 338, 344). An entry in the "Town Records" suggests that Smith tried to avoid paying taxes: "It was voted that the select men shal manage the Case depending between Benjamin Smith and the Town respecting the country rate and the town doe ingage to beare what reasonable charges the select men may have att in managing said case" (1 March 1709/10). Taylor's point may be,

however, that Smith "riggled" out so much that some complainants did not bother to file against him.

[86]Cf. Acts 8.9ff and Exodus 9.25ff.

[87]Taylor is probably referring to the statements in Chap. VII of "The Cambridge Platform, 1648": the Elders are to "*prevent* & heal such offences in life, or in doctrin; as might corrupt the church" (see Walker, *Creeds and Platforms*, pp. 212–14).

[88]Smith received his dismission the following year to the West Springfield Church (see below, p. 278).

[89]A rather telling accusation on Phelps' part. The allusion is to the responsibilities of elders, discussed in I Peter 5.2–3:

> Feed the flock of God which is among you, taking the oversight thereof, not by constraint, but willingly; not for filthy lucre, but of a ready mind;
>> Neither as being lords over Gods heritage, but being ensamples to the flock.

Phelps seems to be suggesting that Taylor's actions were not completely exemplary, although he then withdraws the accusation. But when the Town voted in April of 1723 to call Stiles as minister, and several people dissented and desired their names to be recorded, Phelps was one of the dissenters (see above, note 54).

[90]Phelps is referring to Chap. X, "Of the powr of the Church, & its Presbytery," of the 1648 "Platform": "The power graunted by Christ unto the body of the church & *Brotherhood*, is a prerogative or priviledge which the church doth exercise.... In *Choosing* their own officers.... In *admission* of their own members and therefore...they should have power to Remove" (cf. Walker, p. 218).

[91]Cf. the "Propositions" of the Reforming Synod of 1679: "...The pastor of a church may by himself *authoritatively* suspend from the Lord's-table a brother accused or suspected of a scandal, till the matter may and should be regularly examined. Our Lord forbids the coming of such an offender to his altar....The pastors of the church are the porters of the temple..., and its belonging unto the porters of the church to direct the brethren in the application of the 'necessary discipline;' it is not reasonable that they should be bound in the mean time to declare *practically* what shall be contrary to such direction by administering the Lord's-Supper unto a person against whom the discipline is to be urged" (Mather, *Magnalia*, II, 249).

[92]August 9, 1713, the same date as Meditation II.114. Cf. particularly stanzas five and eight.

[93]Taylor adds in the right margin the following note:

The note I put in the Colonalls hand was thus. Whereas in the past Benjamin Smith being of a fever sent for me & I was at his house I saw his fever so high that I thoug[ht] him in danger of Dea[th] and so advised * * * [144/145] myself to advise him to looke into his life, & soul & se what was amiss therein; & renew his repentance before God & so apply himselfe to Christ by faith. I saw his Spirit rise hereat & he asked me whether I had anything against him. I told him, that I doubted not but if he searched into his life he would find that his life had not been so Even but that he might finde matter of repentance, etc. Now this it seems lay boyling on his spirit till now; & the morning as I take itt before I gave in the matters of his offences to the Church he came up to me as I was in my garden & told me that he had been offended with me ever since that time & he thought he [would] never be reconciled to mee while he lived, & doubled it over again. I told him if God took him in hand he would quickly pull that away, or word to this effect admiring at his Envy: Now this is the matter that the Colonal turn so upon me hard as to revive old matters after I had admitted him to Ordinances. & yet I never knew any thing of this before he spake it now. Thus was Unworthily treated by Colonal making Smiths malice against me to be mine against him, & implicitly turning upon me as acting irregular in not attending that rule, Matt. 18.15,16,17, which respects private offences, & not open, as Smiths was being a publick Slander in the face of the Court. & so ought not to be took up in private & in the open Church his Carriage.

[94]This date should read 3 March 1712/13.

[95]Cf. above, note 91. The "Propositions" of the Reforming Synod are quite explicit on this point: "But the elders of the church have a *negative* on the votes of the brethren; who, indeed, in the exercise of their liberty are under the conduct of the elders. To take away the negative of the elders, or the necessity of their *consent* unto such acts, indeed is to take away all government whatsoever, and it is to turn the whole "regimen of the church" into a pure "democracy." And, if the *positive* of the brethren can supersede a *negative* of the elders, either the elders may be driven to do things quite contrary unto the light of their conscience, or else the brethren may presume to do things which belong not to them" (*Magnalia*, II. 249).

[96]Taylor adds the following note at the bottom of the page: "Sometimes the Pastor Suspends administring the Lords Supper a great while for difficulties arising; its said that Mr. Hooker sometimes suspended * * * for nigh a yeare. For difficulties the Mr. Russell suspended Mrs. Tilton, Mr. * * * Widow Howe, how much * * * * * * "

[97]Oberholzer states that Kellog "offered a confession which was rejected. Another confession, submitted six years later, restored him to fellowship" (*Delinquent Saints*, p. 135). He implies that Kellog was suspended for six years, when in fact the time "set for approbation" was from early summer to October of 1714. The confession six years later is for another case of too much to drink.

[98]Thomas Dewey is the son of Jedidiah, who, with his brothers Thomas and Josiah, was one of Westfield's first settlers; John Ingerson's father was one of the foundation men.

[99]This is the clearest statement about Taylor's refusal to administer the Lord's Supper. But even here he does not say that he suspended the Church, though since the Supper was not administered during the four-month interval, the effect was the same.

[100]Taylor's handwriting here is quite shaky; the spaces between characters and lines are broad, and the lines drift down the page. Because of his recent

severe illness we suspect that he has only recently been able to return to his duties. (See the poem written during this month, "Upon my recovery out of a threatening Sickness in December Ano Dmi 1720," *Early American Literature*, 7 [Spring 1972], 41–42).

[101]We have compared our transcription with the typed copy that Louis M. Dewey made of these records ("Baptismal Records," Westfield Athenaeum). Taylor often leaves blank spaces for names he intended to enter later, or, perhaps, for persons whose names he did not remember. Where possible we have entered these in brackets.

[102]In *The Half-Way Covenant*, Pope argues that "from Taylor's baptismal records...it seems apparent that within two years of his ordination the church was using the half-way covenant" (p. 190). And he notes that a "remarkable increase in baptisms in 1680 probably marks the initiation of the practice." He counts thirty persons as being baptized in December of 1680, and all on the fifth of the month (p. 190, note 9).

Dewey's typed copy of the baptismal records would suggest that this is the case; but the manuscript is not this clear. After the entry for 5 December, a new column begins; at the top of this column Taylor has entered twenty-eight names. But this list is not in the sequence of years and months. It may indicate (as the entry for 20 January does), those children already baptized who came under the Watch of the Church. When the Westfield Church was first organized, Taylor's sons, Samuel and James, were five and two years old; from Taylor's usual practice, it seems unlikely that he would wait so long before he had his children baptized.

We suspect that rather than an indication of Taylor's adoption of the Half-Way Covenant, what this entry indicates is that these children—during the period before the Church was organized—were baptized in other churches, and were at this time formally entered as half-way members, recognizing their baptism elsewhere. Taylor, for example, commonly baptized children whose parents lived in areas where a church had not been formally organized (see entries for 1/25/1683, 3/13/1683, 09/25/1683, and so on).

[103]Abigail was one day old when she was baptized; she died a year later.

[104]This is the first child by Taylor's second wife, Ruth Wyllys Taylor. Ruth was baptized the same day she was born.

[105]Taylor was in his late sixties when his only son by Ruth was born; Eldad was baptized the day after he was born.

[106]This section begins on manuscript p. 307.

Notes: Sermons

[1]The manuscript of this version is carefully prepared, firmly and neatly written, containing few cancellations. The handwriting is that of the early 1690s.

[2]In the right-hand margin Taylor has written "*εν ανθρώποις.*"

[3]For this reference to Ambrose, see above, CR, note 25.

[4]Taylor cites here from Zanchy, halfway down in the right margin. See above, CR, note 26, for this citation.

[5]Taylor refers here in the margin to "Justin de Mor: & vitt. Epist: p. 135." We have been unable to locate this exact source, though the comment is found in a number of contemporary works (see, for example, Samuel Clarke, *The Life & Death of Julius Caesar . . . as also The Life & Death of Augustus Caesar* [London, 1665], p. 89). This same reference also appears in the first version of the sermon.

[6]For this reference, see above, CR, note 28.

[7]Up to this point, the text for both sermons, excepting stylistic changes and minor additions, has been the same. The following material (manuscript pp. 10–14) constitutes the first substantial addition.

[8]Between manuscript pp. 14 and 15, on an unpaginated leaf, Taylor has added the following material; it is in a later hand, perhaps about 1700:

> 1. Instances out of the Old Testament. For altho' it is not to be granted that the Church of the Jews is the Pattern, or modle compleat in all things according to which the Gospell Churches are shaped, & cut out by (for God took Abraham, & his whole house into a Church State: & hence all his seed: & on this bottom did the Church of the Jews stand; Hence their posterity's Church State, & saintship was their birth-right, & Birth-Priviledges; & they could not prevent it, if they would, for if they refused the Externall Rites of the same, they were not permitted to Live, Gen. 17.14, Ex. 12.15,19, & 31.14, Lev. 17.4,5, etc.[)] yet hereby they were brought into Such a Relation unto God as that God saw meet to put his Name upon them: & the title Saints upon them because such they should be, & had the means allowd them to make them such. Whereas in

the Gospell Churches the Case is otherwise. For altho' the seed is given to God according to Gods institution in the Parentall Covenant, yet this is nott sufficient for a Church State unto their Seed. Neither is the title Saints given in all the New Testament to any in a Church State, or Evangelized person but where the Visible sanctifying works of the spirit was the reason thereof, as I Cor. 1.1,2,4,5,6,7, II Cor. 1.1,7, Eph. 1.1,2,3,4,13, etc. & the Censures of the Church came upon such within as visibly sinners. But while the Church of the Jews injoyed their Free state & other Lords did not rule them we have not one instance in all the scripture tho' never so vile Excomunicated: but if the offence was treated it was by Civill sword. But yet I say notwithstanding this greate Difference, We may finde that God Called them to hold out a plain demonstration of the power of Divine Ordinances upon their hearts bringing them up to hold forth their Repentance, & Faith, & this especially with respect unto their approaching unto Divine Ordinances as for instance[.]

[9]Taylor's mark (ℵ) in the right-hand margin refers to Ainsworth and Jackson "on the place." For the Jackson reference, see above, CR, note 29.

The reference to Henry Ainsworth is to the *Annotations upon the five bookes of Moses* (London, 1616), a copy of which Taylor had in his library (*PW*, Item 40): "[The penitent] shall confess laying his hands on the head of the sacrifice, and confessing the iniquity of his trespass; as is noted on Lev. 1.4" (IV, 5–6).

[10]Taylor's symbol in the text refers to the marginal citation from John Cotton's *The Way of Congregational Churches Cleared*; see above, CR, note 30.

[11]Taylor notes in the right-hand margin, "Se Jackson & Hutchinson on the place"; see above, CR, note 31.

[12]The marginal note here reads, "See Poli Synops: in lo:", a reference to Poole's *Synopsis*; see above, CR, note 32.

[13]Taylor refers here in the margin to Poole's *Synopsis* (see above, CR, note 33), and to Arthur Hildersham's commentary on Psalm 51. Hildersham discusses the necessity of "secret confession unto God," as well as a public confession exemplified by David who "made publike confession of his sin to the congregation, and church of God. . . . In this publication of his repentance, he hideth not from the Church his sinne, nor cloaketh it at all . . ." (*CLII Lectures upon Psalme LI* [London, 1635], p. 170).

[14]The marginal reference is to Poole; see above, CR, note 34.

[15]Two citations here in the margin refer to Poole; see above, CR, note 36.

[16]Taylor uses this same citation from Calvin in the first version of the sermon (CR, note 37); unlike the first reference, this one is legible, a citation from Calvin's commentary on I Peter: "*Summa ergo huc tendit, debere nobis in promptu esse fidei confessionem, ut eam proferamus quoties opus est. . . . Idque (meo judico) signifact Apologiae nomen quo Petrus utitur, nempe ut Christiani testatum mundo facerent, se procul ab omni impietate . . .*" (*Commentarii* [Geneva, 1580], p. 29).

[17]The particular edition of Augustine which Taylor had is not clear; of the more than 200 references to Augustine in Taylor's writing, however, the sermon numbers, tract numbers, page and volume references fit most closely the

Omnium Operum, 10 vols. folio, edited by Erasmus, and published in Basil in 1529 (see "Edward Taylor's Library: Another Note," *Early American Literature*, 6 [Winter 1972], 271–73. This reference is to VI, 594).

[18]Taylor refers here in the margin to Jackson and Owen; see above, CR, note 35.

[19]Taylor cites here in the left-hand margin from Poole; see above, CR, note 38.

[20]John Weemse's discussion of Hebrew "Ecclesiasticall Politickes" occurs in the section of *The Christian Synagogue* (London, 1623) entitled "Of their Proselytes." Taylor simply paraphrases Weemse's comments: "Three things made a Proselyte; first, they were washed; secondly, circumcised; thirdly, they offered their sacrifice" (p. 141). Taylor had a copy of Weemse in his library (*PW*, Item 22).

[21]The marginal note lists "Beza, Estius, Grotius, etc.," as cited in Poole's *Synopsis*; see the "*Commentatorum in I Epistolam Petri*," IV, pt. 2, col. 1525.

[22]Taylor notes in the left-hand margin that these two citations are from the *Synopsis*; see above, CR, note 39.

[23]Taylor had this rather expensive set of the *Centuriae Magdeburgensis* (Basil, 1559–1574) in his library (*PW*, Item 11), using large sections of the material in his "Metrical History of Christianity" (see Donald E. Stanford's essay in *American Literature*, 33 [November 1961], 279–97). The reference, cited here in the right-hand margin, is to Cent. I, *Lib.* II, *Cap.* VI, p. 497 (as Taylor notes, the comments on I Peter 3).

[24]After citing the Latin of this account in the right-hand margin, Taylor notes: "Norton Contra Apolo: p. 5–6, ex Just. Mart. Apolog. 1"; for this reference, see above, CR, note 40.

[25]The marginal citations from Victor and Irenaeus are from the *Centuriae*, Cent. II, *Cap.* VI, "*De Ceremoniis et Ritibus*," pp. 111, 112.

[26]Norton's comments, which Taylor paraphrases here, define these categories:

...*Fuerunt ordines & propria habebant intervalla in primordiali Ecclesiâ catechumeni, Competentes & fideles.*

Quando tantum audiebant, dicebantur catechumeni, quando flectebant genua, & petebant Baptismum, & Communionem (idem interpretativè ac apud nos petere admissionem) dicebantur Competentes.

Quando admittebantur ad Sacramenta, dicebantur fideles, & Christiani. Ex Catechumenis fiebant competentes, ex his fideles (Responsio ad... Apollonio, pp. 6–7; see also above, CR, note 40).

[27]Taylor cites this passage in the left-hand margin; like the earlier citations from Victor and Irenaeus, this one is also from the *Centuriae, Cap.* VI, p. 124.

[28]In the first disciplinary sermon (see below, note 70), Taylor identifies the edition of Origen he used as the one edited by Jacob Merlin, a Professor of Theology at the College of Navarre, *Subjecta opera Origenis* (Venice, 1516). The passage which Taylor cites here in the left-hand margin is from Vol. 1, "*In Exodum homiliae*," fol. XLV. Johnson's interpretation of the inventory listing of Taylor's library (*PW*, item 12: "Origens homilies Vol. 2. fol: 4s") is probably

inaccurate, though Taylor may have also had another edition of the homilies alone.

[29]One-half of manuscript p. 23, and eight lines at the top of p. 24, are taken up by this long quote from Origen's "*Homilae II, In Psalm XXXVII*," fols. LVI–LVII.

[30]Taylor cites this same passage in the CR version of the sermon (see above, CR, p. 134), but without identifying the source as he does here. The reference is to the "*Epistola Canonica, Can. 11*," *Opera Omnia* (Moguntiae, 1604), p. 133, a Greek-Latin edition of Gregory's Epistles. Taylor lists the Greek terms for the five "degrees" in the left-hand margin.

[31]This reference, and subsequent ones to early histories of the Church, is taken from a single volume edition, edited by Johan Grynaeus, of the Histories of Eusebius, Pamphillius, Ruffinius, Socratis, Theodorit, Sozomenius, Theodorius, Evagrii, and Dortheius, the *Ecclesiastica Historia, sex propè seculorum res gestas complectens* (Basil, 1570). The marginal reference here to Eusebius ("Euseb. Lib. 6. C. 34.") is actually to Chap. 33, p. 85.

[32]Taylor refers here in the margin to "Heironym: in Epistola ad Oceanum." A contemporary source for this citation is the *Epistolae et Libri contra Haereticos* (Antwerp, 1578), I, Epist. 30, p. 85. Taylor's direct source might have been the *Centuriae*, although he usually identifies the specific passages when he cites from this set.

[33]The marginal note refers to "Sozomonus Lib. 7. C. 16," a reference to the *Ecclesiastica Historia*, pp. 554–55.

[34]When Taylor cited this long account in the CR version of this sermon, he identified the source as Owen's *Discourse Concerning the Holy Spirit* (see above, CR, note 43). Here he cites this account in the right-hand margin and gives the source as "Augustin: Confes: lib. 8. Ca: 2." In the ten-volume Basil edition, the reference is to I, 99.

[35]Johnson lists Theophylact's *In quator Evangelia enarrationes* (Cologne, 1532), as the edition Taylor had in his library (see Item 15). Taylor's citations from Theophylact, however, are always in Greek, and we suspect that the copy Taylor had was the Greek-Latin edition, *Commentarii in Quator Evangelia* (Paris, 1635). In this edition, this marginal note appears in the "*Commentarius in Matthaeum*," *Cap*. XVI, p. 95.

[36]For the source of this marginal citation to David Pareus, see above, CR, note 45.

[37]Taylor refers here in the left-hand margin to "Piscat. in Matt. 3." For this reference, see above, CR, note 46.

[38]Taylor refers here in the margin to the "Bohem Conf. in Harmo Confess, Sect. 13. Cap. 12. p. 44."; see above, CR, note 44.

[39]For this reference to Rutherford, see above, CR, note 47.

[40]The marginal note reads "Socrat: Histor: Cha: 20," a reference to the *Ecclesiastica Historia*, pp. 244–45.

[41]Taylor cites here in the margin a passage from Origen's "*Homilae I, In Matt. 16*," II, fol. II.

[42]The marginal note here is from Augustine's "*Tractatus L, Cap. XII*": "*Petrus corpus bonorum, corpus ecclesiae, immo corpus ecclesiae, sed in bonis: nam si in Petro non esset ecclesiae sacramentum, non ei diceret dominus, Tibi dabo claves....* [... *Si hoc Petro tantum dictum est, non facit hoc ecclesia:*] *si autem* [*&*] *in ecclesia fit, ut quae in terra ligantur...qui cum excommunicat ecclesia, in coelo...solvitur reconciliatus. Si hoc ergo in ecclesia fit, Petrus quando claves accepit, ecclesiam sanctam significavit*" (IX, 252).

[43]The marginal note here refers to Augustine's comments in "*Expositio in Epistolam Beati Joannis, Tractus VI*": "...*Unde discernimus? Intendite, eamus simul corde.... Vigilat ipsa charitas, quia ibi pulsatura est, ipsa apertura...pulsate, tangite vasa fictilia, ne forte crepuerint & male resonent. Videte si integre sonant...*" (IX, 423–24). None of these citations to the tracts is in the CR version, though a number of similar citations occur in the "Manuscript Book" (see above, CR, note 4).

[44]The marginal note here is a citation from Calvin on I John 4.1; see above, CR, note 49.

[45]The following material, from manuscript pp. 29–53, represents the largest body of additions to this version of the sermon; the series of "objections" and "solutions" here added represent Taylor's most direct response to Stoddard's proposals, particularly to his assertion that the Lord's Supper is a converting ordinance.

[46]Cf. Meditations I.14 and 15, particularly ll. 49–52:

Be thou my High Priest, Lord; & let my name
    Ly in some Grave dug in these Pearly rocks
Upon thy Ephods Shoulder piece, like flame
    Or graved in thy Breast Plate-Gem: brave Knops.

[47]John Lightfoot's comments appear in "Hebrew and Talmudic Exercitations upon the First Epistle of St. Paul to the Corinthians," *The Works of the Reverend & Learned John Lightfoot*, 2d ed. (London, 1674): "He [St. Paul] has said before verse 19...*That they which are approved may be made manifest.* And in the same sense he saith, δοχιμαζέτω, *Let a man approve himselfe*, in this place; not so much, *Let him try*, or *examine himselfe*, as *Let him approve himself*; that is, let him shew himselfe approved by the *Christian* Faith and Doctrine.... We meet with the word in the same sense very often" (II, 779). In *A Paraphrase, and Annotations Upon all the Books of the New Testament*, 2d ed. (London, 1659), Henry Hammond makes essentially the same point: "That δοχιμαζέτω, *to prove*, or *trie*, signifies so to examine and prove as to approve, appears by some other places [other than Rom. 2.19] where the word is so used. So I Cor. 11.28, *Let a man prove*, or *examine*, himself, and so let him eat of that, etc., where 'tis certain that, if upon examination he find himself unworthy, he must not eat; for if he doe, *he eats damnation to himself*, v. 29. And therefore it must signifie the approving himself to God and his own conscience" (p. 449).

[48]The Greek here is unclear; the term seems to be some form of ρήσσει, to rend or break asunder; and the Latin seems to signify to suffer anguish or separation.

⁴⁹Taylor refers here in the left-hand margin to Theophylact on Matt. 7.6; we cite the Latin, though his annotation is in Greek: *"Canes sunt infideles, porci autem porcinam vitam agentes. Mysteria igitur incredulis non sunt prodenda, neque clari & margaritis similes sermones de Theologia immundis communicandi"* (*Commentarii in Quator Evangelia*, p. 39).

⁵⁰Taylor transcribed in English Origen's *Contra Celsum* and *De Principiis*; the manuscript copybook is in the Westfield Athenaeum (see Francis Murphy, "An Edward Taylor Manuscript Book," *American Literature*, 31 [May 1959], 188–89). The paraphrase of this material, cited in the right-hand margin, however, is not from the copy book, but from IV, *Lib*. 3, fol. XXXVII, of the Merlin edition, *Subjecta opera Origenis*.

⁵¹This marginal citation is also from IV, *Lib*. 4, fol. XLVI.

⁵²This citation from Chrysostom runs from the right-hand margin of manuscript p. 47 to the left-hand margin of manuscript 48. As Taylor notes at the end of the Latin citation, he is citing from the *Centuriae*, III, Cent. V, *Cap*. IV, p. 398.

⁵³This marginal annotation is also from the *Centuriae*, Cap. VI, p. 670.

⁵⁴Taylor cites here in the margin the following material and identifies the source as "Tract. 11 in Johan": *"Si dixerimus catechemeno, credis in Christo? Respondet, credo, & signat se cruce Christi, portat in fronte, & non erubescit de cruce domini sui. Ecce credit in nomine ejus: interrogemus eum, Manducas carnem filii hominis, & bibis sanguinem filii hominis? Nescit quid dicimus, quia Jesus non se credidit ei.... & nesciunt catechumeni quid accipiunt Christiani? Erubescant ergo quia nesciunt: transeant per mare rubrum, manducent manna, ut quomodo crediderunt in nomine Jesu, sic se ipsis credat Jesus"* (IX, *Cap*. III, 66–67).

⁵⁵Taylor cites here in the left-hand margin from *"Tractatus VI, Cap. I"* in Augustine's *In Evangelium Joannis, Exposito*: *"[Et] cuid ait Apostolus, [qui] autem manducat & bibit indigne, judicium sibi manducat & bibit: non ait quia illa res mala est, sed quia ille malus male accipiendo, ad judicium accipit bonum quod accipit"* (IX, 38).

⁵⁶Taylor enters the following note in the margin here: *"Sancta Sanctus, i.e., Si quis non est Sanctus, non accedat."*

⁵⁷Taylor takes this account, as he notes, from John Foxe, *Acts and Monuments of Martyrs*. Foxe quotes the Bull of Leo X condemning Luther's heretical teachings, and giving him forty days to desist and recant. The first article of Luther's answer is the point Taylor is interested in: "It is an hereticall sentence, and also common, to say, That the Sacraments of the new Law do give grace to them which have no obstacle in themselves to the contrary." Taylor simply quotes Foxe's marginal note on this article (*Acts and Monuments*, 8th ed. [London, 1641], II, 643). Taylor owned a copy of the "Martyrology" (*PW*, Item 2).

⁵⁸Taylor owned a copy (*PW*, Item 107) of William Ames's *Bellarminus enervatus*, a response to the attacks on Protestant "heresies" by Cardinal Bellarmine in *Disputationes de Controversiis Fidei adversus hujus temporis Haereticos*. Ame's rejection of the Catholic view of the sacraments is in Bk. III, Chap. 5 (*Bellarminus enervatus* [Amsterdam, 1658], pp. 42–44).

[59]George Gillespie's *Aarons Rod Blossoming, or the Divine Ordinance of Church-Government* (London, 1646) is not among the books listed in the inventory of Taylor's library, but he was clearly familiar with it. He refers here specifically to Chap. 12, "Whether the Sacrament of the Lords Supper be a converting or regenerating Ordinance," and Chap. 13, "Twenty Arguments to prove that the Lords Supper is not a converting Ordinance." At this point in Taylor's preparation for the *Treatise* sermons and his response to Stoddard's proposals, such arguments as those Gillespie makes in Chap. 13 must have appealed very strongly to Taylor:

That which necessarily supposeth conversion and faith, doth not work conversion and faith. . . .

That which gives us new food, supposeth that we have the new birth and spirituall life, and that we are not still dead in sins and trespasses. . . .

That Ordinance which is instituted onely for beleevers and justified persons, is no converting but sealing Ordinance. . . .

That Ordinance which is appointed onely for such as can and do rightly examine themselves. . .is no converting Ordinance. . . .

That Ordinance unto which one may not come without a wedding garment, is no converting Ordinance. . . .

That Ordinance which hath neither a promise of the grace of conversion annexed to it, nor any example in the Word of God of any converted by it, is no converting Ordinance. . . .

That Ordinance whereof Christ would have no unworthy person to partake is not a converting Ordinance. . . .

That Ordinance which is instituted for the Communion of Saints, is intended onely for such as are Saints, and not for unconverted sinners. . . . (pp. 505–14)

And so on.

[60]A reference to the bed of Procrustes.

[61]Taylor here returns to the text of the CR version (see above, p. 137).

[62]The left-hand marginal note here reads "*Quidquid continetur in genere, continetur in qualibet Specie.*"

[63]This section of Scripture metaphors (manuscript pp. 56–61) is nearly five times longer than the CR version material on the subject (see above pp. 138–39).

[64]This marginal citation, somewhat abbreviated is the same one which Taylor has referred to earlier in this version (see above, note 50).

[65]This right-hand marginal Latin citation, as Taylor notes, is from the *Centuriae*, II, *Cap*. VI, "*De Ritibus et Ceremoniis*," p. 421.

[66]In the right-hand margin Taylor has left a blank space in which to enter the reference to Zanchy; it is the same passage he refers to in the CR version (see above, CR, note 26), and earlier in this version (see above, p. 286).

[67]For a fine analysis of this type of "construction" imagery, and its significance to the New England sense of mission, see Cecelia Tichi, "The Puritan

Historians and Their New Jerusalem," *Early American Literature*, 6 (Fall 1971), 143–55.

[68]For the circumstances surrounding the disciplinary sermons, and the relationship of the dates they were preached to the disciplinary case, see above, CR, note 83.

[69]We have been unable to trace this reference. Taylor seems to have had a Greek text of Theophylact on the Book of Acts; there is no reference to this scripture in the *Commentarii in Quator Evangelia*, nor in Theophylact's *In De Pauli Epistolas Commentarii* (London, 1636) that we have been able to identify.

[70]This is the same reference to Book 3 of the *Contra Celsum* which Taylor cites in the second version of the foundation sermon (see above, note 28). His text, as he notes, is "as Merlin gives it," a reference to Jacob Merlin, the editor of the *Subjecta opera Origenis* (Venice, 1516). This reference is to IV, fol. XXXVII.

Francis Rous, in *Mella Patrum* (London, 1650), an "anthology" of the Church Fathers, includes a number of sections from Origen's *Contra Celsum*. Rous's text (p. 778) is somewhat different from Merlin's, but, as Taylor notes, "nothing as to the matter here in . . . hand."

Taylor's annotated copy of the *Mella Patrum* is in the Yale University Library; unfortunately, the copy is incomplete, breaking off at p. 528 (a full text is 983 pages), and whatever annotations he may have made on the passages from Origen have been lost.

[71]There is no marginal citation here; this long passage, however, does not seem to have been taken from the *Mella Patrum* or the *Centuriae*. In the *Opera omnia* (Paris, 1554), these scattered excerpts from the "*Apologia Secunda Pro Christianis*" appear on pp. 18, 19, 20, 40, 42.

[72]There is no citation here. This long paraphrase is from Tertullian's "*Apologeticus Adversus Gentes*," Cap. XXXIX, "*De Disciplina Christianorum*" of the *Opera* (Basil, 1521), p. 577.

[73]There is no citation here. Taylor also refers to Clement of Rome, supposed author of an *Epistle to the Church of Corinth*, in Sermon 12 of the *Christographia*, p. 395. That reference, unlike this one, is a specific quote from the *Epistle*.

[74]"*Homilae I, in Psalm XXXVII*," I, fol. LIII. As Taylor notes in his earlier citation of this passage in the second version of the foundation sermon (see above, p. 309), Psalm 38 in Origen's numbering is actually Psalm 37.

[75]This is a reference to the public confession of Victorinus, the Platonic philosopher; Taylor refers to this passage in both versions of the foundation sermon (see above, CR, note 43 and RS, note 34).

[76]This phrase is from the "*Apologeticus Adversus Gentes*" (see above, note 72). The full comment is "*Corpus sumus de conscientia religionis, & disciplinae veritate, & spei foedere*" (p. 577).

[77]This annotation is written vertically along the left-hand margin. In "*Adversus Marcionem*," Tertullian speaks generally of the early churches; Taylor adds the names of the specific churches in brackets: ". . . *Sic & caeterorum* (i.e.,

Ecclesiarum Corinth, Galatia, Philponsium, Thessali, Romae, Asiarum] generositas recognoscitur. *Dico itaque apud illas, nec solas iam Apostolicas, sed apud universas, quae illis de societate sacramenti confoederantur . . ."* (I, *Lib.* 3 [not 4], 223).

⁷⁸The reference is actually to "*De Unitate Ecclesiae Catholicae,*" *Opera* (Basil, 1568): "*Adulterari non potest sponsa Christi, incorrupta est & pudica . . ."* (p. 254).

⁷⁹Taylor cites here in the margin this passage from St. Cyprian, "*Epistola XIII: Ad Clerum de Lapsis . . ."* (I, 32).

⁸⁰The reference is actually to Matthew 15.26, the request of the woman of Canaan for "crumbs which fall from their masters' table."

⁸¹Taylor cites here this passage in the left-hand margin; it is from "*Epistola LV: Ad Cornelium . . . sive Contra Haereticos,*" I, 112.

⁸²This marginal citation is from "*Epistola VI: Ad Clerum de Cura . . ."* (I, 14).

⁸³Both these passages are cited in the left-hand margin; they are from "*Epistola LXVIII: Ad Clerumet plebes in hispania . . ."* (I, 164).

⁸⁴At this point Taylor adds the following marginal annotation: "The Councill at Nice thus, *actam ut Episcopus (si fieri potest) ab omnibus Episcopis totius provinciae, ordinetur (Si hic Officilis est) certe non minus quam tribus.*"

⁸⁵In these comments about the authority of the Elders of the Church, Taylor is simply paraphrasing the statements in Chap. 10 of the Cambridge Platform of 1648, "Of the powr of the Church, & its Presbytery" (see Walker, pp. 217ff.).

⁸⁶Taylor makes this same reference to Book IV of the *Contra Celsum* in the second version of the Foundation Sermon (see above, note 50). Here it is cited in the margin.

⁸⁷During the few years of peace for the Church between the persecution of Decius (250) and the Emperor Valerian (257), Cyprian participated in several councils which had been called to deal with the readmission into the Church of those who had fallen away during persecution. Cyprian recounts these matters, as Taylor notes in the right-hand margin, in "Epist. XII": "*Ad Plebum de Rescripto Martyrum . . ."* (I, 30).

⁸⁸Taylor identifies the source of the marginal citation here as "Epist. 44": "*Ad Cornelium . . . sive Contra Haereticos*" (I, 116). There is also a three word phrase written vertically in the left-hand margin; it is illegible.

⁸⁹Taylor's marginal note indicates that these comments, cited here, are paraphrased from "*Epistola LXVIII* " (I, 163).

⁹⁰Taylor cites here in the left-hand margin this comment from "*Epistola LXVIII*" (I, 163).

⁹¹We suspect this is a reference to "blind bayard," a proverbial saying identifying the reckless and ignorant self-confident, though Taylor seems to have a specific legend—which we have been unable to identify—in mind.

⁹²Taylor seems to be mistaken here; the reference to the "Diseased & contagious Sheep" mixed with the flock is from Cyprian's "Epistle 55" (see above, p. 398), though, of course, Origen may have said the same thing.

[93]Taylor cites here in the margin Theophylact's statements from the *Commentarii in Quator Evangelia*, p. 106.

[94]Taylor cites this passage in the margin; it is actually from Chap. XII of *"Tractatus* 50 [not 51]" (IX, 252).

Textual Apparatus

Textual Apparatus

Church Records

Introduction (pp. 3–10):

Emendations and Alterations:

3.7	granted to be] orig: granted by them to be
3.24	their] there
4.3	Minister] followed by canc. "of a min"
4.34	this time] this they
5.21	one] own
7.10	On] on
7.37	laid...Assemblies] orig: laid in the Assemblies
8.24	their] thateir
9.19	build a] orig: build to
10.13	I...Experiences] orig: I shall first give an account of our Experiences

Textual Notes:

4.21	Taylor adds here in the margin, "5th 9m 1674." He also adds "1675" in the margin opposite the reference to Philip's War.
4.34	A blank has been left after "being," as if Taylor later intended to enter a date.
8.9	There appear to be about five lines of text worn away at the bottom of this page. Neither Lockwood nor Dewey transcribes this material, although they do have the missing lines at the top of ms. p. 4.
9.29	Approximately five lines are missing here too.

The Profession of Faith (pp. 10-96):

Emendations and Alterations:

12.25	Parts of] Parts
13.2	God. Where] God. where
14.3	its] it
16.2	ending. Hence] ending. hence
18.5	Puritie] Purtie
22.2	of God are] orig: of God of God are
24.10	Special] followed by ill. canc.
28.7	Affections] orig: Propagation
33.9	them] then
34.3	were] orig: now
35.5	Righteous] Rigteous
35.10	its] it
36.5	Eternall] Eterernall
37.7	Parts] Part
38.7	Christ] Chist
8	extraordinary] extraordary
40.5	whereby] followed by ill. canc.
41.6	Redemption] redeption
42.1	Christs] Chists
45.3	joyn'd] joy'd
46.3	God.] God
8	off] of

47.4   in Christ. . . $\left\{ \begin{array}{l} \text{Principall, \&} \\ \text{Acting.} \end{array} \right.$] orig:

               in Christ $\left\{ \begin{array}{l} \text{faith, \&} \\ \text{Affections} \end{array} \right.$

50.2	consists] consist
7	account] accout
53.5	Particular.] Particular
8	together] togeter
55.8	Ministry is] orig: Ministry is that
11	Apostolicall persons] Apostosicall person
57.5	of the Name] orig: of the thing
58.7	Nature] Sature
12	there. . . Matter] orig: there is the 2. The Formall Cause words,] word
24	Redemption] Redembtion
26	by pronouncing] orig: by passing
33	is ascribed] orig: is used
36	& so] & & so

59.13	God's] God
18	Covenant. Parties] Covenant parties
22	their] there
23	these] thes
36	Christs] orig: Christ
60.31	Circumstantiall] Circustantiall
34	its] it
62.11	things] thing
14	Charge. For] Charge. for
63.2	Christs Passion] Chists Passion
3	Christs] Chists
66.16	men's] men
26	Assise. Its] Assise. its
27	is a day] is day
67.3	Its] It
24	Now] now
68.17	distinguisht] orig: distinguisht with
69.8	of the grave] of grave
10	Christ's] Christ
22	There] Their
27	freckles] freckes
70.19	it. It] it. it
26	there] their
71.10	Affections. All] Affections. all
12	repaired. Hence] repaired. hence
31	its] it
72.21	Wicked] orig: Wicked in which shall * * *
	$\left\{\begin{array}{l}\text{Their Bodies} \\ \text{Their Souls.}\end{array}\right.$
22	shall come] orig: shall rise & come
29	talent. Hence] talent. hence
74.14	toy. But] toy, but
25	Judge. He] Judge. he
27	25.31. If] 25.31. if
75.16	such] shuch
36	Court. This] Court this
76.3	Judgment] preceded by ill. canc.
10	Christ's] Christ
77.20	Extrinsical] Extrinscicall
25	glory. If] glory, if
26	Silver] Siver
27	head] hed
28	shall we] shall, we

78.22   brightness...appeare] orig: brightness of doth appeare
79.30   Inward] Iward
80.26   God. If] God. if
29   Strains.] Strains
81.9   off] of
15   into.] into
82.22   thing.] thing
83.16   ever. If] ever. if
17   place. Oh] place. oh
35   then? Ay,] then? I,
84.11   here. Let] here let
20   as sorely] orig: as highly
28   to force] do force
85.16   Spirits] Spirit
30   troops] trope
86.11   the Phancy] will the them Phancy
21   in...Justice] orig: in revenging God of Justice
24   God's] God
31   way. Thou mayst] orig: way. the Lord thou mayst
38   Soule. Who] Soule. who
87.28   Explication.] Explication
89.6   of the first] of first
91.13   The...thing] orig: The thing Description
92.16   Now] now
94.3   Private. Now] Private now
8   voice. In] voice. in
28   God. Now] God. now
35   name.] name
95.7   frame] fram
8   now] no
31   its] it
32   to the last] the last
96.2   its] it

Textual Notes:
10.18   The following material, to the end of this section on ms. p. 6, is in a later hand.
11.31   Here, as in a number of other places, Taylor has left several blank lines where he apparently intended later to enter additional scriptural references.
12.32   The ms. is unclear at this point. This should be subdivision 3, but the text seems to read 4.
23.8   The following leaf (ms. pp. 17–18) is missing.

29.7   Ms. p. 25 is blank.

38.10   Two leaves (ms. pp. 35–38) are missing; we suspect that they were left out when the ms. was rebound because they were blank.

55.2   Directly below the word "Manner" the word "effects" has been canc.

    6   "Gospell Charges" may have been canc.; the ms. is blurred at this point.

59.30   This paragraph has been extensively revised. It originally read: "The onely...which is a means of Grace applying the Will of God by Censors unto offending members wherefore offences are put them out." In revising, Taylor has canc. some words, changed or canc. letters ("are" becomes "or"), but neglected to change "offences" to "offenders."

62.1   Several lines are left blank here; Taylor apparently intended later to add scriptural references.

65.1   The corner of this leaf (ms. pp. 59–60) has been torn away.

75.37   Taylor uses brackets here instead of quotation marks.

78.1   In the left-hand margin at this point, Taylor has written "Inhabitants." It is a later addition prompted by the blurred heading.

87.31   The remainder of this page is blank; Taylor may have intended to copy more of this sermon in the "Profession."

91.5   This section on Prayer may have also been part of a sermon. It appears to have been hastily and somewhat carelessly transcribed; the numerous blanks in the text indicate spaces for scriptural citations that Taylor never added. Unlike earlier sections, these headings do not run in a single column from top to bottom, but each heading covers both columns before a new head is entered.

96.6   The "Profession" breaks off at the bottom of ms. p. 74; three leaves (ms. pp. 75–80) are missing.
         The Public Relations of Taylor and the foundation men begin on ms. p. 81.

The Public Relations (pp. 97–117):

Emendations and Alterations:

100.19   off] of

    23   account, of] account, of,

    25   Feare against] Geare against against

101.17   it. Yet] it. yet

102.18   here is the] orig: here is that

    19   consists] consist

    32   without it. &] without &

103.1   it. Oh] it. oh
     7   God. Oh] God. oh
     8   Quick] Quck
    12   Shine as] Shine a
    14   to be.] to be
104.10   indeed. Oh] indeed. oh
105.6   sinners] sinner
    12   miserable. A] miserable. a   their] there
106.2   receive] releive
    18   me] my
107.15   their] thier
109.2   praise] paise
    13   much.] much
109.26   wrought] wroug
110.1   with me I] with I
    39   tare it] tare
111.19   & vileness] & & vileness
    23   me] my
    26   seeming] seeing
    36   not but] not
112.1   told me that God had] told me that God had told me that God had
113.9   dreadfull place, a place] a dreadfull place a place, a place
    29   might obtain a] might a
115.24   to come to] orig: to come to come to
    33   State] Stat
    35   preached] preach
116.9   off] of
117.34   if I did] if did

Textual Notes:
    97.22   The phrase "by the fall" is added above the line in a later hand.
    117.36 The last two-thirds of the first column on ms. p. 87 is left blank;
            the foundation day sermon, untitled, begins on the recto,
            ms. p. 88.

The Foundation Sermon (pp. 118–58):

Emendations and Alterations:
    118.3   all mankinde] orig: all men
        13   opposing of the same to] orig: opposing of the to
        17   men] followed by 4 ill. canc. words
    119.10   Citizens of the Saints] Citizen of the Saint
    120.10   Apostles...Foundation] orig: Apostles are found on this
             Foundation

121.5   UP TO BE A HABITATION] UP HABITATION
14   "ye"] [ye]
23   Building] orig: Building where
35   of the thing] of the the thing
122.24   Acts. Its] Acts. its
35   The Actings] orig: The building
123.14   its] it
18   of the Witness] of Witness
28   from above] from from above
124.2   some of] some
12   hold fourth] orig: hold out fourth
24   on. Here] on. here
25   speakes] speake   25.22. Here] 25.22. here
27   in his house] orig: in his Ps.
125.5   1.16. Hence] 1.16. hence
126.23   Expressed] Express
34   Windows are] orig: Gates are
127.10   Stately] Sately
14   makes] make
128.8   & not held in Communion] orig: & must be withdrawn from
13   unto God] unto, God
20   Church. This] Church this
31   Arguments] Argument
129.11   publick] puplick
33   this,] this
133.6   suffice,] suffice
26   others] other
29   testimony.] testimony
35   greatly Confirm] greatly greatly Confirm
134.38   yea] ye
135.5   further] furth
21   words to troops] words troops
24   who] followed by 2 ill. canc. words
136.27   she knows] shew knows
137.11   Hypocrasy. Nay] Hypocrasy. nay   lets] let
15   it.] it
138.10   wrought] wrote
12   Frame or Temple frame] Fram or Temple fram
24   Jews of] jews or
139.2   Further] further
140.28   it. Hence] it. hence
32   it. Hence] it. hence
34   man's] man

141.3   it. Its] it. its
    5   things. He] thing. he
    8   what he hath] what hath   thereof. Its] thereof. its
    14   of it. He] of it. he
    16   glory. Here] glory. here
    35   Spirit. Hence] Spirit hence
142.3   Spirit. Hence] Spirit hence
144.17   Churches. Why] Churches. why
    32   implicitly] implicity
145.10   against the] against the the
    13   below. Oh] below. oh
    22   house. Oh] house. oh
146.6   Steward] Seward
    13   house. But] house. but
    29   shame. What] shame. what
    39   here?] hear?
147.3   God's] God
    8   habitation. Is] habitation. is
    10   Stones? Let] Stones? let
    33   residence. He] residence. he
148.16   Pull. . .down] orig: Pull down
    17   spoke).] spoke)
    22   salvation. By] salvation. by
    34   Habitation. Doth] Habitation. doth
149.1   stones] stone
    3   fould right] orig: fould relation
    18   habitation. Oh] habitation. oh
    31   prepare, prepare.] prepare prepare.
    34   Acts 5. Oh] Acts 5. oh
150.38   hither, turn] hither turn
151.4   guesst] guess
    20   things] thing   Solomon's] Solomon
    23   excellent. Oh] excellent. oh
152.9   Still] Sill
    17   prepared] prepare
    19   habitation. If] habitation. if
    23   It] it
153.31   Christ's] Christ
154.7   things] thing
    19   grace shew itselfe] orig: grace appeare
155.7   Same. For] Same. for
    9   therein. He] therein. he

11	entrance. For] entrance. for
19	Scotfree. No] Scotfree. no
21	Sorts] Sort
29	tremble.] tremble
156.1	unto its] orig: unto up its
8	relation. But] relation. but
21	house. For] house. for
24	thee. He] thee. he
26	house. He] house. he
27	36.8. Are] 36.8 are
31	same. All] same. all
34	God. For] God. for
157.4	allurements.] allurements
15	especially yours] orig: especially unto you
31	man,] man
34	temporary; he] temporary he
36	amongst] amongs you. There] you. there

Textual Notes:

118.24   The following passage has been lightly canc. in the ms.:

> As it respects God. So he sets it out to be that which the Angel made the burden of his Song, Luke 2.14, Glory to God in the highest, peace Good will toward men. [I]ts a State therefore of peace heavenward, & of peace from heavenward, v. 16.
>
> As it respects the People of God, or the Saints.

124.27   Taylor first entered "house" above the line in the text; because it is blurred, he has also entered it at this point in the right-hand margin.

125.17   This scriptural reference is added in a much later hand, and is the only scriptural addition in this version of the foundation sermon so made.

128.1   In the right-hand margin Taylor has written, "*de occultis noti judicut Ecclesiae*," and keyed it to be entered after "Manifestation."

131.38   The final phrase of this sentence is added in a later hand.

132.4   The word "formally" is added in a later hand above the line.

140.6   At this point in the ms., the second column on ms. 94, something over twenty lines have been left blank. Taylor apparently intended to enter the response of the baptized in the primitive church, a citation to one of the early Fathers probably.

144.10   Where possible, when the edges of leaves have been worn or trimmed away, we have filled in the lacunae from the later version, as is the case here (cf. the revised version, p. 356).

150.16 Cf. revised version, p. 364.

154.16 Cf. revised version, p. 368.

The Church Covenant and Admission Records (pp. 159–73):

Emendations and Alterations:

159.9 Messengers] Messenger

10 proceeding. If] proceeding. if

13 If otherwise] if otherwise

16 pronounced us] orig: pronounced up Christ] followed by 2 ill. canc. words.

22 Churches give] orig: Churches give give

34 onely] orig: onely that

161.17 publickly] puplickly

29 experiences] experience

162.7 ourselves] ourselve

172.10 1720] 1620

20 1722] 1622

Textual Notes:

162.10 We have regularized Taylor's methods of entering these dates; from year to year he often inverts the order of the day and month. Where possible, we have also filled in the names of individuals where he has left blanks.

164.26 Following this line, several entries have been canc.

27 Two leaves (ms. pp. 103–106) are missing here; there is, however, no interruption of the chronological order. The leaves were probably blank and were omitted when the volume was bound.

29 An entry for 09/06 regarding Abigail Fowler has been canc.

165.7 Opposite this date two lines have been canc.; they do not seem to be entries.

166.4 For the 26th day of the 6th month a three-line entry has been canc.; it appears to refer to someone's baptism.

167.18 An entry at the top of this page has been trimmed off.

19 The baptismal entry for Jonathan Noble, dated 3/05, has been canc.

168.6 An entry for 4/14 has been canc.; it seems to be a baptismal entry.

169.4 The words "Rebeckah daughter" have been canc. before this entry.

21 An entry for 8/27 has been canc.; it is ill.

170.7 Several baptismal entries have been canc. following this entry.

19 An entry for 2/20 has been canc.

171.7	An entry for 3/9 has been canc.
18	An entry for 9/17 has been canc.; it is a baptismal entry.
23	Two baptismal entries at the beginning of this year have been canc.
172.20	Seven baptismal entries for this year have been canc.
173.33	Ms. p. 124 is blank; the records of the disciplinary cases begin at the top of ms. p. 125.

The Disciplinary Cases (pp. 174–242):

Emendations and Alterations:

177.2	the Town] orig: the inhabitants
178.33	others] other
38	thereby, he] thereby. he
179.27	others] other
31	their] there
181.30	their] there
183.8	the 10,] the 10m
185.3	Alienation] Alienatienation
22	few words] orig: few words words
186.3	him &] orig: him who &
29	humbled] bumbled
187.17	of touching] orig: of touching touching
188.16	as a Bitch] as a a Bitch
189.13	so] followed by ill. canc.
26	principalls] principall
190.9	this:] this
192.21	that...you] orig: that he would go on with you, that he would go on with you
194.5	tuesday] tuesda
7	time] tim
195.33	not their] orig: not their not their
197.35	cost, of making] orig: cost, & Charge of making
198.30	for the four] for they four
199.19	proposalls] proposall
200.12	inconveniency] orig: danger
201.5	State] State State
202.7	these words Sanctify] orig: those words Call
	assembly] assemply
34	fasts] fast
203.26	God's] God
205.8	June] orig: June June

206.2   shame is] shame
  28   expressions] expression
  34   to Speake] to to Speake
207.13   hard] heard
  24   restored.] restored
208.13   1711/12] followed by canc. word
209.38   their] there
210.10   subscribe to] avoid
211.7   (in effect)] [in effect]
212.26   he was] orig: he had
213.11   & in the] & in y
214.6   desired] desire
215.13   being] being being
  27   that wrote] that whot
  37   so. At] so. at
  39   it. He] it. he
216.3   vote of] orig: vote formally of   & the Church] & the Church
         & the Church
  33   & saith] & & saith
217.17   Confession] followed by 2 ill. canc. words above the line
218.21   Elders] Elder
219.4   blaim'd] orig: offe[nded]
220.31   about it] followed by 2 ill. canc. words
221.17   accepted it] accepted
  27   Smith's] Smith
222.26   their] there
223.22   Churches] Church
224.6   before...Admonition] orig: before the brethren had by their
         public Admonition
  11   God's] God
225.2   prove it. I] prove I
227.5   Ordinances. Therefore] Ordinances. therefore
229.30   yielded. This] yielded. this
230.9   Conference. He] Conference. he
  28   out and] out
  34   Officer's] Officer
  35   detaining] detining
232.9   read...wrote] orig: read that which I had read that which I had
         wrote
233.35   note] not   Smith's] Smith
234.3   gathered] gather
  4   others] other
  25   we are your brethrens] you are your brethrens

235.38 length] lenth
238.12 Wife. These] Wife. these
239.7 purpose. Then] purpose. then
  26 do. Then] do. then
240.1 hope] hop
  13 Witnesses indeed] orig: Witnesses indeed * * * indeed
  21 authority. This] authority. this
242.6 further] furth

Textual Notes:

187.11 Several lines at the top of this page have been trimmed off.
196.12 The remaining two-thirds of this column is left blank, as if Taylor later intended to add to this account.
199.20 Two ill. lines have been canc. here. In the margin Taylor has written the passage beginning "have thought it proper..." and ending "Convocation at Boston." The canc. seem to be the result of a scribal error.
212.25 The phrase "greate unrighteousness" is written vertically in the right-hand margin and keyed to this point in the text.
220.2 Between "would" and "me" Taylor has left out a word or more as he moved from the bottom of the first column to the top of the second.
226.16 The following restatement of events was apparently written some time later; the script is firmer, clearer, and the text more carefully written, although the ink has faded badly in a few places.
  23 Written above the line after "Society" is "* * * of the Church."
231.17 Taylor has revised this section several times. The text originally read: "...if they judged Brother Smith had offended in this Case they would signify it by lifting up their hands. Every person lifted up his hand: I propounded it in the negative also, & not a person lifted up his hand."
242.21 Taylor's entries end near the top of column 2, ms. p. 151. The next case, in the handwriting of and signed by Nehemiah Bull, is dated 5 February 1726/27. From ms. pp. 151–243 are various records, disciplinary cases, church meetings, letters, and so on in the script of Taylor's successors. His hand begins again on ms. p. 243 with the baptismal records.

Baptismal and Dismission Records (pp. 243–79):

Emendations and Alterations:

261.2 Elizabeth daughter] Elizabeth son
262.20 Phelps] orig: Fowler

276.12 & send...which] orig: send it after them & send it which
    20 doth wholly] orig: doth hereby wholly
278.22 same, and complied] same, complied
    24 remembred...desired] orig: remembred not to what Church he desired
    28 neglect] neclect
    32 you. Accordingly] you. accordingly

Textual Notes:

245.23 On ms. p. 244, the numbers for the months have been largely trimmed away; numerals in brackets indicate the months (Old Style) for which the dates that remain match the dates of Sundays. It is not certain, however, that they actually represent Sundays.

267.11 The dates for 1716 and the first three months of 1717 have been trimmed away.

268.25 Beginning with 1718, Taylor has again reversed the order of the days and months; we have transposed them to make the entries consistent.

270.9 The handwriting of the remaining years is nearly illegible; the effects of Taylor's illness are clearly revealed in these entries, although the handwriting is somewhat clearer for the years 1723 and 1724.

    19 An entry after 12/12 has been canc.; it is ill.

    23 Much of this entry has been canc.

274.12 Taylor's hand ends about one-fourth of the way down the second column of ms. p. 254. The next entry is in Bull's script, dated 30 October 1726, and begins on the recto of the next leaf.

276.11 The date has been entered in a later hand.

278.15 A final "s" has been added in a later hand on the word "deacon."

279.5 Taylor's handwriting ends at this point, three-fourths of the way down column 1, ms. p. 308. Bull's first entry is dated 5 February 1726/27. There is a section in the "Records" listing the deaths of members, but these entries do not begin until 1781.

Related Sermons

The Revised Foundation Sermon (pp. 283–373):

Emendations and Alterations:
283.15 Favour.] Favour

286.2	Consist. So] Consist. so
32	"You"] [You]
288.4	& Life] orig: & of Life
19	Christ,] Christ
289.6	Service. The] Service, the
29	of life.] of life
290.7	Deacons.] Deacons
291.10	Service are] orig: Service is
14	House.] House
292.20	of, may further] orig: of, doth thus further
293.21	that the Spirit of God] orig: that the Spirit of God that the Spirit of God
294.2	Marble:] Marble
31	things.] things
296.34	Sanctifying. If] Sanctifying. if
37	inlaide] inaide
38	to be laid] to laid
297.24	arguments] argument
299.35	sorts] sort
300.7	Law.] Law
23	& say . . . perverted] orig: & say I have perverted
302.2	Saith] Sath
35	of Sin,] of Sin
304.7	Abrahams] abrahams
13	Witnesses] Witness
16	Word read] Word red
35	forenoon] forenan
305.25	received. Hence] received. hence
31	5. The] 4. The
39	Case.] Case
306.3	Divine,] Divine
10	suffice.] suffice
24	taste] tast
307.11	there . . . unto] orig: there to express unto
15	Christ's] Christ
26	about . . . thus] orig: & about the yeare thus
32	are led] are had
33	necessity he leaves] orig: necessity the Person * * * to baptizing * * * he leaves
309.6	off] of
311.7	confess] confiss
31	him. He] him He

29	Persons] Person
35	Apostle was not right] orig: Apostle was too general
336.27	they were such] orig: they that shall be such
337.7	are yet] are fet
38	saith he,] saith,
338.15	here.] here
339.23	bond] bold
340.5	him,] him & had] orig: & had had
21	Choice] Coice
23	Spirituall] pirituall
27	Costliness] orig: Qualifications
342.10	2. I] 2: I
18	Arguments] Argument
343.24	Good enough] God enough
344.14	Inartificiall.] Inartificiall
345.2	Waste] Wast
346.22	*Forma.*] Forma
28	things] thing
33	be some] orig: be some some
347.8	Covenant.] Covenant
348.13	its] it
15	to an other] orig: to one an other
349.2	Form.] Form
8	Objective.] Objective
24	here.] here
28	Church.] Church
29	Arguments.] Arguments
350.5	Martyre.] Martyre
30	But what] orig: But what what
351.26	*propriety*] Taylor's italics
32	thereby.] thereby
352.9	made.] made
15	God.] God
19	much.] much
353.13	it. I] orig: it. He saith, I
355.9	& Bowls, the Cherubims,] & Bowls the Cherubims
18	habitation thro' the Spirit] orig: habitation by the Spirit thro'
21	hard] heard
32	testimony] orig: Authority
356.3	truth.] truth
5	Affections.] Affections
8	Information] Information
14	them] orig: them himselfe

357.11   Happy] Happ
       17   them.] them
       35   it.] it
358.4   Synogogues] Synogogue
       31   as] a
       39   Prayers] Prayes
359.5   etc., & also] orig: etc. but * * * also
        8   they are, by] orig: they may be, by
       21   you be.] you be
360.10   Sin. Art] Sin. art
       12   What makes] orig: What what makes
361.6   House.] House
       27   this is not] orig: this is up not
362.24   trim thy lamp] orig: trim thyself
       26   *Translationem.*] Translationem
363.2   this Husband] thus Husband
       37   Saints] Saint
364.4   thyselfe,] thyselfe
       19   this house...unprepared] orig: this State. As it is a fault fault
               not to enter
365.8   Stones in] orig: Stones are in
       17   It. Can] it. can
       19   It's] It
366.16   Earth.] Earth
       21   God's] God
       34   gone,] gone
367.17   Motives.] Motives
368.10   wary.] wary
       12   off] of
       13   again;] again
       23   Contest without] orig: Contest lest thou
369.12   God's] God
371.9   thee.] thee
       18   here.] heare.
       37   Hitherto...Exhortation.] orig: Hitherto of the first branch of
               the Exhortation.
372.8   & hath] orig: & hath & hath

Textual Notes:
       283.1   Each ms. page of this sermon is headed: "A Particular Church
               Gods House."
       291.34   The word "visible" is added above the line in a later hand.
       292.19   The word "visibly" is added above the line in a later hand.

307.33 Between the lines Taylor has also canc. another revision; it is ill.
331.9   In the upper right-hand margin of ms. p. 43, Taylor has left a blank space, as if he intended to add some citation.
33   There is a large tear in the center of the leaf containing ms. pp. 43-44.
350.3   Taylor has left four or five blank lines in the text here; he apparently intended to add the citation from Justin Martyr.
373.12 The text ends two-thirds of the way down the verso; four blank leaves follow, and the first disciplinary sermon begins on the recto of the next leaf.

The First Disciplinary Sermon (pp. 375–424):

Emendations and Alterations:

375.2   2. He] 2. he
7   term. Its] term. its
376.24 impenitant according] orig: impenitant may according
29   Conclusions.] Conclusions
34   where] orig: where where
377.10 trespass,] trespass
378.8   Covenanting.] Covenanting
17   cannot.] cannot
379.34 Affirmative.] Affirmative
381.18 intended. But] intended but
24   Doubtless] doubtless
39   Church. Now] Church. now
382.2   agree & would] orig: agree unto them & would
11   Sanhedrin;] Sanhedrin
383.1   derived from] derived
12   12.28. For] 12.28 For
18   in it.] in it
384.26 not be any] not any
385.1   ever was such] ever such
17   6.] 5.
29   7.] 6.
33   tho' they] orig: tho' they they
386.23 not members of it, it] not member of it in
35   unto.] unto
38   none. Now] none. now
387.1   them,] them
11   Societies.] Societies
388.1   dedicate . . . God] orig: dedicate to * * * God
19   truth] thruth

26   according as] orig: according to what
29   Amen. After] Amen. after
34   remission of] remission
389.9   erect in] erect
18   Sums] Sum
25   more;] more
27   Apostles. For] Apostles. for
390.35   whereby] wereby
392.8   Relation to,] Relation to
393.1   that. . .these] orig: gatherd by the Apostles I therefore say that
        we use * * * with
3   *all. . .Confederated*] Taylor's italics
11   Organick.] Organick
394.4   Constrains.] Constrains
396.15   actings.] actings
16   Churches] Church
397.12   parts] orig: Call
20   His] his
398.19   thus,] thus
23   years] year
37   people,] people
399.23   them. So] them so
35   authoritatively,] authoritatively   Table,] Table
400.14   alone,] alone
20   acting.] acting
28   warrantable. Its] warrantable its
401.15   offenders.] offenders
16   These Christ] orig: These you shall
22   examining] examing
402.20   this.] this
39   Officers. The] Officers the
403.5   attended. Hence] attended hence
9   Priests.] Priests
33   Saints,] Saints
405.3   that have such] orig: that have Ruling Elders such
7   Office. Otherwise] Office. otherwise
17   house.] house
18   their] there
23   person being not] orig: person not being
406.10   admit] admitted
33   transgressions] transgression

407.13	Churches] Church
15	accomplisht the] accomplisht
408.21	Admissions, Admonitions] orig: Admonitions, Admissions
409.1	Yea,] yea
31	Call.] Call
410.11	*particulari*.] particulari
411.24	Cleare.] Cleare
412.3	Philippi,] Philippi
4	Colloss,] Colloss
30	therefore are] therefore
413.30	hears] heaes
414.11	there are] there
18	Ecclesiasticall,] followed by 2 ill. canc. words
415.6	of.] of
31	Christ's] Christ
34	thus,] thus
416.7	members] member
28	Church.] Church
417.29	things.] things
418.8	this Death] orig: this death Death
10	me,] me
26	justifiable,] justifiable
419.2	reproved.] reproved
34	it] its
420.2	Church.] Church
24	lower] orig: lowering
33	Promise.] Promise
421.30	repent,] repent
39	hands.] hands
422.9	Rulers] Rulars
12	worke.] worke
19	against] against,
28	*them*] Taylor's italics
29	them.] them
31	discipline.] discipline
32	Sphere] orig: place
423.12	remiss.] remiss
14	Eate with, I Cor.] Eate, I Cor.
16	in,] in
34	you are] you
424.5	members] member

7	they. Hence you] they have you
13	a miss. You] a miss you
19	Churches.] Church.
24	his.] his
26	you,] you

Textual Notes:

380.6	For subdivisions 1 and 2 Taylor has also entered the numbers in the margin.
36	The heading for ms. p. 8 is "Church not the Jewish Church."
381.35	The heading for ms. p. 9 is "Church not the Jews Sanhedrin."
382.27	The heading for ms. p. 10 is "The Jews Sanhedrin not the Gospel Church."
383.19	The heading for ms. p. 11 is "This Church not Nationall, Provincial, Metropolitan."
384.5	Taylor has written "this Church" above the line; because it is not clear, he has also written the phrase in the right-hand margin.
12	The heading for ms. p. 12 is "The Church in our Text no Classis."
24	For subdivisions 1 through 6, Taylor has also entered the Arabic numerals at the appropriate places in the margin.
385.36	An Arabic 2 is entered here in the margin.
37	The heading for ms. p. 14 is "Church in this place is a Particular Church."
387.19	The heading for ms. p. 16 is "Church here a Particular Gospell Church."
388.15	The heading for ms. p. 17 is "The Church in our Text a Particular Gospell Church."
389.13	The heading for ms. p. 18 is "Church here a Particular Gospell Church."
32	For subdivisions 1 and 2 Taylor has also entered the Arabic numerals in the margin.
391.4	The heading for ms. pp. 20-24 and 26-32 is "Church here a Particular Gospell Church."
393.25	The phrase "with any Elder present" has undergone several revisions. Taylor originally wrote: "with the Elder"; he then changed it to read "with any the Elder." Then he wrote vertically in the left-hand margin "with any Elder present."
394.17	Arabic numerals 1 through 5 are written in the margin.
398.10	Above "they are" Taylor has written "by the Church," and then canc. it.
401.25	There are several ill. canc. in this line.
403.16	The heading for ms. p. 34 is "Tell it to the Church."

404.5   There is a blank space after this scripture, as if Taylor intended to enter additional references.

11   The heading for pp. 35–39 is "Tell it to the Church."

20   Here, and throughout the remainder of this sermon, Arabic numerals for all divisions and major subdivisions are also written in the margins.

408.31   The ms. heading for p. 40 is "Why tell a Particular Church."

409.26   The ms. heading for p. 41 is "Why tell the Church."

410.19   For ms. p. 42 the heading is "Why tell it to the Church improved."

411.14   The heading for ms. p. 43 is "Information."

416.13   The heading for ms. p. 49 is "Conviction."

417.5   The heading for ms. pp. 50–53 is "Conviction."

420.7   The heading for ms. p. 54 is "Caution."

421.8   There is an Arabic numeral 2 in the margin at this point; what it refers to is not clear.

36   The heading of ms. p. 56 is "Cautelary Exhortation."

422.32   The heading for ms. p. 57 is "Cautelary Exhortation."

424.27   This sermon ends at the bottom of the verso, ms. p. 58; the second disciplinary sermon begins at the top of the facing page, ms. 59. The sermons are continuously paginated.

The Second Disciplinary Sermon (pp. 425–46):

Emendations and Alterations:

425.18   some working] orig: some offring

22   words of our] orig: words of and our

426.9   Faultt.] Faultt

24   yee. Now] yee. now

29   Publican.] Puplican

32   yee. If] yee. if

427.18   injured, whatever] orig: injured binde, or loose & whatever

26   yea the body of] yea the body

31   Heaven. When] Heaven. when

35   Austin may] orig: Austin one person may

428.25   it by vertue] it with by vertue

429.1   Officers.] Officers

3   is with] orig: is with with

25   forth.] forth

430.23   it is oft] it oft

432.8   told him I] told I

27   Churches] Church

433.20   Captain saw] Captain say

434.20   Earth. First] Earth. first
   24   dutie.] dutie
   28   shall eate] orig: shall eate eate
435.22   Chap. 38.] orig: Chap. Chap. 38.
   31   rise;] rise
   36   their hands] there hands
437.3   Heaven] orig: the Church
   23   informe us] orig: informe us us
438.3   Loosed.] Loosed
   25   order'd] oder'd
   31   own it.] own it
439.8   matter. But] matter. but
   17   to binde.] to binde
   22   paste] past
440.30   judgment is in] judgment in in
441.8   to pieces;] to pieces
   13   Will Christ] orig: Will Christ Christ
   34   ruin.] ruin
443.4   Earth shall] orig: Earth she shall
   6   be loosed] orig: be bound
444.3   Objects.] Objects
   11   Church.] Church
   15   too] to
   18   founde;] founde
445.1   it. Oh] it. oh
   7   hath his sword] hathis sword
   31   repent.] pepent
   35   Sin. If] Sin. if
   37   being prooved] orig: being being prooved

Textual Notes:

426.14   The heading for ms. p. 60 is "Who ment by Yee, or Spoken to."
   38   Here, and throughout this sermon, Taylor has entered the Arabic numerals designating major divisions and subdivisions in the margin as well as in the text.
427.9   The heading for ms. p. 61 is "Who Spoken to here by that term Yee."
   38   The heading for ms. p. 62 is "Who Spoken to by the term Yee in the Text."
428.34   The heading for ms. p. 63 is "Who spoken to in our Text."
429.30   The heading for ms. p. 64 is "What is Binding & Loosing."
430.28   The heading for ms. p. 65 is "What binding & Loosing."
431.20   The heading for ms. pp. 66–68 is "What Binding & Loosing."

434.2   The heading for ms. p. 69 is "Why shall this be ratified in Heaven."

435.5   The heading for ms. p. 70 is "Why Christ will bind & Loose in Heaven Such."

436.6   The heading for ms. p. 71 is "This Binding & Loosing prooved"; Taylor originally wrote "improoved."

437.2   The heading for ms. p. 72 is "This Binding & Loosing improve."

437.38   The heading for ms. pp. 73–74 is "Use of Inference."

439.25   The heading for ms. pp. 75–76 is "Use of Inference improoved."

441.6   The heading for ms. p. 77 is "This Binding & Loosing improove in Reproof."

     37   The heading for ms. p. 78 is "This Binding & Loosing improved for reproofe."

442.32   The heading for ms. pp. 79–80 is "This Binding & Loosing improoved."

443.37   Taylor has written "not" above the line before "right," and then canc. it.

444.13   The heading for ms. p. 81 is "This Binding & Loosing improved as a Call."

445.8   The heading for ms. p. 82 is "This Binding & Loosing improved in its Call."

446.6   This sermon ends at the botom of the verso, ms. p. 82; the first sermon of the series on the Lord's Supper begins at the top of the facing page.

Index